THE MIDDLE AGES SERIES

Ruth Mazo Karras, Series Editor
Edward Peters, Founding Editor

A complete list of books in the series is available from the publisher.

Sisters and Brothers of the Common Life

The Devotio Moderna and the World of the Later Middle Ages

John Van Engen

PENN

University of Pennsylvania Press
Philadelphia

Published by
University of Pennsylvania Press
Philadelphia, Pennsylvania 19104-4112

Printed in the United States of America on acid-free paper
10 9 8 7 6 5 4 3 2 1

Library of Congress Cataloging-in-Publication Data

Van Engen, John H.
Sisters and brothers of the common life : Devotio moderna, self-made societies, and the world of the later middle ages / John Van Engen.
p. cm.— (The middle age series)
Includes bibliographical references and index.
ISBN 978-0-8122-4119-8 (alk. paper)
1. Christian communities—History. 2. Societies living in common without vows—History. 3. Communalism—Religious aspects—Christianity—History. 4. Spiritual life—Christianity—History. I. Title.
BV4405.V36 2008
274'.05—dc22 2008017462

for Kathryn

CONTENTS

ILLUSTRATIONS

Introduction: The Devotio Moderna and Modern History

BEGINNING IN THE 1380s, in market towns along the IJssel River (east-central Netherlands) and in the county of Holland, groups of women and men formed households organized as communes and a lifestyle centered on devotion. They lived on city streets alongside urban neighbors, managed properties and rents in common, and prepared textiles or books for local markets—all the while refusing to profess vows as religious or to acquire spouses and property as lay citizens. They defended their lifestyle, self-designed, as exemplary, and sustained it in the face of opposition, the women labeled "beguines," the men "lollards," epithets meant to mock or cast suspicion. They also spread, toward Münster to the east, Cologne and Liège to the southeast, Brabant and Flanders to the south, and eventually as far as Magdeburg and Rostock to the east and the Upper Rhine to the south. For the most part, in the first generation or two especially, these "Modern-Day Devout" puzzled contemporaries, their zeal surprising neighbors and churchmen, its intensity evoking admiration but also worry. For the Devout it was all the negligent parishioners and self-indulgent religious, the corruption of the ordinary, that seemed worrying. Parish-goers appeared "crude and beastly" in matters moral and spiritual, resistant to anything but required worship,[1] and the professed religious mostly compromised and hypocritical. The Devout resolved—over against indifferent parish routines, over against those who vowed religion but lived in privilege—to embody "piety" in the "present-day," the rhetorical force of their term "devotio moderna."

This seemed admirable to some, annoyingly self-righteous to others. A story from the mid-1430s may help us visualize the tensions. Egbert ter Beeck, head for many years (1450–83) of the men's household in Deventer, was sent as a boy to the renowned school connected to the canons of St. Lebuin. He came from a gentry family in Wijhe, several miles north, and lived as a schoolboy with kinswomen in Deventer. He became drawn to the Brothers in good part by their "collations," talks they offered on Sunday afternoons and feast days. Soon he began to imitate their demeanor, even the cut of hair associated with them. In a city busy with merchants, clerics, and students no one could mistake his stance. Young Egbert, walking down a street with guarded eyes, bearing a plate of food, once failed to see, or to look up and greet, a female relative. She knocked the plate out of his hand, and indignantly quipped, "What sort of lollard is this who walks around like that!" He bore her insult without remark, picked up his plate, and continued on his way. Here was a teenage student, not cloistered in a monastic house, yet somehow not of this world—a "lollard" in his relative's eyes, meaning, possibly a heretic, certainly a "fanatic." His father, too, tried every argument to free him from his fascination with the Brothers, offering to send him to Cologne for advanced schooling and promotion, or to secure him a church post in the neighborhood, even to set him up as an eremetical hermit in a personal dwelling. But Egbert resisted. Most clerics lived dissolute lives, he explained. With his fragile nature he was more likely to get "perverted" by their lifestyle than to "convert" them.[2]

Egbert's story, written by a companion upon his death in 1483, touched on elements common to the Devout experience. The life-passages he worked through were also theirs: conversion (teen or adult); breaking with family, with ecclesiastical promotion, with a career in learning; choosing to join a self-made urban commune sustained in part by manual labor; resolving to internalize and enact devotion in the face of suspicious townspeople and wary churchmen. This experience animated a lifestyle consciously set apart, yet lived out in the midst of urban society and parish routines. It informed stories and proverbial sayings they told and retold among themselves. These they wrote up, often in quite personal ways, in notebooks as well as "sayings" and "lives" (by the men in Latin and Dutch, by the women in Dutch). At the earliest Sisters' house, shortly after 1400, a noblewoman from the county of Mark resisted invitations to join a professed form of this life then getting underway at Diepenveen, an hour's walk outside Deventer. "If I had wanted to become a nun, she protested, I would not have come here."[3] The experience of turning inward (*innigheid*, in their tongue) defined for them a social and religious position awkwardly poised between church and society, religious community and social kin. This awkwardness provoked self-awareness, and that self-awareness expressed itself in writing—a boon to historians, if not always easy for them.

All this comes to us now, however, from a distance of six hundred years. The Modern Devout, whether we regard them as "late medieval" or "early modern," lie at several removes from us, with no direct line back. Too much in their story presupposes socioreligious structures long since gone. Theirs was a world where a single church claimed jurisdiction over virtually every person in society, and where towns extended liberties to, and exercised oversight over, most within their walls. In actual practice individuals had to sort through a host of overlapping and sometimes competing familial, economic, religious, and political ties. "Estates" ("stations in life") delineated groups socially and ethically, including a special class of "religious." That entire world order got upended five hundred years ago by the Reformation, and then two hundred years ago definitively dissolved by the Revolution. Serious scholarly work on the Devotio Moderna began in the aftermath, in the 1830s when churches, nations, and cultures, in the wake of Revolutionary change, sought to reclaim some vestige of the old order, the Devout then initially often envisioned as "prereformers."[4] Subsequent scholars seized upon their "modernity" for larger European narratives, and found in them every likely agenda: reformers before the Reformation, educators before the Renaissance, pious ascetics before Catholic Reform, democrats before the Revolution, laity before bourgeois piety. Each of those views, whatever its insight, stemmed from reading the Devout through the prism of sixteenth-century movements and ideas (or their nineteenth-century representations). Most scholars, to be fair, knew their predilections; even saw it as part of their purpose to pursue agendas old and new, to reproduce in miniature ongoing struggles between Catholics and Protestants or humanists and scholastics. National loyalties, too, drove narratives: The Dutch celebrating the Modern Devotion as their distinctive contribution to spiritual and educational renewal, Germans preoccupied with the coming of the Reformation, and Belgians highlighting mystical expressions (Ruusbroec) as well as a continuing institutional presence in their land (houses of canons regular closed only in the eighteenth century by Joseph II).

In time grand manifestos were issued. In 1924 a thirty-year-old Dutch American of protestant heritage, Albert Hyma, offered a panegyric still influential in textbooks. The Modern Devout, he argued, marked a turning point, perhaps *the* turning point, in European history, partly by their lifestyle, mostly through a cultural program he called "Christian humanism." I quote: "this 'New Devotion,' or Christian Renaissance, between 1380 and 1520, absorbed the wisdom of the ancients, the essence of Christ's teachings, the mystic religion of the fathers and the saints of medieval Europe, as well as the learning of the Italian humanists; . . . assimilated all these ingredients and presented them in a new dress to the old world and the new. . . ."[5] This extravagant claim met with a stern Catholic response forty years later (1968), a long book codifying a lifetime of learning. R. R. Post saw the "Devotionalists" as monastic and quasi-monastic figures, narrowed in scope to the Netherlands, ascetic, sober-minded, safely medieval and pious, devoid of any link to Renaissance, Reformation or the new world.[6] Hyma had projected a grand narrative; Post answered with, as he said, "the facts." Post's has now become a standard point of departure; but Hyma's provocation lingers still. To disconnect the Devout from all larger claims and rubrics is to reduce them to little relevance outside local history. The dilemma is not unique to them. Other groups from the same era have achieved relevance by having them address, or seem to address, contemporary issues: Lollards as subversives embodying the people's voice, Hussites as the spark of Czech nationalism, Brigitte of Sweden and Catherine of Siena as representing the presence and powers of women.

Since about 1970 scholars have begun to imagine alternatives for the Devout.[7] Kaspar Elm has positioned the Devout "between monastery and world, the middle ages and modernity," on the cusp of change, as emblems of transition, if not its agents. For him the Devout came last in a long series of medieval groups living "ruled lives without a rule," even fitting into an accepted social estate: neither innovators nor monks but "semi-religious," like beguines or hospitalers.[8] Anton Weiler has directed attention to the moral psychology of the Modern Devout, their efforts to found a "constitution of the self." For him the Devout anticipated strategies to make and remake the human self, "self-fashioning" if you like, their methods crafted at a turning point between tradition and innovation.[9] Thomas Mertens has highlighted the literate dimension of Devout practice, especially in Middle Dutch: their reading and making of books, from personal and collective notebooks called *rapiaria* through collations (preaching) to prayer books and spiritual tractates.[10] Nikolaus Staubach, director for a decade of a research institute in Münster dedicated to the Modern Devout, has cultivated a vision of Devout book-making as integral to their spirituality, their texts, personal and collective, woven into interior practice.[11] And in Amsterdam a research project initiated by Kurt Goudriaan has focused attention on the women in this story,[12] as Van Dijk and Scheepsma had done a little earlier.[13] Outside the Low Countries or Germany scholarship on late medieval religious culture, preoccupied of late with Lollards in England or prophetic figures on the continent, has paid scant attention to the Modern Devout, passing them over as not very accessible or as not very interesting (the after effect of Post's conservative depiction). This has in part to do with language, much as scholarship on the Hussites has tended to get ghettoized inside a linguistic or regional historiography.

As the Modern Devout had trouble fitting in, so too historians have had trouble finding ways to fit them in. Fifteenth-century historians tried to place them back in the millennium-old framework of medieval religious orders, though they knew that Sisters, Brothers, and Tertiaries did not take vows—but they had no other category. Sixteenth-century princes and prelates, fixated on groups or practices certifiably "Protestant" or "Catholic," found little place for Sisters or Brothers. In 1568, after the Council of Trent, Pope Pius V ordered any who lived in-between, as religious but without vows, to join an order or dissolve their community. A tightening Catholic discipline could no longer tolerate unregulated groups, people "semi-religious" or "semi-lay," at least not in principle. At the same time Protestant regimes energetically closed Devout houses and confiscated their resources, sweeping through the home region of the Devout in 1569–70. To Calvinist eyes the men and women in these "gatherings" (*congregatio, vergadering*) looked too much like medieval religious, not at all like "congregations." Recent study of religious culture in the Later Middle Ages has taken up anew notions of a "premature reformation" as well as a "new devotion." The former, ironically, echoes an approach that goes far back in European historiography, one bristling with confessional polemics that brazenly read history backward to reinforce religious agendas. And the latter too often has tended to presume rather than to isolate what was "new" about later medieval piety.[14]

The Modern Devout inhabited a distinct moment in time. They originated in the 1380s, and were disbanded by Catholic and Protestant rulers alike in the 1560s (apart from those surviving for two centuries more as canons in present-day Belgium). As self-conscious "converts" they undertook to found a new form of community in which to care for their religious selves. This is a book about that enterprise, its community-building and its self-making. It is not a textbook history of the Modern Devotion as such, not in the institutional sense of narrating its houses and their adherents, also not in the cultural sense of surveying "devotion" as an amorphous rubric for later medieval religion. Histories of the Devout movement exist, more and less adequate, as do monographic studies and fine research manuals.[15] This book, keeping the Modern Devout at its center, seeks to think through their story anew and, as possible, to have that story bring into focus not the early modern future but the late medieval present. Few interpreters have read the Devout insistently within their own time and space, the social and religious conditions that marked towns and parishes in northern Europe during the fifteenth century, the widespread upheaval in cultural and religious life between the 1370s and the 1440s. An unmediated reading of the past is hardly possible, to be sure, however laudable the ideal or clarifying the attempt. I claim no exemption, only personal oddities that crisscross older categories, perhaps helpfully: a medievalist who began his studies in the renaissance, an American of Dutch ancestry who has lived in Belgium and Germany, a Protestant who has taught for years at a Catholic University.

The story of the Devout and their households cannot be told from any single viewpoint, nor from any single source. Despite long and fine traditions of writing about the Modern Devout, basic sources still need attention. Indeed Hyma, whatever one holds about his interpretations and however inadequate his editions by modern standards, first made available in print sources crucial to this study, as to many others. But the largest and most informative chronicle, also the latest in date, by Petrus Ympens, remains unedited, though it exists in a manuscript of his own hand; the most influential narrative account (by Johan Busch) was edited more than a century ago in only one of its two versions; memorial lives written by and about canonesses have been published in only one of two known versions; the founding figure (Geert Grote) has just begun to receive a critical edition of his works; and so on. My own work in this field began with a series of discrete projects to get at, and get out, unpublished or poorly published sources. But enough new sources—whether newly discovered, newly edited, or newly read—raise questions about our big picture. The Devout themselves make it both inviting and difficult, inviting because this writing-conscious group generated tractates and documents essential to their self-defense and self-definition, a mix of legal, apologetic, and related materials mostly not well edited or still in manuscript. But they also make it difficult, for as an essential part of their spiritual self-cultivation (*cura sui ipsius*) they took care, even great care, to shape and reshape memory, especially in their memorial lives. It is easy in my view to read Devout texts too naively and also too skeptically. Readers may judge the results here for themselves.

In the spiritual exercises they set for themselves, the Devout strived by way of reading, meditation, and writing to remake their human interiors, and thus too in a sense their public presentation, personal or collective. In the documents they amassed to guarantee and defend their communities, they gave shape to, and monumentalized for themselves and their heirs, a distinctive "estate" (*status*) as their chosen way of life. In the memorials they wrote of departed companions, they remembered those "lives" as a way to kindle and rekindle their own zeal and purpose. All these sources are rich; none can be interpreted straightforwardly. For most scholars the narratives have proved most attractive: remarkably human, written by and for themselves, in their own languages. Documentary materials can prove more difficult of access, not consistently preserved, rarely in completeness, intermittently edited, harder to bring to narrative life. The spiritual exercises that so marked Devout practice can also seem inaccessible, but for other reasons, inadequate editions to be sure, as well as inattention to their handwritten formats (though this is improving). But their relentless self-examining and self-disciplining, even in our "age of therapy," can prove dismaying (or tedious), and overshadow the innovative character of this "self-care," this cultivating of "interiority." Bound up with all three source-forms (narratives, documents, and exercises), even prerequisite to them, was a remarkable drive to write. The Devout took extraordinary care in manuscript production as a way both to nourish the spirit and profit the house. Any serious historical approach must strive to hold all these sources in steady tension.

The aim of this study is to grasp the Devout in their humanity, communities, and religion, all within the urban societies of the Low Countries and the cultures we call late medieval. This confronts us with three words, all charged concepts. The first is "modern." Past scholars tended to claim too much for the term, then in reaction too little. For nineteenth-century scholars it leaped off the page, suggesting incipient new beginnings, a post-medieval future. It projected these fifteenth-century actors onto a larger stage led by Renaissance humanists or Reformation believers, the Devout preparing for either or both. A reaction inevitably set in, mostly from Catholic scholars. They demanded philological precision. In Latin the word "*moderna*" means "present-day" over against a long-ago past (*antiqua*). To speak of "devotion in the present-day" (*moderna*) was, at least implicitly, to recall an "earlier day" (*antiqua*), a better day, of apostles and Desert Fathers, of twelfth-century monks and thirteenth-century friars. The word thus harbored an agenda: to appropriate in this age (*moderna*) the piety (*devotio*) of those neglected medieval ancients.[16] It also cast glaring light on "present time" as inadequate, lax in religion or barbarous in learning, counterposed to those ancients so worthy of emulation. The critics thus were right, at least about the core meaning of the word. But that does not account for its full force.

The term "modern" could also highlight the present-day as newly capable of realizing all that was good in religion or learning, even rivaling the ancients. Henry Pomerius, former schoolmaster and then canon regular at Groenendael outside Brussels, wrote three books on his house's mystic teachers, John Ruusbroec and John van Leeuwen ("the cook"). There he described Geert Grote as the "font and source of present-day devotion in Lower Germany among canons regular" (*fons et origo moderne devotionis*)—the earliest recorded use of this phrase.[17] His introduction conceded the "sufficiency of ancient models of sanctity for some" but insisted upon "new stand-outs" to stimulate devout spirits today (*deuotis mentibus noua sanctorum singularitas*), his prickly word *singularitas* eased into Dutch as "special interiority."[18] By the 1410s Pomerius saw this movement as a force, could even gesture toward it with a short-hand rubric "*devotio moderna*" (Present-Day Piety, Devotion in Our Day). But he applied it to his own order in these newest/latest times (*precipue . . . in nouissimis his temporibus in nouitate spiritus*),[19] not to unprofessed Sisters or Brothers. Twenty or thirty years later Thomas of Kempen, in a highly influential account of the "fathers" of the movement focused on Brothers, staged a dialogue between a "senior" and a "novice," launched by this query: "Although I have heard many splendid things about the old saints, I want to hear good and new things (*bona noua*) about the present-day ones (*de modernis*)."[20] In short, the term (*devotio moderna*), though proudly contemporary, was fluid, a catch-word bandied about, capable of bending to more than one usage. It pointed to people in the present animated with a heady sense of purpose, even of "singularity." At its core the word meant "of this era" as distinct from an "earlier era," thus *via moderna* to designate the newer ("terminist") way of philosophizing in the fourteenth century over against an older thirteenth-century way (*via antiqua*, the Thomist school), these both in the fifteenth century hardening into labels, as would in time *devotio moderna*, first the newer sort of pious or piety in our day, then firming in meaning as a distinctive group.

Equally pesky is the term "late medieval." Fifteenth-century humanists and sixteenth-century reformers successfully smeared as "middle time" a thousand years of Europe's formative history, creating a "dark abyss" that separated them from the light of truth and beauty, whether of Antiquity or the Apostles or both. Medieval historians much later introduced epochs into that thousand years, "early," "central," "high," or "late," though the chronologies and rationales vary to the present day. The earlier period (pre-1000) now usually stands on its own, and the "high" marks a season of new beginnings, the "renaissance" or "reformation" or "revolution" of the twelfth century. But what then of the "late"? Any age accounted "late" is headed almost certainly for interpretive trouble, though the "Late Roman Empire," a downward spiral of decay and disruption, has given way among historians, thanks especially to Peter Brown, to "Late Antiquity," three centuries of creativity with lasting consequences for the shape of Europe, Africa, and Asia. Not so, however, with "The Late Middle Ages," despite, or indeed owing to, Huizinga's influential sketch of its culture and sensibility as an "autumn." Almost without exception the fourteenth and fifteenth centuries (unless humanists are the theme) get represented as in "crisis" or "decline," an age in waiting, the vital forces of "reform" or "renaissance" or "modernity" barely on the horizon. In textbooks and surveys the rubrics appear now nearly automatic, as is the list (plague, war, famine, economic downturn, social unrest, intellectual collapse, cultural morbidity).[21] For Huizinga, and for many writing at the turn of the twentieth century, perceptions of "decline" and "world-weariness" had as much to do with their own "fin de siècle" mood as with the year 1400.[22] But the labels and storylines have stuck, partly because they set up convenient straw men for humanists and reformers to knock down.

Of late some of the evidence adduced for decline has come under scrutiny.[23] But it is not only about questioning evidence; it is a matter of attitude, of expectation. No one doubts the reality of plague or warfare or economic dislocation. At issue is what that meant on the ground, how people dealt with them; and for us how dark the lens through which we look, how smeared with pathos (in Huizinga's case). To keep the tone and narrative consistent we often create quite separate worlds in dealing with these two centuries. We hardly imagine

Joan of Arc, Bernardino of Siena, and Leonardo Bruni as contemporaries, the Hussites and Observants as making rival religious claims, Langland, Chaucer, and Julian as living in the same space and time (or of teaching them together). We forget that Catherine of Siena began to write about the time Petrarch and Boccaccio died, that Savanarola preached hellfire in the vernacular and used the printing press two or three generations after humanists first pushed for moral and educational reform by way of classicizing Latin. Whatever labels we choose for it—a large problem not to be solved in a short introduction—this was the "present-day" in which the Modern Devout lived.

Finally there is the pesky word "devotion." At the moment religious history is flourishing among medieval and early modern historians. But for many piety can appear uncomfortably off-putting, also either uninteresting or unyielding unless made to speak of something else, whether of politics or of sex. Nearly a century ago Johan Huizinga portrayed the Devout disparagingly, as ascetics turning their backs on a world sinking into its cultural autumn (his image of them probably colored by austere Protestant pietists in his home region). Within the nationalist/racialist categories common to his time he saw their sober-minded pursuit of religion also as "typical" of Netherlandish steadiness, unlike the passionate and spasmodic outbursts of enthusiasm he found in Romance lands.[24] To complicate things futher, the rubric "Modern Devotion" is frequently and broadly employed, even promiscuously, to capture the temper of religious culture generally in the later middle ages. That usage, hazy and imprecise, gestures toward an extravagantly expansive world of devotion in fourteenth- and fifteenth-century Europe, so powerful in its impetus as to produce hundreds of vernacular texts and tens of thousands of cultic and visual objects, so diverse as to defy any single rubric or characterization. It still needs adequate historical characterization, and readers may judge by the end whether the Modern Devout represent that world or sit at cross-purposes to it. Links may well exist, but on the whole scholars have not thought hard or clearly about this.

One deserves notice. The booklets that comprise Thomas of Kempen's *The Imitation of Christ*, hundreds of proverb-like sayings in four originally distinct pamphlets, came out of Modern Devout houses, began circulating in the early 1420s, and are extant still in some nine hundred fifteenth-century copies and one hundred early printed editions, with unparalleled print runs in early modern Europe in nearly every language.[25] About those booklets, apart from endless wrangling over authorship (now settled), scholars have only begun to ask basic historical questions: How do we account for this resonance? How may self-made communal societies in fifteenth-century Dutch towns have informed its message or leavened its appeal? Some, moreover, still identify with the forms of piety fostered in those booklets, even strongly so. And the Devout too still inspire a circle of admirers who find in their writings a seriousness about religious renewal that stands as a bulwark against encroaching indifference. But others find all this utterly incomprehensible, the piety naïve or cloying or worse. This study springs from neither restorationist longing nor modern distaste. It aims at understanding, historical understanding first of all.

A last word about terminology. The term "Modern Devotion" arose in contemporary texts and is well embedded now ("Moderne Devotie" in Dutch), and perhaps rightly so. But it has also become overlaid with generations of meaning, the term freighted with connotations and expectations. In this study, to try break the grip of those associations, I generally use the phrase "Modern-Day Devout" or occasionally the "New Devotion."

CHAPTER ONE

Converts in the Middle Ages

Since . . . certain women commonly called "beguines" who—since they promise obedience to no one nor renounce personal property nor profess any approved rule—are in no way "religious" though they wear a habit . . . we, rightly holding them suspect, with the approval of the council hold that their estate (statum) *is perpetually to be prohibited and wholly abolished from the church of God.*
—Cum de quibusdam *(1317)*

Right reason does not suffer that the innocent be judged equally with the harmful. . . . beguines of this kind, not chargeable nor suspect . . . by the advice of our brother [cardinals] we wish and declare not to be included. . . . Nonetheless, the estate of the kind of beguines we permit to be, unless it is ordained otherwise concerning them by the apostolic see, we in no way intend by the foregoing to approve.
—Ratio recta *(1318)*

Geert Grote of Deventer (b. 1340) spent his first thirty-four years, to mid-life by medieval standards, in pursuit of a clerical career, inquisitive about learning, eager for office and income, restlessly underway. The only legitimate heir of patrician parents, orphaned at ten by the plague, he went to Paris in his mid-teens, earned his master's beret in 1358, and stayed on as a regent master in arts. From age twenty-two he applied repeatedly to the curia at Avignon for church incomes (1362, 1363, 1365, 1366, 1371). Named in 1362 the "most celebrated" of those supplicating that year from the English nation, he was identified in 1366 as studying law after "having labored hard for more than seven years in the natural [astrology], moral, and other speculative sciences"—possibly including theology since he resided for a time at the Sorbonne. Meanwhile he kept his house at Deventer, consulted on law, and twice in 1366–67 acted on behalf of his native city at Avignon. Already in November 1362 he had received an expectative for a canon's prebend at Aachen (obtained in the later 1360s), in 1371 another for St. Martin's in Utrecht.[1] In all this Master Geert Grote of Deventer proved a fourteenth-century type. Thousands of "clerics" (a term signifying "book-man" as well as "church-man") made their careers facilitating the business of church and society, having indeed become indispensable to it, whatever resentments that stirred up. But not all proved successful. Many lived on the hunt for patrons or positions. Langland the poet sniped at those from poor parishes who sought "to have a licence and a leve in Londoun to dwelle/ and synge ther for symonye while selver is so swete"[2]—self-mockery in part from a west-country cleric working as a book-man in London. Master Geert, about the year 1374, found this way of life "more unclean" than he had words for.[3] He resolved to make a "turn."

Grote left no harrowing conversion story.[4] He penned notes, "resolutions, not vows," and drew up a reading list.[5] Scholars have read these as a kind of diary, a glimpse inside. They were a first in fact, a convert working out on paper a new plan of life. His resolve to "order his life" now to the service and honor of God proceeded with a mix of intentions and pragmatic reasoning. First, he would seek no more benefices: gaining one only fueled avarice for more and holding several destroyed peace of mind. Nor would he serve cardinals or prelates to gain patronage, or cast horoscopes to win the favor of lords. He would not pursue the lucrative arts, medicine, astrology or law, since such people, corrupted by gain, rarely remained just (*equus*) in their reasoning or at peace (*quietus*) in their outlook. He would give up the liberal arts as useless, and focus on moral arts. He would not seek degrees or write books to curry fame. He would shun as pointless and provocative the public disputations of artists and theologians, such as at Paris. He would pursue no degree in theology since such people thought "carnally"—and he could have the learning without the degree. He would offer no consultations in law or medicine except to help friends or kin, recoiling particularly from horoscopes and reckonings. To Master Geert it all looked tainted with self-interest. He wrote this out amid his turn, most likely in 1374/75 while mainly resident in Deventer and Utrecht.[6] In September 1374 he transformed his family house into a hospice, and by October 1375 gave up his benefices at Aachen and Utrecht.

In the decade between his inner turn and his death of plague (1374–84) he moved piecemeal toward an alternative lifestyle. One letter betrays a painful inversion of relationships. A wealthy young relative (Berthold ten Hove[7]) had made a promise of virginity on some occasion, then grew troubled at the thought of separating from family, also worried that he was not "sensing" the Spirit in his "interior person." Grote saw the young man as "sweet in nature and pliable and inclined to be a 'joiner'." The Spirit of God, he noted, though present, is hidden (*absconditus*). This should not surprise: we barely "taste" our own "cognitive spirit," whence our attraction to palpable realities. Watch out, he warned, for vain circles (*societates*). Frequent the poor friends of Christ. As for kinship, he reassured him, I will not leave you: by the Father's conceiving we are brothers in spirit. This play on words brought scant comfort, and Grote relented: Come visit, and "I will tell you about our father, about mother, the friends in our kinship, from whom we will not be separated into eternity." Agreeing then to converse about family, Grote insisted on pointing toward Father God and "friends" forming a kinship of spirit.

In the fall of 1383[8] Master Geert responded to queries about the papal schism from a Parisian friend thirty years senior in age and much higher in rank. William of Salvarvilla, chanter at Notre Dame and master of theology, now archdeacon for Brabant in the bishopric of Liège, was forced out of Paris in March 1382 for leaning "notoriously" to the Roman claimant.[9] But he grew disgusted with his new "worldly" duties (including driving out partisans of Avignon) in a post sumptuous with housing and banquets and staff. All this resonated with Master Geert, his experience exactly, he said (*Experior hec valde in me*). The "inner person" is "flooded" by the "outer person." William, he warned, should not descend blindly into the "ruin of the church so patent all about them" but stick with the few serious people (*graviores*). He issued a caution: the proper end is temperance and frugality, not strict austerity. He admitted to remaining at odds with himself, fearing to starve his spirit, then taking too much for his body. He hinted that the present state of affairs—papal schism, clergy with companions—pointed toward the prophesied end-times. This "fall" (*casus ecclesie*), this "abundance of evil arising from neglect," might nonetheless prove "useful" if clergy were jolted into giving up their habitual ways and came "to live out of books and truthfully, not absorbed in ecclesiastical busy-work."

Grote's own resolutions had moved directly from his clerical renunciations to a reading list beginning with the Gospel, followed by the lives and sayings of the Desert Fathers—all conceived still as learning (*Revertor ad scientias*). In the later 1370s he went into retreat, spending time especially at the Carthusian house outside Arnhem but in the end joining no order. After roughly four years he emerged as a deacon, and now crisscrossed the diocese of Utrecht on self-made preaching tours (late 1379–fall 1383), making converts. To make sense of this and the Devout communities that soon appeared, we must first put in place the thousand-year history of medieval conversion.

Conversion as a Medieval Form of Life

What "convert" brings to mind for us, persons moving from one community of belief or practice to another, most medieval Europeans rarely saw. They lived in the land of the christened. About infidels they knew mostly legends, storied characters beyond the lands of the churched. In Iberia Christians interacted with Jews and Muslims, but elsewhere—even if some encountered Jews at court or in cities, and a few dealt with peoples beyond the frontier—most spent their lives inside Christian culture. Abelard noted bluntly that Jews and Christians owed their faith allegiances to birth-parents and custom.[10] And yet converts were everywhere to see. For in the experience and language of medieval Europeans this term denoted, often first of all, those who left family and friends to take up a dedicated spiritual life. Converts sought to realize a "perfect" life, implicitly calling into question the adequacy of ordinary religious practice. This deliberate reconfiguring of life toward an envisioned perfect form released a dynamic that energized and upset medieval society for a thousand years.

In medieval history conversion came to represent a life-form in church and society.[11] Already in late antiquity key markers of human life—birth, marriage, property, power, death—had become interwoven with Christian claims and rituals, the social and religious co-opting each other, christening thus meaning at once baptism and naming. Opting out of Christian practice entirely, if exceptionally undertaken by converts to Judaism or Islam, was largely unimaginable. People harbored doubts, and rankled over obligations. But finding fault did not mean moving into a heretical stance—that too, on the whole, was exceptional. People might far more readily slip into neglectful indifference or passive resistance, this not easy to get at, though preachers railed at it constantly. Most people carried out their expected routines more or less (these too varying by place and century), some with heart, some without thinking. For those not content with inherited religious practice, however, haunting questions arose: If everyone was accounted Christian, was anyone truly Christian? How could you tell, especially for yourself? If the privileged (monks and nuns) counted as the religious, where did that leave the ordinary and the poor? If the privileged were hypocrites, what of religion in general? Such questions may have troubled only a few, or most people only on occasion—we have limited ways of knowing. But for some it consumed heart and mind. Preaching to student-clerics in Paris in 1139 Bernard of Clairvaux declared: Converting was God's will (*voluntas eius conversio nostra*), for there was "no true life for us except in conversion, and no other access to a true life."[12]

Conversion first took on additional meanings when a Christian majority emerged in fifth-century Rome. Some now chose to separate from the compromised life of the ordinary baptized. Anthony left Roman Alexandria for the Egyptian desert, as did thousands more around the Mediterranean, their acts paradigmatic for the middle ages. That storied act jolted Augustine into converting (in our sense), followed soon by his converting in the second (leaving city, career, mistress, and betrothed for a country retreat and like-minded group). Throughout the middle ages converts, moved by inner conviction, also by social pressure or material need, turned away from the "world"—sex and family life, goods and private ownership, power and mastery over one's own will—toward "things on high" as well as "things within." By an act of earthly renunciation they gained, if they persevered, heavenly exaltation. They might also attain, a paradoxical inversion, exaltation on earth. For they emerged collectively as medieval Europe's first estate, representing "religion" in all its fullness. In the poem *Piers Plowman* Haukyn the baker, figure of the "active life," is depicted as constantly soiling his cloak, his white christening garb, with every conceivable sin, a filthy mess, only to give it a bit of a scrubbing once a year at Lent. Converts, by contrast, cast off their dirtied outer cloak, the muck of ordinary life in christened Europe, to free themselves for constant cleansing ("penance"), also undertaking an interior scrubbing that went beyond appearances or annual duty. They undertook *metanoia* or change of mind ("penance").

Conversion assumed differing life-forms across historical time. Early on it got institutionalized. To convert was to enter a monastery and take vows under a Rule. Conversion thus entailed, apart from matters of the heart, a change in social estate with lasting human consequences. Like marriage (the analogy explicit), it was a move that might be arranged by others with material conditions attached, especially entrance gifts analogous to dowries. Church lawyers eventually framed the act of profession with definitions, thereby rendering conversion a technical term akin to betrothal. A convert entered into a recognized legal estate, adopted a Rule for life (*conversatio*), gained a measure of social prestige, and looked to a heavenly reward. Like marriage, this was a lasting bond, the one vow impeding the other, unless husband and wife both voluntarily agreed to join the higher estate of religion.[13] Leaving a monastery was as difficult as leaving a marriage. It brought great opprobrium, the person accounted an "apostate," the term itself telltale, conversion's opposite.

The cloister, however, could never fully contain the potency latent in conversion. During the eleventh and twelfth centuries, after generations of recruitment to monastic life primarily by way of child oblation (like child baptism, an expression of parental or group practice more than individual will), adult converts appeared on the historical stage in numbers. Robert of Arbrissel toured the French countryside in outlandish garb haranguing recruits, at least as his shocked critics told it, gathering women converts in particular and so, critics charged, putting them at risk by displacing them from home and family without adequate shelter or control.[14] Guibert of Nogent, writing about 1115, recalling similar stories from his youth, looked back on it all as "the beginnings of the conversions of that time" (*conuersionum tunc temporis extulere primordia*)—his phrase for what we call the twelfth-century reform.[15] Adolescent students, adult clerics, troubled noblemen, interested women—all made their distinctive "turns." Unlettered peasants now did so too, giving the word yet another meaning, "lay brother." Some converts acted as religious innovators to the end; others channeled energy into new forms of organized monastic or eremitic life; still others found their forms and energies disapproved. Churchmen and lay lords also pushed back, privileging conversion and trying to claim its spiritual benefits but also trying to domesticate it. Robert's foundation at Fontevraud, lampooned in the 1110s, became the burial place for Henry II, Eleanor of Acquitaine, and Richard Lionheart.

Conversion's appeal could touch any segment of society, also, perhaps puzzlingly for moderns, the secular clergy. In his early twenties Bernard of Clairvaux left the local secular clergy to join a house of radical monks at Cîteaux. Twenty-five years later (probably All Saints 1139), addressing a crowd of student-clerics in Paris, he lambasted them for careerism and ambition, for entering the church without a spiritual calling. He now urged them to leave school and clerical life for a new monastery like his. He met with little response, and in frustration he turned this sermon into the first tractate on conversion. In it he deployed an image. A person wearing a filthy garment will cast it off. But anyone looking inside at the rank bilge-water of his own memory will find himself caught, for memory is constitutive of the self and a defiled soul cannot cast off its own self. Were he to impose law on this self, it would protest: "What's with this new religion (*Unde haec nova religio*)?" But Bernard darkly warned: "do not be secure" (*Noli esse securus*). Do not confide in a broad (inclusive) net (of salvation); for not all fish are reckoned good or will be kept.[16]

Conversion also took the form of converting the converted. Cistercians challenged Benedictines, and in the later middle ages Observants in all orders called for new strict adherence to Rules and customs.[17] Too many had entered for the wrong reason or lost heart amid cloistered routines, as Thomas of Kempen noted: "we find ourselves better and purer in the beginning of our conversion than after many years of profession."[18] Grote's proposed reading list contained only one "modern" work, the *Horologium* of Henry Suso (ca. 1295–66), a text from ca. 1330. Suso, after entering the Dominican friary in Constance at age thirteen, remained unfocused, distracted (*sin gemute ungesamnet*), until a "turn" in his eighteenth year (*abker*-the final rhetorical word of his introduction). To rein in his unruly spirit (*wilder mut*) he turned away from those in the convent who seemed loftily self-indulgent (*upiger gesellschaft*), though they heckled him about his strange ways (*sunder wise*) and predicted no good end.[19] Suso fell into an immobilizing depression.[20] After emerging he told of raptures, entered into marriage with Wisdom, carved the Name of Jesus onto his chest, pursued ascetic austerities to an extreme. This conversion while within a converted estate yielded the first autobiography written in German, partly for (and with the help of) a nun, Elizabeth Stagel. The book has all the stylistic trappings of romance, adventures, and encounters dared in a hostile world. Conversion here summoned up tones more common in vernacular poetry: No love apart from suffering, no real suitor unless a sufferer, no real lover unless a martyr.[21] Suso's tamer Latin version, the *Horologium sapientiae*, known particularly for its meditative sequence on the passion, is extant still in some 250 Latin manuscripts, 70 Middle French, 70 Middle Dutch, and so on. The Middle-Dutch version in fact circulated primarily among the Modern-Day Devout, especially Devout women.[22]

Medieval conversion played out at two different, if intersecting, levels: life-forms making rival claims to perfection, and individual life-turns eliciting admiration as well as contempt. Johan Busch (1399–ca. 1480), author of the most influential chronicles of the Modern-Day Devout, recounted his own.[23] Born into a modestly well-to-do family in Zwolle, by age eighteen, so he reports, he had learned everything the local school had to teach, disputed successfully with two or three masters of Parisian training, and worked as a teaching assistant for the lower classes. His parents wanted to send him to university at Erfurt in hopes he would become a leader among their kin (*ut caput essem omnium amicorum et cognatorum nostrorum*). But Johan mused inwardly: suppose people do eventually greet me as "Sir Doctor" but I burn in hell, what would I have gained? He resolved to think hard about eternity, apparently in the vernacular (*Hoc enim uerbum "ewelike ende ommermeer" ad hoc me coegit*), and could not resolve his worries. So he decided to give up the world's delights to prepare for eternity. His parents and relatives, utterly dismayed, tried hard to dissuade him, especially his mother. "When you were young, she said, you only wanted to lie in bed and eat. You are not able to fast; do you want to kill yourself?" Or again: "You ought to be our leader, and now you want to abandon us?"[24] Whatever we make of his narrative ego, his story captures human and social tensions of which we must not lose sight.

Converts stirred up trouble particularly when they made their own way, as the Sisters and Brothers would. Margery Kempe did as well, across the Channel at about the same time. In a "little treatise" (*schort tretys*) penned in 1436 (the date it was recopied and polished) she claims the Lord had ordered her (Margery) to write down her "felyngys and revelacyons and the forme of her levying," so other "sinful wretches" might find in it "gret solas and comfort," particularly how the creature "was parfythly drawen and steryd to entren the wey of hy perfeccyon."[25] The narrative is of her "conversacyon,"[26] that word meaning (from biblical Latin's *conversatio*) a convert's "manner of life." An interim confessor doubted that a "sinful woman" could be so suddenly "converted," that God would prove so familiar (*homly*) in such a short time.[27] As nearly always with medieval converts, dress soon loomed up as a marker—to "take the habit," after all, short-hand for joining religion. She was told by the Lord to wear white. But it would make her stand out and bring charges of hypocrisy, she objected; the deity held that the more amazement she caused by loving him the more she pleased him.[28] Margery spent years going round to those perceived as authoritative to set out her form of life, to the anchorite Julian of Norwich, to clergymen, to masters, who all reportedly assured her it was acceptable, not deceitful (*no disseyte in hir maner of levying*).[29] She even laid it before the archbishop of Canterbury (*he fond no defawt therin but aprevyd her maner of levying*), only to find her confessor threatening to leave owing to all the ill talk.[30] At issue was not the possibility of conversion but the reality of it, here in an extraordinary, self-made, and (to many) annoying woman, and the anxiety her life-form generated, even apparently for her.

Conversion's meanings in the middle ages—from the personal experience of a life-turn to social estates as privileged life-forms, from turning laypeople to reconverting the professed—points to a socioreligious reality not reducible to a formula, also varying by time and place, class and gender. Herbert Grundmann drew attention to it with the label "religious movements." This modern term brought into focus medieval phenomena previously located too narrowly inside orders (a history written then mostly by professed men) or defined too exclusively as heresy (a history written mostly by protestants or critics). Grundmann knew he was dealing with "conversions" but reserved that term for extraordinary individual cases. He had no taste for institutionalizing or any turn to orders, and generally treated heresy apart, as born of a questing impulse.[31] Constable, with the term "reformation," has sought to capture the sweep of conversion in the twelfth century, especially its diversity, with its individual and institutional expressions treated together.[32] Foucauld, with little nod to medieval conversion but reared in a Catholic environment, reproduced elements of the older dynamic in intriguing ways, the fragmented person in tension with an oppressive collective environment, forced or moved to construct an alternative "care for the self."[33] But few modern accounts (Constable excepted) capture the continuities between the personal and the institutional. Most indeed dispute it. Medieval conversion certainly engendered contradictions, Francis, for instance, wanting a Rule but hardly an order. Still, medieval converts did not see a life-turn and a life-form as necessarily at odds (as we post-Revolutionary, post-Romantic moderns tend to do). Sisters and Brothers introduced an unusual life-form (communes) to support the ends of their life-turn.

Master Geert was not the only "unquiet soul" in the fourteenth century.[34] Catherine of Siena gathered a mixed lay and clerical circle, chiefly through teaching and letter-writing in Italian.[35] Lollards in England repudiated all professed converts as "sects" and "private religious," hoping to assemble "true Christians" around "poor priests." In Bohemia such teachings precipitated open rebellion and a fiery destruction of religious houses, but also lay religious communes. Within every religious order reformers called Observants formed separate networks to pursue their ends, generating the next generation of religious leaders (San Bernardino, Savonarola). Notable is the synchronicity. These phenomena got underway mostly in the 1370s, then gathered momentum into the 1410s/20s and beyond. Elsewhere I suggested that all this constituted a crisis in the received notions of medieval conversion.[36] However helpful that interpretive angle, the word "crisis" gets bandied about too easily, masking more than it reveals. The Modern-Day Devout were self-conscious converts, anxious to convert others, who knew implicitly the medieval tradition of conversion, and found it wanting in their own day. Here we might summarize those earlier life-forms schematically: New monks and canons after the year 1100 withdrew for prayer and contemplation; new mendicants after 1200 set up shop in cities to preach, teach, and hear confession; new mystics, Free Spirits, and spiritual Franciscans around 1300 yearned for a realm of freedom beyond matter and duty. The Devout ended up contesting with friars, dissociating from beguines, and fearing Free Spirits; and yet their vision silently incorporated elements from all three.

Converts in the Low Countries

In the years 1190–1230 a revolutionary wave of converts convulsed Europe. Friars transformed the religious and social landscape of thirteenth-century European cities, as did beguine women in the Low Countries. Their forms broke with a centuries-old commitment to *stabilitas*, the pledge to cloister one's self for life. They also espoused religious poverty in new ways, whether disavowing ownership and endowment (Franciscans) or incorporating it (beguines). Francis acted penance out in public streets rather than a cell. Dominic organized a band of mobile brother-priests dedicated to preaching, confessing, and studying, with an eye to bringing back the wayward.[37] Marie d'Oignies pursued fulltime spiritual life as a married woman, separating herself from fleshly commerce with her husband while engaging in charitable activity and spiritual guidance, the first of many female recluses in the Low Countries,[38] comparable to the "living saints" of Italian towns.[39] Waldo and his followers established preachers and communities alongside or within parishes, while the "good men" and "good women" called Cathars pursued an intense spiritual ascesis apart from an earth-bound church, these Cathar leaders circulating locally (and clandestinely) to teach and guide. Friars and beguines became, selectively, allies, beguines held up as, thus Jacques de Vitry introducing Marie's life, an alternative to Cathar "good women." In Rhineland towns beguines frequently located near a friar's church (especially Franciscan), or arranged for friars to serve as their preachers and confessors. Friars and Waldensians, by contrast, competed fiercely, the latter driven into mountains or remote villages; and friar-inquisitors turned viciously on Cathars. Friars themselves emerged as the new image of conversion, ubiquitous agents of religious culture, in schools as well as neighborhoods (sermons, devotions, images, vernacular texts). Reliant locally on patrons, they acted internationally in networks. They instituted a collective decision-making apparatus (general chapters), prepared themselves intellectually in *studia*, and acted under an umbrella of papal protection.

By the 1310s friars had founded nearly three thousand houses, half of them Franciscan. Dominicans tended to locate in larger cities or more well-heeled quarters closer to commercial or political power, Franciscans in smaller cities or craftsman's quarters closer to middling and laboring peoples, though a major city could support both and perhaps two or three others as well (Augustinians, Carmelites, Sack-brothers until they were banned). Committed in principle to living from alms rather than landed endowments, friars proved adept at urban investment, taking gifts in exchange for spiritual services (prayers, masses, burials). Recent scholars, mostly in Germany, have traced their exploitation of urban economies to support ever more complex operations.[40] Friars had entered the Low Countries from the south and east in the 1220s, their houses and support networks well-studied in Flanders.[41] Most towns in the north acquired one or the other, Utrecht welcoming both by 1240. Franciscans went to Dordrecht, to Groningen in the 1240s, Kampen in the 1290s, Deventer about 1300; Dominicans to Haarlem and Zutphen in the 1280s, to Groningen about 1310.[42] Their immense churches competed with town parishes (in this region frequently a single church, St. Bavo in Haarlem, St. Walburg in Zutphen, St. Michael in Zwolle), especially over burials and fees. Townspeople welcomed mendicants as offering spiritual opportunities beyond parish routines. Thus Geert Grote arranged for a private "box" in Deventer's Franciscan church near his family home. There he could follow the office, see the Eucharistic consecration, and make confession.[43]

By the later fourteenth century, five generations along, friars were wearing their welcome thin: a pretense of poverty while constantly begging for money and investing in city bonds, intellectual arrogance, international connections, inquisitorial interference. Antimendicancy, present from the beginning, sharpened in tone, while satire abounded in the vernacular (Jean de Meun, Boccaccio, Langland, Chaucer). Secular clerics rejoined the battle. Richard FitzRalph's "Defense of Curates," preached before the curia at Avignon in November 1357, ruthlessly attacked mendicants for economic hypocrisy and pastoral intrusion, a reality he had confronted about 1348/50 as archbishop of Armagh. His tractate/ sermon, derived from a longer work on "the poverty of the Savior," gained audiences across Europe, translated into English amid the Lollard affair.[44] The *Reformation Kaiser Siegmunds*, a vernacular cry for reform at the Council of Basel (1439), advocated enclosing friars (contrary to their whole way of life), though with their worship services and ministries still open to laypeople.[45]

With the same conversionary fervor as the early friars, and in the same years (1190–1240), urban women entered upon lives of spiritual intensity in phenomenal numbers, most unprofessed, living as recluses and in quietude, though also active in hospices and alms-houses. In Italy no single name prevailed. In the Low Countries, German-speaking lands, and Provence these unprofessed converts came to be called "beguines."[46] The label was generic, a word that designated or smeared or both,[47] derived from a word for "mumbling," according to Gysseling,[48] thus not unlike "lollard." This suggests that their private prayer particularly caught peoples' attention, lay women saying under their breath the Psalms or little hours of the Virgin, not the ordinary layperson's "Our Father" or the cleric's Latin office.[49] Beguine life varied by region, even within towns. Not an international order, not free as women to pursue university learning, they relied upon private resources and struck agreements with town magistrates and parish priests.[50] In Montpellier and Narbonne such women (*beguins*) formed close associations with radical Franciscans, in Strassburg with mystic teachers. Individuals might live in private houses, in a "convent" housing several women, and in various private arrangements (five sorts in Neumann's typology for Mainz[51]). In the Low Countries they set up self-enclosed court complexes with their own church and priest.[52] The founders were often women of means with access to power (gentry or patrician). But the life attracted ever more of lesser means, so that beguine settlements came to mirror social conditions across the urban spectrum: some women owning their own places and living off rents, many working for a living (usually textiles), not a few on the dole. Walter Simons, drawing upon sources across three centuries, has suggested persuasively that up to a quarter were moderately well-off (some very well-off), half poor, and a quarter indigent seeking a semirespectable life.[53]

Most astonishing were the numbers: 205 documented foundations in the southern Low Countries between 1220 and 1320, 14 in the county of Holland, 70 or so in the city of Cologne, 85 in Strassburg, 28 in Mainz, nearly 120 for the area around Lake Constance. Reichstein counted a grand total of 636 (!) in three hundred towns or localities across medieval Germany.[54] The house at Paris, said to hold a thousand women, attracted distinguished preachers from the university, their sermons for the year 1271–72 recorded.[55] The beguine courts at Brussels and Louvain may have held as many as two thousand persons each (the same number claimed for Strassburg in 1318)—this reckoned from a letter of the 1270s counting prayers for a departed soul. Of a city's population, Simons reckons, they could represent between one and seven percent.[56] Local city councils oversaw statutes, the women still lay, a town thus not losing people or property to clerical immunity nor the parish its members to religious houses. Beguines lived in towns, yet made up their own "city of ladies" (so called at Dendermonde in the 1270s);[57] independent, yet locally regulated; near family, yet separate from the lay world. They brought their own bed and cookware if they had them, possibly a prayer-book, often working in textiles. They also took in young girls, forming them in manners and morals, occasionally in letters—this highly valued by townspeople, cited in their defense at Ghent.[58] In 1245 the parish priest at Tongeren, acting on the beguines' own request, established a walled enclosure, and permitted them to receive spiritual services at a nearby hospice chapel. Attending the parish had required that they walk through crowded streets and marketplaces; their purpose, however, was "contemplation of the divine," distance from "the disorder and clamor of laypeople."[59] The beguine estate, in short, offered a place of refuge for urban women, for the singularly pious but also for the widowed, orphaned, jilted, or destitute.

Beguines occupied a fragile but recognized place in these urban societies. In the middle of the world's sea, a cardinal legate at Cologne said in 1251, these women risked dangerous waves of temptation, unguarded by cloister walls, unbound by a Rule.[60] The Dominican friar Humbert of Romans saw lay women, unprofessed, focused on things spiritual. In a model sermon he took as his text "those who fear the Lord convert their heart to him" (Sirach 21:7), and praised these women who in the middle of a perverse people led a holier life than most, solicitous for their souls while others sank into worldly busyness.[61] But beguines also met with scorn, lampooned as "gray" (wordplay on their garb), also as hyperpious.[62] Critics also worried about the talk or teaching that went on inside their communities in the vernacular.[63] In 1274 Gilbert of Tournai (the bishopric responsible for Bruges and Ghent), complained that beguines loved "subtleties and novelties," even discussed in public places a French Bible (himself possessing one full of dubious glosses deposited with stationers in Paris for transcribing).[64] In 1439 the author of the *Reformation Kaiser Siegmunds*, still another take, thought they represented "idle mouths." They accepted alms, flattered Franciscans with attention, hid under the guise of Franciscan Tertiaries, lit candles, paraded before people in the guise of holiness. They should be placed under a Rule and enclosed—or forbidden, all this a century after they had already come under official censure.[65]

Throughout the thirteenth century the church dealt piecemeal and contradictorily with these "converts commonly called beguines" (*sorores conuerse que begine uulgariter appellantur*).[66] Churchmen noted particularly their voluntary turn to virginity outside vows (*uirginibus . . . per Teutonium constitutis*), whence the incipit for a papal privilege from Gregory IX in 1233 (*Gloriam uirginalem*) granted occasionally to protect local communities.[67] But at Fritzlar in 1244 a synod held that women not enter this estate until age forty, thus past childbearing if not marriage,[68] apparently wary of women who might change their minds (as they could in principle, with no vow). At Osnabrück clerics and laypeople attacked the women for their dedication to chastity (*cultui castitatis opposita*), and an episcopal privilege of 1251, while echoing *Gloriam virginalem*, recognized the estate as properly coming under local bishops.[69] Still beguine foundations and numbers grew steadily, and we must be careful of generalizing about them. We have bare-boned legal documents attesting to foundations and properties. We have the lives of eleven women, all from the thirteenth century, much used in modern research but hardly read, so far as we can tell, among beguines. We have statutes agreed to by civic or parish authorities, on the whole not well studied. And we have three writers, Hadewijch, Mechthild of Magdeburg, and Marguerite Porete, extraordinary thinkers in Dutch, Low German, and French, who led lives in tension with ordinary beguines.[70] Jan Ruusbroec of Brussels wrote a small treatise "On Twelve Beguines."[71] Ruusbroec's mother lived in Brussels' large beguine court, and he may echo talk he overheard there. He began in rhyming verse, portraying beguines as speaking variously of their lover Jesus, some pining, some feeling abandoned, some knowing him. Ruusbroec presented them with vernacular teaching on what he called "pure contemplation" (*scouwen*). Such "heavenly conversation" graced "the estate of good beguines" as they once were, some still living so "in these years" (mid-fourteenth century). Too many of "ours" have gone off the path, become a scandal to Jesus, he says.[72] By this he seems to have meant in their practice as much as in teaching, too many who were arrogant or stubborn or complaining or easily angered, conduct "not befitting this estate."

Beguines made no formal promise of chastity (as, say, a proper recluse did), nor any commitment to poverty as such. Meersseman first documented converts in thirteenth-century Italy with no name or Rule as such but statutes, "penitents" neither religious nor fully lay.[73] As Pope Honorius III put it in 1221, certain persons in Italy widely called "brothers [or, sisters] of penance,"[74] inspired to this "*affectum*" by the Lord, "converted to penance within the world, assigning to it [penance] their whole time."[75] Engaging in penitential acts lifelong, not just at Lent or after a public crime like other laypeople, they were freed by this papal privilege from duties in civic life—bearing arms, swearing oaths, serving in public office—and exempted as well from interdicts, though bound still to parish priests and tithes. Gregory IX (1227) referred to this form of life as "their religion" and a "way of perfection," and he impugned "worldly people" who "vigorously attacked" them and their privileges.[76] Town leaders were in fact not pleased. Florentine authorities reportedly forced (*compellit*) some to act nonetheless as ambassadors, swear oaths, or undertake civic acts.[77] In Tuscany Osheim found converts sometimes suspected of dodging fiscal or civic responsibility.[78] At Bologna by 1251 some were attempting to bequeath the exempt status of "penitent" to sons and grandsons, taking it as a group privilege.[79] Penitent converts seemed model semi-lay Christians to some in their day,[80] scam-artists to others. The middling way was never easy.

Around 1300 people called Free Spirits, as well as mystical teachers and a party of Franciscans called Spirituals, came on the scene. Though usually treated as representing forms of false teaching, they too sprang from deeply conversionary impulses. Spiritual Franciscans held that only conversion to poverty on the model of Francis made one Christ-like; more, that the corrupted church, as Joachim and Olivi foresaw, would be converted wholesale by divine force in the endtime, and soon.[81] Free Spirits and mystics sought utter union with God. For them what began in conversion as a loving yearning came to transcend all love and will so a person's "within" (the soul) merged indistinguishably with the "beyond" (the deity). Such a self could be turned inside-out only if, paradoxically, all striving, even the subjective will itself, was annihilated. Advocates of this position were said to travel about, gathering groups into "conventicles," teaching an ennobled state of freedom beyond ordinary obligation, even, in bolder formulations, beyond religious rites and moral virtues. While Spiritual Franciscans operated mostly in Provence and Italy, Free Spirits and mystics circulated in the region of the Modern-Day Devout.

Scholars have reached little clarity on the people called Free Spirits. Legislation first formulated at the Council of Vienne in 1311, publicly promulgated as law for teaching in October 1317 (*Ad nostrum*), described persons in "Germany" claiming a state of contemplative perfection such that ordinary obligations impeded their freedom of Spirit; if, for instance, they were to descend from contemplative heights to reverence the eucharist with bodily gestures. They also need not wait for the next life to enjoy beatific vision, need no longer pray or give alms or obey, and might use the body indifferently as a thing external.[82] Whether actual claims or misrepresented teaching, they share points with Marguerite Porete's *The Mirror of Simple Souls.* Its author likely came from Valenciennes (a French-speaking part of the medieval Low Countries), and had been burned in Paris a year earlier (June 1310) after refusing to answer for fifteen propositions drawn from her book and condemned by twenty-one Parisian masters. Six of them took part in the discussions at Vienne. Tarrant found, however, that the original conciliar version of 1311 was aimed at "Beghards" with no mention of "beguines." In a precocious and influential book Lerner depicted the Free Spirit phenomenon, on the whole, as a terrified projection of prelates, inquisitors and theologians. By ruling against matters they heard rumored, or feared, or failed to grasp, they in effect invented it, providing inquisitors with teachings and people to look for (and find).[83] Wehrli-Johns has proposed to find Beghards arising instead from a wing of Franciscans, Italian in origin, called "Apostles" or Fraticelli, whose critique of a material church issued in a vision of the human spirit set free by radical penitential poverty.[84] For this scholar the defining moment came not in *Ad nostrum* but an episcopal letter generated at Strassburg in August 1317 (*Lecte coram nobis*).[85] The bishop had reported on an inquisition carried out in his diocese against a worrisome sect of "beghards" and "swestriones" (such people also condemned at Mainz in 1310 and at Cologne in 1307), Franciscan Apostles in fact, she suggests, just entering the German Rhineland.

Marguerite Porete was tried first in Cambrai, the bishopric to which Brussels (and Jan Ruusbroec) belonged, her book consigned to the flames sometime between 1296 and 1306. In it she imagined a soul moving through a conversionary turn to a point beyond turning, "annihilated" in God. She imagined descent and ascent all at once: "she has fallen from grace into the perfection of the work of the virtues, and from the virtues into love, and from love into nothingness, and from nothingness into the illumining of God, who regards himself with eyes of his majesty, and who in this has illumined her with himself. And she is so wholly dissolved into him that she sees neither herself nor him."[86] Such a soul's will, she states, possessing no will of its own, lives in total freedom, ennobled in God. She posited seven stages of spiritual progress, beginning with folk tied to the virtues and sacraments, much of her book focused on a fifth stage where the soul confronts its "nothingness" in the face of the "allness" of God. Souls so illumined make up the tiny "Holy Church" over against a "larger church" of clergy and parish observances. "It is, she says, a very long journey from the land of the virtues, which the forlorn possess, to the land of the forgotten and naked and brought to nothing or the illumined, who are in that higher state of being where God is, abandoned by himself in himself." In this book

Marguerite self-consciously set herself against two dominant false ways, learned clerics who believed they could come to God by reason rather than love, and the masses pursuing God through duty and striving, not just parishioners but also earnest converts like beguines. About people avid to cultivate spiritual affections, whether ardently or anxiously, she remarks: "those who love are deceived by the tenderness of their affection, which prevents them from ever coming to true knowledge." As for the freed and ennobled, "such a soul has attained to the greatest perfection of life, and has come nearer to the Far-Near when Holy Church can take no example whatever from her life."[87] That is, even saintly exemplarity, for which all converts in some sense strived in word and deed, impeded union. Hers was, arguably, the most radical critique of inherited conversionary conceptions in two centuries or more. And some churchmen including Godfrey of Fontaines understood it, even regarded it as not unorthodox, if also not easy reading and not for everyone. She—like Eckhart and the circles at Brussels and Strassburg treated below—represented a radical turn inward, away from activity in the world, after a century of its opposite led by friars and beguines.

Those charged at Strassburg in 1317 included some actual or apparent Franciscans, some married and single people, some living in apart "conventicles." They called themselves "Children" or "Brothers" or "Sisters" given to "Free Spirit and voluntary poverty." And they held that the Christianity of their day was utter foolishness (*Christanitas est fatuitas, et sic in vulgari "die Cristenheit ist ein toerin"*).[88] Some likened themselves "truly and by nature to Christ himself"; some held that a good layman could confect the eucharist as well as (or better than) a bad priest; that a person should trust in the "heart" or "interior instinct" more than the Gospel as then preached; while some excused themselves from normal practices ("fasting on Friday, obeying a husband, praying aloud regularly, earning their bread by labor"). Bishop John ordered that these conversionary partisans put off their unusual garb, their households be seized and given to poor-relief, they recant and live like "other mendicants" or "normal Christians," and his own people cease listening to their songs or using their writings. He also distinguished "Free Spirits" from Third-Order Franciscans and "upright lay beguines in the world" (*beginis honestis secularibus*).[89] Eckhart, resident in Strassburg during the years 1313–22, possibly played a role in the investigation.[90] Intriguingly he had resided at the Dominican convent in Paris the year after Marguerite's burning and almost certainly knew her work. He was absorbed by similar questions, what it meant to empty one's self, how the "grounded" soul and the divine were ultimately one, how Christ was born in the heart.[91] Of the three sermons by Eckhart translated early and often into Middle Dutch, one

(*Beati pauperes spiritu*) contained his most daring formulations on "poverty of spirit," several of those manuscripts from Devout houses.[92]

Free Spirits and Beghards haunted the later fourteenth-century church. Their ideas enticed. An anonymous fourteenth-century work written in Middle Dutch between 1325 and 1340 called *Master Eckhart and the Layman* staged a fictitious dialogue between a serious-minded "layperson" posing questions and a "Master Eckhart" offering answers. Its author was annoyed by arrogant "habits" (professed religious, *abiten*) and proud priests (*paepscap*). The "layman" asked "Eckhardt" about Beghards and Sisters who, he says, the "habits" and "priests" were persecuting, even forcing some back into the world and into sin. This scandalized "good people," defined as those living by the highest reasons of their soul. Beghards and Sisters, the layman claims, travel around Cologne, though he had not seen them nor wished to. They wandered the land seeking their bread, unashamedly doing great penance, illumined with heavenly wisdom and godly knowledge, if sometimes speaking too boldly and openly before people who did not comprehend. "Eckhart," interestingly and unusually, ducked this question, instead berating evil men for persecuting or disparaging the good simply because they were different.[93] The "layperson" also reported once hearing a Dominican preach before the Benedictine sisters at Rijnsburg (outside Leiden), denouncing Beghards and Sisters as heretics. This seemed to him disgraceful: better to talk to the Sisters about becoming illumined. Even if some Beghard or Sister on occasion fell (as do many "habits") or spoke unguardedly of God, he added, this was no reason to account them evil. The "habits" were jealous of the good reputation (*den goeden name*) these people enjoyed, annoyed that, as laypeople, they talked of God.[94] Holiness and godly wisdom have nothing to do, he insisted repeatedly, with being "lettered."[95] The one complete manuscript, very late (Brussels, Royal Library MS 888–90), belonged to a house in the Devout tradition (Bethlehem at Herent outside Louvain), where the dialogue was copied with mystical works of John "the Cook" from Groenendael. Of the eight manuscripts with fragments, often excerpting the juiciest "Free Spirit" bits, one, a miscellany probably from the Delft region, includes sayings ascribed to Geert Grote.[96]

For Geert Grote and his contemporaries Free Spirit teachings hung ominously in the air. In the expanded version of statutes for Sisters in his house at Deventer, those women were forbidden to stay there who held to or taught any of the eight articles ascribed to beguines (*Ad nostrum*) or the "twenty-eight" charged against Eckhart or who possessed books of such teachings (said to be "plentiful" in "German" lands) or who pursued God in "naked emptying out" (*in bloter ledicheit*) rather than in virtue and penance and works of mercy, this sort supposedly "found all around here in German lands." Authorities were to watch out for Sisters who hung out with or entered into "secret association" with Beghards.[97] Whether or not these additions came from Grote himself (a contested point), and sprang from a real incident or vague fears, it comported with his own wary stance. Midway in his short preaching career he attacked an Augustinian friar from Dordrecht preaching at Kampen, charging him with "Free Spirit" ideas, for instance, that "perfection was founded on pure nothingness." This move only earned him the anger of local residents, whereupon he urged the bishop to shut down this friar as an "ignorant pseudo-preacher." He concocted a plan to sneak into the audience, along with a notary, while the friar toured through Zwolle, to take down suspect declarations. The friar initially evaded charges, but Grote confronted him in court at Utrecht, then reportedly with success.[98] For him these ideas represented the false way to conversion, misleadingly inviting, avoiding penance. The Modern-Day Devout were consistently wary of the perfect life conceived as a free and limitless emptying into God, transcending penance and discipline.

Circles of Converts at Strassburg and Brussels

From the 1380s the Modern-Day Devout would form circles of converts living together. A generation earlier in Strassburg "Friends of God" had gathered around Rulman Merswin, and in Brusssels around Jan Ruusbroec and his writings. The first reveals some intriguing parallels to the Devout, the second was of direct influence. At Strassburg and at Brussels we find writings in the vernacular, the quest for a satisfying form of life, struggles to sustain it outside parish or convent, along with mystical literature moved still in part by the aspirations of the generation around 1300. The lands at either end of the River Rhine existed in a kind of polar complementarity, each a region with a distinct language and culture: the Lower Lands (*Niderland*) of the Rhine delta spreading outward from Cologne and Utrecht, the Upper Lands (*Oberland*) extending from Constance and Basel to Strassburg. Contact was comparatively easy, and cultivated by spiritual circles on either end. The Devout would eventually acquire knowledge of Tauler and Eckhart as well as Merswin's *Nine Rocks.* Tauler, a Dominican preacher and disciple of Eckhart, came to visit Ruusbroec, possibly already in 1346, as reputedly did other "masters and clerics from Strassburg, Basel, and the Upper Rhine," finding at Ruusbroec's Groenendael "the experience of true wisdom."[99] By 1350 a team had translated Ruusbroec's "Espousals" and "Temptations" into Oberland German.[100] Other visitors to the Low Countries took Hadewijch back with them (chiefly the Letters), as they also acquired Mechthild's *Flowing Light of Divinity* and translated her Low German into our only surviving vernacular text.[101] The Friends' library in Strassburg in addition possessed a key 1366 copy of Suso's *Exemplar*, though, interestingly, no known copy or translation of Marguerite. In short, much of the mystical vernacular literature that has gripped scholars this past generation passed through, was translated by, or preserved in, the tiny circle of converts in Strassburg and Basel called "Friends of God"—including Henry of Nördlingen. We see there—with Ruusbroec's circle in Brussels—self-made communities and self-designed reading circles.

A century ago these "Gottesfreunde" gained lavish attention for their imagined exoticism, as well as their searing critique of medieval religion, interpreted as "pre-reforming" and "lay." Scholarly sobriety has since reduced them to a mostly literary phenomenon, some thirty vernacular texts of limited distribution, many fairly derivative[102]—perhaps not altogether fairly, but no fresh historical approach has yet been attempted.[103] Rulman Merswin (1307–82) came from the merchant elite in Strassburg. About age forty he came to the "single-minded view" that he "wanted to do penance," a "turn" (*ker*) away from the "natural pleasures" of society as well as trading and profit-taking.[104] Initially he launched upon such debilitating austerities as nearly to ruin his physical and mental health. Tauler restrained Merswin lest he "go mad," and their careers evolved together. Merswin suffered through bouts of real religious doubt. Only in his fourth year, about 1351, did he gain "a peace in the Spirit beyond nature." He immediately felt "forced by God" (*van gotte betwngen*) to write "little books to aid his fellow humans."[105] This conversion had resolved itself in calling a lay merchant to write. "A man in the upper lands" (*einen menschen in obber landen*) came to visit him, heard his story, and enjoined him to write up his conversionary years, Merswin's work then sealed until his death.[106] This comes to us in his own telling, reputedly in his own hand, a manuscript quire discovered in a small chest after his death and kept by the community as a relic (*heiltume*).[107] The booklet appears never to have circulated outside the community, though Merswin had addressed it to "all Christian people."[108]

This book set the tone for the Friends (the quire itself inserted into the community's "memorial cartulary"). The writings they generated often turned on conversion, tales of merchants, knights, recluses, priests, theological masters, or Jews, in a tone closer to "lay." One ("Zweimannenbuch") recounted the meandering "inner turn" of two men, construed as Merswin and the confident who had enjoined him to write. Another ("The Five-Man Book of the Friends of God") told how the "man from Oberland" retreated with four others (a knight of long-standing acquaintance, a knight whose wife had just died, a converted Jew, and a practitioner of church law) to set up a society of Friends.[109] But the most famous and influential piece recounted in dialogue form how an unlearned layman converted a hypocritical cleric (*pfaffen*) and master of theology, the cleric said to be Tauler (falsely), the layman Merswin's "Friend of God from the Oberland." Bits of this "Meisterbuch" would come to preface early printings of Tauler's sermons, giving it a wide reading. When this converted master of theology began to preach anew, his first words echoed the opening of Ruusbroec's *Espousals.*[110]

The Friends produced no sermons or ascetic exercises but stories and dialogues shot through with mystical ideas.[111] They focused repeatedly on the negative dialectic in the conversionary dynamic, deep dissatisfaction issuing in ardent critique of their era. Many writings were ascribed to the Friend from Oberland,[112] described as "entirely unknown to the world but thereafter my [Merswin's] "*heimellicher*" friend."[113] The medieval word *heimellicher*, often translated "secret" or "mysterious," meant (also in Dutch) what came from the household (*heim*) rather than the public sphere (*offentlich*), thus "private" rather than "public," much like the older English word "privy" as in "privy council." This "privy friend" was perhaps, as Steer suggests, Henry of Nördlingen in fact or in model,[114] or possibly an alter ego to lend authority to lay religious writings. The only work certainly by Merswin to gain wider distribution, also in Middle Dutch and Latin, is called the *Book of Nine Rocks*, signifying nine elevations moving from the world to the heights of God.[115] The book uses a dialogue format and is made up of "discourses" (*rede*). Its central portion (more than a quarter of the whole) relentlessly critiqued church and society, estate by estate, beginning with popes, bishops, friars, clergy, and beguines, working through to secular rulers and ending with women and marriage. It turned entirely on the faults (*gebreste*) of Christendom "in these times," its ordinances in total ruin,[116] perverted rather than converted (*alle ordenungen in der cristenheite sint umbe gekeret*).[117] Not in several hundred years had Christendom been so wicked. Would not a pious and simple Jew or a heathen be more pleasing to God than all these false Christians?[118] Only a few were making their way up. The first rock held people not in mortal sin, a divider familiar to laymen. Those caught below this rock, swirling in deadly sin and misery with only the name of Christian, outnumbered those on the first rock, according to Merswin, by more than a hundred to one.[119] Those who had climbed to the second rock were people who disciplined their natures (*ire nature twingent*) to turn from the world, yielding their wills to a Friend of God who knew the way.[120] Seven more elevations loomed upward toward the few clinging to a tiny ledge in the presence of God. Were it not for them, Merswin asserted, God would have allowed Christendom to perish, and their number was fewer now than only a short time ago.[121] What Christendom most needed, what every church or civic leader should be seeking, was a teacher, a guide to the true spiritual life (*einen lerer fundent der ein lebbemeister were*). Hence the opening words of the book: "All Christian people should hear the warning teaching" found therein and improve their lives (*mus sin leben bessern*).[122] Such teachers could be found, the book contended, if heads of state and burghers in towns would only look in earnest[123]—a not so subtle plea for people to turn to Friends to serve as *Lebmeistern* (spiritual guides: a term widely applied to Tauler).

Merswin, while portraying himself as called—or "forced"—to write, remained a doer, the merchant-patrician. In the 1360s Merswin purchased a dilapidated convent in the middle of the city called "Green Isle" and rebuilt it for himself and for "friends of God" with permission eventually of the bishop and Pope Urban V. It was to be a "house of refuge (*ein husz der flucht*) for honest, good-hearted men, lay or clerical, knight or servant, who desired to flee the world and improve their lives (*ir leben zuo bessernde*)"—echoes of language found in his *Nine Rocks*. As founder and owner Merswin underwrote the facility, while Friends spent their own money on meals.[124] Initially four secular priests provided spiritual leadership. About its in-house life little has survived, though, as several scholars have pointed out, the *Five-Man-Book* hints at, or projects, the ideal. The "ordinance" these "brothers" kept was like that of "secular priests" living in a communal society (*in einer gemeinen geselleschaft*, echoing Ps. 133:1).[125] The term "Friend of God," scriptural in origin, used by Eckhart, even more by Tauler, had pointed toward special spiritual intimacy, not to be confused with theological learning or ecclesiastical rank.[126] Now it came to designate as well an inner circle. Among them divine "ordinances" would be kept, setting them apart from those supposed to be the "religious." Merswin turned neither to friars nor beguines, despite their prominence in his city. Of mendicants he said in his *Nine Rocks* that "very few knew the right way and followed it in how they lived," now being too people-pleasing, mostly too easy in confession and penance, too eager for gain.[127] As for women's houses, they had sunk so low that a real Christian had to flee them.[128] As for beguines, they "ran about" and "chattered" a good deal but had no inner seriousness (*indewendiger zufugender ernest*), being consumed in self-possession (*eigenschaft*), meaning something like religious preoccupation or vanity.[129] What Merswin envisioned were "ordinances" and a circle of people prepared to observe them. From the Friends gathered in Strassburg around Merswin during the 1350s–60s we have a *Memorial* compiled after 1382 to record and ground the community's history.[130] Its present redaction passed through the hands of Merswin's co-worker and successor, Nicholas of Louvain (1382–1402), again a figure from the Low Countries.

This gathering of Friends was soon pressed to regularize. Merswin did not lose control, however. After considering his options, he entered into a contract with the Knights Hospitaler in 1371, the conditions supposedly "revealed in a remarkable document to the privy friend" and agreed to by Merswin (copied into their *Memorial*). This would be a house for both "honest knights" and upright citizens, largely of knightly or patrician status. [131] Three lay administrators (*pflegere dez huses*)—initially Merswin and a relative and another patrician—oversaw it and retained absolute veto power, each *pfleger* to be replaced by a comparable person on death. Property dealings, an annual account of goods and finances, and admission of any brother needed their oversight. The Knights were to supply as many priests as deemed necessary. Should these Knights gain some imperial or ecclesiastical privilege, the house and its goods returned to the three administrators or their heirs. In effect, Knights Hospitaler afforded the status of a religious house and a guarantee of religious services—but on contract from Merswin and his fellow lay administrators. The actual negotiations in the 1370s–80s remain a little inscrutable since we have mainly the *Memorial* as redacted in the 1390s. But life there was to be conducted "according to the godly ordinances and intentions of the beloved illumined Friends of God and the founder, following the express saying of this document."[132] Its inhabitants saw themselves as an elite, the intimate "friends of God," their circle keeping the "ordinances," standing between almighty God and a punishing destruction of Christendom. Into their library and reading circle they gathered many of the finest vernacular writers, from Mechthild and Hadewijch to Henry of Nördlingen and Jan Ruusbroec as well as Suso and Tauler, not to speak of the nearly thirty booklets the Friends themselves composed. As a house of converts the Green Isle lasted only through the lifetime of its founder (d. 1382) and his co-worker (1402), then as a commandery of Knights into the eighteenth century. Self-made circles of converts outside a cloister were not easy to stabilize—or even accounted altogether permissible.

From the 1340s Jan (John) Ruusbroec (1293–81) ranked as the most prominent spiritual teacher in the Low Countries, and he too established a "friends" circle, a recent study has argued, comprised of readers and hearers scattered around Brussels who looked to him for counsel.[133] Ruusbroec grew up a student-cleric in the house of Jan Hinckaerts, across from the west front of St. Gudula in Brussels (now St. Michael's), schooled in chapter and ordained a priest at age twenty-five. As a chaplain he formed a household with Hinckaerts and a master named Frank van Coudenberg. He wrote first a school-like review of religious life called *The Kingdom of Lovers* (whose circulation he claimed to regret), then ten more works, two very lengthy, his masterly *Spiritual Espousals* and *Mirror of Eternal Salvation*.[134] With no university education or link to an international order, a lowly secular cleric writing with such power in the vernacular—this was a highly unusual achievement, and disciples ascribed it to inspiration, the Spirit speaking as he went for walks in the woods with his wax tablets. All of his work addressed converts, some professed (Franciscan nuns in Brussels), some unprofessed (beguines), some "falsely" converted (followers of Bloemaert and Marguerite). More, those outside orders who turned inward toward unity with God (*inkeer ende eenecheit behouden in gode*), while also serving fellow believers charitably, he ranked higher and nobler than those who pursued contemplation only for themselves.[135]

Ruusbroec did not write or preach for ordinary parishioners. In a work on the eucharist he gestured toward them, people he saw every day in the street, sometimes in church, parishioners who made their confession and communion once a year at Easter, who tried to avoid mortal sin and obey the teachings of the church, who "wanted to receive the holy sacrament according to the law and custom of good christian people."[136] But all his effort was focused on six other types, all converts, true or false, professed or unprofessed, their lives in order or disorder, each worried about how and how often to approach the altar. It was for them alone that he wrote, as he explicitly noted, those who wanted to live in the spirit (*ghi die inden gheeste leven wilt, want niemen anders en sprekic toe*).[137] He had no single word for such people, though he often characterized them as "turned within" (the *inghekeerde*). To become such a "sparkling stone" (Rev. 2:17) a person had to separate from sinners, typified as five-fold: people full of themselves and material life; knowingly in a state of mortal sin; unbelievers or false believers; shamelessly persistent in mortal sin; hypocrites giving only the appearance of living well.[138] What interested him were the spiritually intense.

Marguerite Porete and Jan of Ruusbroec lived in the same medieval diocese, Cambrai, she in the French-speaking town of Valenciennes, he in the Dutch-speaking town of Brussels. He was seventeen when she was put to death in Paris. He knew her case and work, whether in the French original (intelligible to him?) or in Latin or a lost Dutch translation.[139] Marguerite likely had come from a well-to-do household. Jan came from a village outside Brussels, of obscure parentage, possibly the illegitimate son of a cleric, entrusted early to the patronage of a burgher family active in Brussels' city council and collegiate church, the Hinckaerts.[140] Both Jan and Marguerite wrote exclusively in the vernacular, though conversant with teachings in Latin; both explored ultimate spousal union with God; both came under suspicion, she forced to burn the first version of her book and finally burned herself, he attacked posthumously by Chancellor Jean Gerson at Paris in 1399. Both knew and interacted with—he certainly, she presumptively—women called beguines. He reacted fiercely to Marguerite's work. Was it in part too uncomfortably near his own notions of a union apart from means or intermediaries (*sonder middel*)? Did he know people attracted to her "self-nihilating" way, even promoting it?

Ruusbroec was even more intensely aware of Heilwig Bloemaert just down the street from him, a potent woman teacher, attested in records between 1307 and 1335, a benefactress of beguines, with personal connections to the duchess of Brabant.[141] Bequeathed a house by her patrician family, Bloemart created a hospice for twelve women, her last will handled by the cleric with whom Ruusbroec lived, Jan Hinckaerts. This woman, according to an account written some eighty years later at Groenendael by Pomerius, enjoyed a wide following, went to communion with great acclaim and display, taught her followers from a special chair, and issued writings that had the "appearance of truth." When Ruusbroec took her on, he met stiff resistance locally from "numerous" adherents, some claiming healings after her death. She loomed unavoidably large in his mental and personal world into his early forties. Her teachings likely turned on notions of "free spirit" and "spousal love," with much reportedly about a spirit of liberty and a carnal love called seraphic (*de spiritu libertatis et nefandissimo amore uenereo quem et seraphicum appellabat*). Pomerius claimed to have seen her writings, and conceded that on first glance they seemed orthodox enough, so one could hardly lay bare (*denudare*) the truth about them unless you were graced, like Ruusbroec, with an ability to penetrate the "smoky text" (*fuco, scripta fucata*).[142] Her presence and circle, as much as anything, drove Ruusbroec to write. As for the writings Pomerius saw, some have suggested Hadewijch, a poet who used erotic imagery, her works definitely preserved in Groenendael circles; others, a version of Marguerite Porete given the talk of "smoky" and "seraphic" writing. Pomerius may also have confused either of their writings with stories of Bloemaert in Brussels. Or indeed Bloemart may have built her writings and teachings on Porete's.

In Brussels the contestation for adherents must have been tough, a patrician woman and a minor cleric, each speaking to the nature of conversion and divine union. Ruusbroec closed the second book of his *Spiritual Espousals* with a pointed attack just as Bloemart disappears from our records (dating of Ruusbroec's work itself being somewhat insecure). Certain people seek "rest," he says, as all creatures do, and find natural rest inside themselves, a state with no external sensible images, no activity in the higher senses, stillness without exercises inside or out. But this is mere sinking into emptiness, he objects, forgetting of self and God, not itself a sin but producing self-satisfaction and spiritual pride. Such persons may lead a hard life in penance and appear holy, but their state turns on self-possession and reward. Persons in such inner emptiness and self-preoccupation, he maintains, are fixedly "un-convertible" (*vaste blivet ombekeersam in eyghenheiden*). They cannot enter into union with God because they do not live in charity (his term for the love-bond with God as well as service to others).[143] It leads to perversion (*verkeertheit*) rather than conversion, these people thinking they are true contemplatives (*godscouwende*) and the "holiest alive," holding that they are "free" (*dat si vri sijn*) and one with God "apart from means" (also his chosen term), hence above the exercises of holy church as well its precepts and virtues. They, he explains, passively suffer (*pueren lidene*), allowing God to work in them, without any striving upward (toward God) or downward (toward neighbors), since to work would be "to impede God's work in them." So they think themselves not only free but poor in spirit (*arm van gheeste*)—a likely echo of Eckhart's sermon. They are not subservient to priests and prelates, though they appear so outwardly, and are inwardly subject to no one. They say that those striving after virtue and yearning toward God are still "imperfect." In short, circles of independent converts and readers in Brussels were not limited to those Ruusbroec initiated or approved.

Ruusbroec returned to the theme in his last major work, *The Mirror of Eternal Salvation*. He attacked "evil devilish" people who say they are as Christ or God, elevated above the sacraments, with no need of church practice. They, after driving out the fear and love of God, discover inside a state above reason without features or faculties (*onwise*), and think that all creatures, good and bad, angels and devils, will in the end become a single being without faculties, without knowledge or will (*een wiselooes wesen, een eenvuldege substantie der godheit*)—a strong echo here of Porete. Ruusbroec was emphatic: this "is the stupidest and worst notion (*opinie*) that ever was from the beginning of the world, and yet in it and things like it many people get deceived who appear religious/spiritual (*gheestelec*) and are worse than the devil." To people imagining they exist in an absolutely empty state (*ledig*) one should never give the sacrament or bury them as Christians, but "rightly burn them at the stake"! This plainly alluded to Porete, though also to Bloemart, her "ostentatious" taking of communion, her saintly cult after death. In a battle over true conversion the differences were breathtakingly close. For in speaking of people who came to communion he described approvingly some "turned within" (*ingeheerde menschen*) who walked before the face of God with "elevated free spirits" (*verhaven vrien gheeste*), masters of their own spirits and natures (*gheweldegh haers gheests ende haerre natueren*), having found "true peace."[144] Ruusbroec struggled to make clear how conversion in its liberating and unifying encounter with the divine differed from a featureless dissolving emptiness—his view of Bloemart/Porete.

For those who "who want to live in the spirit" he multiplied distinctions owing directly or indirectly to Bernard of Clairvaux's *On Loving God*. "Hired servants" do good, but in fear of hell, out of law and custom, for (heavenly) reward, whereas "faithful servants" act with true intentions, knowing the "law of love" and coming to feel grace and favor.[145] The church he knew in Brussels, Ruusbroec implied, harbored far too many hypocrites and hired servants. "Privy friends" (*heimelijcke vriende*), by contrast, moved beyond fear and precept to cleave to the "living counsels of God" with a loving inwardness.[146] His term, predating the community in Strassburg, must be grasped in its metaphorical fullness. It imagines a princely household with hired servants, faithful servants, and a circle of privy friends who honorably share in the inner counsels. "Privy friends" were, spiritually, not of two minds or conflicting allegiances (*van herten ghedeilt*) but totally turned inward (*gode gheheel ende te male inghekeert*).[147] "Rough" and uncomprehending souls, "those turned outward," Ruusbroec noted sharply, "reproach and judge" those "turned inward" as merely idle or empty (*ledig*)[148]—a glimpse here of perceptions and talk, as well as tensions, around Brussels. More intimate still than "privy friends" were "sons," the "secreted children of God" (*verborghene sonen gods*). Privy friends knew or cultivated inwardness, but with possessiveness (*eyghenschap*) still, a willed clinging. But hidden children "go over into the presence of God singularly in nakedness and with no means at all," a "singular staring into the godly brightness in a wide-open mental state."[149] "Privy friends" likely made up the largest portion of those with whom Ruusbroec dealt or for whom he wrote. They were held back from sonship, he suggests, by failing utterly to let go of their own busyness in seeking. Some may also have turned elsewhere for guidance, to Heilwig Bloemart, for instance. But her disciples, as he saw it, stared only into themselves, not into the brightness of God.

The person who wants to live in the "most perfect" estate of holy church must be "inward and spiritual," "raised up on high and contemplative," a state he calls "outflowing" and "common" (*ghemeyne mensche*).[150] But this had its social counterpart. In 1343 Jan of Ruusbroec, entering his fifties, already living in common with two clerical companions in Brussels, gave up his post, and retired into woods southeast of town, a "green valley" (Groenendael) with a history of hermits (also a chapel and dwellings), a site subject to the duke of Brabant. They abandoned the city—to the dismay of many, we are told—to pursue a quieter life. They found the people of Brussels noisy and distracting, had also suffered from a fellow chaplain with a bearish voice who sang off-key, forcing them in good conscience to reread their office or to do it in private.[151] The duke made the property over to Franco of Coudenberg, a canon who brought a substantial income to the venture. This was to be a "hermitage" for up to five men[152]—a term we find later in documents associated with the Green Isle. But for a group of men to live in common while still in secular habit, even priests, only provoked "scandal and derision." The duke's men, moreover, disrupted the woods with hunting and dogs. Pressure mounted to regularize. Under the leadership of Franco (who formally held the property) they agreed that their "way of life" could not be "stable" unless in their persons they made profession under some religious habit, also unless their properties went into the hands of a lay guardian while protected as "ecclesiastical" goods.[153] A commune outside religion, even of priests, seemed unworkable, or at least unstable, a scandal to many. Franco and Ruusbroec, under pressure, decided to take the habit of canons regular on the model of St. Victor in Paris.[154]

After his conversion (ca. 1378) Geert Grote traveled the hundred miles south to meet and talk with the elderly Ruusbroec at Gronendael. Later, recommending someone for acceptance at Groenendael, he declared it the healthiest and surest (*sanius, securius*) place he knew for religious life. He also passed the first part of "On the Twelve Beguines" (treated above) to a woman convert.[155] Grote read deeply in Ruusbroec, his Dutch glosses on the Psalms echoing the mystic's vocabulary. He undertook to translate the *Spiritual Espousals* into Latin, "word for word" he claims, over against one made by William Jordaens ca. 1360 in cooperation with Ruusbroec. In his prologue Grote noted that some of its teaching lay beyond his experience (*suam experientiam excedentibus*). Nonetheless he criticized Ruusbroec for showing more interest in the love of God than the fear, and silently redacted the text, correcting or eliminating certain terms or phrases.[156] Grote wrote Ruusbroec to warn that certain words had to be changed (*reformanda*) or expunged (*reprobanda*), that they were both in trouble with at least two theological masters for this text, further noting that he had "said this repeatedly to him" and even offered to help make changes.[157] All the same, Grote translated two more of Ruusbroec's works and a text on the virtues with materials from Ruusbroec and Eckhart.[158] And when a wealthy merchant asked Grote for help in setting up a religious house, he recommended the model of Groenendael.[159]

Converts Under Suspicion: Legislating Against Beguines and Free Spirits

The Modern-Day Devout entered a world suspicious of self-made religion. Families worried about losing sons or daughters to forms deemed out of the ordinary or undignified; town magistrates about losing lands, incomes, or personnel (taxes as well as watch and militia duties) to the dead-hand of the church; bishops and parish priests about jurisdiction and income lost to groups separating off as religious; the professed about prerogatives lost to those who claimed religion freelance; inquisitors about groups taking authority into their own hands. Regulating conversion was hardly new, but it first assumed church-wide forms in the thirteenth century. In 1215 Pope Innocent III declared that "lest too much diversity in religious orders bring serious confusion upon the church of God" no one hereafter was to "found a new religion" (= order). Any "convert" to "religion" (*quicumque ad religionem conuerti uoluerit*) was to submit to an approved Rule in an approved house.[160] This principle, though upheld to the end of the Middle Ages, and also against the Devout, proved problematic at once, most obviously with the rise of Franciscans, soon medieval Europe's largest religious order. At the general council of Lyon in 1274 churchmen acknowledged that new groups continued to emerge, most obviously mendicants and beguines. Yet they reiterated the ban (*Religionum diuersitatem nimiam*) and formulated a new catchphrase, that no one take the habit of a new religion (*habitum noue religionis assumat*).[161] In effect churchmen positioned a drive for order and control over against ever-burgeoning forms of conversionary *metanoia.*

The next general council, at Vienne in 1311, focused on religion-like groups, "Beghards" and "beguines," "Free Spirits" and "spirituals." The law (*Cum de quibusdam*) was confusing from the outset (quoted in the epigraph), its target unclear, though the ordinary gloss of 1322 (by an Italian) saw it as a blanket condemnation of the "beguine" way of life.[162] More than a century later Friar John Nyder, while taking laws against "beguines" for granted, noted that the term was widely used to smear pious people, especially any who remained chaste.[163] The prelates assembled at Vienne had left to Pope Clement V (previously archbishop of Bourdeaux and far from experiencing "German" beguines and beghards) the drafting of its final form, which emerged after March 1314, sent to universities for teaching late in 1317 by Pope John XXII.[164] It spoke of an estate of "women popularly called beguines" who promised no obedience, swore no poverty, professed no approved rule, were in no way "religious," and yet wore a distinct habit and clung to certain religious who favored them (friars). Some, an act of "insanity," also talked nonsense about key teachings of the faith. On the basis of "bad things heard about them" the pope and council herewith resolved to ban the "estate" (the word used four times: *status beguinagii*): women forbidden to enter it, friars to support it. Still, the law ended with a sentence declaring that it in no way barred faithful women doing penance from living uprightly in their dwellings with or without a promise of chastity.[165] An earlier version, Tarrant has shown, banned "convents" of beguines (thus a quasi-house) but not single women setting up independently.[166] A key concern plainly was full-scale convents or beguinages, outstripping religious houses in size in many towns, operating increasingly apart from parish oversight.

With *Cum de quibusdam* came *Ad nostrum*, damning eight teachings ascribed to Beghards and beguines in the German kingdom, beguines included only as an afterthought. It now also enjoined bishops and inquisitors in "German" regions to make inquest into this form of life.[167] A third document (*Sancta Romana*) followed in December 1317, wherein John banned groups associated with Spiritual Franciscans in Provence and Italy (*beguin*). Its scattershot wording impacted others as well, for it referred to suspect groups as "taking on the habit of a new religion," forming congregations (*congregationes et conventiculas facere*), electing their own superiors, setting up houses to live in common—a treasury of charges ripe for deploying later against the Devout. *Sancta Romana* also struck out at those who sought cover as Third-Order Franciscans or Penitents.[168] These laws have been treated in recent scholarship as together provoking a decisive turning-point, as shutting down beguines. In fact they brought no wholesale dissolution or destruction. Archival study shows nearly the reverse: a spike in foundations in the early fourteenth century prior to the coming of plague in 1348/50.[169] The lay author of the *Reformation Kaiser Siegmunds* would complain in the late 1430s that beguines, banned a century earlier, were still thriving and insufficiently regulated.

New papal law mostly enabled adversaries of these women to act out their rivalries and resentments. More, at issue was not only the standing of "beguines" and "Free Spirits," but the writ of papal law, how far it ran. Almost at once the papal court at Avignon heard about the confusion and its consequences, especially from Rhineland bishops. John XXII issued a quick response, a fourth document dated August 1318 (*Ratio recta*): "Right reason does not permit that the innocent be judged along with those causing harm" (see the epigraph). Evil-teaching beguines existed in Germany, he insisted. But "upright beguines" also existed: women dwelling apart (*segregate*), living together (*insimul*) in parental or rented houses, attending church even at night, obeying church authorities, not usurping a right to teach or preach, not mixed up in false teaching. These, he declared, should not be held in suspicion or harassed to the point of putting their chastity at risk—some apparently having already been driven into the street by local thugs or assaulted in the name of "banning." Such actions, he warned, only multiplied troubles in the present (*moderna*) church.[170] He then multiplied confusion anew, "permitting this sort of beguine" (*statum beguinarum huiusmodi . . . permittimus*) but "in no way thereby approving" the estate as such, he said, or in any way contradicting earlier rulings.[171] In practice beguine communities subjected to pressure now sought a formal declaration from authorities that they were not the evil sort, in Holland from the count, in Brabant from the duke.[172] With money or connections enough they might even, ironically, seek it from the pope. By December 1320 John or his court had worked out a standard document (*Cum de mulieribus*), a pastiche from earlier laws and letters (especially *Ratio recta*). Its first known instance was sent to the dioceses of Tournai and Cambrai, dense with towns containing beguinages.[173] This document also used the term *beghinagiis*, even though the pope had explicitly not rescinded his ban on the estate—making for a truly anomalous situation.

Bishops reacted variously. In Utrecht, by October 1318, Bishop Frederick (d.1323) declared the estate of beguines "reprobate" and attacked Franciscans for ministering to Third-Order women who, he said, seemed no different from beguines. He required that such women be severely examined, put on probation for a year, and made to live according to various stipulations (beginning with garb), in effect making them a form of "religious."[174] Everything changed in the first year of Bishop John of Diest (1323–40). Noting that the pope had "damned the beguine estate" but not faithful women who lived honestly, he declared that in his city these women were entirely above suspicion. They had petitioned him for protection against those molesting their persons and goods. The bishop now placed local Dominicans in charge of overseeing their lives and acting as their defenders, enjoining the friars to call on city magistrates if civil help were needed. To the women he granted the garb they wished to wear, the use of a bell, and the ministrations of a chapel, so long as the parish rector's rights were not abrogated, also a right to bar entrance to any undesirables.[175] This letter was subsequently reissued at Utrecht three times by successive bishops in much the same language (1343, 1364, 1380), now addressed to city magistrates—and it was deployed in other cities subject to the bishop such as Groningen. Magistrates were to protect beguines especially from physical harassment or hooligans breaching their outer wall at night.[176] Invoking the new laws in all their contradictions, this bishop had dexterously turned the legal threat into an occasion for lasting privileges.

Strassburg's story in all this gains in importance for its documents and its precedents. At first (22 July 1318) Bishop John spoke against mendicants but not beguines. By early August, however, his parish priests had united around the new laws to take on friars and beguines alike—as we know from a cache of documents preserved by an administrator (Henry of Saxony) and later partly entered into a copy of Friar Nicholas Eymeric's inquisitorial manual.[177] The bishop then queried Pope John directly, who responded (*Lecte coram nobis*) in a letter independent of *Ratio recta* at virtually the same time (August/September 1318). At Strassburg, the pope was told, there existed as many as two thousand beguines coming from every social class, nearly all of good reputation, living in their parent's homes, rented dwellings, and other apart arrangements. Adversaries had used the new law to force recluses enclosed for more than fifty years out into the street[178]—likely the incidents alluded to in *Ratio recta*. The bishop had not as yet set the new law in motion, an administrative act called *executio*, the law being effectively a dead letter until a bishop moved to "execute" or administer it locally. He had hesitated, he says, for "probable and special reasons," most likely his assessment of its fairness, or the futility of taking on this entire estate of women converts. But he learned by "experience," he reported a few months later, that by wavering "scandal and danger only mounted for us among the people."[179] This matter had touched a raw nerve in the city.

Yielding to mounting pressure, he resolved in January 1319 to ban the beguine estate as such on the strength of the new law. It had released forces he could not resist, parish priests who resented women turning to friars for spiritual care, laypeople hostile to their hyperpiety or apart status. The women had now to make it publicly manifest, the bishop declared, that they were giving up this estate, putting off any special habit or garb, attending their local parishes, "conforming in all matters to other Christian women." The letter, addressed notably to diocesan clergy, in effect yielded to them, a ruling they could read aloud in their parishes.[180] An apart status for hundreds of laywomen converts was to disappear, everyone to act and dress like other lay Christians—this to satisfy parish priests and annoyed neighbors. A second letter of the same date, addressed to mendicants, absolved friars of potential excommunication if they ceased to "favor the estate of beguines."[181] Through January and February a tense and even riotous scene ensued, for, as the bishop conceded in a further letter on February 19 in ironic understatement, "about the altering of this estate (*status mutacione*) different people feel differently." Parish rectors tried to force conformity in garb. Hints allude to passive or artful resistance; poor or widowed women claiming to have no ready change of clothes.[182] Soon the bishop allowed friars to minister to the women under certain conditions, then four months later (June 18) without restriction to those called "Third-Order." In retrospect the laws precipitated a change in legal form (from beguines to tertiaries), but not in social realities. Phillips showed in 1941 ago that communities of women converts continued to expand, indeed at a phenomenal rate, most taking cover now under the rubric of Third-Order Franciscan.[183] This formal legal move went back at least a generation. It was an old complaint of Dominicans, also of diocesan clerics, so it was said in 1284, that by way of this fake title (*ficto sermone "de tertia regula"*) the "nerve of church discipline was everywhere being dissolved"[184]

Relative peace followed, even some growth. Then forty years on, in the mid-1360s, trouble started again. The initiative came now from an enterprising corps of inquisitors, mostly Dominican, especially Walter Kerlinger.[185] They gained formal authorization from the highest powers, Pope Urban V (1362–70) and Emperor Charles IV (1346–78).[186] With access to the papal as well as imperial court, Kerlinger got himself named papal inquisitor, then Saxon provincial from 1369 to his death in 1373. From 1372 onward, moreover, five Dominicans would fill permanent inquisitorial posts, an innovation.[187] Pope Urban V's document only hints at what lay behind this initiative. He had heard things from others (*sicut accepimus*) about Beghards risen up (*dicatur exorta*) to threaten parts of Germany. Churchmen in those parts, busy with temporal matters, had paid no attention, he was told, and inquisitors had been inactive there for years.[188] As for Emperor Charles, strongly taken with his sacral duties and with no experience of beguines in Prague, his document of 17 June 1369 refers to Walter as "our chaplain," also as "at our table" and "in our *familia*."[189] Not an agent of the pope either, Kerlinger had worked his way into both courts to persuade them of the dire need to root out heretics and enforce the law, and began by turning fiercely against beguines in his home town, Erfurt.[190]

The social realities had not changed in these cities, and the resentments against apart women converts boiled over anew, Dominican inquisitors now enabling them. A prolific writer named Konrad of Megenberg, a secular churchman, also stirred the pot, notably in a poetic lament called the "tears of the church" where he contrasted laws banning the estate with their flourishing presence.[191] Johan Wasmud of Homburg, a master of Heidelberg and episcopal inquisitor at Mainz, penned a diatribe in 1396/98, expressing passionate sympathy with local clergy frustrated over protected beguines.[192] In Basel Friar John Mulberg, a Dominican, allied with local clergy in 1405 to win over the bishop and set off a fierce battle with the beguines' Franciscan protectors, which ended in 1411 with beguine houses getting closed.[193] The beguine estate stood under ban, each in his way vociferously declared. How could such women call themselves "spiritual" when they refused the sworn obedience of "religion"?[194] As Master Johan saw it in Mainz, most townspeople, "hostile to the clergy in any case," were taken in by this pious guile, the powerful even offering support.[195] Ordinary townspeople had over time (*cumulatim decipiuntur*) become deceived by beguines and Beghards.[196] These women insisted that to achieve "poverty of spirit" (a loaded term in mystical and Free Spirit teaching) a person had to exercise bodily poverty. But how then could prelates with massive temporal holdings possibly achieve perfection?[197]

Strassburg again became a crucible, also indirectly for the Devout. Its Bishop Frederick (1375–93) would become bishop of Utrecht (1393–1423) and make the crucial early decisions there. In August 1374 Bishop Lamprecht of Strassburg (1371–75), an ambitious aide to emperors Charles IV and Wenceslaus, set in motion a "process" directing all preachers in the diocese to pronounce from their pulpits the full set of anti-beguine laws, warning "each and every woman in the diocese" to desist or face inquisitors.[198] This directive was likely the work of an assistant, Martin of Prague, a secular cleric, later infamous in Bohemia as an inquisitor.[199] Someone, intriguingly, also prepared a document instructing these parish priests how to handle announcing the process and any questions it might provoke. Some might say: If these "Sisters" were so bad, even banned, why have the bishop and clergy tolerated them for so long? You need to say back: We and our bishops (plural) did not know about all this (the women's practices), and the friars say they did not either; these women can be terribly secretive. After all, few people bother to read papal law on this point![200] Anti-beguine laws were in actual practice a dead letter, "unread"—unless of course someone chose to invoke them, from outside (Dominican inquisitors, a new bishop) or inside (local rivals). But already local parish priests had seized upon this new process to exclude Tertiaries and beguines from churches and sacraments. This time, however, all local friars took counsel together, despite their rivalries, and in a diplomatic but firm document refuted all charges as false, noting that the very pronouncement was wreaking havoc on people's lives. Less than six years earlier, they added, an inquisitor had declared the women "innocent" and confirmed them in their "estate."[201] The interrogatory designed for this inquisitorial process reviewed twenty-one items of belief and practice, mostly standard, with a final enquiry about Merswin's *Book on the Nine Stones*.[202]

No differently in church than in civil affairs, these cases finally got contested by legal claims and counter-claims. Accordingly, four *pauperes*, beguine sympathizers, forced the episcopal court at Strassburg on 30 December 1374 to take cognizance of yet another papal letter, Gregory XI's *Ex iniuncto*, issued on 7 April 1374.[203] This ruling had arisen in response to complaints from Liège and Trier about new pressures applied to "good beguines," a similar complaint at Cologne in 1375. Gregory XI (1370–78), a lawyer famed for supporting inquisitors, here proved balanced, striving to reestablish "tranquility," his letter addressed to the archbishops of Cologne, Trier, and Mainz, as well as to Brabant and Flanders. He acknowledged "good *pauperes* of both sexes [avoiding the term "beguine"] in their cities and dioceses," and to define them borrowed language from *Ratio recta* as well as *Cum de mulierbus*. These were people, he specified, "who lived humbly and uprightly in poverty and chastity, who devoutly and frequently attended church, reverently obeyed their curates and the prelates of the Roman church, involving themselves in no [doctrinal] errors, but with inner charity served one another, desiring above all, together and as one, to serve the Most High in a spirit of humility."[204] This statement, whether or not it corresponded to any social or religious reality, became now the working definition of a "good" convert, also what the Devout would invoke twenty years later.

Conceding outright that the curia had no real knowledge of these groups' lives or estate, Gregory XI additionally charged local bishops with making inquiry and empowered them with extending protection, indeed papal protection, to those found above reproach. This created the very real possibility that papally authorized inquisitors and papally authorized bishops might clash over a given group—as they soon did. But for a time the pope's tergiversation worked. Actions against beguines slowed. But tensions among local rival parties hardly abated, nor did the ardor of Dominican inquisitors cool. Twenty years later, on 31 January 1395, the zealots succeeded in getting Pope Boniface IX to reaffirm in *Sedis apostolice prouidencia* the mandates of Pope Urban and Emperor Charles, and categorically to "revoke" any "exemptions" such "Beghards, Lullards, or Swestriones" might claim to have gained from the apostolic see itself[205]—a reference to privileges such as *Cum de mulieribus* and the force of Gregory XI's *Ex iniuncto.* When Master Johan wrote at Mainz in 1396/98 he specifically and triumphantly invoked this newest papal letter as warrant for his objecting yet again to "protected" beguines.

When new converts appeared in the Low Countries in the 1380s–90s, they entered this charged atmosphere, two centuries of groups approved and disapproved. When Sisters got labeled "beguines" and Brothers "lollards," people were reaching for available language, partly to label them as unusual, partly to smear them as suspect. All the suspicion surrounding Free Spirit notions of union with the divine, all the laws and charges brought to bear upon beguines, came instantly to life again—even though the Modern-Day Devout would protest that they were entirely innocent of such illicit turns. That confrontation will be the story of Chapter 3. First, we take up the Modern-Day converts in their first twenty years.

CHAPTER TWO

Modern-Day Converts in the Low Countries

*The condition of this land (*status istius terre*) forty years ago was known to me, and there was then not so much knowledge of God in Kampen, Deventer and Zwolle as there is in the least of you.*

—Wermboud of Utrecht to the Brothers at Deventer, ca. 1404

Sometimes she [Kathryn of Arkel, d. 1421] would speak sharply to great and powerful people about their faults and reproach them for things wherein they appeared to act against God. But she had such grace that each held her in reverence and dignity.

UNLIKE HIS FATHER and uncles before him who sought profit at trade and advantage in politics, Master Geert Grote of Deventer poured his energy into converting fellow citizens. People marveled that a man of learning and connections should give up goods and prestige for a self-imposed pursuit of souls. He preached in squares before town churches, sending an assistant ahead to post broadsheets, sometimes carrying books around in a barrel to refute critics. At Zwolle, where Grote stayed with his mother's family, a prominent citizen confronted him: "Why, Master, do you trouble us, and introduce new customs? Stop this preaching, this terrorizing of people." Master Geert calmly replied: "I would prefer that you not go to hell." To which the town father retorted, "Let us go down to hell in peace." And Grote: "I will not! If you do not wish to hear, others will gladly listen."[1] A generation later comemorative poems intoned his success. He had "turned inwards after pouring himself outwards so long," and for this was derided as a fool (*stolidus*). But he converted fully, not feigned or half-way, and daringly addressed all, learned and unlearned, powerful and poor. The result was: "holy gatherings flourishing in our time" (*congregationes sancte nostro florentes tempore*).[2]

No sermons survive, if they were ever written down. Grote's style could be painfully scholastic (like Wyclif's). But he was also capable of rhetorical appeal. Johan ten Water,[3] the scion of a patrician family in Zwolle, became drawn to Grote and his circle while attending the local Latin school. But he was encouraged by city fathers to continue study at the university in Cologne. Master Geert saw this as a fall (*lapsui*), a lure away from spiritual resolve (*bono proposito*) on the "guise of study." In a passionate letter he warned of the university's worldly distractions, urged him to read the chapter in Suso's *Horologium* on death as well as Ruusbroec's *The Faith* on glorified saints and the pitiable damned. The Devil alone thought that student-clerics should learn all manner of things (as he had done at Paris). Worst of all in society today, he said, was the "learned man with an evil will." Johan should learn to know his risky spiritual state; also that he was not up for advanced study, having had difficulty with boyish things—this likely came by way of John Cele (d. 1417), schoolmaster in Zwolle. Grote cried out to the young man from his "innards," his heart "bursting" for him, holding up a life of "sincerity, exaltation, certainty, and uprightness" over against one in the world of "anxiety, sorrow, fear, labor and grief." Johan would eventually join—but twenty years later (November 1403), whether with Grote's letter still ringing in his ears we do not know. The story goes that he invited friends and relatives to a wine-pub (*vinarium*), and then out riding. When they arrived at Windesheim (a few miles south), he declared his intention to stay—his announcement greeted with both dismay and acclaim by his companions.[4]

Grote sought converts but was tortured about conversion as a way of life. A letter of 1380 encouraged a disciple, Matthew of Tiel, then a novice somewhere, to pursue this estate with the "intent" that it was a choice pleasing to God, more secure than any other he could find. But he also warned at length of trials and temptations that would come inside a cloister.[5] Indeed Matthew soon encountered troubles. Grote, a secular deacon, pleased, he says, to hear of the profession, quoted Job: Life is a battle; there is no "place" (house) or "religion" (order) where a person can lead a spiritual life (*militare*) without a fight.[6] A rigorist, he upheld the force of law. Once a person had taken vows there was no turning back. A priest he knew, a learned man who had served creditably in four towns (including Rhenen where early Sisters emerged), joined the Carthusians, then found eremetical life too austere and confining, and wanted out so he could minister to people and reap a harvest of souls. Master Geert declared it no longer an option. God had not asked for the former sacrifice, and was not now asking him to join a preaching order.[7] Such rigor placed religion almost out of reach, a burden too great to bear—like Grote's stance on the holiness of priesthood, and his own remaining a deacon.

In practice Master Geert dissuaded close allies from profession. William of Salvarvilla, after being driven from Paris by the Great Schism, had flirted with joining the Carthusians at Gertrudesberg and came away "burned." Master Geert advised against overreacting: they would likely receive him if he still desired. But as I told you, he went on, this is not the right place for you. As for your separation from the world, begun in such a storm, God will provide, something you are not allowed yet to see.[8] To John Cele, schoolmaster at Zwolle, he wrote dismissing the man's scruples about "promises" he had once made to Franciscans, these mere "whispers of the Devil," all the more real-seeming for his trying now to counter them. Be happy, he says, outside a vow or habit! Grote demanded that promises "vowed" (*uota uestra*) to himself over the past three years be honored instead, a prospect/promise far preferable to taking vows with Franciscans[9]—presumably some pact between them to lead a certain way of life. In a letter to William oude Scute in 1383/84, addressed as the "oldest inhabitor of my heart," he recommended against joining a religious order. His own "foolish heart" preferred to remain in the world but not of it (John 15:19), though many in the world, and also many professed religious, will hate you for this, he warned. The truly religious seek the whole world. He advised staying close (*sitis uniti*) nonetheless to Groenendael.[10] Another letter to the same man, along with Gijsbert Dou (who heard Grote's general confession) and Johan van de Gronde (who joined him in Deventer and succeeded him in his house), set out to these priests (then in Amsterdam) a mission to multiply "servants of God."[11] Concretely, Grote was asking for help, since no priest of "our purpose/promise" (*nullum talem ad uotum nostrum habemus*) existed in Deventer, he being a deacon. This is how far he had come roughly ten years after his conversion, admiring what Ruusbroec had created at Groenendael but counseling friends to foster religion outside professed religion. Within a year (possibly months) he died of plague at age forty-four. Converts inspired by him had now to figure out their own way forward.

To hear the story told retrospectively, Master Geert preached and new converts formed in his wake.[12] But what Grote may have intended and what the Devout actually became, even in his home region, must not be blurred—a historical problem not unlike that of Master John Wyclif (also d. 1384) and the Lollards. In reality a network of converts and organizers sprang up semi-independently across Dutch towns during the 1380s/90s. We begin by situating them in their own world. In the late 1450s Johan Busch wrote a book "on the origin of the Modern-day Devotion (*de origine moderne devotionis*) of all the devout priests, clerics, and sisters or beguines in our entire homeland (*tocius **nostre*** *patrie*) in the germanic region."[13] The word "our" was inserted in his final version (ca. 1464) completed far from home. In a second work he took up "illustrious" Devout figures, and strung similar terms together, culminating rhetorically in "homeland": Just as Master Geert Grote was the source and first father of all the people of the modern-day devotion in this homeland (*origo fuit et pater primus omnium hominum moderne devocionis huius patrie*).[14] The Devout saw this as a story about their land and their day. Prior John Vos preached a valedictory sermon at Windesheim in 1424 recalling those who had first fostered "this devotion and way of life throughout this our homeland,"[15] and the next prior, William Vornken (1124–55), a native of Utrecht, likewise surveyed the "new devotion in our homeland."[16] The latter, then around eighty years old, closed with a rhetorical flourish. If Cato could thank his gods for living at a time and in a place where he was allowed to see the Roman Empire flourish, why should not the Devout thank God for living in this time and this land?[17]

The Low Countries

The homeland of the Modern-Day Devout went by no single name. Pomerius, writing from Brussels, referred to the Devout in Deventer as in "Lower Germany," this rendered subsequently in Middle Dutch as "beyond the IJssel River."[18] Vornken, writing midway between Deventer and Zwolle on the east side of the IJssel, placed "our land" in "regions of the lower earth,"[19] echoing the vernacular *Neder landen.* The Middle Ages, however, knew no kingdom called the "Low Countries." Blockmans has defined this term as embracing generically all lands between the Somme River in northern France and the Ems in western Germany.[20] Commonly referred to in the Middle Ages as "Lower Germany," sometimes as "Flanders" (after its most populous and vibrant region), these lands came to assume a distinct place in the world surreptitiously, more in the Later Middle Ages as central power weakened in the German Empire and French Kingdom. Only from the 1530s would the term "Low Lands" definitively designate a language and a region, though both had existed in practice since the thirteenth century. In the 1560s an Italian based in Antwerp, Lodovico Guicciardini, nephew of the Florentine humanist, offered an influential description of these *Paesi bassi, alterimenti detti Germania inferiore.*[21] The point of the work, he wrote, was to inform others about "this province, so illustrious and such an important part of Europe."[22] But only after more than a generation of battling the Habsburg crown did printers in the region, though pioneers in cartography, dare feature their lands as a distinct unit. Pieter van den Keere, of Ghent, Antwerp, Amsterdam and London, published a foundational work, his *Germania inferior* (Amsterdam 1617), with a humanist text by Montanus.[23] History since has not simplified things. Modern arguments about the medieval shape of these lands have turned as much on national (Dutch-Belgian-German), linguistic (Dutch-French-German), and confessional (Reformed-Catholic) divisions as on the medieval evidence.[24]

The medieval "Low Countries" embraced notable anomalies in modern terms, Dutch-speaking Flanders subject to the French king, Romance-speaking Liège and Cambrai and Hainaut to the German emperor. Its salient characteristic, Huizinga suggested, was a "mediating" role between the "French" and "German" worlds, its delta-lands and few natural barriers making it a crossroads.[25] This region, first converted to Christianity by Carolingians working with Anglo-Saxons (Willebrord), annexed to the East Frankish Kingdom as part of the Lotharingian "middle kingdom," belonged in good measure to the medieval German Empire, whence the name "Lower Germania." Frederick II's broad privileges for ecclesiastical lords in 1220 and secular princes in 1231 rendered these territories quasi-independent, himself also pawning off a large domain in and around Nijmegen on the Rhine in 1247, the last imperial base in a region his predecessors had frequently visited. Towns marked the region, initially serving as bishoprics and administrative centers, then as commercial centers large or small. Counties and duchies nonetheless remained significant, unlike in Italy. When Van den Keere described the region of "Lower Germania" in 1617, he did so by way of its principalities. The Devout too were instinctively alert to borders and competing jurisdictions, moving from one town or principality to another in times of troubles. In broader practice Devout influence traveled east (to Münster and Cologne) as well as west (Holland) and south (Arnhem, Louvain, Liège), not slowed by the Dutch/Low German/French divide or by political borders. It was to the southwest, to the great cities of Flanders, that they came late. They would also penetrate German lands, especially far up the Rhine, but not the kingdom of France and not England as households, though to a degree by way of translated works.

The term "Low Countries" has, as I use it, a broader and a narrower meaning (see Figure 1 for a map). The larger sense encompassed the northwest corner of Europe. We should imagine a wide angle, its point more or less in Cologne, opening out to the sea, its southern and western line following more or less the border of the French Kingdom (but including Flanders and Artois), its northern and eastern line passing west of Münster toward Frisia and Emden. This is also the image we find in the earliest maps, with England close by.[26] Most of the land within this wide angle was drained by rivers flowing west or north. Movement up and down those rivers, of staples, commerce, people, and culture, bridged regional particularity and, via the Rhine, IJssel, Meuse, and Schelde,

Figure 1. The Medival Low Countries, 1400/1500, locating frequently mentioned houses of Brothers, Sisters, and schoolboys, along with the major medieval principalities and selected important towns. Map drawn by Gordon Thompson.

connected to North Sea and Baltic ports, also to England via the Channel.[27] Cologne on the Rhine, though, strictly, an independent territorial power (Westphalia), was the largest city and riverport, also the most significant ecclesiastical capital (with Utrecht, Liège, and Münster suffragan). Forms of Dutch or Low German predominated as the native tongue, though obviously not in the Romance-speaking imperial bishoprics of Liège and Cambrai or the diocese of Tournai (each of which included Dutch-speaking parts to their north) or the counties of Hainaut and Artois. Guicciardini remarked that many people in his experience (centered in Antwerp) knew more than "Teutonico," as he called it, especially French, but also German, English, Italian, and Spanish.[28] He described these people as among the first in Gaul and Germany to accept the faith, and to reverence and practice it still, as one might see in their "infinite" writings and buildings. He was struck that men and women were relatively literate and learned, able to write clearly, many knowing at least some (Latin) grammar but also their own tongue. These "Low Landers," clever in matters of the sea, quite intent upon commerce, were also fine artisans. As for character, they were naturally "cool" (*freddi*), "accepting fortune with wisdom and the world as it came, without too much visible distress" (*alteratione*). Easily inclined to sadness (*dolore*), even overwhelmed by it, they seemed rarely openly moved. And in general they were not excessively ambitious—this, like many observations here, offered as an implied contrast with his Italian kin and comrades, serving moral as well as anthropological purposes.[29]

"Homeland" in the narrower sense hinged on person and place, where you were born or lived, where on the ground you stood and looked out from. For contemporaries what counted emotionally, also politically, was a particular region, city, or diocese.[30] The Devout were regularly identified in texts by their place of origin. Modern-Day converts, while present early as well in Utrecht (the Nedersticht in medieval terms) and the county of Holland, originated in a principality called the Oversticht, a region subject temporally to the bishop of Utrecht. Towns and houses associated with the Modern-Day Devout figure centrally still in Van der Keere's map of this province from about 1600 (Figure 2), especially Deventer, Zwolle, and Kampen. The chronicler Johan Busch, at home in the IJssel River valley (Zwolle and Windesheim), spoke of Devout monasteries and congregations as spreading "throughout this our homeland" (*per totam istam patriam*), and named eleven territories surveyed in concentric circles beginning in Salland (the heart of the Oversticht), with regions to the east (Westphalia) coming as quickly to his mind as to the west (Holland) or south (Brabant).[31] Thomas of Kempen, born in the lower Rhine valley in the diocese of Cologne, resident as a schoolboy and cleric in Deventer and Zwolle, then as a canon for sixty-five years at Mount-St.-Agnes outside Zwolle, described

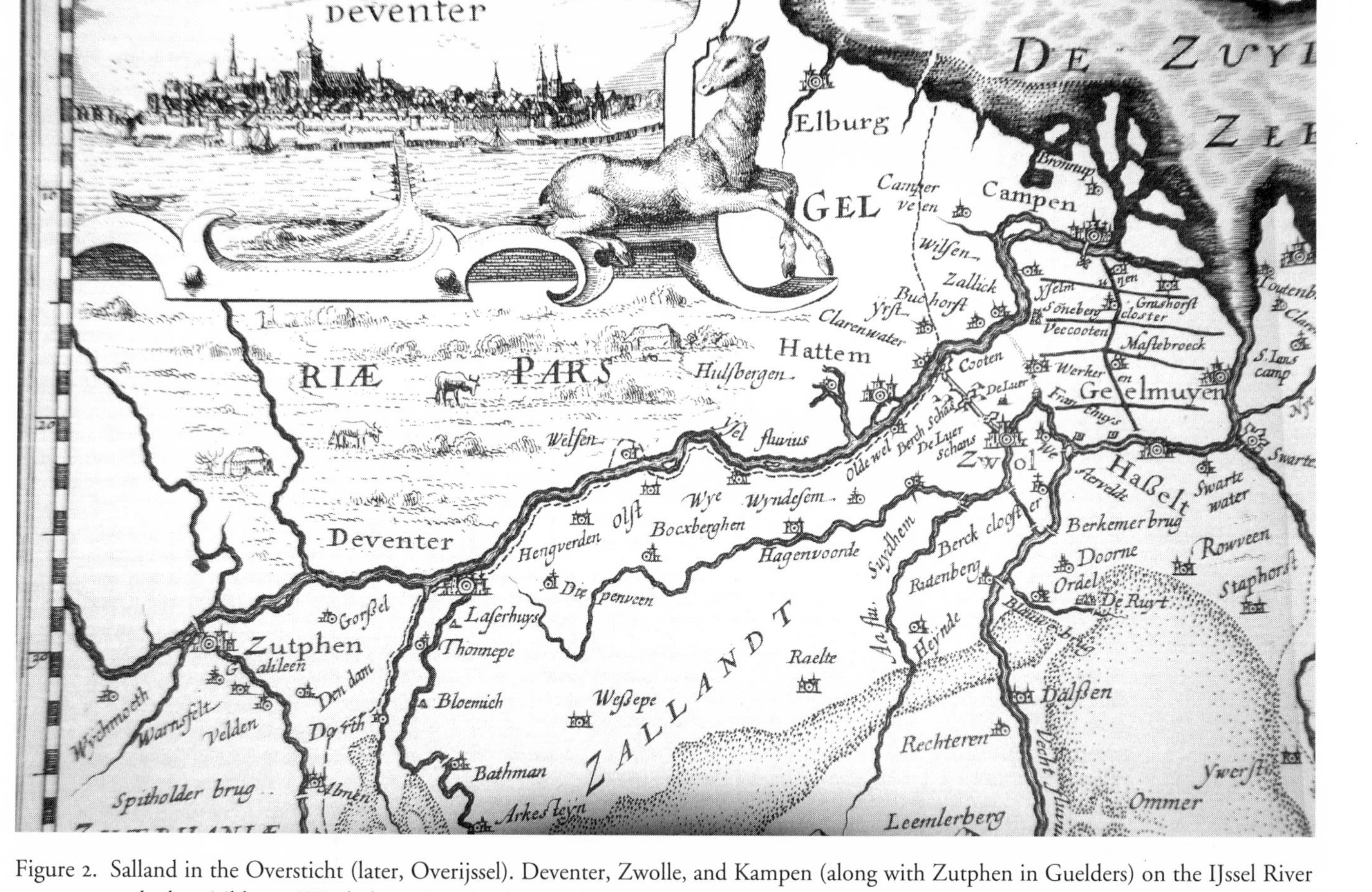

Figure 2. Salland in the Oversticht (later, Overijssel). Deventer, Zwolle, and Kampen (along with Zutphen in Guelders) on the IJssel River appear central; also visible are Windesheim (mother house of the canons regular), Diepenveen (first house of canonesses), Hulsbergen (third most important house of Brothers), and "Berck clooster" (Thomas of Kempen's house). Detail from Pieter van den Keere, *Germania Inferior* (Amsterdam 1617), reprint edited by C. Koeman (Amsterdam: Theatrum orbis terrarum Ltd., 1966).

Master Geert as preaching first in cities temporally subject to the bishopric of Utrecht (Deventer, Zwolle, Kampen = Oversticht), then Utrecht itself (= Nedersticht), next in nearby territories (*proximas regiones*: Holland, Guelders, and Brabant), and still farther afield (*dehinc ad remotiores partes*: Flanders, Frisia, Westphalia, and Saxony).[32] If you looked at the world from the south (Brussels) as Pomerius did, however, Grote was active "across the IJssel," thus "in Lower Germany," and it was Ruusbroec who launched the Devout and in his own homeland, Brabant.[33]

Dutch scholars have often treated regions across the IJssel, especially the Oversticht and Guelders, as more "German" than "Dutch," both anachronistic terms.[34] The local language was Dutch, the regional dialect "eastern." To the Burgundian court in fifteenth-century Brabant, or the republican rulers of seventeenth-century Holland, this region might have seemed a backwater.[35] But in the year 1400, in the northern Low Countries, the Oversticht was vital. Deventer, the first town in the region rebuilt in brick after a disastrous fire in the fourteenth century, was, Guicciardini noted in the 1560s, "truly grand and spacious, full of good and beautiful buildings, both public and private, also densely populated, and the metropolis of the entire region."[36] The city gained importance first as a center of ecclesiastical administration, its acclaim and size (up to 10,000 inhabitants, though probably less) subsequently expanding as a commercial entrepôt with its five annual fairs, also the first city in the region incorporated into the Hansa League.[37] North-south traffic passed through on the IJssel River, downriver (north) past Kampen into the sea and thence to Scandinavia and the Baltics, or upriver (south) to the Rhine and Cologne. As for east-west traffic, Deventer sat astride a major overland route, west to Utrecht and the cities of Holland (Amsterdam, Haarlem), east to Westphalia and the prince-bishoprics of Münster and Osnabrück, ultimately to Hamburg.

Forty years ago Hugenholtz argued that the distinguishing mark of the Low Countries was "particularity," towns and villages able to maneuver at a remove from great political courts or ecclesiastical centers, allowing space for local initiatives.[38] The Modern-Day Devout too were mostly people of towns, even if they turned their households into quasi-recluses. They wrote in Middle Dutch and Latin. They traveled east, but more readily to towns south and west. They might single out a companion as "a hard man" owing to his "Westphalian" birth, but a person from towns in Holland or Flanders or the Lower Rhineland (Thomas of Kempen) as never other than themselves. They told an amusing story about a brother who haled from Liège, roundly cursed by his father for joining this odd group—most ears spared, however, because in Deventer, where this scene transpired, people could not understand his tongue (Romance).[39]

Other scholars have made Utrecht's role central to the northern Low Countries, its temporal powers around the city and in the Oversticht extensive, its spiritual powers stetching across the diocese. Except in the far south, the modern Dutch state is notably close in outline to the medieval diocese.[40] Within that diocese Deventer ranked as the bishop's second seat. Its mighty church on the IJssel was dedicated to Lebuin, an Anglo-Saxon companion of Willibrord. The provost of the collegiate chapter lived in a mansion just down the street from where the Devout would set up their households. A school in the same complex drew young men in hordes from as far away as Holland, Cleve, Liège, and Westphalia. The bishop visited on occasion, en route to his castle in Vollenhove north of Kampen, but he mostly governed by way of surrogates (a "schout"). From the later fourteenth century the three towns on the IJssel along with Groningen came to operate ever more independently, their population density rivaling Holland's. The bishop's powers nonetheless remained a factor, also for the Devout. When in the later 1380s they moved to establish a house of canons as a front or shelter (*securum haberent recursum*), the bishop refused approval until they gave up a site across the river in Guelders and found one inside his own temporal jurisdiction (= Windesheim).[41] The interactions could be personal, at least with bishops' officials. In the cartulary of the Brothers' house at Deventer there exists a note written into its margins by the rector, Godfrey Toorn (1410–50), disputing an income. Godfrey wrote beneath one document, "I then went to Deric ten Vorde sheriff at Colmschate [residence for the bishop's 'schout' outside Deventer] to speak with him about it, and he responded that he knew about this document and the rye, but. . . ."[42] To form and sustain communities Devout leaders had to move dexterously among town aldermen and episcopal officials without setting off suspicious friars.

As for locating their region and project in the world at large, the Modern-Day Devout expressed spiritual excitement about their land, as noted above, but also held darker and more restrained views. They often perceived themselves as far from centers of power or culture, whether the Empire (Germany), the church (Rome), or universities (Paris, Prague), even at the remote ends of the inhabited and inhabitable world, in a low and watery place (thus in a charter for Third-Order Franciscans in Gouda, county of Holland),[43] or as mere feet at the extremities of the world (*et pedibus et in extremitatibus mundi*).[44] People in the Low Countries, not least Master Geert, nonetheless knew how to act in that larger world, their young men sent off to Cologne and Prague and Paris for university training, their agents dispatched to papal or episcopal or princely courts when business needed doing. Theirs was a world of decidedly local ventures and tongues, but this local was now ever more entangled with the international—in which we glimpse, in my view, a primary characteristic of the Later Middle Ages.

What we find in fact is a shifting of the balance. For nearly two centuries creative energy had sprung primarily from drives for centralization and internationalization: the curia in Rome with its overarching "common law" and institutions spreading across Europe, universities with their intellectual forms and products, religious orders with their general chapters, international commerce and Lombard banking, monarchy on large scales and small. Between the 1370s and 1450s, however, new impulses of all sorts appeared nearly at once, surprising and challenging, to be understood first of all locally: Bridget in Sweden and then Rome, Catherine in Siena, Wyclif and the Lollards in England, Hus and the Hussites in Bohemia, humanists in Italy. Not only did they pursue circumscribed ends locally, but also ever more insistently in their own tongues—a tendency sometimes linked in the past to an incipient "nationalism" or "laicism." These initiatives, however local in origin and purpose, entirely presupposed the international, however, touching them by way of law, the papal court, princes, religious orders, universities, inquisitors, political claims (Burgundians), commerce (the Hansa League), language (Latin). Local groups, moreover, availed themselves of those international links when they served their purposes, tried to fend them off when it did not (inquisitors, new papal laws, English dynastic claims to French territories). No account of the later middle ages, not just the Modern-Day Devout, makes historical sense apart from this creative tension. Its emblem, also its frequent facilitator, was the general council, called for from 1378, meeting at Pisa (1409), Constance (1414–18), Florence (1423), Basel (1431–49). There new figures and initiatives represented themselves (also the Devout), there texts and ideas were circulated, there new initiatives also put on trial. Here we begin with the local initiatives, then in the next chapter bring in the friars, inquisitors, and papal court.

Households of Devout Women

Beginning in the 1380s, and for the next two generations, households of women converts multiplied across the Netherlandish landscape. Only in the last decade or two have Dutch scholars turned their attention fully to this phenomenon. Some now call it a "second women's movement" (echoing Grundmann for the twelfth century).[45] The totals were astonishing, an expansion on a very large scale, hardly registered until now in general accounts of women's religious life. I refer to them collectively as the "Devout," though they soon took varied institutional expressions, of which "Sisters of the Common Life" was only one. Records of their ventures were made and kept locally, in each town—and subsequent archival losses have been great. Historians must finally approach them case by case, each foundation and town slightly different. Such study was undertaken for Amsterdam as far back as 1941, more recently for Zwolle and Leiden, now across the diocese for Tertiaries. In Amsterdam, still a modest town, the number of women's communities expanded from one in 1379 to more than a dozen by 1420; in Leiden they came to total twenty-one houses, in Zwolle seven.[46] Overall, new houses of women outnumbered those of men by four or five to one, and women converts their male counterparts by as much as ten to one. New households formed across the whole of the Low Countries but especially, at least initially, in Utrecht, the Oversticht, and the county of Holland. Our earliest evidence goes back to 1379 at Deventer, 1380 at Delft, 1386 at Leiden and Gouda.[47]

Most houses formed as local and private arrangements; and even if the women eventually shifted status to gain legal protection, as beguines had done in Strassburg and Basel, the originating provisions often retained influence. Scholars have only begun to approximate a full and accurate list. An early list (1941) counted 106 houses called generically "Sisters of the Common Life."[48] In fact all houses of Devout women, just in the Netherlands, far exceeded that number. The majority of these, under pressure, would seek cover as Tertiaries, eventually numbering about 150 houses, a document from 1439 claiming seventy with about 3,000 inhabitants.[49] A new study of Tertiary houses in the southern Low Countries puts the total number there at eighty.[50] In addition eight communities took vows as canonesses associated with Windesheim, while several more assumed Augustinian status in the general chapter of Sion,[51] a few also becoming Birgittine or Cistercian. Still another set of houses, between twenty and thirty, remained closer in form to their originating status, and these we now call "Sisters of the Common Life," a mostly informal rubric, attested in the fifteenth century but never as an official title.[52] For them much archival work remains to be done in the Netherlands (though records are sparse). For northwest Germany Rehm did a study close to the archives (which survived better) of roughly sixty houses, several of his in medieval terms in Netherlandish territory.

Women converts between 1380 and 1420 mostly did not turn to orders. Tertiaries too started out as local and lay, their status and claims evolving slowly in the direction of "religious," though the early claim of a "Rule" effectively protected them from inquisitors, as it had beguines initially in the Upper Rhineland. In the Late Middle Ages orders were difficult of entry for all but the most privileged women, requiring social status and entrance fees. More, they were often not held in high regard. These new converts also showed no interest in forming beguine convents/houses or joining beguine courts, though they were themselves often labeled "beguines" in early days. Five generations along beguines increasingly seemed an established way of life in these towns, not a center of fervor or innovation. At the upper end of the social scale, from the beginning, beguines set up in their own houses. Beguine convents by contrast housed several women, maintaining something like a community of goods or consumption within such a house-convent.[53] In Amsterdam in 1389 city magistrates confirmed that a beguine living in the beguine court could not sell her house to someone outside the court, or rebuild it, nor could her heirs, without the consent of the other beguines (*consent der ghemeenre beghinen binnen den hove*),[54] thus fiercely defending the distinct character of their "court" and its common interests. A beguine (or her family) might still sell the house, or rebuild and refurbish it—those common urban rights. But aldermen conceded a collective right to oversee ownership in the beguine quarter in the face of willy-nilly family interests, even though these houses remained private property.

The Devout lived in houses, not in courts or whole streets. Each community presumed someone with adequate means to set up an independent household, and a "gathering" of women zealous to join. They had to negotiate with local authorities for its legal status and form of life. In nearly every case these arrangements got registered sooner or later before town councils—as they had been for beguines. Devout households came and went, some proving quite transient, others evolving into long-term communities. New houses sometimes sprang from old, owing to expanding numbers or differing religious visions or personal tensions. In trying to get at these Devout houses historians possess six sorts of evidence, though never all six for a single house. We have foundation and property documents, prized and more likely to be kept, even when the status of a house changed. We have narratives, nearly all coming later, even much later, and in two forms, house chronicles and lives of sisters. We have internal statutes or ordinances, these rarely preserved and mostly late. We have inquisitorial charges from early days, primarily about a single house (though with implications for others). We have a few book lists. And we have liturgical materials, especially for those that moved into or toward full religious status. This section draws primarily on foundation documents, with attention to the inquisitorial record. At the risk of anachronism, however, and of approaching it all through a retrospective veil of holy memory, we will note first representative stories of women converts.

Kathryn of Arkel, who died in 1421, lived at Master Geert's House house in his lifetime, thus going back to the early 1380s, and became instilled herself with a burning desire to "convert good people and draw them toward the virtues," as her memorialist wrote a generation later. Of a reasonably well-off family, though she claimed to be a "peasant," she was put in charge of tending pigs until welcomed fully into the household. Gifted with conversational and spiritual skills so people sought her out for advice, she was able to interact with them relatively freely. Charged with the house's external affairs, she traveled to towns or farms on business and carried with her a little book (*boexsken*) of devotional materials. From it she read to those with whom she stayed and ate, even addressing them sharply on points she thought they needed to hear. She, perhaps more than Master Geert, attracted the young ardent converts that he, at least among women, often did not or could not.[55] Kathryn's story must stand in for others. Cecelia van den Toorn, styled by Busch a "spiritual daughter" of Master Geert, formed (*instituerat*) a house at Kampen in his lifetime (later relocated to Bruneppe outside the city-walls). He had preached there, and also stirred up citizen resistance. Cecilia nonetheless formed a gathering of like-minded women (*devotarum sororum congregationem*) who resided first in a house near the parish church of St. Nicholas.[56]

Lady Zwedera came from a powerful family (Van Rechteren: the castle stands outside Dalfsen), married well (Van Runen), and in youthful days joined her husband in the pleasures of the hunt. She reportedly grew troubled at the damage done to peasant lands and goods, especially by dogs, and tactfully restrained her husband and their entourage. He died young, as did their only son. Besieged by forceful suitors, she retired to the nearest town, Zwolle, and then to Deventer. With the permission of the bishop of Utrecht (her temporal lord) she set herself up in her own house, intent upon withdrawal and distributing alms to the poor. While establishing her own religious life, she became drawn into the orbit of Devout leaders who lived close-by, especially Florens Radewijns and Johan van den Gronde, the heirs, literally, of Master Geert. She allied herself with them, on her terms. For her inner life she came to rely upon a small scroll (*rotula* = *rulle*) written full with "good points." She reportedly liked especially this saying: "Poverty apart from true want is like a letter (document) sent to a great lord without a seal"—that is, bearing neither authenticity nor authority. She, along with a socially privileged companion and a serving woman, considered joining the community of women in Master Geert's house. But they feared her rank and wealth, and refused her entrance—as they made Kathryn tend pigs. About the year 1400, women converts in Deventer, under growing pressure, resolved to set up a safe house, so to speak, of canonesses in Diepenveen, an hour's walk north of town, as the men had done a decade earlier at Windesheim. Lady Zwedera was invited to join, and participated physically and financially in its building, the chapel built by the women's own labor still standing (Figure 3). She died there in February 1407, fellow converts gathering round her bed and asking for a (spiritual) testament. She reiterated her "points" and added as virtually her last words: "These points [the virtues and marks of the converted life] you must request in prayer from our dear Lord, because they are given to no one, even if the person turns to God with their whole heart, unless God gives

Figure 3. Chapel of the canonesses at Diepenveen, built in part with the women's own labor digging trenches and laying brick, 1400/07, when they were still Sisters and an extension of Master Geerts' house in Deventer (an hour's walk away), prior to their subsequent vows and enclosure as canonesses; since the seventeenth century preserved as a Reformed church. Author's photo.

them."[57] This may sound platitudinous, but her words betray real inner struggle. This was a strong-willed and privileged woman who fought her self and her upbringing for twenty-five years to devise ways physically and spiritually to live as a convert.

Two brief chronicles in Middle Dutch from houses in Delft (ultimately Tertiary: St. Agnes and St. Barbara) deserve attention. In the account of St. Barbara, written down in the sixteenth century, women acted as agents of change after devotion was said to have wasted away. Moved in their hearts to live an apart life, several came together to rent a house, pooling their goods, working for their upkeep. They went to a priest of their choosing to act as confessor and teacher. They also discovered that life together could generate tensions. One woman failed to get on and was put out, whereupon she rented her own place and took several along to set up yet another house.[58] The chronicle of St. Agnes, written already in the 1440s, tells of a priest, a vice-curate of the city church, whose sermons around the year 1380, "moved many good people toward the virtues, especially poor young women who wished to live according to his counsel." He, together with a layman, bought a small house for them, and brought a widow from Flanders to oversee it. What the women could not earn for themselves in the way of food and upkeep, they begged from sympathetic townspeople. Years later the priest bought a larger house, then exchanged it for another closer to the church so the women could more easily visit it and he them. One woman, with the assistance of a lay man, bought yet another where they lived for ten years until they moved again—and so on. Here, with a vice-curate (a lowly clerical position) as prime mover, we see local arrangements, a secular priest and a layman working with women converts, even relatively poor women, to set up households.[59]

A household of Devout women required legal recognition, a founding document acknowledging their right to live together as converts. Whatever burgher parents made of adolescent sons caught up in religious enthusiasm, they mostly did not, or could not, stop them. Women too, in large numbers, were not stopped, or could not be. But unless they were widows or spinsters and of means, they faced greater obstacles, also in the Low Countries where women enjoyed more freedom and leverage than in places like Italy. Ordinarily they needed familial support to enter into marriage or undertake life-transitions, though their own independent powers were growing.[60] In the case of conversion much depended upon a family's attitude toward religion, also its degree of economic neediness. Women ordinarily acted at law in conjunction with a male advocate or guardian called their *mombaer*, be it their father, brother, husband, or another appointed man. To change legal estates, to engage in a property transaction such as resigning goods to a religious house, required his presence or compliance.[61] We must bear these gendered realities in mind as we take up the foundation documents of male aldermen.

On 21 September 1374 Master Geert turned his patrician home on Beguine Street into a kind of alms house for "poor women to serve God." Nothing in the document of 1374 indicates that Grote had any clear notion except to establish a house "for the needs of poor people who wanted to serve God." Still a canon of St. Mary's in Aachen, he went before the town magistrates in Deventer (*scependom*), where his father had figured largely twenty-five years earlier, to transform the family mansion into a hospice for poor people (*herberghen ende woninghen*), reserving, with elaborate stipulation, rooms for himself until death, with a right to oversee any form of life instituted there (*so sal he dat regiren, visitiren, ordiniren, beginnen, inzetten, end uytzetten*). On his death the house and its form of life would fall to the magistrates' jurisdiction, as they oversaw the town hospice and another alms-house (Stappen) near Master Geert's.[62] As it turned out—according to a later life written by, or for, the Sisters—in early days he housed mostly elderly women in the house, because he could not attract (literally, "get") young "virgins."[63] In effect the house served the city's poor and needy initially, exactly like hospices and beguine houses, whatever his hopes. Contrary to most narratives, this was not the self-conscious founding of the Sisters of the Common Life.

In general, at least three parties claimed an interest in a founding document, the end-point of a negotiated agreement. Town aldermen expected to oversee and approve any lay converts setting up on one of their city streets, the document issued in their name or registered with them.[64] Master Geert would provide his house with a set of arrangements, in effect statutes, dated July 1379, the document (in both versions) concluding with the same words: "All these things are instituted with the knowledge and input (*toedoen*) of the aldermen (*Scepene*), being read out to them and set out openly (*openbaert*) in their council (*raet*) where it was found pleasing to them without contradiction."[65] Women are absent, at least in the document, and in this case likely also in reality; it was the work of Master Geert Grote and the aldermen of Deventer, setting up public guidelines for life inside his house. The "ordinances" may disclose Grote's expectations for a Devout community in 1379, certainly what aldermen in Deventer would agree to, but in this case little or nothing about women themselves forming a community.

Second among interested parties were local churchmen, the rector or vicar of the town parish. Women converts remained subject to him for sacramental ministrations as well as parish obligations, laypersons still in church law. These rights were jealously guarded, priests often proving more troublesome than aldermen, who might well look after the interests of kin in a new community.

Aldermen and parish priests were at one, however, in wanting these women and their houses kept from becoming "religious," whereby they might escape jurisdictional and financial claims altogether, and also in keeping them free of any scandal.[66] On 23 April 1409 the vice-curate of St. Mary's, the main parish church in Deventer, issued a document patently meant to counter charges abroad in the town about the New Devout. Within the parish, he declared, are now many households of "Sisters or beguines" (*plures sunt domus seu congregationes*), women who, though living devoutly, are in truth lay persons subject to city and parish. They attend church "in remarkable numbers," especially on Sundays and feastdays, and there, not in their own households, receive the sacrament and make confession.[67] Whatever rumors or worries had sparked this intervention, its testimony had to come from the parish, the vice-curate himself surprised that laypeople would prove so devout.

The women themselves, third, had a large stake and might formally be the petitioners, if sometimes harder to see, for the world of documents was largely a male world. Still, much of the energy, and not a little of the agency, may be attributed to these women. They could and did go before local aldermen or a priest to seek approval of their status and way of life. But we tend to see them along with two other presences. Family members might participate in the negotiations, a father, say, setting up his daughter and her companions, at the very least agreeing to it or helping, in Lady Zwedera's case male kin after the deaths of her husband and son. We also see male figures from the Devout network. Koorn reconstructed the careers of three such activists, one in Amsterdam and a close associate of Grote (Gijsbert Dou), one in Utrecht and a close associate of Florens Radewijns (Wermbold of Buscoep), one a layman, an accomplished goldsmith, who on his wife's death became a priest in Haarlem (Hugo Goldsmit).[68] They acted, it seems, as facilitators, supplying the women and aldermen with templates or exemplary agreements to use as points of departure for their own negotiation. Later, Rudolph Dier of Muiden (d. 1459), memorialist of the men's house at Deventer and father-confessor for twenty-five years at Master Geert's House, recalled a series of early households simply in terms of their priest-guides, listing towns in Holland (Amsterdam, Purmureynde, Hoorn, Medenblick, Haarlem, Leiden) and Gelderland (Zutphen, Arnhem)[69]—however unfair to the women who actually formed and made up the communities. In sum, we must recognize a whole series of competing interests and local actors at work in the making of any one of these gatherings.

Founding charters survive in limited numbers. Of the dozens that once existed, less than a dozen likely remain, though we cannot know for certain until the *Monasticon Trajectense* has completed its work and a comparable survey is undertaken for Sisters' houses. At Gouda, twenty miles to the west of Utrecht, just inside the county of Holland, a well-to-do woman named Machteld Cosijns gathered several women around her after her husband's death, and in 1386 gifted her house to this joint undertaking.[70] From Rhenen, a town on the Rhine twenty miles east of Utrecht, comes the earliest I know, dated 1388 (see Figure 4 for a near contemporary map of this region). The inquisitor would descend upon this community five or ten years later in all his investigative ire.[71] In both cases, so far as we can tell, the initiative lay with the women, roughly in the mid-1380s, and both households struck written agreements with their city aldermen, Rhenen's dated to 1388, Gouda's to 1396. The documents, though issued by the respective aldermen, read similarly in wide patches. Gouda, we might conclude chronologically, borrowed from Rhenen; more likely both drew upon a common model adapted by negotiation to their locales, the template probably from a community in Utrecht called St. Cecilia, founded about 1383.[72] The leading figures there were its priestly leader Wermbold of Buscoep, chaplain at the Buurkerk (downtown parish), and the local "Martha" or head of community, Alijt Cluten. It was the community in Rhenen, however, not those in Utrecht or Gouda, that the inquisitor specially went after.

The house in Rhenen stood near its parish church (St. Cunera), not far from a local commandery of Knights.[73] The mayor, aldermen, and city council referred to the women as "sisters," their house freed from watch and wall (moat) duties and certain taxes, their persons firmly still under civil jurisdiction. As women, "not empowered in, or understanding, of civil law" (the only time I have encountered that formulation) they might call upon a *mombaer* as needed. No woman might join unless she was free of religion and marriage. This community might assume no religious order or unusual way of life, and also had to remain subordinate to the local parish priest. The women should do work appropriate to their estate, inside the house, never begging in the streets unless driven by necessity. Sisters were to be people "whose way of life was truly above all rumor and immorality, living in purity, humility and all kindness . . . moving together toward the good apart from all useless worldly matters, living among themselves in sisterly love and in community of all things." This last point (*in ghemeynheyd alre dinghen leven*) meant, concretely, this: Once a sister had joined the house and brought goods into it, they remained with the house for the "needs" of the sisters even if that person left the society (*geselscap*) because she wanted to or had to (*woude ofte soude*).

As for organization, the wisest and most prudent among them in material things and most sought-out in spiritual matters should be named Martha. She should make decisions with four or five others, or indeed all, about assigning people to spin or sew or shop, also about admitting or admonishing women. The Martha, with a majority, could remove a woman on certain conditions:

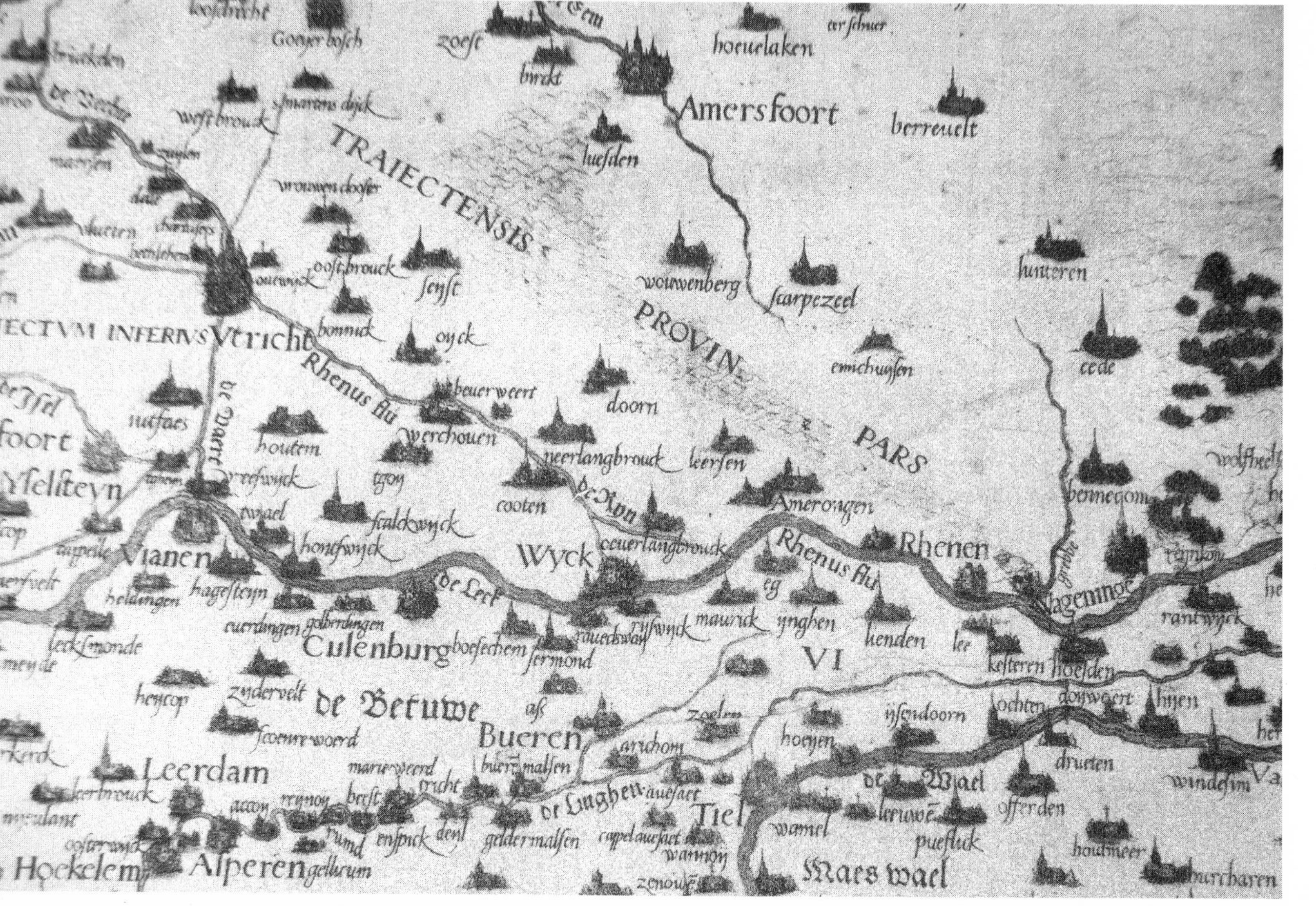

Figure 4. Utrecht, with Rhenen and Amersfoort, the sites of key early Sisters' houses, roughly twenty and fifteen miles apart respectively. Detail (ca. 1540) from *Gewestkaarten van de Nederlanden door Jacob van Deventer, 1536–45: met een picturale weergave van alle kerken en kloosters*, ed. C. Koeman (Alphen aan den Rijn: Canaletto/Repro-Holland 1994).

lack of chastity or inappropriate socializing, leaving the house all the time or wanting to, an obstreperous nature, a "mad" disposition. As for the kind of woman they were to admit, her "deepest intention" must be to serve God, to improve (*beteren*) her life and regulate it according to community life (*ghemeinswisen*). Futher, if the sisters as a group became quarrelsome or immoral, the aldermen stipulated, they would lose this privilege ("freedom," *vryheyt*). As warrant the aldermen and regional civil judge appended their seals and, "since it involved a religious matter," compelled the local parish priest, Roloff van Muden, to append his as well. The document issued at Gouda eight years later manifested differences, most notably an elaborate stipulation at the end about how women joining the community had to resign their goods through a public notarial action. For aldermen and local families it was, beyond public propriety, property issues that weighed, regulating who held what and how and whether a Sister or her family could subsequently reclaim goods (they could not, though no vow was taken). The women obviously had a stake too in whether property could be recovered if they decided to leave; hence drawing up such a notarial instrument represented a big step for them. Upon joining all decisions about goods would be made consensually and communally, under a Martha, though not under sworn obedience.

On 1 April 1389, roughly a year after the agreement reached in Rhenen, a large group of women came before the aldermen of Amsterdam to register their household (Figure 5).[74] Single and poor by choice (*willigher armer joncfrouwen*), they had built a house, endowed it with their own goods and those gifted by parents and kin (*vrienden*), all to support a way of life whose provisions (*voerwaerden, punten*) and customs (*ghewoenten*) they here set out for legal confirmation. Two women were named as having given most toward the building, four as the initiating "principals," but all forty-five (!) who presently lived there now appeared before the magistrates, each individually named, including one mother and daughter (visible in the last lines of the document in Figure 5). This group proposed a different legal and organizational model, perhaps owing to the aldermen, perhaps to the size of the group, perhaps to their priest counselor, Gijsbert Dou (d. 1420). The women made inventive use of four chosen *mombaers*, including Dou, employing them as Franciscans did their cardinal protector, namely as custodians. The *mombaers* constituted a society holding the properties and rights as a collective for the forty-five women, who legally stripped themselves of rights and goods, or rather handed them over to this collective (*si ghaven over wes goet dat si daeran gheleyt mochten hebben ende so wes recht*). No position in the house could be sold or bought. Only the voluntary poor (*willighe arme menschen*) were to live there, those wishing to serve for their salvation (*die tot salicheden dienen moghen*)—that is, neither owners nor the indigent, unlike

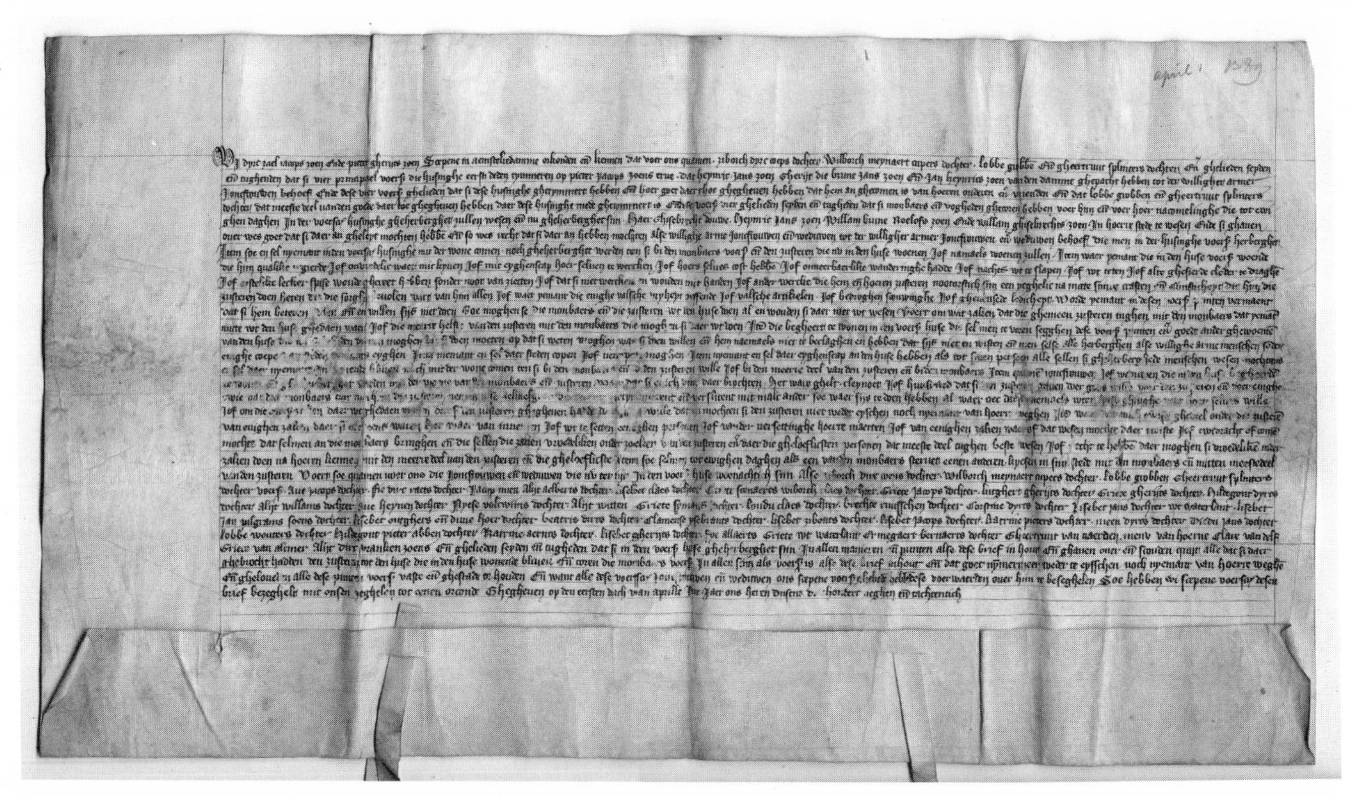

Figure 5. Recognition of a women's house in Amsterdam, the future Mariënveld or "Oude Nonnen,"1 April 1389, with the names of forty-five sisters, introduced (ninth line from bottom) as the women "who now live in this house and came before us." The Sisters sought and obtained this document with the confirming seals of two city aldermen, hung from the parchment strips still visible: Amsterdam City Archives, archief Gasthuizen, reg. no. 36, ed. P. H. J. van der Laan, *Oorkondenboek Amsterdam* no. 528, pp. 348–50.

with beguines. Nor could anyone live there except by permission of the *mombaers* and a majority of Sisters. A young woman or widow who wished to join, if she brought anything with her, had to hand it over as alms to the Sisters before at least two of the *mombaers*, with no further claim on it. The document set out several other points key to life in the house: that no one but Sisters and custodians could dwell there, and that the unfit could be removed, the obstreperous, also any who held or handled personal property and any guilty of false teachings including deceptive forms of contemplation and a fictive "emptiness." If there was no consensus among the Sisters on their form of life or whether to accept someone, they were to present the matter to the *mombaers*, who were to investigate and follow the views of the sensible majority. If one *mombaer* should die, another was to be chosen in his place by the other three along with the majority of Sisters. While the four *mombaers* served as custodians, decisions nearly always involved a "majority" of Sisters.

Still another model is found in the foundation document for a house in Alkmaar, dated 23 December 1394. Here the guiding hand may have been that of Hugo Goldsmit of Haarlem, though he is not mentioned.[75] The action was represented to the aldermen by a local priest and two laymen, *mombaers* for the community. The two laymen (with others) made a free gift of the property and buildings, located behind the parish church and running alongside the churchyard to the city wall. It was to be a "hospice" for "virgins and widows" who wanted to live religiously (*gheesteliic leven*) and consume together (*te samen verteren willen*) what they possessed or earned with handwork. Any goods a woman brought remained permanently behind. Once a woman joined, she was not to go out to eat or out overnight or out to market without permission of the overseer (*bewaerster*). Again, if a Sister proved troublesome and would not improve, she was to be removed. This document, simpler, said little about internal matters beyond overseeing visits in town and goods consumed in common. Now, all this may seem a whir of detail. But in the 1380s/90s, and this is the point, we find several different models for setting up women's households,[76] and a genuine inventiveness at work across these Dutch towns. Nearly all stipulations focused especially on the status of goods in town law and a community of goods in the household, along with control of admission and removal.

The inquisitor's findings at Rhenen offer an indirect glimpse at their internal life, or at least into those items that provoked others and were judged worthy of his attention. Many were crying out against these Devout households, it is claimed, particularly for forming a gathering without papal permission—a charge, if true, likely to have come from clerics rather than laypeople. The friar-inquisitor interviewed an unstated number of witnesses including a local curate, possibly the Roeloff van den Moelen made to seal the charter of 1388, or possibly his successor, but also some women who had left the house. Of his findings we have two versions, both summaries rather than transcripts.[77] Almost none of the items can be found in the foundation charter, not in itself surprising. Civic authorities paid minimal attention to internal practices so long as the house remained above ill rumor. The inquisitor found, then, a self-made religious life, with maximal authority invested in the Martha (contrary, if true, to the consensual emphasis in most documents), gatherings of women also supposedly virtually independent of the parish "like professed religious" (*per modum religiosorum*). What the aldermen approved and the inquisitor perceived may neither capture the lived reality inside these houses. The women reportedly assembled for meals at the sound of a bell, stood in a circle and asked a blessing in Dutch, and listened to readings in Dutch during the meal. Each day they gathered at the sound of a bell in a room set aside as a chapel, the Martha seated, they standing in two parallel lines—like nuns in choir, we might say. One after another they fell to their knees and said aloud their faults, or reported those of another, then waited to hear the penance she assigned.

Sisters reportedly might not leave the house for the parish church to make confession or attend mass or hear a sermon without her permission—this, it was claimed, bringing them greater merit for acting under obedience. Sisters, further, might go only to preapproved confessors or preachers, because some priests were considered unfavorable to this way of life and tried to turn women away from their "resolve" (likely the local curate). Sisters, very remarkably, were said to "check out" priests by going to them in disguise, as if seeking counsel about joining a household, then reporting back his replies. As strikingly, Sisters were said to confess to the Martha first, before they left the house to confess to a priest—this done, it was explained, because young women might stray into trouble conversing open-endedly with priests. Lay married women also confessed to the Martha at times, just as openly (*nude et aperte*) as to a priest, a practice encouraged by Wermboud of Utrecht. All these house customs or ordinances (*obseruationes, ordinaciones*) were set out, reportedly, for each new inhabitant point by point. The women promised to observe them, then allegedly were forbidden to reveal them to anyone outside the Devout network, even to a confessor. Whatever the truth of that charge, these ordinances evidently caused nervousness or tension. Certain Sisters went to the Carthusian prior in Monnickdam outside Arnhem, then to church lawyers in Utrecht, taking written copies along (*secum obseruancias predictas portassent in scriptis*), and were informed that the practices probably would not hold up in law. When Wermboud learned of this, the head Martha (Alheyde Cluten) went out from Utrecht to reinforce the Sisters, warning them reputedly to talk only with him about this, to deny everything, even under oath if pressed, so as to avoid further trouble (*turbacio*) from the outside.

These same worried Sisters eventually left the house, we learn, almost certainly becoming crucial informants in these proceedings against the others.

How skewed all of this was by the friar-inquisitor's preoccupation with priestly and religious prerogatives, how distorted owing to internal rivalries or tensions, or how independent and subversive indeed these women proved to be—this we cannot ultimately know with any clarity. But the findings correspond to the energies and agency revealed indirectly in founding documents: converts setting up their own lifestyle with an incipient network of Devout loyalists to sustain it. All involved, including the women, presupposed the mores of late medieval towns: matters negotiated out, written down, warranted by aldermen, with decisions made, if possible, consensually or communally, a senior administrator ultimately in charge. Among those forming households we find, not surprisingly, some patrician daughters and kin. The women remained under civil and parochial jurisdiction, not taking vows as religious, nor setting up independently as recluses, nor entering a beguine court either as indigent or propertied. Plainly they modeled their households to varying degrees on what they knew of organized religious life, but did so substantially on their own initiative, agreeing themselves to the terms of membership.

Societies of Devout Men

In matters of religion (and of marriage) men could generally act on their resolve more easily than women; likewise priests, gentry, or patricians more easily than artisans or peasants. Busch tells the story of William Vornken, his prior at Windesheim (1425–54). Son of a well-to-do burgher family in Utrecht (*ciues Traiectensis diuites et delicati*), he and another young man (*adolescentes*) heard about the converts at Windesheim from a mature follower (*ueterano deuotario*) in the mid-1390s,[78] and were independently moved to forsake the city and seek a better form of life (*melioris uite propositum*). After first keeping thoughts to themselves, each decided to open his heart to the other, and supposedly met in the street at the same time—a story this prior apparently loved to tell of his own conversion.[79] Men among the Modern-Day Devout, able to act more independently in law, formed "societies" as well as households (not the same thing). In the house of women at Amsterdam the four *mombaers*, all men, formed a society and the forty-five women the communal household. Master Geert, who knew instinctively how to make things happen, never joined a household but was part of several societies—these distinctions explained in due course.

We begin with a document Grote drafted in the year 1382. Its recipient, according to the rubric, was Henry Voppenz, originally of Gouda. The piece, lengthy and technical, was a legal instrument, and its subject the conversion of a worldly priest named John, more precisely the handling of his person and goods.[80] The whole reveals Grote in all his moral earnestness, but also in his inventiveness and command of procedure. Henry was to execute this document, possibly at Vollenhoven, the bishop's residence, since it was overseen by the bishop's "commissar." This priest had acquired considerable wealth by way of church office, enough to own two houses in Deventer. In a letter to co-workers in Amsterdam in late December 1382, Grote sent this document along for them to examine, noting it was drawn up on his advice (*de consilio meo*) and that the man would probably act on it before Lent, thus in early 1383.[81]

A brief word first about the chosen executor of this instrument, Henry of Gouda (born near Schoonhoven), later father-confessor to several households of Sisters in Zwolle. As a secular priest he had heard of Grote and sought him out, then converted and joined the household of Florens at St. Paul's vicarage in Deventer, thus 1383/84. Soon he was sent on to Zwolle, likely Kampen as well, to serve as a preacher and organizer of households, especially women's, also men's.[82] He became a trusted figure. When the house of canons at Windesheim unexpectedly needed a new prior only four years after its founding, he and Florens brought the case to the bishop in 1391.[83] Thomas of Kempen, who spent his early twenties at Zwolle (1399/1406), recalled him as a man of some learning, an able preacher with a strict conscience. He also told this story. Henry, away from Zwolle on business, wearing an undistinguished long gray tunic, felt boys yank on it from behind and heard them mock. "Ah," he said, turning back but speaking to himself, "This is where I should be. In Zwolle they all say 'lord, lord'."[84] The story reveals more than it tells. Would boys have dared yank on the vestments of some well-costumed priest? Devout leaders evidently could appear gravely authoritative and yet noticeably odd. On another occasion Henry observed to a young canon (possibly Thomas himself) that the cloister was a safe and quiet place. He by contrast daily confronted worldly people and worldly ways, and to such "rude people" he could preach only "crude sermons"[85]—presumably a rougher, more admonitory message, suggesting the difference between their sense of the "world" and their own inner circles.

The priest John, a man of the world, had resolved to repent. His "holy intention" (*sanctum propositum*) was to live as a poor priest, with "no more than the simple food and clothing with which apostolic priests were content"—a striking parallel to ideals expressed by Wyclif and Lollards at the same moment across the channel.[86] At issue for Master Geert was how to effect this legally and institutionally. First the man was to be asked if he "freely resigned" all his goods in compensation for past wrong-doing, this done formally into the hands of the episcopal commissar, who was then to redistribute them according to the dictates of divine and human law and the "will of a good man" (*secundum arbitrium uiri boni*), meaning effectively one of the converted, Henry being the agent on the scene. The priest, second, was to "grieve" his contemptuous handling of the sacramental mysteries, his sordid seeking (*questus turpissimus*) thus made publicly manifest—a public shaming in essence. Third, he was to be enjoined never again to act symoniacally. Fourth, he was counseled to avoid any occasion that might draw him back in, whatever might pull him back into the church as business. Fifth, in executing priestly offices (sacraments, preaching, and the like), and especially in any future change of office, he must now deeply (*medullitus*) examine his intentions. And sixth, he should flee any appearance of evil, show himself a true spiritual minister (the language gets intense here) and set himself off from all the merchant clerics (*alios mercenarios questuosos*). As for his private sins (presumably sexual), he should reveal those only to privy friends and spiritual doctors so as not to scandalize the public. He was, in short, to convert from a "worldly" to a "Devout" priest.

Now the question of goods. What the man had acquired came by way of the church, and must be restituted. But the point was not simply to refund. Within a time set by the commissar he should agree to resign all ecclesiastical incomes (as Grote had in 1375, roughly seven years earlier); give up ownership of his books (as Grote also had), books in general, it's noted, being granted to a "poor" man's use only for his lifetime and a set purpose; also to sell his land and put the money into the "manifest construction of a spiritual church" (in effect, the Devout community). The same held for household belongings and clothing, retaining nothing precious or superfluous, only enough to support himself, one other priest, and a housemaid. As for his houses, the commissar should assign these, the property itself of the first, the usufruct of the second, to "holy ministers of the church" (*sanctis ecclesie seruitoribus*), the second retained by John for life as a residence should he return to Deventer to live as a poor priest serving God (*sicut pauperi et indigenti presbitero Deo seruienti*), just as Grote had done with his house. Otherwise it was to be left for the use of "ministers of God" and the "fully converted" (*seruitoribus Dei et plene conuersis*). The rents, each year after Easter, should go to them, either to subvent their present rental (that is, their household) or to buy a dwelling or purchase books, especially a Bible and a *Summa confessorum*. He might have "use" of them as a "poor priest needing" such books, but ownership resided with the "ministers of God and the manifestly converted." This document takes us close to Grote's own actions post-conversion and to his ideal for converted clerics, that is, how to set "ministers of God" off from "clerics on the take."

Behind this loomed a larger project: to construct a spiritual church through material means (*realis ecclesie spiritualis constructio per temporalia*). The mechanism was what I call a "joint-holding society," two to four persons holding title to incomes or a house dedicated to Devout purposes.[87] Those committed to this endeavor were "Christ's spiritual poor," called ministers (*servitores/dieners*), the funds in this particular case specified for "ministers" in Kampen and Deventer. Each group formed its own society, Florens and Geert being joint-holders of the assets for the men's household in Deventer, a woman (Celia) and a man (Henry) for the women in Kampen.[88] Ownership of John's goods (houses, books, utensils) now resided with the joint-holding societies, John himself retaining no further rights, even in his last will (*eciam in testamento*). As for any additional rents that might come in, from lands or elsewhere, Henry of Gouda (the addressee of this letter, the "good man" at the beginning) should dispose of them for "ministers of God" with the aid of Celia, granting a certain amount to John as a "poor priest" should he need help getting through the year ahead. In all these arrangements Master Geert was the visionary, Henry the agent, and the "ministers" and communities in Kampen and Deventer the beneficiaries. As for what happened to John, we do not know, though a story about Grote's "prophetic" powers might allude to him. The story concerns four priest converts holding a frank talk among themselves about their shortcomings. To one named John Grote reportedly remarked, "I know what you're really thinking in your heart, about leaving, apostating"—which is what eventually happened.[89] Possibly this was the same John.

To underwrite materially the larger enterprise—establishing "spiritual ministers" amid "rude people"—they formed joint-holding societies. Grote employed the mechanism of a "society" (*societas*), a form taken over from civil law, in effect a private contract to receive and administer incomes. This joint-holding, interestingly, may actually have begun with books, Master Geert's most precious possession. He resigned his substantial personal library to a "society" (the original document no longer extant) when he gave his books (*communicavit*) to Florens Radewijns and Johan van den Gronde in an agreement that the joint-holders should always number three,[90] forming a "commune with respect to books" (*communia quoad libros*)[91]—what by December 1382 he demanded of the priest convert John. From 1382/83 the mechanism was everywhere in evidence. On 28 June 1383 a citizen of Deventer and his wife, Henry and Gheze Bierman, deeded over a sizable annual income drawn from newly reclaimed wetland, the dorso marking this a part of their will. At that moment the income was handled by Johan de Hoyer, an alderman active between the years 1371 and 1399,[92] and it benefited a cleric named Johan Peterszoen, whose small house stood on the Enghestraat, near those of other clerics and vicars appointed to St. Lebuin's.[93] De Hoyer and Peterszoen, together with Geert Grote and Johan van den Gronde (d. 1392), acted as joint-holders of this income (*verwaers ende be-*

hoeders deser rente), with a provision that if one died, he be replaced by another selected "within three months from among the very best, most conscientious and inwardlydirected men in the city." They were to distribute said monies to "two or three good inwardly directed (*ynnighen*) poor priests who served God and set themselves apart (*afghescheydenheit*) from the world." Chosen from among the "humblest and most godly of priests," men "poor and without ecclesiastical income in Deventer," they were to act as "mirrors" for others, hear confessions, and pray for benefactors.[94] The language suggests what Grote foresaw for the repentant John: to act as an independent poor priest, a model of conversion in his locale. Such "inward" free-standing (that is, untainted, unbeneficed) priests needed material support, however, whence this income-holding society made up of one layman (an alderman), two clerics, and one priest to oversee its incomes.

A year later in Zwolle a different situation unfolded. At the inspiration of Master Geert three laymen had begun to lead a spiritual life together in a house alongside the local Franciscan convent. To prevent relatives from claiming their pooled goods or ousting them, they sold the house to Geert Grote on 5 July 1384, who in turn made it available, or gave it, to "inwardly-directed people" (*ienighen menschen*). Eight days later (13 July) he "gave" the house to two priests, Johan van den Gronde and Master Florens Radewijns, with the understanding that the three of them constituted joint-holders, each to be replaced on death; also that the wishes of two among three would prevail in decision-making (see Figure 6, with Grote's name and seal). Twelve days later (25 July) Grote, Radewijns, and Brinckerink, the joint-holders or custodians, "loaned" (*doen ende lienen*) the house and goods back to the three laymen, for them to dwell in and thus to serve God (*te bet to dienen*).[95] In this case three clerics made up the society, with no citizens from Zwolle; three lay men living in common were its beneficiaries, forming a household. A later chronicler described it as a "hospice for receiving devout men."[96]

This same mechanism was employed in still other ways in other towns. In 1392 a society was formed in Hoorn to support a small house of priests located near the parish church and a larger womens' community forming up behind the church. The joint-holders there reveal the extent of networking, a priest and a layman from Hoorn, Johan van den Gronde and Gisjbert Dou from Amsterdam, and Paul Albertsz from Medemblick, along with, in 1397, Hugo Goudsmit of Haarlem. At Hoorn they would eventually hold as many as seven little houses.[97] In Purmerend (1392–99) a society involved several of these same men. In Leiden three societies were contracted with Pieter Danielsz uut den Pol, Florens acting here once (1396) as a joint-holder.[98] Societies, in sum, acted as the private legal holders of books, incomes, and houses, each one distinct, each

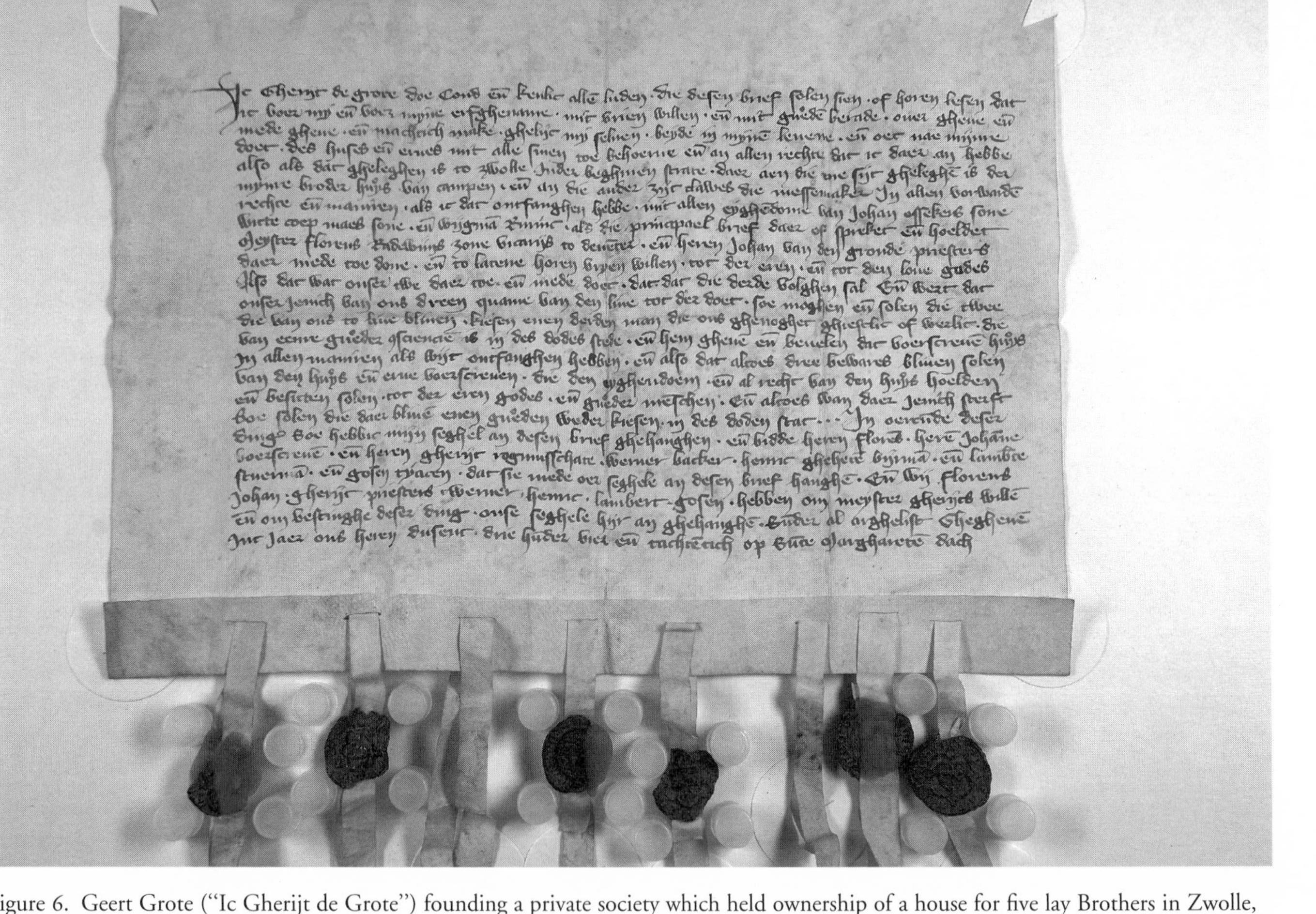

Figure 6. Geert Grote ("Ic Gherijt de Grote") founding a private society which held ownership of a house for five lay Brothers in Zwolle, dated 13 July 1384 (a month before his death), with the personal seals (from the left) of Grote, Florens Radewijns, Johan van de Gronde, and four others, the only extant document with Grote's name and seal: Historisch Centrum Overijssel in Zwolle, A.V. Mensema, *Inventaris van het Stadsarchief Van Zwolle* (2007), inv. nr. 13544; ed. Schoengen, *Narratio*, pp. 282–83.

comprised of varying combinations of people and holdings, their membership potentially spread across varying towns.

Societies and households, as noted, were not the same thing, though the two could merge. In 1391 the society that formed the house in Deventer identified its joint-holders as those chosen to act as the custodians of Master Geert's and their own books.[99] That house, the headquarters initially of the Brothers, stood on a smaller street (Pondes steghele) around the corner from Florens' vicarage and the house of Johan Peterszoen. The Devout acquired it by exchange in January 1391. According to a document negotiated with the aldermen, the priests who guided Lady Zwedera (and jointly held the house of Peterszoen: Florens, Johan van den Gronde, and Johan Brinckerink) proposed an exchange of her larger property for that of the recently departed Peterszoen, small and nearby.[100] Her house lay further back from the street, more suited for a society of inwardly-directed priests and clerics dedicated to "serving God."[101] Rudolph of Muiden subsequently described Zwedera as their "partial founder," though her stately income of 300 gulden annually went mostly to the house of canonesses founded at Diepenveen.[102] Nearly six years later (November 1396), the two surviving joint-holders (Florens and Johan Brinckerink) and Lady Zwedera had a notarial document drawn up in Latin, done in the house itself, to confirm that exchange. Already called "Florens' House," it was for (*pertinere*) Florens, John and companions (*socios*) who lived a "companionate life" (*sociali vita*) there.[103] When this society purchased its first income-producing property in February 1397, the four priests and one cleric who made that agreement identified themselves as those chosen to preserve and possess Master Geert's and their own books, as well as—this new after 1391—the house in Deventer "now called Florens House," originally the house of Lady Zwedera.[104] That income was to support "priests and clerics who continuously lived with them, whether inside or outside Deventer."[105] Societies did not exist, in other words, to found a house as such but to fund the "ministers" who lived there, wherever they served, and to hold in common their books and material necessities. These "societies" represented private legal arrangements negotiated with town aldermen, or at least under civic law, though they generally involved clerics as well. In the 1380s/90s nothing as yet was fixed except their purpose, and the centrality to that purpose of books, incomes to support "priest ministers" or a female household, and increasingly a house in which these "companions" could dwell.

Modern-Day Conversion

What drew people into Devout communities and societies is not easy to discern at this historical distance. Retrospective narratives cast Geert Grote and his preaching as the driving force (*pater, propagator*). But the springing up of so many new converts in all different towns, and for a generation and more after his death, far exceeded one man's preaching. Often it must have arisen from personal conversation or the attractions of a fervent community or personal questing or deep social need. Nor should we imagine Grote's as a lonely voice in a silent church—in the metaphor of his heirs, the only font of spring water in an arid landscape. The scenes in these towns could be lively, with rival preachers at work. Master Geert attacked Friar Bartholomew for teaching Free Spirit ideas in Kampen, and most citizens, it seems, inclined to the friar's teaching. He also attacked a Dominican from Haarlem named Frederick who, he said, proved amazingly harmful to the Devout in Kampen (*nocuit Deo deuotis mirabiliter*) by preaching the "old golden mountain" (*ueterem aureum montem*), an obscure reference, probably to some kind of merchant spirituality, religion trading on material goods. Master Geert in any case preached against it (*feci sermonem contrarium*).[106] In this one city, a river-port with a women's Devout community forming up around Cecilia, he did battle by way of sermons with two friars. For those drawn to the Modern-Day Devout, however, what were they hearing? How might it have differed from what they heard from their parish rector or a traveling friar or an Augustinian with "Free Spirit" sounding ideas? What might have touched them?

In religious terms the parish was for most people the focal point, coming fully into its own in the Later Middle Ages.[107] Here we can only approximate what ordinary townspeople experienced, what moved them, what bored or annoyed them. Divine claims had long since settled into routine observances: weekly services, confession and fasting at Lent, communion at Easter, confession with alms and restitution-making at death. For many this fully engaged and fundamentally sufficed.[108] For some—it is hard to know how many or how fitfully—it was not enough. In the later fourteenth century hunger for a palpable sense of the divine moved many into ever-swelling rounds of devotions, at chapels, in private societies, as lay associates to religious. They participated in new practices from the stations of the cross to the rosary, a devotional busyness represented in painting and sculpture, thousands of pieces for side altars or private alcoves. Some did so with a kind of anxiety, a desperate search for assurance; others, we may assume, peacefully and with satisfaction. Right alongside it—and not always treated by scholars in tandem—fundamental literacy worked its way more deeply into townspeople and gentry (a point also noted by Guicciardini), no longer the exclusive reserve of clerics and students or a tiny elite. As one scholar noted, "The desire for English vernacular books of moral and spiritual guidance seems to have begun in earnest among the laity in the mid-fourteenth century."[109] Estimates have it that 80 percent of the prose produced in fifteenth-century German was devotional in character, and 70 to 80 percent of the Middle Dutch.[110] Both vernacular books and devotional artwork, moreover, would have been aimed especially at women. For all that, we must not sidestep equally strong indicators of an intense pleasure in things earthly, a relative indifference to, even cynicism about, things religious, a jaundiced sense that all things spiritual had been rendered material, what Langland represented poetically as the reign of "Lady Meed" (corruption and greed), with "Lady Holy Church" almost wholly disregarded. In a world where religion could seem humdrum or privileged or corrupt, the Devout looked to carve out a new private world, one that turned on the "interior person" and "care for the self," pursued outside the cloister by way of individual resolve and communal households.

We may begin with John Brinckerink (d. 1419), the man who assisted Grote on his preaching tours. In this way we also begin in a sense with the women themselves. A sister (Liesbeth of Delft, d. 1423) took notes on wax tablets as he preached in Dutch at Diepenveen, those notes assembled into eight "collations," the text representing what they/she heard.[111] The first collation dealt with conversion (*bekeringhe*). It was heard as an appeal to the young, not the aged or widowed or indigent. The heart of a young woman is like an unwritten wax tablet. If she does not write "virtues, inwardness, and good thoughts" upon it, the Devil will write bad, and in old age she will find these hard to "unwrite." She must make a "great book" in her heart now, from which she can later read; otherwise she will find no "peace" in old age. All this begins with a "goodly desire for spiritual progress," and freedom from unruly passions: "Authentic interiority is a humble, fiery desire for God and for all things godly." But it must mature into a good resolve (*een goed opset maken*). For this is a call to the service/ministry of God (*toten dienst godes gheroepen*)—not just a matter of wearing gray vestments. Those who so act may become "enlightened servants/ministers of God" (*verlichte dienren Christi*) and can know "peace of heart." The collation ends with the apparent reversal of a key mystical teaching going back to Beatrice of Nazareth (*Seven Manners of Loving*) and Eckhart, namely, that a truly spiritual person acted without a "why" (*sonder enich waeromme*).[112] Here the final sentence read instead: "For in all our work we should keep an eye on our purpose [our "why" (*waerom*)], and so we may come to see our reward."[113] The reward envisioned was not so entirely different, however, to be "enlightened" and "at peace." But rather than abandoning the will or liberating the spirit, the Devout were to resolve, to focus, to write a book of virtues on the heart.

At the men's house in Deventer, Florens Radewijns and Gerhart Zerbolt together produced several manuals for devotion in the 1390s: a florilegium (*Omnes inquit artes*: not edited) ascribed to Florens, a summary (*Tractatulus*

Devotus) ascribed to Florens,[114] a devotional book on the "reform of the human faculties" (*De reformatione virium*) ascribed to Zerbolt, and another on "spiritual ascents" (*De ascensionibus spiritualis*). The books are deeply interrelated in theme and text, sprung from a commonality in intellectual labor as well as life. The latter two became virtually required reading in Devout circles, the *Tractatus deuotus de reformacione uirium anime* extant still in some forty manuscript copies, the *De spiritualibus ascensionibus* in some 125 (including fragments).[115] "Reformation of the church in head and members" was the general cry of the age, the slogan itself going back generations but now on everyone's lips amid papal schism and swirling corruption. In the Late Middle Ages this word (*reformatio*) simply became standard for reform, as in the *Reformatio Kaiser Siegmunds*, a point sometimes obscured by its later use to designate Protestants or an entire historical epoch. Zerbolt appropriated the term for what needed tending in the human interior, an appeal to remake the faculties of the self. A good decade earlier William of Salvarvilla, anxious about the papal schism, had written Grote for advice, how to think about it, what to do. Do not fret so much about the external schism, Master Geert wrote back, but about your own internal schism.[116]

The present condition (*status*) of the human spirit, as the Devout saw it, was inconstancy and misery (*mutabilitatis et miserie*), humans having lost "peace and tranquility, joy, happiness, quietude." To return to the "estate from which you have fallen" required diligent "spiritual exercises" designed to reform the faculties of the soul (*vires animae*). Simply put then: "Truly and spiritually to be converted is to convert, reduce and reform the affections and powers of the soul . . . to their rightful state."[117] The return was ultimately to a state of inner tranquility (*statui illi tranquillitatis interne*),[118] but it came only with a struggle. Progress in these exercises, Florens noted at the outset, borrowing from the Franciscan David of Augsburg's "On Composing the Inner and Outer Person," was an "art" acquired like that of a "skilled craftsman"[119]—a metaphor resonant for an urban audience. What needed honing, the powers to be re-formed, were a person's faculties of intellect, memory, and will (the latter also called the affections), the Augustinian triad. The intellect, dealt with expeditiously here, was to be reshaped through spiritual experience, reading, and the counsel of others. Memory was reformed through recalling one's sins and especially by constructing mentally (*cogitacionibus*) a series of meditations on subjects ranging from death and hell to heaven and divine benefits, and especially the life of Christ in its passion sequence. In practice this meant "filling your soul" with the nourishment of texts (*diuinarum pabulo scripturarum*).[120]

Then came the remaking of the will, the heart of the matter: by penance, by obedience, by manual labor, above all by doing battle one by one with the vices. Many, Zerbolt conceded, could not sustain the spiritual pace required and simply returned to the world. Others wanted to be "spiritual," or to seem so, but grew lax and tepid.[121] The aim was to become one in experience with what one read and worked at, then to console others who were also "depressed/ weighed down" by similar pressures (*alios in pressuris depressos consolaretur, ita et tu*).[122] Again the contrast with the conversionary ideals of two generations or so earlier, partly in ends, more markedly in means. Where mystics threw themselves finally into the spiritual abyss and onto the favor of God, their nothingness sinking into God's all, the Devout called upon urban neighbors to take charge of their souls, to remake their inner powers and affections, like an expert craftsman. For them the energy was to go into recrafting rather than escaping or transcending the self; hence, making the turn, taking up the resolve, doing the exercises, checking on one's progress. The way worked out by the Modern-Day Devout was at once hands-on and anxiety-producing. In thinking about sin, for instance, they were instructed to recall the inscrutability of God's judgments: "You do not know if you are in grace, do not know if you are truly converted, do not know what may lie hidden in you that is not hidden to God but offends him, do not know if you will persevere."[123] The point ultimately was not to frighten people (though this happened) but to shake them out of their complacency, to stir up in them a resolve for making spiritual progress. And the work, though lifelong, was not pointless; it was finally to know peace.

John Kessel (d. 1398), a lay Brother in the house when this was written, is known to us through a memorial penned by Thomas of Kempen, who as a young man shared a room and a bed with him for one year.[124] Kessel was born in Duisburg on the Rhine, and became a successful merchant in Flanders and Holland with a grand house in Dordrecht (a port city). At midlife he came to think better of it and went to Deventer to study Latin for the priesthood (even ordering luxurious vestments in advance). After encountering the Devout he resolved to give up learning and the priesthood to join their household and serve as cook, neither a patrician merchant nor a lordly priest but a household servant. Thomas records him saying from time to time, a striking play on words, "Have I not become a great priest and prelate, I who 'communicate' twice a day with the Brothers?"—that is, serve them meals morning and evening.[125] Kessel left behind "exercises" written in the privacy of his cell. He appears there a man weighed down by his fragility and waywardness, to the point of depression. Crucial among things he had "truly learned" was this: that nothing displeased God more than despair, for the Lord wanted penance (a "turn"), not death. The former merchant, now a cook, sought to fix God before his eyes at all time, to think good things within (*ab intra*) as he went about his work in the kitchen, show obedience, foster silence, read useful books, examine himself at the end of each day. His exercises concluded with the words "thorough improvement of myself" (*me utique emendare*).[126]

No attempt to get at the spirit of the early Devout can bypass Thomas of Kempen (1379/80–1471). He spent his teenage years around the Brothers' house in Deventer, then seven more around the early Brothers in Zwolle, before joining the canons at Mount-St.-Agnes in 1406 where he would remain for sixty-five years. The Agnietenberg, an hour's walk or so northeast of Zwolle, had first been founded by Brothers, four clerics and fifteen lay men, who in 1395 resolved to live away from the town's noise and distraction. When some in the community agitated for regular status, perhaps to counter outside pressures, the city aldermen in turn resisted and battled two years with the bishop (the temporal and spiritual lord) before yielding permission. Several early founders and laymen then departed for Vollenhove, to set up an unprofessed house.[127] Throughout his formative years, then, even into his thirties as a professed canon, Thomas lived in a spiritual atmosphere shaped entirely by Brothers. When he was made novicemaster for would-be canons in 1425 at age forty-five, he chose, not so surprisingly under the circumstances, to present the lives of Brothers in Deventer (Grote, Radewijns, and nine of the latter's disciples—nearly all people he had known personally) as the exemplary "fathers" of the Modern-Day Devout.[128] He had begun even earlier to compose little spiritual pamphlets, each comprised of dozens of proverb-like sayings of the kind that circulated in these Devout houses. Four of these pamphlets eventually would travel together as what we call *The Imitation of Christ*. The first of these ("Admonitions Useful for Spiritual Life") was written by ca. 1420 already (two extant manuscripts from 1424). It represented a straightforward call to conversion, directed in this instance particularly at young student-clerics. It concluded with a chapter (25) on "the fervent emendation of our whole life," the same point on which his one-time roommate the layman John Kessel had concluded his exercises, at least as reported by Thomas in his book on the "fathers" of the movement.

In the short second pamphlet ("Admonitions Drawing to Things Inward") the end of a converted life was portrayed as constructing a *homo internus*, an "interior person."[129] Equally important was the making of a *homo pacificus*, a "person at peace," able to bring peace to others (*alios pacificare*), such a person "more profitable" than someone very learned.[130] In Thomas's simple and supple prose, the appeal was straightforward:

> Turn with your whole heart (*Conuerte te*) to the Lord and forsake this wretched world, and your soul will find peace. Learn to despise outward things and to give yourself to inward things, and you will see the kingdom of God come in you. . . . As iron placed in fire loses its rust and

> is rendered brightly aglow, so someone converting truly (*integre*) to the Lord puts off torpor and is changed into a new person.[131]

Such a converted "interior person," one "simple in intention and pure in affection," would also place "care of himself (*cura sui ipsius*)" ahead of all else, consequently so "intent upon himself and God" as to be largely unmoved by what went on around him.[132] This turning inward toward peace nonetheless came only by way of a lifelong effort, its solace mostly divine, only occasionally human. This was, if I may put it so paradoxically, a passionate, hard-fought, self-conscious quietism. That stance, though seemingly contradictory while potentially integrating, deeply informed the spirit of Modern-Day Conversion. This word—"quietude" or "living quietly"—is scattered all through their documents and apologias and memorial lives.

This understanding of conversion presumed, and also set itself off from, earlier forms. The Devout pulled back from the activism of friars and some beguines, certainly from any begging and lively interaction with the world, also from any ambition to lead the church (none of their people ever were promoted to important prelacies)—and yet not entirely, for they still saw preaching and spiritual guidance, gaining a harvest, as central, to be carried out in their own ways (almost immediately contested). They were also wary of the heights and depths of mystical and Free Spirit yearning—and yet remained sensitive to its allure. Beyond Grote's translations of Ruusbroec, we find it in some of their writers, especially in Gerlach Peters (d. 1411), Hendrik Mande (d. 1431), and Alijt Bake (d. 1455), even in Thomas of Kempen. In his third and longest pamphlet, on "inner solace," he described peace this way: "If you know to annihilate yourself perfectly and to empty yourself of every created love, then I [Christ] may grow into you with great grace." Again: "Child, so much as you are able to go out of yourself, so much are you able to go into me."[133] This particular vision of solace (*consolatio*) echoed Ruusbroec indirectly, and more distantly notions ascribed to Free Spirits. The Devout vision of conversion, in short, was not made out of whole cloth. It appropriated elements old and new, remaining sensitive to the conflicting desires of their age, while establishing over time its own paradigm. The Devout were self-conscious compilers, excerpting from writers and models they esteemed, usually late antique or twelfth-century (though also Bonaventure and Suso). Whatever originality the Modern-Day Devout generated in their understanding of conversion—originality is not what they were striving for—rested more upon practices than teachings.

At issue was how to be "spiritual" or "religious" while also being in the "world" or "lay" (same word: *secularis*), the Sisters entirely lay, the men mixed, as we shall see. Grote was already struggling with that, for himself and for others.

He was once asked whether it constituted simony to purchase a place (*ene stede or ene provende*) in a beguine convent, probably in Kampen (St. Agnes), possibly in Zwolle (Oude Convent), a not uncommon practice. He penned a thirty-page legal and spiritual response for the women in Dutch.[134] Fees for entrance into religious houses, legally banned since the twelfth century, continued in social practice, often masked as a gift since women's houses in particular needed endowments. Grote, a stickler for an upright conscience, raged against it, though he conceded that the church was mostly quite indifferent. But the law itself proved only the starting point here, for the women's query came with legal sleight of hand. If beguines were still lay, the law was moot; a "place" in their house was not "ecclesiastical" and hence could come with a fee attached. This twist became the crux for Grote, eliciting passion and originality. These beguines—any indeed who treated community life as a social good open to material exchange—had to understand that a "place" in their house was something "spiritual," even without vows. Grote argued his point from principle rather than law: the more spiritually a person acted within and without, the more she acquired the virtue of religion even without entering the estate of religion. This principle applied equally and fully to persons choosing companions (*gheselynnen*) for a society (*gheselscop*) such as theirs:

> This [sacrifice of "tongue, life, and material goods" to religion] a person may well have as perfectly outside a community and outside a cloister and outside wearing vestments in a cloister, because perfect love and perfect hanging on God, to the best of our ability in this misery below—that is the fullest religion. This a person may have, and also may find, many times over, outside established cloisters. . . . This society, this brotherhood, this sisterhood, this community, this friendship, this sharing (*communicatio*), this helpfulness, this life, this estate, these offices, these exercises—these are spiritual things, and no upright person doubts that within. For . . . the Holy Ghost is given in the brotherhood, and Christ says that where two or three are gathered in my name there I am in the middle of you [Matt. 18:20]. Whether one exercises the virtues of religion perfectly or imperfectly, so long as the work and virtue are upright works of religion and proper virtues in love, then the companionship and the brotherliness are spiritual.[135]

For Grote and his beguine enquirers the word "spiritual" (*gheistlic*) came with a double-edged meaning, ecclesiastical (thus subject to this law) but also religious in the broader sense, making for a "religion" outside the professed estate. Even if they were lay, Grote insisted, thus outside the laws about simoniac entry into religious life, they and their community were properly spiritual/religious, for that hinged on their inner disposition.

The modern-day challenge was for people to take charge of their own souls, including responsibility for their inner powers and disposition, and thereby to reorient themselves toward an inner peace. Taking responsibility for themselves religiously—as aldermen did for town government, craftsmen for their shops, women for their households—could energize and also satisfy. As self-made converts they were freed of family life and routine parish life while not shackled by obedience to cloistered observances. Still, they were expected to join in the all-encompassing expectations of a communal household. To account for interest in this life, we should factor in social considerations (see Chapter 4) but beware of slipping into reductionisms.[136] The recurrent threat of sudden death by plague certainly induced a self-consciousness about life's purposes and the nearness of death; but in many it demonstrably also occasioned a new luxury and lust for life, not spiritual panic or asceticism. Indeed devotional manuals called on people to think first on death and judgment—as if they needed the reminder. Family life likely remained the first point of reference, an individual's prospects for work or marriage, also personal relations within a household. Disrupted family life, as we shall see, opened the way to at least some conversions; but hardly all. Some simply chose to enter this new sort of household. This conversionary movement also presumed the greater social maneuvering room which townspeople increasingly enjoyed, their negotiating capacities already noted. The Modern-Day Devout proposed an alternative community, not just a house for the widowed or needy (the role fulfilled by alms houses or beguines), also not a religious house with all that it entailed. This was to be a place where in peace and quiet one could cultivate an internal life, where you could have God ever before your eyes, "make progress in the virtues," take charge of your own spiritual life. But not alone, as a recluse would, a common figure in the later medieval world, but in a gathering of like-minded people who lived in a total sharing of goods, like the early church.

CHAPTER THREE

Suspicion and Inquisition

*At that time Master Eylard was the inquisitor of heresy [in this region]. He seriously harassed (*multum molestabat*) the Devout sisters in Utrecht. But Father Florens and Father Wermboud resisted him.*

But this does not fall to their [the inquisitor's] office because it is not heretical. Nay rather it is meritorious and licit so to live freed from the chain of religion, because so did the faithful in the primitive church also live.

So many new converts appearing in such a short time stirred up talk of "zealots" and "beguines." How widespread that talk was, how dangerous, how merely mocking, is hard to discern from this historical distance. For twenty years nonetheless their status—exactly the bishop's word (*super* **statu** *quarundam personarum nostre dyocesis*)—hung in the balance.[1] The Modern-Day Devout remembered it as harrowing. Tempting as it may be to reduce these clashes to broad binaries (clergy versus laity, authorities versus Free Spirits, men versus women), these disputes played out locally and in all varying combinations, with allies and adversaries face-to-face in city streets and public squares. We scholars tend to focus, understandably, on those instances when clashes exploded into violence, thus in Montpellier or England or Bohemia, or when inquisitors intervened with brutal force. Just as often, though, also in England and Bohemia, confrontations played themselves out less dramatically, in the slow-moving and complex apparatus of a multilayered church, in contestations over rights and privileges and truths. Parties sought to take advantage of complexities in church law, to find spaces in late medieval society or church for their own groups. Cases played out unpredictably. Marguerite Porete was burned at Paris in 1310, outside her home jurisdiction, despite favorable recommendations from three churchmen, while Bloemaert enjoyed a cult-like status in Brussels in the 1310s–30s, the same diocese (Cambrai). Birgitta of Sweden was put up for canonization and inquisition in turn, nearly at once, and more than once. Wycliffe, though forced out of Oxford, died peacefully in a country parish, while some of his disciples were pursued into hiding or to death. Hus was put to death, but Hussites battled to a negotiated compromise.

The story that follows, of the 1380s–90s and the diocese of Utrecht, involves a host of actors, many unnamed. Some were annoyed townspeople and neighbors: in Deventer an alderman favorable to the Devout (de Hoyer) was smeared as "priest-like." From the beginning Master Geert and the aldermen there reached an agreement that Sisters "were to remain and be called 'lay people'," not to be "specially dependent on any professed religious," and to "stand before aldermen in secular law like other laypeople."[2] Parish rectors too jealously guarded their rights. Those same revised house statutes specified that these women remain "subject to the curate like other parishioners."[3] For their parts most professed religious looked askance at self-made converts; an inquisitor's oversight could be relatively open-ended if matters of faith appeared at risk; and a bishop's jurisdiction equally opened-ended in nearly all local matters. All these figures became players in this story, one the Devout did not choose to recount apart from glancing references to hostile critics or a savage inquisitor. Our knowledge of it, as with fourteenth-century campaigns against beguines and beghards, derives in good part from surviving official or quasi-official documents. Actualities must be eked out from between the lines, with details of time, place, and circumstance often frustratingly elusive. The story that follows has been reconstructed from four sorts of materials. We have some official documents, three at least newly discovered. We have two inquisitorial reports, previously known in poor editions and studied apart from the context in which they were preserved. We have a series of *consilia*, professional legal advisories procured by the Devout, probably for a fee, to represent their interests and positions at the bishop's court. And finally we have a massive defense of the Devout, a hundred-page tractate divided into eleven contested "questions," the work of Gerhard Zerbolt of Zutphen. His heirs took care to preserve this dossier and pass it on, but anonymously, whether out of self-protection or humility or in a guise of officious impersonality.

Reconstructing this story, essentially from 1385 to 1401, serves two purposes, quite beyond its inherent interest. First, it allows for a more nuanced and complex picture of the confrontation between new groups and old interests, Sisters and inquisitors, than what sources and our standard narratives often allow. Second, in defending these households and practices the Devout generated arguments of more than tactical import. They moved toward reassessing "religion" itself in medieval society, toward something approaching rethinking social and religious theory—to be worked out in subsequent chapters of this book.

Suspicion of Devout Practices

From the beginning women's foundations spoke of consuming their goods in common, potentially threatening property rights as well as social propriety. What it meant in practice got little written explication, and doubtless varied locally and widely. The statutes for Master Geert's House were expanded on two telltale points after 1379, a warning against heresy and heretical books, but also with extensive rulings on the handling of property. Of the goods a woman brought to the house, a part was now to go to its fabric, a part to "shares" (*deelinghe* = portions in the house), these to be the same for all. A woman could initially retain private incomes (*renten*) unless she had no heir, but was required to leave one year's return to the house on her death, along with unspecified amounts in her will[4]—this also presuming at least some women of means. While certain practices may have aped precedents known from beguine convents, the emphasis upon commonality and household control of goods appeared unusual enough to raise suspicion among locals.

On the men's side, Florens Radewijns first introduced community of goods at his house in Deventer. As a teenager Thomas of Kempen "visited and looked on every day" (*cotidie et inspexi*), remembering the men gathered there as "remaining quietly at home" where "they devoted themselves to the copying of books." Florens, he reports, instituted a practice that "each one place together in common what was their own."[5] Rudolph, who first saw the house as a fourteen-year-old in 1398 and joined a few years later, rehearsed its communal beginnings with equal simplicity. "Father Florens kept the monies of those living with him. Seeing how fully these men were converted to the Lord and how amenable and adaptable, he poured their coins together, and coins that had been separated according to individuals he made to be of all, and thus they began to live in common."[6] Busch, long after, told a more dramatic story. Master Geert, attempting to renew religious life among secular clerics, gathered books from monastic libraries and paid students to copy them. One day Florens proposed that these student-scribes pool their weekly income and live from a common purse as equals. Grote reacted in alarm: "A commune? A commune? The friars will never allow it."[7] The scene in fact echoed later troubles but also captured the social novelty contemporaries perceived in these communal gatherings. Any offended Dominicans would have come from Zutphen. Their house maintained a preaching station on the New Street in Deventer, and belonged to the province of Saxony whence the inquisitor would come.[8]

For instituting a communal life the Devout were "publicly attacked and privately reproached," Busch had "frequently heard" from "the fathers" and read in "certain ecclesiastical documents."[9] Master Geert, as he tells it, mounted the pulpit in Deventer (presumably St. Mary's, the parish church), and refuted any charge that this way of life contravened church law (specifically the anti-beguine legislation). This he did "juridically," and the text Busch relates here corresponds to no known tractate or *consilium*,[10] nor the sort of text he was likely to make up whole-cloth himself. But it also read as a sermon, with a punchy ending: Would that these friars ceased reproaching the simple lambs of Christ living together! It is the professed living as the propertied who are the truly damned![11] A scholarly cataloguer at work around 1600 (Possevinus) listed a lost or unknown work of Grote's titled *De cohabitatione et exercitiis devotorum* (On the living together and exercises of the Devout), the work itself supposedly found in the library at Zevenborren (Septfontaines) outside Brussels.[12] Busch must have seen some such work, however accurately he understood or reproduced it. Mounting the local pulpit to defend people living together in a self-made community of goods, while consonant with Grote's fiery nature, would have drawn only more attention to the community. Complaints accelerated, more about women than men.

A year after Grote's death, by late 1385, things had gone further. Parish priests were denying new converts the eucharist and other ministrations, or threatening to do so. Now we first see Florens Radewijns assume leadership. He tried the same tactic those *pauperes* had deployed a decade earlier in Strassburg, that is, invoking the papal constitution *Ex injuncto* issued by Gregory XI in 1374. It, remember, provided for local investigations and also potentially local approvals. Radewijns lobbied the bishop of Utrecht, Florens of Wevelinchoven (1379–1393), to put it into effect across their diocese. From the converts' vantage point the strategy was to keep any investigative procedure in the bishop's court, out of the hands of either resentful locals or outside inquisitors, and also to gain confirmation for their way of life. Bishop Florens was accordingly petitioned by Florens Radewijns, along with perhaps other Devout colleagues, and he duly had this papal constitution instrumentalized or set in motion (*executio* is the technical term), also claiming that an earlier bishop had already done so (Arnold of Horn, 1371–78). Florens then had a copy of the order and constitution drawn up by a public notary at Deventer on 29 November 1385.[13]

The bishop's *executio* was addressed to all priests, clerics, and faithful in the diocese, and came with a fresh preamble. Appropriating the language of the papal constitution, he instructed his priests to allow the "upright" to attend divine office and receive communion and participate in common church affairs. Indeed he directly ordered his lower clergy: We admit them (*ut . . . licite faciant . . . recipimus et admittimus*). Some local clergy had patently resisted the Devout with the one power they had (sacramental ministrations). But the bishop added a catch in his last line: until we specifically instruct otherwise—putting the priests on notice but also the Devout. Nothing was settled yet. Radewijns nonetheless exploited his advantage. He had multiple copies of the *executio* made up, one by a public notary two weeks later on 15 December 1385 in the choir of St. Lebuin's, with two fellow vicars acting as witnesses. Himself identified in full title (priest, master of arts from Prague, perpetual vicar of St. Paul's altar), he held in his hands the original with the bishop's seal. Notarized copies were sent out as needed to the Devout network. We know of one surviving transumpt (authenticated copy), sent to Haarlem, presumably to help Goudsmit protect "beguines" there.[14]

Troubles had only begun. But before continuing we must introduce Florens Radewijns, the "most fervent propagator" of the Devout according to Thomas of Kempen.[15] Rudolph of Deventer named him the "founder of our house and administrator of the Devotion in this entire land," while Busch, though a Windesheim canon, repeatedly called him the "father and patron of the Devout in the entire homeland."[16] After Grote's untimely death the Devout had "humbly submitted themselves" to Florens, Thomas claims[17]—obscuring thereby the networks active in Utrecht and Holland. Still, most of the next generation's leaders were trained by him, or came out of his house. Florens drew Thomas of Kempen too into the "service of God," and from him we have an admiring portrait, the largest section (Book III) in his *Dialogue for Novices*. Sent for schooling to Deventer about 1392 as a young teen, and drawn into the Devout circle like his older brother John, Thomas came to know Radewijns well (*apertius eum agnoui*), served him at table, and lived in his house for one year (1397/98), witnessing personally his generosity to the poor and to schoolboys. Thomas had once given a book in pledge against fees he owed his schoolmaster, and received from Florens the money needed to redeem it, the master then refusing the coins on learning their source.[18] When Florens was present for office at St. Lebuin's, Thomas dared not "tell stories" (*fabulari*), he says, and Florens once put hands on his shoulders so he dared not even twitch.[19] When Florens grew ill, Thomas acted as a messenger (*internuntius*) to the women, reporting on his condition.[20]

This portrait, though affecting and very influential, does not account for a movement leader. Neither cantankerous nor brilliant like Master Geert but firm and effective, Master Florens Radewijns of Ledderdam (ca. 1350–1400) possessed an inbred sense of how to get things done, how to handle income, how to interact with authorities—this anchored in his family, his training, and early preferment.[21] He came from a gentry family in the lordship of Arkel, not far from Utrecht, and secured a canon's position at St. Peter's in the episcopal capital very early. With parental support he went off to university in Prague, listed there as a bachelor in 1375, a master in 1378, also as starting the study of law.[22] Many from the Low Countries at that time went to Prague for university, Moll counting 180 Netherlandish graduates between 1361 and 1409.[23] Prague, a recent foundation (1347), emerged as a place of intellectual refinement and advancement, also now the imperial capital. At age twenty-seven or twenty-eight Florens earned his master's beret as a relatively older man (Grote was eighteen at Paris). After returning to the Low Countries, just over thirty, he heard Master Geert preach (Thomas says, at the main parish church in Deventer), and began rethinking his career. They conversed, and he resolved to move closer, this about 1382,[24] possibly at Grote's suggestion. Florens exchanged his prestigious post as a canon in Utrecht for that of a lowly vicar of an endowed side altar in Deventer. Altars and chantries proliferated in the later middle ages, patrons endowing masses for families or groups. Chantry priests often came in for mockery in literary jibes or reformist pamphlets as sinecures with little priestly piety. For Florens, however, this marked a transition into a more self-directed form of life, also a move into priesthood (which Grote himself had avoided). St. Paul's, one of ten vicarages in St. Lebuin's, required its occupant be ordained.[25] The post came with a small house on the Enghestraat, soon the base of operations for Devout converts.[26]

Florens may have gotten the bishop to authorize *Ex iniuncto* and order priests not to harass converts in later 1385, but the next year he felt compelled to take another step, suggesting the pressures had not eased. In 1386 he and his allies in the IJssel valley proposed to establish a religious house in the full sense, an institution above suspicion. Ruusbroec and his companions had been forced to go this direction five years into their solitude, and Merswin in Strassburg as well. In this case however Florens remained leader of the Devout, and his house in Deventer the nerve center of the movement. Thomas of Kempen as well as Busch, both canons, claimed later that the plan itself went back to Grote, his dying intention.[27] For this there is no evidence. The decision was taken in 1386 as pressure on the Modern-Day Devout mounted. Prior William Vornken (1424–55) articulated the founding conception: a house conceived as a "refuge" in whose "shadow" all Devout could find relief from the "assaults of the hawks."[28] Busch's swollen narrative of Grote's death-scene states the same purpose: to institute an irreproachable "refuge" for all Devout of both sexes, a "secure recourse," a "much-desired fortress," to which all could turn for counsel, help, and defense, offering aid for God-fearers throughout the province.[29] And a later prior of Windesheim, Theodoricus Graviae (1459–86), simply named

Florens as founder, citing the documents.[30] This was a strategic move (*causa mouens*), as it was also remembered in Deventer. Those living in a communal lifestyle feared persecution, Brother Rudolph says, and the unprofessed majority hoped to "hide" under a few professed.[31]

To secure the founding of a house of canons regular, Florens again went personally to the bishop (*pater omnium deuotorum in propria persona*), three times in fact in the mid-1380s according to Busch.[32] In July 1386 the bishop conceded their right to seek suitable land, rejecting a site near Hattem across the River IJssel (thus in Guelders) and insisting upon a location within Salland, his own temporal jurisdiction.[33] Busch's language here (probably echoing a document) suggests that Windesheim too began as a "society," with seven people named, Florens and Johan van den Gronde at the head. Berthold ten Hove, Grote's kin, eventually "gave freely and totally" properties and incomes at the "hof" there worth 3,000 pounds, all hereditary rights duly foresworn by him and his heirs.[34] A lay member of the society, then a citizen of Kampen, took over the feudatory homage attached to these lands. The foundation was referred to as a *collegium* with an *oratorium*,[35] the language of a secular college of canons, not that of a full religious house. The chapel and basic buildings at Windesheim were dedicated in October 1387, and a privilege establishing the house's organization and full ecclesiastical immunity in December 1387, it issued notably at Deventer. The founders sent two members to St. Victor in Paris to learn about statutes and customs for canons regular,[36] and the first six professed members, all disciples of Florens, to Eemstein to learn the customs of Groenendael. As for their choosing to become canons regular, Busch projected certain musings onto Grote. The only two religious orders respected in his day were the Carthusians and the Cistercians, but the first he accounted too far removed from society and other Devout converts, the second too inflexible in its form of life. They needed an order with high standards but flexibility, open to new converts, including women and men.[37]

If Windesheim, in the country and under ecclesiastical immunity, was projected as a place of refuge, the Brothers residing in the house in the middle of Deventer remained on the front lines. Their nunbers continued to grow, whence the exchange (already noted) for Lady Zwedera's larger house in 1390/91. This too met with resistance. The aldermen in Deventer, we are told, took a "hard and unfavorable stance against these clerics," whom "they would not permit to hold any property"—fearing its permanent loss to the "dead hand" of the church. Lady Zwedera's nephews and heirs, Wijnelt van Arnhem and Swieder van Rechteren, intervened, and the magistrates eventually yielded, sealing an agreement that allowed for four priests and nine clerics to live in the house.[38] Their joint-holding society, however, had to accept the addition of two members from the city council (*wille wy toe voeghen twee van onsen rade*). And, as with women's households, they were forbidden, without the aldermen's consent, to profess religion (vows) so long as they lived in the house. If they acted moreover in any way "contrary to the honor of God and our city," the city counsel could throw them out.[39]

Charge and Counter-Charge in the Mid-1390s

Ten years after Florens first employed *Ex iniuncto* to protect new Devout communities from hostile pastors, illrumor and critique reached new heights, and the fate of these gatherings fell under the sway of a new bishop. Bishop Florens had died in April 1393. The papal schism, fifteen years along with no end in sight, enabled rival allegiances and candidates, especially in border regions like the Low Countries, to play off two popes. Utrecht, politically subject to the German Empire, suffragan ecclesiastically to Cologne, followed the Roman obedience, though well aware of its French border to the south, and with its own people divided.[40] Regional powers had a major stake in this as well, even campaigning in person to try sway the electing canons in Utrecht, for the bishop was a territorial prince. In lands temporally subject to the bishop (the Sticht and Oversticht), lords and towns maneuvered as best possible, Deventer itself now becoming more of a player. In the spring of 1393 the count of Holland favored the brother of the lord of Bronkhorst, a man then treasurer of Cologne's cathedral. The duke of Guelders preferred an Alsatian named Frederick of Blanckenheim, kin in some way, a man about forty years old but bishop of Strassburg already since 1375/76. The canons, divided, opted for Frederick. Of a powerful family, Paris-trained in law, a bishop in his twenties, a political activist, he also knew firsthand the tensions in Strassburg over beguines and Tertiaries. Pope Boniface IX agreed to "translate" him, his entry into Utrecht staged on St. Martin's day (11 November) 1393.[41] Frederick ended up reigning for thirty years, a commanding presence. He worked to regain temporal control of his territories, including distant Groningen,[42] proved an active church administrator,[43] a benefactor of the newer Observant movements, and a supporter of those cardinals who tried to end the schism at the Council of Pisa in 1409. As for the Devout, he was not hostile, unlike Arundel's stance toward Lollards at precisely the same time. Busch, writing more than a generation after Frederick's death, celebrated him retrospectively as a great supporter,[44] partly in the wake of troubles that would follow, partly acknowledging the bishop's openness to reform-minded regulars like the Windesheimers. Had there been open hostility across those pivotal thirty years, the Devout could well have been driven out or into far more radical stances. Frederick was cautious about converts, in fact. For nearly ten years he allowed the Devout and their critics to battle in charge and countercharge.

Things came to a head initially in 1395, as suggested by three pieces of evidence, two certainly from 1395, one possibly. We begin with the last, an undated *consilium* from Master Evert Foec (d. 1418). During the fourteenth and fifteenth centuries *consilia* emerged as the primary form in which lawyers did their written consulting work. Given a disputed case (most often marriage or property or wills), or some other contested matter, a lawyer would draw up a set of arguments bolstered with supportive legal authorities. This was done for a fee, signed by the lawyer himself (usually a "handwritten-seal"), with other jurists sometimes adding their handwritten agreement to strengthen it in the eyes of a judge.[45] In the diocese of Utrecht Master Evert Foec was the foremost ecclesiastical jurist, a position he had inherited from his uncle Gerard (d. 1383), the latter son of the mayor, one of the first Netherlanders to graduate in civil law from the University of Orléans, longtime dean of the chapter (1349–74), a position then passed to his nephew. Master Evert also graduated from Orléans, and inherited his uncle's house in the cathedral precinct along with his books and networks. In his lifetime he would hold multiple ecclesiastical posts, but from 1364 he lived and worked primarily in Utrecht as a cathedral canon at Oudmunster, a post obtained very young.[46] Deacon Evert served as dean of chapter for forty-four years, introducing measures to discipline and improve liturgical worship, and playing an important role in building the gothic sanctuary that still stands. On 8 March 1402 Foec was empowered to handle the legalities of all benefices in the bishop's gift, a lucrative and powerful position. Of the dozens of *consilia* he must have written, only a few survive, two concerning the Devout (preserved by them).[47] In his testament Evert made a gift to the Devout women's foundation in Utrecht (St. Cecilia). But the main object of his benefactions was his own cathedral chapter, along with a large gift setting up its almonry in 1407, allowing them to feed fifty poor people in the city, a practice that survived into the nineteenth century.[48]

Foec would have been a figure familiar to Grote and Radewijns from their days as canons in Utrecht in the 1370s. About 1382 Master Geert recommended that the fledgling foundation at Eemstein seek his juridical help in private (*secrete consiliarius*) on a certain matter, and "grease his wheels" with money. Foec would have ways to work out the business, Grote noted bluntly, but no mind for matters of conscience, these legal *consilia* in general tending to the superficial, he opined.[49] Around early 1395 the Devout in Utrecht and Holland nonetheless sought his advice in a written consilium, suggesting a matter of some gravity. Tensions had apparently advanced beyond loose street-talk. Someone was publicly preaching against "suspect beguines," that is, the new women's communities, even lodging written complaints. This priest (*dominus*) would not refrain his slippery tongue or silence his pen but in words and writings was busily attacking the "estate" of people living together.[50] Foec warned him to stop his clamor, his empty and boring words (the *consilium* begins "*omissa prolixitate uerborum inanium*"), lest he become legally liable for ill fame (a lawyer's threat). He referred to the man pointedly as "inferior" in jurisdiction. This priest, "whoever he was" (a put-down, but Foec may have known the case only by report), had intervened in a matter beyond his competence.

Master Evert spoke from ironic distance. He revealed no inner engagement with, or much personal knowledge of, Devout communities, these *pauperes*—Foec himself having once gone off to Orléans on a horse worth more than a hundred pounds.[51] But he knew how to set out the law. It was simply wrong, he began, to say that the "estate" of beguines was banished, a misreading of the legislation, not applicable to "beguines of these parts." The critic had apparently invoked *Cum de quibusdam*, and Foec dismissed it: not pertinent because these women held to none of the odd teachings proscribed there. Nor did they fall under the sanctions of John XXII's *Sancta Romana* because they had formed no new religious order and elected no religious superior. Benedict XII's *Recta racio*, he continued, simply glossed and made operational (*est constitucio declaratoria*) the earlier *Cum de quibusdam*, and it "today expressly approves or permits" communities of the type found "in these parts," that is, stands as the ruling law on this matter. Foec also knew and cited Gregory XI's *Ex iniuncto* of 1374, pointing up that it conferred on a local bishop authority to "investigate" and "license" the "devout and innocent poor," also to constrain them, or any objecting to them. Foec's contempt for the accuser was palpable: The power to examine such people belonged to bishops, not "inferiors."[52] Someone, probably a local pastor, was trying to move against the new women's communities as banned beguines, he thus "preaching" and "disputing" and citing church law. The threat worried Devout leaders enough to secure a terse written response from one of the most prominent jurists in the diocese.

The pressure was consistently greatest on the women's communities, but the men's too were were coming under pressure, and they tried a different tactic. In March 1395 they engaged in a kind of legal flim-flam. In 1392 two more houses of canons regular had been founded in Arnhem and Hoorn. Now the priors of all three gathered at Windesheim, Florens likely present as well, though deliberately not mentioned.[53] All were his disciples. Formally speaking, the former Brothers, now professed canons, affirmed in writing the respectability of the current Brothers (implicitly including Florens, their effective leader), an ingenious circularity. The group had prepared the document in advance (*cedula in papiro conscripta per ipsos*), likely under Florens' direction, now presented to a public notary. The canons stipulated that they had lived in the house in Deventer for many years, still regularly visited it, personally knew it to be above reproach, and stood ready, if called upon, to act as witnesses under oath against any detractors—suggesting some kind of formal charge or court appearance could be in the offing. They declared the Devout innocent of all rumored charges: that they housed a schismatic sect or conventicle, engaged in preaching outside church pulpits, disputed articles of the faith, formed a religious order illicitly, adopted a religious habit, vowed obedience to a prelate of their own making. These points were derived in good part from anti-beguine legislation, but also echoed public perceptions of Devout practices: the men's household a "sect," their collations a kind of preaching, their teachings in the vernacular dubious, their following Florens a kind of "obedience." To declare the house's lifestyle licit, the canons took over for themselves *Ex iniuncto*'s language, its formula for the good convert (as quoted at the end of chapter 1). But on one point they differed, the first practice named: that the men in Deventer led a common life, living together from labors and income that they pooled.[54]

As for the canons themselves, they resolved, also in early 1395 and doubtless with Florens's agreement, to form a general chapter, thus a new religious order, and gained approval from Rome officially on 16 May 1395.[55] This effectively rendered them even less vulnerable to critique, now a religious order, not a simple *collegium*. The person who acted as their facilitator at the papal court was a canon of the cathedral chapter (Oudmunster: like Foec) named Gerrit of Bronckhorst (d.1412), belonging to the family just denied the bishopric. Schooled in church law, busy for many years (ca. 1359–ca. 1374) at court in Avignon, he lived in a large house just off the cathedral square (today the "Wed"), and was treasurer of the cathedral chapter until 1402. Though based in Utrecht, he served the provost (head) of the chapter in Deventer for a time as vicar for matters spiritual.[56] There he would have worked near Florens's House, though himself living in a palace. Bronckhorst would emerge as the key inside player for the Devout. He attended Windesheim's founding in 1387, the document authenticated in Deventer.[57] In 1394 Bronkhorst witnessed and sealed the setting up of the joint-holding society for what became the Brothers house in Zwolle (though not himself a member of it).[58] As the scion of a wealthy family, he made benefactions to a host of Devout communities, men's and especially women's, his will offering a virtual guide to the movement, the largest bequest going to St. Cecilia's in Utrecht where he asked to be buried.[59] When Mount St. Agnes started out (Thomas's house), he donated two cows, one of which died, the other "wondrously" giving more than enough milk for the Brothers.[60]

On a visit to Windesheim he reportedly remarked that only the pigs there seemed well-fed.

Amid growing pressures in the spring of 1395 someone undertook a further step, an expensive one. In July 1395 Bronckhorst was back in Rome, formally at the behest of Bishop Frederick. Among other things he requested from the papal chamberlain a true and proper copy of the papal letter *Ratio recta*, this to be taken directly from the papal register. (Parenthetically, it is intriguing to consider administratively how Rome had access to registers drawn up at Avignon seventy-five years earlier, with a papal court still at Avignon.) The request was agreed to, a notarized copy elaborately collated and double-checked, all dated 19 July 1395 in the papal chamberlain's office. The law was identified as an issuance of John XXII, not Benedict XII, "as was frequently said."[61] Foec, remember, had invoked this text as reigning law on converts, but as "Benedict XII's *recta ratio*," in fact a reissuance a decade later. Someone had caught the mistake (different popes, a reversed *incipit*)—and perhaps challenged Foec's opinion. Or the bishop had accepted Foec's argument that this constituted reigning law on all these burgeoning converts and now wanted an accurate text from Rome. Most revealing, in any case, was the preamble to this authenticated copy of *Ratio recta*. This particular text was badly needed now in Utrecht (*plurimum indigebatis*), it explains, to help "adjudicate converts" appearing in their diocese (*aliquibus conuersis interdum occurentibus sanius et facilius* **terminandis**). With it they hoped "more wisely and easily to decide their cases" (*in terminandis conuersiis iudicialiter*). The dispute had reached the bishop's court, which also accounts for Foec's opinion on behalf of the women and the canons' testimonial on behalf of the men. We may also detect at work here the mind of a bishop trained in Paris at law, familiar with the interminal disputes at Strassburg, wanting a reliable text before moving himself toward deciding judicially these converts' cases.

Two generations earlier a wit a Strassburg had quipped that no one paid any attention to these papal letters, or even knew about them. And indeed these constitutions only truly came alive when parties on either side, those trying to condemn freelance converts or those seeking legislative protection, invoked them. But they were transparently a live item at Utrecht in 1395, of interest to the Devout as well as the bishop. This document with its Roman seals was checked and notarized again on 15 November 1395 by the Benedictine abbot of Egmund, Johan Weent, perhaps in preparation for going into court. But this notarized copy was also duplicated for use in other local situations, one such preserved in Hoorn (a center for communities in that part of Holland), another transmitted by the Devout with their apologetic materials.[62] How many more went out to key Devout leaders or communities in late 1395 we cannot say.

Whatever the state of the court battle on "adjudicating converts" in 1395, exchanges also multiplied now concerning certain practices, eliciting two tractates probably datable to about this same time (1395/96), one on clothing, another on vernacular books. Gerhart Zerbolt of Zutphen, a Brother at the house at Deventer, emerged now as the Devout's inhouse thinker and writer. Of him too we have a personal portrait from Thomas.[63] The son of burgher parents in Zutphen (his father "Zerbolt" perhaps an alderman), Gerhart (1367–98) came from a religiously inclined family, with two half-brothers, Helmut (d. 1441) and John (d. 1445) born of a father "Minne," they joining the Crosiers at Huy and Namur respectively. These houses stayed in close contact with the Devout and came to possess important early manuscripts, also of Zerbolt's works.[64] Zerbolt attended Deventer's Latin school and studied at Cologne, but was largely self-taught in the disciplines of law, theology, and devotion. An ardent student, he was consumed with books, reportedly grieved when classes were suspended for holidays, never left his cell as a Brother, not opening a window for fresh air or sweeping out cobwebs, given entirely to copying and writing books, well beyond the time allotted in the household. He loved well-made books, and was named house librarian in his mid-twenties (early 1390s), thus taking charge of Master Geert's and the communal books. When consulted on something, he made a note and read or asked until he found a fitting reply. Florens came to rely on him for aid in "disposing the house's affairs," and worked out with him "anything concerning legal matters." Zerbolt in turn consulted with local experts, especially Arnold Willemz (abbot of Dickeninge), another leading jurist in the diocese.[65] Though not a jurist himself, Zerbolt could, as other petitioners did in the Later Middle Ages, draw up a dossier of authorities and arguments to represent his case to jurists or judges. Thomas would later note Zerbolt's two influential spiritual manuals prominently, but said not a word about his four tractates: a hundred-page defense of the Devout (*Circa modum vivendi*), a lengthy apology for clerics not seeking ordination (*Scriptum pro quodam*),[66] a defense of clerics' not wearing costly garb, and a defense of vernacular books—all key markers of the Devout lifestyle and disputed in the 1390s. On his early death in 1398 one Devout leader remarked that it was just as well: So many people would have come running to consult him in years ahead that it would have harmed him and his household.[67] But Florens was devastated: the "pillar" of our house taken from us, my "other hand" in house affairs (*altera manus in negociis pertractandis*).[68] Zerbolt's writings, according to Revius in the 1650s, were gathered up in the house into a single volume (since lost).[69]

His tractate on clothing was composed in Latin, first of all for fellow clerics, and translated into Dutch the next generation.[70] Foec had alluded to this matter (*deferentes habitum*).[71] In the Middle Ages clothing (*habitus* can refer broadly to apparel or more narrowly to the special garb worn by religious) signified status.

In older canon law "wearing the habit for a year" or "assuming the habit" constituted profession. Sumptuary legislation too attempted to define apparel appropriate to certain estates, as well as to restrain luxurious spending and inflammatory display.[72] The Devout initially adopted simple garb, something "middling," they said, neither lay nor clerical, distinctive nonetheless in its cap or hood,[73] also in its deliberate "abjection" or refusal to follow status norms. Florens, for instance, deliberately embarrassed Thomas's brother John, a man considered all too quick (*abilis et ingeniosus*), by having him wear "abject clothing" and "overlarge shoes,"[74] one of many such scenes in the Brothers' lives. The Brothers did not look properly like either clergy or laymen, and the Sisters, though lay, looked as if they were adopting a kind of religious dress.

Zerbolt proceeded in three parts, his defensive punch coming at the end. Certain persons, he says, judge it "no sin to wear expensive clothing, indeed wrong or vile (*uiciosum*) to wear something humble or less expensive." This assertion of a right to wear finery, whether as clergy or laypeople, implictly countered Devout practice, perceived doubtless as hyperpious. Zerbolt adduced authorities first to show that it was sinful and sin-producing to fuss about or to sport costly clothing. Then, at twice the length, he defended wearing clothing that was neither expensive nor vile, only what sufficed for human need and induced inner humility. "Private persons," he says, "act with merit and virtue if out of personal humility and contempt for the world they wear humble clothing, humbler even than their station in life would ordinarily require."[75] "Public persons," this distinction drawn in part from Thomas Aquinas, were expected to wear clothing befitting their estate (such as clerics or religious), something Devout clerics failed to do. A third part (twice as long again) applied these principles to the case of certain persons now speaking or preaching in favor of expensive clothing (*informacio uel predicacio illorum qui inducunt populum ad deferendum uestimenta preciosa*).[76] With this (*ammonicio uel exhortacio de bonis uestimentis*) they in effect "taught and inspired common people (*vulgus*) to procure for themselves expensive clothing beyond what befit their estate," since these commoners had taken in from this debate only that "it was licit and not a sin to have fine clothes."[77] Here then was a "preacher"—a local rector, canon, or friar—piqued with Devout practice or rhetoric. True preachers (*veri predicatores*), Zerbolt countered, exhort people not only to what's licit but also to what is expedient, not only to commands but also to the counsels.[78] They set a higher spiritual standard, and also with respect to garb.

Zerbolt placed five arguments in the mouth of this adversary, which suggests an active exchange. This stance on finery was taken, first, not simply to justify inordinately expensive clothing but to commend garb befitting an estate in life. This was a common argument among churchmen, also a reformer like

Gerson. Others, second, were scandalized by an abject habit of this sort (*huiusmodi*: the sort worn by converts, presumably): "it is not similar to the rest," to which "they should simply conform."[79] Laypeople should look like other laypeople, clerics like clerics, priests like priest. Virtue, moreover, and third, was a matter finally of the heart, not of clothing, and a humble heart could reside in expensive worldly clothing. Indeed the critic pointed out, fourth, citing Augustine, persons making a fetish of wearing clothing different from those around them were "superstitious." And, fifth, Christ, our informant in all things, wore expensive clothing; otherwise the soldiers would not have cast lots over it.[80] People manifestly were taking exception to the Devout, in this case the male clerics in particular, and saw their garb as odd and sanctimonious, causing scandal.[81] Zerbolt's stance, like that in his general apology, was assertive, and employed a favored turn of phrase: "The use of abject clothing is not blameworthy but to be praised, because it is licit and meritorious."[82]

Critics objected as well to the use of books in the vernacular. Zerbolt's pamphlet "on germanic books" (*De libris teutonicis*) survives in three Latin forms and more than one Middle-Dutch form, it too densely argued and full of authorities.[83] The Latin text likely came first: his authority apparatus tends to confirm that, as does incidental evidence.[84] But one does not write a treatise in Latin to bolster laypeople in vernacular reading; one does so to counteract charges arising from churchmen. Zerbolt set these out in his opening sentence: Some people, with little understanding of Scripture and little reflection on the fathers, say that it is illicit for laypeople to read or exercise themselves in holy writings, also that to provide them with devotional books in the vernacular or to have books translated specially for them is deserving of reproach, to be avoided, indeed stopped.[85] Circumstantial allusions are rare here, making it difficult to tease out an exact context. These objections had arisen locally. But in 1374 Gregory XI had issued *Ad apostolatus nostri* responding to reports of "dangerous" books of sermons in the vernacular infected with heresy, now being read out to laypeople and thereby "usurping the office of preaching." He had accordingly authorized friar-preachers in German lands to investigate and curb this—the initiative in fact arising with them.[86]

Women converts in the Low Countries acquired vernacular religious materials from the beginning, especially Geert Grote's translation of liturgical hours and prayers, of which some 2,000 manuscripts survive.[87] In addition, Wermboud in Utrecht "had many books of sacred theology copied out, and he translated certain sayings of the saints into the Dutch vernacular for the use of faithful laypeople."[88] These "sayings of the saints" most likely included sermons and devotional writings ascribed to Augustine, Anselm, Bernard and the like, authors and writings which, Zerbolt said, laypeople often understood better than learned masters.[89] In Deventer the women of Master Geert's house came under severe criticism, probably a little later, from the canons of St. Lebuin's for using books in Dutch, works such as David of Augsburg's *Profectus religiosorum* (a Franciscan manual), the "thoughts" (*gedachten*) of Bernard, and other "good books."[90] Indeed the women were sorely accosted on the street by canons as they went out on business (*zeer lestich ende pynlick . . . om der boken willen*).[91] But it was the hearing of books as well, as the tractate makes clear, books read out and explained, that elicited objection, possibly readings at meals, certainly the Devout practice of collation. Talks were held in the men's houses, open to all comers, with texts read out in the vernacular, biblical as well as sermonic and devotional. Books were rendered "legible" in the medieval sense: read out and glossed (explained, discussed) in public and in the vernacular.

This situates the dispute but does not fully account for its intensity. The translation of Scripture, as of devotional writing and saints' lives, represented, as such, nothing new in the 1380s, not in the Low Countries, also not in England, France, or Germany. The basic legal issue was settled in principle by a ruling (*Cum ex iniuncto*) going all the way back to Innocent III, it regularly cited in this dispute too.[92] But two practices were concretely at stake here: reading religious materials in the vernacular (or hearing them read aloud); and praying biblical or liturgical materials in the vernacular. Three more general phenomena heightened tensions in this era: an exponential increase in religious materials moving into the vernacular, challenging a comfortable clerical monopoly; a core of activists promoting these materials, not friars (who had done so to a degree in sermons and devotions for five generations), also not local rectors, but self-appointed spiritual guides; and widespread fears about content, greater in the wake of Marguerite Porete and Eckhart, these having become ciphers for dangerous teaching, the latter especially in the "germanic" world (explicitly in both Master Geert's statutes and this treatise).[93] New groups were stretching linguistic boundaries all across Europe in the Later Middle Ages, if not all in the same way and with the same intent. Purposes must be read group by group. Here, though the issue ultimately turned on women's vernacular practices and the men who supported them, it was a Latinate dispute, a quarrel among clerics about lay reading and praying.

Zerbolt dealt explicitly with two major questions.[94] His first point was straightforward: It is useful, not prohibited, indeed recommended, that laity read or hear books issued in the vernacular or translated into it, so long as these do not treat of high or subtle doctrine and are not at odds with church teaching.[95] The qualifiers sprang in part from defensiveness, but were also consistent with the general Devout posture, more oriented to devotional than mystical or theological writing. He offered fifteen arguments buttressed with authorities.

This pamphlet argued broadly but pointedly for an estate of people, including laypeople, who were "exercised in the spiritual life" and thus better able to grasp, even to teach, also in their own tongue, matters that carnally minded clerics and masters could not truly understand. This half of his text would remain largely the same in all known versions, and will be treated in Chapter 8. Even here the underlying dispute breaks through, however. Divine writing, he bluntly asserts, "does not inform and enlighten (*erudit*) a single estate [namely, the clergy], but teaches and instructs each person in their own estate." Why make people come to church and listen if they may not themselves read the same material? What people hear preached once every two weeks or so (his summary of practice in his day) they rarely retain: so why not let them read it for themselves and take it in? It will only render them sharper in listening and in self-disciplining, thus more able to teach others![96] In general, he added, the laity are preoccupied with worldly affairs, fogging over the light of their conscience and natural reason; so why shouldn't they read devotional books to focus and brighten that light? More, they are already constantly reading worldly poems that inflame them to carnal love; it's irrational to deny them devotional books inspiring divine love.[97] Zerbolt's second large point, also reserved for treatment later, was to distinguish between books risky for laity ("high" and "obscure" and "disputacious") and those to be encouraged (the "plain" and "devotional"). With this theoretical foundation in place (itself quite original), he turned to the matters under dispute in the mid-1390s.

As in the pamphlet on "expensive clothing" Zerbolt arrived last at the most contested point.[98] At issue, it seems, was the psalms (along with other prayers and chants) used in daily prayer.[99] Devout women prayed these in the vernacular rather than in Latin, unlike, it was objected, "the general custom of the church." Nuns and clergy, any professed religious, used a Latin liturgy, indeed learned their Latin by way of singing the psalms. But these new converts, especially the women, used the vernacular. The psalms, Zerbolt explains, can be difficult, and so it is better to put them in the more accessible language of the people—which Grote had done in a set of standard liturgical offices, complete with glosses for elucidation. No one could doubt, he went on (this rhetorical turn of phrase always an alert in his work), that it is better for laity to pray with understanding in their own tongue than to recite with non-understanding in Latin. A person expressing her desires or laments to God more ably in her own tongue is herself more enkindled or inspired.[100] Then a final point, perhaps the true issue in contention: should lay people pray in prayers drawn up in ordinary words (*per oraciones planis et usitatis uerbis compositas*), or in psalms and antiphons provided in translation? Zerbolt allowed for either "so long as the affect of the heart is fervently raised aloft to God." But the "more devout," he claimed, often preferred the psalms, as more enkindling (*maxime deuociores sepius magis accenduntur et afficiuntur*), and they therefore possessed little prayer-books (*libellos oracionum*).[101] These books and their usage had provoked the clerical objections. The Devout would in fact make the copying of them one of their principle occupations (see Figure 7 for a palm-sized example from about 1450). While the tractate concludes with a series of citations, the last words that are Zerbolt's own drove the point home: It is licit for the laity to pray the psalms in their own tongue.[102] This might apply to any layperson using Master Geert's book of hours. But Devout women in particular sometimes prayed the psalms together in the vernacular, from their little books of hours, sometimes brought along, sometimes made there, sometimes passed down. In any case this looked to canons or friars like a self-instituted liturgy, competitive with their divine office in Latin.

We may round out our picture of the tensions that now haunted Devout gatherings and practices with two documents from the end of 1396. The first confirmed Lady Swedera's exchange of houses with the Brothers in Deventer almost six years earlier, now in Latin and notarized, with no magistrates involved, on 17 November at the house in Deventer. While claiming simply to set things out more clearly than the aldermen had in 1391, and before any more participants died, the move was defensive and also constitutional.[103] This document now stipulated that there be four or more priests and eight or more clerics along with an unspecified number of laymen who together would lead a companionate life (*sociali uita*) in pursuit of the virtues and in service of the Most High (deliberate echoes of *Ex iniuncto*). Permanent inhabitants in the house were to be of two kinds: those not fit in body or soul for professed religious life, and those not choosing it (*secundum suam uoluntatem inspirati, religionem ingredi non proponunt*). Further, the society reserved a right to house any Devout of good will, and "especially" to serve as a prenovitiate for some who might go on to Windesheim or elsewhere. A second document issued at Windesheim a week later (24 November), after offering a history of the house, had the prior, subprior, and two canons (all products of the house at Deventer) describe it as priests and clerics "living together in a loving society" to flee the dangers of the world, and Windesheim as their main refuge (*pro refugio, utilitate et aditu*). The house in Deventer served those not fit for religion or those of another inclination, "since there are a diversity of callings."[104] They, "serving God together outside religion" (*insimul extra religionem*), were to inspire other clerics and laity to forsake the world. Important in the Windesheim version is this characterization of the house as a way-station, a portal to professed life. Already a gap between the professed and nonprofessed was widening, the canons coopting the house and its history for their "higher" ends.[105] But amid rising tensions this

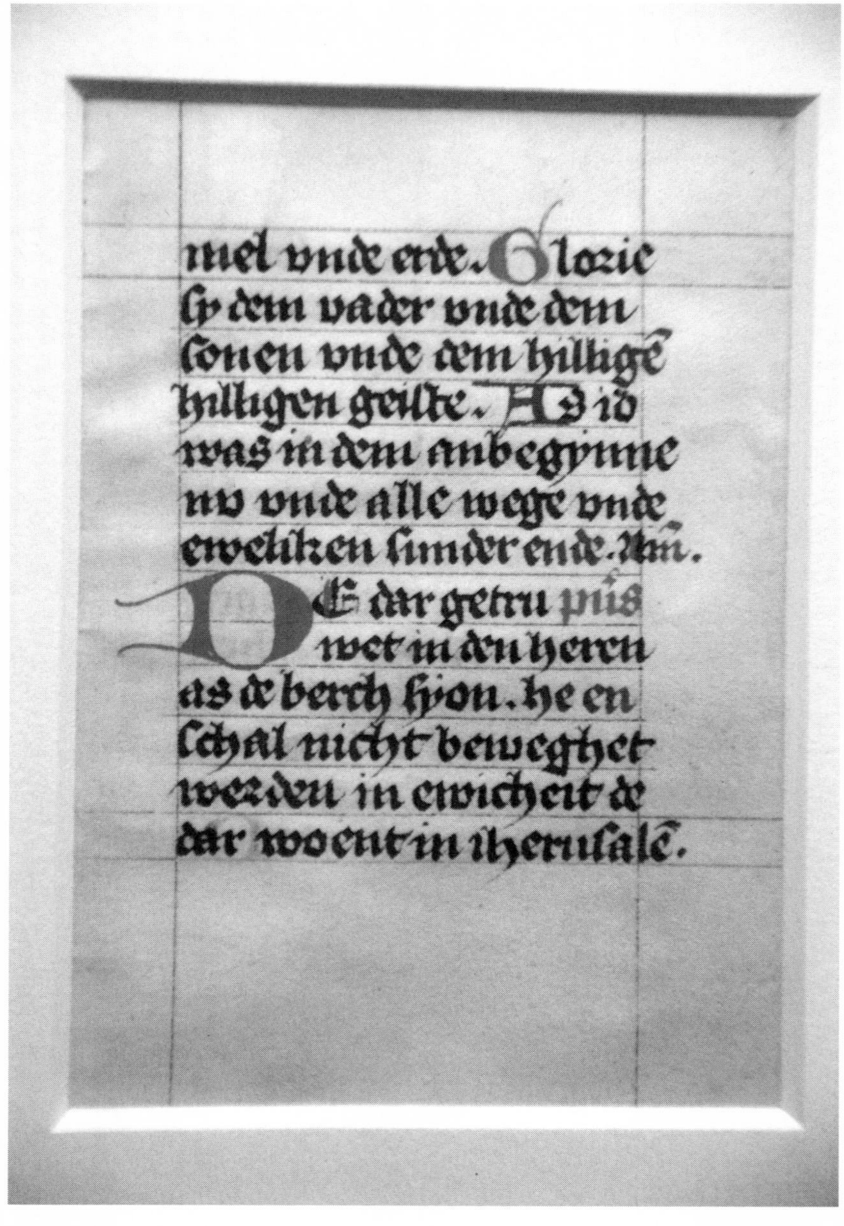

mel vnde erde. Glorie
sy dem vader vnde dem
sonen vnde dem hilligē
hilligen geiste. Als id
was in dem anbegynne
nu vnde alle wege vnde
eweliken sunder ende. Am̄.
DE dar getru ps
wet in den heren
as de berch syon. he en
schal nicht bewegthet
werden in ewicheit de
dar woent in iherusalē.

Figure 7. *Book of Hours* in Dutch, copied ca. 1450 at the Brothers' house in Cologne, with the "Gloria" and beginning of prime. It is "palm-size," just over two by three inches, thus very small and in parchment with red and blue initials. Leaf owned by John Van Engen and Kathryn Kerby-Fulton.

also was meant to satisfy local clergy, portraying the house and its purposes in clerically intelligible terms. And even if it was becoming harder to sustain the brave language of acting religious as private or laypersons, of being in the world but not of it, both documents, written under or by Florens and Zerbolt, nonetheless recognized explicitly a "diversity of callings," some preferring a religious life outside cloistered profession.

Sisters Under Inquisition, 1396–97: Friar Eylard Schoneveld Intervenes

A petition addressed to Pope Boniface IX in Rome, dated 7 January 1394, pleaded in behalf of certain devout persons of both sexes scattered throughout German towns "from of old." These people, not in violation of *Cum de quibusdam* or *Sancta Romana*, they held, suffered nonetheless from charges (*gravamina*) brought by papally deputed inquisitors, these indictments set in motion by local bishops as well as hostile locals.[106] The papal court found itself caught between inquisitors sometimes egged on by unhappy locals, and "beguines" with their own advocates and protectors. Pope Boniface IX reissued a form of Gregory XI's *Ex iniuncto*, addressed as before to the metropolitans of Cologne, Trier and Mainz, but especially bishops in Germany, Brabant and Flanders. Again, it instructed them to investigate and confirm the innocent but now, contrary to the original wording, with the help of inquisitors.[107] The Dominicans, with better access, perhaps discovered in Boniface IX a different pope. A year later (31 January 1395: *Sedis apostolice*) the pope issued a new letter, speaking of his "beloved brothers the inquisitors" and the "cancer of heresy" infiltrating those parts. He had also learned (*sicut etiam accepimus*) that such "Beghards" and "Lollards" and "Swestriones" were now protecting themselves with papal law (meaning *Ex iniuncto*). So he revoked those laws, and called for the guilty to be punished.[108] The incipit of his letter echoed one issued to Kerlinger in 1371 (*Sedes apostolica*),[109] leaving little doubt about the origin and intent of this fresh initiative. Ten months later, on 1 December 1395, "humbly petitioned by the Dominicans," Pope Boniface reissued Gregory XI's *Ab exordio nascentis* (under a framing incipit *Meritis uestre deuocionis*), the bull that had first established five permanent Dominican inquisitors in German lands.[110] In short, a new generation of friars was taking up the initiative originally launched by Kerlinger and his band. When Friar Eylard went to work on communities around Utrecht less than two years later, he labeled them "Swestriones."

Little is known about Friar Eylard Schoneveld (d. 1404/07), stationed in relatively distant Soest, a Dominican papal inquisitor for the Saxon region.[111]

When exactly he intervened in Utrecht, and why, also eludes us, and he may not have operated alone.[112] By December 1397 (when dated *consilia* explicitly raised questions about the rights of an inquisitor in this case) his investigation was well underway, but whether for months or a year or two we cannot say. In Devout circles Eylard was remembered as ruthless with the women, especially around Utrecht[113]—as he would prove even more so in the north German/Baltic region in 1401/03.[114] We possess two overlapping but distinct reports, both drawn from his lost *acta*. One came from Hinrich Schoenvelt, the inquisitor who directly succeeded Eylard in Saxony about 1401, it written in his own hand in a passage added to a codex with Eymeric's *Directorium inquisitorum* of 1376 and Gui's *Tractatus de potestate inquisitorum*, two key Dominican inquisitorial manuals.[115] Friar Hinrich had this section begin with twenty-one items copied from anti-beguine legislation (labeled "a" through "u" by Patschovsky), the last being Boniface IX's new version of *Ex iniuncto* of 1394, identified as the "*noua bulla Beghardorum*." There followed, in a fresh writing campaign, a legal brief pertinent to the Devout, then, after a break but in much the same hand, Hinrich's account of the Devout case. He claimed to have drawn it from the *acta* (*de actis inquisitionis*), an investigation carried out by Friar Eylard in "13__," the last two numbers left out. Friar Hinrich wrote soon after, perhaps ca. 1405, and his reason was simple: the case had been stopped, and wrongly so he believed. He entered this note into the inquisitorial manual personally as a protest and warning, to alert future inquisitors to this still threatening sect (*Notandum pro detecione figmentorum secte* **Gherditarum**). He was frustrated that the "sect of Geert's little women was growing daily stronger in towns throughout the diocese."[116] Their continued presence and strength annoyed him, a situation still ripe for investigation. It also puzzled him that the case had not advanced fully to trial and sentencing despite reliable testimony against the women.[117]

The second report came from, and was written in the hand of, Friar Jakob of Soest, also a papal inquisitor active in the Saxon region, appointed there in 1409. We have from him two folio manuscripts (Soest, Stadtbibliothek 14a, 14b) datable to 1410/15 or earlier, both also copies of Eymeric's *Directorium*.[118] The first includes various inserted additions, including anti-beguine legislation down to Gregory XI's *Ex iniuncto* of 1374 and records of the process at Strassburg in 1317 (ff. 39r–44),[119] together with other items like the condemnation of Wyclif at the Blackfriars council of 1382 (f. 101r). A second copy of Eymeric concludes with Jacob's own notes, instructions, and summaries on recent cases, the last being this investigation into Devout women around Utrecht, it inserted without title (ff. 98v–100r), followed (ff. 101r–103r) by notes drawn from church law regarding two main topics, the appeal of a case and the office of inquisitor. He too provided a summary description of suspect practices (the only part that has received attention), identified as "things declared to the inquisitor under oath." He provides in Dutch the oath itself and the interrogatory that was to be followed, and ends (missing in editions) with ten points wherein the women were held to have contravened church law. The charges are repetitive, essentially that the women have founded a new religion, assumed a new habit, taken up a banned estate (beguines), and generally acted contrary to anti-beguine legislation including the decrees of Charles IV. This version appears relatively closer to Eylard's own, the case as it stood in its initial stage.[120]

What triggered this inquisitorial investigation is not known. Friar Eylard Schoneveld may have followed up on rumors. More likely he was prodded or alerted by disgruntled churchmen, such as the *dominus* dismissed by Foec or those clerics preaching about clothing or still others worried about vernacular religious books circulating among the laity or Sisters praying the psalms in the vernacular. The enlarged statutes for Master Geert's house stated explicitly that Sisters were to open themselves to the inspection of the *Kettermeester* (heresy-master).[121] Aldermen too could get restless if faith or church appeared to be tainted by unusual groups operating in their town.

An inquisitor, according to standard formularies, was to announce an investigation by posting notice at the local church, calling upon everyone within a certain radius to stand ready to testify, notifying all that they could be put under oath, and threatening excommunication if any failed to comply. Friar Eylard focused his attention on gatherings (*congregationibus*) associated with Wermboud of Utrecht, these drawing women in "large numbers" he labeled "Swestriones." Many people were crying out against them, he claimed, for forming gatherings without papal permission. For his part Eylard apparently proceeded altogether properly, getting his *acta* notarized, for instance, with proper witnesses. How closely the two summaries we have from Jacob and Hinrich are based on the raw *acta* and the witnesses' testimony, how many witnesses there were, how many communities got examined, over how many days—all this is impossible to know. He investigated the household at Rhenen for certain, and gathered information from the curate there, also from women who had left the house. The findings make these Devout women appear to emulate practices standard for professed women (antiphonal prayer, confession, a form of obedience, readings at meals, a chapter of faults), also to manipulate their way round local priestly authority (presented in Chapter 2).

After gathering testimony under oath, the next step for an inquisitor was to take his findings to the bishop (or his official), the ordinary judge for a diocese, so they could agree upon how to proceed, whether to leave it all to the inquisitor. This could be a formality; it was often a source of tension. Papal law mandated that lay lords cooperate fully, basically ceding jurisdiction to an inquisitor, though its iteration suggested resistance, active or passive. This we can occasionally document, increasingly in the later middle ages. The friars' power rested ultimately on local compliance and cooperation, and that could not always be had, not in Italian towns for instance.[122] Also not in Spanish towns: In June 1388 Friar Eymeric was publicly and formally "taken exception to" (*recusare*) as inquisitor by a city council in Valencia.[123] And Friar Jacob was blocked twice in Cologne, once when a case devolved into wrangling over the two competing papal obediences, again when it touched a dispute between seculars and mendicants, his jurisdictional competence challenged in both cases.[124] Even in Lollard England, a new study argues, inquisition hinged upon the social relations, or resistances, engendered by episcopal visitations and calling for witnesses.[125] The Devout were not alone in trying to resist an inquisitor.

Bishops moreover were often jealous of their ordinary jurisdiction. Boniface VIII (1294–1303) had first decreed that a papally deputed inquisition should not be derogated, turned back, by an ordinary bishop; they were to work together and remit differences to the papal see[126]—intimating deep and recurrent troubles. At the Council of Vienne the "complaints of many reached the ears of the apostolic see that some papally delegated inquisitors were exceeding their bounds," thereby "burdening the innocent" to the "detriment of the faithful." This lengthy new decree (*Multorum querela*) tried to curb inquisitorial excess. It also ruled that either bishop or inquisitor could take people into custody and make inquiry of them, but neither could advance to sentencing, let alone torture or harsh imprisonment, without the agreement of the other.[127] As even Friar Bernard Gui conceded a decade or so later in his on "the power of the inquisitor," this "restriction" produced some "inconvenience" in the "free exercise" of the inquisitorial office.[128] This papal constitution, though constantly complained about by inquisitors, stood as church law, and was among the rulings copied into Friar Jakob's copy of Eymeric.

In 1397 Friar Eylard would have had to present his findings to Bishop Frederick (or his official). By then much already had transpired: the hearing of local witnesses under oath, the drawing up of charges, and most important a claim now that the women's case be delegated to him as papal inquisitor. If that was agreed to, any Devout Sister he chose could be placed under oath and forced through the proposed battery of questions, also threatened with torture or incarceration if they did not cooperate. Exactly at this point, probably earlier, Florens and Wermboud got deeply involved. They sought ways to block the inquisitor, and in the end succeeded. The Modern-Day Devout were never released to Friar Eylard for trial, interrogation, or sentencing, which might well have extended to dissolving these communities. This blocking of his predecessor's case was precisely what frustrated Friar Hinrich. In his last sentence he declared that these Devout Sisters could still be proved false if the interrogation were only allowed to proceed.[129] Earlier historians, as I see it, missed the crucial distinction in an inquisitorial process between an initial gathering of evidence under oath (as in an American grand jury) and an actual prosecution and sentencing, to which a bishop had formally to accede. No one could stop the former undertaken by a papally authorized inquisitor who was ostensibly pursuing charges or practices that appeared to fall under one of his rubrics; hence the widespread fear of these "heresy-masters." One could, however, contest jurisdictions, even if our evidence of it (also not looked for all that carefully by historians) comes often in the form of indirect grumblings or papal mandates to cooperate. Bishop Fredrick, we must remember, knew his rights and knew about converts, whether or not he had himself, as a later Dominican claimed, gone after Waldensians and beguines in Strassburg.

Resisting the Inquisitor: Legal Tactics

Florens and Wermboud assumed leadership, remaining in close touch it seems, though based in different regions, Florens in Deventer and the Oversticht, Wermboud in the Nedersticht and county of Holland. Wermboud, a parish priest, was dubbed the "father of the Devout" in Utrecht and also "apostle of Holland," largely for his activism, a public preacher, a mover and shaker, going from house to house among the new women's communities, indefatigable.[130] The Devout leaders turned to jurists in Utrecht for legal counsel, as they had earlier, and this time also to university jurists in Cologne. They also set Zerbolt to writing more apologetic tractates. By this time a papal inquisitor had already gathered sworn testimony and laid claim to his legal competence to put the Devout on trial for their households and practices as heretical. Exact chronology remains frustratingly unclear, the only certain dates being those of several written advisories (*consilia*), two from Utrecht jurists dated to December 1397, all those from university jurists in Cologne to January 1398.

First we must introduce Zerbolt's work, most likely written in pieces, probably across 1396/97. His "Concerning the mode of living of certain devout persons who dwell together in their homes or rented dwellings" constitutes a vast dossier of apologetic materials organized around eleven "questions," these written in part as issues arose with questions within questions, suggestive of its expanding and responsive nature (See Figure 8 for one of nine extant manuscripts, this one copied from materials close to the action since it includes supporting legal documents.) The entire assembled dossier, complete with several of the *consilia*, dates from 1398.[131] A cursory summary here may serve to indicate

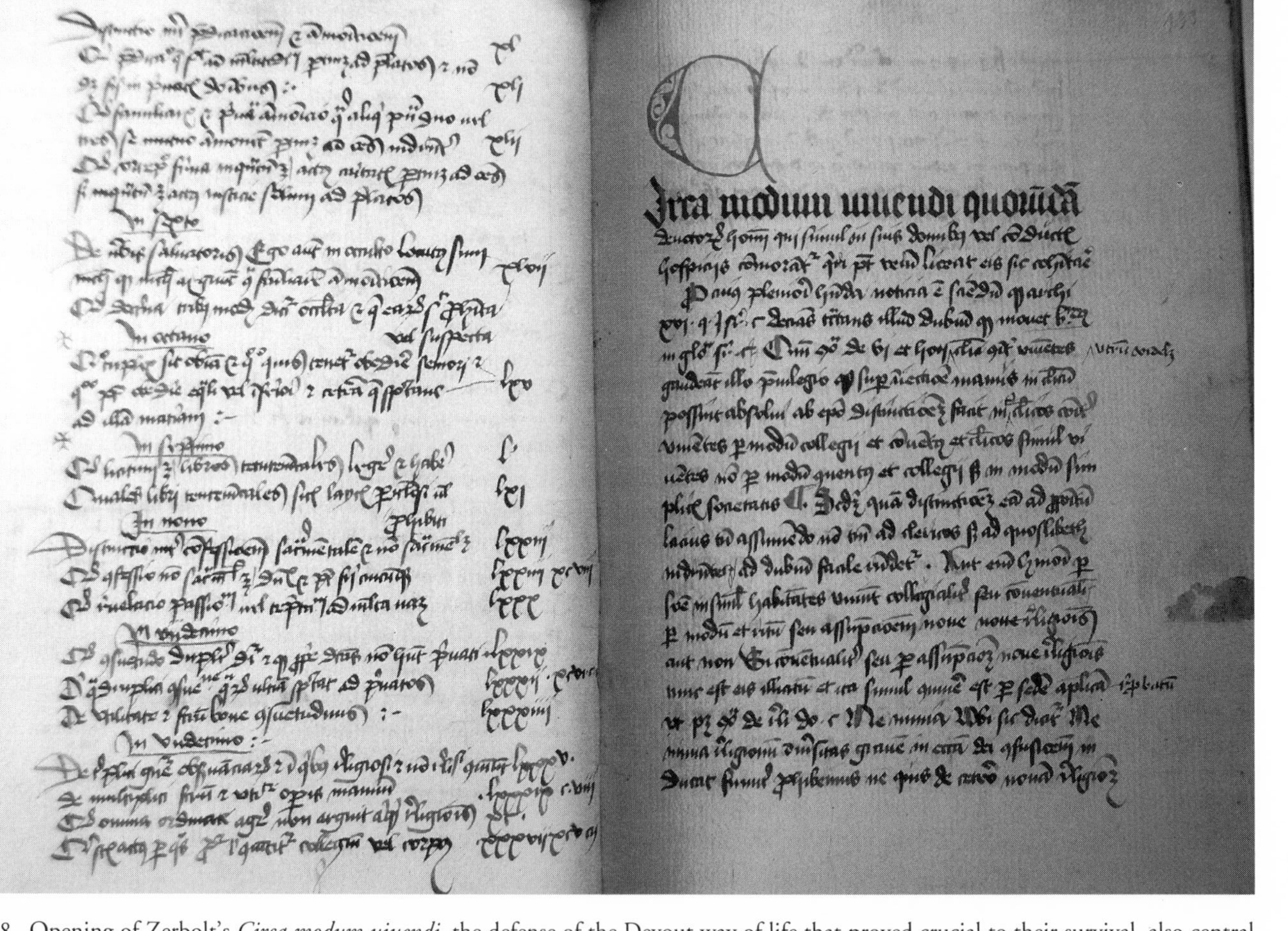

Figure 8. Opening of Zerbolt's *Circa modum uiuendi*, the defense of the Devout way of life that proved crucial to their survival, also central to this book, with an index/table of contents as an appended bifolio on the left: Liège, Bibliothèque du Séminaire Épiscopal [formerly, Grande Séminaire], MS 6 F 2, f. 199, one of nine extant copies.

what issues the Devout perceived to be at stake. Questions I–IV, forming nearly half the total, deal with community of goods and life, and charges arising from anti-beguine legislation. Questions V–VI take up practices of "admonition" and "correction," that is, forms of public teaching and private guidance. Two manuscripts, out of the nine known to me, contain only these questions, the core issues of communal goods, anti-beguine laws, and public teaching—whether this represented a first distributed form of the work or simply one particular selection of material. Question VII offers a slimmed-down version of the tractate on vernacular books. The remaining four questions take up matters central to the internal life of Devout societies, practices said to emulate religious houses: obedience (VIII), private counsel approaching confession (IX), and customs observed in a household (X–XI). The full dossier offered to the public and the jurists from mid-1398 (anonymously, though mainly the work of Zerbolt) would consist of the *Circa modum vivendi*, together with a summary of the university jurists' advisories, two *consilia* from Master Evert Foec, one from an unnamed figure, and occasionally one from Abbot Arnold. If the inquisitor generated documents from his side or local churchmen from theirs, they have disappeared.

Of the legal advisories procured, two stand apart, their authors unnamed, their texts not dated. One remains unedited, essentially unknown, and of it we have only a concluding fragment. But we begin there for what it reveals about the situation, tactics, and mood. It comes from a manuscript of St. Katherine's in Nuremberg, a women's house overseen by Observant Dominicans including Friar John Nyder. The materials must have circulated in Dominican circles in the aftermath of the fracas, Nyder's knowledge of the case possibly linking him to this codex.[132] It contains our only Latin copy of Zerbolt's "on vernacular books," and also a previously unidentified copy of Foec's opinion.[133] A third text filled out this quire, the center bifolio missing, hence also its rubric and opening sections (which might have named the author or occasion). This text, as we have it (ff. 273–75), dealt entirely with the crucial question of the inquisitor's jurisdiction, presenting a lengthy, passionate, and legally informed repudiation of his claim. It shows no dependency on Foec, though it was likely someone from Utrecht, possibly John of Arnhem, another prominent local jurist with whom they met.[134] The text had opened apparently with six reasons why Devout persons and practices did not fall under the inquisitor's purview. With the missing bifolio we begin well into the fifth.

Charges of living together and sharing the fruits of their labors did not render these people so ill-famed (*diffamos*), this jurist notes, as to fall under an inquisitor's scrutiny—*fama* (rumor) being just cause in church law for an inquisitor to investigate. Communal living made these people, on the contrary, Christ-like, the man asserts. It was brash to threaten inquisition rather than submit their case to proper judges,[135] this last prompting a critical blast citing *Multorum querela* on inquisitorial abuses. Sixth and last, power was given the church to seek truth and edify, not to destroy. This jurist then drew up advice in the appropriate formula: these people have every right to take legal exception to (*recusare*) an inquisitor proceeding against them.[136] His text went on to explain. They begin with a demand that any charges be made in writing and time allowed to deal with them.[137] If the main charge really is a communal lifestyle, the inquisitor must show how this is criminal or touches on heresy. Even if a crime is charged, one can still legally query the inquisitor's jurisdiction (objecting that it is rather an episcopal or civil matter).[138] As for the bishop, he can procede extraordinarily only if there is serious ill-fame (*grauiter diffamatus*). So too with inquisitors: It would be most disruptive if an inquisitor could simply drag a woman (*eam*) in and defame her.[139] He cannot procede to inquisition on whispers and rumors, especially since in this world the good and holy are often despised by the carnal and worldly.[140] The writer went on to warn inquisitors at length against acting on "trivial indicators" (*signa leuia*). The copyist of this text, quite possibly a Dominican, did not complete the work but at the end of the quire (f. 275vb) simply said "etcetera"—enough for him. Most striking in this advisory is the rhetorical power deployed, and most informative its direct reference to what the Devout were now in fact up to, raising legal objections (*recusare*) to the inquisitor's jurisdiction.

A second *consilium*, stripped of name and date, was transmitted as "a devout and learned man" speaking for "devout persons" in the province of Cologne against "the inquisitor," "those unfairly molesting them."[141] Its opening line went to the heart of the situation. "They" want to proceed against these people as heretics (*uelle procedere contra istos pauperes*), and on the strength of three papal constitutions, *Sancta Romana, Ad nostrum*, and a certain *bulla*. They invoke *Sancta Romana*, but it fails to apply because the estate described in it, though condemned, is not technically "heretical," thus not within an inquisitor's purview. To this came the retort (*cauillatur*): these people can be held suspect and judged "by analogy" (*a simili*).[142] But such an argument (suitable to philosophy or theology) could not hold, the jurist responded, when a penalty came entailed. Second, and "most importantly," they invoke *Ad nostrum*. Devout practices, however, do not fall under its provisions. Mere name-calling, smearing them as "beghards," will not do. Third, they have cited a papal bull, unnamed (*ex bulla*), most likely Boniface IX's *Ex iniuncto* of 7 January 1394, the one added to Friar Hinrich's list as "*nova bulla Beghardorum*." The writer dismissed it as a gloss on *Ad nostrum*.

Overall the chief accusation turned on their communal consumption of goods (*Maxime . . . calumpniari communem uictum*).[143] This raised eyebrows and generated complaints: would not such a lifestyle, it was objected, lead to the ruin of Christian teaching and good morals? But that practice was in itself hardly heresy, the jurist retorted, and therefore not the inquisitor's business (*officium*). To sustain a common life apart from religious vows was rather an act of merit, an imitation of the early church[144]—the same point the other jurist had made. The writer went on about this at length, and ended with a flourish: Why bother to muster up more authorities when this practice was authorized by Christ and the apostles, it being simply a point of perfection to live a common life, "even outside religion."[145] The authorities he invoked here on behalf of a common life overlapped with materials worked up more extensively in question three of Zerbolt's *Circa modum* ("*Queritur utrum liceat extra religionem in communi uiuere sine proprietate rerum uel dominio*"), the two texts at points very close. Both note complaints that a common life outside religion was unusual, and deployed nearly the same rhetorical language in rebuttal.[146] The tone of the *consilium*, however, was distant ("*uidentur*" to introduce the situation, "*pauperes*" to designate the Devout, "*prouincia coloniensi*" to name the region), more that of a lawyer (though possibly an intentional formality). That said, he almost certainly borrowed this lengthy justification in part from *Circa modum vivendi*, that section possibly circulating independently or in an early form. The central thrust of both jurists in any case was clear: whatever these *pauperes* practiced (it in fact laudable, an imitation of the early church), it did not fall under the scrutiny of an inquisitor.

These advisories were not enough, or the situation looked increasingly threatening. So the Devout next sought formal counsel on six questions—in the expectation of supportive answers, the whole reason one paid for *consilia*. The issues were exactly those dealt with by Zerbolt in his *Circa modum vivendi*, though not in the same order or wording: (1) community of goods and life (= Zerbolt's I, III); (2) obeying an elected superior (= Zerbolt's VIII); (3) disclosing temptations and passions for confession and guidance (= Zerbolt's IX); (4) reading and owning vernacular books (= Zerbolt's VII); (5) mutual admonition and correction amounting to preaching and a chapter of faults (= Zerbolt's V–VI); and (6) adopting common household statutes in matters such as manual labor, table-reading, and the like (= Zerbolt's X–XI).[147] A key seventh question followed: whether an inquisitor had the right to investigate people choosing to live a communal life. These were all now posed to Utrecht's top two jurists, Evert Foec and Abbot Arnold, the second conincidentally being Zerbolt's main consultant all along. We possess Arnold's response in two forms, dated respectively 2 and 24 December 1397.[148] The seventh question notably was not part of the first, but included on Christmas Eve. There he put the question broadly, perhaps in his own language, whether an inquisitor could investigate these "articles," and his response seems an abbreviated version of Foec's. Master Evert was finished then before 24 December, and Abbot Arnold had access to his advisory. For the Devout, in legal and political practice, this matter of inquisitorial jurisdiction for now precluded all quibbling about other practices.

The legal argument—tactic, really—was to hold that an inquisitor possessed no jurisdiction. The Devout were not heretics, nor suspected of heresy. The inquisitor had no right to investigate unless he had received a specific mandate on this matter from the pope—and he had not. Law indeed forbade inquisitors to exceed their expressed mandates, thus specifically *Multorum querela*. If, moreover, he proposed to intervene and dissolve these households—our only indication of how great the threat actually was—simply on grounds that individuals were living in common, he had no more legal competence to do so than to pursue, say, adultery—none, that is to say, in "morals" cases apart from some specific papal mandate. Third, Gregory XI's *Ex iniuncto* had ruled quite specifically that in the bishoprics of Cologne, Utrecht, and Münster judgments about such groups lay with the bishop and his staff as the ordinary judge, not with an inquisitor. The inquisitor must manifestly back off and leave the matter to local churchmen to work out, that is, to the bishop's court,[149] within which Foec and Arnold were leading players.

Not content with getting the two leading jurists in the diocese to write on their behalf, Florens and Wermboud also took their case to university jurists in Cologne, eight of them in fact, all identifiable as members or former members of the faculty. The key response came from two professors of civil law, Johan of Neustein canon of Aachen and Johan Bauw canon of Malines, their opinion dated and sealed 18 January 1398, then approved by two further lawyers, Radulphus Rivo dean of Tongeren and Tylman Eckhart, both advocates at the archbishop's court—all this transmitted as a single document. Further documents offered affirming opinions from the provost of St. George at Cologne, Herman Stakelweg, also a civil lawyer, and two canon lawyers, Gerhard of Groningen and Johan Furburg, and the same Rudolphus Rivo, these briefer and dated 21 January 1398. A third opinion, also short, came in the name of Johan Furburg and Rudolphus Rivo.[150] Common to all was the name Rudolphus Rivo, a friend to the Devout, subseqently a liturgical scholar, manifestly some sort of intermediary in the acquiring of these written *consilia*. These university jurists, at a remove from the strife inside the diocese, argued their positions almost entirely in terms of civil law, with little indication of knowing Zerbolt's massive apparatus.

Consilia were about cases, not abstract principles, and this is the way the first and longer opinion formulated it:

> The Case: In certain places many people betake themselves to withdraw and live together, some, being clerics, in a single house in which they copy out licit books for a fee, others, not able to do copy-work but knowing various mechanical crafts, exercise them for a fee in another house, or also do some other manual labor. These persons, being thus together in their houses, work and live from their labors which, together with the personal property they possess, they share with one another amicably and to achieve greater harmony. They also eat together and do not beg. They also have among them a single rector who has the care of the house, whom they obey as proper students do their master. And they divide up the hours of the day, laboring in some of them, being free for God in others, and they organize similar good things for one another so they can live quietly together. This way of living together they do and carry out principally not for material gain but in the hope that by so living they may better please God and serve him.
>
> About all this the question is asked, whether a "college" of the aforesaid is licit, and whether in living so they may elect a rector and make ordinances among themselves, and may do and have various other things which are permitted in law to licit colleges? Likewise, what in law is the standing of women who, separate from the men, likewise live together in their houses, who sew, weave, do textile work and other female occupations, from which they live? Do they likewise have a licit "college"?[151]

The second two opinions described the situation similarly, though less legalistically:

> Whether it is licit for several people to live together in the same house outside religion so they may more safely (*securius*) serve God and live more easily (*commodius*), may eat together, and if they have anything they acquire by labor share their own with one another and live from these things, so long as they do not beg; and for now have one honest person who has care of the house, in whose good counsel and admonitions they acquiesce without promise or vow and voluntarily obey as good students do their master.

For lawyers, especially civil lawyers, but also Foec and Arnold, the issue of "living together" turned on the legal status of these gatherings. Had they in effect created a *collegium* (the word used of Windesheim in the bishop's privilege), a public corporation, or instead an illegal gathering or association? According to Foec, critics charged that these houses represented a *collegium*, the term suggestive again of local churchmen.[152] This they might not do, not without proper authorization, especially not if it assumed the aspect of a clerical house or a new religious order. Friar Eylard even labeled it heresy, as in violation of the anti-beguine laws.

There was no impediment in church law (*impedimentum canonicum*), Foec countered, which would block people from living together and in common from the fruits of their labors; that seemed rather to follow the example of Christ.[153] The jurists at Cologne, all civilist (Roman law) in training, took care to distinguish a *collegium* (a body living together) from a *corpus* (a contracted association), while admitting that this might on occasion also be called a *societas*. Roman law, while very nervous about illict or subversive associations (*collegia illicita*), had allowed for *collegia* on grounds of poverty (pooling resources) or of religion. The Devout, they noted, would fall under the latter rubric.[154] Canonists, following Hostiensis, were more comfortable in saying that groups might form what lawyers called, going back to Roman civil law, a *societas*, a private incorporation of individuals joined for an agreed-upon and licit purpose, that society dissolved when its purpose passed, the most common examples being a merchant company or a body of students gathered round a master. While the rationales differed slightly, either set of lawyers was prepared to recognize the right of these groups, the men and the women, to form an association of their own contracting, so long as it did not fall into an "illicit" category or constitute the founding of a new religion (order).

On the practical rather than theoretical plan Foec's opinon counted most in Utrecht, and of it we have the most manuscript witnesses. In terms of prestige, however, the university jurists counted most, their opinions subsequently preserved in a notarized transumpt, one also later presented to Cardinal Pierre d'Ailly and entered into the cartulary for the Brothers' house in Zwolle. Parties would ordinarily present these juridical *consilia* to a bishop's or inquisitor'court. The originals, as often, are now gone. Foec's text exists as the Devout copied it into their dossier; Arnold's the same, with one independent copy. As for the *consilia* of the jurists in Cologne, the Devout secured and actively distributed them—and for this we have an unpublished witness. The text must have first reached Wermboud in Utrecht (indicating both his role and the threat to the women's communities there), and then Amersfoort, this roughly three weeks after the opinions were sealed in Cologne. The Devout in Amersfoort had close ties to Deventer.[155] On 13 February 1398 a subdeacon named Tydeman Cluten appeared before a notary public to have proper transsumpts made of the original opinions (*tres litteras patentes*) complete with seals of the persons (jurists) there mentioned, this done near the altar of St. Nicholas in the church of St. George in Amersfoort. Safe and authorized copies were needed, Cluten said, because the originals could not be carried round owing to dangerous roads and great distances. Willem Hendriksz, a notary, was rector of St. George's and vicar of St. Nicholas, and then joining the men's household in Amersfoort; this subdeacon worked for him, and the notarial transaction was done in his church.[156] That subdeacon bore the name "Cluten," same as the Martha of all women's households (Alheyde Cluten), possibly kin. We do not possess those transumpts. But a copy was entered into those quires now in Nuremberg, labeled a *determinacio* on "laypeople living in common,"[157] the same manuscript with a copy of Foec and of the jurist who advised on handling an inquisitor. The point for the Devout was to get multiple notarized copies made in preparation for possible looming battles with the inquisitor.

Sometime after February 1398 someone additionally drew up a dense summary of the three opinions issued at Cologne blended in with Abbot Arnold's. The "solutions" expressed, he added, stood in agreement with Master Evert's and "many others." It set the case out in the way the first opinion in Cologne had formulated it (translated above), with no query about the inquisitor's competence. While the person clearly had access to the whole file, suggesting one of the Devout, possibly Zerbolt himself, the result provided a useful summary, an aid in argument, though it was not a notarized document with legal standing.[158] Of all the materials generated by this case it was most frequently transmitted, perhaps most legally useful. Friar Jacob, the later Dominican inquisitor, even included it in his compilation, with an assertion that this statement had been drafted "in defense of Beghards," meaning heretics.[159] Wermboud also had a text translated into Dutch and distributed among women's households, and this was likely it. That undertaking—translating legal counsel into the vernacular, equipping women with authorities and arguments—irritated Friar Hinrich quite especially.[160] The Sisters, he reports, clung to these and brandished them, an act he regarded as utterly brazen (*satis impertinenter*).[161]

Awaiting the Bishop's Decision, 1398–1401

The Devout stategy succeeded. Friar Eylard was blocked, the decision about converts living a common life reserved to Bishop Frederick. Exactly when, where, or how this happened, unfortunately, we do not know. A few years later Friar Hinrich referred obliquely to it as a "false" and "improper" reading of the masters' juridical advisories, as "twisting" (*detorqueri*) them against their rightful intentions.[162] That of course was sour grapes, and hardly the case. These *consilia* were meant precisely to defend Devout practices and challenge (*recusare*) the inquisitor's jurisdiction. We can place all this, by indirect evidence, at the bishop's court sometime between late February and early June 1398. In February the Devout were notarizing and distributing juridical opinions for use in defending themselves against an inquisitor; in June they were at the bishop's court trying to gain recognition from him for their communities and practices. The focus had shifted, and a new campaign was underway. It hardly proved a sure thing, and ended up lasting nearly three more years. Neither Florens (d. 1400) nor Zerbolt (d. 1398) would live to see it through.

Bishop Frederick, in not ceding jurisdiction to Friar Eylard, may have been moved by a territorial instinct, perhaps a distaste for outside inquisitors. But we should take seriously the legal arguments deployed, and their consequences. When a bishop and an inquisitor failed to reach agreement, church law specified, the matter could be referred to the papal see. There is indirect evidence that Eylard tried, whether or not the bishop paid any attention. Roughly a year later, on 6 June 1399, Boniface IX reissued *Ab exordio nascentis*, reauthorizing the system of standing papal inquisitors in German lands. More to the point, on 16 June 1399 the pope directed a letter to German churchmen and secular powers demanding complete support for Friar Eylard in carrying out his inquisitorial office.[163] This was a form letter basically, nothing specific about Utrecht or Cologne. And Eylard was in fact about to turn his attentions eastward, this time with grisly success. But it is striking that he sought reauthorization, and especially that the letter got entered as the last item in the list of papal issuances copied out as pertinent to the Devout case. He could muster a general letter of papal support apparently, but not a reversal of the bishop's decision in Utrecht. This rebuff stung Dominican zealots, his successors Friar Henrich and Friar Jacob in particular, a reality that would haunt the Devout a decade later when another Dominican, Matthew Grabow, settled in the diocese as a lector.

In all this Deacon Foec had proved prescient, perhaps the real master of the situation on the ground. From the beginning he had argued for local jurisdiction, ardently defending the rights of his bishop. He had also given the Devout rather direct advice, even somewhat patronizingly. Because diverse opinions persisted on this matter of "communal life," he said, with people "whispering" about them and their ways as giving offense, they should in prudence make work of seeking special permission (*licentiam*) from the bishop to live in this unusual way.[164] This is exactly what they now set out to do, making repeated trips to Utrecht in June 1398, even dining with Foec himself and John of Arnhem. But success did not follow. People at the bishop's court continued to oppose them, possibly the Dominican inquisitor still a factor,[165] more likely the same unnamed churchmen who had raised objections all along. Importantly,

Bishop Frederick himself, while upholding his jurisdiction and warding off the inquisitor, had not made up his own mind about the Devout.

If the inquisitor had sparked fear, delays at the bishop's court engendered frustration, palpable in letters written during the summer of 1398. On Friday, 21 June 1398, Zerbolt reported to other Brothers that he was in Utrecht and hoped for final word on their business (*negocium*) yet that day. He had gone on Monday. But through the week nothing got settled. Most items in contention, he opined, might perhaps be agreed to (*forsitan bene admitterentur*), except, "as we feared and everyone is saying," permission to have a private chapel, a privilege difficult to obtain. Yet nothing was certain, and their business would need further promoting (*agitari*) in the Oversticht with the help of expert allies such as the church lawyer Abbot Arnold.[166] Not long afterward Zerbolt left Utrecht in frustration, his patience exhausted, his presence there, he said, making no difference at all.[167] A month later, about 24 July, he was back, this time accompanied by Florens Radewijns. But the "business of the Lord," he wrote, only ran up against more obstacles. Florens and Zerbolt, aggrieved and astonished, communicated bitterly how they had become worn down "eating and drinking with the supposed chariot-drivers of the divine raceway," meaning officials in the bishop's court, "supposed to be about the Lord's business, but who stand against us."[168] In December Zerbolt went to Dickninge to consult yet again with Abbot Arnold, only to die suddenly of plague on his way back, aged thirty-one, the skillful apologist of the Devout now permanently silenced.

Even if the inquisitor was kept at bay, it offered scant comfort to all the men's and women's houses still facing local criticism and unable to gain episcopal recognition. Wermboud and leaders in the west (predominantly in Holland), not Florens or leaders in the Oversticht notably, turned in 1399 almost in panic, at least hurriedly, to the option taken by beguines in the Upper Rhine, namely to secure recognition as Tertiaries, as living under a kind of rule—an option Bishop Frederick, it turns out, was happy to support (next chapter). Two more full years on (30 April 1401), a year after Florens too had died, Bishop Frederick finally issued the "license" the Devout had been seeking. His was a cautious privilege, but decisive. It took its stand, notably, explicitly on the basis of the jurists, their having found this way of life "licit and meritorious," wording that partly echoed Zerbolt's *Circa modum vivendi*. The bishop "consented" to that judgment and "approved" Devout communities so as to grant them "peace," and now warned off any who would hereafter attack this "licit way of life." More, he explicitly invoked his own ordinary jurisdiction, which had earlier blocked the inquisitor, and also Gregory XI's *Ex iniuncto* that conferred on a local bishop the power to investigate but also to confirm—Foec's position from the beginning. Why Bishop Frederick granted this privilege then is not known.

The petitioners here, not named, must be distinct from the "devout persons" whose status still hung in limbo. Those who mediated the privilege (probably Bronkhorst or Foec) had "humbly proposed" this agreement and pointed out to the bishop that these Devout persons had "frequently" been subjected to legal and theological scrutiny.[169] The bishop, notably, named no Devout persons or houses in the privilege. Though not unsympathetic to them, he kept his distance and invoked the jurists' opinions.

The privilege referred to, and implicitly accepted, several key practices: (1) to live together (*simul plures in eadem domo cohabitare*); (2) to share meals and labor (*adinuicem libere communicare*) in a common life; (3) to acknowledge one or two "heads of household" in whose counsel they acquiesced without obligation or vow, as students to a master; (4) to organize their day in "customs" fostering devotion and labor, without becoming a new religious order with a Rule; (5) to admonish and correct one another, so long as they remained subject to curates, (6) to seek spiritual guidance from an "expert," so long as they did not contravene priestly confession; (7) to read books in the vernacular, so long as they avoided problematic material. Amelius of Buren (1400–1404) meanwhile had succeeded Florens as head of the men's household in Deventer. On 26 August 1401, four months after the privilege was granted, he had copies drawn up by a notary public, the same William Henrici who had prepared documents at Windesheim a few years earlier and also at Amersfoort, this done in Deventer by way of the "officialis" of the archdeacon's court there.[170] Amilius, we learn, possessed the original bishop's charter with its seal. But he needed notarized copies because—almost the same phrase used at Amersfoort in 1398—the document pertained to persons in a variety of places, and the roads were not safe for carrying the original around.[171] How many copies went out, and to which gatherings, we do not know. It was effectively the foundation privilege for the Modern-Day Devout, and never rescinded, though challenged, and more than once.

CHAPTER FOUR

From Converts to Communities: Tertiaries, Sisters, Brothers, Schoolboys, Canons

It happened once that she [Sister Fye (d. 1454)] traveled to her family for some things she had to do there. Because she was friendly and pleasant, her family was virtuous and kindly toward her. And because she was still young and had not visited in the world much . . . she never again, after she returned to the house, had such a love for this life as before. For from then on she became sickly in body and declined from day to day, and finally died.

It is not a small thing to dwell in a monastery or a congregation and to live there without complaint and to persevere faithfully until death. Blessed is he who lives there well and ends his days happily.

THE WAY OF the convert, so Grundmann held, was to be co-opted or marginalized, become a professed religious or a heretic. In actual practice, Elm argued back, converts found their way to various options outside heresy or religion, as beguines, hospice workers, or recluses, all forms of life that also gained recognized standing in medieval society.[1] This view, though not wrong, fails to account for real pressure brought to bear on beguines and the Devout, indeed on nearly any new or unusual form of converted life.[2] For women in high-profile cases such as Birgitta of Sweden the line separating canonization and inquisition could prove perilously thin.[3] Yet the Modern-Day Devout, despite pressure, formed communities, even large and successful communities, and their transition from converts to communities involved inventiveness, not just stifling conformity. We must beware of falling back into a simplistic either/or. The medieval world was surprisingly complex, the later middle ages even more so. Possibility and inventiveness were not dead in the fifteenth century. After 1401 the Modern-Day Devout steadily expanded, proliferating into several wings, even as they faced suspicion or scrutiny, the expansion continuing into the 1480s or 1490s, scrutiny into the 1450s. This chapter puts the communities and the people first. Then we turn to the form of communal life they created (Chapter 5) and their scrapes with authorities (Chapter 6), though it was in fact all happening at once.

The religious world of the later medieval ages bewildered, a spectrum of institutions and practices that embraced still the entire population of Europe. Church structures reached deep into the social fabric, into marriage, testaments, and "estates" (sociolegal status), all administered by churchmen with legal expertise, a pattern two centuries old by the 1380s. Medieval law and institutions cut two ways: they stipulated but also privileged; they banned but also protected. Converts understood that fully. Church administrators acted with caution in issuing written approbations for new converts, thus Innocent III's handling of Francis, or Bishop Frederick's of the Devout. Prelates knew how these documents would be used, as did the people who sought them. Recent approaches to medieval religious life have focused less on matters of socioecclesiastical status, more on religiocultural authority (who could speak or act, how, on what basis). This has opened up historical space for women and nonpriestly males, also for heavenly visions, holy lives, personal revelations, and innovative readings as distinct from, or over against, ordained hierarchies. This approach has predominated for a generation, and helped render intelligible and empathetic lives and practices often dismissed earlier, especially women's, this most influentially by way of Bynum's *Holy Feast and Holy Fast.*[4] But scholars have tended to forego the institutional dimensions of community-building, partly compensating for earlier historical predilections, partly because such acts tended to be maledominated, and partly too to open avenues into the experiential and bodily in human experience. But institution-building was central to the later medieval experience, and itself potentially creative and inventive.

Historians routinely distinguish as well between charisma and institution, an authentic insight canonized by Weber. Of late we have focused especially on manifestations of charisma, extremes of asceticism, persons gifted with visions or revelations, self-made writers or teachers or preachers. This leaves still the question of the ordinary, even of the majority. Either we pass them over (as no longer accessible), or we draw assumptions from charismatic practices. We have noted this of beguines: our attention to the remarkable eleven lives of early beguines and to the extraordinary writers Hadewijch and Marguerite, with astonishingly little to say about thousands of others, whether or not we account them "ordinary." The divide between charisma and institution impacts our work on medieval religious communities in still another way. It introduces a hidden or not-so-hidden narrative of cycles whereby institutions move from spirit to establishment to decline, the very expectation predetermining interpretation, the institutional phase accordingly marking the beginning of decline. But inspiration and inventiveness were not limited to a single point in a community's history, nor were they excluded from the making or maintaining of organized communities.

Tertiaries "Living the Common Life"

The largest number of Modern-Day Devout became Tertiaries, most of them women, more than 150 houses in the end, a truly astonishing number.[5] Under pressure from the inquisitor and hostile churchmen, looking for creative ways to sustain their gatherings, several houses moved at Easter 1399 to adopt the status of Third-Order Franciscans. They did so at the urging of Wermboud of Utrecht (d. 1413) and William Hendriks of Amersfoort (d. 1413), with legal advice from Bronkhorst, Foec, and Abbot Arnold, and the cooperation of Aleyd Clute as head Mother. All doubtless were aware of beguine houses that had made the same move over the past three generations to seek legal cover.[6] But they did not forsake their identity. A copy of their statutes names them "Brothers and Sisters of Penance" (the proper name for Tertiaries) "who lead a common life" (the Devouts' own distinctive mark): *Status fratrum et sororum ordinis sancti francisci de penitencia nuncupati in communi uita degencium*).[7] The Franciscan connection was a ruse, bitterly complained about earlier in Strassburg and Basel. Legal commentators had conveniently found that Tertiaries were not included in anti-beguine laws such as *Cum de quibusdam*.[8] Resisted in the Upper Rhine, the move worked in the Lower Rhine. That owed something to the adroitness of the Devout leaders, more than a little to the eventual favor of Bishop Frederick and something too to the affirming support of the counts of Holland. In addition, and even more innovatively, Devout Tertiaries from the beginning created a supporting network, the Chapter of Utrecht, an "order-like" unit. Papal recognition, no less, was secured for it already in 1401 (*His que diuini cultus*) and 1402 (*Apostolice sedis equitas*). The latter specified that only those Tertiary houses associated with this Chapter enjoyed these rights and protections[9]—in other words, no other people calling themselves Tertiaries who might happen to exist in the diocese. The Chapter of Utrecht would eventually incorporate 164 houses (150 women's, 14 men's), with 3,000 women members claimed already in 1439.

The "Rule" these women now claimed originated in fact among thirteenth-century Italian penitential societies, and was falsely linked to Francis by the Franciscan Pope Nicholas IV in 1289 (*Supra montem*). On entering this estate Devout Tertiaries promised (*promitto, loeve hoechlic ende openbaerlic*) to keep God's commands (expected of any good Christian) and to "do right by" (not "obey": *satisfacturum ut conuenit, ghenoech te doen alst betamet*) the statutes for this "way of life." They also "promised" to preserve "eternal purity of body,"[10] their own addition to entrance formulas otherwise derived from the Italian penitential rule (where many were probably married). This promise was registered, importantly, by a notary public, binding them to this estate publicly in civil law. There followed a ritual investing, initially undertaken by local churchmen, later by representatives of the Chapter. It all stopped short of formal vows, with no promise of poverty or obedience, their goods too handled in a civil transaction. This general stance would hold largely for three generations. In 1480 Pope Sixtus IV (*Ad Christi vicarii*) declared, amid questions and confusion across Europe on the subject of Tertiaries, that their promises had the same force (*uim et ualitudinem*) as a solemn vow, rendering their promises and their persons in effect ecclesiastical.[11] In 1488 the promise was extended to include obedience and poverty (recognized by papal bull in 1499).[12] A full century along, in other words, they became virtually the equivalent of a religious order, though still promising, not vowing, their way of life.

A hundred years earlier, at Amersfoort about Easter 1399, Wermboud, Dou, Goudsmit, and William Hendricksz first agreed to transform the men's gathering there into a house of Third-Order Franciscans. By September of that same year women's households began doing the same, including St. Cecelia in Utrecht, the mother house of the contested communities. Theirs was plainly a coordinated strategy, for, we also learn, Devout Tertiaries secured a first papal privilege already on 26 September 1399, one that designated them specifically as houses with a communal life (*in communi uita sub obseruantia eiusdem ordinis*), wording that could only have come from one of the community leaders. Who went to Rome to obtain this privilege we do not know; but Bishop Frederick charged Bronckhorst with administering it.[13] This cut Franciscans out; it also subordinated Devout leaders to a trusted canon from the cathedral. The document noted further of these communities, perhaps defensively, that they possessed no chapels but were allowed a portable altar, and a provisional right to choose their own priest, even though this marked a breach with standard law and parish rights. Devout Tertiaries in the event would always choose priest-guides from among their own men or from the Brothers, never Franciscans.[14]

The prologue to the statutes of 1401 noted explicitly that these women all came out of local houses.[15] Each local foundation needed convincing that the move to Tertiary status and a common "Rule" was useful or safer. A house in Delft, for instance, was persuaded that previously they had had no "ordinances or rule or profession or 'mother' like the 'common sisters'."[16] The formal document authorizing the Chapter in January 1401 (*His que diuini cultus*) has the Sisters lament "formlessness" in their observances (*difformitatem*), a source of "danger" and "scandal"[17]—whatever the source or truth of that language. Adopting a "rule" and a chapter came with trade-offs, even one without vows. Not everyone would find a move toward more regimentation easy or desirable, even if it brought benefits like protection. In 1406 Bishop Frederick authorized the Chapter's ministers to close houses that did not abide by the statutes, even to hand them over to the secular arm. In 1408 he admonished his parish priests (under whom these women still stood) to warn and even excommunicate those who proved recalcitrant, this repeated in 1414 about women who left a house and so brought "shame" on the newly founded Chapter. In the same year the count of Holland ordered his officers, if requested by a priest, to arrest such women and return them to their houses.[18] The transition from self-made communities to a religion-like Chapter had gone quickly, in a moment of anxiety and pressure. How freely or eagerly household foundations took the step is nearly impossible to discern at this distance, though these measures hint at second-thoughts and resistances. Their statutes likely incorporated, or permitted, practices already begun (certainly communal life), including some the inquisitor had found objectionable as too "order-like." Bishop Frederick and his juridical advisers understood in any case, even with cunning, that an "order-like" rule and chapter was within the law and above reproach. He approved Tertiaries notably a full two years before he did the more ambiguous Devout. When in 1418 he authorized certain houses to become Augustinians (the Chapter of Zion), his document noted explicitly that he had earlier offered "favor" (*paterno confauentes affectu*) to Tertiaries, thereby "protecting" them from those "barking against them"[19]—alluding to the real situation on the ground.

Complexities followed when a self-made women's gathering became a more formal house. There was, first, the local parish. Tertiaries were not a religious order, despite the "Rule" and Chapter, and remained subject in principle to local spiritual jurisdiction. In practice agreements were struck whereby the women could work mostly with their preferred confessors and overseers ("visitors"). When parishes or patronage rights were multiple in a town, this may have come about more easily, Tertiaries possibly exploiting implicit rivalries.[20] In fact, as H. Van Engen found, agreements struck with rectors abounded in the first decade or two of the fifteenth century, worked out individually, which suggests local bargaining, if including common elements (the questions of an oratory, of burial, confession, and so on); and always agreement came in return for a fee, the rector compensated. These also survive in large numbers, an indication of their perceived importance.[21] Formally and indeed actually, they originated as petitions from the Tertiaries themselves, acceded to by local pastors, then by the bishop. Many have a common arenga, which suggests, H. Van Engen has rightly argued, a basic template supplied by Chapter/Devout leaders—possibly Gijsbert Dou of Amsterdam.

With respect to town magistrates there was the question of property. True to their statutory origins as lay penitents, not sworn religious, they made no promise of poverty. But Sisters "shared" goods and incomes inside their households, the statutes declaring that persons "should not appropriate goods or rents for personal use."[22] This was not the same as resigning all goods or giving up all claims to property or inheritance. Bishop Frederick in 1407 and the minister general in 1424 made it clear, especially to a skeptical public, that women and men could enter such communities and not give up their claim on family properties or inheritances. This definitely raised hackles, referred to as "troubles and disputes" said to arise from "ignorance of the law and lay simplicity." After consulting further with jurists the episcopal court corrected and narrowed its ruling: Tertiaries could indeed still legitimately inherit, the same as laypeople or secular priests; but such goods or rents, the minister-general clarified, they would subsequently buy or sell on behalf of the community, not as individuals.[23] Later, Tertiaries were represented to the Council of Basel in 1439, interestingly, as living primarily from the labor of their own hands, another practice that linked them in spirit and act to the Modern-Day Devout.[24] All the same, as people promising chastity and claiming a rule, also sharing goods, they looked like, even thought of themselves as, "ecclesiastical persons," while also inheriting or handling properties like a layperson, not a happy mix for town aldermen or heads of families. To lay authorities—and we should take this perception seriously—it could look like converts (mostly women) trying to have it both ways.

As members now of a Chapter they obtained, apart from protection, articulated organizational rights: that a superior be elected, that the "ministers" (father-confessors) as well as "persons deputed by each house" meet annually in chapter with full power to make and correct statutes in an ongoing way; that they might, if they wished, also take a vow of permanent chastity (*uotum perpetue continentie si uelit*); that the clerics among them be allowed to keep benefices up to a certain value.[25] The minister general was a secular priest, all initially Devout figures, beginning with the William Hendriksz who had also served as a public notary. St. Cecilia in Utrecht joined nearly first and served again as headquarters, while Rhenen and Gouda (St. Margaret's) also joined early. To what degree the move to Tertiary status grew simply out of panic, to what degree it was pressed by Devout leaders as well as churchmen or the count, to what degree it was chosen by the women themselves—this we cannot easily discern. But it worked. More than that, women from these Netherlandish towns joined in the thousands, arguably the largest women's religious movement (with its 150 houses in the north, 80 in the south) in the Later Middle Ages.

Houses were open, this means, to people of little means who could find refuge there, to widows or the abandoned (whereas Sisters consistently required "virgins"), also to people with means who might still hold or inherit goods and share them inside the house. These communities manifested little service orientation. Theirs was a life of prayer and work, or work and prayer, modeled at a distance on Carthusians or Cistercians, this too mediated by the Devout. Evidence about actual practice is surprisingly and disappointingly scarce. Some number of these women would have been illiterate or nearly so, and they made use of repeated Our Father's, along with a few other memorized prayers, much like lay sisters and brothers in orders,[26] while those who could read used Geert Grote's translated hours. But that is hardly the whole story. Some houses, including that first house at Gouda, left behind stunning libraries (Chapter 8). So particularity still reigned, and houses, though belonging to the Chapter, in some sense still set or maintained their own tone, that coming out of their origins (as in Chapter 2). What they sought was clear enough, if one may generalize: shelter from the public life of congested late medieval towns, from burgher and marital and merchant expectations, from the dangers that came with being a woman in the world. They sought peace with independence, and they sought it in religion, without the hindrance of taking vows, while also thinking of themselves as "religious."

Sisters of the Common Life

Women consistently outnumbered men among the Modern-Day Devout, in persons and in houses. After an initial explosion of Devout female communities reaching well over two hundred houses, the largest number became Tertiary, others joining orders (Augustinian canonesses, Birgittines, Cistercians: between thirty and forty in all), though quite a number of these operated as "Common Sisters" for a generation or two.[27] In northwest Germany all of the roughly sixty houses Rehm located evolved into Tertiary or Augustinian foundations,[28] none remaining "Sisters of the Common Life" in the stricter sense after the 1460s. Yet personal, spiritual, and structural continuities deeply informed their later life-style, this inadequately studied. In the Netherlandish region about twenty-five houses persisted in a form of life closer to the originating impulse of the 1380s–90s, and these we call "Sisters of the Common Life." No list exists, nor is there any accepted agreement among scholars.[29] These communities also left frustratingly sparse materials. Each retained local status and was known by a particular name, often that of a founder (Master Geert's House). Any complete list must await scholar/archivists who undertake the kind of *monasticon* we now possess for canons, canonesses, and Brothers, and is underway for Tertiaries. Cohesion and identity came from belonging to the Colloquy of Zwolle (or Münster), an annual gathering of all rectors for men's house and all father-confessors for women's; belonging signaled their status. But the records of the Zwolle Colloquy disappeared after 1570.

Of those houses that persisted as Common Sisters, we can point to five in Deventer (two eventually united),[30] four in Zwolle, three in Zutphen,[31] one each in Groningen, Doesberg and 'sHertogenbosch (Ten Orten), one possibly in Gouda and Utrecht. Some scholars see regional trends, the west (Holland) inclined to Tertiaries, the east (Oversticht, Guelders) to Sisters.[32] Differences more likely sprang in good part from political conditions on the ground. In Holland the count intervened early to monitor these women's houses, and expected institutional coherence and oversight. In the Oversticht, formally subject to the bishop, towns were largely independent de facto, leaving aldermen free to oversee local houses. This produced, ironically, a climate in the bishop's territory more conducive to independent Sisters' houses. Gender was also at work. Women found it harder to set up communal households entirely on their own, and nearly impossible independently to create a network. The Brothers became key, and were mostly empathetic, unlike many professed religious (Cistercian, Franciscan, even Windesheim canons). From these Sisters we have documents, though achingly few overall, and also statutes, though distended between the very early case of Master Geert's House and a very late set ('sHertogenbosch). Most important, we possess in-house memorial lives written by the women themselves in the vernacular, a source, intriguingly, with no counterpart among Tertiaries or Augustinians (except two houses founded directly out of Master Geert's: Diepenveen and Emmerich). Further, we have "collations" (addresses, talks), given by Brothers but taken down by Sisters.

Drawing upon documents and especially lives, this section outlines the Sisters' world: their social origins, numbers, the women themselves, who entered, why, and at what age. About social origins, first, scholars have offered mostly impressionistic remarks based on chronicles or lives.[33] Rehm asserted that in "German" houses women came from all social strata, with burgher families predominant.[34] Van Luijk, researching Leiden and Zwolle, could locate only a third or so of her women socially, even going deep into the sixteenth century. Of that third, three-fourths came from urban patrician families, the town elite, out of which Master Geert had also come (as did someone like Margery Kempe), the women's fathers, uncles and brothers attested as aldermen and urban officials.[35] At Emmerich fourteen of sixty-six memorials noted family goods, some holdings extensive.[36] But this leaves two-thirds of the women unaccounted for, and many would have come from lower social origins. Devout houses specifically forbade entrance gifts, opening the way in principle to women of all economic means.[37] Many in the 1380s–90s at Master Geert's House came initially from "poor families," we are told, including peasants from the "country."[38] Heylewich (d. 1418) tended the Sisters' cows along with other hard and dirty work, they seeing her as a pearl within even if she was not regarded as such by the world.[39] The house at Emmerich took in initially (1420s) all willing souls, thus one woman who spent much of her time combing out wool:

> Mechtelt [d. 1482] was born in Kalkar. Before she came to live here, she was there a maid of little means (*schemel maget*), and content whatever her hardship (*noetdroefte*). When this house first began, Mother Jut and Sister Griet accepted all the women of little means they could get.[40]

Sisters took pride in their poor, and in their house's social mix. The in-house chronicler at Deventer pointedly left it to others to tell of the "wealthy and noble" (meaning, the canonesses of Diepenveen); hers would be a story of virtue flourishing despite mixed and lesser origins. Spiritual quality was played against social status, manifest virtue over against the crudities presumed of poor or rural women. At Diepenveen, by contrast, of twenty-seven canonesses portrayed in social detail, Weiler found, fourteen came of noble or knightly lineage, five of patrician, two of wealthy burgher, four of "upstanding" families, along with two servants.[41] Well-to-do Devout women gathered there in part by choice, but also after being barred from Sisters' households, their wealth and servants feared as ruinous of simplicity. Still, social distinctions (urban/rural, wealthy/poor) persisted inside gatherings, these sometimes self-consciously reversed, a person of relative means or standing preferring a lowly job, or a nonliterate woman named as the first Mother at Emmerich. Bringing women of such varied backgrounds together to share resources, meals, and a common dormitory, even if it did not erase all social difference or personal tension, created a novel community atmosphere.

About the number of inhabitants in a gathering we have scattered information. Of thirty-three German houses for which Rehm could find numbers fixed by charter or otherwise reported, the average size ca. 1460 exceeded thirty-five individuals. Houses could range in size from twelve to a hundred, with several at fifty or sixty. A house in Coesfeld (lower Rhine, Cleve), eventually Augustinian, kept precise numbers, climbing from about twenty women in the 1420s to seventy-five in 1500, then declining through the sixteenth century back to about twenty. Where Rehm could also estimate town size (nineteen localities), Sisters represented 1–1.5 percent of the population in nine cases, ranging up to an estimated 6 percent in one, with Coesveld coming in at an estimated 3.75 percent.[42] In these compact medieval towns Sisters might thus represent one in a hundred people, sometimes more. Numbers are harder to come by for the Netherlands. The largest house in Zwolle (Cadanetershuis) had forty-two in 1461;[43] that in Zutphen (Adamnanshuis) thirty-nine members in 1464.[44] In 1458 plague claimed sixty-two Sisters (!) from houses in Deventer.[45] Even afterward its houses retained large populations. Aldermen ruled in 1463 that Master Geert's House could serve sixty women, "as it now is," while other houses should "decline by natural deaths" (*versterven*) to sixty for the combined Kerstkens-Brandes', twenty-eight for Buyskens', and twenty-four for Lammens'.[46] Owing to its generous endowment, Diepenveen was licensed for fifty canonesses in choir, though their number in the 1460s was actually about sixty-six.[47] In sum, even after a severe round of plague more than 175 Sisters in Deventer and another sixty canonesses outside the city would together constitute between 2.5 and 5 percent of the population in an important commercial and ecclesiastical center. Most houses were eventually assigned a fixed number of spaces (*stede*), determined by beds as well as workplace positions, this set formally by city aldermen. Compared with men's houses (averaging twenty or less), women's were generally twice as large, often more. For the larger pattern of Devout female recruitment Coesfeld's record fits what fragmentary evidence we otherwise have. Devout women (and men) expanded their numbers for roughly a century after the 1380s, reaching their highpoint in the 1480s/90s, then declined, slowly or precipitously depending upon circumstances, to the 1560s/70s.

These houses, we must further understand, were in origin simply that, houses on an urban street given by a founder or benefactor. Over time, as they attracted dozens of women, the house itself would be expanded, and to it would be added workhouses, stalls for animals, and gardens. Where remnants remain, it is usually of the house itself or the chapel (always late, usually 1490s). In Deventer, while Master Geert's House is entirely gone and a house that stood alongside the Brothers' House (the Lammenhuis) retains only a wall fragment, the complex that once made up the Buiskenshuis survives partly in the town library (Athenaeum), where the former chapel now houses rare books, and more extensively the house itself, now the city archives (see Figure 9). In Zutphen the complex that was once the Adamanshuis survives far more extensively, subsequently restored, including the inner courtyard, which would have provided the women some quiet and safety from the street (see Figure 10).

Master Geert wanted young willing converts of any social class in the early 1380s, we are told, but initially could attract only needy older women, Alijt

Figure 9. Remnants of a Sisters' house (Buiskenshuis) in Deventer, one of five in that city, now the city archives. Author's photo.

Figure 10. Sisters' house (Adamanshuis) in Zutphen, from its courtyard. This house was founded in 1397/98, became one of the larger and more successful of surviving Sisters' houses, one of three in Zutphen, and received its pastoral care from the Brothers' house in Deventer. Author's photo.

Crauwels (d. 1417) being the first of his true "converts."[48] Bollmann has pointed to intriguing evidence that in early days the converts and the needy dwelt in separate houses, suggesting a conscious distinction between the involuntary and the voluntary poor.[49] In-depth evidence about Sisters comes mostly from the two houses with surviving memorial books, Master Geert's at Deventer and St. Agnes at Emmerich.[50] At Emmerich half the Sisters came from the town or its immediate environs, half from outlying villages or towns.[51] The evidence for Deventer, though less clear, comports with this. Houses could recruit from farther away, thus in Deventer two daughters of an alderman in Arnhem, steward to the duke of Guelders. Inside the house all, high and low families (notable in any era, certainly in the Middle Ages), dwelled together[52] and engaged in common customs and labors. Social difference might be made to serve community needs, a farm girl put to tending cows, an only daughter of wealthy parents made keeper of books, presumably because she was privileged to grow up literate.[53] Family connections surface widely in these memorials as well, sisters or aunts, or cousins in the same house.[54] At Emmerich one-third of the sixty-six lives refer to such relations (nineteen sisters, three aunt/nieces, a sister who left, a sister at Master Geert's House).[55] At Deventer a prominent figure with an especially rich life, Stijne Zuetelincks, was Florens's niece, another woman a sister of Van den Gronde (the father-confessor who succeeded Grote), another a sister of the Mother, and so on.[56] All this made the emotional ties within even more complex. The same held for emotional ties outward. One woman deliberately moved to Deventer to escape the tug of her natural family. But another at Deventer, a vibrant young woman, visited home for family events, then grew deeply divided in mind, eventually dying young in a kind of nervous breakdown (see the epigraph). The memorialist added a warning against emotional allegiances causing confusion between the familial and the communal household.[57]

About age of entry we also have a surprising amount of information, Emmerich's memorial providing data for twenty-one of its sixty-six lives, six more described as either "young" or "adult." The median age was 15.5, four entering at 14, three at 17, and so on. Four who entered at ages 9–12 were described as young,[58] a woman of 23 as adult.[59] The lives in Master Geert's House provide less specificity but fit the same pattern, a woman older than twenty regarded as "old," a girl of nine as "very young."[60] The women entering, then, were typically between fourteen and eighteen. In human terms they had entered puberty, and were now to begin marriage and/or work—or life in a Sisters' household. One woman, of a well-to-do town family in Emmerich, later serving as Mother for twelve years, fled marriage at age eighteen to enter the newly founded house.[61]

For some 125 of these women (along with scattered *vitae* otherwise transmitted) we have lives written in-house in Dutch upon their death. A brief word here (more later) about these memorials. The intent was edifying, but their tone presumed a genuine human honesty, one of the significant markers of these lives. One young woman (with a sister already in the house), eighteen years old, "light and lively by nature," in "blooming youth," full of "lust for life," found it hard, we hear, to "conquer and break" her self for community life, then was frequently put to hard penance by superiors.[62] No less, a girl said to have "taken on this apart life willingly and with great desire," found it in fact "altogether contrary and hard," a person by nature "light and pleasant" who had to apply "great force" to bring her nature round.[63] On the other hand, Sister Eefce (d. 1423), fighting off her mother's efforts to make her a canoness, deliberately roughened her white gentry hands with sun and work, and on her deathbed insisted upon having her gown removed. Surely not in the presence of the father-confessor, her attending Sister said. But, Eefce retorted, "a naked bridegroom wants to have a naked bride!"[64] The keenness of human observation in these lives rested ultimately upon the spiritual climate fostered within Devout gatherings, a subject to which we will return.

Sister Stijne (d. 1445), Florens's niece, herself of gentry offspring, had a tough time at first because she was by nature, they noted, not pliable, deeply unsettled and impatient (*gestuert end onlijdsom*) when sent from one task to another. Fondly remembered in the end, she was never still, always working, always thinking, also teaching. Her memorial reports a variety of sayings and teachings, perhaps taken from her personal scrapbook by the memorialist. In any case she is said to have described three sorts of people present in their gatherings: Those put there forcibly by parents or relatives, people "taken on" by the Lord, she said, even if they did not take the life on themselves; second, those joining the house to escape a hard life in the world, people "nailed" to the Lord, trying to turn necessity into virtue; and third, those who chose the life out of love, even giving up plenty or sufficiency in the world, women "glued" to the Lord.[65] Her insights were born of daily observation of tens of women in close quarters.

Sister Stijne described as "taken on by the Lord" those who of themselves "had no love for an apart spiritual life" but entered the house under "compulsion" (*bedwanck oere oelders*) because "parents and relatives wanted it so"—young women chosen by God before they chose him, as she put it.[66] At Emmerich the memorials name fourteen girls, or just over 20percent, as brought by parents or relatives,[67] this arranged, it often says, to keep them "unstained by the world."[68] More cases too fit this rubric, rising to a quarter of the women. Most, also those entering under duress, were remembered nonetheless as having "willingly given themselves over" (*gaf hoer willick auer*) to superiors and house ways, some even proving "easy to lead toward a good life."[69] We may allow for the edifying gesture here, but must also contextualize "coercion" in a world where social roles often were inherited or imposed. In some cases a measure of human and social complicity must have existed between parents and teenage daughters, even if parents held the upper hand—daughters interested, parents agreeing, the latter then accounted "god-fearing" for raising their child to love things spiritual.[70] Some situations at entry, however, were heart-rending.

In at least two cases, we are told, parents simply had too many children at home.[71] In five cases one parent died and the survivor remarried, creating stepchild issues. The Sisters' house appeared a respectable and handy way to clear space at home for a fresh marriage, or to protect a child from a stepparent. Thus relatives brought one girl so she could "serve God in this good life without care and anxiety" [at home]; a father brought his daughter precisely so he could remarry. Another girl of fourteen acceded to her father's wish that she enter the house on his remarrying.[72] A father died and the mother resolved to visit Rome in the jubilee year (1450); so she offered up one daughter to the house as a sacrifice, intending to offer all her children. One of these daughters placed with relatives, both angered by and resistant to her mother's leaving, was later taken to the house as too naïve (*onnosel sijmpel kijnt*) to remain in the world, she later, however, becoming Mother of the house (Ide Prumers).[73] On the other hand, a prominent couple in Emmerich, the father a city judge, "offered up" their daughter to pray for them, and she "gave herself over diligently, to the degree of her ability."[74] Most dramatic perhaps is a story at Master Geerts House. Sister Hermen (d. 1453) was promised to the house by her parents, a life for which she had little inclination, making it hard for her (*soer*, literally "sour"). But she was kindly to her parents and struggled daily to break her own nature, often becoming sick, simply saying with a certain nonchalance: I was forced to enter (*Ich mach wal seggen, dat ic gedwongen bijn in te gaen*). In the month before she died she said to another Sister: This life is so contrary to me that I think if I had returned to the world I would probably have become healthy again[75]—remarkable for its insight, no less remarkable for its retelling in writing. For a host of familial and human reasons, then, up to 25 percent were "taken on by the Lord" before they "took him on"—this "good society" a respectable alternative to social or familial troubles at home.

To Sister Stijne the second of her types looked hardest, those "nailed to the Lord." These were young women who had suffered dark and weary days (*droeve*) trying to survive in the world by hard labor, and finally took up this estate to meet bodily necessities. To live now as a Sister would require a makeover in spirit and attitude.[76] One woman, an "adult," was urged by a natural sister already in the house to join; then that sister left to care for their parents, and the newer sister suffered "bitterly at heart," this "spiritual life hard for her beyond measure," her nature and it being like "fire and water."[77] But necessity did not always end in unhappiness. A poor girl, put out to work by her parents and beloved by her employing family, was helped by the latter to enter the house, fulfilling her "wish to serve God."[78] Often those in hardship were "adults," past age twenty. One was a baker's daughter, heavily tempted in the flesh once she joined herself to life in the house; another a maid pursued relentlessly by a would-be husband; two others physically strong and grateful for a safe place.[79] Nearly all these poor "adults" were illiterate, and considered too old now to learn, therefore often put to hard work in the kitchen or the workhouse. For them it was a trade-off between a secure home among the Sisters and uncertainty in the world, a calculation that then had to evolve into a spiritual calling. Those driven by economic need represent a smaller group of the lives, interestingly, under ten percent. They were not what these gatherings of converts sought—alms-houses being for that, and perhaps beguines. Among Tertiaries their numbers were likely far higher, even as Tertiaries also accepted widows or the jilted, not just "virgins."

The ideal for Stijne was a woman "glued" to the house by love for God and the way of life. These were women, in her words, who chose it out of their own free will, under no compulsion, having enough to live on in the world had they so wished.[80] If the foregoing percentages are valid, they comprised as many as two-thirds of Sisters at Emmerich, certainly more than half, which fits with what we can also infer from Master Geerts House. These were young women mostly in their teens, up to a third with means and connections, another third of more humble background. A Sister Alijt (d. 1431), who entered Master Geerts House about 1423, had to fight off her parents and relatives, especially during the time of interdict, hiding where she could when they angrily entered the House grounds looking for her, finally falling on her knees before them saying that she had resolved (*ic hebbe opgesat*) to live and die with the Sisters for better or worse, also had promised her chastity (*reynicheit*) to the Lord. If they forced her out into the worldly wilderness (*bijsterheit*), they would have to make their reckoning with God.[81] If we use the median age worked out above, she was eighteen or nineteen at this point, dying five years later of plague, still "young," the memorialist noted. It was these women of resolve who made up the core of the Sisters. Their male relatives found themselves in a ticklish position. Some resisted losing daughters to houses lacking in social prestige; some also found the religious earnestness at odds with their pride in social or familial achievement. They wanted security and "good society" for their kin. A Sister Griete (d. 1422) at Master Geert's House, of a gentry family, with two natural sisters professed at Diepenveen, forcefully resisted her mother's efforts to move her to profession with her sisters as a canoness.[82] In them we see free will, expressed as spiritual intent, exercised by women from families attuned to decisionmaking.

Routines inside the house are harder to reconstruct, at least in detail. The lives take it for granted, and written customaries have nearly all disappeared, apart from one, late and fragmentary, followed here. Sisters were to rise at four, arm themselves for the day with prayers in the chapel, then take up their labors (*hantwerck*), these interrupted by set prayers and mass (which over time became more institutionalized) and a midday meal. Afternoon brought a nap, more work, and another meal before they broke off at six or seven for reflection or reading and self-examination before retiring at nine.[83] The day was more or less common to all. As for basic organization, beyond a Mother, each house appointed a procurator to deal with material affairs and the external world, also a librarian, an overseer of the kitchen, and so on, offices analogous to religious orders, especially Carthusians and Windesheim canonesses.[84] The lives from Emmerich regularly noted specially a Sister's diligence in labor (in textiles), also in the common labors of tending to the house, working in the garden, and so on. Among general virtues consistently noted most often were: saying/reading their prayers (*gebedeken*), openness in confessing fault, correcting others fittingly, seriousness about keeping house customs, a humble bearing, devotion at mass. Individuals might also be remembered for spiritual sayings, exceptional kindness, and generosity in aiding or tending to others.

An elected Mother ruled each community, the first at Master's Geerts House (Beerten, ca.1398–1449) for fifty years, she brought from Zwolle ca. 1393 to organize their bread-winning labors and eventually elected head. Her confident leadership stabilized the gathering, we are told, and grew it with daughters from "good families" (*gueder lude kinder begonden to comen*). Though rough in manner, also austere with goods and tough in correction, her collations (addresses) were remembered as kindly, as to children; and she steadily mediated between the women and their father-confessors.[85] These features come up more often, a Mother's ability to act as a buffer between the Sisters and the father-confessor, and her own skill in addressing them, in effect teaching or preaching. At Emmerich the first Mother, Jut (d. 1469) ruled for forty-two years, herself not literate but taught from within by Christ, her life says.[86] By the time Emmerich's book was compiled in its extant form (1503) it began with the lives of three father-confessors and four Mothers, then treated Sisters in the order of their deaths, this order betraying a formal sense of deference within the house. As the communities grew, a Mother came to rule over a minor religious complex, if still a large house at its core. Beyond the house itself with its dormitory, refectory, and gathering room for collations and mutual correction, there were also a "work-house" (where wool was combed and weaving looms set up), a "spin-house" (where the wool was spun), a prayer-house (*bedehuys*) or chapel (eventually with a portable altar), and stalls for animals.

We close by considering the Sisters' literacy. Their use of vernacular books was attacked early on, and their copying sermons and sayings became basic to in-house spiritual life. The formal evidence is thin, what statutes remain setting aside only a possible hour a night for reading, though Sisters also engaged in daily prayers and table-readings and frequent collations.[87] With their large numbers and relatively poorer incomes, Sisters slept in a common dormitory, whereas Brothers each had their own cell/room, complete with a writing-desk. A Sister could ordinarily read or write only at the foot of her bed, a more or less public space, and only during times when the community was in the dormitory. But some made other opportunities. Sister Griete (d. 1444) at Deventer was in charge of the "cutting room" (*scheerkamer*: where the raw wool was undone and combed out, a burdensome job, involving much interaction with lay suppliers), but on holy days she sat by her bed reading or praying.[88] Mother Ide at Emmerich kept a life of Jesus next to her as she sat and spun, turning to it when she became distressed.[89] A sister at Emmerich, Geertuijt (d. before 1451), came from a modest family as an adult and so could not read "holy writing," nor did she ever learn to.[90] Their noting this, however, suggests that others came either with basic literacy or young enough to acquire skills in the house. In society at large girls had no public access to schools, though noble and patrician parents might have their daughters tutored. Indeed by the mid-sixteenth century Guicciardini remarked on the relative literacy of women in the Low Countries. The Sisters took in mostly teenagers, and forming them in community life must therefore have included reading skills.

A girl from Emmerich was said to love "reading and studying holy writings," which in turn she told to and taught others. Accounted "smart,"[91] on her deathbed she had her favorite book brought and read from it.[92] Sister Griete (1413–22) made notes and resolutions on wax tablets (*taeflen*). Sitting with others in chapel, she suggested that each say "something good" from what they had been reading. She also had a rather nice bookmark, and felt compelled to confess her inordinate pleasure in it. Among notes she wrote out was this: that "even though she made no profession of obedience, chastity, and poverty, this [life] was her 'betrothal-gift'(*trouwelschat*)," her offering, to Christ.[93] Also at Master Geert's House a Sister Griete Otten (d. 1452), served as librarian, remembered as an excellent manager of books, so given to "holy writings" that she seemed never to get enough.[94] Sister Metten (d. 1452) liked to read in the "Soliloquy" (probably of Augustine), as well as a book on "divine *mores*" falsely ascribed to Aquinas. She and another Sister gathered up and wrote down the "points" their father-confessor, Rudolph (memorialist of the men's house), made in his collations (these lost).[95]

Of some sixty lives from Geert's House ten or so include remarks about reading or study, suggesting that at last fifteen or twenty percent, probably more, may have come from tutoring at home, the rest exercising prayer and meditations with more minimal literacy and acquiring skills in the house. Most Sisters probably initially made do with a minimal ability to construe letters and familiar words in their prayer books. A Sister Armgert (d. 1463) from modest parents in Zutphen was remembered to have read her prayers out heartily, like a trumpet.[96] Reading after all was to be purposeful. Sister Wijce (d. 1417) had an exceptional capacity ("grace") "to retain what she heard or read" and winsomely to strengthen younger sisters in virtue.[97] At prayer, it is said, they put aside being "busy with their books" to "exercise themselves inwardly in good thoughts."[98] Sister Alijt (d. 1428), though in charge of the wool for their textile production, a heavy job, was gifted in "reading and studying holy writings," which got her through. In fact she was accounted highly intelligent, a person who knew her own mind, that independence also making trouble for her at times.[99] Sister Gertrut (d. 1434) read "high books" such as the Song of Songs and Ruusbroec's *Espousals*, and as death neared said: "Away with the high books, only the passion of our dear Lord, because only in it now do I feel peace."[100] The Modern-Day Devout in effect made it possible for women to reach the same end as literate men or professed Latinate women. Those purposes were built out of the raw material of young women—mostly teenagers, half or more entering willingly, a third or so placed there by relatives, a tenth or so in dire human straits—who committed themselves to prayer, labor, mutual discipline, shared goods, and reading, all as lay persons.

Brothers of the Common Life

Brothers represented a smaller group, in persons and households. Documents about them, however, run far deeper, and so do scholarly studies.[101] The tone in these houses was predominantly "clerical." One memorial noted in 1492 that "extra caution was needed in accepting lay brothers," though this man's relative, also lay, was admitted in 1494 (*confraternitatem*) with no probation at all.[102] To understand what "clerical" meant in this case we must fit that term and its social reality back into the Later Middle Ages.[103] It referred to "book-men" as much as "church-men" (also in the vernacular: *clergie*), and included all sorts of people (Petrarch, Langland) we often place under other rubrics (humanist, poet), quite especially students, civil servants, and ecclesiastical secretaries. A generation of scholarship on popular religion, projecting churchmen wholesale as its oppressive opposite, has obfuscated a far more complex social reality. In the countryside the social distance between peasants and parish priests was small, the intellectual distance often only slightly greater. Such nearness could foster mutual sympathy, most famously Chaucer's idealized rendering of his Parson, brother to his Plowman, his Clerk (student), notably, also coming in for gracious treatment. In towns and courts schools and universities generated a whole new class of "clerics" servicing a host of administrative and ecclesiastical needs, also a new class of "clerks," here meaning students. This yielded a large body—a proletariat may not be too strong a word—of young clerics seeking education and jobs. These clergy in the world (hence the term "secular") acted amphibiously, pursuing careers, enjoying female companionship on a regular or intermittent basis, owning homes (as Grote did in Deventer), yet also falling under the ecclesiastical legal umbrella, and often struggling for survival. They could become as cynical and worldlywise as any layman, if not more so. It was this class of people especially that Devout men sought to reach, and out of which most of them came.

Memorials written for Brothers accordingly reveal different social patterns. Nearly all who joined the houses at Deventer and Zwolle came from the local Latin schools. At Emmerich, a house founded out of Deventer, nine of fourteen memorialized were recruited first from the school at Deventer, then sent on to found Emmerich, with others soon joining from its school.[104] Sometimes former comrades in school joined together. Most were drawn by the collations and spiritual advising and "home-like" milieu of a Brothers's gathering, thus Egbert in the opening scene of this book, also Thomas of Kempen and a majority of cases we know about. Because these Latin schools, especially those in Deventer and Zwolle, drew from the entire Low Countries, Brothers also came from all regions. Consider the rectors at Deventer: Florens from Arkel (south of Utrecht) and study at Prague, Amilius from Buren (Guelders), John from Haarlem, Godfrey from Moers on the Rhine (near Duisburg, Germany), Egbert from Wijhe (north of Deventer), Jasper from Marburg, Godfrey of Den Bosch. Half or more of a gathering of Sisters came from the local town or nearby, but very few Brothers did. For Brothers, then, beyond accomodating differences in social rank, a household might embrace varying regional types and accents. The leaders were quietly, or instinctively, sensitive to this. Thus, though Emmerich in the Middle Ages was "Dutch"-speaking and belonged to the diocese of Utrecht, nearly all those sent there from Deventer came from towns west of Cologne and Bonn, thus the Rhineland region.

The memorials describe them as "youths" (*iuvenes*) but rarely give exact ages. Peter Horn, later librarian and chronicler at Deventer, joined at eighteen,[105] probably close to a median age. In social practice this meant upon finishing Latin school (whether or not they reached the "first" or final class). They then faced options: going to university (if they had money), seeking a position in church or court or town (if they had connections), prowling for a job requiring "clerical" skills, seeking entrance to a religious order. Beginning around 1400, another option was to join a Brothers' household, free of vows, freed of seeking a job in the world, settled in a quiet spiritual community. Nearly no men, in striking contrast with the women, get described as entering out of social necessity or awkward circumstances, though plainly student-clerics with poor prospects may have fit that description. Choosing this form of life took a certain resolve, because its status was widely adjudged humiliating, if not downright strange or suspicious, especially compared to what clerics would ordinarily hope or aim for. They even had to engage in manual labor, not the mark of "bookmen."

Closer to the Sisters in social origins were the lay Brothers, who frequently held the positions of cook, brewer, baker, and tailor.[106] We must be clear, however, that all Brothers, clerics and priests included, engaged in the "common labors" of the house, thus its ordinary maintenance, work in gardens or fields, carrying in wood, and so on, a constant motif in their memorials and a marker of their virtue. Clerics too, moreover, by choice or assignment, might serve as cook or brewer. And a lay Brother might prove as effective at offering admonition or working as a scribe (in Dutch) or counseling youth as any school-trained cleric, one of them acting as a virtual priest, as it was said.[107] Still lay men, compared to school-boy clerics, ordinarily came to the house with a different mix of devotion and need. Brother Tyman at Zwolle lived as a day-laborer and a busker (street musician) before joining, proving a "very good worker," though a man uncommonly untroubled, they said, in mind and body by sexual desire. He played his instrument and led them in song, especially at Christmas.[108] Brother Helmicus, a "hard and inflexible peasant," came to the house for help, vexed by bodily difficulties and demonic temptations, a man easily angered, who calmed himself by working as a cook for the students.[109] At Doesburg about 1453 a layman left, unable to bear the daily disciplines of the house, and married but only to live in great poverty.[110] At the other end of the spectrum was Brother Matthew at Deventer who fled a woman pursuing him in his hometown of Zutphen, served in nearly all the posts from brewer to baker to cook and tailor, and was so admired that a priest companion wrote up his life as that of an ideal Brother. Though lay, he was fully as capable as house clerics in writing and reading and offering spiritual counsel.[111]

Individual houses, as with the Sisters', went by differing names, a local name (Florens' House), also frequently the "clerics' house" (*Clerckehuus, domus clericorum*) or "gathering of priests and clerics living a communal life."[112] Stipulations in early days at Deventer foresaw four priests, eight clerics, and an undefined number of lay men (four to six).[113] Extant documents at Zwolle name three priests and twelve clerics in 1415, seven priests and fourteen clerics in 1465, the lay men in this case uncounted *familiares*.[114] The chroniclers for the house at Doesburg consistently provided detailed lists: for 1440 three priests, six clerics, and one laymen; for 1443, three priests, seven clerics, and seven laymen; for 1493 nine priests, six clerics, three laymen, with six priests serving outside the house as father-confessors to Sisters; and so on.[115] Modern-Day Brothers, in short, gathered priests, clerics and laymen into a single household, an unusual mix. No standard descriptor emerged except that of "common" (*gemeynre*) "brothers" or "fathers," their collective eventually the Brotherhood (*fraternitas*). Erasmus, who spent eight formative adolescent years under their care, described them as a *medium genus inter monachos et laicos* (a middle species between monk and lay) and as *semi-monachos*.[116]

The heart of the matter lay in each individual's resolve (*propositum*), the set of spiritual exercises (*exercitia*) he undertook. Initially these appear to have been truly individual, several written out, also by the laymen, that impulse having come from Master Geert himself. On his turn away from the worldly life of an ambitious secular cleric, Grote wrote into a "book" what was to order his state in life (*hoc ordinat statum tuum*), read through at a set time each day (*hora ad perlegenda*). This highly novel move found deep resonance in the Devout community, spawning imitators. Pledging himself to no religious rule (also, obviously, no municipal or guild or university statutes), he devised, in writing, his own rule for life, to guide his present "estate." We must imagine a handwritten quire or two filled with resolutions, read and consulted each day, added to from time to time. We have the text only as filtered by Thomas of Kempen.[117] Its title—*Determinations and Resolutions, not Vows, in the name of the Lord*—characterized the program of a man "intent upon (*intendo*) ordering his life to the glory, honor, and service of God," as he declared, "placing no temporal good of body, honor, fortune, or learning ahead of the salvation of my soul." Later writers referred to it (and texts like it) as "points" (*puncta*). Master Geert spoke of intent (*intendo*). His spiritual heirs would resolve (*propono*) these points.

So what did Grote resolve in order to privilege soul over body and career? The answer came almost entirely in negatives (the word *nullus* over and over again), ways to extract himself from the clerical life he had pursued for twenty years. He must give up the pursuit of more benefices or income-yielding clerical posts, also serving churchmen or temporal lords to gain such posts. The argument is practical: multiple posts bind a person, robbing him of "liberty of spirit, the principle good in the spiritual life" as well as of "peace of heart." He must also give up casting horoscopes and the pursuit of all "curious sciences" and "secrets of nature," because they had brought neither peace nor moral improvement. He would also take no degree in medicine, since he sought no gain (though he practiced both medicine and astrology, closely linked in this era), also no degree in law, its only end being material gain. He would pursue nothing (craft, book-writing, journey, learning) to enhance his fame. He would neither attend nor participate in public disputes in arts or theology, these all empty and for show and harmful besides; nor engage in private disputes unless they achieved some good end. Nor would he pursue a degree in theology because it was a carnal subject, its disputatious and self-absorbed speculations drawing one away from prayer and quietude; he could have the learning without the degree. He would intervene in a law case only if it was a pious cause or he could help the poor, also be cautious in representing friends or kin, "for peace of mind is disturbed if you go and let yourself in for the clashes and shipwrecks of the world." Nor would he seek vengeance on behalf of injured kin, only peace, and thereby set an example.

He wanted above all to flee the noise and stress (*strepitus*, repeatedly) of a clerical way of life, to gain "liberty of spirit" and with it "peace of mind" and "quiet." His positive program had essentially three components: reading, attending mass, and fasting. The dietary program was comprised of things "good to do but not promises" (*Videntur bone sed non promisse*), that is to say, no obligatory fasting as with professed religious. The program for mass called for daily attendance if possible, church law requiring that for clerics, he says, but only Sundays for laypeople. He also noted devotional gestures, sincere intentions, reverencing the sacrament—these in themselves nothing exceptional. His reading program, unique and influential, he placed first, a list of books centered in Scripture as well as in monastic texts going back to Cassian and the desert fathers, along with church fathers and "devotional" books, Suso's *Horologium* being the only recent work. As for church law he should only "run through" it to check the basics for piety and avoid obvious faults, not absorb it (*non ad incorporandum*).

Many at Deventer early on set up similar schemes, some copied out by Thomas of Kempen. These "exercises," under various rubrics (*propositum, exercitium, resolutio, puncta*), underlay the lives of all the Modern-Day Devout, even those who eventually took vows. They fully shaped the life and writings of an early figure and eventual canon like Gerlach Peters (d. 1411), but remain visible still in the later Windesheim prior Dirk of Grave (1459–1486).[118] Busch added to his chronicle an example of one said to be used by all lay brothers associated with the canons.[119] By the time that Henry of Ahus (d. 1439?) was codifying house customs for the Brothers at Münster, Wesel, and Cologne in the 1420/30s, to the description of statutory offices a resolve was added (*Collectum pro qualibet persona*), a generic exemplar one might say for use by any entering Brother. This one began with a personal resolve to live in community of life according to the early church, to keep the precepts of God and church, to observe chastity, to avoid banqueting, to pursue simplicity in clothing and utensils, to keep a schedule of prayer-life through the day, to retain no coins or jewelry without knowledge of the rector, to focus each day on meditation materials as a directive for the heart (*directio cordis mei et meditacio*), to confess once a week, to write out the day's faults each night—and so on through a long list, all this drawn up as a personal resolution, in practice thus adjustable by each individual. The text from Münster proceeded to "notable points for my emendation": thus, not to swear, to speak plainly and honestly, not to be noisy, to take good care of books, and so on.[120]

Within a generation Brothers had also drafted a working set of customs to guide their common life inside the house, these in principle distinct to each house, though much borrowing went on and a certain commonality emerged. A few basics may be noted here. Brothers were to say the divine office, this for clerics an obligation. They began around four in the morning, the priests together, clerics in twos, laymen as their work (cooking, for instance) permitted. Mostly, it seems, they followed the hours of the Cross and the little hours of the Virgin, as did many of the Sisters. Next came an hour of private reading and meditation, each in his own room/cell with a book or notebook. They then heard mass, whether at the parish or in an oratory with a portable altar. A huge portion of the day, three hours before the first meal (*prandium*) and then another three hours afterward (essentially the whole afternoon), was spent in manual labor, interrupted after the meal by a mid-day nap. After the evening meal (*cena*) they were to return to their cells/rooms for an hour of private reading, self-examination, and writing. Bedtime came roughly at eight. These customaries included a set of offices for governing the house: the rector (always a priest), procurator (financial administration), librarian, scriptor (book-copying), tailor, cook, and so on—a structure taken over with adaptation from religious orders, especially Carthusians and Cistercians. In the Colloquy of Zwolle the same offices appear (the texts had actually originated at Deventer or Zwolle) but came interwoven with materials on the purpose of this way of life, the structure of the day, materials for meditation, mass, manual labor, collations, and on expected virtues such as humility and chastity.

Unlike for Sisters we possess in the *Monasticon fratrum communis vitae* a marvelous research guide to the Brothers' houses and their extant sources, even if the volumes' use of present-day boundaries (Netherlands, Belgium, Germany) can be historically misleading. The Houses in Münster and Emmerich ("German") and in Louvain and Liège ("Belgian"), for instance, were founded out of Florens' House in Deventer. More pertinent to the actual history are filiation schemes, which house was founded out of which,[121] as well as the colloquies (Zwolle or Münster), meaning to which network a house eventually belonged. To offer a brief history, with apologies for the flurry of names and places, Florens Radewijns at Deventer was the indisputable founder of Brothers' houses, and remembered as such. After his death (1400) Dirk at Zwolle (1409–57) emerged as a de facto general leader, most "Dutch" foundations in the next generation growing out of his work, as did the colloquy. In "German" lands early foundations sprang from Henry of Ahus (d. 1439) in Münster just after 1400, as did the colloquy there a generation later, with five houses added after his passing, at Hildeshim (1440), then Kassel (1454), Rostock (1462), Magdeburg (1482), and Merseburg (1503). In Netherlandish regions Egbert at Deventer (1450–73) assumed de facto leadership in his era, adding foundations at Gouda (1456), Emmerich (1467), and Utrecht (1475). In Brabant and Flanders Louvain was founded out of Deventer, and Geraardsbergen out of Zwolle, but Ghent out of Louvain, the houses there, including Brussels, possessing broadly common founding privileges. All this, along with a distinct late burst in the Upper Rhine under the leadership of Gabriel Biel, yielded approximately thirty-nine houses. If we consider this history over time, we find an initial strong burst of activity in the Netherlandish and north German regions down to 1410, persisting despite troubles to about 1440, then only scattered additions in both regions in the next half century, but a whole new set of foundations late in the Upper Rhine. To all this we might add the Collège de Montaigu in Paris (1490), not a Brothers' house but under the influence of their way of life.[122]

Brothers aimed at an unusual mix of withdrawal and reaching out. Living a common life but in individual rooms, they operated as a band of committed priests, clerics and laymen, a contracted society. They were decidedly book-men but acted much of the day as artisans copying books. They themselves chose who among them would be "priested" and honored laymen as equally effective in spiritual guidance. In general Brothers frequently served as spiritual guides or father-confessors to Sisters and schoolboys while professing to prefer the contemplative life, reading and writing and meditating in their own room. In the colloquy of Zwolle, of the sixteen Brother's houses that lasted six took Jerome as their patron, as had the house in Deventer, and six Gregory, as Zwolle. The Brothers placed themselves thus in the penumbra of the early church and its doctors, Jerome copying Scripture in his cell and writing letters of spiritual guidance, Gregory preaching and teaching the contemplative life by way of scriptural reading and study.

Schoolboys

By the late fourteenth century many Netherlandish towns had schools (that is, Latin schools for teenage boys), be they capitular (Deventer), municipal (Zwolle), or parochial (city/church: 'sHertogenbosch), their schoolmaster, often a relatively prominent local figure, appointed and paid by chapter, city, or parish.[123] The capitular school at Deventer and city school at Zwolle were particularly famed, drawing in adolescents from the entire region, from Liège, Holland, Westphalia, and especially the lower Rhineland and Cleve. A text celebrating Deventer in the later fifteenth century focused attention mostly on its townspeople, their commerce and qualities, but noted that the footsteps of students (*scholarium clericorum pedore*) filled the town squares in almost uncountable numbers.[124] Alone at Deventer and Zwolle the schools offered all nine classes, counted in reverse: the oldest boys being in the second or first class and serving as teachers (lectors) to the lower. The third class rounded out the fundamentals of grammar and logic, whence most local schools stopped there. The two higher classes went on to the basics of philosophy, preparing students for university. Parents paid, and sometimes dearly: education enhanced their sons' prospects and prestige. Brothers saw this large body of schoolboy-clerics differently, however, as teenagers about to lose themselves in a world of vain ambition and careerism. Schoolboys aged between twelve and nineteen almost from the beginning came to form another important wing of the Modern-Day Devout.

Connections between these Latin schools and the Brothers ran deep. Of Master Geert's eighty or so extant letters, a good fourth (21) involved exchanges with other university masters, but especially schoolmasters in Deventer (William Vroede), Zwolle (John Cele), and Kampen (Werner).[125] Florens Radewijns drew schoolboys into his circle as copyists, and cultivated good relations with the local schoolmaster.[126] Thomas of Kempen's brother John, remembered as a fine scribe, collator, and editor, joined this way.[127] Busch devoted a loving portrait to his teacher John Cele, a close friend of Grote's, the headmaster at Zwolle (1378–1417) when that school boasted eight hundred or more students.[128] Godfrey Toorn, rector of the Brothers at Deventer (1410–50), first excelled in school there and served as a lector for a time; so too the first rector at Amersfoort was formerly head of its Latin school.[129] What comes into view is a circle of like-minded schoolmasterly comrades. This world of late medieval minor clergy has tended to get either overlooked or caricatured, but at London (Langland, Hoccleve, Gower) it drew men into civil service and legal jobs, at Avignon (Petrarch) into papal service, at Rome in time into a humanist curia—and in these Dutch towns into self-made religious communities.

Schoolboys arrived in their early teens needing lodging and care, quite vulnerable to price-gouging and abuses of various kinds. American readers in particular, perhaps some European as well, must remember that education and housing were distinct, the first organized and overseen by schoolmasters or university masters for a fee, the second in principle a private affair, in practice taken up in part by colleges (endowed dormitories, in American terms), referred to as *bursae*, funded spots in a house for students. Already in the 1390s laypeople sympathetic to the Devout in Deventer began to take boys in virtually for free as an act of charity, providing lodging or meals and of course security. One man took in eight at his expense and another four who could pay, a woman eight whom she provided with at least one meal a day. Indeed the dean of the Chapter, Rembert, arriving at his high post in Deventer with the intention of keeping three horses, instead resolved to meet the full expenses of six students, including fees and clothing.[130] Many such students, referred to as *scholares deuotes*, came to hang on Florens for guidance, filling his house on feastdays.[131] Already in 1398 a "new house" was built in Deventer to accommodate them, especially any attracted to a devout life with no place to go as their school days drew to a close, some, we are told, even giving up school to sit at the feet of Florens and earn their bread as copyists.[132]

Of the twelve "Dutch" and four "Belgian" houses of Brothers that endured, thirteen would sponsor and oversee care for students by way of *bursae*, houses for poor student-clerics (*domus pauperum, domus parva*) called in English "hostels." Hyma and others saw in them a seedbed for Renaissance or Reformation intellectual life, while Post found only pastoral care and austere discipline. Over the last generation a moderating consensus has set in (led by Weiler), but as yet there has been no focused study of this phenomenon.[133] Some were small: Delft had a house for twelve (dwelt in by the future Pope Adrian VI); Utrecht sixteen positions limited to future priests only. Others grew into expansive operations, Deventer's housing seventy students or more, Zwolle's about two hundred in 1514, 'sHertogenbosch's 225 in 1526.[134] These student houses too began as private societies, attested at Deventer in 1398. The "new house," at some remove from Florens's house but next to the Brothers' garden, was set up to receive benefactions and dispense burses, like the societies set up to support "inward priests."[135] The two (Brothers' and schoolboys') kept their legal boundaries (and cartularies) distinct, even though overlapping individuals were involved, an act of 1447 stipulating for instance certain incomes as belonging to the New House, reserved in this particular case for student-clerics preparing for entry into religious life.[136] The house itself was subsequently named after its longtime procurator Otger (1440s–60s), a signatory to this document—and is likely the house where Erasmus lived for a time ca. 1480.

Brothers' hostels soon gained a reputation across the Low Countries. Sometimes town magistrates invited them in, thus authorities in Liège already around 1410 to take over a troubled house (*Bons-Enfans, Bonorum Puerorum*), and still a century later the canons in Cambrai (1509).[137] Such a "poor" or "small" house elicited gifts from citizens or landed gentry prepared to give alms in support of needy students, a benefaction of the house itself at Gouda, a layman underwriting "poor student-clerics (*armer clercken*) who lived there to attend school."[138] By the mid-fifteenth century Brothers had devised as many as three different housing complexes according to student need. Some schoolboys were lodged and fed entirely on endowments (the "poor"), some in payment for services (the "rich"), with a "middling" option also emerging, all three present in Zwolle and 'sHertogenbosch, possibly in Deventer.[139] In Zwolle at least, where some of the complex survives, we can see still a dense complex of urban buildings (see Figure 11). The "middling" house abutted the Brothers' own, and the "rich" students house (see Figure 12), rebuilt, stood on the site of the Brothers' first house, all joined by a gateway and a common courtyard. This complex stood roughly a good city block (in modern terms) from the town parish (St. Michael's) and the town Latin school (now gone). The "poor" students' house (Figure 13) was roughly a block away, but closer to the Latin school. In general, town aldermen saw these schoolboy hostels as a good thing, bringing paying students to their towns, while also providing order and safety for the boys. Whatever these town fathers may have thought of the Brothers' religious intentions (mixed, as we shall see), the hostels offered a crucial and welcome social service. Erasmus, always sour about his upbringing in the Brothers' hostels in Deventer and Den Bosch, noted acerbically that it was all a money-raiser for them[140]—a heartless exaggeration, but a point worth bearing in mind too. In any case these complexes—the Brothers' own house and the student hostels and sometimes an associated women's house—sat densely packed into the narrow streets and courtyards of these medieval towns.

At a hostel one Brother was assigned to supervise, usually called a *procurator*, sometimes a *rector scholarium*, not to be confused with the rector of the Brothers' House. According to Zwolle's chronicle, its extant version by Jacob of Utrecht, himself a co-procurator in the 1480s, few Brothers escaped interaction with students. Rutger of Doetinghen (d. 1478) oversaw and cooked for fifty student-clerics, "fervent about the care and advancement of these youth." This was a role as much "lay" as "clerical," requiring hard work at cooking, sewing, cleaning, and the like. Rutger, for instance, did all the shopping and cooking and gardening for these student-clerics while also managing to relate to them personally.[141] A friendly man, he could be sharp about transgressions of household custom and good conduct, even with a whip—he the overseer of the young Wessel Gansfort, later a reform-minded theologian.[142] His successor, Arnold of

Figure 11. Overview of the remaining Brothers' complex in Zwolle, near the main parish church and the city Latin school, also adjacent to a former beguine convent. Visible still are remnants of their own houses (lower right) the "middling" hostel (lower center), and the "rich" (paying) students' hostel (upper left), the site where the Brothers first began. Brothers' houses were nestled deep in the urban cityscape on ordinary streets. Author's photo.

Figure 12. Site of the first Brothers' house in Zwolle, later rebuilt as the hostel for "rich" (paying) students. Author's photo.

Figure 13. Back wall/gable of the hostel for "poor" (nonpaying) students in Zwolle, built around 1500, holding as many as two hundred students. It stood just down the street, or through a walkway, from the city's Latin school (since demolished). Author's photo.

Emmerich (d. 1484), was beloved by students as well as schoolmasters, reverenced for his serious demeanor, yet "putting up with a lot."[143] So flourishing was this operation that Brother Reyner of Maastricht (d. 1489) rebuilt the house for poor students (see Figure 13 for the surviving gable), remembered for "teaching them in all sorts of ways with nuance," also for being "proficient in learning (*scholasticalibus*) and good *mores*" as a resident once himself.[144] While "schooling" and "character-formation" were distinct ends institutionally, they inevitably became interwoven. Brothers in practice helped with schoolwork. Beyond supplying poor boys with paper, pens, and associated needs, they helped with lessons. The boys, after going out to school in the morning, returned to the hostel for "drill" (*repetare*) in the afternoon, that mastery of material by mind and heart so integral to medieval basic education.[145] Brothers hereby acted in effect as tutors, whence their facilities could be referred to as a *schola clericorum*. Over time a transition to teaching themselves or setting up schools did not seem altogether unnatural.[146]

Latin schools in these Netherlandish towns preexisted the Brothers' hostels, and tended to be jealous of their rights. If schoolmasters or lectors joined the Brotherhood, they had to give up their teaching post with its attached income. Quite a number did: at Deventer Godfrey of Meurs and Henry of Wesel ca. 1400, Bernhard Meyer in 1455;[147] at Zwolle Henry of Herxen ca. 1436 (who would then serve as procurator for forty-seven years and rector for four) and Nicholas of Middleburg ca. 1440.[148] All the same, clear and absolute as the distinction was between a Latin school and a Brothers' hostel, personal connections overlapped. Florens at Deventer and Dirk at Zwolle had a hand in the appointment of local teachers.[149] The procurators of student hostels routinely dealt with the boys' schoolmasters, and vice versa. Further, in Zwolle, and elsewhere too, the two buildings were just down the street from each other. As the Brothers' reputation grew, attitudes toward their schoolmasterly role changed. To the south the Brothers' house in Geraardsbergen had a school of its own from the beginning (1440s, founded out of Zwolle), that in Ghent from 1463 with eventually two hundred students,[150] that in Liège from 1496, that in Brussels from 1504 with sixty students, that in Cambrai from 1509. At Liège a contemporary document reports that the Brothers were called in by the city's leading churchmen and burghers (*les bourgeois de ladicte cite*) precisely to set up a school of instruction and character-formation (*instruire les enffans en sciences et bonnes moeurs*).[151] In Brussels the Brothers' school amalgamated with the chapter school, and in Ghent it became the leading city school, responsible for introducing humanism to this wealthy Flemish city.[152]

In Utrecht, the episcopal capital, no Brothers' house was founded until 1475, but then with a school, set up in the face of four parish and five chapter schools, it soon emerging as the city school. There Johannes Hinne Rode devoted his attention in the 1520s to the New Testament (including a vernacular translation), and its rector George Macropedius (1530–56) became a famed humanist writer.[153] We can detect something of a pattern, Brothers providing a way to establish a city school (overseen and financed by aldermen) in the face of established ecclesiastical schools. No less interesting is what transpired at Deventer, a capitular school. With the appointment of Alexander Hegius (Sander Heck) as head (1485–98), the school opened to humanist impulses, Hegius himself learning Greek from Rudolph Agricola (ca. 1440–85). Earlier Hegius had studied in Rostock (1456–63) and was Latin master at Wesel (1469–74) and Emmerich (1474–83), all towns with Brothers' houses and hostels, thus a manifest connection. He now allowed Brothers to teach in the school, including Johannes Sinthen who taught Greek.[154] Erasmus experienced this school and the Brothers on the eve of that change (1478–83), later crediting Hegius and Sinthen with improving the literature taught there.[155] The Brothers received mixed reviews for their roles, sharp criticism from Erasmus, lavish praise from Rutger of Venray, both referring specially to 'sHertogenbosch where the school did not reach to the second and first classes. Venray praised them for their production of books and conversion of students. He also noted, mostly with approval, that they tried to shield students from Latin texts considered risky or obscene, Ovid in poetry or Livy and Sallust in prose, though they welcomed new authors like Baptista Mantuanus and Jacob of Wimpheling. Above all they taught Boethius, particularly the *Consolatio*.[156]

For the Brothers, founding hostels (and eventually schools) aimed finally at winning souls, turning young clerics away from rampant careerism to a more spiritual life. John Brugman, the most famous Franciscan preacher in the region, addressed the Brothers and boys together at Deventer in the summer of 1460. The manuscript rubric for his sermon characterizes the Brothers as "diligent in correcting, composing, and directing the character (*mores*) and affections of young student-clerics."[157] This task specially energized them, he claims, and took the form of offering "collations" (talks) and spiritual advising, also one on one. Brothers also acted as confessors, a right claimed early and upheld, though requiring the consent of the local curate. As a mendicant Brugman saw the talks and confession as the heart of their work, and urged the boys to take advantage—which suggests avoidance was possible.[158] Rutger of Venray wrote an oration in praise of their work, and claimed to have seen sixteen of these hostel/schools (all named).[159] When Brothers managed to turn someone from a worldly clerical career to a religious one, he noted (as if it were not all that often), they rejoiced as if they had just freed a soul from the maw of the devil.[160]

For life inside these houses we have few sources. Statutes likely once existed—Brugman appears to refer to them (*illas pias consuetudines quas habetis*: addressed to the schoolboys).[161] For some late medieval colleges and *bursae* statutes survive, thus from Erfurt in 1447.[162] Karras drew creatively on such material to trace how schoolboys were to be fashioned into university men, with much emphasis placed upon manners and decorum as well as moral (especially sexual) restraint.[163] The Brothers would not have disagreed. Schoolmasters and town authorities, too, might have been content on the whole with their instilling order, fostering a maturing dignity, and providing a climate for learning. This matter of educational and moral formation was in fact attracting growing attention across Europe just in this era. In Italy Vergerio's tractate on the "character (*moribus*) and studies" of a young man (*adolescentiae*), dated to 1402–3, represented the fullest expression of the early humanist program. Addressed to the scion of a ruling family, it, as its most recent editor put it, "has a distinctly moralizing flavor: education must make the student virtuous as well as learned."[164] Vergerio addressed first the character of the young (*iuuenum mores*), recognizing the abundance in them of heat and blood, hence the need to correct, specially restraining any premature sexual activity. The young for their part had to open themselves to critique and admonition. Religion, above all (*ante omnia*), needed cultivating in them.[165] That said, for humanists it was preparation in the liberal arts newly informed by classical texts, as well as training in physical prowess, that was chiefly to guide, an outlook that reached schools in the north only in the 1470s/80s. Humanists wrote these tractates moreover primarily for an elite lay clientele, grooming them for roles in society at large (even if many ended up in church posts), while Brothers focused on student-clerics and their possible roles in reforming the church.

Jean Gerson took up these issues too, in April 1411 proposing a plan for schoolboys at Paris, he then head of the cathedral school in Paris. He imagined a regime like the hostel, indeed a society of boys (*puerorum societas*) as potentially the most "beautiful and flowering" part of the church.[166] Schoolmasters should act as models of virtue (again plainly in matters of the body and sex). More, they were to go beyond teaching and exhort students to the love of God, warning them of hellfire, keeping them from sin, even with whips (though gently, he specifies). One master should always stay with them. One should lead them in the hours of the Virgin (the Psalms that Sisters and Brothers prayed). Further, beyond teaching the standard grammar and logic, these masters should set aside time to expound the Gospels and Epistles, this also and thoroughly in the vernacular to make sure they understood—as Brothers were doing in their collations. One boy should read at meals. Boys should also report on each other's faults: whether, for instance, they spoke in the vernacular (enforcing an early use of Latin, also common in Brothers' houses), whether they swore, lied, struck someone, touched someone intimately, and so on. They were also to avoid any dice and games that led to raucous noise, personal anger or mutual envy. Boys could not go into another's bed at night, or form little "societies" among themselves. But, interestingly, Gerson advised setting up a "nightlight" for their comfort and bodily necessities: a candle burning before a statue of the Virgin.[167] He envisioned, in short, a full training (*instituendo*) of schoolboys, not just in schoolwork but in body and character.

For the life of schoolboys inside Brothers' hostels we may approximate a picture, I would suggest, by inference from Gerson's plan for Paris but also more specifically from two other sources. In 1469 a part of Cardinal Nicholas of Cusa's substantial legacy was dedicated to founding a *bursa* in Deventer. Its statutes survive, drawn up by Cusa's executors, and specify that this hostel was to follow the pattern set by the Brothers (*ad instar scolarium in domo clericorum*).[168] Cusa's foundation (*bursa*) was to house twenty students, each in their own bed, aged between twelve and eighteen, poor but free, not professed but in the first clerical tonsure, good enough to start in the seventh class (4). There, cared for by two *provisores* and a housemaster, they were to eat, sleep, and do their "school exercises" (1–2). The master was to get them off to school in the morning and then tutor them (*repetare*) on their return, instructing them in learning as well as modesty and humilty, all under a common discipline like that kept up in the Brothers' hostel.[169] Also as in the Brothers' hostel, the boys had to promise obedience to the master and submit to his correction, thus to preserve "concord and brotherly love" (6)—a typical Devout phrase. These schoolboys, like the Brothers, were to walk two by two to school or church, never beg, keep to the house regimen in matters of conduct and schoolwork, say set prayers after meals, and listen to admonitions from the hostel's rector on "increasing in virtue," (8) another Devout formula. They were to wear a gray outer cloak, falling to halfway below their knees, and a black hood (9), likely modeled on the Brothers'. Besides room, board, and clothing, the foundation was to supply their school needs and pay school fees, all together reckoned as roughly fifteen gold florins per student per year (7), a substantial amount—indicating why the Brothers' hostel over time acquired a healthy endowment. Local citizens were allowed to present three of the twenty boys (5), a way of "making friends" with aldermen. In November 1470 the executors made a Dutch translation of these statutes and presented them to the city council in Deventer.[170] The statutes for Cusa's burse provide unnoted glimpses into the customs that governed life inside a Devout hostel, and attest as well to the high regard given the Brothers' paradigm for schoolboy formation.

Brugman's sermon of 1460 was addressed to student-clerics at Deventer. From it may be gleaned something of what he expected, allowing for the fact that he was an Observant Franciscan advising as a guest, not a Brother tending schoolboys on site. He invited the boys to enter Jerusalem with its twelve gates, each a specific virtue, each applied to schoolboy life. As for faith (the first), they were not to write their notebooks full of charms and figures, the sacrilegious stuff of old women. And so he went on through charity, humility, and all the rest, urging them of course to enter religion. Then he portrayed twelve gates leading to hell, also with practical injunctions attached: to write no letter without showing a superior, not even to parents, for it could open the way to apostasy (leaving the house); never to go out without permission, for it could lead to flesh and the devil; not to bear correction badly or hide things in confession but lay temptations out nakedly before the Brothers. The schoolboys should find an hour a day for praying, examining themselves, and holy reading—it would not take away from progress in your schoolwork, he assured them. As for poverty, they were to be content with gray garb (like the Brothers), and to beware of ecclesiastical benefices, lest in future they got burned by them. So too with study at university, a good thing in principle but in practice rarely cultivating virtue. Brugman says he might better himself have spent time in Deventer, where learning (*sciencia*) came with character-formation and virtue, than in Paris.[171]

From the Brothers' side around 1470 an anonymous work pointed to their labors among students (*iuuenibus maxime scholaribus*) as their most signal contribution to the region: the "innumerable" young men they had grounded in religious life and many others simply counseled to a better life.[172] Erasmus, himself a canon regular at the Brothers' urging (as he later told it), more sarcastically observed that Franciscans and Dominicans so loved the Brothers because without their conversionary efforts convents would simply have emptied out.[173] All the same, towns would not have invited them in, or benefactors supported them, or parents sent their sons, or past students remembered them fondly, had not these hostels/schools fulfilled an important and widely appreciated service. They emerged as a large presence in Netherlandish towns during the fifteenth century, a crucial source of learning, moral formation, and reforming religious for two or three generations—also the key source of recruitment for the Brothers' own houses.

Windesheim Canons and Canonesses

Only a brief word here about the canons and canonesses of Windesheim, a major topic in their own right. The Congregation of Windesheim proved arguably the most successful new religious order in the fifteenth century: papal approval of their general chapter from 1395, numerous privileges in 1413 mediated by d'Ailly as cardinal legate, an ever expanding network of houses reaching a hundred in all, revised common statutes from 1434, annual decision-making in their general chapter recorded serially from the early 1430s, a membership reaching perhaps 2,000. Women as professed canonesses were artificially cut off in 1436 after the incorporation of thirteen houses, owing to their demand for pastoral help (as so often with earlier orders), though subsequently many women's houses still associated informally with the Congregation (see Chapter 7). The Windesheim canons soon presented themselves to the world as the official face of the Modern-Day Devout, a stance reinforced by influential chroniclers (especially Busch and Ympens), and indeed with a kind of triumphalism. In the year 1464 Busch, then aged sixty-five, already forty-five years a canon, looked back "seventy-six years," as he said, to the origins. He saw their expansion in his lifetime as a modern-day wonder.

> We have known great and wondrous works of divine power, done in our days and a little before us, deeds placed squarely before our own eyes, multiplied and expanded vastly in this whole surrounding region. And we see them still, to this day. There was at one time in our land, then a sterile and unfruitful desert, no place of refuge in which souls might be saved, where they might work out their own salvation, either in the world or in religion. . . . [But now] throughout this province hardly a city or town can be found but where, all around, monasteries and congregations and numerous dwellings of the Devout have been newly founded or been re-formed from existing houses.[174]

Busch, a reforming administrator, liked numbers. He reckoned, quite accurately, that more than eighty houses of canons and canonesses were founded in his lifetime, more than fifty gatherings of Brothers and Sisters, more than a hundred houses of Tertiaries—some holding a few persons, some twenty or thirty or forty, some, he claimed, two or three or four hundred. This did not count, he added, thousands of lay people touched by them. Who could imagine, he exulted, such a "multitude of holy people" arising "through the whole germanic world"? Who dared think "in these our times" of a "new miracle of the early church," of all that had followed from that first "commune"?

Busch saw the succession as passing directly from Florens (d. 1400) to Prior John Vos (1391–1424).[175] Windesheim's public ecclesiastical status inevitably overshadowed Devout energies; what had begun as a "front" became the approved public face. Still, Windesheimers in the northern Low Countries never entirely lost their links, keeping up friendship with Brothers, offering spiritual care to Tertiaries, the Brothers from Zwolle indeed buried in Windesheim's churchyard. Still, Busch's book on "illustrious men" treated communal life, so central to the Devout, as particular to religious orders, with no mention at all of gatherings.[176] In the south Groenendael and five other Brabantine houses of canons joined the chapter of Windesheim in 1412/13, and they retained a resistant sense of distinct identity and prior origins. Their writers had the story begin with Ruusbroec, Groenendael, and canons regular, Brothers and Sisters thus reduced to supplying recruits or training potential novices.[177] To the east the chapter of Neuss, under Devout influence from early days, joined along with ten other houses in 1430, another distinct presence. From the mid-1450s expansion would take place almost exclusively in German lands.[178] With canonesses now restricted, canons dominated the Congregation, whereas Sisters outnumbered Brothers, and Tertiaries outnumbered everyone.

The Brothers saw things differently. If a community began as a household and shifted to regular status, as sometimes happened, this insulted the inherent perfection of their own communal ideal. At Doesburg in 1465 Rector Henry of Grave, twenty years into his rule, persuaded the Brothers there to make this move and secured permission from the bishop in advance, the ratifying document still extant.[179] The Brothers had also to agree in writing since they had earlier resigned their goods to the society. Initially they did so. But a Brothers' house stood still in the civil world, and the duke of Guelders as it turned out would not agree apart from the pastor and town aldermen, who refused consent. Egbert, rector at Deventer, showed up in Doesburg just as the Prior of Windesheim (Dirk of Grave, 1459–86) came to try invest them. He enunciated the complete outrage of the Brotherhood,[180] not opposed to religion as such, he said, but to this seizure of "their place," this disparagement of their estate, this utter violation of charity, canons appropriating a house set up for Brothers, erected by their labors, sustained by their incomes and purposes.[181] The house in the event remained in the Brotherhood, its rector moved out, though whether Egbert's remonstrance would have prevailed without the local pastor and aldermen's resistance is not clear.

The Windesheimers were deeply indebted to the Brothers, and not just owing to early days under Florens. Though canons also produced writers,[182] the authors who most shaped the order's spirituality came notably from among Brothers and Sisters. Theirs was the foundational experience. Gerlach Peters (d. 1411) began in Deventer, his writing the product of a half-way stage between the Brothers and the canons, assembled after his death and then circulated widely through the order.[183] On the women's side the leading teachers, such as Salome Sticken, began life among the Sisters. Their *vitae* also became the model for those written later at Diepeneveen. The key exercise for meditating on the life of Jesus, circulated widely in the vernacular and then by Busch in Latin, came, whoever its originating author (John Vos or even Zerbolt), likely from Deventer.[184] Thomas of Kempen's guide for novices would focus entirely on the Brothers in Deventer as the "founding fathers." His sermons for novices referred to gatherings as well as convents, as his chronicle included the history of both, the Brothers always as present to him as his own canons. The booklets that came to comprise the *Imitatio* breathed the spiritual energies and insights he first acquired during his years in Devout gatherings.

An Option for Enclosure: Male Canons and Female Tertiaries

One final unusual feature deserves attention, a further mark of Devout inventiveness: enclosure as a voluntary option for nonprofessed female Tertiaries and, much more strikingly, for professed male canons. Going back to 1399 at St. Cecilia's in Utrecht, some women's gatherings chose enclosure (*inclusorium*, *slot*) along with Tertiary status, possibly as a further way to ward off suspicion or recrimination. Across the early fifteenth century fifty-one houses would do so, a third of the total.[185] This might at first glance befit a drift toward regularizing, also fall in line with papal demands for *clausura* after 1298,[186] but we must be careful. Tertiaries, not being vowed religious, did not fall under *Periculoso*, or any rule or statute about enclosure. As persons otherwise operating ambiguously inside and outside the world, they were choosing to live, as I see it, as recluses or anchorites, a common type in the Late Middle Ages. Novel or inventive here was the adoption of a reclusive or enclosed form of life by whole households collectively. This raised issues both practical and principial.

Like the enclosure of recluses, this was an act that came under a bishop's purview and liturgical enactment. Bishop Frederick and his court drafted a common documentary understanding early on, seventeen instances uncovered by H. Van Engen,[187] who has also argued convincingly that the petitions actually came from the women, and voluntarily. Their requests met with little resistance from parish priests, though some from aldermen. The Chapter, especially the ministers who directed it, must have played an enabling or encouraging role, but evidence is not at hand. These women, as the document expressed it,[188] wanted to live more freely and quietly for God (*liberius et quietius Deo uacare*) and to preserve their bodies' chastity. Both the document of enclosure (*speciosus forma*) and the statutes underscored the high premium placed on virginity (or chastity for widows), celebrating the spiritual ideal but also hinting at a social role for these houses as offering refuge. Enclosure, as they put it, removed occasions for lust or misconduct (*lasciuiendi*) in heart or body, drew a line in effect around the ambiguous situation in which the Tertiary status functioned; it likewise protected them from social or familial pressures, even personal violence. But constricting women to a house was not possible unless they had sufficient income to survive without going out to work agricultural lands or trade in the market. This sparked steady worry among lay authorities. Scattered references to manual labor indicate that textile production still went on, with mediators presumably handling goods and bringing necessities. Town aldermen also feared that enclosure would move their persons and properties definitively over into ecclesiastical "freedom" (*fryheid*) or immunity. In practice this was partly so, perhaps what these women partly sought. In legal principle, however, their status remained unclear until at least 1480, if not 1499, so long as their ability to hold or inherit property, the status of their "promise" of chastity, and no promise of obedience left them outside the privileged circle of "religion."

Tertiaries still required access to religious services, normally their parish church since few houses were granted a private chapel or had the funds to build one until late, generally the 1490s. Anchorites, remember, often attached their dwellings to a church. Here the Devout proved ingenious too. H. Van Engen has gathered photographic images of, for instance, enclosed passageways built to link their house to the parish, whether overhead or underground. In Rhenen, where the women chose enclosure by 1420, a tunnel was dug from their house to their own space in the church.[189] The expressed purpose of enclosing Tertiaries was to "separate themselves from the stormy waves and great spectacles of this world for a holy converted life (*sancta conuersationis*) and the sweetness (*dulcedine*) of contemplation." This presumed, unspoken, the din of the streets—merchants, families, markets, animals—and the bustle of families, also perhaps the pain of troubled or broken families, all aspects of late medieval urban life they aimed to free themselves of in the peace and quiet of their own enclosure.

Still more striking, and not part of any general historical discussion as yet, is the case of Windesheim canons who chose enclosure,[190] men voluntarily confining themselves like women for religious purposes. The move originated in the south, especially Brabant, and gained support from lay benefactors, who in the later middle ages increasingly favored austere foundations (thus Observants too) for their order and decorum (and supposed enhanced intercessory powers), Carthusians being the paradigm. The Devout house at Corsendonck swung for a time after 1395 between canons regular and Carthusians, then between Windesheim and Groenendael, and chose enclosure in 1432. The first house to adopt it fully was Bethlehem outside Louvain in 1414. Its largely unpublished chronicle from nearly a century later, Petrus Ympens' *Chronicon Bethleemiticum*,[191] offers the fullest account, including a rhetorical laudation. The ideal, as he relates it, is a solitary life (*solitudo*) for men, marked by "silence," casting off "distractions of the world" in order for the soul to "cohabitate with God." This solitude, even "constraining one's body to a particular place" (*corpore locali angustia coartato*), represents the true guardian of religion (*uera custodia religionis*), for it removes all ability to wander abroad. It also exposes as illicit all the ploys religious have found to render their travels and recreations licit—a sharp dig at the *refugia* (vacation houses) and trips outside a cloister then common. True solitude defined a person who actually found it punishing (*pena*) to go out into the noise and tumult of people in the world—a sentiment probably intelligible to enclosed Tertiaries as well. The ideal, we must remember, was not peculiar to the Devout in this era. Ympens actually closed with a quotation from Petrarch's widelyknown "On the solitary life."[192] The humanist's plea had been written more than a generation prior to the beginnings of canonical or Tertiary enclosure, in his case imagining a life not only for religious (like his Carthusian brother) but also for clerics like himself choosing leisured and literary solitude.

But what would enclosure mean for men already professed as canons? It required an additional promise, that of perpetual enclosure following the form of a given house (*promitto perpetuam inclusionem secundum formam huius domus . . .*). In actual practice it meant a sworn promise never to leave a delineated precinct, its boundaries and accompanying conditions set out singularly in each enclosure document. Here I note representatively the still unpublished agreement for Leidersdorp outside Leiden. This act explicitly went beyond ordinary vows (*ultra professionem emissam*). Boundaries were set out first: what street or wall or river they might never again cross, an invisible fence around the house. This they could cross only with permission of their prior, that not easily given, though the prior and procurator were themselves free to move around to fulfill their offices. Canons sent out to serve as father-confessors were also dispensed, but had to return to enclosure on completing their office. If anyone crossed the boundary apart from fire or war, he was to be incarcerated. Neither the prior nor the general chapter, moreover, had any right to violate this agreed-upon enclosure, in effect to dispense from it, once the vow was taken and the document ratified.[193] Enclosure also involved a special rite beyond profession. According to Busch, each canon would approach the altar during mass with a candle in his hands, make his profession of enclosure, sign a confirming document and place it on the altar, and then in the presence of the whole body pronounce his promise aloud.[194] For men, plainly, enclosure did not mean life confined entirely behind walls and restricted to a "talk-window" for outside communication, as it did in principle for women. But any freedom to travel, preach abroad, visit relatives, or see friends was deliberately lifted. In the north twenty-three men's houses eventually took this option in the 1430s/40s.[195]

Busch devoted only one chapter to this phenomenon, the last in his chronicle (completed 1464). He was skeptical, even if its supporters regarded it as a higher form of devotion (*ampliori deuocionis amore*). As Busch saw it, the General Chapter had condescended to the demands or needs of weaker brothers. Enclosure, he noted, provoked hot debate. Partisans argued that too many professed canons, close to family and friends, left the house frequently on visits, claiming that they were going out to speak about salvation. But others countered that except for blood-letting (a medicinal act at appointed times in the year, followed by a day of "recreation") and common labors in fields or gardens, many had not left the house in ten or twenty years. In the spirit of Brothers and Sisters, moreover, some houses resisting enclosure claimed greater virtue for their acting freely and not under constraint. Busch snidely remarked, for his part, that the precincts were drawn generously, lest "the spirit become exhausted by overmuch devotion."[196] In this ongoing tension between contemplation and contact ("winning souls"), more than a quarter of the Windesheim canons swung radically in one direction, and tried to make enclosure inviolable by legal contract. The impulse had originated in Brabant, moreover, houses formed in the spirit of Ruusbroec, always more contemplative in orientation. Resistance came from figures like Busch, houses formed by the Brothers with their "in the world" stance.

No one has yet reconstructed the full debate or edited the treatises it generated. Ympens claims that mendicants too mocked the canons for enclosing men.[197] Proponents drew deeply from antique monastic traditions. Stability, the first of the old Benedictine vows, along with dwelling contentedly in one's cell, they said, was the source of all good things, wandering outside producing all things evil. Outside a convent, daily experience showed, according to this apologist, one is exposed to multiple phantasms and dangers, one's devotion worn down by an excess of sights, sounds, and idle words. What they aimed for was mental solitude; to persist perpetually in enclosure moreover was to participate in the passion of Christ and in his heavenly kingdom. But, critics retorted, why do all this with a vow, and so abandon God-given liberty? The apologist cited Thomas Aquinas's argument for higher merit in acting under vow (see Chapter 7). So why not, came the response, also fast under a vow? Why create obligation? These enclosed men exposed themselves in fact to greater danger, critics charged, falling into despair and other sins. Moreover, no inherited rule called for such enclosure; it was a novel and brash act. But in "these modern times," the apologist responded, when "devotion is cooling," it is licit and salubrious and prudent to vow enclosure, to annul any freedom to go out or even ask to go out; better than to claim freedom and risk failure. As for novelty, did not Cluniacs and Cistercians, still praised in the church, add new things to inherited rules?[198]

Canons found themselves here in an intense debate about whether it was solitude they most wanted or an active spiritual presence in society, whether to act under obligation or in freedom, whether as men to enclose themselves as an act of higher devotion. Sisters and Brothers consciously preferred "resolutions" to vows, liberty to necessity, a self-made interior cloister to an obligatory walled enclosure. How they brought that off is our next topic.

CHAPTER FIVE

Inventing a Communal Household: Goods, Customs, Labor, and "Republican" Harmony

I resolve to institute myself according to the form of life which is written about in the Acts of the Apostles [4:32]: "The multitude of the believers were of one heart and one soul, and none said that anything was his own, but all things were common to them."

A good society is like a tower of strength in the face of an enemy. There a person lives more securely; there is help from many. And if on occasion he is troubled by someone, he is in turn consoled by another.

THE LATE MEDIEVAL church was big business. Extensive material holdings and a vast clergy made it collectively the largest land-holder and employer in Europe. In the fourteenth century papal ideologues articulated theoretical claims to it all as one great monarchical state. In actuality clerical land and office came complexly interwoven with lay and princely powers, and clergy remained inextricably linked to local families, the web of interests, and of competition, labyrinthine. Princes funded churches while exercising patronage and skimming income; clerical office funded princely administration. Ecclesiastical banking enriched prelates as well as bankers, and also greased the economy at large. Church office opened paths to honored careers and purveyed needed services. Many complained that material interests steadily corroded spiritual purpose; at the same time most who could availed themselves of this apparatus, itself constantly expanding in the fourteenth century. The papal court, exiled from its Italian lands, centralized ecclesiastical administration at Avignon, partly a matter of control, more a matter of revenue. The theologian Matthew of Cracow, in a tirade against the "squalors of the curia" in 1402/03, found the entire upper leadership suspect of simony, the first crime in the church's law book.[1] Pleas to curb all this dealing in offices and properties would only multiply after the outbreak of papal schism in 1378.

Between the 1380s and 1440s multiple solutions were proposed, and none found. All possibilities were put on the table, if not all accounted licit or doable. At the councils of Pisa (1409), Constance (1414–18), and Basel (1431–49) reformers proposed measure after measure; yet could never agree upon how to proceed. Often fully entangled themselves, they proved variously anxious to protect their own stake in how things worked. Two generations earlier Pope John XXII had condemned as heresy the Spiritual Franciscan teaching that Jesus and his apostles held no property individually or collectively. For souls empathetic to this vision the only solution now appeared apocalyptic, a divine intervention to sweep away the whole carnal church. Within religious orders critics lambasted those they labeled *proprietarii,* people professing poverty while basking in collective wealth and ever grander buildings and personal luxuries. Strict Observants proposed now to impose a new draconian regime, to enforce religious rules to the letter. This proved realizable only in scattered houses, those, however, attracting stellar recruits as well as lay admiration and support.[2] Other critics, lay and ecclesiastical alike, proposed total disendowment, the church stripped of lands and goods, handed back to temporal powers, the church itself reduced to a society of poor priests and voluntary alms. Wycliffites and then Hussites favored this approach, and have caught the attention of modern scholarship, though Marsilius of Padua's vision a full generation earlier was not so different. Rumors and attitudes of a similar inclination, broadly labeled anticlerical, circulated widely, if denounced by most churchmen. The embrace between the material and the spiritual seemed complete and destructive and unavoidable. It elicited many imagined ways out, some thoughtful, some angry, some apocalyptic, some wishful thinking, some perhaps workable. The Modern-Day Devout projected their own small-scale solution: communal gatherings set up in the spirit of the earliest Christians.

Claiming the model of the early church was nothing new; it happened throughout the Middle Ages. Of interest was how groups imagined that original community, and how they meant to implement their vision. For a thousand years religious orders had monopolized claims to the community described in Acts, confining religious perfection and the Jerusalem model to men and women taking vows and entering convents—even if monks and mendicants disagreed about who fit the model best, the more prayerful monks or more apostolic friars. The Modern-Day Devout, equally dedicated to prayer and outreach, set up a community of goods (*vita communis*) in private "gatherings" (*congregatio, vergadering*) outside a vow of poverty. Contemporaries saw them as people "living together" (*cohabitantes, commorantes*) to share housing, food, labor, and resources. This made little sense to many contemporaries at the conceptual or practical level: families lived as families, convents as convents. To some it even appeared impermissible. In this study I use the world "commune" or "communal" for this activity, at which readers should not be unduly startled. For many this calls up notions of groups from the 1960s or social experiments in nineteenth-century America or a kibbutz in twentieth-century Israel. But that same combination of idealism and social inventiveness applied as well to these fifteenth-century Devout. They set up civil communal houses, initially outside ecclesiastical law: an "intentional community," to use a phrase current in sociological circles; a "dynamic utopia," to borrow from Schehr's title; a non-obligatory "amicable society," to invoke one of their own formulas.[3] They anticipated an impulse realized differently by Taborites at roughly the same time in Czech lands[4] and by radical Reformers at Münster and elsewhere in the sixteenth century. That life, we must understand, was a total life, proving inventive in its legal approach to a community of goods, earnest in its commitment to sustaining a "society of spiritual friends."

The Modern-Day Devout also—important and for the Middle Ages unique—produced a theoretical apologia. Roughly half of *Circa modum*'s hundred-page defense focused on the common life, or rather communal gatherings as such, which raised four questions: whether it was licit to live this way ("together"), whether theirs was a "new religion," whether it was licit to live with no individual ownership or property outside professed religion, whether this constituted a forbidden "conventicle."[5] Zerbolt's work in 1396/98, stuffed with authorities and arguments, written in the heat of conflict, proved amazingly innovative, an unappreciated work of social theory. *Circa modum*'s exposition stood up to the inquisitor in 1398, helped convince jurists and local bishops (Utrecht, 1401; Cologne, 1417/1422), bolstered the dossier for Constance (1418), entered Dirk of Herxen's book of collations,[6] and influenced Gabriel Biel after 1469/70.[7] In this book its theoretical positions will be interwoven with documents, customaries, and lives to set forth the Devout way of life.

Two points to close, one about the Devout, the other about the world they lived in. The Modern-Day Devout fit badly into the binaries we too often rely upon to frame medieval religious history. They accounted themselves true Christians (as did most Cathars and all Lollards), and quite loyal ones too, even as they brought an inquisitor down upon them and met with local hostility. But Sisters and Brothers also resisted being fully drawn into the "Ruled" center (like Cistercians or Franciscans), or being pushed into heresy or the margins (like

Waldensians and Lollards). They were an alternative community, always perceived as slightly odd, often somewhat on the defensive, at the same time that towns came to take their presence and work more and more for granted.

The European-wide religious establishment survived too, and not only by inertia and power. Its survival rested in part upon a sensibility that was widely shared despite all the complaining. We may illumine it with a series of questions most would have regarded as rhetorical: Should the first estate (the clergy and professed religious) not carry itself with all the dignity befitting their role as society's premiere estate? Should those who minister in the place of Christ look and live like the homeless? Was the work of God honored by shabbiness in its houses of worship and ordained representatives? A spiritual office required material income to function, and that income should befit the office's rank, as Gerson argued with respect to the papacy in his tract on simony (*officio pape debeatur beneficium sufficiens et condecens*). This principle filtered down to cardinal and priest, monk and nun, even parish priest.[8] This was a matter of estates, stations in life, what material and legal and cultural status befit a given spiritual task or office. Reformers and converts, to be sure, tried to reverse the linkage: the poorer the social estate, the higher the spiritual.[9] In actual practice these two stances or sensibilities often overlapped, even in the same person: expectations came attached to social rank, then mixed variously with spiritual disgust or idealism. This disruptive tension kept medieval society from ever settling entirely into a system of impermeable or unchanging socioreligious castes.

Living Together Without Personal Property

A community of goods and life was present nearly from the beginning, though it would mature in complexity over time. In itself sharing goods and table was not entirely novel, this also found in some beguine convents. The founding document for Rhenen specified that what a Sister brought in should thereafter remain in the house, that for Gouda in 1396 as its second provision that if a Sister possessed goods or income these should be "consumed in common" (*int ghemeen verteeren*). Among men it emerged first under Florens Radewijns at Deventer, probably about 1383/85.[10] The documentary mechanism for it was employed at Zwolle already in 1395,[11] probably taken over from Deventer, though the mind behind it (Grote? Florens?) remains unknown. What we find among the Devout is a widely shared zeal to break with possession and its associated greed, to emulate the earliest Christian community, to share consumption. The chronicle of the house at Zwolle would actually begin with the words "common life" (*Communis uita*) as the heart of their story. The practice, it claims, had all but died out but was now revived. At Zwolle it had a double beginning, first with five lay men whose society Geert Grote helped set up in 1383, then again in 1394 when a knight (Meynold) from the bishop's court, converted by Master Geert, set up a house for clerics and sought help from Florens in Deventer (*sicut Daventrie clerici in communi uiuentes instituebantur*).[12]

A gathering was constituted in law as a "society" (*societas*) with its goods and incomes located in the persons of its "joint-holders" (*provisores*), each, it was further stipulated, to be replaced on leaving or dying. This society was a personal or private venture; it lacked a corporate seal. To any agreement struck the seals of the three or four *provisores* would be attached (see Figure 6). That society might jointly hold books (thus at the beginning with Master Geert) or incomes or a house or goods. But it was moveable, and sometimes did move. So how then could a private society become a communal household? This required two further and ingenious elements. Upon joining a Brother (occasionally a Sister, though the evidence is far thinner and more mixed) resigned all goods and incomes to the society by way of a *donatio inter vivos*, a civil transaction publicly notarized. The earliest original document known to me to survive comes from Alberghen in 1420, the resignation of goods expressed in Dutch (laymen in this case), but the whole framed by the notary public's confirming Latin (see Figure 14). Thereafter, he or she had no further claim on these goods or properties, nor did their families; and if they left, they might take only everyday clothes. We must imagine the house's chest holding as many of these documents as there were Brothers in the house. Here Devout communal gatherings differed pointedly from beguines (though our information on them is more limited) and also in part from Tertiaries, who shared consumption (thus a "common life") while still holding or inheriting family incomes (the ways things probably were at the beginning for Sisters and Brothers as well). Brothers also frequently made out a last will and testament declaring all their companions or the society their heirs—we find this already at Alberghen in the 1420s–30s—in order to foreclose any familial claims. These documents were then carefully kept in a chest by the procurator, the business administrator of the house.[13]

As late as 1509, a full century later, the formula at Zwolle, now swollen to three pages of dense legalese, made a resignation of goods by way of a *donatio inter vivos* the condition for acceptance into a society and its goods (*ad eorum numerum et societatem gratis acceptati et talem incorporationem et bonorum domus participationem sint adepti*). The person joined the "estate of those leading a common life" in material terms and in spiritual "resolved to improve" (*statui communis uite et emendacioris propositi*). The whole hinged upon a *donatio inter vivos*, glossed as a valid and irrevocable transaction (*donatione quidem ualida, perfecta et irreuocabile*) made utterly freely, and construed as alms conferred on

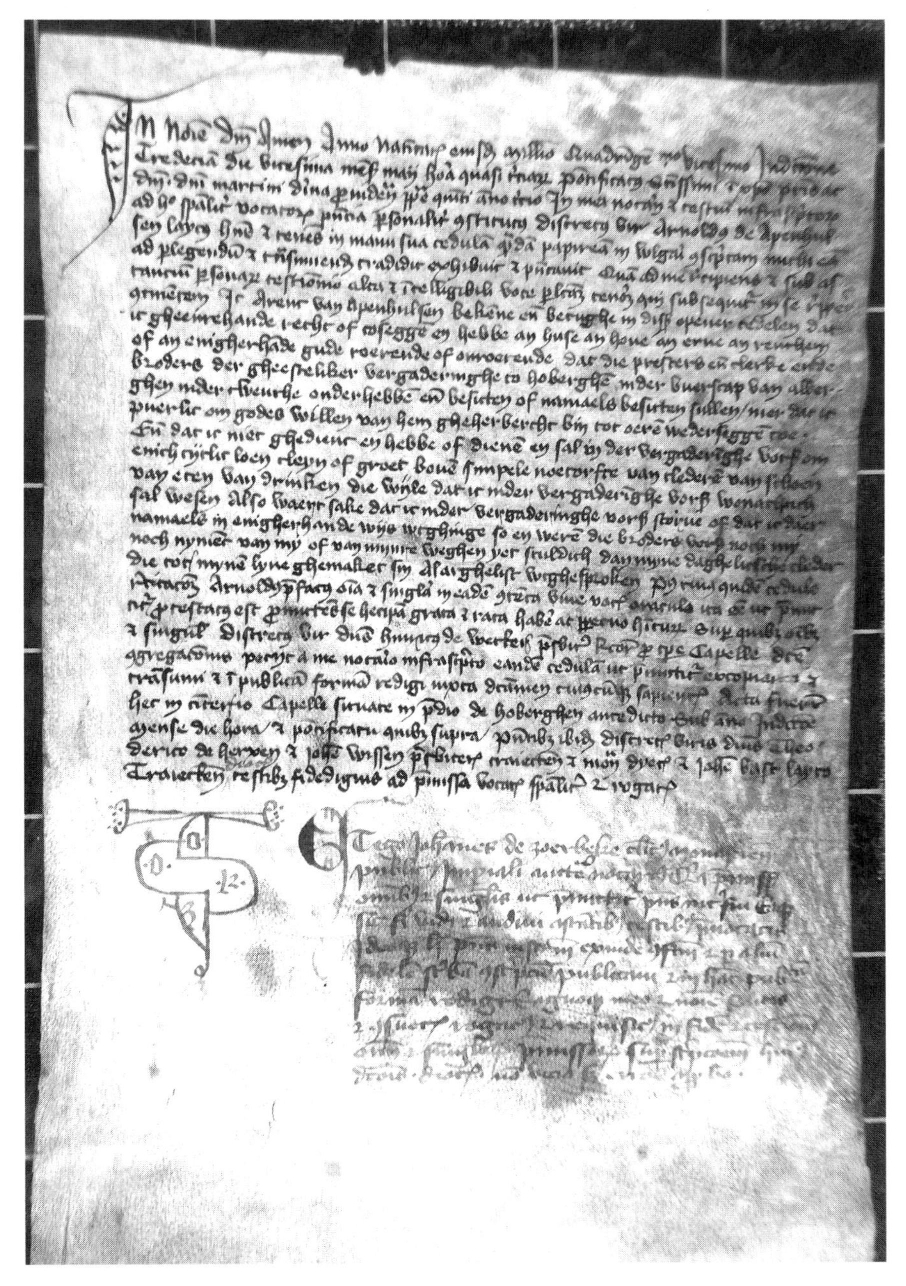

Figure 14. Notarized resignation of goods by a lay Brother Arent at Albergen (30 September 1420), the notary's framing language in Latin, the Brother's resignation in Dutch. All Brothers would have been expected to prepare such a document. This is, to my knowledge, the earliest surviving original. Historisch Centrum Overijssel in Zwolle, Albergen, Inv. 19-1.

the "priests and clerics of the house." No further claim was possible on those goods in civil or ecclesiastical law, the community itself thereby empowered to use them as it should decide. This was all duly drawn up in a notarized instrument. Its model was written into the house cartulary under the rubric "*Formula resignacionis fratrum domus nostre*" and dated 4 May 1509.[14] From 1395 (likely earlier) until 1509 (and later: Herford in the 1530s[15]) the basic mechanism, despite increasingly sophisticated legal terminology, hardly changed. This is what constituted a gathering in law, what every Brother, rich or poor, cleric or lay, went through to enter. About Sisters we have little surviving evidence, many perhaps less able to represent themselves and their goods in an independent legal forum.

Zerbolt, presuming this mechanism, had to deal with more fundamental questions: Their "congregating," the right of individuals to assemble in a house and live together. While Devout women as laypersons could seek approval from town aldermen, for Zerbolt and Florens this meant clerics and some priests and some laymen living together in a private house (*simul in suis domibus . . . commorantes*: the opening title of *Circa modum*). To skeptics this looked like a would-be order or self-made clerical house ("collegium") or subversive sect ("conventicle"). But, Zerbolt asserted, it was "licit" to live together. Objections were nonsense so long as the Devout lived in a privately contracted arrangement as a "simple society" or "fraternal union" and did not illicitly form a public corporation or a new religion.[16] To make this claim stick he stretched a distinction in law made with respect to clerics: those living together in "college" might claim benefit of clergy (ecclesiastical status), but not, it was widely held, merely by virtue of living in a "simple society," though with an ambiguous concession possibly for those observing a "common life." Zerbolt proposed now to extend this notion (*eam tamen ad propositum lacius assumendo*) to any estate or set of persons (*non tantum ad clericos sed ad quoslibet indifferenter*),[17] going beyond his glossators, even contradicting them, and drawing out a positive claim.[18] Where these juridical glossators defined living from a common table as one possible mark of individuals in a protected clerical status, Zerbolt inferred the principle that communal life itself was therefore simply licit, and indeed for all. Lay and clergy, men or women, could live together as a private "society"; this infringed upon no laws regarding any public religious corporations. A few pages further on Zerbolt conceded that the text was about clerics living a common life, but pointed up that the jurists had not explicitly objected to anyone else living together in a communal society.[19] That is, he knew at some level that he was finding or making law where there was none.

Key to all this, also in the juridical advisories, was the difference between a "society" and a "college."[20] He returned again and again almost verbatim, as did other jurists, to a passage in Cardinal Hostiensis's *Summa* (it drawing upon Roman law) and to Pope Innocent's apparatus on *Dilecta* (as reported by Johannes Andreae and the standard gloss). The lawyer-pope had carefully laid out permissible forms of public corporations. To it jurists contrasted a contractual arrangement they accounted "voluntary and not required" (*uoluntaria et non necessaria*), and offered the example of Latin teachers or bakers or students who chose to make up a *societas*, becoming *sodales*, terms taken over from a passage in Roman law concerning illegal corporations or gatherings (*de collegiis illicitis*). Roman and canon law both recognized these private societies as contingently legitimate, particularly if members acted for religious ends (*causa religionis*).[21] One term for them, borrowed from Roman law by way of Hostiensis, was a "society of friends" (*amicabilis societas*), meaning voluntary or private actors. Moreover, "any could legally form such a voluntary society together" (*licite quicumque simul contrahere societatem amicabilem*), Zerbolt asserted. As always he concluded with a rhetorical appeal: If a society of friends is permissible in law, how much more a society to foster devotion![22]

To what degree Zerbolt worked this out for himself, with what measure of help or advice from his jurist consultants (especially Abbot Arnold), remains difficult to discern. But we should not overlook his passion or originality. The jurists' advisories were by contrast consistently drier, more careful, less expansive, protective of the Devout but not reinventing theories to justify a right to live together or communally as private persons. Foec dismissed any charge of suspicion, and labeled Devout gatherings "an entirely licit charitable gathering living in a common life" (*congregacionis caritatiue omni iure licite in communi uiuentis*)[23]—a way of making a similar point without the broader claims. The technicalities fascinated some jurists in Cologne, with civilists and canonists approaching the core issue somewhat differently (as noted in Chapter 3). At the end of tractate III Zerbolt returned again, more defensively, to a fuller exposition of the differences between a "society" and a "college," suggesting this had met with resistance. Copying definitions from standard law-books he reiterated the "great distance" between a public corporation and a personal society, even one with communal goods (*simplicem seu amicabilem societatem, eciam omnium bonorum*).[24] Some churchman likely had challenged his merging of the legal notion of a voluntary impermanent society with that of a voluntary gathering leading a common live.

In medieval tradition Innocent, and Hostiensis after him, had tried to distinguish four units by way of Roman law, a *universitas* or collection of many/all bodies, a *collegium* or collective of persons living together with a name (the canons of St. Victor), a *corpus* or grouping of persons such as bakers, and a *societas* or grouping simply for commercial gain. Innocent's commentary, a veritable *sic et non*, made it clear that distinguishing public corporations (*collegium*) from private contractual arrangements (*societas*) was provoking testy debates already in mid-thirteenth-century Italy. Hostiensis a generation later and then Johannes Andreae two generations later settled on certain distinct markers for a corporation, above all a common or corporate seal. Three further points emerge as crucial, all in some way spun out of Roman law but adapted to medieval practice: a *collegium* required the warrant of a superior authority, while a *societas* privately entered into did not; a *societas* could be initiated and also dissolved simply by its members, in fact ordinarily died with them (unlike a public corporation); and a *societas* for purposes of religion (a prayer confraternity, a group for redeeming captives, etcetera) was in law ipso facto licit.[25] The Modern-Day Devout, with Zerbolt in the lead, exploited this opening. What had originated in Roman law and its medieval interpretation as a mechanism for commercial ventures and in Christian law additionally for charitable enterprises, they turned into an independent, privately contracted set of persons who jointly held books or incomes or a house, thus standing outside civil or ecclesiastical corporate bodies, needing no superior warrant, but fulfilling a religious purpose, the communal life perhaps even a further enabling marker. The Devout moreover deliberately avoided the chief marker of a public corporation, a common seal. For any documents or agreements their leaders or *provisores* employed their own individual seals collectively (see Figure 6).[26]

Zerbolt moved freely from the legal to the personal to the religious and back again, focused obviously on the latter two but surprisingly skillful in manipulating law. At the personal level he dismissed it as nonsense to say people could not live together in a dwelling. It was hardly forbidden in law for people to assemble or congregate or act; nor was anyone so "foolish" (a favorite word) as to say living together was prohibited.[27] This would cast most people into damnation since most do not live alone. But his rhetorical point came attached to a legal one: about people free to live together in a house as a free or private society (*in una domo et simplici societate conuiuere et cohabitare*) in a form of life neither professed nor collegial (*modum uiuendi extra religionem non collegialiter*).[28] He held, further, that it was indeed "altogether customary" (itself a legal term) from the time of Christ for church-people to live together (*simul conuiuere et cohabitare*). He assembled instances from the early church through the Desert Fathers to Ambrose and Augustine (citing the *Confessions*), reaching to the life of Bernard and Marie d'Oignies (the first "beguine"). Saints and doctors had "recommended" this way of life too. He offered an ingenious reading, uncommon in medieval exegesis, of Paul's greetings in his epistles as directed to "households." Living together was "licensed" by popes as well. He cited the passage from Gregory XI's *Ex iniuncto* that the Devout wove into all their privileges and statutes, and also cited canons from church law, five in particular,[29] all texts, most interestingly, that had entered church law in the era of Pope Gregory VII amid efforts to reform worldly clergy by encouraging a common life. He had patently hunted these out, and now drew upon them to defend Devout communal gatherings. This form of life, moreover, was "useful," advantageous to those walking in the way of God, here, quoting spiritual advice from Jerome and Augustine. And living together was materially easier, reducing anxiety, enabling people to fulfill commands or counsels, helping them know themselves, fostering the exercise of virtue, building up fortitude and common caring.[30] The beauty of it was precisely not to live alone or wholly for one's self.

Papal legislation against new orders, to come finally to the sticking point, he observed, surely never intended to forbid licit forms of spiritual life. It was "foolish" (*fatuum*)—his core emotions erupting here—to deploy, as adversaries were in fact attempting, papal (anti-beguine) laws against people living voluntarily together (*socialiter uiuentes*), withdrawn from the world so they could live "more religiously than other lay/worldly people." Indeed no one could be forbidden to live a holy life![31] He turned for support first, as others had, to Hostiensis. Already in the mid-thirteenth century this influential cardinal-jurist had recognized people in Italy who lived "more religiously" than others without being bound to a Rule, people he called religious in a "broader sense" (*modo largo*).[32] Zerbolt for his part noted some commonly accepted cases: a secular clergyman living more religiously than ordinary laypeople, a devout widow in her home, a lay *confrater* or *donatus* joined to a religious house by goods and life. He now extrapolated a new case: Nothing prevented this from applying as well to people who chose to live together apart from the world. Such "companions" were also "religious." But in fact Zerbolt and the Devout had steadily to fend off charges arising from the papal legislation against new orders and beguines. This he did by holding that if these "companions" did not assume any of religion's markers—vows, superiors, habits—they did not fall under the proscriptions.[33] It was a very narrow line.

Living together was one thing, pooling all their goods and incomes to create a "friends' society of all goods" was another. Tractate III dealt conceptually with notions of ownership and religious poverty, on which there existed at least two centuries of disputation already. Zerbolt's method was consistent, to turn to reigning encyclopedic definitions, earlier to Hostiensis and Innocent on societies, here to Thomas Aquinas for definitions of ownership (*Summa*, II II q. 66) and especially to Henry of Ghent for notions of possessions and poverty. Henry declared these to be different for different estates in society, an articulation that may well have caught Zerbolt's eye.[34] But as he here intimated, his case only partly drew on them. Zerbolt first distinguished ownership from administration and usage, a point crucial for Franciscans, then noted six forms of communal goods moving from worst to best. Most evil was a total sharing of everything including wives, an antique example passed down in church law.[35] In his own day he found evil, second, a greedy ownership that ceded nothing to the common good, burgher neighbors in effect, whom he held guilty of mortal sin on this front.[36] In the middle ground came two acceptable and more flexible forms of ownership, namely, ownership with goods ceded to the community at large in times of necessity (a part of church law as well),[37] and ownership with usage ceded in charity to the community (what the Devout understood themselves to be doing). The third form he described as sufficient for salvation, the fourth (his) as extraordinarily meritorious.[38] Then came the renunciation of goods in religious poverty, professed who possess goods in common but not personally. Franciscan "simple usage," no ownership at all, represented finally the "highest and most perfect" mode in his view. Zerbolt had invented the fourth option for the Modern-Day Devout, conceived as "owners" still who could possess and alienate goods but yielded to common usage as "need" or "charity" required, its defining mark being "friendship" (*proprium est amicicie*).[39]

For it Zerbolt mustered nine arguments, the core rationale for communal gatherings. The Gospel admonished it ("Go and sell all . . ."). For those taking vows this counsel became obligation. For everyone else, Zerbolt argued, it appealed to a personal "disposition," his a self-conscious stretch of prevailing notions of the "counsels of perfection." To deny this counsel to the nonprofessed, he added emphatically, thus to any impaired or not literate or otherwise indisposed, was to impede the Gospel injunction—unthinkable, Zerbolt feigned to protest.[40] Natural law, second, recognized an original community of goods in the primeval human state (this set out at the beginning of Gratian's *Decretum*),[41] a point elaborated, third, with texts from Giles of Rome's well-known *Regimen of Princes* and Seneca's *Letters*. As for ownership, fourth, it had come about by sin and greed, a familiar teaching, though Pope Innocent IV (in his legal commentary) and Thomas Aquinas had argued that ownership served society by reducing disorder and neglect. Zerbolt added that some owners (i.e., the Devout) put communal life above personal interest and thrived in "charity and friendship," this not a lesser but a more meritorious state.[42] For, as Aristotle taught in his *Ethics*, community of goods lay at the heart of "friendship." All human acts moreover were to be informed by Christ's example, and according to Augustine, sixth, the Lord had lived in community of life. The perfect, seventh, were to imitate the early church, where a common life existed long before any religious orders, it going back to a time when there was as yet only a basic "Christian life"(*nondum erant religiones alie quam uita Christiana*)[43]—an original formulation, importantly, that predated Gerson's twenty years later at Constance. The founders of monasticism, eighth, would never have adopted community of life had it not already been exemplified by the apostles and widely observed outside orders. So no one, including the professed, could now prohibit it to others![44] Nature, to conclude, teaches that human life is social and communal, Scripture that all people should be members one of another, extending to a total sharing of goods. The tradition was clear in law, Scripture, and historical precedent, and not limited to the professed. The implicit argument throughout was that the orders imitated an original Christian life, indeed a primeval communal life, not the other way round, and this way of life was still open to all. What Zerbolt presented as the fourth category, or middle ground, appeared closer to lay ownership than religious renunciation.

Someone apparently objected to this communal ideal that the pope himself seemed quite content with clerics who made no pretence of adopting a common life, thus tacitly accepting prevailing practice. In truth, Zerbolt responded, we should take care in making any such judgments apart from recovering authentic customary law, the genuine usages of the ancient church. Community of life was in reality widely practiced from the beginning of the church, indeed from the beginning of human creation, quite especially by the most upright, those practicing charity and friendship. Its unusualness in their own day was no defense. Community of life was, to be sure, rare in "our day," even, Zerbolt sternly noted, among the orders. But because the counsels (poverty, chastity, obedience) were no longer customary this did not make them less meritorious for any who did practice them—and in whatever state of life.[45] Still other critics (likely townspeople) objected that communal life was simply odd, different from other Christians. This elicited a burst of anger. If the Devout lived truly odd lives, say, walking around naked or not talking to people or not attending church, they might rightly be called to account—but not for living together devoutly and in charity and observing the teachings of Christ more strictly than others.[46] "Living together" was marvelous in fact, foreshadowing life as it would be in glory, above the evil of their day.[47]

Living in common was justified, thus, from a host of sources, not least being the church canon *Dilectissimis*, a ninth-century forgery ascribed to Clement, Peter's successor, which offered a full endorsement of a communal lifestyle, especially for clerics.[48] The customary at Wesel later invoked this canon immediately after Acts 4:32 as warrant for their household.[49] For Zerbolt the sharing of goods and resources went back to natural law and Gospel injunctions, to precedents in the early church, to saints who lived it, doctors who taught it, popes who licensed it. This opened it, and thus also "religion" and the "counsels of perfection," to all. The orders and vows of poverty had sprung up later, resting on that earlier and more basic foundation, not the other way round.

Theory, however, was one thing, practice another. House customaries exhorted members ("Let us . . . let there be. . . .") to live together in "charity, peace and concord" without "ownership" (*proprietas*).[50] This came down to concrete particulars: a common chest, a common purse, a common table.[51] Personal ownership undercut community. The Herford statutes allowed no private or locked chests without permission.[52] The Emmerich statutes, coming after two generations of experience, enjoined each to say "our tunic," not "my."[53] Members quickly learned, to judge from the customaries, what sorts of people might not work out so well in a communal "society of friends." They should not take in recently divorced people (especially young ones), nor elderly priests not prepared to resign all goods and take up an ascetic discipline (old men, that is, looking for "retirement"). Further, no Brother should accept any benefice unless prepared to resign its income at once to the whole community, and none should take on bonds or other financial instruments. No lay or clerical person should live in the house for more than a half-year unless prepared to stay. These points hint at fluid rather than rigid practices in actuality. Brothers also should not teach to others their skills in copying, illuminating, and binding, nor should they take in such craftsman except as members.[54] This was to protect their trade and source of income, but also, quite interestingly, to distinguish their society from a guild some might wish to join. To some at least—the recently divorced, retired priests, craftsmen seeking a trade—a Devout society could look advantageous.

With communal life came a series of practical measures: the right of a rector to ask a Brother simply to change rooms; an annual visit of each room at the beginning of Lent to see what in the way of books and utensils a Brother held; no locked chests; no money on a person. It also meant bearing with one another in failures of body or conduct, not giving offense or being derisive, avoiding special friendships, cultivating a common charity. And to prevent the house itself from accumulating common or corporate wealth (like many monastic houses), a cap was placed on annual income, any surplus dispersed one-third to the library, two-thirds to the poor. The issue all the same was ultimately not things but affection for things (*ab amore rei familiaris affectum nostrum suspendere*).[55] This went far beyond property. In Münster separate rubrics enjoined Brothers to "watch out for the vice of discord" and to "preserve concord," the paradigm being their image of the early Jerusalem community, what they pledged to revive: being of a "single heart and a single will."[56] Strikingly, however, their spiritual manuals say not a single word on communal life as such. It hinged on household practices, the stuff of customaries.

For women we have no comparable sources. The little we find in their statutes emphasizes that all things were meant for common usage (*gemeynen orbaer*), that no Sister was to keep anything secretly, and the Mother could on occasion examine a bed and what was under it.[57] Statutes in Germany meant for Sisters moving into regular status declared that all was to be held in common, nothing personally, and that gifts from family or friends were to be resigned to the Mother who might return it or use it for the community.[58] At Emmerich a Sister Gerberch (d. 1461) was remembered for special kindnesses to the poorest members, those with no other resources or connections, intimating, as many texts do, that individual and familial means still played their role. She shared anything she might receive, as did Sister Alijt (d. 1478), especially caring for the young with no relatives or friends.[59] Sharing goods and table and personal resources was the crux of the matter. When first admitted to this society of goods (*ad societatem bonorum*), a text from the men in Deventer observed, new people often might seem malleable and contented—enthused, we might say. But after a while "simplicity was subverted" and they wanted things for themselves. It all depended on personal disposition, or as they usually articulated it, "personal humility." Otherwise trying to regulate (*ordinatio*) clothes or goods by constant mutual admonition proved pointless, and a person became useless to themselves as to others.[60]

Above all, it remained an animating ideal. Dirk of Herxen compiled a set of collations in both Latin and Dutch, exhortations on key topics of the religious life. For the most part his texts represent excerpts compiled from earlier writers. The only exception I have found came, remarkably, as an exhortation to the common life, entitled "in praise of a good society." He offered a rhetorical paean, interlaced with warnings about the danger of leaving it. It advanced by a constant reiteration of the word "there" (*ibi*), meaning the communal society itself. Along with two sentences quoted in the epigraph more follows here, still less than a fourth of the whole:

> There he finds those he fears and has those he loves, and thus profits from all. There the correction of another should be as his admonition, the danger of another made his mirror. There one is the keeper (*custodia*) of another, and one tests the other in patience. There a person carries and is carried; there he hears and sees much by which he should be taught. . . . There a man is not permitted to grow lazy, nor to act according to his own will. . . . There tasks are diverse, and many works of charity are put on display. For there they all have time and each goes to his work in obedience. There it is conceded to no one to be idle, and to each is enjoined a measure of work. There the sick person is upheld by the stronger, and the healthy person visiting the sick delights in serving Christ. There when one is failing another takes his place;

> there the healthy members are solicitous for the weak. There the able person works in place of the absent one. . . . There he leaves as heirs, on death, sons of God, constantly in the mean time remembering him; their pious zeal in the cell will be his happiness. There his effort and good way of life will not be swallowed up in oblivion but profit many who come after by way of example. There whatever in the way of good is done is believed to redound to all those living together quietly (*quiescentium*) at that place.[61]

This same text also appears as the second of nine sermons Thomas of Kempen addressed to novices, there under the rubric "in praise of a good gathering," but framed by additional sentences at the beginning and end to render it an exhortation to persevere.[62] Both Dirk and Thomas were compilers as well as writers, and neither acknowledged a source.[63] Thomas's first sermon had treated the "concord of brothers" with an exhortation to "fraternal charity and unanimity," and had also addressed not only professed canons but as well "Sisters and Brothers in gatherings." He ended with three exempla, two about Brothers who left and fell into serious trouble, one by falling in with dicing and gambling.[64] Almost certainly Thomas took these sermons over from the Brothers and Sisters (and adapted them), whether they originated with Dirk himself, or a third party.

House Customs and Personal Exercises

Communal life itself, Zerbolt innovatively argued, had arisen outside the cloister, not inside. And the key to it was a voluntary gathering, an *amicicia* of private individuals who shared all goods, a *societas omnium bonorum*. But living together without personal property patently needed ways to order such a life, agreed-upon practices. In the earliest days Devout men wrote up personal plans for the conduct of their spiritual lives, "resolutions" (*propositum*) that consisted in part of spiritual "exercises," three from Deventer reproduced by Thomas of Kempen as useful also for novice canons.[65] Klausmann has argued that Florens' own resolution or exercise subsequently became custom for the whole house.[66] However that may be, a gathering plainly could not organize itself communally as a dozen personal plans; they needed common customs. As for women's houses, Master Geert had set down ordinances for his, authorized finally by aldermen. In Rhenen and elsewhere the inquisitor, remember, complained about internal ordinances, some written down. To begin to untangle all this we must distinguish between personal resolutions and house customs, also between founding charters and internal customs. Founding documents regulated a house's legal position, gained authorization ultimately from aldermen, and usually alluded to basic moral or disciplinary expectations. Internal ordinances by contrast governed the way of life led inside. From a legal as well as practical perspective the matters were distinct, if overlapping: Who had the right to set up a community? Who might establish ordinances for its way of life and with what prescriptive force? In Master Geert's case, he, working with the aldermen, did both. In Rhenen and Gouda the founders were local, the second a widow; but internal ordinances seem to have come from the Devout network in Utrecht. Tertiary houses likewise had individual founding documents and solved the problem of internal ordinances by acquiring technically a "Rule" for their way of life along with statutes and a General Chapter that annually updated legislation. But it was different for Sisters of the Common Life, and Brothers too, much more ambiguous, also much harder for historians to reconstruct. By setting up statutes they appeared to appropriate church authority for themselves, or simply to emulate an order. The women at Wesel declared that theirs should be understood "not as statutes but good customs" intended simply for bettering their community, plainly a defensive pose.[67]

For professed religious a Rule defined their life or rather their religion, what made them a Benedictine or Dominican. They vowed to become molded by it, and parts were read out daily in "chapter" (the meeting and room named after a practice going back to Benedict). On the lay side too in the Later Middle Ages, guildsmen, aldermen, knightly orders, and nearly every other form of social solidarity articulated rights and duties in ordinances or statutes which they mutually pledged to uphold, often in formal rituals. In perception and expectation these ceremonial pledges and readings fostered a symbiosis between the defining ordinances and the social estates they represented. But what of a private gathering? The Devout needed internal regulatory coherence if their societies were not to fragment. But who could draw them up, and on what authority? It came down to the binding status of customs established by "private persons in private houses" (*priuati in domibus priuatibus*), as Zerbolt put it repeatedly in the last two tractates (X–XI) of his *Circa modum.*

Zerbolt conceded outright that a communal gathering could not set up for itself ordinances like those for ecclesiastical corporations ("colleges"), nor did it possess civil power, a "people's right bearing the authority of law" (*ius populi habens legis auctoritatem*). Private persons in private societies, with no coercive or superior jurisdiction, could not establish binding ordinances.[68] But private persons in private homes could, first of all, mutually propose to keep among themselves as law (*constitutiones*) items already "instituted" publicly in the church, for instance, that clerics wear certain garb or that laypeople attend mass on Sunday. Indeed they should do so; better still, should keep them together (*uel pocius debent simul obseruare*). Resolving together to keep such already instituted ordinances was not only licit but meritorious.[69] Zerbolt next surveyed four forms of custom defined in the summist legal tradition. He fixed on the last, its most particular form (*specialissima*), the custom that governed local settings, a household run by a paterfamilias or, alternatively, as he put it, "private persons living together."[70] A household of people living together could introduce customs, as nearly all households do, Zerbolt asserted rhetorically, each specific to itself, household customs differing for poor craftsmen or wealthy landholders, for a tailor or a farmer.[71] Such customary practices (*assuefactiones, ad bonum usitaciones*), altogether permissible, even expected, claimed no status as public law and infringed on no civil or ecclesiastical rights. But for "private persons living religiously in private houses" they regulated and enabled a common life lived in virtue, such customs becoming "second nature," hence again meritorious rather than illicit.[72]

Churchmen objected, and with irritation: the household customs of the Devout came far too close in appearance and practice to those of a religious order.[73] Zerbolt turned for help to Bernard of Clairvaux's work on religious precept. Among religious, this Cistercian observed, injunctions to primary virtues such as not to kill or steal or lie were "incommutable" and "inviolable," and keeping them could bring salvation to all persons in all times (*omni tempore, omni persone*).[74] Zerbolt enlarged on that idea. These injunctions deriving from natural and divine law applied to every Christian of whatever status, thus were hardly reserved for those in orders. More, all the various teachings about cultivating interior virtues too were not restricted to the professed. Likewise precepts commonly thought of as peculiar to ("attached to") professed religious such as fasting on Friday or manual labor were hardly forbidden to private persons in private houses; the latter too might, for instance, rise in the night to pray. Zerbolt conceded that some practices might be specifically restricted to religious corporations, certain forms of fasting or ritual worship, for instance, as well electing a superior or promising obedience; also the right to erect a chapel and sing the office publicly. Private persons also might not conduct a "chapter of faults" under the aegis of a superior applying discipline, though they could "take counsel" together with one another like any other group of private persons.[75]

Then came the twist, and the core of his argument. Practices that religious undertook as a matter of obligation (*ex coactione uel statuto*), such as fasting, any other person (*quicumque alii ex caritate et consilio*) might pursue voluntarily as a matter of charity or counsel. Those who did so—prayed regularly or fasted or sought spiritual guidance—thereby turned voluntary virtue into customary usage (*assuefactionem et usitacionem uirtutum*).[76] This was a silent but deliberate twist on Bernard, who had spoken of monks, upon making profession, transforming a voluntary choice into a required obligation.[77] The Modern-Day Devout subsumed themselves to no Rule but to accustomed practices. Zerbolt nonetheless appropriated wholesale practices widely held to define the status of religious in medieval society, thus "meditating on scripture at certain times, reading aloud at meals, keeping vigils, fasting, and so on." To do these things in an organized fashion at stated times, critics were objecting, was to adopt the life of an order. But all virtuous people, Zerbolt retorted, do things in ordered ways. What's illict about that? It's especially not surprising that people should so do in a household, rising or eating or sleeping at the same time. In some cities, he noted, artisans in the same house started and stopped work in response to the ringing of bells. This alone, he added pointedly, did not make such artisans "religious," nor did common usages make the private Devout "religious" (*Nec propter hoc dicendi sunt religiosi; sic eciam nec isti*)![78] With this assertion the redacted form of *Circa modum* ended.

Throughout Zerbolt had to deny that theirs was in any way a Rule or a law infringing upon legislative authority they did not possess as private persons, while at the same time arguing that they could observe common customs, the connective tissue of their collective households. It was an ingenious argument, and it presupposed that they had such customs. For historians the difficulty is to know what they were, and how they evolved. These customs came to be written down fairly early, Dirk in Zwolle said to have adapted his from Florens in Deventer. We possess seven complete texts of men's statutes and one incomplete[79]: that of Zwolle from 1415/25 (though our copy is much later), of Münster from 1425–31, of Wesel from ca. 1436, of Herford from 1437, of 'sHertogenbosch from the 1440s (or later?), of Gouda from after 1456,[80] of Hildesheim from after the 1450s or 1520s,[81] of Emmerich ca. 1560. Each is distinct, as befit local societies and private houses; yet all complexly interrelated, with rubrics and patches of text in common. For women's houses we have very little, and the only serious study has questioned whether they ever existed, which is in fact mistaken.[82] The inquisitor at Rhenen reported on written statutes (lost) he regarded as illicit, and hinted that they came from the father-confessor (Wermboud of Utrecht) or the head Martha (Aleyde Cluten). At Master Geerts House in Deventer the lives claim, in remembering Mother Beerten (ca. 1393–1449), that a true common life was introduced under her and John Brinckerink (1392–1419), along with such practices as manual labor. Before that each Sister did what "seemed good to her."[83] The only Sisters' statutes to survive are early from Wesel (in the sphere of Henry of Ahus) and late (at least in their extant form: 1554?) from Den Bosch. Both set out a pattern of internal life (eating, sleeping, working, liturgy, and so on), with nothing about constitutional or organizational matters.[84] But we have a set of instructions (ca. 1435) from a prominent early female figure, Salome

Sticken of Deventer/Diepenveen, on setting up a women's house, which alludes directly to such customs and entirely presupposes them, in effect following them in outlining her ideal for a house.[85]

What we possess in these scattered surviving remnants are various pieces of a lifestyle, definitely not a Rule. In the cases of Münster and Wesel, for instance, we find gathered into the same quires: a quasi-constitution for the house, a resolution each Brother could make his own, exhortations to key virtues and practices, sets of exercises also called "points," and decisions taken in common. All this they "resolved to keep" in order to preserve peace and charity among themselves.[86] The quasi-constitution outlined the offices and customs that structured household life, the personal resolutions the commitment each made on joining a gathering, spiritual exercises the personal plan they worked out or adapted from a model, all supplemented by various decisions that arose from the experience of community life. In the tradition of those customaries represented by Deventer and Zwolle (and also Herford), by contrast, constitutional matters came interwoven with exhortatory passages (on common life, charity, chastity, and so on) but with no personal resolutions (those existed separately), and no record of common decisions taken. In short, these were malleable texts, distinct to each house, including multiple genres with multiple usages. In the extant written customaries the voice can slide between "I" and "we," personal and common resolutions. At Herford the customary begins with a "we have resolved" (*proposuimus, uolumus*) to live in community of life, and so on.[87] The authority of the customaries lay not in themselves but in the intent of those undertaking this life, and the exercises by which they personally animated that life, the same we find in Sticken's example for women.

We can certainly imagine an early and conscious effort to draft something like statutes (this attributed to Florens), with elements borrowed in part from religious orders (especially Carthusians).[88] But the texts sprang as well from experience and practice, usages reduced to texts and circulated on to new houses. All this involves complexities of text and function that will require more space to sort out elsewhere. But their role and status require a word still. A sentence in the customs surviving from Zwolle and Deventer/Gouda refers to them being "written up" so their keeping would not be forgotten. Then the point of tension: observance aimed at household peace and spiritual progress, yet was not vowed, though a person would not be held "without guilt" if neglectful or disobedient.[89] It was a very narrow line to walk. At Zwolle there followed immediately a paragraph on the legitimacy of common household customs, with several arguments and authorities taken over in fact from Zerbolt. That defensiveness was not present, interestingly, in texts from houses overseen by Henry of Ahus, who as paterfamilias gathered up these materials to serve, he said, as a "moral directive."[90] The appeal was not to obligation but conscience and spiritual progress. From the beginning the Devout had been very self-conscious about inculcating a particular way of life, this noted by Florens in a letter of 1398. Amid grievous plague losses and opposition to their gatherings he had worried whether enough were now being trained in their "way of thinking and seeing" (*instituti in sentire et uidere pro utilitate domus nostre*), whether the newly joined were "feeling" and "talking" and "teaching" the same disciplines and exercises.[91]

A certain intensity, even anxiety, entered into the keeping of household customs (*gewoente, consuetudines*). In the memorial lives personal resolve and mutual commitment came up repeatedly, a worthy Brother or Sister distinguished by scrupulous observance. A Brother at Deventer, suffering from various illnesses, was unable to keep up general practices (*communes mores seu consuetudines domus nostre*) but made sure to do his part in the common labor.[92] Customs, likened to *mores* (conduct, practices), referred here to matters such as the hour at which they commonly rose (4:00 a.m.), the fasts they commonly kept, all the liturgical routines and spiritual exercises and community gatherings they observed. Amilius, the rector (1400–1404) who succeeded Florens, was most "diligent in behalf of keeping the customs of our house," and assured all that whoever persevered in the house and properly kept (*competenter conseruauerit*) its customs would be saved.[93] Peter Hoorn (d. 1479), longtime librarian at Deventer, was remembered as extraordinarily zealous, not able in conscience to allow any slippage to go by without a word of admonition, himself preserving house customs as if they were "laws and divine precepts which he could not violate without grave damage to his soul."[94] Key here was "as if" (*quasi*), for these were finally self-imposed, not a Rule to which they had sworn their souls, not a legislative document that any bishop or pope had approved.

We find the same among Sisters. At Emmerich Sister Griet (d. 1479), longtime procurator, exhorted Sisters on her deathbed "above all" to uphold the house customs or institutions (*die guede gewoenten ende insettinge des huijses*).[95] Here customs were likened to "ordinances" and the subject of deathbed talk, thus at the core of what held a community together. Sister Mente (d. 1468), who at first had a hard time adjusting to life in the house, urged others to stick to its "good customs" and admonished any who ignored them; customs in fact helped a person hold fast.[96] Admonishing another for straying from house customs could rank moreover as highly as correcting their personal vices.[97] We also find joint endeavors, thus three young women led by Sister Fenne (d. 1456) resolving to admonish one another in trust when any broke from house customs, covenanting together to uphold a point on which any was found wanting.[98] All this earnestness bespeaks loyalty to a common life; it also betrays a looming chasm. With no authorized Rule, with different forms in every house, only personal resolve finally upheld the common life of a house. These practices were, in Zerbolt's words, "private customs" for "private persons" in "private households." And if they failed, there would be, soon enough, no house, at least no orderly house, and thereupon churchmen or aldermen to intervene. What comes through—from Zerbolt's defense, from the exhortatory language in customaries themselves, from the attitudes articulated in lives—is the large role that house customs actually played in these gatherings. That was not reduceable to a constitutional document; it encompassed the whole way of life, its organizational forms, personal resolutions, common observances, jointly made decisions. And yet within it the Modern-Day Devout could each undertake a certain self-styling. For the customs depended finally upon their resolve and their exercises to exist at all.

Obedience and Humility in a Voluntary Community

When Master Geert negotiated statutes at Deventer in 1379, he specified to the aldermen, as did most foundation charters, that the house would not evolve into a "new religion."[99] Roughly a hundred years later Gabriel Biel said plainly (*simpliciter et cum omni libertate fatemur*) at the outset of his defense of their peculiar estate: We are not an order, for we do not profess vows or wear a habit. To us "it suffices for all perfection to stand and live in the freedom of Christian law under Abbot Christ."[100] At issue was what in the Middle Ages constituted religion as a distinct legal and religious estate. Vows, Biel conceded, were fine for those so inclined but never if less than freely chosen. Zerbolt drew his definition from Thomas's *Summa* and a quodlibet of Henry of Ghent.[101] In the early thirteenth century popes and lawyers had turned the estate of religion into a legal caste system, partly by way of a decretal letter of Pope Innocent III to Abbot Joachim of Fiore. The two inherited markers had been living the life in habit and a ritual blessing. Church law now defined licit vows as sworn obedience to a superior and submission to a Rule.[102] Or as Zerbolt put it contrariwise and in self-defense: The strictures of *Sancta Romana* did not apply to "people living together as companions" so long as they did not "promise obedience to anyone, assume a Rule, make profession, or don a distinct habit."[103]

Companions in a communal household had nonetheless to live in harmony. In any age, certainly in the Middle Ages, that meant someone had to lead, set the tone, assign the tasks, make the hard decisions. From the beginning an elected "Mother" headed Sisters' houses; an elected "rector," always a priest, Brothers'. In early days a leader may have evolved somewhat naturally, centered in the great figures that loom so large in the narratives, Florens in Deventer, Dirk in Zwolle, Henry in Münster. But critics immediately challenged their rank and legitimacy, and the Modern-Day Devout had themselves to come to terms with what kinds of authoritative structures they expected or could live with in their gatherings. Where did personal resolve stop and yielding to an authority figure begin? When Florens's sucessor Amilius (1400–1404) neared death he called the Brothers to his bedside and addressed just this point. To whomever the care of the house was entrusted next, he said, no matter how young or inexperienced or unread, they should "obey him as the vicar of Christ," each thinking rather "how he might humble and subject himself to the other." No heap of devotions would profit them so much as their obedience in carrying out assigned tasks. If someone said he was prepared to obey in all but one thing (certainly thinkable, given no vows), Amilius recommended "removing that person from our house and society rather than bear such rebellion." This is how he articulated his central point: "Let us support one another mutually as members, for if we choose not to, our enterprise (*res nostre*) will quickly perish and each pursue his own life." If each "subjects his heart to the other's feet," no harm will come and we "will persevere in our estate."[104] The narrator, Rudolph, was present at that bedside. It made an unforgettable impression, or he rendered it even more dramatically to make the point for his own time (1458/59), or both.

Hardly by accident, obedience was the only vow common to Benedictines and mendicants. It was the constraint that held medieval communities together, and for jurists a marker to locate individuals in society (who was superior to whom). This held not only for religious herarchies; it rested upon attitudes deeply embedded in a rank-conscious society, endowing princes, prelates, and religious superiors with at times quasi-divine authority. The Modern-Day Devout proposed an alternative. Zerbolt took it up as his eighth tractate (*Circa materiam de obedienca*), again a work of social theory as well as defense, the theory in this case entering directly into the customaries. Structures of authority as such, of prelacy and obedience, should not be overthrown, he conceded straightaway; church and civil society were owed obedience. Thus persons living together in a communal gathering remained subject to their given superiors, laypeople to civil authorities, clergy to prelates, for they had not altered their original estate on entering this society (as someone making profession would).[105] A private society, he also granted, could not simply concoct an alternative vision of obedience—the point here being to fend off libertine charges, the kind ascribed to "Free Spirits." They made no claim to transcend obedience by way of any pseudo-perfection, nor did they cease to recognize and attend their parish churches.[106]

A third principle, however, was peculiar to private gatherings, he insisted. Members, as equals, did not obey a superior as such; that obligation attached to orders or corporations whether civil or ecclesiastical. Forming a "society" assumed rather equality (*equalitas uel paritas*).[107] The conceptual dilemma that now loomed for Devout societies looked something like this: Could these companions, all at the same time, act as a society of equals, keep up all ordinary obligations, and form a community with its own leadership—and not encroach upon religious obedience? To solve this Zerbolt turned to Bernard of Clairvaux's *De precepto and dispensacione* but read it through a distinction made by Thomas (*Summa* II/II q.104 a.5) in his exposition of obedience. Bernard, writing (ca. 1140) a generation into the Cistercians' new literal-minded obedience to the Benedictine Rule, was attempting to balance severe notions of obligation with charity and dispensation, lest vowed submission seem, and become, a terrifying necessity.[108] With his characteristic rhetorical command Bernard projected a series of paradoxical steps, a monk's move first from a voluntary to a necessary obedience and then from a required to a loving submission, this interior movement presuming an exterior obligatory frame. Zerbolt read past all these rhetorical and casuistic distinctions to construct a new version befitting a non-obligatory structure. He posited two kinds of obedience, one of necessity and one of charity. Necessary obedience arose by virtue of either a person or a precept.[109] As for the need to obey persons, even in a society of equals a priest might be obeyed *qua* priest, or a paterfamilias obeyed *qua* his position as head of household.[110] As for obedience owed precepts, members in a society of equals were also obliged to keep the general commandments, and thus would be obliged to obey if, for instance, one member acting in fraternal charity reproached another. This also held if the admonition came from the elected paterfamilias. None of this obeying among equals rested upon any claim to jurisdiction anchored in vows. This alternative form of obedience, based upon precept or person, held particularly—here he invoked the jurist William Durand—if some act of disobedience might endanger the society as such or its members.[111] Conceptually, the argument ran parallel to that by which Zerbolt projected members answering to counsels and commands without setting up unauthorized statutes.

For the Devout, Zerbolt argued, the crux of the matter was an obedience born of charity rather than precept. Bernard's monks, on taking vows, turned voluntary obedience into an obligatory necessity.[112] But in a society of people living together, their gathering resting fundamentally upon love rather than authority, obedience might properly be offered to equals or even an inferior.[113] Domestic peace and concord grew alternatively out of a mutually loving obedience. Who could doubt the legitimacy (*licitum*) of someone yielding in love to the good counsel of another?[114] This rhetorical move prepared the way for a strategic move toward defining community leadership. He noted two kinds of prelacy, one anchored in office and duty (the standard medieval type), another in love. Those bound together in love would find themselves, he observes, engaging in a kind of "care of souls," namely, for their companions. All that Scripture and tradition said about the good shepherd as pastor Zerbolt applied to a paterfamilias presiding over a household.[115] With this sleight of hand he proposed an alternative power of prelacy. A child's obedience toward parents or a wife's toward a husband might properly be construed as "charity," not law (quoting Augustine), as voluntary, not obligatory.[116] Not all among Zerbolt's contemporaries would have agreed. One of the legal advisories from Cologne perceived precisely what was afoot, and suggested instead a nuanced alternative from Roman law. Such a society could not establish a rector with obligatory powers. It could however agree upon someone with "fraternal preeminence" possessing powers only of reproach—especially in a society founded for religious ends (*causa religionis*). Its members could not be compelled to obey; they could however simply leave if they chose. Such a leader functioned more like an administrator in a household (*maior in aliqua domo qui dicitur dominus domus*), the jurist noted, or in a society of the poor—not (silently) as a paterfamilias.[117] Zerbolt never cited civil law texts in his tractate, nor did Deacon Evert Foec. Zerbolt's tractate "on the matter of obedience" foresaw rather a care of souls based theoretically on people yielding to one another in love, a voluntary community. So too with its leader, who acted like anyone else who ought to exercise rule over his household by word and example (*ita* ***quilibet*** *uerbis et exemplis debet preesse sue domui*).

The customary tradition instituted by Florens and Dirk reflected exactly the distinction Zerbolt made. Brothers personally resolved (*proponimus*) to keep the "laws of obedience" with respect to church, prelates, and the sacred canons (that which was generally "necessary"), and also to yield voluntarily (*uoluntarie acquiescere*) to the admonitions and counsel of the priest who headed the household (*patrisfamilias loco regimen domus habet commissum*). They were additionally to have recourse to him four times a year for private conversation and in times of trouble.[118] In the tradition instituted by Henry of Ahus this appeared as a firm personal resolve to uphold the precepts of God and church and superiors (Münster: *propono de gracia dei precepta dei tenere . . .*), or a more general resolve to live in the ways of the community (Wesel)—with, intriguingly, no talk of obedience as such.[119] Both betray the precariousness of this issue in law and society. House customs proposed forms of "resolve" each member should undertake personally upon joining a community, but no vow of obedience; thus a voluntary act sprung from love, no positioning of one's person in an authoritative hierarchy.

In the memorial lives as well as the spiritual manuals, and also in their perception of human practice, the notion of mutual loving obedience came very closely linked to humility (*oetmoedicheit*). Sister Heylewich at Deventer (d. 1418) tended cows and did external errands, a person of little note in social terms (the "world's" eyes) but eager to help, especially with hard or dirty work lest the Lord find her a disobedient grumbler.

> Obedience loomed so large for her that it seemed all the same whether she heard mass or carried cowdung. . . . and all her *mores* and everything she had, such as clothes or books or what she had to watch over, was ornamented with the virtue of humility. Because as cast down and humbly as she went about externally, so zealously and religiously she carried out the work assigned to her, such that she seemed to take no notice of herself.[120]

In human terms, and in community dynamic, the two virtues hung closely together, obedience as a virtue, or loving submission, requiring a person to lower the instinctive boundaries of the egoistic self, to make the self in a sense porous in order to flow out into the community and the community in turn into the self. Their stories, for all their edifying tone, betray a realistic notion of how varied people interacted, what made communities work. A Sister Trude (d. 1438), friendly by nature, always with a smile on her face, always answering "happily" (*geerne*) when asked to do something, nonetheless found it "extraordinarily hard" when assigned to the kitchen, not because she disliked serving the Sisters but because it allowed no time for the prayer and spiritual exercises she could keep up while spinning or combing wool, that is, for following her personal preferences; but she acquiesced.[121] What would not work in a communal household was a person "full of herself," those for whom mutual obedience and humbleness came hard. A Sister Alijt at Emmerich (d.1478), probably its longtime procurator, was remembered as someone of very independent mind (*een mensche van voel siens*) who therefore had often to constrain herself (*moeste si hoer oec wacke bracken ende bedwijnghen*) in order to fit into the community.[122]

Humility came up more often, also for the Brothers, than any other virtue. This was not just a deferential religious notion (that too) but a necessary human stance for a voluntary communal gathering. It was also self-consciously pursued, Sisters and Brothers outdoing one another to undertake the vilest community work, for instance. Salome Sticken admits "many indiscretions" have arisen from that. But she also herself understands it her job to "afflict, exercise, and reproach" Sisters, and claims they love her all the more for it.[123] On the Brothers' side this tended to take forms socially apt for clerics. Thomas of Kempen's older brother John, regarded as "able and bright," was deliberately humiliated among his peers, clerics and students at Deventer, by being asked to wear shabby clothing wholly unbefitting a rising cleric.[124] This fostered a related and key spiritual faculty, the ability to break one's own will, as their texts regularly put it (*frangere propriam voluntatem et in sensu suo non habundare*). Loving obedience required as its counterpart that the individual will be tamed, opened to mutual obedience. But it was even more complicated than that, for the "loving obedience" was not only mutual as among equals. It was also to be shown the head of household. Sticken "asked graciously" (*desidero cordialiter*)—she cannot command—that Sisters submit themselves totally to their Mother (*totaliter uos subiiciatis matri uestre*), that they strive to have their will become one with the heads of the community.[125]

It cannot have been easy, and the lives note that it often wasn't. We find a remarkable and pithy saying-like declaration of what was at stake in a collation of Brinckerink as written up by the Sisters in Diepenveen:

> If you give yourself to a humble simple obedience, and guard yourself from being wise in your own eyes and co-ruling, then this house will remain standing, and you will arrive at genuine wisdom. Obedient persons become much more enlightened than others; our dear Lord speaks to them within (*meer insprekens*) more than others. . . . A person that gives herself to obedience in a gathering comes to share (*deelachtich*) in everything that the whole gathering does.[126]

But it required "going out of yourself," the freedom of belonging solely to God. And they made claims for it reminiscent of religious obedience generally. Any act sprung from obedience—eating, drinking, sleeping, working—constituted an act of prayer. Anyone who acted out of her own will betrayed herself. With obedience came all other virtues—and so on. This same collation, as copied down by the Sisters, intimates that many had not yet reached (or wanted?) anything like the submissive obedience recommended here. The lives make it clear that the personal struggles were all too human. The key was humility, defined as "going out of yourself," the opposite of the proud (high-spirited: *hoemoediche*) who wanted to rule themselves or co-rule. In practical terms it was also vital to sustaining a viable communal gathering. The key to learning humility, they said, was labor, steady humbling work.[127]

Labor: Living from the Work of Their Own Hands

Those who professed religion lived off others. That, along with their perceived arrogance and hypocrisy, deeply irritated late medieval townspeople. Beguines came under attack as able-bodied beggars, monks and nuns as leisured gentry, friars as inveterate fund-raisers. The Modern-Day Devout, whatever their distancing from worldly laypeople, resonated to this social mood, and determined from the beginning to support themselves, to live by the work of their own hands. Work, often prominently noted in the lives, especially the women's, dominated these gathering as both material necessity and spiritual practice. Clerics normally did not lower themselves to manual labor, this left for centuries in religious orders to lay-brothers or lay-sisters. So too women coming from gentry and patrician families did not ordinarily work alongside the poor at combing and weaving and spinning. All this too Biel would feel the need to explain early on, himself a university master. The Devout engaged in manual labor to sustain themselves, he noted, so they might be "less burdensome to the people and citizens among whom they lived."[128] Virtually every reference to the Modern-Day Devout lifestyle noted explicitly that they did not beg. This was a deliberate stance in these late medieval towns. Begging earned only contempt, and people had had enough of mendicants. It was a neuralgic point. At Deventer the procurator John of Hattem (d. 1485) drew up a remarkable text offering an account of all the house's holdings and buildings, which began with insisting that these were acquired entirely with their own income, not from anyone else, not by begging or panting after gifts or rich endowments but with their own goods and labor.[129]

Zerbolt offered six reasons for doing manual labor in *Circa modum*. Work with the hands restrained concupiscent desire, quieted the heart, made someone self-sufficient, humbled a person, benefited others in need, removed occasions for temptation. It was recommended or practiced by Paul, Augustine, Martin, Ambrose, the Desert Fathers, and "Bernard" (William of St. Thierry). Moreover, no person could be continuously engaged in spiritual labor; hard labor from time to time suppresses false spiritual yearnings.[130] The statutes ascribed to Master Geert stipulated that each woman healthy of limbs and able to work should live from the work of her own hands, to avoid idleness as well as empty contemplation (that is, heretical forms), and the return on her work belonged to the house. Nor should she beg for bread at the church, or eat out at mealtimes.[131] The men's customs held that daily manual labor was required because "human fragility would not permit a person to be wholly and continuously occupied with mental exercises," also rendering them "free, lest we find it necessary to pant after the gifts of others."[132] In the Münster tradition, of a more "clerical" caste, this topic interestingly did not come up. In general, though, it touched upon a neuralgic point, especially among townspeople, land and income flowing into clerical hands.

The tenor of this commitment permeated the lives. Peter (d. 1479), born near Hoorn of parents who bore the name "tailor," was schooled at Deventer and soon named house librarian. Though weak by nature, he was prompt to do his part in baking and brewing as well as the spade-work at their farmsite and carrying wood into the house. Never excusing himself from these common labors, he was first to go and last to leave. Though librarian, copying manuscripts actually proved difficult because he had a shaky hand not apt for writing—the pen reportedly springing out of his hand in the winter cold. Yet he always persisted in it until his death in his fifty-fifth year.[133] Stories of this sort, sometimes amusing, sometimes troubling, appear in nearly every life. Heilwich, who tended the Sisters' cows at Deventer (considered heavy, dirty work), was asked why she never grumbled. "Lord God, how dare I do that? The cows never scold me or fail to mind," she replied.[134] A teenage woman at Emmerich, who self-consciously chose life at the house over marriage despite a well-to-do father, threw herself into the hard work of the workhouse (wool preparation); thus, the life simply says, the household earned the necessities from which they lived together.[135] Sister Foube (d. 1479), also of well-to-do parents in Emmerich, chose this life at twenty, was placed first in the workhouse, then took up heavy farm labor, including slaughtering animals and preparing meat, because, the text explains, they had no money for a hired hand (*knecht*) and lived from the labors of their own hands.[136] Such stories can be multiplied almost indefinitely, a Sister's work carefully noted, also her strength and ability and degree of zeal. They were also all to engage in what gets called the "common labors" of a house. We have stories of Brothers cutting down wood on a distant property, of Sisters working alongside laypeople in fields, of Brothers and Sisters working alongside each other in adjoining fields or gardens. Indeed they were occasionally warned against becoming light-hearted during such tasks (suggesting they did), instead to utter short prayers or sing hymns. The women at Diepenveen, eventually canonesses, initially did much of the "men's work," digging foundations, carting and lifting sand and mortar, Sticken noting particularly their carrying rocks and so on for the foundations of their new house.[137] Similar accounts exist regarding the founding days of the Sisters and then the Brothers at Emmerich. The Devout rubbed shoulders in the street with merchants and artisans, along with clerics and students, though, as with many inhabitants of small and medium-sized medieval towns, they also worked occasionally in gardens and fields.

Manual labor consumed their day and energy, Sticken saying simply that it was the custom in Sisters' gatherings to work from morning to evening, apart from spiritual services, and indeed with alacrity.[138] Sisters worked at textile production, while Brothers were to engage in labors befitting a cleric such as copying. The hours of the day were divided up in such a way as to allow for sustained labor three hours before and three hours after the midday meal, two hours more on fast-days—this not counting their various common labors undertaken to maintain the house and its needs. In their assigned work, copying or cloth-production, they were to prove constant, but not so driven as to extinguish the spirit, the customaries warned, remaining all the while in a meditative and affective frame of mind, readily turning to God in prayer, working quietly or in silence. Men wold ordinarily not leaving their room during work hours, and then every Friday show the scriptor/librarian what they had finished that week. Women stayed at the wheel or the loom or busy preparing the wool more or less through the day.[139] No Sister might leave her "hand-work" without permission, and if she was called away to share in common labors or something extraordinary, she was to return at once.[140] Indeed if they did not work, their food or drink could be withheld.[141] Work was for all of them, the women perhaps somewhat more intensely than the men, in some sense the normal condition, carried out in silence and prayer. While religion dignified the work, it is hard to escape a sense that attention to work could become compulsive. The lives suggest a need to prove themselves in outdoing their companions as well as in offering full support to the house.

These communal houses, as economic enterprises, had to remain viable, and they dealt in commodities, textiles and books. At Master Geerts House the Sisters were set to work beginning in the 1390s. At the outset of the schism in 1425/26 aldermen denied them the right to sell their textiles, making it hard since "outside work was necessary for their bodily necessities." In exile in Arnhem they were denied access to looms and had to get by on even lower and harder work.[142] In general, dozens of women producing textiles could look like competition to local guildsmen; and while clerics making books rivaled no local craftsmen, their services even welcomed, it looked socially and culturally odd. Textile production on a large scale indeed risked repressive actions from local producers and merchants. Sometimes restrictions were written into founding charters, more often into subsequent regulations. At Deventer in 1463, besides regulating the size of houses, city aldermen set the number of permissible looms in each house at six, which seems to have been about average.[143] In German houses, according to Rehm, the number was set as low as four, as high as eight, but more often about six.[144] How the wool was purchased and the cloth sold, what interactions with merchants and markets Sisters normally maintained—about all this we have almost no information.[145] But they and their operations were fully a part of these towns. Over time Sisters might acquire some landed endowment, gifts from family or benefactors, though in the case of Emmerich they quite specifically did not have enough such income (*renthen*) to hire a male worker to do the heavier jobs around their place until two generations along.[146] All Sisters, whatever their social origins, unless assigned to another household task, joined in. It was hard work, even drudgery, which some sought to relieve by keeping a book of prayers or meditations beside their wheel.

Brothers filled a different niche, one partly invented by them, as learned artisans offering a book service. In time they advertised themselves as able to prepare texts in at least four hands of differing orders of luxury (and price).[147] They set up a system comparable to a shop. Someone who wanted a book would come with a request, anything from a deluxe liturgical book for a church to a personal copy of devotional writings, especially books of hours, in either Latin or Dutch. The house "scriptor" would show the customer sample hands, and quote a price per quire. The customer would agree and mark a register. A Brother was set to work, the book copied, and the customer could claim the book upon payment—this too duly recorded in a reckoning book.[148] Brother Dirk of Kalkar (d. 1475), for instance, appointed librarian (scriptor) at Zwolle before he was elected priest, was remembered for his conscientious and kindly handling of all customers, whether they came to order or to buy.[149] In the lives Brothers were also noted for how long they could sit at their work-seats copying, how many quires they could do in a day or a week. They offered a service largely unavailable in later medieval Europe outside stationers' shops in university towns. They also threatened no lay rivals, therefore stirring up no resentment; indeed at Zwolle they quickly became the official copyists of laws for the city council. Among those seeking or needing books (there being as yet no self-evident way easily to procure them), the Brothers won admiration. In a famed work Jean Gerson wrote a kind of laudation in behalf of the scribe.[150] He noted the need for this service in his age (*defectu quem patitur aetas nostra*)—a deficiency the printing press would meet a generation later—and declared the work not "servile" but worthy of eternal life for rendering the teachings of salvation accessible, a work thus of preaching and of prayer. Gerson specially named the Devout, in his mind apparently the leading exemplars in his age.[151] Boys who learned this craft should rejoice, he said, and be glad of a way to draw their minds away from contemporary evils and tumults.[152] So manifestly was this not servile work but labor honoring the church that it could be done on feast-days (against the usual church laws), better to write out books or devotional tractates then than, as he put it, multiplying prayers or pounding away at (*inculcatio*) masses.[153]

"Work is holy" (*labor est sanctus—heylich is vanden handen te leven*), thus Master Geert Grote. Theirs was not the privileged leisure of the professed religious, nor the layperson's battle for subsistence or advantage. Though it contributed to subsistence, it was approached as something holy.[154] As the Sisters gathered up Brinckerink's collations, they also devoted one (VII) to work. Striking is that it mostly assumes hard labor (*uutwendighen arbeit*) as their condition, and focuses primarily on an equally earnest "interior labor" that should accompany it.[155] The insistence on manual labor had its edgier side, born of attitudes in these towns. Grote proposed that women's houses should accept no one not prepared to work (echoing a Pauline proverb), warning away anyone coming with land or to beg.[156] Still, a remarkable degree of defensiveness persisted about how artisanal work could be holy, how living from handwork dignified people with a contemplative calling. Early on after the Brothers set up a house in Emmerich one of them (John of Münstereifel) found himself defending their way of life before a learned canon in Cologne. When there are so many well-provided religious houses all around, the canon queried, why would parents allow their son to join a house where he had to work with his hands in order to live? What about all the time and expense that had gone into his education? Would it not be better then simply to keep him home and put him to work there?[157] The earliest Sisters stood out too, some of them from gentry backgrounds, for they did not only household and farm labor but actually the hard work of building, even at Diepenveen the trench-digging and dirt-hauling and brick-laying (see Figure 3).

Less clear is the degree to which the Devout actually lived off the work of their own hands. This would have varied from house to house. They kept records, but few have survived. For Brothers we have now an important study by Kock, the first to explore whether it is truly credible that they supported themselves by copying books. Rejecting exaggerated and unsubstantiated past claims, also conceding a dearth of hard evidence, he concluded that Brothers came to live predominantly in fact from inherited incomes (their own or benefactions). Book-copying served more, he argued, as their spiritual ideal, this manual labor a form of preaching by the pen (a Carthusian tag).[158] The resources Brothers brought and resigned to their house, also the landed rents they acquired over time, certainly loomed large, often at the center of the archival record, this evident in a study I undertook for Deventer and in records Weiler edited for Doesberg.[159] But we should not discount the Brothers's claim. We have no extant "register" of contracts and incomes for book-copying, some ambiguous materials from Zwolle apart.[160] We have however direct assertions that book-copying was necessary for survival at Gouda and Emmerich in the early days.[161] But those same texts intimate that book-copying alone barely guaranteed survival. In the only instance where Kock could locate hard figures, for a half-year at Wesel in 1487, it seems that copying generated something under twenty percent of the house's total income, not a small sum, and this coming well into the house's history after its rents would have accumulated.[162] A global claim from Herford—what the house collected for book copying over a century's time—suggests an even lower percentage.

Book-copying retained significance, I would argue, important indeed not just for early days or spiritual discipline but, at a minimum, for weekly cash-flow. The incomes or goods each Brother resigned at entrance, this clear from Deventer's record, were applied to specific community purposes or building needs[163]—with no mention of funds from book-copying meeting those larger expenses. But for the weekly needs of a household in food and clothing and basics, a steady fifteen or twenty percent of income drawn from book-copying would have made a huge difference, also one of which they would be highly conscious, like a shopkeeper following the daily exchange of goods for income. This fits with the anxiety that seems to attach to this matter, the earnestness of the lives about it, as of the women working in textiles. It is fair to say, however, and this also corresponds to the weight of evidence in the lives, that the women's work in textiles contributed more substantially and vitally to the household economy than did the men's book-copying. All the same, Brothers worked hard too. A young Brother, suffering from pleurisy, coughing up blood whenever he moved around too much, still kept up his copy-work as best he could.[164] Brothers too, let me note only in passing,[165] weathered relatively well their most severe economic-technological crisis, namely, the invention of printing. By the 1470s many Brothers' houses became involved with, or themselves set up, print shops, some eagerly and as pioneers, some reluctantly, hesitant to abandon the religioartisanal regimen they had fostered and lived under for three generations. On his deathbed in 1475 Brother Dirk at Zwolle regretted that he had gotten all caught up in this issue (*tam multis implicaui me*), and counseled his successor to "watch out for that tumult" and take care rather to "stay quiet"[166]—most easily done, of course, as copyists in their room. And copying, we must also remember, retained its importance as a source of books into the 1480s–90s and beyond.

Communal Gatherings and a "Republican" Impulse

We close by considering the spirit of these gatherings. With no vow of obedience to a superior and no formal submission to a rule or order, the life of a gathering hinged finally upon its terms of membership. This meant first the right to oversee its boundaries, admission and removal. Acceptance in a house depended on available space, rooms for men, beds in the dormitory for women, along with sufficient house finances. But the key was suitability: a person's health, age, fervor, previous life, and fitness for household practices, described as their customary exercises (*aptus ad consueta exercicia domus nostre*), and if clerics, whether they were competently literate and could write.[167] "Guests" would reside in a house for ten or twelve months, and then Brothers would decide collectively whether the person had "pleased"; if not, he was sent out at once to avoid future trouble. If he had, he was examined as to his intentions, meaning in effect his spiritual disposition, whether he could suffer correction and reproach, would obey if assigned vile tasks, be open in revealing his passions and temptations. If all seemed promising, by a majority vote (in medieval terms: *de communi consilio fratrum uel maioris et sanioris partis*) they could move him from guest status (*de hospite*) to household companion and brother (*socium et fratrem domus nostre*). He had then to sign over all possessions and incomes, confirmed in a public document as soon as possible, this to prevent "vexations" in future from kin.[168] In the Münster/Wesel texts assembled by Henry of Ahus the person was received into "our house and society" to share in all "temporal and spiritual goods."[169] For the Sisters' houses, unfortunately, we do not have customary or documentary evidence about the formalities of admission.

Just as important in guarding the well-being of a community was its right, if necessary, to remove an obstreperous member. The Devout became exceedingly defensive about this point, often noted in documents and apologias. The reason is clear: with no sworn obedience or hierarchical constitution, the right to cast someone out could appear quite arbitrary, particularly since the person had irrevocably resigned all future claim on his own goods, creating potentially a very prickly human and familial situation. But lest one bad sheep infect the whole, and since (as one customary put it) the Modern-Day Devout had no prisons (as orders did), they reserved the right to decide, again communally, that someone should be expelled, normally for resisting house customs or betraying his own resolve. Their word for problematic members, often and tellingly, was "rebellious," with overtones of a family or a political community. Its first mark, notably, was "staining the society with the infidelity of ownership," another powerful metaphor. To it were added sins of the flesh or other grave scandals, along with indebting one's self or the house through financial instruments without the leaders' knowing. The tradition spawned by Henry of Ahus affirmed that each house was established for its members to live in common in chastity and harmony; any who violated that was to be expelled from their society and household (*de nostra societate et habitatione expellere*). It listed ten specific grievances: heresy, rebellion against leaders [second after heresy], sins of the flesh or other scandal, staining the society with ownership, secret correspondence, secretly opening chests in the house, spending the night in town, starting lawsuits without knowledge of leaders, a person socially in bondage or married, a person entirely discontented with the exercises and ways of the household.[170] Such a person lost all rights, including all goods resigned to the society. This point was noted already by Zerbolt: Any departing member had no further claim on goods given to the society.[171] In reality Brothers often proved more charitable. At Deventer a departing priest was put on an annually decreasing stipend for a number of years after his departure, drawn in effect from the goods he had resigned to the house.[172] When an unworthy Brother was removed at Doesburg in 1461 (*demeritis exigentibus*), they restored his large patrimony (350 gulden) despite, as they noted, his having freely resigned it to their society (*sua libera resignatione non obstante*).[173]

Only one set of memorial lives, that of the Brothers in Doesburg, took note of departing members, recording fourteen between 1443 and 1522, about one every five or six years. Their stories offer further insight. In 1443 the first rector offered to resign after protracted internal difficulties over leadership style, but only if granted an annual income of fifteen gulden; he then went to serve as father-confessor at the local house of Sisters, recently become Tertiaries. A Brother in 1458 gave up a post he had been assigned as father-confessor, having proven unsuited for it, and thereafter lived on his own from a benefice he accepted. Another ran off with one of his Tertiary charges, only to serve thereafter, with her as his companion, as priest in a country church.[174] A layman left in 1453, unable to bear the daily disciplines.[175] Another Brother, an inconstant soul, fervent, then burdensome to himself and others, left to stay with his parents, only to return more than once, finally settling with the Teutonic knights.[176] In 1470 a Brother left unwillingly over a case of conscience. He had earlier seduced a family maid and now became persuaded that only entering a religious order would assuage his guilt. They sadly restored most of his patrimony too.[177] In 1479 a Brother left, initially fervent, later unable to bear their "quiet and solitude," his demands and stubbornness and discontent having cast their whole house into confusion.[178] A layman, their taylor, was thrown out the next year, unwilling to submit to house customs and disciplines, then found sleeping with a woman.[179] A priest in 1496, accounted "perverse" and impatient of discipline, rumored to be unchaste, left for Utrecht and there sued in court for the return of his goods. The Brothers won (indicating the validity of these resignation agreements), though, they wryly noted, court costs exceeded the value of his goods.[180] Finally in 1522 another Brother, weary of their house, unable to bear inwardly its "solitude and subjection," fled home, probably at the instigation of his mother, and subsequently served as a village pastor.[181]

Over time the process of admission would grow more institutionalized, manifesting a concern to "form" (*instituere*) people in order to avoid "grave damage to internal peace and brotherly concord." What the community sought most was a malleable person (*tractabilis*), responsive to their ways (*promptus*). New Brothers were instructed in how to conduct themselves, what voice to use, how to adopt a humble stance and guard their eyes, when to pray aloud or silently. They had to alter their old worldly ways, confess openly, mortify their will, live in complete commonality, never judge others, not insert themselves in others' business. They were now to live entirely for God, quietly in their cell, intent upon sacred reading and meditation.[182] Not so many people were fit for this, in fact, and when an able person died young, as at Zwolle in 1465, the outpouring of grief was immense, the Brothers even at odds with God (*gemuimus et quasi querulose Deo diximus*) for taking such an ideal recruit from them.[183]

The women's lives speak to these struggles as well, perhaps more humanly and honestly. It made a great difference, they observed, if a person entered with a "free heart" (*mijt enen gueden vrien herten*).[184] Earlier we noted the mix of circumstances that brought young women, willingly or unwillingly, and the struggles they often worked through in adapting to house customs, even learning to "break their own natures" in order to persevere. By contrast Sister Heilwich (d. 1481) at Emmerich, the oldest member of the community, a person of noble nature (*rechte edel guede nature*), was "ready and willing" for the ways and work of the house (*willich ende bereit*, the Brothers' *tractabilis*), beloved by God and humans, never at odds with anyone; but even so she suffered mightily because she found it hard to get up at the expected hour, typically about 4:00 a.m.[185] Even a woman who chose it might find "this apart spiritual life extraordinarily hard," thus a chamber maid who repudiated a persistent lover, rejecting his offer more than once, preferring a greater heavenly reward, it was said. Her mother tried to visit and to dissuade her and reportedly cried out in protest, "Oh, that one Christian would advise another to take on this life!" Yet the young woman stayed and met her death of plague twenty-one years later reportedly with inner peace.[186] Because entering and staying hinged so on personal resolve, complicated by issues arising from personality and fit, the inner anguish could be intense. These Sisters were not afraid to record it, and saw it as a grace when someone persevered.

The spirit inside a house must have depended a good deal on the tone set by its leading personalities, its three or four senior positions (rector/mother, procurator, librarian), these often prominent in the memorials. Apart from a certain malleability of character, their ceding to one another in "loving obedience" and humility, no communal house plainly would have survived. But still another factor entered importantly into the spirit of these gatherings, the high positive premium they placed on counsel and consensus. In the customary tradition that originated with Florens and Dirk, two rubrics spoke to this, one on a monthly colloquy, the other on "taking counsel."[187] At the beginning of each month they were to discuss what pertained to the gathering's "estate" (*colloqui de his que deseruiunt statui nostro*).[188] Any member might speak or raise a point, especially pertaining to neglect in upholding house customs or caring for its goods, also collations or reprimands delivered by the rector, and any signs of dissension in their midst or persons fixed in their own ways. The rector could respond, then all brothers (*vota fratrum*) were to be consulted, and important matters (*principalioribus negociis*) had to bow to the judgment of the "majority" (*maiori et saniori parti fratrum*). Matters major enough to require "counsel" included: appointing or deposing the rector, appointing or changing a *provisor* (those who legally constituted the society), accepting or expelling members, buying or selling incomes and land, ordaining someone to the priesthood, appointing or deposing a procurator or librarian, a building project beyond a certain value. If disagreement persisted, the rector could delay a decision, or choose two respected brothers to help him decide. Real contention could and did occur. To spare the innocence of newcomers (*permaneat simplicitas uerecunda*) young clerics were not required to "vote" for a year or two, laymen a little longer—thus at Zwolle. At Gouda—its statutes more than a generation later—this became several years for clerics and possibly never for laymen. For Sisters, again, our information is scant, though they too were to take counsel, even weekly or bi-weekly on all major community affairs.

Striking by medieval standards is what got discussed and decided: all matters of leadership and membership and even promotion to the priesthood. Already in letters of 1398 Brothers voted among themselves as to who should be ordained next as they lost priestly members to the plague.[189] Two generations later Brothers at Zwolle spoke of electing people to serve as librarian or for promotion to the priesthood.[190] They expected thus that questions of electing new leaders or accepting new members or even promoting new priests—clerics and laymen weighing in too—should be the decision of the community, a remarkable and little-noted feature. It arose in part from a conviction that the priesthood, while revered, should never personally be sought, a position Zerbolt also defended in a major treatise, quite widely distributed, a tract against "the arrogance of seeking the priesthood."[191] All this bespoke, or arose from, another feature informing the spirit of these communties. Where male religious houses, whether monastic or mendicant, had long since become almost entirely priestly, the tone of Brothers' houses was instead clerical, in its medieval sense, meaning students and clerics in minor orders, book-men and liturgy-men. Where priests commanded a certain inherent authority in the Middle Ages, clerics expected by contrast, from schools and especially from chapters or collegiate churches, that business be done collectively. Chapters upheld rights against superiors (bishops or priests or provosts), whether of property or elections, and students through their colleges or nations could on occasion uphold theirs. The Brothers' term for a "majority" was that used in ecclesiastical elections ("the larger or wiser party"). But the tone was not just clerical. Laymen were members too, as all Sisters were lay, and all of the Modern-Day Devout engaged in, and lived from, manual labor. They could also think like urban artisans.

As important thus was a civil way of doing things, the collective arrangements common to towns, from craft guilds and city governments to neighborhood watches and pious confraternities. Any agreement Brothers and Sisters struck with city aldermen required them to proceed in this way, as did their own retailing of books and textiles. On the human level Master Geert's father was a city treasurer and alderman, and many early leaders came out of this class, as did many of the women. Their families dealt necessarily and routinely with town governments, municipal laws, and merchant societies. In their own writings they sometimes spoke of religious exercises as a craftsman's art, often of their gatherings as a household with a paterfamilias and domestic customs, no less their houses and persons as "private," their societies as legally comparable to those of students or merchants. More, all about them they saw, we must remember, practices of consultative government, lay as well as clerical, and they lived through a time when the church on a grand scale was abuzz with conciliar talk, heady proposals to govern the whole church on a consultative rather than monarchical model, this partly actualized at Constance and Basel. The Modern-Day Devout intentionally avoided the status ("arrogance") of the ecclesiastical hierarchy and professed religious, but no less the self-serving greed and pomposity of the laity. At a local and private level they aimed to mount an alternative.

The style they developed was "republican," another unusual term, requiring explanation. It is a term found in customaries coming out of the Zwolle colloquy, invoked to clarify the position of the rector, the head of community. "Any republic great or small (*in magna et in parua qualibet republica*)," it began, "needs a presiding figure in order to preserve the community . . . and [ours] thus, with the common counsel of our Brothers, assigns one priest to stand in the place of a paterfamilias."[192] In medieval terminology the notion of a "republic," ultimately antique, could take in communities large and small from cities to kingdoms, but also a small society (*parua qualibet*) organized as a household. Theirs was a "republic" modeled on a private household, whose governing spirit fostered "taking counsel" and "preserving domestic peace," submitting themselves obediently and humbly to, but also working consultatively with, the paterfamilias or mother. Republican notions were visible mostly in practice, especially in towns. Theorists were few. Marsilius of Padua, a Paris-trained schoolman and Italian townsman, was one, and found its spirit best represented in the general assemblies of Italian towns, which he stridently counterposed to an interfering monarchical papacy whose temporal powers, he thought, should be stripped. The Brothers were more cautious. From Grote onward nonetheless they approached society as a place of consultation, participation, contract, and negotiation, in the clerical as well as the civil spheres. The outlook I call republican may be grasped as falling between two other later medieval attitudes toward governance. This was an approach, despite a deferential society, that did not unilaterally accept monarchical authority, preferring to work outside hierarchically organized courts. At the same time, however, it held itself aloof from the mob, the indistinguishable *vulgus*, commoners in city streets or parish churches, who acted far too readily, so they saw it, outside law or reason or negotiation. People animated by a republican spirit knew how to contract a legal society, to constitute a freely assembled organization, to defend it in law. They cast their purposes into written form as a legal document, a set of statutes, maybe with an oath or a pledge to bind each to each and all to their common ends. Aldermen, for instance, had to swear an oath of office upon taking up their posts in Dutch towns. But Modern-Day converts made resolutions (*propositum*, *opsaet*), agreed upon customs, and entered voluntarily and contractually into a society, to which they then submitted themselves humbly and obediently to sustain.

We close with a depiction from someone inside their own circle, likely in the mid-fifteenth century. He portrayed them as an "amicable society or companionate friendship" (*societate amicabili seu amicicia sociali*). It is one thing, he explained, to live well, another to live well together (*bene uiuere, bene conuiuere*); one to be a good person, another to be a good citizen, friend, companion, or monk. A good person lives virtuously with respect to himself, keeping his vices in check; to live well together means also to live well with respect to a group. But there are different ways of living together (*diuersus respectus et modos conuiuendi*). It could mean civil society, thus living justly with others according to common laws and statutes. It could mean monks living under obedience to a superior and in charity with their fellow professed. But to live together in a companionate society (*modus conuiuendi socialiter seu amicabiliter*) was yet a third way. It meant living according to "friendship," proving profitable to others in aid and counsel, being sweet and malleable (*tractabilis*). More, this living together in friendship and harmony failed unless members suppressed their own vices, needs, desires, and ego.[193] The point of this address was actually to call Brothers and Sisters back to personal virtue and communal harmony as basic to the well-being of their community. But the speaker chose to open by deliberately positioning their community over against two other prevailing models in later medieval society, urban citizenship or professed religion. Theirs was to be an alternative, anchored in restoring to life early Christian Jerusalem, realized here as a freely contracted society, a communal household, a private gathering, a "tiny republic."

CHAPTER SIX

Defending the Modern-Day Devout: Public Expansion Under Scrutiny

> *With his whole heart [Peter Horn, d. 1479] loved not only our house but our entire estate (*totum statum nostrum*). Therefore he could not bear it with an easy spirit if anything was said or done against our estate, but with words, if he could do so comfortably, or in writing if he could not, he strove to defend both. He was made very anxious, even up to the end of his life, if anyone seemed to threaten any danger, especially spiritual danger, to our house.*

RELIGION IN THE Middle Ages was public. New forms of conversion almost inevitably provoked fresh arguments over what was permissible: what practices or teachings stretched the boundaries of the licit, what forms of religion could be recognized without infringing upon the rights of others, what rulings (or inquisitorial interventions) narrowed the range of the possible. Participation in this debate hinged as much on society as church, on social and educational status as well as gender and kinship. But lines also ran crooked. In the majority Christian religion any person might potentially be recognized as gifted with a divine calling or a divine word because, Scripture taught, God was not a respecter of persons. Public authorities, however, might well query that call's authenticity or submit its manifestations to a discerning of spirits, here too women or the uneducated or those further down the social scale often possessing less bargaining room. New groups could nonetheless, more than we sometimes credit, maneuver, religion being in effect a public commodity in which different people and groups held shares of differing sizes and values. Beguines had long negotiated for rights or property, those far better attested in surviving records than their spiritual intentions. After nearly fifteen years the Modern-Day Devout had obtained an episcopal privilege in 1401 allowing seven practices as licit (Chapter 3). Over the next three generations their communities would mature and acquire more privileges, and would also meet more resistance.

Odd as it may sound, new religious movements in the Later Middle Ages routinely issued in legal contestation. This held as well for the more spectacular contests. In 1395 Lollards tacked up "twelve points" for deliberation, calling upon parliamentary lords at Westminster to legislate, a provocative broadsheet, satirical too, serving public notice that religion needed fresh policy-making. Six years later harsh legislation directed against them sought to cut off any negotiation, to foreclose certain practices as out of bounds.[1] Vernacular religious texts continued nonetheless to get written and to circulate.[2] Jan Hus, though in danger, went to the council of Constance in the fall of 1414 under a promise of safeconduct in the conviction that he could freely represent actions undertaken at Prague, even persuade others to agree, his efforts ending at the stake in June 1415[3]—an unforgivable betrayal to his disciples. Lollards and Hussites dared take positions on the eucharist and the church (ecclesiology), matters going to the heart of later medieval religion, as dangerous to touch as a third rail—yet touch them they did. Moreover, Hussites managed finally to negotiate, even after open warfare, for the privilege of offering the eucharist in their preferred form (both species). How far one might go in critiquing or subverting the estate of professed religion, whether this was as dangerous to touch as the eucharist, remained unclear, a more ambiguous case. From the beginning, with the founding of Windesheim, the Modern-Day Devout had hedged their bets.

Most negotiated privileges focused on specifics, often of practice or rights, as had those for the Devout, though a person or group might seize upon any recognition as blanket approval. Some among the Devout also worried that any accruing of privileges meant ease or even decline. Godfrey, head of the men's house in Deventer (1410–50), warned against getting many, even to protect their own hard-won customs.[4] Privileges were particular, and the word particular here is a form of Zerbolt's oft-repeated "private." Not entirely separate from the "public," as in our instinctive understanding, it represented a distinct right or "liberty" conferred upon a person or group, not one that inhered in their status or estate or corporate standing. For a comparative sense of the way this public religion and particular privilege actually worked, we might look briefly at the more or less contemporary case of Margery Kempe across the channel.[5]

Once Kempe had launched on her convert's way with white garb, chastity, and weeping, she went to the bishop of Lincoln with her husband, waiting three weeks to meet him, and sought permission specifically to wear her garb and ring. The bishop, uncertain, sought advice, then put her off: "I have take my cownsel, & my cownsel wyl not gyf me to professe yow in so synguler a clothyng wyth-owtyn bettyr avysement."[6] The verb here, whether the bishop's or hers or her priest-scribe's, indicated that she was seeking an approbation, as all understood, which would privilege her peculiar way of life. This bishop hesitated, but Archbishop Arundel (1399–1414) granted her certain rights by "letter and seal," namely to choose her own confessor and to receive weekly communion, this in effect, in her telling, approving "hir maner of levying."[7] When a hostile cleric arrived in Lynn, this document was invoked.[8] Margery herself remained troubled by doubts all the same, and repeatedly set forth her self-designed/Spirit-enjoined form of life, that is, "hir maner of governawns," before various clerics, also before Julian of Norwich, and was reportedly assured by all that "ther was no disseyte in hir maner of levyng."[9] Nonetheless in Leicester lay magistrates as well as the abbot made her attest to certain articles of the faith, especially her views on the eucharist (Lollardy), and her practice of chastity. She challenged them in return, and they worried aloud that she, with her white garb and unusual ways, "art comyn hedyr to han a-wey owr wyvys fro us & ledyn hem wyth the." Town patricians were wary about unusual religion appearing in their sphere, especially its potential for stealing away wives or daughters. With the help of mediators she again obtained a "letter," this time from the bishop of Lincoln. It directed the mayor not to "vexyn her" and to "lettyn hir to gone & comyn whan sche wolde."[10] These "letters" were privileges, written and sealed, more specific and cautious about particulars (communion, confession, freedom of movement) than the narrative suggests. Margery, like many of her contemporaries, understood perfectly the role of public religion in medieval society, but more specifically of particular (private) privileges within it, whatever convictions she also harbored about the extraordinary nature of her own inspiration.

Women's Houses and Converting Schoolboys: Burgher Critics at Zwolle

Tensions over the Modern-Day Devout erupted early at Zwolle.[11] This commercial center counted 666 taxable hearths in 1404, also a flourishing Latin school serving as many as eight hundred schoolboys.[12] In a single generation women's houses had multiplied there from one older establishment to five, those five steadily expanding in size.[13] In 1407 patricians and aldermen reacted and revised municipal law to rule that "religious" people had to sell off any inherited property or, if they wished to live from it in their lifetime, bequest it to laypeople[14]—that is, could not hold property and act as religious like Tertiaries and some

Devout. In 1413 the guilds (led by their *oldermannen*) achieved unprecedented power over an older patriciate, and struck an alliance with the new rector of the town's single large parish, St. Michael's.[15] This Henry of Compostella, himself licensed in canon law, insisted now that Devout women attend the city parish on high feastdays and confess to chaplains of his choosing, and that schoolboys do the same. When Dirk of Herxen, head of the men's house (1410–57) tried to protest, he met with hostility in the street and was denied an audience with the rector, then as well with the provost and chapter of St. Lebuin's in Deventer (patron to many parishes in the region). To make matters worse, from about 1410 John of Haarlem, former rector of the men's house in Deventer, now confessor to the women's households in Zwolle, had preached "boldly and authoritatively" against the city council and its vices, even on occasion in the city church. He was beloved of the people, it was said, but not the aldermen. He came into open conflict with them over the one older women's house, which he wanted to reform and also to relocate,[16] and he was later banned from the city.[17]

On the Devout side Dirk of Herxen (1381–1457), though just over thirty years old, now assumed local leadership, and we begin with a word about him. Born to wealthy landed parents, he grew up under the care of his mother and two uncles, one (Meynold) counted among the founders of the men's house in Zwolle. Schooled in Deventer, he considered joining the Carthusians at Monnickdam or the canons at Windesheim but was counseled by prior John Vos to take his talent and wealth to the nascent and needy house in Zwolle, this lesser socioreligious estate (*cohabitandum in humiliori et abiectiori statu*) and poor house where he could be of more use and win more souls.[18] Within a few years,[19] at age twenty-nine, he was elected head, eventually acclaimed "father of all the Devout" in the land, as Florens was in his day[20]—though often little appreciated, the in-house chronicler remarked, by some citizens in Zwolle.[21] Of all the Devout leaders he turned out to be the most significant in the first half of the fifteenth century, and he is the only Brother or Sister of whom we have still the surviving gravestone, a gray sandstone slab, the grave (and stone) originally shared with his predecessor as rector, the stone depicting him as a priest (see Figure 15).

On 13 January 1415 aldermen, driven by the enraged guildsmen, took action. They forbade new religious foundations as well as gifts to existing houses (except the one pre-Devout house), halted three households from accepting any more women (and another only with their agreement), likewise any more gifts to the houses without their ratification, and the making of any new policies (as well as documents) with respect to the houses apart from their oversight. Any violation risked severe penalty, even loss of citizenship. This was read out by the city herald before the central parish church, only a block or so from the men's

Figure 15. Gravestone of Dirk of Herxen, head of the house in Zwolle (1410–57) and de facto leader of Devout Brothers and Sisters in his lifetime, buried at Windesheim with his predecessor, Gerard of Kalkar (d. 1409). Sandstone, with the etching of a priest-figure with chalice. This gravestone, long left outside, was recently placed inside the only remaining building from Windesheim, perhaps its former brewery, since the seventeenth century the local Reformed church. Author's photo.

house.[22] Earlier, the aldermen had taken to hiring Brothers to make fair copies of their laws—a recognition of how quickly this service had gained recognition. But not this time; these policies were written in the hand of one of the guildsmen.[23] The guildsmen intended to regulate the Devout literally to death. Two months later, on March 9, Dirk went to Utrecht and protested these ordinances to the bishop's legal advocate in Utrecht (*officialis*), calling for their revocation, or a hearing at the episcopal court, or a hefty fine—the bishop being temporal as well as spiritual lord of the city. A hearing was set for March 26. The aldermen, with help from a local master in law, cleverly protested it as falling in Holy Week. It was reset for 18 April, but only the Devout appeared. On 26 April the bishop laid a massive, thousand-pound fine on the city, also placed it under excommunication and interdict, and had its legal rights suspended until the fine was paid.[24] For Bishop Frederick his temporal powers as overlord of the city were as much at stake as his spiritual powers; indeed he may have seized on this opportunity to reassert rights then fast devolving on municipal governments. The city's leaders, also grasping what was at stake, appointed nine lawyers to appeal the interdict to the Council of Constance, thus going over the head of their spiritual and temporal lord.[25] Two months later, however, on June 30, the new laws were removed from the books, the fine paid, and the interdict lifted; the city had backed down.[26] Several months later tensions spilled over within the town council itself, and now the bishop felt strong enough to intervene militarily, which he did, stealthily and powerfully, on St. Lucia night, 12/13 December 1415. The radicals were removed, some banned, a few reportedly beheaded. It would require most of 1416 for the city to settle down again.

Amid this fearsome test of power between bishop and city, and city council and new converts, the men's house was compelled to reflect seriously on what they were about. This produced a document notarized on 2 May, less than a week after the city came under interdict—this a known text, though not yet read in context.[27] Such rethinking, even redocumenting, may have gone on in the five women's houses as well, but no record remains. Dirk of Herxen with two priests and a cleric as the four joint-holders (*provisores*), along with eleven other clerics, all residents (*incole*) of Zwolle, drew it up, all fourteen residing in the house. Their house had been built on a lot made available to them in 1394 by the then curate of St. Michael's, Reynold van Drynen, offering it in perpetual lease (the site of the building in Figure 12). Aldermen were suspicious already then but could not touch it since the property was legally ecclesiastical. In May 1402 the Brothers moved to have the house formally declared ecclesiastical property, while specifically ruling out a "college" or "new order."[28] A good decade later the guildsmen, with a now cooperative rector, pounced. They read the agreement of 1394, so they said, as allowing for only three or four inhabitants;

but now there were fourteen, and so the Devout stood in violation.[29] The novelty of a joint-holding society had given the aldermen an opening. This house had been built in good part with funds supplied by Dirk's two uncles, Meynold and Witte of Windesheim, and he now declared this a misreading of their original intent: the "three or four" referred only to the joint-holders, not all the residents, the house and its goods given, he further explained, for the use of the entire "gathering" (*ad usum totius congregacionis*).

This misreading came about, he surmised, because certain people were now "hostile to devotion and to multiplying spirituals," this emerging amid evil times and various events (*propter diuersos occurrentes casus*)—a veiled allusion to the new laws and the interdict. But the troubles had "unsettled the harmony and unity in the house." Hence the need now for a careful restipulation of their rights and purposes, which in turn generated this first miniconstitution. The document closed by declaring that all the goods each had brought and resigned to the society, movables and immovables, inside or outside Zwolle, belonged to it; and were also portable because the point was adherence to the community, not to a place (*magis attraxit nos bona societas quam locus*). So if they or their successors faced burdens or oppression such that they could not "hold out" in Zwolle, they reserved a right to move the society, with the consent and advice of the prior of Windesheim and the head of the men's house in Deventer. Plainly Dirk was not yet sure they could outlast the present regime. When the new parish priest had angrily pronounced at mass that Sisters were henceforth to receive communion in the parish, some people had shouted at Rector Dirk: "Throw that beghard in the water!" Any move would be to another town (*in ciuitatibus mansionem preelegimus*), however, since the purpose of the society was to serve God by reaping a spiritual harvest among clergy and laity.[30] "Clergy" here meant especially student-clerics, "laity" any drawn to the Devout lifestyle, especially women. This written declaration of their society's nature and purpose was drawn up in their house before a notary public, with two clerical witnesses.

In the aftermath of the crisis and the bishop's reassertion of power, but only a full three years later, the local parish rector Henry had finally to climb down (pressure from the bishop?) from his hostile stance. We may understand his antipathy if we note that already in 1406 Pope Innocent VII had ceded to the "house of the gathering of clerics in Zwolle" a right to use a portable altar "in their and other houses," meaning those of local Sisters. This was a transaction negotiated by intermediaries we no longer know, the persons who handled it, for pay, being an "L. de Temperiis" and a "Francinus" (*Solvit michi Francino*),[31] plainly preempting powers ordinarily reserved to the local rector. In any case in December 1418 Pastor Henry issued a document in his name and under his seal, full of innuendo, ceding what he had to, preserving what he could. He "wished to make manifest," he said, fearing lest he offend the Lord, that he meant to proffer "favor" to these fellow "workers in the harvest" who, he noted wryly, "seem connected" (*assciti*) to him, "devout priests and clerics" who pooled all goods (*sua in communi conferre*). They held the rights to hear confessions from students who came to them (so long as the students confessed once a year to the pastor); to read Scripture and hold "talks" (*colloquium*) with students or interested citizens (so long as these did not conflict with divine office or parish sermons, and so long as it was a simple exhortation, not a sermon); and themselves to receive last rites from one of their own if a curate was not available.[32] The tension was still palpable.

A pamphlet by Dirk of Herxen, recovered only in the last twenty years, but now known to exist in at least six copies, grew directly out of this crisis and its aftermath, as I read it.[33] It sprang ostensibly from discussions with a citizen, a special "friend" (*amice dilecte*), possibly one among several who reportedly would join them for a relaxed meal after their medicinal "bleedings."[34] The work, listed among Dirk's writings,[35] bears the marks of everything from a quasi-private letter to a public sermon and general tractate: it begins with a salutation, is laced throughout with the friend's charges, and ends with a sermon-like phrase. The final text likely grew out of more than one public intervention and usage. Lengthy and rambling, replete with quotations from Latin authorities, it was meant for churchmen or other Devout, and ended on an inauspicious note, with the Devout still under a cloud: it was better for spiritual persons to face mockery and troubles than to be revered, lest they become soft, he said.[36]

Lay sentiments drove the structure of this pamphlet. Dirk articulated and then rebutted them, whether those of a real person or general talk from the street. The lay critic sees the Devout as "monks" and "beguines" and beghards." In Dirk's language they were rather "spiritual persons," "devoted servants of God," "good people given to divine service"[37]—terms from the earliest days of the Devout. The townsman raises a host of complaints: Of what use are so many monks and beguines? Who will defend the homeland (*patria*)? Better one strong man in battle than a hundred beguines. Then as pointedly: are those alone "good" who live like these people? Were not beguines condemned? Was not marriage instituted by God, all the biblical patriarchs married? After all, if we all remained virgins, the world would disappear. Does this not broadcast (*sonare*) a message that only monks and beguines serve God, us lay people the Devil? There are, besides, simply too many now in our region, all going under one or another dishonorable (*indigno*) title.[38] Then the critic adopted a line seemingly traditional, but actually quite pointed: We could tolerate such types perhaps, if they were not so avaricious, clinging to goods (meaning able to hold and inherit still, also as Sisters). Near the end he also alluded to the Devout legal mechanism. Persons resigning their goods mutually to spiritual households and societies should not be able to receive inheritances, he objected, since they were unwilling to produce heirs.[39] Moreover, they do not distribute those goods to the poor (as in urban alms-giving) but to one another (the legal mechanism again), and then build larger houses.[40] It was the concrete issues of inheritance rights and expanding religious houses that most offended the burgher ethos.

Dirk was smart enough not to respond with a sermon on contempt for the world. The *patria* must be looked after, he conceded, but even more so the commandments and worship of God. People should look to the common good of the homeland (*huius patrie communem utilitatem*) in a way that does not neglect the soul's eternal well-being.[41] Trying to meet these townsmen half-way, he noted benefits the Devout brought to the *patria*, to an urban republic, even as he characterized his counterpart as mostly moved by "worldly prudence" (*O amice, hec . . . dicere et sentire est prudencia secularis*).[42] Over against fortune and fate or felicity in the presentday, he asserted, the Devout clung to a providential God ordering life to eternal ends. As for their multiplying numbers, these served in actuality to mitigate the anger of God: "The evil live better and more comfortably (*commodius*) in this world because of the good." God is "sparing the world," protecting the republic, because of all the good "who live and flourish now."[43] Dirk conceded to his lay critic a goodness among people in the world, though hinting broadly at plenty impious hypocrites, but also set their status in the church lower (*status eorum . . . infimus est*) than any who kept the counsels of perfection. This was a traditional position, the point for Dirk being to keep the counsels, not take vows. He agreed nonetheless that in his day (*modernis temporibus*) most laypeople were put off by "spirituals," convinced they were "of no use."[44]

Starkly in play here were two contrary worldviews, the spirituals' and the townspeople's, and much of it turned concretely on marriage and property. Dirk accepted marriage as a good but upheld the virgin state as primary, buttressing this elaborately with authorities, especially Jerome. He launched a minor diatribe against parents who withheld their sons and daughters from joining spiritual life. God could more easily forgive someone who burned all the churches between Utrecht and Rome, he says, than a person who willfully and knowingly became the "cause of perdition of a single soul." Think how many, he declaimed, by their "threats, blandishments, violence, bad advice, or even harmful laws" (*siue eciam nociuis constitutionibus*) "obstruct or restrain so many from conversion, and thus from salvation"[45]—the battles of 1415 still echoing and alive here, with a hint that many women or schoolboys may have been scared off by the civil threats. Dirk also was not prepared to credit that some burghers might hand off one child to spiritual life simply in order to marry the others more handsomely, or force an unwilling child, or a child physically or mentally indisposed, into the spiritual estate. Summing up, he tried to retrieve the high ground: this was not about disparaging marriage but lauding virginity, that infertile fertility (*ad laudem infecunde fecunditatis*) incomparably superior to fleshly fertility.[46] Little in all the Devout literature conveys quite so vividly the dialectic between converts and their married and propertied neighbors, all members, coincidentally, of the same local parish.

Property and goods represented the other fundamental divide. Townspeople found this spiritual estate different and odd (*uitam eis difformem*), he says. Their lives effectively turned on riches in the world, the Devout on the price of a single soul. But for the Devout wealth was not so much at issue as unguarded interaction with the world.[47] As for the resignation of goods to communal households, Dirk answered with a question: What do you say about town drunks and indulgent folk who only spend through goods and not endow their children? More, you hold it to be godly and honorable (*deificum et honorificum*) to bear five or six children and leave worldly goods to them. But what if a person chose to remain chaste and bore five or six children in the spirit by converting them to God, and left goods enough behind for them to live in divine service? Is that not better (*melius et excellencius*)? And if a person lacked the grace of converting others, could she not sustain those whom others have converted with the gift of her temporal goods?[48] As for building larger houses, lastly, they simply had to, because smallish ones did not suffice for holding so many all together. The houses were larger, he granted, but also plain, and suitably appointed for persons who rarely left to go out into the world. By comparison, he jibed, we now see churches lavishly decorated (doubtless the pride of aldermen and the curate alike), and people barely willing to stay inside them to the end of mass.[49] In the aftermath of this attempt to shut the Devout down Dirk was unflinching, clear about the divide that came with conversion, clear too that theirs was, though now protected, a minority stance.

He also wrote another tractate, harder to date, still unedited, again in Latin, thus also for ecclesiastical ears, whatever vernacular exchanges it may presume, this one defending the care of schoolboys. Again it took as its point of departure unhappy townspeople, parents and aldermen frustrated to have their sons lured away from school to religious life. In Zwolle and Deventer, we learn, people dared not attack openly (*non impungent manifeste*) but disparaged or dismissed this conversion operation (*eorum conversione derogant uel non magnipendunt*), the disciplined care and recruitment of schoolboys. Adolescents were too fickle and inconstant to make such a choice, townspeople protested, too young and inexperienced to be straightjacketed—the word was "yoked," taken from Scripture and Gerson—under religious discipline at this age. It wouldn't even make for good religious later on. They cited a proverb: You cannot avoid evil unless you know it. Those with experience of worldly life would prove nobler and wiser in spiritual life. Dirk found this "possible but rare." Mental knowledge (*cognicione intellectuali*) sufficed. Numerous people innocent in their youth became saints, including Willibrord (evangelist of the region) and Lebuin (patron of Deventer's church and school). A stronger objection then arose: this push for conversion simply insulted the state of people in the world. But let them simply open their eyes and look round at the state of Christians today (*status modernus christianorum*), Dirk retorted.[50]

Gerson, remember (Chapter 4), had made similar arguments a little earlier, and he too, it turns out, met with strong opposition in Paris. He subsequently drafted a passionate, even wounded, defense dated October 1406, this work partly inspiring Dirk's.[51] Jean Gerson believed that if the church was to be repaired it had to begin with the young (*paruulis*). Parents and schoolmasters, he asserted, now cared little about oversight and conduct (*eorum disciplinata custodia*)[52]—rather, only about the education and what it could bring. Further, university clerics had whispered and mocked, even calling Gerson and his partisans insane, in part regarding "all piety as nothing but foolishness and the stupidity of old women." Why should a master of theology, an ecclesiastical prelate, a university chancellor, belittle himself with tending and training children?[53] Ignoring such taunts, Gerson proposed four ways to effect this task: public preaching, private admonition, schoolmasterly discipline, and confession. He regarded the last as the form "proper to the Christian religion" and focused on a serious confessional regime for the young, not any once-a-year quicky with over-worked pastors at Easter (his description).[54] This too met resistance, people warning him off, also warning the young off. "The disparity [between priest/master and schoolboys] was too great."[55] They insinuated charges, including sexual ones, and suggested he would do better sticking to public preaching. His proposed approach they found novel, not then the accustomed way to handle schoolboys. But what could be more fitting, he protested, than their religious formation (*religiosa bonorum morum disciplina*)?[56]

Dirk, knowing Gerson's work, generated four pamphlets: "On drawing the young to Christ," "An exhortation to preserve innocence," "A response to those who disparage (*derogant*) the conversion of the young," and "On the praiseworthy effort (*studio*) of those who try to train the young (*nituntur instituere iuuenes*) in the good life."[57] The first (*De iuuenibus trahendis ad Christum*) was printed in the heyday of the schools and hostels (1479), about the time Erasmus's mother took him to Deventer as a nine-year-old child (1478). The yoke of the Lord, Dirk argued, should be borne by a "rude soul" from an early age so the "discipline of divine servitude" could constrain the innate urges of unrestrained desire (*concupiscentia*).[58] Negative as this sounds, Dirk mostly expressed positive attitudes toward this "flowering age of most pleasing youth," a time "most apt for beginning and exercising good studies."[59] He relied upon a kind of science, that the "natural heat of the blood" had not yet been infected by lust, nor the soul hardened into habits. Like a new plant (an image from Gerson) it was capable of growth, "docile and flexible in taking in good instruction (*bonas informaciones*)," a *tabula rasa* not yet written on by carnal images and experiences. As for notions of it as a wild age, that referred to its abusive form, arising from immature powers of deliberation.[60] Three social figures, as Dirk saw it, should be informing those youthful powers (parents, church prelates, and schoolmasters)—and all were failing. Few parents cared, Dirk claims, about guiding their children in a God-fearing way, interested more in opening to them the ways of the world. Schoolmasters instructed them mostly in puffed-up learning rather than edifying charity, curiosity rather than beatitude, thereby confusing the means, learning, with its end, a good life. And hardly any pastors could be found who were not out for themselves, the whole church infected in the present day with ambition and greed. Hence a need, implicitly, for Brothers to act as instructors (*instructorem et institutorem*, the latter word meaning in medieval Latin spiritual prose "forming"); otherwise, "very few of the young would be saved."[61]

The longest of Dirk's four tractates defended the efforts (*studio*) of those who undertook this care, rescuing schoolboys (*eruere*: pluck them out) from spiritual death, a work of charity. Despite "most dangerous" times God was pleased by those who acted—and for eight reasons. Dirk denied explicitly that Brothers sought any material gain or worldly honor, and insisted that they accepted boys without consideration of family or wealth.[62] As for the means employed, Dirk saw private admonition and conversation as more effective than preaching, since the latter was often all air and no act. Whence his anger at those who tried to block it, as if mutual talk (*mutua collacione*) was "presumptive preaching." This was aimed almost certainly at the parish priest Henry. Example was the best talk (*sermo*), Dirk suggested on the Brothers behalf, deeds speaking louder than words. Brothers also supported any whom they rescued, that is, in the houses for poor students. As for the confessional, though potentially effective, it depended upon the disposition of the person. Too often those who confessed acted no better afterward—an important difference in emphasis here with Gerson. Indeed the most effective tool in Dirk's view, never mentioned by Gerson, was the mutual encouragement of fellow youth. All this finally, here playing off Gerson again, could be undertaken at any site with schools and enough young students and the proper personal guides, not just in Paris.[63]

In retrospect, the objections at Zwolle to multiplying women's houses highlighted utterly divergent stances on conversion, marriage, property, and inheritance—illumining the lay ethos, but as well as the women who joined. Equally striking, evident as well in the reaction to Gerson's program in Paris, was the hostile critique of care for schoolboys, this also partly clerical. What would become in fact standard practice in the later sixteenth century, and into the early twentieth, struck laypeople and university masters alike in the early fifteenth as novel, inappropriate, unbecoming for serious adults, even out of bounds. But the young could be rescued, as Dirk and Gerson saw it; that was the point. Adults hardened in their ways hardly ever got turned around. Somewhere amid all this, we learn, an Augustinian friar stationed in Zwolle was reportedly going around preaching against the Devout and their estate (*statum nostrum*), stirring up "worldly" laypeople against them.[64] Dirk's critics were town leaders, but the friars too were not prepared to yield ground so easily to new forms of religious life and pastoral care, their bailiwick for nearly two centuries.

Friar Matthew Grabow and the Council of Constance

Yet another Dominican friar set in motion what the Modern-Day Devout came to see as their greatest threat, and retrospectively as their greatest victory. This clash originated around 1415 too, escalating into a dispute that reached the Council of Constance and drew in European-wide luminaries such as Jean Gerson and Pierre d'Ailly.[65] The driving figure was Friar Matthew Grabow of Wismar in Saxony, appointed lector (principal teacher) at the Dominican convent in Groningen after 1410.[66] The town of Groningen, key politically and commercially to the north, had a decade earlier been subjected to firmer control from the bishop, a point Frederick had insisted on in law, and nearly with troops. Grabow arrived there aware of his confreres' growing success in the Upper Rhine in pressuring beguines and Tertiaries, even suppressing them at Basel in 1411. Allied with secular priests, a bishop and certain laypeople, Dominican zealots had turned on beguines and Franciscans there, abetted by burghers irritated with "able-bodied beggars."[67] But in the Lower Rhine at the same time new communities were expanding everywhere, what can only have struck Friar Matthew as astonishing, even an affront. He also knew about Eylard's frustrated investigation, having procured or seen its findings, referred to obliquely as the Devout's "bad and enormous doings."[68] The "Olde Convent," one of three former beguine houses in Groningen, had already come under Devout influence, its women turning to a "common life" and then Tertiary status. To make matters worse, their house stood more or less across the street from his priory.[69] They also fought for pastoral independence, securing a legal advisory from one of the jurists of 1398 (Gerard Radink), seeking (and winning) the right to choose Devout guidance.[70]

In the diocese of Utrecht Grabow saw, quoting from a later document, converts gathering in communal households apart from any vows, some as Tertiaries, forming "conventicles," assuming a kind of habit, choosing superiors, drawing people in with a "pretense of piety," building large houses with lay gifts, entering them with self-made rites[71]—and, though he does not say it, a bishop passive or approving and an inquisitor blocked. Later he smeared these houses (called by them "houses of God") as expensive, large, and pleasant,[72] not unlike the charges alderman were making in Zwolle. Friar Matthew, a trained scholastic and teacher, commenced to think hard about these communities (*apud semetipsum ardenter cogitare*), and wrote a think-piece referred to as a little book (*Libellus*). According to its *incipit* he meant to query their way of life, proceeding in the manner of a schoolman (*tantum scolastice inquirendo procedere*), producing a disputation, now gone, that ended with "through this is evident the response to the tenth [proposition or objection]."[73] Such tracts were now the ordinary way for educated men publicly to treat contested issues.[74] He probably hoped to rally the diocese to his cause, as Mulberg had done in Basel. There, beyond pushing and shoving in the street and negotiating in ecclesiastical circles, the controversy had featured public disputes. A sympathetic Franciscan on All Saints Day 1400 had argued for the women converts (charged with begging, or receiving support).[75] Then in June 1405 Dominican Friar John Mulberg had rebutted all this before the assembled clergy, his presentation issuing in a written tractate.[76] Grabow might even have read there a claim that Frederick as bishop of Strassburg had once moved against beguines as subject to excommunication under papal law.[77] In any case, the Devout in Utrecht did not perceive Grabow's disputation as a scholarly debate. They saw a tough-minded attack and entitled it a "tract against the Brothers and Sisters of the Third Order," a rubric Friar Matthew indignantly called "invented."[78]

Grabow put forward, he says, seven principle "conclusions."[79] What survives from his tract are twenty-four "propositions" or "articles" or "conclusions" excerpted by his Devout adversaries, seventeen of them subsequently defended by Grabow as more or less his, the other seven discounted as their doing.[80] The latter, mostly pointed attacks on communal life, were perhaps not so much "invented" as raw asides excerpted out of context. In most medieval cases of culling out suspect sentences (think of Thomas in the 1270s, Marguerite in the 1300s, Eckhart in the 1320s), opponents seized on sensational items and strung them together. Grabow complained that the excerpting, and especially the ordering, had destroyed the inner logic of his case. But from him we have a later apologetic response in which he reconfigured the seventeen sentences into a précis of his argument, it now our only access to the tract on his terms (also suggesting the Devout had not completely misrepresented him).[81] Where Friar Eylard, and Mulberg in good part too, went after "illicit" converts legally, that is, as in violation of anti-beguine legislation, Grabow attacked them theologically. For him the matter hinged on the integrity of socioreligious estates, their status rigorously deduced theologically from vows. He built upon what Thomas Aquinas had worked out a century and a half earlier defending mendicants.

The fundamental point, Grabow argued,[82] was that no one could licitly and meritoriously, indeed truly, fulfill the counsels of obedience, poverty, and chastity outside professed religion. On this premise he aimed to destroy any pretence to "religion" on the part of beguines or Tertiaries or Modern-Day Devout. For a lay person to act in such ways (wholly giving up goods or conjugal sex) would constitute sin, indeed mortal sin and a form of murder, for it would cut the person off from carrying out those tasks essential to their own estate, namely bearing children and supplying material needs to those in their care. Indeed this would—confusingly, even contradictorily—make a "lay" (*secularis*) person a "religious." Other conclusions followed, those less easy now to reconstruct. One struck at the heart of Devout households, and was meant to. Resigning all goods as a layperson was wrong, even mortal sin and heretical, because it was likewise inimical to the nature of that estate. The Devout listed first in their presentation of his excerpted propositions a claim that property was "essentially" attached to the lay estate, a necessary marker. Grabow, to be clear, recognized that a person might undertake one of the counsels as a private initiative, thus chastity or a measure of poverty, but denied that all three could be pursued fully and properly apart from vows.

As with the inquisitorial intervention of the 1390s, we are left to reconstruct what happened next from scraps of evidence and disjointed stories—this worked out elsewhere and summarized here. Grabow's tractate was written sometime between 1410 and 1415, probably 1414/15.[83] He claimed later to have passed it around, not trusting his own understanding. But someone swiped it and brought it to the Devout, he says, and they overnight made a copy and alerted their network. However cleverly distributed by these professional copyists—Grabow also alludes to this (*quibus diuersimode communicatis hincinde*)—the work provoked a harsh stand-off between the friar and the Devout, first face-to-face in Groningen. They then took it to episcopal court, a tactic they had employed successfully against Eylard fifteen years earlier. Grabow, a foreigner, feeling surrounded there, trumped them by taking his case to the council of Constance for a "fair" hearing, going over the head of Bishop Frederick. The date is uncertain and we may wonder about linkage with the aldermen's appeal to Constance in early 1415. At Constance, in any case, after the flight of Pope

John XXIII on 20 March 1415 and his deposition on 29 May, the assembled conciliar delegates were effectively running the church, with Jean Gerson their intellectual and ecclesiastical leader. Importantly, Grabow approached the council not as an appellant but as a *sollicitator*, petitioning for action.[84] This *sollicitatio*, fully in the spirit of a long line of Dominican inquisitors, called on the council fathers to banish utterly (*funditus extirpare et radicitus euellere*) these beguines and beghards long since condemned by the church, especially those now hiding as Third-Order Franciscans,[85] the Tertiaries in Utrecht specifically in his mind. He charged the Devout with preaching, deluding simple people, proffering an appearance of holiness, and especially fogging things over (*fucatis excusacionibus*) with excuses that their "religion" (here, Tertiaries) represented a recognized estate approved by fathers and popes.

Word of this action reached the Devout by the end of May 1416. They grasped its seriousness. With a fractured church, themselves neither prelates nor masters, and belonging to no order represented at the council, they felt threatened, entirely uncertain of the outcome. They resorted to an earlier strategy, gathering seven priors including John Vos of Windesheim to attest to their uprightness. This produced a lengthy testimonial focused on the legitimacy of communal life (as if it were the heart of Friar Matthew's objections, whether or not that was accurate), which spoke mostly (five paragraphs) about men's households, briefly about women's (one paragraph), perhaps missing what most annoyed Grabow (Tertiaries). The Devout here pleaded with the reformers and luminaries gathered in council (*reformatoribus, luminaribus*) not to cut off (*abscindant*) healthy members of the church amid so many others so diseased, a hint of the fear, even panic, that Grabow's move had generated. The document was sealed by all seven priors on 13 June 1416, the Saturday after Pentecost, then reaffirmed by their jurist ally Abbot Arnold and the prior of the Carthusians in Monnikdam, and three days later ratified by Bishop Frederick in response to their petition. He also affirmed that he had never heard of any heresy among these "devout people dwelling in gatherings"[86]—still here a sense of discreet distance.

Grabow's *Libellus* and petition got processed at the council as a matter of "faith," not "discipline," theology, not law. If accepted, it would affirm Eylard's original contention that these religion-like communities represented heresy. The matter was eventually taken up in the appropriate committee, and the Devout too appeared there with speeches and materials.[87] One Devout spokesman pointed out that the friar's move represented a global attack on a type or estate, not just a critique of certain individuals (*sollicitator materie illius non in singulares personas sed in uniuersitatem retorsit*).[88] He described by contrast the "many and large gatherings" of men and women living holy lives without vows in his home region, so many that housing could hardly be found for them—that issue again.

He begged rhetorically for sense and good judgment over against a "most iniquitous petitioner."[89] A second spokesman claimed that all this had arisen at the bidding of "private individuals" (*a priuatis personis sub spe certa*) with vague hopes, presumably of turning the tide against the Devout (suggesting critics such as the guildsmen in Zwolle). [90] After this first flurry, however, things stalled out for nearly two years. Grabow later complained that he was required to stay in Constance (*arrestarunt*) while they deliberated, himself reduced to "extreme poverty" and never called upon, whereupon he finally left. In November 1417 Martin V was elected and enthroned, ending the schism, and Grabow petitioned the new pope to have his case entrusted to a cardinal for action, Martin committing it to the cardinal of Verona, Angelus Barbadicus.[91] Someone from the Devout side also petitioned for a hearing. But as he set forth the situation, Friar Matthew had already fled twice, once from Bishop Frederick (*citatus contumaciter recessit*) when he turned to the council instead and again when he left the council in secret, only to return with demands and "conclusions." The Devout petitioner now presented all this, in a key reversal, as mounting a case against the friar.[92] Grabow had called upon the council to banish the Beguine-Devout-Tertiary estate as illicit and fomenting heresy; the Devout and their partisans two years later pressed the case forward as a challenge to the orthodoxy of his *Libellus*.

The official managing the commission for the cardinal, a Master Olavus Jacobi, had before him a large pile of oral transcripts, texts and assertions (*inquisitiones, positiones, et articulos facto realiter et in scriptis*). From the Devout side Evert Swane (the fourth named in their delegation) presented the cardinal's commission with various items (*iura, literas, instrumenta et munimenta*), presumably whatever testimonials, privileges, and juridical opinions the Devout had mustered to date, with a demand now that Friar Matthew be made to respond to these, not they to his material.[93] The next step was crucial. Grabow was asked in fact to respond under oath to certain "positions and articles" (no mention of "inquisitions"), items excerpted from his tractate by the Devout.[94] This he did between December 1417 and March 1418, summarizing or "expounding" his *Libellus* in an *expositio* (summarized above) of the seventeen excerpted articles he accepted as his own.[95] Master Olavus then asked experts for opinions on the twenty-four articles along with Grabow's *expositio*, all examined as a "matter of faith," Grabow's *Libellus* too, though the experts seem to have had little or no access to it. Olavus also asked these experts how best to proceed, an indication perhaps of the confusion the affair had generated with its charge and countercharge.

Jean Gerson wrote out his advisory on this matter, the most crucial as it turned out, in his own hand on 3 April 1418. By then he had seen d'Ailly's, and concurred with it.[96] D'Ailly, expert in law as well as theology and a former chancellor at the university of Paris, was striking in his advice on procedure. The cardinal in charge should convoke all masters of theology present at the council for a free discussion. They should together determine what here conformed to Scripture, the matter to be settled not in the dark and by individuals but in the light and by all. That was how, he said, he handled matters of "faith" (*causa fidei*) assigned to him at council[97]—a striking instance of free university debate extended to conciliar decision-making. In all eleven other masters were consulted, none of their names preserved, and their opinions only indirectly.[98] The deliberations, following the theological advisories, turned decidedly against Grabow and his propositions, finding them brazen or heretical.[99] Probably armed with this (though it is not explicitly stated), Evert Swaan, advocate for the Devout, petitioned the cardinal to have the tractate declared "in error" as well as "scandalous" and therefore burned, Friar Matthew himself imprisoned until he returned to the faith and his senses, also banned from any preaching in the province of Cologne and diocese of Utrecht, and handed over to the secular arm if he refused to recant.[100] If accepted, this demand turned the tables entirely: from banning the Devout estate to banning Friar Matthew and his book. And it was accepted, finally on 26 May 1419, the papal court by then having moved to Florence. A subsequent report claims that Grabow died in prison in Rome two years later, himself never released, also never relenting.

For the Devout, what began as a dire threat ended in affirmation, or so they chose to remember it. Unlike the encounter with Friar Eylard, however, or even Dirk's with the guildsmen in Zwolle, this contest produced no apologetic writings. Perhaps there was no Zerbolt to undertake it, or they considered his *Circa modum* statement enough. We must be clear, however, about what did and did not happen. The council soundly rejected Grabow's theological conclusions as extreme. It did not license or affirm the Modern-Day Devout as such, about whom they would have known or understood comparatively little—even if the Devout subsequently chose to construe things differently. They now appropriated Gerson's advisory as their own, and made it foundational to future affirmations of the legitimacy of their way of life.[101] His little consultation traveled only in their circles, though it entered an early imprint of his works. As for the theological issue at stake, in response to Grabow's "conclusions" Gerson set out six propositions. The only truly Christian religion was that Christ perfectly observed. Second, that "Christian religion" did not make the counsels of perfection obligatory, with or without a vow; otherwise they would be commands. Third, it could be kept most perfectly without vowing the counsels; Christ did so, as did the apostles and early Christians, several of whom were married. Fourth, its observance did not require any "added-on religion" (*superaddatur aliqua religio, religiones factitias*) such as the Augustinian. Those added-on religions were arrogantly and distortedly called the estate of the perfect (the position of Thomas Aquinas); they are "aids" or "ways" (also Thomas's position). This "Christian religion" can and must be observed by popes and prelates apart from vows or profession. Grabow's position, he contends, is "stupid, heretical, and blasphemous," denying to Christ, the pope, and church prelates (all of whom took no vows) the perfect keeping of an estate of perfection. He and his defenders were to be constrained and punished, though not going so far, Gerson cautioned, as to give license and comfort to beghards and beguines.[102] In good part this marked for Gerson the revenge or return of the secular clergy over against the overweening claims of professed mendicants.

With Friar Matthew Grabow's condemnation in May 1419 the incident was closed. But it echoed for a generation, and not just among the Devout. Friar John Nyder, a major reformer and writer among Dominicans over the next twenty years, had access to the documents, even as he knew all about Mulberg in Basel. The basic issue unsettled him: what was one truly to make of beguines, Tertiaries, Devout, recluses, hermits, secular canonesses, and all the rest? Were they lay or clergy? Secular or religious? under civil or ecclesiastical law? permitted or illicit? Grabow had a point, even if he had driven it too hard and too far. In a work on "the religions of laypeople" (*De secularium religionibus*: his title possibly suggested by one of Grabow's propositions), he tried to sort through all these types, and in another on "laypeople practicing poverty" he tackled issues both Mulberg and Grabow had raised (the "able-bodied poor"), concluding the latter with Grabow's case. Nyder sided with the council, even quoting (without identifying them) Gerson and d'Ailly. But his stance was cautiously inbetween.[103] With respect to the point the Devout listed first, Grabow's "conclusion" that property is an essential mark of the lay estate, he agreed with council theologians that, so extremely overstated, it was potentially subversive, offering an opening to Wycliffite disendowment, since the church too had a rightful and necessary tie to property (*subuersiua possessionum temporalium ecclesie que diuinitus equaliter approprientur statui spirituali sicut seculari*). But the larger outcome of all this was to provoke, alongside Wycliffite and Hussite challenges to the eucharist and ecclesiology, a wide-open debate about the nature and prerogatives of "religion," taken up in the next chapter.

The Sisters and the Aldermen in Conflict at Deventer: The Women's Narrative

Bishop Frederick died in 1423. The battle over his succession divided the diocese for ten years, fueled by rivalries between Holland and Guelders, as well as by two princely families within Utrecht and by the collegiate and cathedral canons in the episcopal city.[104] This directly threatened Devout communities a generation into their existence; it also dispersed them, and indirectly spread them. All parties immediately pressed for their favored episcopal candidates, including now the towns and princes of the Oversticht. An attempt was made in fact, though in vain, to move the election to Deventer. Canons in Utrecht split among four candidates, a majority emerging for Rudolph of Diepholt, favored by Cleve and Bentheim as well as the towns and princes of the Oversticht. In Rome Pope Martin V unexpectedly opted for someone else entirely, the then bishop of Speyer. In the Low Countries the majority party stuck by their candidate, and made plans to appeal to a council; the bishop of Speyer then eventually refused the appointment; and in February 1425 the pope, again unexpectedly, named instead Zweder of Kuilenburg, the candidate favored by Holland, the one initially with the least votes, now backed by the powerful duke of Burgundy. Zweder gained control in Holland and Utrecht more or less but met stiff resistance in the Oversticht. On 14 September 1425 the pope placed Deventer and Zwolle under interdict, suspending public ecclesiastical ministrations. Some canons at Deventer sang the office anyway but most stopped, and the two parish priests left town. In the city magistrates and people resisted, however, deeply resenting this suspension of divine services over a "political" matter, and determined to find clerics or religious who would stand with them. Their candidate Rudolph, moreover, gained in following over time; so a genuine schism emerged, at times virtually a war. This went on for years, with no resolution possible until Eugene IV succeeded Martin V as pope in March 1431. In the summer of 1432 the interdict was lifted, in September Zweder went to the council of Basel (it already at odds with the pope) for reconfirmation of his election, and in October 1433, Zweder having meanwhile died, Rudolph was confirmed as bishop, the man, ironically, first elected by the canons in 1424.

All this created a prickly situation for the Devout. Their gatherings answered to the aldermen in law, especially the women's. The dilemma, as the women put it, was whether to betray their spiritual estate and good society (*enen geesteliken staet ende guet geselschop*), and as well to act against a command of holy church in order to please the temporal magistrates who oversaw and licensed them. For them it was not about a given episcopal candidate, but honoring a church interdict despite aldermen. So long as the interdict continued, however, and they honored it, they had no access to the sacraments, even on high feast days, thus Easter, Ascension, and Pentecost 1426. So tangled did this issue seem that once again—we know, though yet unstudied—they turned to lawyers for advisories. In the end most of the Modern-Day Devout left the region of Zwolle and Deventer to escape those pressures, and spent roughly six years in exile. Societies and households were indeed moveable, as Dirk had said. But they also had to abandon houses they had just fought hard for, and find refuge in territories not under interdict (Zutphen, Guelders, Bentheim, Friesland), there to live in cramped quarters apart from work and resources. When they returned in 1432, it was to houses desolate or plundered, to a bishop they had not recognized, to aldermen whose candidate in the end won out.

Our most interesting record, written out by the women and in their own tongue, comes from Master Geert's House, twenty dense and dramatic pages inserted into a book of memorial lives.[105] In a codex given over to lives, listed one by one in the table of contents subsequently placed at its head, this chapter gets listed too, the last item—"how the Sisters were driven out—on the first page (see Figure 16). Here we listen to their story first, then look back at its meaning. As the Sisters tell it, the encounter began with repeated flattering visits from the aldermen, promises of support and privileges in extending their house (reversing recent attitudes in Zwolle!), even the offer of a complicit auxiliary bishop to absolve them of any supposed sin in cooperating, so long as they "bowed to the town and did like other good people and went to church."[106] Services were apparently going forward in some way, and attendance by the Devout, high-profile local converts, would have greatly bolstered the magistrates' stance in facing down an interdict. When the women's father-confessor then left the city, along with nearly all the Devout men, the aldermen felt sure they could bring the Sisters around, and apparently mostly did in the four other Sisters' houses in town. The women at Master Geert's resisted, however. With this began a series of dramatically escalating confrontations. Around Easter 1426 the aldermen forbade them to accept any new member or to sell textiles, their key source of income. Then on June 15, nine months into the interdict, they were given an ultimatum: go to church, or leave town. Those deciding to stay would get the goods of any that left.[107] On another day several aldermen entered the house itself to harass them, poking into all corners to look for secret worship, also getting the younger sisters apart to pressure them—but to no avail. In the other four households in Deventer, it seems, the aldermen had found the women generally more pliable,[108] and so became all the more enraged at those in Master Geert's House, threatening now indeed to drive them out, with no right of return, no claim on their goods. The women came virtually to despair (*soe droeuich weere, nouwe troesten conde*). As rumors spread through town their families showed up and tried personally to reclaim daughters and kin, fearing the poverty and worse that awaited women put on the road and driven into exile.

One woman, especially "persecuted" by her family, secretly traveled with another ten miles upriver to Zutphen (in Guelders, outside the interdict), and

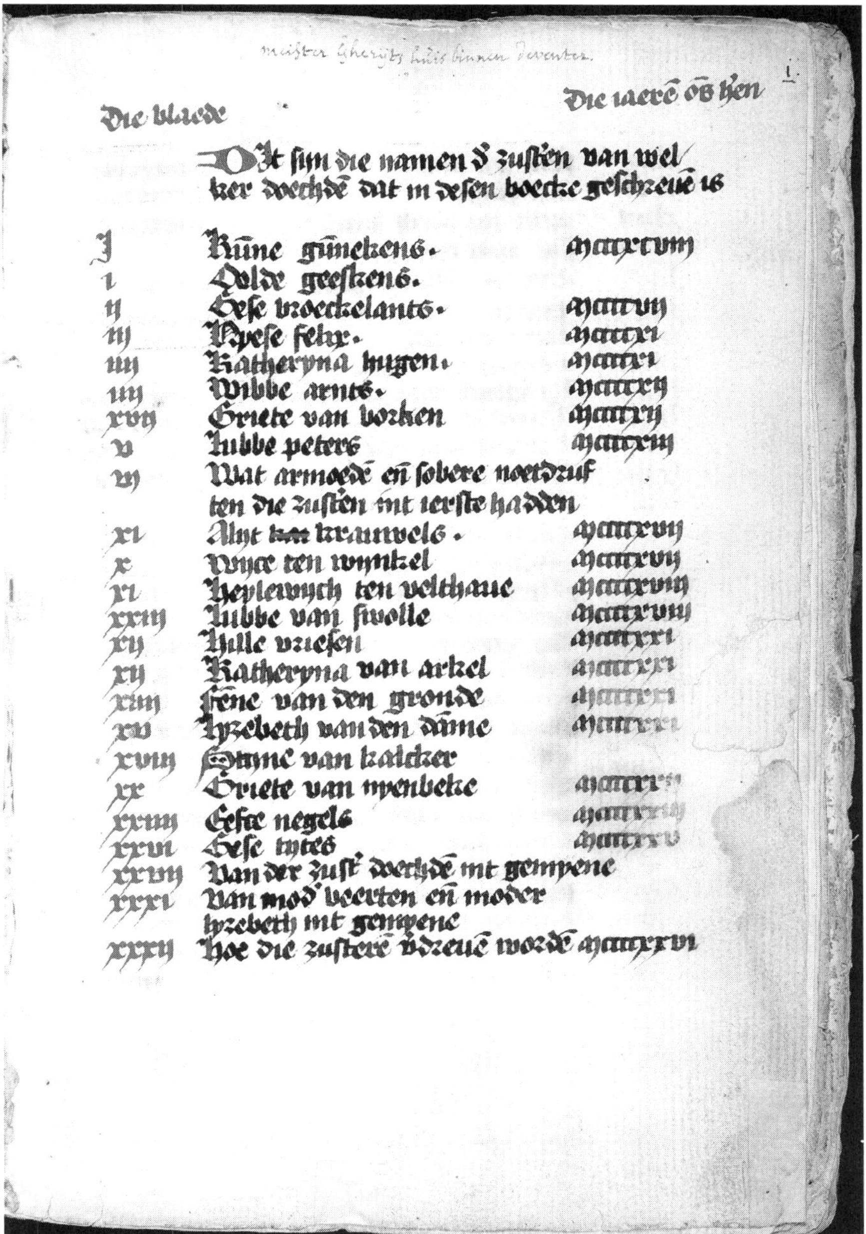

Figure 16. Sisters' Lives, Master Geert's House, copy made by a Sister in the 1480s of a collection of lives written in the 1460s/70s. Here the opening of the table of contents, appended at the beginning ("These are the names of the Sisters whose virtues are written in this book"), with the "exile episode" separately noted (as f. 32 in the year 1426). Deventer, Stadsarchief en Athenaeumbiblioteek, MS. Suppl. 208 (101 F 25), f.1r.

there certain aldermen agreed to receive them. So they resolved to act. The two Mothers hired wagons and Sisters outdid one another in loading things up, then moving toward the dock to take ship for Zutphen. At that point the indignant relatives of one Sister got a city official to stop them and confiscate all goods until she was returned home; there she was subsequently held a virtual prisoner by her family for several years. The rest of the women could neither stay, because they still refused to attend church, or go, because their goods were confiscated and they had nothing. A sympathetic townswoman, with a dwelling above one of the city gates (Zandpoort), took them in, and there they stayed for a week. During this time townspeople mocked, called them names ("devils"), even said they should be burnt as "infidels."[109] Two of the gathering's members, it turned out, were daughters of the steward (*rentmeister*) to the duke of Guelders, a fairly high-ranking position. When news of all this reached Arnhem, the duke of Guelders wrote to the city of Deventer asking mercy, and sent a ship to fetch the women (thirty miles). But the aldermen turned it back without reply or notice. The women, then getting desperate, on the advice of other townspeople, decided to face down the aldermen, who were also in a tightening spot, and so reclaimed and reloaded their wagons. This brought angry blasts from more townspeople: these women were not "converted" but "perverted," the young as well as the old, all fixed in their strange ways. The next day the aldermen ordered the women out of the city, blaming them for bringing trouble from an outside lord (the duke of Guelders), and demanding the key to their house. As the Sisters boarded ship, more epithets were hurled at them, about thick-headed stubbornness, women worthy of being dumped in the river to drown, indeed out of their minds (*bijsinnige*).

At this point the narrator stopped to recall other hostilities they had suffered for pursuing their way of life. One sister, joining the house against the will of her family, was reading at meal when her family came in and hauled her off in leg-irons, never to allow her to return. In another case a brother-in-law came to fetch a woman home to her sister, met resistance from a man who sympathized with the Devout, and both drew knives inside the House.[110] But we return to the scene at the dock. The Sisters were so bound in love to one another, the narrator observes, that they preferred loss and poverty with fellow-Sisters to remaining with parents: better to go into eternal life in strange surroundings than into everlasting ruin with kin.[111] But not all the women went along to Arnhem, we learn indirectly. Some remained behind, forced by families or owing to a "poverty of spirit." These then made free with the goods left behind in the house, at least as the hostile narrator tells it, holding banquets, inviting people from town, including chaplains who were serving despite the interdict. But these women subsequently fell out with each other, were hauled before the aldermen for lack of discipline, and finally thrown out in exasperated anger by the magistrates, leaving the house totally empty.[112] The house itself was plundered, but a relative of Master Geert (a nephew or grand-nephew on his mother's side) locked and protected their oratory (*bedehuys*).

In Arnhem the duke's steward made his house available. But it was overrun with knights and civil servants surrounding the court, making it difficult for the women to sustain a quiet and dignified life. They also had difficulty setting themselves up in work, since they would end up rivaling local textile producers. After six years they returned, on 15 August 1432, a month after the interdict was lifted (July 15). The house was a wreck and recriminations continued. The aldermen were reluctant to allow the most determined of the women to return; several found places in houses in other towns, two sneaking back to another household in Deventer. The head of the men's house was allowed back only three months later (30 November), and their own father-confessor never, dying in exile. In his case the reason was, apparently, a letter of advice he had sent to the women during the troubles. They had asked what to do if a Sister died (a huge issue during interdicts). He suggested they bury her under the mulberry tree in their yard until the interdict was lifted and then later have her properly buried in a consecrated churchyard.[113] Repeatedly, these disputes came down to points of public practice, crucial to both sides—whether the women would attend church, whether to bury a Sister in the churchyard during interdict. The town aldermen were determined to have compliant Sisters and a compliant church. Converts who resisted were "crazy," perversely stubborn.

This narrative was written in-house in Dutch by an unidentified Sister a generation after the events.[114] She told the story impersonally but with a nearness to the events that seemed personal, speaking either from experience or as a gifted writer or both. This was "tribulation" for them, a demonic testing, hard to bear. She even alluded to their "martyrdom" but repeatedly as well to their acting on "obedience to God" and to their mutual love and solidarity.[115] This was not a tractate, but a narrative, a record of mutual allegiance to a society of converts, and told as such, a quite remarkable piece of women's prose that has gone almost entirely unnoticed. They, or at least an important majority of them, were prepared to face down the aldermen who oversaw their house, also those relatives who thought them stubborn or extreme or "crazy," along with the townspeople who mocked them as "devils." The also found themselves (this nearly unstated) opposed by those women and chaplains who were inclined to work with the aldermen. For, plainly, women in four other houses, and some in their own, did not resist to the point of exile. The divisions were political too, especially for local citizens: one name Sisters got called was "Kuilenburger," that is, partisans of the bishop appointed by Martin V. Stirred up across the city were political as well as personal antipathies, and all of it with a gendered undertow, whether these women would submit to the bidding of the town patricians who oversaw their house. The Sister-narrator describes the aldermen as frequently "enraged" at them (usually *toernich*). For the women, however, it was a religious matter, their loyalty to God and to holy church and to each other.

Institutionalizing Under Scrutiny

As the years passed the Modern-Day Devout struggled to stay true to their originating vision while also stabilizing their peculiar institutions and warding off external pressures. To uncover how we must take account of two larger contextual realities. First, their houses remained independent, though umbrella networks (colloquies) also developed. Names offer an important clue. Where we use, not entirely incorrectly, a general rubric (Sisters or Brothers of the Common Life), they went by all differing names: the local house, the "Common Sisters," "Collation Brothers" (after their public talks), the "clerics' house," and "hooded Brothers" (*cullatti, Kugelherren*).[116] This independence required that their status be worked out anew in each town (as we have seen) and also in each diocese. Bishop Frederick's "license" of 1401 applied only to communities in the diocese of Utrecht. The repudiation of Grabow in 1419 offered no general warrant for Devout gatherings, even if they trumpeted it as such. At Cologne, metropolitan see to Utrecht and Münster, a society of six clerics had existed at Weidenbach near St. Pantaleon since 1402. But it took until 7 March 1417 for the archbishop to grant them a "special license" to live communally (*simul stare et uiuere in communi*) and engage in spiritual "exercises." Of the privileges he conceded, the most important were a right for these "companions" (*socii ydonei*) to choose their own confessor, also acting as their paterfamilias; to decide which among them might be ordained priests (notwithstanding synodal statutes to the contrary); and to remove from their society any unworthy member. He granted this finally, he said, on the strength of *consilia* drawn up by the university jurists.[117]

Five years later a fresh approbation dated 31 January 1422 was co-signed by eleven masters of theology and law.[118] The archbishop, petitioned by the Devout, again granted extraordinary permission (*approbacionem specialem licenciantes*), here underscoring that they had not violated the anti-beguine laws of John XXII. He pointedly forbade anyone from impugning this way of life or harassing their persons but specified that they be visited once a year, at their expense, by an Augustinian prior. It happens that at Cologne in the year 1420 a crusade preacher against Hussites had pointed to a women's household in St. Gereon street and decried: Why march to Prague when you have heretics in your midst? Charges like this stirred up enough trouble, we are told elsewhere, to have the case brought before the archbishop and university masters. Henry of Gorcum, a theologian, investigated and found on behalf of the women.[119]

We have an independent witness to how matters might proceed in a new place or a new diocese. A Sister named Fye of Reeden (d. 1429), a woman of commanding presence said to be of prudent but pointed speech, served as companion to a knight's wife in Cleve before she converted to Master Geert's House.[120] Brinckerink had bargained with her to try the house for a year, promising her a hundred gulden if she disliked it. She stayed, and proved so able she was sent to Xanten to head up a new household, even later accounted the "apostle of Cleve" for her work there. The women's estate or way of life (*state ende maenier van leven*) also came under attack in this new environment, and she was hauled before an inquisitor in Cologne (whether in connection with the previous incident is not known). She grew anxious, the Sister-memorialist reports, because she knew no law, and a priest she consulted with became so nervous and cowardly he refused to accompany her. As it turned out, relying on God speaking to her inwardly (*inwendelike toesprack*), as the narrator puts it, she found words and wisdom (*mont ende wijsheit*) to withstand her accusers. The encounter this time, about 1420, was between a woman with no knowledge of canon law and charges from an inquisitor in Cologne, and she stood up to it.

Beyond the issue of local houses and diocesan approbations, privileges in the later Middle Ages were by their nature particular, the subject of individual negotiations. Privileges or "liberties" in medieval understanding conferred rights on groups or houses or individuals, in part dissolving public authority into specific privileges while also lifting such "private" individuals or groups into the realm of those enjoying a publicly recognized right. When such privileges conferred rights on whole groups, say, something like clerical immunity from civil prosecution, the privileged group could emerge as a distinct estate, as with the special rights enjoyed by anyone accounted a town's citizen. This is a world still too little explored, though Kaminsky set it out well, he too emphasizing the notion of estates as crucial along with an intersection between the "public" and the "private" in ways foreign to modern expectations.[121] Thus when papal law attacked the "estate" of beguines, it set up a conflict between global recognition of their form of life, now explicitly denied, and whatever particular privileges a houses or beguine court could nonetheless secure, some ironically from the papal court. We may complicate this still further by returning to the notion of late medieval religion as, among much else, a public commodity, of which groups or individuals tried to secure pieces for their own purposes. In effect the curia in Rome became in the fifteenth century a great exchange center. Petitioners pursued their interests, and rights in turn were conferred, usually facilitated by a figure called a procurator, these rights coming ordinarily with a fee. There was nearly no aspect of church (and society, in so far as the church reached into it) untouched by this. We have now a study, for instance, of the right to advance to priesthood despite an impediment such as illegitimate birth (very common for priests' sons wishing to continue in their father's trade, and awarded in the tens of thousands).[122] We must think of the papal curia neither as the focal point of all carnal corruption nor as the spiritual center of the world (though there were those—and we tend to study them—who held strongly to either). It was a legal clearinghouse where spiritual and ecclesiastical benefits of all kinds were administered and exchanged. Bishops and princes did the same. When Bishop Frederick finally ruled on the *status* of certain persons in his diocese who were living together (*insimul in suis domibus commorantur*), he conferred on them "special approval" licensing (*licentiam, concedentes*) certain specific practices (Chaper 5), in this case by virtue of powers devolved on bishops by Gregory XI's *Ex iniuncto*.[123]

The Modern-Day Devout had to decide whether to avoid this world of privilege altogether or make it work for their purposes. They cautiously exploited its possibilities, even as they had used lawyers and the courts to protect themselves, and as Master Geert had appealed his diocesan preaching suspension to Rome. Sisters, to begin there, with aldermen overseeing their lay status, sought control above all over securing priests who were understanding of their spiritual intentions. Van Luijk found that in Leiden they secured rights to chapels, churchyards, and their own father-confessors relatively quickly, while in Zwolle Sisters gained almost no straightforward privileges at all.[124] They commonly also sought permission for a portable altar so they could worship within the house without walking across town or mixing with worldly people. This liberty was granted, even confirmed by the papacy, at 'sHertogenbosch in 1431 and at Emmerich in 1436, along with choosing their own father-confessor (*possitis eligere confessorem*), and confessing to him except at Easter and last rites (reserved for the parish rector)[125]—by way of what procurators or intermediaries we do not know. At Emmerich the right to a chapel was granted by the dean and chapter of St. Martin's in 1448, apparently under pressure from the duke of Cleve, and for a churchyard in 1458.[126] The bishops of Utrecht by contrast remained notably aloof from awarding such privileges. In the Oversticht this left matters in practice to the chapter of St. Lebuin in Deventer, also resistant to parceling out parochial rights.

Brothers' houses too acquired privileges, always specific, the earliest from Pierre d'Ailly, in 1113/14 when he was papal delegate and bishop of Cambrai, granted after he was shown the juridical advisories.[127] Already in 1424 the Brothers at Münster under Henry of Ahus obtained a papal privilege permitting its priests and clerics to hold and distribute incomes in a "common life," to use a portable altar, and to function independently as priests.[128] In December 1431, while Brothers from the Oversticht were still in exile, Pope Eugene IV issued a document to Cologne, Utrecht and Münster that protected, as he put it, men (*uiri*) who lived a communal life supported by the work of their own hands. Neither their life nor their lifestyle were to be disparaged (*detractoriis sermonibus*), Deventer and Hulsbergen (third most important "Dutch" house) specially named here as exemplary. It too confirmed a right to celebrate mass with a portable altar and have members ordained without a benefice or title (a violation of church law).[129] This was the work of Henry of Ahus, though it aided threatened Dutch Brothers then in exile.

Churchmen, when not resisting Brothers, worked instead to fit them into some accepted public form. For men's gatherings this meant recognition as a *collegium*, an enduring public ecclesiastical corporation, not a privately contracted society. In 1437 a declining Henry of Ahus sent a colleague to Rome to obtain a more general privilege for the Modern-Day Devout. On 18 April 1439, two months after Henry's death, Eugene IV "raised" (*erigi*) their persons to the status of "canons" and their houses to "colleges," reportedly to shield them and their way of life thereby from hostility (*inuidos*). They might accordingly elect a provost and adopt statutes, set up bells and a cloister, and account themselves freed of parochial jurisdiction.[130] To the curia it was a concession (apparently won only after two years of bargaining). The only way they could conceive of a general privilege for these odd Brothers was to "raise" them to public respectability as "canons" and "colleges." For the Brothers this looked quite wrong, putting their purposes entirely at risk. At the Münster colloquy the next year (1440) they simply tabled the Roman privilege without any discussion (*omnino taceamus*).[131] The Brothers at Hildesheim, a new house founded that year, unanimously rejected the title "canon," explicitly preferring, as they said, the manner of life and lesser prestige that had originated with the Dutch ("western") fathers. Even if their way met with "suspicion" and "derision," and the title of canon appeared more familiar and exalted, they did not want it. It all remained a "poisonous" (*infectum*) business, untouched until the death in 1457 of the Brother who had spent two years securing it at the curia.[132]

Truer to the Devout sense of themselves was their development of an organizational network that fell outside the lines of standard ecclesiastical recognition. To the skeptic it would have looked like a general chapter, and it plainly emulated that. This regional network had originated in personal bonds among early leaders, then in the 1430s assumed regularity as an annual meeting for mutual talk, the Colloquy. In time there emerged a "western" one based in Zwolle for "Dutch" houses (Dirk of Herxen's leadership), and an "eastern" one in Münster for "German" house (Henry of Ahus' leadership). The Zwolle Colloquy met on the second Friday after Easter, just before the Congregation of Windesheim's general chapter on the following Sunday.[133] Based on an "obedience of charity" like the houses themselves, it possessed only as much power as members agreed to. The house at Hildesheim—ironically, the source of our most complete surviving record—ardently resisted any real subjection. All records of the Zwolle Colloquy, moreover, have disappeared. The founding agreement for Münster was dated 1431, its initial group the rectors of three Brothers' houses (Münster, Cologne, Wesel) and the father-confessors of four Sisters'. They agreed voluntarily (*sponte et uoluntarie de pleno consensu et uoluntate nostra*) to meet once a year for at least two days of talk about what served the Brothers and Sisters' "advancement and utility" and their common "peace." The protocols were much like those for a general chapter: a formal reading of their agreement, a remembrance of the departed, a minute made of any decisions.[134] Visitors sent to individual houses were to ask members (men or women) whether they agreed to abide by the Colloquy and its consensus, that assent noted in the house customary—though we have no evidence of it, only Hildesheim's dissent.[135] The rector of Amersfoort was present at Münster in 1433, and in 1437 it was agreed that two people from Zwolle (*colloquium partium inferiorum*) and two from Münster should attend the other's meeting as a recognition of solidarity. Bishop Rudolph (1433–55), the opposition candidate during the interdict, at some point, the document now lost, granted (*concessit*) a right to hold this Colloquy, more specifically to meet annually and make visitations regularly, all for the "preservation of their estate."[136]

Not every rector or father-confessor attended regularly (complaints about this multiplied), but over time the Colloquy played varying roles, reducible here somewhat arbitrarily to four. One or two outsiders from the Colloquy came eventually to attend the election of a new rector/Mother in a house, to insure decision-making would not dissolve into personal wrangles. At Doesberg in 1443, for instance, the Brothers secretly took counsel and called in Dirk of Herxen who, accompanied by Godfrey of Deventer, oversaw an agreement removing the house's first rector, a man whose leadership had come to be deeply resented.[137] The Colloquy, second, decided which new gatherings to admit to their ranks, in effect certifying the viability of a new society and sometimes aiding in its set-up. This caught the eye of aldermen who turned to them on occasion if they sought such a house for their town, usually for its role in fostering a local school and caring for schoolboys. Devout leaders were practical men, as we have seen, not so different from aldermen. At Gouda, for instance, after initial interventions failed in 1453, they refused to support the house as viable, though it would later gain recognition and prove successful.[138] Houses, third, were to receive visitors from the Colloquy from time to time, affording each Brother or Sister a chance to say in confidence what needed attending to or improving. This was voluntary, however, and seems to have happened only sporadically, possibly regarded as an infringement on the independence of each local gathering. So in 1485 the rectors of Deventer, Zwolle, and Hulsbergen got an injunction from the bishop of Utrecht to force it, apparently in the belief that it needed doing in some communities, even gained support in 1486 from Pope Innocent VIII.[139] Whether these visitations were ever carried out is not known. Fourth, the Colloquy oversaw the assignment of father-confessors to Sister's houses. This represented a major commitment of the Brothers' relatively limited manpower, and took considerable decision-making time to judge from the record of the Münster Colloquy.

By the 1440s Devout houses had stabilized. In Deventer, however, great tension arose just after Egbert (1450–83) took over as its young and inexperienced head. Cardinal Nicholas of Cusa was touring German lands as papal legate, settling cases, urging reform, granting privileges. He came through Deventer in August 1451, preaching at Diepenveen (the first house of canonesses), staying overnight at Windesheim (21–22 August, a Saturday/ Sunday, octave of the Assumption), granting a full plenary indulgence (jubilee of 1450) for exercises undertaken without leaving the cloister or making pilgrimage to Rome.[140] Someone at Deventer, said to be a regular canon, raised formal objection to the Brothers, whom obviously the Cardinal did not visit. Fear spread among them that Cusa would shut them down—what in fact "they were threatening." In the week of 15–21 August Cusa heard out the complaint, then called in Rector Egbert, and in the end offered good words for their way of life (*commendauit statum*). He also offered to privilege them as "canons" (*priuilegia pro munimento obtulit et canonicatum cum priuilegiis*), exactly as Pope Eugene had done twelve years earlier in 1439. Egbert steadfastly refused, the estate of "canon" being contrary, he held, to the resolve of their founding figures.[141] This was a bold stance, for fear was real. Later John Brugman, a Franciscan, reminded them of this incident: how they had called on God amid tribulation, how their knees shook in zeal for their estate.[142] Whether the accuser was a canon regular (as stated), or a canon (say, of St. Lebuin), is impossible to know. But in 1451 some churchmen had seen this powerful papal legate as the perfect opportunity finally to shut down these anomalous gatherings.

An apology for the Brotherhood, first uncovered twenty years ago by Elm (which I edit and treat more fully elsewhere), was written about this time, perhaps growing out of this incident.[143] It survives in a single manuscript that ended up at the Brothers' house in Emmerich but originated almost certainly in Deventer, part of a package of materials sent along to help the house set up there in 1469.[144] One Brother drew up this apology for another (*Petis a me, karissime*) to counter unnamed people who had "disparaged" their communal way of life.[145] His letter-tractate presumed all the arguments and approbations already in place (*tractatus sufficientes ac determinationes . . .*). This way of life had originated, it says, "seventy years ago." Devout narratives usually reckoned from the beginning of Geert Grote's preaching ca. 1380 ("1377" in the chronicle of Zwolle), which would place this work roughly in 1450. "Scoffers" had charged that they were an "illicit estate" (*obiectu status illiciti*) lacking papal approbation,[146] precisely the sort of point an adversary might raise with a papal legate. The work reviewed a series of objections, many now familiar: that communal life and the counsels of perfection should be pursued only inside orders, that these households had elected their own superiors, that Brothers wore a distinct habit instead of conforming to other clerics, that the Brotherhood operated outside a Rule, and so on.

As the author saw it, three different sorts of people were making these accusations. Simple and ignorant folk assumed unthinkingly that this way of life must be wrong since it was out of step with what usually got counted as Christian, the reaction of townspeople who did not truly appreciate, as this author put it, that "narrow is the way" to salvation. The learned, by contrast, heard or read various disparaging things about the Devout and assumed a dismissive stance. John Brugman, before he became an Observant Franciscan, had, he later confessed, instinctively held negative views of the Brothers.[147] For both the simple and the learned taking time now to correct false impressions seemed potentially useful. But a third group, described as "holding the worship of God in contempt," had resisted making any concessions, sought only victory, and were therefore simply to be contradicted. These, not identified in any way, were probably churchmen, despite the description, for his only direct address was to them (let those churchmen beware: *caueant, queso, ecclesiastici uiri*), his point of departure being their hostility. Because the Devout constantly held up the early church as their model, some construed that as disparaging of other clergy including parish priests. Others charged that, like Hussites, the Devout administered sacraments and preached outside ecclesiastical approval—a reference to their alternative spiritual services. Members of an order, this apologist revealingly observed, will often tolerate people in other orders but not the strict observants in their own. To some clergy the Brothers looked like "observants," the stern folks others could not stand, while to the apologist the Brothers appeared as reformers within this "clerical order" (*sui ordinis, idest clericalis, cooperatores in huiusmodi reformatione*).

This letter-tractate—whether it took up commonly circulated rumors, responded to an otherwise unknown clash, or spoke to the atmosphere surrounding Cusa's visit—adopted a mostly conciliatory tone. It invited critics to look inside the house if they wished to see for themselves, and pointed up notable advances in regional religious life owed to the Devout, particularly their care for students. It even attempted a flourish in the form of a rhetorical question: With the whole church, particularly by way of councils, calling out for reform in head and members, why should people not rejoice at this local reform advancing in a lowly and far-away place? As for his written "explanation" (*satisfactio*), the author concluded, "pious hearts" should receive it in the right spirit, not as disparaging of anyone (thus, other secular clerics). But he added a stinging barb to close: Those who could not see purity were themselves the impure.[148]

The attack of 1451 was the last to threaten the entire estate. In the 1450s these societies and gatherings, now some two generations along, consolidated into standing houses. As Dirk's end approached a new generation of leaders emerged with Egbert in Deventer (1450–83) and Albert of Kalkar (1457–82) in Zwolle. About the same time a new resignation of goods was drawn up and publicly notarized, beginning at Zwolle and Groningen in 1455, then at Deventer in June 1457, and probably throughout the Colloquy. It carefully restated the provisions that constituted their societies and gatherings: resignation of goods by way of a *donatio*, those goods then accounted common to all, the foreswearing of any future claim by the Brother or his kin, his commitment to live in common and to labor, his foreswearing any future claim on goods except daily clothes should he leave, and the right of the society to remove him should he prove rebellious or obstreperous—all because communal life was for them the first priority (*In primis quia communis uita semper in promptu fuit his*). This particular resignation of goods was enacted, however, or rather reenacted, by the whole community together, not an individual agreement struck at joining. It was a collective reassertion of first principles, presumably to keep communal societies from easing into established houses (or "colleges of canons"), also to remove any ambiguity about future property claims by members or relatives. These documents, though not wholly uniform because carried out house by house, referred to each still as a dwelling and society (Zwolle), or a dwelling, society, or brotherhood (Deventer).[149] These actions were accompanied by still others to protect their peculiar estate. At Deventer eight days after that house acted (6/14 June 1457) the bishop, at their request, issued a privilege placing their persons and goods under his protection along with all their accumulated rights. For the first time the list of privileged acts included acquiring a common seal (*sigillum eciam commune habere et obtinere)*, in principle the marker of a "college," along with a right to administer the sacraments within closed doors during an interdict,[150] elements previously unthinkable. Whether the right to a house seal was sought by the Brothers, or simply granted by the bishop's court routinely thinking in "collegial" terms, the first extant document employing a house seal at Deventer dated only from 1466, a full nine years later.[151] In February 1462 all these same privileges, notably, were confirmed by Pope Pius II. This set of documents taken together, importantly, would thereafter form the core of materials deployed at the founding and privileging of any new house.[152]

The papal curia meanwhile offered again what it knew, the title of "canon"—under what circumstances we do not know. Calixtus III issued such a privilege for Amersfoort in 1457, not implemented, if ever, until after 1469; that same year one issued as well for 'sHertogenbosch,[153] then to the Brothers' houses in Ghent, Geraardsbergen, and Brussels.[154] To what degree any Brothers in the Zwolle Colloquy ever claimed the title "canon" is dubious; there is no evidence for it. But it is how the church tried to make sense of them without banning them. From 1463/64 Brothers in Germany, by contrast, began to accept these titles, persuaded they could do so without subverting their way of life. Later in the 1460s the new houses in the Middle and Upper Rhine launched under the direction of Gabriel Biel all accepted this rubric, and eventually formed their own chapter, distinct from the Münster Colloquy, even though also Biel identified fully as a Brother and with societies going back to Deventer.

Pressures to regularize increased more for women. Nearly all the houses Rehm studied moved into Augustinian status in or by the 1460s. At the house in Emmerich this occurred in 1463, thirty-four years into the house's history, under pressure from the duke of Cleve. The Mother, Mechtelt of Diedem, who had become head only two years earlier, resisted, as did many Sisters, but in the end capitulated. The lives hint at resistance or difficulty, and some Sisters kept up their old patterns and exercises as best they could.[155] Even after regularization statutes for houses in northwest Germany had a new member, interestingly, request to become part of *vestram confraternitatem*, received then by the Mother into their "fraternity"[156]—the language still of communes and companions. From the lives, if indirectly, we sense nonetheless what changed: stricter cloistering (where Sisters had plainly interacted to varying degrees with the surrounding urban community), common liturgical and ascetic practices (where most had practices to some degree of their own preference); more time devoted to liturgy; and acting now strictly under obedience. We have an intriguing account of how one Sister (Beel, d. 1481) dealt with the impending transition in 1463. She had entered at fourteen, urged on by a mother who had remarried, the parting extremely hard for her. "Lively and happy" by nature she had now to "constrain" herself, so that at first her heart nearly broke—her nature and this disciplined communal life, the memorial noted, like light and dark. But she gave herself fully to it, a hard worker, a compassionate and beloved companion, especially sympathetic to the bruised and disconsolate. She emerged central to the community. But she could not bear the prospect of a further yoke, and resolved to leave; no "religion" and "obedience" for her. First, however, she consulted with others in Nijmegen, women and men, and finally ended up going forward. This she did, notably, by way of a new resolve (*si maecten nu een nije opsaet*), that is, a *propositum*, the term for a Devout commitment, but quite precisely to give herself over to the will of God (not, the will of the order). Thereafter she reportedly experienced a "greater fiery inwardness," to the point where she would lose consciousness (*ontgeisten*) in God. To her last illness she "did good for the community (*gemeynten*)" as she could, though she also suffered a final crisis over not having proved more "fruitful."[157] Taking orders midway through was for her an impediment, though the suffering brought a new religious intensity. Her religion still sprang from "personal resolve."

Sisters enjoyed greater freedoms than the cloistered, and that came to vivid contention in Deventer in 1470, here over against the Brothers. Egbert, now firmly in the lead of his house and the town's five Sisters' houses, undertook to tighten discipline, the women charged with wandering abroad too freely (*libertate euagandi*).[158] He joined two houses (Brandes and Kerstkens) into one, and obtained, first from the local parish priest, then the bishop, then the pope, the right for Sisters to have masses celebrated in the house, freely to hear collations there, to have the Sacrament and holy oil reserved, all to be overseen by the father-confessor, who would have come from the Brothers' house, at times Egbert himself. Here a privilege was not a liberty (at least from the Sister's standpoint) but a means for closer oversight. Sisters reportedly had used the excuse of going out to church to meet relatives, see friends, look about the town, even visit the houses of male friends. The new privilege largely obviated any need to go to the parish church across town. The Sisters promptly complained to their powerful relatives, and the city council, under whose authority these houses still stood, at once ordered the two houses separated again and the new rules rescinded, the women freed to visit the parish church when and as they wanted—unless Egbert could show cause otherwise. He appeared before the council with Otgher, procurator of the New House for students (plainly the other leading Devout male figure in town), and delivered this speech, at least as his heirs recorded it:

> Honorable lords, it is a fact well known to your honors that the Sisters of this city, among whom are your daughters, sisters, and nieces, have up to this time been preserved by ourselves and our predecessors in chastity, good discipline, and the exercise of all the other virtues by diligent care and solicitude to the honor of your city. But now . . . we have discovered great scandals arising by way of visiting the churches,

> wandering abroad, and all that then follows. . . . It seemed therefore necessary to our fathers and ourselves that the Sisters be kept in their houses and provided there with masses, sermons, and all the rest under a good and faithful watch, a mandate to this effect having been granted to us by our superiors. Therefore, having thought through with due diligence what we have received from you, if your honors decide to persist in the prior decision declared to us, we hereby exonerate our consciences and commit their care to your consciences because we cannot do otherwise. You govern them then, or have them governed as it pleases your will.[159]

The aldermen asked Egbert to step out, deliberated for a time, and yielded. While we cannot know what considerations went on inside their chambers, they plainly would not take on responsibility for the spiritual care of these their own citizens and kinswomen.

While Egbert is shown here as taking a high tone, things inside the house may not have looked so promising. The aldermen had ordered Egbert to stop "under a certain penalty" (*pena*). For this reason, maybe others we do not know, the Brothers in Deventer felt seriously beleaguered again in late 1470. Their dark mood reaches us indirectly through two letters sent by Friar John Brugman from his sick-bed in Nijmegen not long before he died, the first to Peter Horn (librarian), dated 6 September 1470, the second to Egbert (rector) dated 14 September. The first dealt more generally with the Devout estate. Horn had apparently asked for a spiritual testament from the dying Franciscan.[160] It must have been a plaintive request, Brugman characterizing it as a resonant lament (*matura lamenta*), truly downcast (*Nec deiciamini, obsecro*). The Franciscan, formerly a scoffer himself, reviewed the troubled points one by one (*articulatim*). The Devout were still looked down upon (*portio uilis atque despecta*). As "little ones" they only wrestled with other little ones, meaning schoolboys. Some among them were not content and sought higher status. Even Brugman had somewhere referred to them as "lesser" (*fratres minores*), this heard by Horn as a disparaging Franciscan pun. Friar John, ever glib, quipped that as the term "philosopher" meant Aristotle and "apostle" Saint Paul (and so on), so "brother" equated them with any truly good Christian (*quilibet bonus christianus*). Moreover, by leading lives apart from the carnal, they of course would appear very earnest (*graues*). And the Devout in effect had an implicit Rule (*formulam implicite obseruatis*): purifying the spirit and loving one another (1 Peter 1:22). Yet Brugman added, very interestingly, that he had himself come to accept them owing to the advisories issued at the Council (Gerson's and the others').[161] Brothers now represented, in his view, God's stand against the ruin of the orders. And yet for all this smooth reassurance, this Observant Franciscan, a famous regional preacher, never once equated their way of life to the prestige of orders, only gave them high praise as a stopgap in ruinous times. As for their role, he saw them as important mostly to convert schoolboys to religious life; at this he declared them "best in all Germany." Brugman marveled: they had converted numerous people, he said, and he hardly one.

A week later Brugman wrote to Egbert. Probably the rector had thanked the Franciscan for his testament, and then poured out his fears and worries. Egbert felt threatened, probably by the city aldermen. Brugman alluded to the "rage of the barbarians" and "floodwaters of tyranny and impiety" now flowing out of Deventer, also to "stupid people" (*popule stulte insipiens*) who put pressure on the Devout and "hold hands with the non-devout and irregular," thus to the "tribulations about which you write."[162] The situation must have appeared threatening: I firmly hope, he wrote on 14 September 1470, that the mother house of Florens will not finally perish![163] This suggests the aldermen were threatening some very stiff penalities indeed. Brugman assured Egbert that the role of Brothers, his "order," was to stabilize and advance the "clerical way of life" (basically a reference again to caring for schoolboys).[164] In the letter to Horn he had warned against the "arid stuff of acquiring privileges." The Lord might abandon them if they came to rely on such.[165] This might well allude to the privileges Egbert had acquired, even waved in the aldermen's faces (also in his speech), and which the Sisters and aldermen now resented—and a discrete warning from the cagey Brugman not to insist on them. We may finally perhaps relate one more little text to this threatening moment. An anonymous few paragraphs written about this same time into the codex containing the *Satisfactio nostra* insistently pointed to all the privileges they had acquired over time, even noting that the first, in 1431, had come to them from Pope Eugene without their laying out money. People should presume good rather than ill of us, it insisted, but then ended on a more sanguine note: Since they had survived unshaken nearly ninety years (ca. 1470?), and were still generating spiritual exercises and the conversion of many schoolboys, they could hardly be viewed as a bad tree yielding good fruit[166]—an oddly defensiveness way of expressing the Brotherhood's position in the world after three generations. The situation around Deventer for Brothers about 1470 must have seemed surprisingly unnerving.

The perception that Brothers did not quite fit persisted, even ninety years along, and rendered them susceptible to malcontents or the suspicious, particularly whenever they moved into a new region. Gabriel Biel (ca. 1410–92), possibly the most distinguished fifteenth-century theologian of a "modernist" philosophical bent, master of theology at Tübingen (1484–92), got to know the Brothers in Cologne, became one himself first at Butzbach, then eventually helped found three houses in the middle Rhine region (1460s) and six in the Upper Rhine (1477–92).[167] He had reason to think hard about this communal way of life for clerics (*ecclesia presbyterorum et clericorum communiter uiuentium*),[168] and wrote in fact a full defense.[169] This work was in reality—scholars have overlooked this—a kind of *consilium*, its phraseology found at the beginning (*sub correctione cuiuslibet*), the work formally "submitted" at the end (*correctioni cuiuslibet sanum sapientis humillime submittenda*), though subsequently copied in the only surviving manuscript as a *tractatus*. Someone had raised questions (*questionem propositam*), though Biel in fact enjoyed the patronage of powerful lay families, in Wurttemberg indeed the regional prince. So he prepared a miniature *Circa modum*, twenty pages rather than a hundred, drawing upon Zerbolt and especially Gerson (whom he treated as foundational). He offered first a short history of origins, and then reviewed the main contested topics, hardly different from what they were in the 1390s: the notion of a religious order, communal life, the desolation of religious life, manual labor (especially book-copying), an elected superior, chastity, a distinct garb. Christ, he insisted with Gerson and Zerbolt, instituted the common life. Had it been kept, religious orders need not have been founded. Communal life itself assumed form at once in the early church, with the Spirit as its teacher. Should not this form of life also exist among upright clerics (*nonnullos obseruatores clericalis honestatis*)?[170] Biel presupposed all the legal formalities houses had long since worked out, thus no one accepted without a formal resignation of goods, a written pledge (*cautio*), the community itself here called a *consortium*.[171] Amid "many ranks of perfection," high, middling, and low, theirs, he suggested, was a middling way (*medius uiuendi modus*).[172] Yet it was these Brothers and Sisters, the unprofessed, he asserted, that had restored religion, however ungrateful and unremembering the professed.[173]

We conclude by noting one final shift in institutionalization—at least as visible in the historical record. It came a generation later, just as the Modern-Day Devout reached their maximum growth in houses and persons. In 1487–89, under Rector Jasper (1483–1502), the house at Deventer acquired additional property, added buildings, and generally transformed itself into a religious complex. Most important, in 1501 the Brothers struck an agreement with the chapter of St. Lebuin whereby they were finally dissolved from the parish and allowed to set up their own chapel (to which the remains of Geert Grote and Florens Radewijns were then moved).[174] At Zwolle an altar and churchyard were dedicated in July 1498, and all Brothers and Sisters' houses there separated from the local parish in May 1501. At Hulsbergen outside Hattem (in Guelders) a chapel was dedicated in 1488 already. The Tertiaries too in Holland by 1490 began to build their own chapels. A good hundred years along, the notion of a private and independent gathering with continuing obligations to the local parish was rapidly evanescing. And yet their names and sense of identity did not change (society, estate, Common Brothers and Sisters). One bit of evidence comes as a formulary, undated, though probably later rather than earlier, whereby people could enter into the prayer network of the Brothers' Colloquy, its houses labeled "gatherings of the Zwolle Colloquy of those living a communal life" (*congregationum colloquii swollensis in communi uiuentium*).[175] Little changed, not in the memorial lives from Doesburg which continued deep into the sixteenth century, not the formula for resignation drawn up at Zwolle in 1509, nor the privileges confirmed by Bishop Frederick of Baden in 1514 and Bishop Phillip of Burgundy in 1517. That of 1514 in particular reviewed all the key ones awarded since 1401, stipulating again the particular practices and rights allowed for Brothers, concluding with their right to remove obstreperous members from their gathering, that of 1517 noting specially the rebellious, contumacious, and propertied.[176] The way of life remains identified here as an "estate," never an order or a college. More than a century along, Sisters and Brothers were recognized and privileged; yet they never entirely fit in the eyes of some, maybe of many.

CHAPTER SEVEN

Proposing a Theological Rationale: The Freedom of the "Christian Religion"

The Gospel law . . . is the rule of the "Christian religion" and is simply free.

The Christian religion can be most perfectly observed in all its perfection through the liberty of the Holy Spirit apart from any vow of religion.

Many presume that whoever does what is written in the Gospel should immediately possess the charity written by God on the heart. They do not note how great is the difference between doing the good and doing the good well.

THE MODERN-DAY DEVOUT invoked canon law to defend their way of life, copied books for a living, oversaw young students, sometimes taught basic Latin arts, kept scrapbooks to aid their spiritual lives—all with inventiveness. But they were wary of theology. For them it meant idle speculation. They were bookmen by trade, and temptation lay in losing their heads in scholastic disputation. Grote dismissed theologians as thinking carnally (*carnaliter*), their arguments oriented to show or ambition or intellectual self-satisfaction. Florens too repudiated books of learned speculation and focused on devotional books. When the men's society in Deventer rebuilt their house in 1441, Rector Godfrey (d. 1450), a former lector in the Latin school, insisted that the library be accessible only through the librarian's room: Brothers should not wander in to read just any book, especially not scholastic books. Scholars have often viewed all this as insipid anti-intellectualism, piety played off against learning, and have pointed to the famous lines near the opening of Thomas of Kempen's first pamphlet:

> Of what profit to you is it to dispute high things about the Trinity if you lack humility and thus displease the Trinity? Truly, high words do not make a person holy and just; but a virtuous life renders one dear to God. I would much prefer to feel [*sentire*: can also mean "think"] compunction than to know [*scire*] its definition. If you were to know the whole Bible [by heart] and the sayings of all the philosophers, what would all that profit you without the love and grace of God?[1]

Theology signified preferment and prestige, learning leveraged for advantage; it was not the way to interiority. Thomas set experience over intellect, devotion against cognition, charity against learning. But we must not be misled. The Devout thrived by way of local Latin schools and drew their male recruits mostly from schools. Wariness about intellectual life sprang from operating on the same turf, the nearness of temptation, intense rivalry to win students away from careers in church or university.

Tensions between learning and piety must be contextualized, not reduced to an oversimplified grand narrative (common in studies of the Later Middle Ages). Franciscans fostered devotion to the passion and also wrote abstruse philosophical theology (Scotus, Ockham); Dominicans reigned as "scholastics" and as "mystics," even in a single person (Eckhart). Master Geert gave up his house and his clerical career but not his books; he set young students to copying more. He attacked priests with companions, but turned a reformist sermon into a dense legal apology, this text, notably, the most widely distributed of all his works and the only one to make it into print (1504). The Devout too would produce theological writers, despite their wariness. Gerlach Peters (d. 1411) wrote on religious life and mystical union, as did even more audaciously Alijt Bake (d. 1455), she upsetting her own Sisters and then the General Chapter who saw converted life more in ascetic terms. Gabriel Biel (ca. 1410–95) shifted from the arts faculty at Heidelberg to theology at Erfurt and Cologne, then to diocesan preacher at Mainz (1457–65), and emerged a founder of Devout houses in the Upper Rhineland as well as a professor of theology at Tübingen. In a collation written to praise and defend communal life, he concluded with a plea for the Devout to study theology, to train Brothers and care for people.[2] Wessel Gansfort (ca. 1419–89), a native of Groningen, was schooled in close association with the Devout in Zwolle, then lived in old age with Tertiaries back at Groningen. Never out of touch with the Devout milieu, he went on to study at university (Cologne, and perhaps elsewhere), and wrote widely on disputed theological topics such as indulgences, always with that edginess, or standing out of the mainstream, that characterized the stance of the Modern-Day Devout.[3] At Louvain too bonds between the Devout and university masters, extending into theology and humanism, deepened into the sixteenth century.[4] The very nature of the Modern-Day Devout left wide scope to individual initiatives, which adherance to an order might have curtailed, and most theological writers among the Devout emerged along those edges.

Brothers and Sisters might be able dexterously to defend and stabilize their distinctive form of life with negotiated privileges and legal inventiveness. But their lifestyle also raised issues that were finally theological: what was the status of "religion"? How did the "counsels of perfection" for religious relate to the "commands" for all the baptized? Was there greater merit simply in acting under a vow? How could they justify their "estate" in terms of the gospel? Zerbolt instinctively drew upon theological arguments from Bernard or Thomas when he needed to. Consider too his most oft repeated line: that their practices were not only "licit" (thus acceptable in law) but also "meritorious" (a theological claim). One Brother, John Pupper of Goch (d. 1475), who lived the latter part of his life outside the Brotherhood but as a father-confessor, took up this theological challenge, his themes arising from the heart of their enterprise.

Place in Society: Taking on the "Estate of the Perfect"

The Middle Ages had many ways of thinking about society. All those schemes, whatever they owed to social empowerment or the mental imaginary, sprang from perceptions of difference, those differences then hedged round by rights and privileges, and often made manifest in clothing. From the twelfth century thinkers and writers had begun to employ the notion of "estate" to distinguish groups (knights, monks, bakers, and so on). This category enabled them to define distinct rights but also to exhort people to fulfill their particular duties, also eventually to satirize their failings. The notion appears everywhere in later medieval preaching and literary work, the material also compiled in "mirrors" as paradigmatic literary expositions of a given estate in life.[5] The Latin word *status* (and its vernacular equivalents) took in a wide compass of meaning from "station" and "status" to "estate" and even "state." It "placed" people in medieval society, socially and conceptually. The noton of "place," however, defined a person from multiple angles, these sometimes coincident, sometimes at odds: one's place before God, here and hereafter; one's place in a sacred community (Christendom), especially locally (parish, convent); in a political entity, also locally (town, village, lordship); in educational status (illiterate, working literate, university trained); and in society broadly (family, gender, occupation, wealth, age). A person might be noble and professed and male and universitytrained, thus privileged in several distinct regards. But all varying combinations were possible. Late medieval religious, for instance, were commonly accused of being more preoccupied with their noble or university status than their vows. The notion of estate took on over time, in addition, the connotations of an abiding quality, designating not just how things were (social description) but how they ought to be, what rights an estate entailed. Thus a university master remained so in title and claim with or without a good position, a nobleman noble with or without significant wealth, a monk professed with or without virtue, a woman a female person whether or not she had power or education. That was the theory at least. The abiding claims and the contingent realities could well clash in reality, part of the complaint about the estate of the perfect.

Beginning in the thirteenth century thinkers began to speak of an "estate of the perfect" (*status perfectorum*). In a society defined overwhelmingly by religious markers much was at stake conceptually and also concretely in just how this station in life was conceived. Its theological underpinnings went back to late antiquity, grounded in gospel images that converts variously claimed. Christ had enjoined a rich young man, already keeping the commandments to sell all he had and come follow if he would gain treasure in heaven (Matt. 19:16–22). Again, the parable of the sewer described good seed as enjoying a thirty-fold, sixty-fold, or hundred-fold return (Mark 4:20), projecting heavenly rewards for, respectively, laypeople, secular clergy, and the professed. And again, those "apostles" who renounced family on behalf of the kingdom would sit with Christ on the last day as judges, not themselves among the judged (Matt. 19:27–29).[6] The measure of perfection, from Augustine and Gregory to the twelfth century, corresponded to their degree of withdrawal, the married and propertied being tied to the world, the chaste and poor separated for God, the eremetical potentially highest. Twelfth-century reformers reemphasized this withdrawal from worldly society (including traditional monasteries) but also explored the human interior more boldly than ever, William's *Golden Epistle* and Bernard's works continuously influential thereafter (also with the Devout). Choice in religious life also emerged as a reality now. Monks and nuns might move (*transitus*) from one group to another, but only if it were "stricter."

In the thirteenth century friars envisioned a religious vocation not withdrawn from the world, if still apart, a mixed life pursued in the heart of the city, this, they argued, "truly apostolic." They broke with the centuries-old ideal of pure contemplation, only recently reinforced by Cistercians and Carthusians, to conceive religious life as serviceoriented (preaching, teaching, confessing). The three Benedictine vows (stability, obedience, conversion of *mores*) gave way to "poverty, chastity, and obedience," a shift so successful that the latter became known simply as the "three essential marks" (*substantialia*) of religious life. Franciscans forced a rethinking of poverty: True followers of Christ lived hand to mouth. Dominicans introduced new forms of governance, more representative, with legislation generated from the ranks. Revolutionary as was this rethinking of the "perfect" life, it applied almost entirely to males, women (also Dominican nuns) still expected to withdraw into cloistered prayer. Beguines and hospiceworkers engaged in service in the city while living apart religious lives, but with no vows, rendering them vulnerable. Those attacks, as we have noted, were led in part, ironically, by Dominicans. Within two generations mendicant writers molded their vision onto existing rationales in works that entered the mainstream of religious literature as fully as twelfth-century thought had, thus the Dominican master general Humbert of Romans' exposition of the three vows, the Franciscan David of Augsburg's three-part tract on how to "advance" (*Profectus*) in religious life without being confined to a cloister (this highly influential among the Modern-Day Devout).

The friars' challenge provoked surprisingly little response from monks and canons who, admittedly, did not compete in the same sphere and for the same people. Conflict came with the secular clergy, repeatedly and lastingly, in nearly very parish and diocese, over preaching and confessing and burial rights. Popes, after hesitating in the early 1250s, sided with the friars, creating an extraepiscopal force in the church, a well-organized network outside the traditional hierarchy of bishop and parish, also making of medieval friars ardent defenders of papal leadership (or, ardent critics). At the university of Paris, when in the 1250s friars came to occupy three of eight faculty chairs in theology in the 1250s, William of St. Amour, a secular, confronted them head-on: they represented the spearhead not of Christ but of anti-Christ. But friars would largely win this battle, and soon come to dominate faculties of theology at Paris and elsewhere. In 1256–59 and again in 1269–72, however, when the very existence of friars and their redefinition of religious life seemed still on the line, the task of defending them theologically fell to the young Dominican Thomas Aquinas. His arguments, formulated in three apologetic tractates, would gain foundational status. Even more influential, however, was the second part of his *Summa theologie*, which closed with questions on the status of "religion."[7]

Thomas had to define a position that could weave its way through critics attacking from several angles: other religious who located perfection in monastic withdrawal or Franciscan poverty, secular clerics who resented the friars' pastoral and magisterial interference, bishops who saw themselves as head of any hierarchy of perfection. He took as given the notion of estates ordering social life. While his discussion focused on "prelates" and "religious" as the two exemplary estates, the "perfect," he always had the civil forms in mind as well, or even first of all. He defined "estate" accordingly as a life-form sealed by a public solemnity, such as the dubbing of someone into knighthood. He cited etymology ("standing") and law (*Decretum* C.2 q.6 c.40) to interpret estate as representing no accidental attribute—a knight remained a knight whether rich or poor—but a fixed quality to be defined by its inherent obligations or its legal standing. Thus an estate did not refer to acts (which derive from an "office") or to rank (*gradus*) within a group, but to an "abiding condition." Among humans it had first of all, indeed most basically, distinguished persons as either free or in bondage.[8] In spiritual life it then referred to persons either "free of sin" or in bondage. But Thomas also saw in present religious life a gradation from beginners through the advancing to the perfect. In his argument perfection was to be defined and measured ultimately by charity, the love of God and neighbor mandated in the commandments. Hence a definition: an estate of the perfect will be made up of persons who bind themselves by a solemnity to that which makes for perfection, the full pursuit of charity.

This entailed "secondarily and instrumentally" the counsels of perfection, for they helped remove impediments to perfect charity, thus marriage or property getting between a person and love of God.[9] All this rested upon a presumed distinction between commands (*praecepta*) and counsels (*consilia*), the first being precepts enjoined upon all Christians, the second (poverty, chastity, obedience) expectations for the perfect. The notion, though adumbrated earlier, first coalesced in mendicant teaching, not without serious critiques from secular theologians and deep divides among friars themselves.[10] Franciscans wanted to merge the counsels with their own Rule (thus as embodying poverty), while Dominicans struggled to define the exact relation of counsels to commands, some thinking Thomas had gone too far by making counsels "instrumental" rather than "essential" to perfection. He was trying to avoid a singular focus on poverty (Franciscans), while leaving an opening still for prelates and recognizing commands as that which was "essential" for all Christians. To bind one's self to the estate of the perfect, crucially, was no claim in itself to possess perfection but a commitment to pursue it, the three counsels thereafter undertaken under vow (*ideo religionis status requirit ut ad hec tria aliquis uoto obligetur*).[11] As Thomas readily conceded, bad religious and bad prelates existed in each of the estates he counted as "perfect," while people not belonging to either might achieve measures of perfection.[12] He insisted nonetheless that the same act was better and more meritorious (*melius et magis meritorium*) when done under a vow, and for three reasons. It represented prostrate worship (*actus latrie*), but also a person thereby offering more than the act, the whole tree (i.e., person) and not just the fruit, and it thereby hardened the will toward the good (*per uotum immobiliter uoluntas firmatur in bonum*).[13] Persons in the two estates he identified as "perfect," moreover, were not free to leave: prelates being bound to things pastoral, and religious to fulfilling the three counsels. Because others, including priests and deacons, could leave their posts, theirs was not a perfect estate. Since religious, however, were vowed to implement a life of perfection, and pastors only to help others in implementing the good life, the estate of professed religious ranked finally highest.[14] This intricate and ingenious (and self-serving) rationale entered into the mainstream of later medieval thought, becoming vitually a kind of orthodoxy.

From the 1380s onward, however, fundamental objections arose not just to specific practices or institutions (that a medieval constant), but to the very rationale for a separate estate of the religiously perfect. Whatever the simmering disgruntlements of anticlericalism or antimendicantism, it had never boiled over into an attack on the religious estate as such, and never, outside Hussite territories, provoked governments into overt hostile action against them. But the challenge was profound in theory as well as practice. We begin with the secular master at Oxford, John Wyclif (d. 1384).[15] Nearly twenty of his tractates assailed religious, both friars and "possessioners" (monks or other endowed clerics), with ever increasing virulence. This was not an attack upon conversion—living in penance and poverty, in fear and love of God, alms-giving and charity—but upon its perversion by a caste who had turned a public charge into private privilege. About English Wycliffite sermons Gradon and Hudson concluded: "The most frequent subject of polemical attack in the sermons are the new sects, four sects, new religious orders, and the attacks are undoubtedly the lengthiest single subject in these sermons."[16] Not, we might note, the theologically explosive issue of the eucharist or the politically explosive issue of disendowment. The latter, admittedly, was basic: stripping the church materially so it could function spiritually, in practice a proposed handing over of ecclesiastical wealth to civil lordship. "True Christians" articulated their complaint in the Disendowment Bill of 1395, a broadside spread abroad in Latin and English, in this case an attack upon prelates as much as professed religious:

> all the true commoners desire for the worship of God and to the profit of the realm that these worldly clerics, bishops, abbots and priors that are such worldly lords be made to live by their "spiritualities," for they do not live so now, nor do they perform the office of true curates as prelates should, nor do they help either the poor or the commoners by way of their lordships as true secular lords should, nor do they live in penance or by manual labor as true religious should by their profession. . . . the life and evil example of all these has been vicious so long that all the common people, both lords and simple commoners, are now become so vicious and infected through the arrogance (*boldeship*) of their sin that hardly anyone fears God or the Devil.[17]

Wyclif and his followers both presumed and attacked the system of estates, claiming here that the common estates were rendered "vicious" by the vices of what were supposed to be the leading and exemplary estates. Wyclif in time turned decisively against religious orders as such, friars in particular, as "private sects" forming a "private religion" over against what he called a "common Christian religion," assuming here still that more particular notion of "religion." Of this common "Christian religion," he says, Christ was the chief patron, the founding abbot (*Christus abbas tocius christiani ordinis*); any other (Benedict, Francis) merely caused destructive divisions,[18] and came as a Rule added on to the Gospel (*preter religionem domini expressam in ewangelio adinuenta*).[19] Not only added on, their founders were at odds with the only Rule, the "Law of the Lord," essentially Scripture. They even dared to label as heresy any efforts to make them conform to that one pure law.[20] This theme carried into Lollard vernacular sermons: "Sects" put their Rules above the law of Christ (*and so mannys lawe groweth and Godus law is lettyd, and specially by lawis of these newe ordres*).[21] Accordingly, feigned holiness and these private Rules were to be avoided, indeed adjudged "heretical," since their effect was merely to justify privileges in this life.[22] Lollards understood themselves and their "Christian religion" by contrast as the "meek" walking in uprightness with "poor priests" as chosen leaders.[23] Their stance represented at once a critique and a challenge. It repudiated a special estate of the converted or perfect but also assumed and appropriated it—now as realizable in each parish, with Christ as abbot and Gospel law as Rule.

There might conceivably be, Wyclif then conceded in one work, a "private religion" given to this truer end. But a Christian observing Gospel perfection outside the cloister should not then be labeled "worldly" or "lay" (*non dicitur secularis*), for indeed Christ and the apostles had lived this way, in their own personal/private religion outside the cloister (*religio privata secularis sive exclaustralis perfectorum*)[24]—and religion inside or outside the cloister was then in principle equal. Professed religious, he explained, abandoned the "liberty of the law of the Lord" to take on orders and all their accompanying customs.[25] They ought rather now "freely to leave those chains and put on freely the sect of Christ."[26] In the language of Wyclif, then, no other "sect" than Christ's, no other "law" or Rule than the Gospel.[27] Many of those who had entered these "new orders" were in fact, he asserted, unfit for keeping the law of God.[28] So the aim must now be to "convert" the orders to the true sect (*ad puram sectam Cristi . . . convertantur*). This would require a miracle, however, like the conversion of Saul/Paul; better then to "purge" them out (*vel illas evacuet*) and keep the body healthy.[29]

One text, transmitted as both a disputed question and a sermon,[30] went to the heart of the matter. In it Wyclif confronted head-on the command/counsel distinction, arguing instead for a religion of commands foundational to that of counsels (*prima religio sit . . . substrata fundabiliter ad eandem*), with both mandated for any who wholly loved God: thus chastity for each (*cuilibet christiano*), a poverty grounded in the first beatitude, an obedience subject to God, authorities and fellow humans. Private religious had no right to steal the counsels or their rewards from secular priests and the laity. He vigorously attacked their "crappy" arguments (*merdosas argucias*) as to excellence, Thomas being here the target. The "common Christian religion" was what Christ had instituted, the other being established by "uppity false religious" (*religiosiarche*, a term modeled strikingly on heresiarch, a founder of heresy). This "private religion" (orders) was not found in the Gospel. Christ did not mean to cloister his disciples but to send them out. Further, these religious increased anxiety for people with all their extra obligations. The "common Christian religion" (*communis cristiana religio*) was actually more certain, better, lighter.[31] In all this, however, the command/counsels distinction was so firmly in place that Wyclif too essentially emulated it. He considered this "common Christian religion" to include chastity, poverty, and obedience, kept by people as best they could in their circumstances, and dismissed all rival private sects as false. Thirty years after his quiet death, the Council of Constance condemned forty-five errors in the teachings of John Wyclif on 4 May 1415, then damned by papal bull on 22 February 1418. Beyond matters getting prominent attention such as eucharistic teaching (the first three items), papal or episcopal authority and disendowment, five more items, more than a tenth (21–23, 35, 44), singled out his repudiation of religious orders, or as they put it, that "those in private religions are not of the Christian religion (35),"[32] whether or not they really understood his position. This play on words could cut both ways.

Also at the Council of Constance, we must remember, Jean Gerson and Pierre d'Ailly (and eleven others) condemned Friar Matthew Grabow's *Libellus* in April 1418 for, in effect, taking the opposite tack, making "religion" too exclusive. As it turned out, ironically, Gerson more than any other would legitimize the phrase "Christian religion," understood more or less in the sense Wyclif gave it. Gerson too had concerned himself with this question off and on throughout his life, in his case primarily to defend the secular hierarchy, and especially parish priests, his position shifting only slightly as he came to deal first with Wyclif and then Grabow.[33] Very early on, possibly 1393, he issued a quodlibet on the nature of the counsels, drawing from and disagreeing with Thomas, the only academic quodlibet by Gerson to survive.[34] His stance undercut mendicant claims and privileges. "Charity and its commands," he held, "constituted the perfect Christian life." The counsels, he continued, here further exploiting Thomas, were instruments, not ends in themselves (*non intrant essentialem constitutionem uite christiane*). But, turning on Thomas, he insisted that "essential and final perfection" lay in acts rather than in estates or vows.[35] Behind this question probably was some Franciscan claim, for he further insisted that if poverty were essential to Christian perfection, any person with wealth, including popes and prelates, would by definition fall short, as would anyone moving from "strictest poverty" into an office like bishop. The point, he says, was not "usage" (their key term) but desire (*libido*). In Paradise humans were perfect and yet acted as lords. Abraham and Lot too were perfect, and had wives and children. Poverty, abstinence, fasting, and all the rest should be called "punishments" (*penalitates*) rather than virtues.[36]

Gerson then contradicted Thomas even more fundamentally but without naming him. Since essential spiritual perfection consists in the keeping of commands and exercising of virtues, that obligation surpasses and is more efficacious than any obligation attached to vows. The counsels are useful but not required since "perfect people" are found in every estate, gender, and rank. Vows are mere "instruments" to "Christian" life[37]—an ironic twist on Thomas. Gerson was traditionalist enough to concede one key Thomistic point, however, that there was greater merit in acting under vow. But he also held that a pope could dispense from a vow of religion.[38] The reverse opinion was widely held, especially by lawyers, and employed as a powerful argument for the superiority of religious life: even popes could not dispense from vows. Next Gerson the secular theologian silently and daringly reversed Thomas again to rebut nearly two centuries of mendicant preeminence: The estate of those "exercising" perfection as sacerdotal ministers was more perfect than that of those "acquiring" it as religious; hence the "most perfect estate" in the church was that of bishops. It afterall required a "perfect man" intent upon radiating good to others, not someone still acquiring it for himself.[39] A further reversal followed: since curates stood next in rank to bishops, they were also more perfect in estate than religious, also requiring a more "perfect man" to fulfill them. More, they held a kind of ordinary jurisdiction within their parish, which oriented them to the common good while religious looked only to their private good[40]—an unprecedented elevation of curates with respect to vowed religious.

The estate of curates, he further held, quite innovatively, was instituted directly by Christ (that is, not mediately by the pope). Therefore, while religious vows could be dispensed (being an ecclesiastical arrangement), the pope could not abolish the estate of curate, nor suspend rightful subjection to them. Christ himself had authorized (in the sending of the seventy-two disciples, Luke 10:8) that parishioners be "hierarchized" by their curates.[41] Gerson thus elevated the "estate of curate" to a place of perfection second only to bishops (an estate, incidentally, hardly noted in canon law as such, the word itself "curate," common only from the fourteenth century). As with Wyclif's poor priests and true Christians across the channel, the enemy were the vowed religious seeking private good and having the effrontery to call their estate perfect. The perfect life, the keeping of the law and exercising of the virtues, sprang from parish life and the curate.

Gerson returned to this theme twenty five years later (1418) when he wrote his advisory against Grabow at Constance, fulminating against the friar and elaborating upon the same basic arguments. Five years later still (1423) Gerson was still brooding on this, now in a dialogue between the "soul" and a "theologian" on "purity of heart."[42] He now declared that everyone baptized and in a state of grace was in the "estate of eternal salvation and the Christian religion, that estate . . . to be held as perfect."[43] As with Wyclif, the counsels could not simply be avoided, however. Every priest by his promise of chastity was in an estate of perfection; no voluntary vow added anything more to it or to the baptismal vow. As for obedience, everyone owed it to "the supreme abbot Christ"[44] (same phrase as Wyclif!). As for poverty, it was a matter of the heart; that is, of intention or desire, most religious in any case abusing ownership in one way or another, as he saw it (and many in this era, also among the religious: Observants). This yielded one estate of the Christian religion under one abbot, thus also one estate of the perfect.[45] All Christians from baptism entered an estate of "exercising" and "acquiring," this not peculiar to the professed religious—a direct rebuttal of Thomas, as was the idea that curates were bound to their charges by vow.[46] Gerson applied this to the laity as well, they pursuing chastity within marriage, being poor in spirit, obedient in ways appropriate to worldly affairs.[47] Indeed he explored this even more explicitly in some ways than Wyclif had. Gerson pushed harder than anyone before him, entirely within orthodoxy, for a singular "Christian religion" under Abbot Christ as the "perfect estate."

About the time that Wyclif had taken up this theme, Coluccio Salutati, the first humanist chancellor of Florence, wrote a lengthy work in 1381/82 "On the world and religion," an exposition setting out the woes of this world and the advantages of life in religion, this particularly for a friend who had entered the Camaldulensian house in Florence.[48] The work, once dismissed as a rhetorical exercise, linked by Witt to a dark time in his circumstances, in fact endorses the traditional case for religious profession as a superior form of life. Few make it safely through the "perverse customs" of our time, he says—these set out by Salutati with an eye to the temptations of Italian cities and political or literary ambitions—even though the promises of baptism alone could lead perfectly to God (*plene quidem, si rite servetur, via perfectionis ad deum*). Obligating one's self as a cleric is an ampler way (*plenior*). But amplest of all (*plenissima perfectio*) is to take vows and offer up a sacrifical holocaust of the self, the way to a hundred-fold harvest[49]—a full echo of Thomas and the tradition. Doing good apart from vows is good; doing good under vows more meritorious, offering the whole tree with the fruit[50]—still another echo. Interestingly, Salutati knew, and dismissed, countervailing voices, here labeled "raving" (*delirantes*), people arguing that more is actually owed someone acting out of free will than anyone acting under religious obligation.[51] Salutati as a lay humanist—unless we are to read this as entirely tongue-in-cheek (which the rhetoric really will not support)—upheld what Wyclif and Gerson, from slightly different angles, were trying at the same time to undermine.

Another Italian humanist, Lorenzo Valla, wrote a dialogue "On the Profession of the Religious" about 1441, probably directed against Observant Franciscans, possibly San Bernardino. This work, addressed to a lay magistrate, attacked the estate of the professed as such, in sharp and elegant prose. The professed were not "religious" but a "sect," people who withdrew to think and live apart from others, the term here echoing schools of philosophers in the antique world. What is a "religious" if not a "true Christian"?[52] Why add a "second promise" to that made at baptism to live an upright and holy life?[53] Why beg from others for your living? Better not to give up all you have, and carry out your duties in society![54] Valla fully understood what was at stake. He disputed any view that vows entailed greater merit and a greater reward. The vow itself was only an oath creating a legal bond. The professed may in fact deserve less reward, for they pursue virtue entirely under obligation (the position Salutati dismissed as crazy). What can be the point of vows except to bind the bad?[55]—a witty jab at his mendicant adversary. Valla also challenged the friar's individual vows. Afterall, the apostles, for instance, were married. And he poked at their sense of privilege.[56] True "brothers," Valla concluded (playing on the Franciscans' title), were those whose "declaiming" called men and women from vice, freed them from bad views, led them to piety and learning[57]—what Valla and people like him could do as well or better without vows. We must allow here for witty jibes at religious, for rivalry between humanists and friars. But Valla held these views on conviction, and reiterated them when called to account for them three years later: "I think that all who observe the Christian religion are 'religious', and the professed are not right in saying that they alone are 'religious', when others may well be, indeed are no less than they."[58]

During the same years the Modern-Day Devout emerged (1380–1440), then, a searing critique of religious claims to perfection arose across a wide spectrum, articulated by, in our terms, a heretic, an orthodox reformer, and a humanist. The Devout fastened on to Gerson's position, knowing little specifically about Wyclif's, and generally acted more than they theologized. But John Pupper was an exception.

John Pupper of Goch (d. 1475)

John (Johan, Jan) Pupper came from the town of Goch, then in the duchy of Guelders, born into a burgher family called "Capupper."[59] Our only personal account describes him as a good scribe, an excellent illuminator, a good cleric (meaning, a "learned book-man"), and an outstanding preacher. He likely came into contact with the Devout through schooling at Deventer or Zwolle, but appears first as one of four clerics who together with three priests constituted the men's society at Amersfoort in 1442.[60] After a decade in Amersfoort, perhaps more, John was ordained a priest and in 1451 sent to Gouda, a house not yet part of the Colloquy but in need of a good preacher. There a society had been founded in 1425 when a priest left his house behind the main city church to two to four persons charged with preaching to the city's people on feast days and after Sunday vespers (whence its later name, the "collation-house")[61] City magistrates confirmed this arrangment in 1447, invoking the model of Deventer and Zwolle.[62] Hendrik Herp, rector at Delft (1440–46) and then at Gouda (1446–50), an eloquent and industrious man, made a success of it, his sermons well received. The house itself expanded by six rooms (*cellulas*), though it remained poor, and they engaged in copywork for survival.[63] In the jubilee year (1450), however, Herp decamped for Rome and there became an observant Franciscan.[64] Those left at Gouda saw his change of estate as "weak-souled."[65]

John Pupper, the new head (1451–54), had a hard time. The one remaining senior priest found him unsuited for the job and left for Delft, lest the "cart be pulled badly by two unequally yoked oxen."[66] The house was desperately poor, demoralized by Herps's departure, not yet formally a part of the Brothers' Colloquy. John himself began to doubt, persisted nonetheless, and personally worked hard at copying books.[67] His preaching, however, upset the local clergy and people, quite in contrast to Herp's.[68] Dirk of Herxen tried in November 1453 to intervene: The Brothers needed clothing, food and drink, their daily necessities, he explained to the city aldermen, John being now the only person capable of real labor. As for any tensions, John was only doing, as they heard it, what was expected of him.[69] In the house meanwhile one fellow-priest died of illness, one cleric went home sick to his parents, another left to join Herp and the Franciscans. John alone remained, now truly despondent. He had arrived in mid-June 1451 and departed in late June 1454. His last public sermon lashed out at the people of Gouda for their lack of support.[70] He then left to do other things (*transferens se ad alia*), the chronicler says. By December he had matriculated at the university in Cologne as a law student.[71] How long he stayed, a year or two, is not known. He subsequently served as father-confessor to a house of Tertiaries, presumably in Sluis.[72] During this time he also came into control of the family residence in Goch, its proceeds subsequently left to a house of canonesses where his sister (probably) had professed.[73]

In 1459 John Pupper—Brother, preacher, university student, father-confessor—moved with thirteen Sisters to Malines, where they set up an enclosed house of Augustinian canonesses called Tabor (the Mount of Transfiguration), dedicated as well to Augustine (John's favorite theologian) and Agnes (common among the Devout). A local citizen handed over the site—a house and property on the city wall just outside the Nun's Gate, purchased from the head mistress of the beguines—in November 1359, the women were granted the right to choose their own priest.[74] In 1463 Pope Pius II awarded it all privileges associated with Windesheim though it was not formally a part of the congregation, this arranged by the head of the Brothers' house in Brussels, presumably at John's urging. In 1470 the founding citizen tried to limit the original endowment to local Sisters, thus to exclude John and the thirteen women from Sluis. Whatever had sparked that action, John in fact died and was buried there, in November 1375, though remembered still in Amersfoort as one of their Brothers.[75] According to one chronicle, during his sixteen years he had professed sixty-six nuns, along with nine *conversae* and four *donatae*, with five novices and ten "schoolgirls" present at his death.[76] Whatever his occasional personal troubles in Gouda or Malines, he must have proved an inspiring organizer and preacher.

John was gripped by theology. In Malines, free beyond his duties to the women, he wrote assiduously, though, alas, no manuscripts survive. Foppens (1739), mostly relying on Valerius Andreas (1623), who built on a lost work of Johannes Bunderius (d. 1557), ascribed six works to him.[77] One complete work, one incomplete work, a letter, and various fragments exist in early editions, some printed in the 1520s already by a humanist evangelical, Cornelius Grapheus. As a result John Pupper of Goch is known to scholars, if at all, almost exclusively as a "pre-reformer." This is unhelpful. He was a Brother through and through: member of a society, copying books for survival, ministering to women, preaching to people, living an ascetic life probably from schooldays onward. John, fascinated by a range of current theological issues, was utterly driven by ideas, also by the issue of status or estate in "religion."[78] What we have, however, is fragmentary, with all evidence about his work internal to it.[79]

The only complete work still extant is a *Dialogue* (*Dialogus de quattuor erroribus circa legem euangelicam exortis et de religionibus facticiis*). Its preface refers to a "brother" (*uestra fraternitas*) who had alerted him by letter to querulous types contending that any perfect observance of the evangelical law, indeed of apostolic life in the early church, required an obligatory vow.[80] This Brother urgently sought (*expostulare*: a strong word) a written response to an issue described here as once buried but now again current (*recentes*).[81] John's work, written as a fraternal aid (*modo fraterne informationis*), and in dialogue form to make it easier for readers, offered a strong rebuttal which would not, he knew, please all. We may find an interpretative key in its dialogue format: "soul" (*anima*) asking short questions or raising objections and "spirit" (*spiritus*) supplying lengthy and learned answers. The soul's queries expose the issues at stake.[82] Four sorts of error now obscured the proper realization of Gospel law, John contended. Some people would impose a "Mosaic law" on Christ's liberty; but observing Gospel law alone, he countered, sufficed to achieve perfection—this probably a jibe aimed at overly rigorous and coercive churchmen. But others say that faith and baptism alone suffice, a view often attributed to the easy-going baptized; people must however, John insisted, also *will* and *do* the good, exercise *interior* and *exterior* acts of faith, the Brother speaking here.[83] Still others imagine they can do good by natural virtue and effort alone (*potentia naturalis*), his rendering of certain Free Spirit or related ideas. Such false teachings, he says, have "poisoned" many, especially women (*multas*) who "display an insupportable rigor" in their practices, offering extravagant promises and an impetuous spirit, driven by a "reasoning appetite" more human than divine, in reality comprised of a natural love; and who thus "burn out their labors in vain."[84] How then to discern proper love (q. 5)? When love appears sufficient to itself or makes a great display, it is human and mercenary.[85] When it is born aloft by something greater than natural power, forgetful of itself and of reward, dissolved (*resoluitur*) into the one it loves, that love has taken on divine form—this a place where John seems to speak from his own experience or desires, and yet ironically to echo not only Ruusbroec but distantly, as the Devout did from time to time, other aspirants from the generation around 1300.[86]

All this leads to the fourth error, it being, he says, the error of our time (*error nostris temporis*), and "comporting in many ways with the Pelagian heresy." These people recognize interior and exterior acts of faith but impose on the interior (and its liberty) an obligatory vow, claiming that Gospel law cannot be achieved perfectly apart from vows—a pharisaic superstition.[87] John had an opponent in mind (*sicut uos dicitis, quero a uobis*), alluding to Thomas Aquinas as "your false leader" (*princeps erroris uestri*) for holding that a vow hardens people in the good.[88] In truth, John says, it only constrains the will under law and destroys gospel liberty. Will (q. 6) is the way to God, not the intellect as Thomists say; and humans conform more closely to the divine will the more they act in freedom of will.[89] This extended to seeing God (*non intuitiuam cognitionem intellectus quam fruitiuam cognitionem uoluntatis*) as well as to human knowing, a wisdom born of the affections here set against a science of cognition.[90] But can this hold if God in fact comes to humans with commands and vows, thus even the yoke that bound Jesus to death on the Father's will (q. 7–10)? John Pupper here boldly set a "liberty of spirit directed by the yoke of charity" (*libertatem spiritus iugo charitatis dirigatur*) against any "thousand vows" as well as any form of "monastic discipline." Like "feathers on a wing" this "yoke" would elevate to God in "true liberty."[91] It referred to what Zerbolt had called the "obedience of love."

But why the objection to vows? Were not Christians already uniformly obligated by baptismal vows (q. 11)? Promising the faith and keeping the commands were required for salvation, but John pointed beyond to a free offering (*libera et spontanea oblatio*) which "no more diminished gospel liberty of the will than did the obligation to observe gospel law."[92] It was essential to distinguish an "obligation of the will" undertaken by vow, with or without grace, by sinners as well as the virtuous, from an "oblation of the will," choosing the good in a free offering moved by grace. This was the fundamental point of opposition, and it was the church, John asserted, not the Saviour, that established vows binding the will (q. 13–14). So how can "doctors" say that obligating vows may "improve" people and generate good? In truth this happens only when people offer themselves in freedom, through a love informed by grace. Coercion as such (*necessitas coactionis que fit per obligationem uoti ad bonum*) was not necessarily bad, John actually conceded, but less good than whatever is done in freedom (q. 16), a "supernatural and free conversion of the will to God."[93] After setting out his central point he treated "nine conclusions," in practice cases pertinent to the "freedom of the Christian religion." Were, for instance, religious not more perfect than simple priests since they renounced all property (q. 17–18)? Could the highest rewards of Christian religion be earned in every estate when chastity could not be exercised in the state of the married (q. 19)? John appended last a discussion of communal life, probably independent in origin since it alone was not cast in dialogue format.

By contrast John Pupper's *Freedom of the Christian Religion*[94] has a more formally theological character, its "books" referred to internally as "*distinctiones.*" First published in 1521, it lacks roughly two and one-half books. At least in the version that went into print, it came with no prefatory letter, was written in sequence (he refers back within it), and broke off part way into the fourth *distinctio*, just after setting out his most novel claim. Six parts were planned, announced in the introduction (future-tense verbs: *erit*).[95] He meant this work—given its scope and ambition, its structure and language—as a theological testament, a learned summing-up (expository, not disputational) of his stance on religious life. To understand the work, it may usefully be approached in reverse.

The sixth part was going to refute the tractate of a Friar Engelbert (see below). The fifth was to treat, as the culmination of his theological argument, difference or sameness in the acts of vowing and not vowing, his rubric provocative in itself, given common assumptions about the radical distinctness of those acts and their resultant estates and rewards.[96] The fourth (partially extant) treats vows as such, the third the nature of merit, the second the will and human acts, and the first the authority of Scripture. The point of the work was to resist false teaching, and the proper way to do that, John contends, was not through disputation but with a word from Scripture, not with philosophical questions but fraternal admonition, something he claims to have learned from Paul and Augustine.[97] His argument about Scripture has often been made a focal point of interpretation (looking forward to the Reformation), but it was prefatory (*ea que premissa sunt placuit anteferre*), meant to pull the rug out from under "modern doctors." His treatment of nature and grace (II) argued for the unity of the human soul, the primacy of will, the identity of charity and grace, and the need for grace ("acceptance") in meritorious acts—positions that put him on both "modern" and "Augustinian" sides in contemporary debate, without his belonging overtly to any school. The third book, on merit, refuted the view ("philosophical opinion") that merit was an act for which reward is justly owed, this position attributed explicitly to Thomas. From "canonical truth" John offered his own teaching, a mix of Augustinian grace and Franciscan "acceptance." The fourth turned finally to vows as a "special act of the human will," and here objections raised by "Thomists" appear often, directly and indirectly. This, theologically, is what he was moving toward refuting or replacing.

Beyond these two major works (and a host of fragments) John wrote a *Letter,* printed twice, first in 1520, that edition possibly based on a manuscript copy in his own hand.[98] As he tells it, he had been sent a *libellus*, a "little book" written by a Dominican "against the liberty of the Christian religion." John's response, ten dense pages, proceeded in two substantive parts. He asserted the authority of "canonical truth" over against teachings and opinions from philosophers and masters, a position developed systematically in *distinctio* I of *De libertate*, aimed in part at Thomas, apparently cited repeatedly in the little book.[99] Aristotle did not possess the "light of truth" and "modern-day masters" (*doctores moderni*) strayed, he noted, leaving the writings of friars mere opinions resting on philosophy. John then refuted the erroneous view, an effort to submit Gospel liberty to the necessity of obligation, what we have already encountered as systematically explored in both the *Dialogue* and *De liberate.*[100] All hinged on his core theme: "Gospel law was instituted from the beginning in liberty of spirit, and has never been meritoriously kept by anyone except in liberty of spirit." To fulfill Gospel law, to gain acceptance from God, one must act in the same liberty of love with which Christ redeemed humans, not out of any necessitating obligation.[101]

We have three vague internal clues to the chronology of these works. Toward the end of part I of *De libertate* John alluded to a theological battle at the university of Louvain in "our time" (*nostris temporibus*).[102] Its topic was future contingents: did Jesus's knowing that Peter would betray him make that event inevitable? The dispute pitted a master of theology (Henry Someren) against a master of arts (Peter de Rivo), with hints of a double-truth charge (things true according to "faith" but not according to "Aristotle"), all this launched by a quodlibet in 1465, the controversy crescendoing into the 1470s. In July 1470 the rector of the university intervened to try clear away the quarrels (*materia iurgiorium*) and especially to halt "scandal" and "rumor."[103] This, though hardly the end of the matter, was roughly what John echoed in *distinctio* I (widespread agitation, with most masters aligned against Someren). So John was at work on "Freedom of the Christian Religion" sometime after 1470/71 and would complete at least three and one-half more distinctions before his death in November 1475. Second, Grapheus reported of the *epistola* in 1520 that it was written "forty-six" years earlier, thus in 1474 (n. 98 above). This claim likely reflected a colophon in the manuscript, or possibly some detail omitted in publication. Most scholars agree, third, that the Friar Engelbert whom John intended to refute in the sixth part of *De libertate* was Engelbertus Cultificis. Engelbert (ca. 1420–90/91) "Knifemaker" (Messemaker) came from Zutphen, belonging to a burgher family as his name suggests. He and his brother John both joined the Dominican house there, probably in the 1440s, if not earlier.[104] In 1461 he was resident there as a bachelor in theology, and from 1465 served as its lector and promoted the introduction of strict Observance. In 1468 he was named prior in Groningen, a convent he helped found. In short, Engelbert was an educated local Dominican active in the home region of the Devout; his writings and stance would have come to their attention. Two of his works survive, both later and not directly pertinent to what John sought to refute. Any work John meant to rebut has not survived or not been identified. But it plainly defended vows as such with the help of Thomas, and to the Brothers appeared an actual or perceived threat.[105] Since Clemens' work more than a century ago, no one has tried seriously to unscramble or recontextualize all this evidence. I will propose a new ordering of the works.

Apart from broad swipes at philosophizing "modern doctors" and "Thomists," John tended to use differing words for his adversaries. The Letter referred to a "*Libellus*" by an unnamed Dominican friar, the *Dialogue* to "falsifiers of

Scripture" and "recent errors," and *De libertate* to a "*tractatus*" written by a Friar Engelbert.[106] Both the *Letter* and the *Dialogue* were addressed to a "brother" (*uestra fraternitas, fraterne informationis*). While "your brotherhood" and "your charity" were common enough medieval address-forms, it seems quite likely that the *Letter* and *Dialogue* were addressed to the same person, a Brother in the Devout network. This man knew Scripture (*canonica scriptura nota est*) but was shaken by the *Libellus* and had turned to John for theological help (*fraterne necessitatis subsidium postulatum*). The "*Libellus*" may be none other than Matthew Grabow's, a copy resurfacing some fifty years later with or without title and author. It fits the description: a work "upsetting" to the Brothers, described here indeed as "volatile and foolish," based on Thomistic authority, with the beginning of the *Dialogue* capturing Grabow's argument well,[107] as does the allusion to a "poison" once buried and now rising again. John also protested that he meant not to go against any determination of the church or better understanding (possibly echoing his knowledge of Constance), but spoke here only as one brother instructing another.[108] Between the *Letter* and the *Dialogue*, moreover, we have one verbal link, his bold phrase about a "thousand vows" counting for nothing if not done in "liberty of spirit."[109] Neither derived from the other; this was a phrase in John's head, pithy in the *Letter*, worked out and contextualized in the *Dialogue*. The *Letter* may have represented John Pupper's first reaction to reading the *Libellus*, the *Dialogue* a more considered response at greater length written in a more accessible format.[110] The latter work also appended notes on the "common life," which would be pertinent to Grabow's attack.

But what then of Friar Engelbert and the "Freedom of the Christian Religion"? With no prefatory letter, written in a far more formal theological style, this work represented a deliberate effort to respond to someone who was, remember, a bachelor in theology (from Erfurt, it seems) and the lector in a convent. Here John did not write to aid a distraught or troubled Brother, not in dialogue format, but to speak as one theologian to another (though he lacked formal training), one "tractate" answering another on the subject of vows. Engelbert may himself have been set off by a revived reading of Grabow's *Libellus*. Or, amid so many Brothers and Sisters and Tertiaries in towns all around him, he may have resolved to write anew on vows and their theological legitimacy and necessity, this then likely in the later 1460s. John Pupper's "Freedom of the Christian Religion" was written in the last three or four years of his life (1471/75), his latter years thus consumed by the question of what was required to fulfill "Gospel law" perfectly, in particular what form of life.

Gospel Law and the Freedom of the Christian Religion

When John Pupper referred to the "Christian religion," like Wyclif and Gerson he engaged in a play on words. The immediate point of comparison was not "Jewish" religion but "Franciscan" or "Dominican" or "Benedictine." Even more complexly, where we refer to "the religion" of Christians or Muslims or Jews, later medieval writers in nearly all languages would have referred to their "law."[111] That term signified the divine norms inherent in the universe and especially their written articulation, Torah or Koran or Scriptures. For medieval Christians this was God's own lawbook, trumping human law, even papal constitutions. Wyclif and the Lollards therefore invoked the law of God or Christ (*lex Dei, lex Christi*) to impeach all they found wrong with church and society in their day, as did John Hus (usually *lex Dei*). What came with the Gospel in other words was "law" (*lex*), a way of life with its set of defining expectations, for John Pupper "Gospel law" (*lex euangelica*). Whether "law" referred to the religious community as a whole together with its norms (thus the "law" of the "paynim" meaning Muslims and their religion), or more particularly to its authorizing holy book, was often ambiguous. Medieval Christians came under this law (both senses) as infants by virtue of the "sacrament of faith," baptism obligating them to the biblical commandments together with church prescriptions.

Friar Thomas Aquinas saw law in general (eternal, divine, natural, human) as "ordering human conduct (*conuersatio*) to a certain end." He treated "old law" (Moses), then "new" (*De lege noua scilicet euangelii*), before taking up grace and merit to round out section one in the second part of his *Summa*, as "religion" would subsequently round out section two, the culmination of each part.[112] "New law," according to Thomas, was principally the grace of the Holy Spirit which disposed a person to believe and act upon the New Testament, itself the written expression of "new law" (q. 106 a.1). Here Thomas drew extensively on Augustine's *On the Letter and the Spirit*, as John would. The "estate of the new law" (*status noue legis*), Thomas held, was more perfect and lighter than the old (q. 107 a.4: "My yoke is easy"), indeed most perfect since the grace of the Spirit would never be more perfectly present in any other *status* (q. 106 a.4), thus sharply ruling out a third estate or law of the Spirit as Joachim had envisioned. Even if Paul called the Spirit free (Rom. 8:2, 1 Cor. 3:17), certain acts still came with this new law. The Spirit's grace was present in people fundamentally, however, as an enabling "habitus" infused within, disposing them to act rightly.[113] While this new law could in itself "sufficiently order" acts inwardly and outwardly to secure a person's eternal end, Gospel law nonetheless proposed specific counsels (poverty, chastity, obedience) as ways to attain that end better and more efficiently (*melius et expeditius*), not necessary commands but options (*in optione*: q.108 a.4).

The truly meritorious, John Pupper declared by contrast, operated out of gospel liberty; it was the weak who acted under vow. His *Letter* articulated the key themes in all their complex tensions:

> No one can keep the Gospel law meritoriously except in liberty of spirit—and no wonder, because the Gospel law is the law of love. But no one is able to love except in liberty of will, for no one can be compelled to love. Someone can be compelled to live in continence, not to possess anything of his own, to obey someone's command. But no one can be compelled to love, for love proceeds from will and grace, which are its generative principles, and especially free, and therefore what comes from love cannot be otherwise than free. Yet it is necessary for each to love who must keep the Gospel law.[114]

The early Christian community, as he read the book of Acts, had moved to a "perfect keeping of the Gospel law and a charitable sharing of all property in a communal life" solely by the grace of the Holy Spirit, with no vows.[115] Gospel law worked fundamentally as a law of the heart or the intentional will (*lex cordis, idest deliberatiue uoluntatis*), not as a "Mosaic law" of deeds or an enslaved will. Even if the term refers to deeds written up by the evangelists to teach the "life and way of life of the faithful in the Christian religion,"[116] one should not confuse a law of charity written on the heart with, as he says, works of charity written in dead letters. This failed to grasp the enormous distance between doing something good on command, and doing the good well in love.[117] A person truly pursuing Gospel law cannot operate out of fear or subjection, only out of charity and from within, "and this charity is none other than God the Holy Spirit," thus a law "not written or writable" (a direct attack upon "Thomists").[118] To this Gospel law all are called, not just an elite, and it is a law of love, of "perfect liberty" which cannot abide "necessitating obligation." Put simplest, Gospel law is the will of God in Christ and the "rule of the Christian religion"; arising from the free will of Christ, it is by definition free.[119] Amid the density of theological argument his vision of the converted life as a free and gracious act permeates the whole, set against a perceived world of privileged lawful religion.

There follows the other key point: Only a will informed by charity and acting in liberty can win merit, merit, especially eternal merit, still being an essential consideration. Vows, with their obligating necessity, could not yield merit except incidentally, by providing an occasion for acting well.[120] John Pupper challenged, beyond his Dominican adversaries, any assumption that taking vows was *per se* meritorious.[121] Vows were nothing but a law added (*superadditum*) by the church (*positiua constitutio*) to the original "Christian religion" to force exterior observance,[122] whereas "Christian religion" was most perfectly observed without vows in liberty of spirit.[123] The founder (*institutor*) of this religion was Christ; what got generated was the Gospel law; and its end was to have human wills conform to the divine.[124] To keep the Gospel law according to the "perfection of a made-up religion" (*secundum perfectionem religionum facticiarum*) hardly represented the highest perfection, which was to cling to God as an act of will and love. The former was merely fulfilling a Rule.[125] Likewise, to possess nothing of your own, or like Franciscans nothing personally or in common, was not the perfection of Christian religion. To have no will to possess anything at all, a will liberated from earthly affections and dissolved in God, that was the perfection of the Christian religion. Such a will was possible, moreover, in every estate in life, whence the highest reward, eternal beatitude, could be merited in every estate.[126] For an "interior act of preparation" was possible in every estate, and it brought reward.[127] Merit was not the privilege of the vowed.

John Pupper, though theologically engaged, was a man nestled in devotion and preaching more than the disputes of the schools, with a sense of the supernatural closer to the *via moderna* than the *via antiqua*. For him the will, not the intellect, was the determinative human faculty. Here he stood with Franciscan theologians and Italian humanists, and also with the assumptions that drove Devout practice. Evil impulses in the flesh were in themselves not worthy of punishment; an evil will (*malum uero uoluntatis*) conjoined to them yielded sin.[128] Grace liberated the will from evil desire and rendered it fit for the reward of eternal beatitude.[129] This grace, he argued repeatedly against "philosophers and logicians" on the strength of "canonical truth," was no habitus planted in the soul to generate virtue but the very Holy Spirit poured into hearts as "charity" to animate the will, invoking here, as had Augustine, Rom. 5:5 ("the love of God is shed abroad in our hearts by the Holy Ghost which is given unto us").[130] Grace was the same as charity (*gratia est idem quod charitas*: a debated point, known to all theologians by way of Lombard's *Sentences*), infused in the soul directly by the third person of the Trinity.[131] John, deeply and consciously indebted to Paul and Augustine, especially the anti-Pelagian works, derided those "in our times" who thought they could "cooperate" in effecting justifying grace.[132] This may seem paradoxical for a Brother determinedly holding out for a converted lifestyle. But he also imagined a free Almighty at work directly in individual hearts, not a world with the divine embedded in metaphysical and ecclesiastical structures, in vows or in habitus. The result of the human-divine interaction as he perceived it was an "ingratiated will" (*gratuita uoluntas*), instilled with supernatural movement free of coercion and sin, a liberty to love with a power to act.[133] He wanted, or perceived, two spiritual realities at once: an act of offering to God that was entirely free, not necessitated by a vow or an estate in society, coming from the heart, a deliberating will; and the direct presence of the Spirit as the third person of the triune God "gracing" that heart with the love and power to act.

As for acts as such, some are purely good (if they arise from charity), some purely evil (if they arise from concupiscent desire), many somewhere inbetween, to be judged entirely by their "inner intent," not their "exterior act"—this last especially true of those making a great show of religion with their vows and orders.[134] Recent historians have made much of a certain "reckoning-up" mentality in late medieval religion, amassing prayers or relics as a heavenly wager or divine insurance policy. John Pupper denounced this merchant mentality. Reward came only, he said, from an "ingratiated will" and intent.[135] Taking a vow did not make an individual act a rewardable good or of greater merit, no matter what people commonly said (*solet uulgariter dici*)[136]—this aimed directly at Thomas (or Engelbert or Matthew), but also at widespread popular attitudes which underpinned an estate system. No one can truly "merit," John Pupper asserted, unless acts of will were entirely free, done under no coercion—the theological underpinning for the Devout way of life. Yet, ultimately, this was fully possible for only one person, Christ. Merit therefore rested finally upon divine acceptance. This actually placed John Pupper closer to the "modernist" and ultimately Franciscan wing of late medieval theology.[137] Here we find in reality a mix, perhaps peculiar to the Later Middle Ages, of anxious effort and ultimate reliance. Given the paltriness of human acts in the face of the divine, all hung upon the sheer will of God. For most the mix of effort and reliance produced—and also reflected—uncertainty, whether a person was worthy of love or hatred from God, rendering the spirit anxious and the heart troubled, as John Pupper himself eloquently articulated it.[138] After looking into that abyss, he insisted still upon the centrality of an acting subject. No one would be rewarded with eternal beatitude who had not done meritorious acts of virtue, given faculty and opportunity, even if Christ was the only one who could truly merit it as owed justice (*ex condigno*).[139] This was the spiritual world of the Modern-Day Devout. Life turned on a resolution and continuing conversion in an act of willing love; yet the ultimate outcome rested with God, his acceptance.

John Pupper of Goch was driven by the question of vows, together with freedom, grace and merit, but he first caught the attention of nineteenth-century scholars for his supposed "reformation-like" stance on the authority of Scripture.[140] His *Letter* spoke of a "single canonical and catholic truth founded on prophetic and apostolic foundations," and set it against writings that confused and divided the mind, chiefly scholastic authors.[141] He intended to speak only from eternally guaranteed witnesses.[142] But there was nothing new about asserting a "primacy" for Scripture. Masters of theology taught Scripture as their ordinary textbook, along with sayings of the fathers organized topically (Peter Lombard's *Sentences*). What that meant in practice varied by time and institution; but scriptural teaching enjoyed a revival in the fourteenth century, marked by Nicholas of Lyra's massive commentary (used by John), also Wyclif's resolve to comment on the whole of it.[143] As for Scripture's position in the church, nearly all discussants (also John) took as their point of departure the exposition of that issue in the textbook for canon law. The first quotation in his *Letter* was a direct citation from it, unacknowledged (also unrecognized by editors).[144] John would have learned it as a student of canon law in Cologne. The failure to recognize that John was citing canon law to prove the authority of Scripture has produced some ironic historical interpretations. In any case, Gratian had set out a hierarchy of authorities, equating Scripture with the divine will and divine law, all other laws therefore yielding to it, as did commentators on Scripture.[145] Marginal glosses from the twelfth century—known to all students and practitioners of church law—became even firmer in distinguishing canonical scripture, which could not err, from other writers including Augustine, who could.[146] This still left unresolved many issues both practical and principial: If Scripture was the principial source, what were people to do about other "traditions" not attested there (thus, vows)? Who determined Scripture's meaning for the church, masters of theology (= professors of Scripture) or bishops as apostolic successors (the pope as vicar of Christ)?[147] John Pupper, neither master nor bishop, here undertook to interpret Scripture independently on an issue that moved him and indeed all Sisters and Brothers, that of vows and Christian freedom.[148] For him scholastic and devotional writings acquired authority only as they could be "brought back" (*reductio*) to Scripture, it alone having "unquestionable authority," even as philosophical teachings, he analogized, were brought back to truth by checking them against first principles.[149] In practice this rendered an accepted medieval principle edgy and polemical. Amid a welter of opinions, blamed partly on exegesis, mostly on philosophers, he sought "certitude" and the intent of canonical scripture.[150]

Already as a brother at Amersfoort and Gouda John Pupper would have sunk deep into "holy writings" (*sacra scriptura*). Master Geert's reading list began with the Gospels,[151] and in house customaries treating "the study of holy writings (*sacre scripture*)" Brothers were exhorted: "Let us therefore be diligent and constant in the study of holy writings, each of us having with him some book from the Bible (*canonica*) or some other genuine and approved writing (*aut alias autentica uel probata scriptura*)," to read every day, setting aside at least an hour for this.[152] We find among the Devout an impulse, attested since Grote, to have "*originalia*," whole texts of authors, not just excerpts. At the core of John Pupper's reading stood the Bible in Nicolas of Lyre's giant gloss along with works by Augustine, referring at one point to what could be found "throughout" one book (*Augustinus per totum librum de littera et spiritu diffuse prosequitur*).[153] From a "literal reading" (*litteralis expositio*) of Acts on the early church he found no vows.[154] At issue, he said repeatedly, was how to read Paul and Augustine, and he read them according to their "intention." Seeing himself in a cosmos of potentially unfettered divine power and nearly unfettered ecclesiastical power, amid confusions wrought by modern masters on issues as sensitive as grace and merit, he sought an "infallible source" for knowing.[155]

John opened his "Freedom of the Christian Religion" by citing and elaborately reinterpreting the text (*Vovete et reddite* = Vow and render unto the Lord, Ps. 75:12–76:11) standardly invoked as giving warrant for vows. But religious vows did not originate in Gospel law or canonical truth, he countered: he found no mention of them at all in the New Testament. Rather, when the Holy Spirit was poured out the early church came to live in common in perfect observance of Gospel law (*perfectam obseruantiam legis euangelice*).[156] This came down to a dispute, as he saw it, about the meaning of John 13:34 (the "new command is love"), Pupper taking off from Lyra's gloss, insisting that no act, however great and arduous, could bring a person to newness of life unless the Holy Spirit had poured into their heart a love of doing right.[157] Then, conceding outright that it would startle readers, John repudiated any argument (meaning especially Thomas's) that counsels had been added to commands as a better and more efficacious way.[158] But in wholly dimissing this two-century-old two-tier system John did not lower the bar; almost the reverse (this implicitly true for Wyclf too). In Gospel law counsels thereby functioned as commands and became necessary for all.[159] Gospel law, its "new commandment" centered in love, was delivered to all as a command, not counsel, with each to observe it according to their time and place. What other Gospel perfection could there be, he asked rhetorically?[160] With that John began a reinterpretation of the standard Gospel text for vowed religious life (If you would be perfect. . . .)—whereupon the entire work broke off, whether lost, silently censored by a copyist, or never finished.

Distinction Five was supposed to take up the difference between professing and not professing, the conceptual end-point of the argument. We may infer some points from the *Dialogue*. He labeled as the "error of our times" any view that in fulfilling Gospel law liberty of spirit would not suffice.[161] Vows achieved nothing without animating charity—this evident especially, he said, among mendicants.[162] He also rejected the widely held view that vows effected a second baptism. "I do not see it," he remarked. They live in no greater conformity to the will of God. This "higher warrant" for vows had come quite simply from the church (*quoad iudicium ecclesie*), not God.[163] As for the argument that vows "hardened" one in the good, widely taken over from Thomas, and probably cited directly by the adversary, this could hardly apply to the predestinated, John countered, since God did not need the help of vows to save people. Nor did it in fact truly harden the vowed, as one might readily see from their present state. So how should we think about things instead, the Brothers' and Sisters' alternative in effect?

> In the single gathering [note the Devout term] of the church there are some, it seems, who, called to the supper of eternal beatitude, come of their own volition (*sua sponte*), but others who, to come, are compelled. . . . some, following the movement of grace in the liberty of the Spirit, move toward (*tendunt*) eternal beatitude according to Gospel perfection, but others arrive at it compelled by obligation, vows being the cause by accident.[164]

John deliberately, even mockingly, reversed a thousand-year presumption about estates within the church. So why then are there professed? Mother church, like all mothers, has more affection than intellect, John says curtly, and allows obligation as an occasion for good, not as a good in itself.[165] It's for those who could not otherwise be brought to fulfill the "Christian religion"[166]—whence they have no right in their superstitious pride to claim theirs as the "estate of perfection." This is of course exactly opposite to the way even the Devout in desperation had defended themselves in the 1390s, describing theirs then as a lesser estate for the weak, taking "refuge" in the shadow of Windesheim—though that too was silently arranged by Florens, not professed.

John also took up priesthood and its traditional place in the hierarchy, another Devout theme. The priestly life, he declared, is truly apostolic (not that of friars or bishops), the most perfect expression of the "Christian religion," the highest estate in the church militant[167]—so high in the Devout view that only a few should be called to it and that by the election of their peers. This was a stronger version of Gerson's position, which John knew. John saw Christ, or at least presented him, primarily as a priest. Borrowing from Pseudo-Dennis he defined the priestly role as that of ascending to the divine in contemplation and descending to people in prayer, sacraments, preaching, and mercy (this also used by Thomas and the friars, by the way).[168] Whence a priest need transfer into no other estate to advance toward perfection, if he lived worthily (*digne conuersari*),[169] need take no vows as a religious—friars again being the adversary here, and John in effect describing his own state as a Brother and father-confessor. Rights now conferred on bishops, he further protested, had derived from ecclesiastical law or custom, and taken away powers once bestowed on priests (reserving major crimes to bishops, for instance). As for the common notion that bishops ranked as successors of the apostles, this too was true only in church custom and with respect to jurisdictional authority.[170] Originally, bishops lived with priests in a communal life, ranking above them only in administrative labors (like the rector in a Devout household). John Pupper argued strongly, and correctly, that Augustine instituted a commune around him as a community of priests, not religious, modeled on the life of Christ and the apostles, the perfect Christian religion.[171] John lived in a community of priests at Gouda, and served the nuns of Tabor as an independent priest. Repudiating church custom, he claimed for this way of life the most authentic apostleship, an estate perfect in itself.

But priests, the soul objects, can own property and make testaments; so religious renouncing all property must be more like Christ.[172] John countered: But Christ and the apostles had necessities such as clothes; so having temporal things makes for no lessening of holiness.[173] The real issue was intent and love. He then posed a series of cases like the canonist he in part was. Take the case of a poor person who joined a house to meet material needs, then eventually converted. The conversion could not make the previous intent and years "good"; but the original self-seeking intent could not render the conversion null, nor keep the remaining years from being "worthy of reward."[174] Another case: someone who copied books to earn their keep in a religious house—as John Pupper did at Gouda and probably Amersfoort—acted in a way that was good and worthy of reward owing to its end, that is, to serve God quietly (*ut quietius ualeat deo seruire*).[175] But someone who preached to gain money supposedly to give to the poor (meaning, friars) did not act well; neither the act nor the ultimate intent saved it from subordinating a spiritual to a temporal good.[176] These were all matters patently near to John's own life and heart.

John closed his *Dialogue* with "notes" on the common life, amounting to nearly a tenth of the work. Written in an argumentative mode, not in dialogue format, the text may well have arisen independently. Communal life represented the perfect fulfillment of Gospel law, he held (*Vita communis quantum ad omnem legis euangelice perfectionem fuit in fidelibus in primitiua ecclesia*), giving ultimate theological expression to the animating ideal of the Modern-Day Devout. Against Grabow's *Libellus* and Dominican adversaries, John described the early church as observing a common life freely and out of love. To hold the opposite, he asserted, and stubbornly (Grabow again?), was heresy.[177] Christ instituted Gospel law to be observed in the liberty of charity; but the church, on instituting religious orders, bound people in order to secure faithfulness.[178] Poverty and begging (Franciscans) had nothing to do with Gospel perfection, even if they helped some individuals. Better to retain goods and give to the poor[179]—an attitude echoing many late medieval burghers, and also Valla.

Ownership of things may nonetheless comport with the highest Gospel perfection, he added paradoxically (witness, he says, biblical patriarchs and many saints and bishops). Things were not finally the issue here, but the love for or inordinate use of them.[180] This he aimed at monks and friars: What's the use of giving up personal things and becoming zealous for communal goods?[181]—a critique found implicitly already in Zerbolt. Perfection does not require resigning proprietary ownership but giving up proprietary love. Living a common life now requires a vow of poverty only owing to weaklings.[182] But Brothers too were required to resign all goods on entry, something he would have done on joining at Amersfoort, though in his present independence (and unhappy experience in Gouda) he may have looked back on that too as a concession to weakness. Or, in his zeal to undo an estate of the perfect he may have pushed his own logic to the outer edge. He was now almost certainly a holder in the property of the women's house, at least before it achieved corporate ecclesiastical status, and he may have held, again legally, family goods. It was not about goods, he insisted, but about loves. More, he could concede, vows need not be wholly abolished, since they proved useful for the weak. Is that how he thought about the sixty-six nuns he served as father-confessor? Vows were in any case efficacious and merit-worthy only in so far as they sprang from love and an authentic will. And they did not create an estate of the perfect. True merit and authentic Christian life came with the outpouring of the Spirit that spontaneously created communal life in the Jerusalem community.

CHAPTER EIGHT

Taking the Spiritual Offensive: Caring for the Self, Examining the Soul, Progressing in Virtue

If every year we were to root out one vice, quickly we would be made perfect. But now on the contrary we often feel that we found ourselves better and purer at the beginning of our conversion than after many years of profession. Fervor and progress (profectus) *ought to increase daily. But now it seems a great thing if someone can retain even a part of their initial fervor. If we would do a little violence to ourselves in the beginning, however, afterwards we could do the rest with lightness and joy.*

Put yourself first at peace, and then you will be able to bring others to peace. A peaceful person is of far greater profit than a learned one. . . . Have zeal therefore first of all concerning yourself, and then justly you will be able to have zeal as well for your neighbor. . . . It is more just for you to accuse yourself and to excuse others. If you wish to be carried, carry someone else.

THE MODERN-DAY DEVOUT aimed ultimately to build souls, not structures or theologies. Their tone was intense and practical: a call for people to convert, make progress, eliminate one vice after another, add virtue to virtue, never leave off examining the self. This was the way to purity of heart and peace with God, conceived not as rapturous union but as a confident quietude in the dread presence of the divine. The Devout shared certain assumptions with townspeople and clergy, including that life at its best was not endurance or giving in to fate but looked toward progress (*profectus*). At issue, however, was the nature of gain (*lucrum*). The Modern-Day Devout called on people to turn away from short-term material gain, the wealth and honors and progeny of this world, the opening appeal in Thomas's pamphlet offering "Admonitions helpful to a spiritual life" (= *Imitatio Christi* I.1). They projected alternatively a never-ending progress in virtue that would open out into everlasting gain. Few phrases appear so often in their lives and spiritual treatises as "progress in the virtues" (*profectus uirtutum, in doegeden voert te gane*), truly the *leitmotif* of their program.[1] Crucial too was a sense of choice. Clerics or merchants, burgher daughters or students, also the striving poor, were as converts to focus their energies spiritually on what they could do (*facere quod in se est*). Late medieval theologians debated whether "doing what you could" sufficed for grace and divine acceptance.[2] Among the Devout this never arose as a formal issue for theological reflection. It was a practical matter. It required, another favored expression, caring for the self, the interior self (*cura sui ipsius, een ynwendich mensche sijns selfs sorghe*), and that first of all.[3]

Devout methods could occasionally seem harsh, their interiority probing, their ascetic discipline unrelenting. Sisters and Brothers lived in an intricate balance between apartness and interaction, interior examination and exterior example. They abandoned family and personal property to enter a communal spiritual life, while dwelling still in the middle of densely populated towns and reaching out to others in written texts, spoken exhortations, and personal guidance. For they aimed to care as well for the souls of others:

> At that time many citizens of Deventer, and even those from beyond, frequently went to Father Florens and his Brothers, seeking counsel from them about how they might save their souls, confessing their sins to them with the permission of the parish curate. Especially on feast-days they gathered at the house of Father Florens to hear sacred readings, which were read out and are still today in Dutch, also to hear ardent admonitions delivered by the Brothers. Whence those good people, rendered remorseful, converted to the Lord.[4]

Zwolle's chronicler, Jacob of Utrecht, described the Brotherhood in terms of several inter-connected exercises: praying, studying, writing, being available to students.[5] Any "diligent practitioner of our exercises," he elaborated, was faithful in the "work of copying" (*opere scripture*), "fervent in the study of scriptures" (*feruens in studio scripturarum* = holy writings of all kinds), as well as a "humble and penitent (*compunctione*) person devoted to life in his cell (*bonus cellita*).[6] Thomas of Kempen, who "daily attended and observed the way of life" at Florens's House during his teenage years (1390s), claimed never to have seen people so devout and fervent, yet living among the laity (*seculares*), free of worldly life. His description, retrospective, glowing, meant to entice, offers an eyewitness account from an outsider who became the ultimate insider:

> Remaining quietly at home they solicitously gave themselves to the work of copying books. Busy frequently with sacred readings and devout meditations, they had recourse to short uttered prayers (*iaculatas*) as solace during their work time. In the morning they also went to church to say the morning hours, and during the celebration of mass, pouring out the firstfruits of their lips and their hearts' sighs, with bodies prostrate, they lifted pure hands and the mind's eye to heaven. . . . Having thus one heart and one mind in God, each placed what was his own in common (*conferebant in commune*), and accepting simple food and clothing gave no thought to the morrow. Freely dedicating themselves to God, they were content to obey the rector or his vicar . . . and strove with all their strength to conquer themselves and resist their passions and break the motions of their own will, fervently asking as well that they be earnestly reproached.[7]

Fifteen years later or so he wrote the first two booklets that would make up his *Imitatio Christi*, and there turned this into a general appeal: for souls to follow the converted life (*admonitiones ad spiritualem uitam utiles*), for converts to pursue an interior life (*admonitiones ad interna trahentes*).

A century later Erasmus described the people with whom he lived from his ninth to his eighteenth year as a "medium type between monks and laypeople."[8] A Brother from Hildesheim described their way of life positively as the golden mean, engaged in neither the excessive austerities of some professed or the vain worldliness of the laity.[9] This chapter explores that spiritual life, and especially how it was sustained "inbetween." One important way to position the Modern-Day Devout as historical figures in their own time is by way of clothing. In the Middle Ages clothing marked people: rich or poor, knight or merchant, cleric or lay, Benedictine or Franciscan, Dominican nun or unprofessed beguine. Some accused the Devout of appropriating religious status by their dress. In response Zerbolt took from the jurist Johannes Andree a technical definition of the habit as garb worn by those living together in the same "college" and professing the same religion. The Devout, he argued, did neither, and so did not wear habits, also in fact nothing of a common color or fit. Instead they donned garb that, admittedly, set them apart from the laity but only by its simplicity and poor quality.[10] Precisely here Zerbolt chose to cite that influential passage from Cardinal Hostiensis often invoked to describe the "semi-religious." Beyond the formally professed, the jurist had noted in the mid-thirteenth century, some other people adopted a lifestyle "more religious than the laity" and thus found themselves in an "inbetween state" (here Zerbolt's term: *status medius*), thus certain widows or virgins or members of confraternities. Such people also wore "inbetween" garb, neither a religious habit nor the trappings of lay worldliness, but-something simple, even vile. Merely "wearing such humble garb, however, Zerbolt asserted defensively, should not be said to make someone a 'religious'."[11]

Sisters for a long time wore no strictly common garb, their memorials noting only that a woman wore "simple" clothes. As late as the 1470s Biel would take this up, still defensively. We do not assume a habit or profess religion but return spiritual life to its original integrity, he declared. What difference does it make if our garb is slightly different, mostly simpler? We have no solemn investment of novices; so what's the issue?[12] By then, however, Brothers had in fact adopted a distinctive marker. While they wore simple black or gray tunics, they employed a headpiece running down to the neck, a distinctive hood (hence, in German, *Kugelherren*). This, Biel asserted, served simply to protect them from the cold, and was simpler in any case than what most priests and clerics wore. Brothers dressed, in other words, more like clerics than merchants or aldermen but ultimately like neither, men in gray with a special hood. We have in fact, and notably, no contemporary images of either Brothers or Sisters, only a later attempt to visualize them (see Figure 17) and one late carved bust of a presumed Brother in an Upper Rhine house, from the group more comfortable with the title of canon.[13] In any case none of it was really about dress for the Devout. It was about dressing souls. All turned finally on inwardness, the intentions of the self. Whence, interestingly but fittingly, garb received no attention in Devout customaries. What did receive attention, in Zerbolt's apologia or in the customaries, and certainly in the lives, were the practices meant to cultivate that interior self, practices that also roused criticism: sacred writings circulated in the vernacular, exhortations that looked like preaching, guidance that looked like confession.

Reading, Writing, and the Lay Tongue

The Modern-Day Devout made spiritual reading central, for prayer, for meditation, for personal reflection. While labor consumed the largest portion of their day, reading came in second, often combined with labor, reading while spinning, reading while copying. Reading here must be grasped in its functional dimensions, enabling prayer, meditation or reflection without precluding intellectual exploration. For women and the lay men in their circle, also for the laypeople who attended collations or came for advice, all this transpired in the

Figure 17. Image of a Brother, from Philipon de la Madelaine, *Histoire complète et costumes des ordres monastiques* (Paris 1839), vol. 2, Pl. 32, drawn from textual descriptions, not contemporary images.

vernacular. Contemporaries including the inquisitor took note, probably reacting most immediately, as set out in Chapter 3, to women praying the hours translated by Master Geert, this perceived as no straightforward domestic exercise (as might go on, say, among the pious well-to-do) but as a communal and proselytizing endeavor. This took place at exactly the same time that Lollards, just across the channel, contended for the right of people to read Scripture and holy writings in English. In the Low Countries, led by the Devout, a defense of vernacular reading generally won out. The practice continued, and challenges largely went quiescent. Neither the English nor the Dutch case may be entirely paradigmatic, or rather both may reflect that localism which is a mark of the Later Middle Ages—the Czech or Italian or French offering slightly different cases again. But the English Lollard case, though spectacular, has held center-stage for too long, or rather that version of it which served first Reformation and now modern agendas.

Translation into Dutch of Scripture and religious literature (such as the Golden Legend, Gregory the Great, Bonaventure) preceded the Devout by a generation, beginning in the 1360s, going back in fact to the third quarter of the thirteenth century with Jacob of Maerlant.[14] In the 1390s the Devout further fostered the translation and distribution of the New Testament and the Psalms in Dutch, one of their own, Johannes Scutken supplying Windesheim lay brothers with Scriptural texts.[15] The Windesheim canons, true to their Devout heritage, made a great effort early to construct a library, and especially to secure a correct text of the Scriptures and the main liturgical books, even acting as editors and correctors.[16] What spread most widely were texts guiding worship such as the Psalms and the Gospel pericopes (with glosses translated from Peter Comester and Nicholas of Lyra), above all Grote's translation of the hours, it present still in as many as two thousand manuscripts.[17] Other texts too spread in the vernacular, and especially in Devout circles, thus the *Golden Epistle* of William (ascribed to Bernard) and the *Profectus* of the Franciscan David of Augsburg, the latter providing the springboard for Devout reflections on "progress in virtue."[18] Alijt Bake (d. 1455), eventually a canoness in the Devout circles, read so deeply in Tauler that a manuscript, a copy of work in her own hand (Brussels, Royal Library, MS 686–89) wove Tauler's sermons in with her own.[19]

Zerbolt's defense, nearly unique on the continental side, was ingenious and careful. He and the two main jurist-consults, Foec and Abbot Arnold, conceded at once that heretical matters should not be read or translated. But it was simply absurd (*nullum istorum potest dici, inconueniens est*) to hold it as illicit for laypeople to read holy writings or divine scripture in the vernacular.[20] Zerbolt took up the key legal ruling on this point, by Innocent III in 1199 (*Cum ex iniuncto*, treating Waldensians in Metz), and exploited an opening he found in its initial clause ("though the desire to understand holy scripture and to exhort from its understanding should not be reproached but rather commended").[21] This (not the main point of Innocent's ruling), he declared, blithely turning a concessive into a declarative clause, was the central stance of the church. Still, he summed up his case in contorted double negatives: "it was not illicit for the laity to read books put out (*editos*) in the vernacular on grounds that it was illicit to possess or read holy scripture in the vernacular"[22]—that is, the issuing of vernacular books could not indicted on the grounds of people possessing or reading them. He inserted a string of lengthy but deft quotations from Augustine, Gregory, Cesarius and others,[23] noting that they had themselves written extensively for the laity, and on biblical matters. So long as these texts did not contain heresy there was nothing evil about the laity reading them in the vernacular (since they were an aid to knowing how one should live), nor was it prohibited in law or theology. Deacon Foec, a jurist, said simply, though also in a double negative: "I do not think it is likely to be called into doubt, since indeed it is licit to have and read books of sacred writings published in or translated into the vernacular." He also treated it as a matter of little interest to civil law.[24] Abbot Arnold summarized the case Zerbolt made (or they constructed together, since they consulted).[25] This issue likewise held little interest for the professional jurists at Cologne. In effect the fact—widespread distribution of vernacular materials in this era—was invoked rhetorically as a principle: what's illicit about it? The double negatives, the implicit uneasiness, issue plainly from the immediate circumstances (charges raised against them) but as well from the relative newness of this phenomenon, the lingering assumption that religious writing was enclosed first of all in the sacred language of Latin.

For English-speaking readers this pro-active stance may seem startling after a generation of intense work on the proscription of Lollard books. In part it represented a strategy of the "best defense is a bold offense." But we must also recognize that in later medieval Europe religious books in the vernacular, whether prayerbooks, or devotional books, or sermons, or guides to confession, or saints lives, or summaries of theology, or Bible translations—were indeed ever more common, their production now reaching explosive levels. So-called Lollards Bibles too continued to be produced, and in great numbers, some marked for liturgical reading—suggesting devotional purposes too. To suggest that such books could not be possessed or read would have seemed absurd to most people, even if some churchmen preferred their monopoly on sacred texts and some laypeople too, apparently, found it novel. This expansion had moved in parallel with, or actually a good generation or two behind, the writing of legal documents and town or guild statutes in the vernacular. As people grew accustomed to their own tongue being employed for all manner of material and legal claims in writing, they began to turn to it ever more naturally to pursue religious aspirations as well. Still, the reaction of the inquisitor and of local churchmen, including the canons at St. Lebuin's, and Zerbolt's treatise on the subject, indicate that it was not all so simple. There was an uncertain sense of moving into new territory, manifest in the double negatives.

Above all there was the question of Scripture itself, the holy book of the church, the preserve of the clergy. The translator active in the 1360s–80s, just before the Devout, had introduced his "History-Bible" with an explanatory defense, offering an interesting parallel to the preface to the Lollard Bible. He claimed to undertake the work for "those un-learned in clerical matters" (*die ongheleert is van clergien*), and for any people (*enighe lieden*) who might make use of it on established holy days.[26] His first group presumed the inherited association of Scripture with clerics, though "clergie" also meant simply Latin learning, thus taking in anyone, including priests and minor clerics, whose Latin was poor. But the second opened up hopeful possibilities for lay practice, exactly what the Devout did in their collations, reading the Scriptural texts in the vernacular on feastdays and explaining them. This man claimed that he would procede "word for word" and "sense for sense" in his translation, in hopes of rendering it understandable to the people (*lieden*) within the customs/mores (*sede*) of "our land." Further, because the biblical text was so "dark" in many places (a common metaphor), he would explain it by way of Comestor's *Historia*, though keeping the two texts distinctly marked.[27] This man worked in part at the bidding of a patrician in Brussels, Jan Taye, and alluded to the fact that "mad dogs" (meaning, certain clergy) would "grumble" and "murmur" that the "secrets of the Scriptures should not be unfurled before the laity."[28] This Bible translation would not enjoy wide distribution until two generations later, then accompanying Devout materials, the real engine behind the proliferation of so much religious material in Dutch during this era. So it is to their defense we must turn.

First, Zerbolt amassed evidence that the Bible was originally written in the people's tongues, and was also read and preached in those tongues, thus Hebrew, Greek, Latin, and more—a point also made by the Bible translator. At Pentecost in the early church, moreover, the Spirit had spoken to people in their own tongues. Scripture was put in Latin not to render it inaccessible, he asserted, but accessible, being then the most widely used tongue.[29] So why should Holy Scripture be denied to people in the Germanic tongue?[30] Scripture was not given to one estate in the church (clergy) but to "all people in every estate" (*generaliter omni homini in quocumque statu fuerit*).[31] Scripture itself commanded that it be known and taught, and did not mention only priests. More, the church ordered the laity to convene for its hearing and preaching, thus making it absurd to deny

Holy Writ to them. The doctors of the church also commended it to the laity, Jerome "even to a married woman, to whom it might seem less fitting."[32] The laity, too, otherwise so caught up in the world, also so ardent about reading and learning worldly poems (he says), should be intent upon learning heavenly business, and were in any case expected to know the commandments, the seven mortal sins, and so on.[33] But some laypeople objected to the reading of vernacular books too (*illi qui in laycis reprehendunt lectionem et studium librorum teutonicalium*), strikingly. They would be far better off reading their duties in a vernacular text, Zerbolt informed them, than drinking in a tavern.[34] Even the poor, he says, citing Chrysostom and Gregory, should not plead poverty but "read Scripture and study devout books."[35] In sum, to deny access to Scripture and devotional books in the vernacular was nonsense. It was not evil, he asserted, to know the good or about evil. It was rather meritorious.[36]

But there were other and outside issues. In 1369 Emperor Charles IV, then in 1374 Pope Gregory XI, both urged on by Dominican inquisitorial zealots, had banned "certain vernacular books of sacred writing."[37] To Grote and Zerbolt the emblem of this was "Eckhart" or what traveled under his name, Zerbolt also explicitly forbidding heretical materials and carefully alluding to that papal constitution. Here we must note a point often obscured. Neither Marguerite Porete nor Eckhart, Arnold of Villanova nor John Hus, were critiqued for writing in the vernacular; they were condemned for the positions they took. Zerbolt commended material that was "open" and "plain," not "obscure." Readings should "treat plain material openly" (*plana materia aperte*); the laity should avoid books which "cannot be understood on the first hearing of the words."[38] Certain Germanic books in particular, he noted, use obscure and difficult words, and though there may be much good in these books, it comes mixed with erroneous material. From reading such books laity may even learn themselves to talk in this distorted (*abusiue*) way.[39] Still, Zerbolt complicated the picture. At first he suggests that books on the divine essence and predestination and such were not fit reading for the laity, too "high." But Augustine had recommended studying the Trinity, and Thomas held that the articles of the faith were required of the laity; what subjects could be higher than those? So he distinguished between setting things out simply for the laity (*tractantes docentes simpliciter*) and those books engaged in "massive disputation." Yet works proceeding "disputatiously" toward "clarity" could also prove useful, especially in teaching or explicating the articles of the faith.[40]

Conceding limits, then opening up possibilities, this tactic came most startlingly to expression in Zerbolt's setting out of what to read. He granted that books proceeding entirely according to reason, that is, in the science of the university man, would not be useful or even intelligible to the laity. But people "exercised in spiritual life, expert in devotional exercises, and rooted in the virtues," he countered, may well understand books to which they have conformed their lives far better than people who were deeply learned but led carnal lives (Grote's word for theological thought). Laity often grasped devotional books which, he says, learned clergy found incomprehensible. Through the affections and experience they had tasted and understood the text, even if they were not learned.[41] This was the same technique Zerbolt had employed throughout, conceding the obvious, then exploiting an opening. The result was a passionate defense of the laity owning and reading spiritual books in the vernacular, holy writings of all sorts including Scripture, extending to books on the articles of the faith if properly and clearly presented, but preferring books that were "moral" and "devotional" and "plain," intelligible on first hearing or reading, even if if intelligible only to the spiritually expert, not necessarily to the clerically learned.

For the Devout the heart of the matter lay not in these arguments but in the way reading and writing informed their way of life. "Holy writings" (*sacra scriptura a sanctis doctoribus conscripta*) instructed people in the way of God, the men's customary explained, inspiring the affections and will to a love of the virtues. Therefore, it went on, "let us be" (*simus*) constant in study. It was to come early, middle, and late, especially for men, also for women, beginning with an hour or more in the morning after rising and saying prayers.[42] Brothers were to engage in "reading" and "prayer," or resolve to do so (at Wesel to "read something pleasing for devotion") until roughly 7:00 a.m. when the signal was given to hear mass or begin work (book-copying).[43] In winter the reading took place by candlelight, in summer after dawn. Their labor, moreover, consisted in copying books much of the day, done in the quiet of their room/cell at a special writing chair. Some lives tell of Brothers who hardly ever left, one Brother, a former teacher, dying by choice in his chair.[44] At the midday meal they listened to readings. At collations in the evening they heard and discussed holy writings. After the evening meal and compline they were free to do what they liked in their room, including more "study."[45] At Münster Brothers were enjoined to spend time until retiring in their "study" (*studium meum*).[46] The statutes for Hildesheim, completed later, emphasized the meditative aspect: their "recollecting materials" at the beginning and end of each day to re-form their interior (*reformando interiori homini*), echoing the title of Zerbolt's spiritual manual.[47]

The spiritual manuals set all this out by way of Augustine as well as *The Golden Epistle* and David of Augsburg. Florens set the tone: this was not reading for the sake of knowing (*propter scire uel propter scienciam*) but to root up vice and plant virtue, declared the whole aim of Sacred Scripture (*tota sacra scriptura est propter uirtutes*).[48] Florens and Zerbolt followed *The Golden Epistle* broadly, twelfth-century advice for Carthusians: one should not read capriciously, should set aside an appointed time, ruminate on readings, direct them toward the affections.[49] The Brothers, presuming books, tried to convert "book-men" into spiritual readers. Reading was not the fleeting or curious stuff of busy clerics but meditative, refreshing for the soul. Not hurried, not skipping about, they were to read whole books to inform *mores*.[50] Florens positioned his discussion early, setting out the three-fold way to exercise purgation, by reading, meditating, and praying, a scheme borrowed from Bonaventure.[51] Zerbolt saw the mind remade by "experience," a spiritual cleansing that opened it up to grasp Scripture like a "Christian philosopher" and then as well by "teaching," interpreted as purposeful reading.[52] Reading, meditation, and prayer underlay all religious exercises, but reading was most basic, Zerbolt argued, informing all the spiritual ascents that followed.[53] The Modern-Day Devout set out an approach that, while experiential and devotional, was text-based.

For Sisters the formal evidence is thinner. What statutes remain set aside only an hour a night, though they too engaged in daily prayers and table-readings and frequent collations.[54] Still, they opened up this text-based spiritual devotion to a host of women for whom it would otherwise have been out of reach (this set out in Chapter 4). In a late text (still unedited) from 1510/12 Jan de Wael, a father-confessor to Tertiaries in Amersfoort, drew up an "instruction book" (*Informierungsboek*) with three distinct lists for reading, going from beginning to mature Sisters. It contains mostly the same texts we have encountered right along, David of Augsburg's *Profectus*, Zerbolt's *Ascents*, Bonaventure's *Three-fold Way* (basic to Florens and Zerbolt's understanding of the spiritual life).[55] Three book lists survive from late fifteenth-century women's houses, all Tertiaries. That from St. Barbara's in Delft, with over a hundred titles, refers to "study books that belong in our library" (*studier boeke die in die liberie horen*), and began with the Gospels and Epistles, possibly in Latin, followed by the Gospels with a concordance and the Gospels explicitly in Dutch (*een vlaems ewangeli boec*).[56] For St. Margaret's house in Gouda, treated with Rhenen in Chapter 2, eventually Tertiary, we have a sixteenth-century fragment listing books in Latin with eighty-two titles, again beginning with the Bible, then, like Grote's list, proceeding to the Desert Fathers and Suso's *Horologium* before materials from the church fathers and the twelfth century in particular, concluding with volumes of sermons.[57] This entire way of life presupposed, also for the Sisters, books and libraries.[58]

Master Geert had set schoolboys to copying for him,[59] and told the schoolmaster at Zwolle that to build up the church they would need lots of "knowledge and books."[60] Over time the core collection of Master Geert and Master Florens' books grew to a library of some one-thousand volumes, a library with its own wall catalogue, nearly all of it lost after the closing of the house.[61] Those books, held in common, might be distributed generously, according to the customary, but once a month the librarian's assistant was to gather all except those in a Brother's room, and once a year in the summer every book for careful examination. Beyond a list of the books they held communally, at Münster/Wesel/Herford the librarian was to keep three more lists, of books employed for table-reading, books in Brothers' "studies," and books leant out to others. In Deventer/Gouda books could not leave town without the rector's permission, at Hildesheim for no longer than four months, and at Münster/Wesel/ Hildesheim not without a pledge if valuable. In the German region, but not the Dutch, the librarian was enjoined not to circulate books in the vernacular to laity unless they were "devout" and "plain" materials—a cautionary and interesting echo of the battles of the 1390s.[62]

The Devout stance toward study as such was ambivalent. They presumed it, even found it essential to their text-based enterprise, yet saw it as opening up the dangerous possibility of learning for its own sake. So too with books. They defended vernacular books but insisted on devout ones, warned against "high" schoolmen's books while also employing them in their own defense.[63] Books were overseen by the librarian, and no Brother could simply take one out, at least in principle, a matter of deliberate design at Deventer when the house was expanded in 1441.[64] But we also have no anecdotes to suggest any disputes over a Brother's preferred reading. About these books we possess scattered evidence from Geert Grote's proposed personal reading list (which proved precedent-setting) to reading lists compiled in 1526 at St. Martin's in Louvain to a still unedited general catalogue from the late fifteenth century of several Devout libraries (still unedited).[65] The list Master Geert constructed for post-conversionary reading began with the Gospels, followed by the lives and conferences of the Desert Fathers (Cassian), then the Epistles of Paul, the "devout" books of Bernard and Anselm together with Suso's *Horologium*, going on to a mix of biblical books and spiritual writings, ending with the biblical book of Kings, all of this "sacred writing."[66] Just over a hundred years later, when the rector at Zwolle oversaw the founding of a house at Culm, a region devastated by poverty and warfare in 1481 and now in need of "spiritual workers," he recommended the lives of the Desert Fathers, Cassian, Climachus' *Spiritual Ladder*, Bernard (probably meaning *The Golden Epistle*), and David of Augsburg's *Profectus religiosorum* as offering the way to "full conversion" and "healthy training" (*sanam institucionem*).[67]

Spiritual formation, in short, drove the Devout reading program. Notable, and in its way comparable to the humanist impulse, was their return to origins, to Scripture, Cassian, and Augustine, with Bernard and Anselm counted as fathers. As important, no readings were specially assigned—also not Thomas's *Imitatio* (as it would be among Jesuits). Each Brother was to make his own way through what pleased, what spoke to him in his own room. This permitted, and encouraged, a self-styling of religious life. Medieval orders had come to foster formation by way of distinct reading programs, Bernard and the *Golden Epistle* for Cistercians, Francis and Bonaventure for Franciscans, and so on. But the Modern-Day Devout offered an eclectic choice: Scripture, Cassian and the *vitae patrum* (Desert Fathers), the *Golden Epistle* (Cistercian/Carthusian), Bonaventure's *Threefold Way*, David of Augsburg's *Profectus* (Franciscan), Suso's *Horologium* (Dominican), along with Augustine's *De opere monachorum* and Jerome's letters to women. This held as well for the canons of Windesheim. The closest Brothers came to fixing upon a common formative instrument was the work of Zerbolt, his two spiritual compilations, the "Reformation of the Powers of the Soul" and "Spiritual Ascents," these recommended for the canons at St. Martin's as, strikingly, post-profession reading. At the Brothers' houses in Münster and Wesel one suggested personal resolve was to secure copies and divide the texts up for daily reading[68]—almost certainly taken over from Deventer. At St. Martin's outside Louvain sixteen different works got listed as reading matter for novice canons or young student-clerics, beginning with a Dominican manual, then a possible letter of Geert Grote (the *incipit* is ambiguous), a Franciscan work, one by Hugh of St. Victor, and so on, concluding with the *Horologium* and four works by Thomas of Kempen, and above all as most useful the four books (*utilissimos*) of the *Imitatio Christi*. After profession these young canons were suggested thirty more books to choose from including Zerbolt, but beginning with the Carthusian Ludolph's life of Jesus and concluding with the works of John Chrysostom.[69] The reading program of the Modern-Day Devout represented both a return to classics, so to speak, of spiritual teaching, but, as important, was open-ended, allowed for personal self-styling. It grew out of a deliberate effort to draw students and clerics into religious reading, away from the Aristotle and school authors they presumed these young book-men ordinarily to be consumed with.

Brothers and Sisters were makers as well as readers of books, including personal scrapbooks called *rapiaria*. Brothers spent up to six hours a day copying books, at once manual labor and spiritual exercise; and some student-clerics were taught to do the same. The early hand of Erasmus is like that of the Brothers. But the Devout were also encouraged to keep a scrapbook, in effect the future commonplace book. Here, on left-over scraps of paper and parchment, they copied out favorite passages encountered in their reading, or made notes to themselves, yielding over time a diary of religious reflections or a program of spiritual exercises. So standard was this that the customary of Herford noted the *rapiarium* among items a rector might examine in his annual room-check at the beginning of Lent.[70] One Brother at Emmerich carried his around in his tunic.[71] Nor was this limited to Brothers, though it came more easily for them with individual rooms and daily copy-work. Sister Katherina of Master Geert's House (d. 1421) read edifying passages aloud from her little book (*boexsken*) to the lay families with whom she stayed or did business.[72] The practice continued among professed canons, explicitly on the model of Florens at Deventer.[73] John Brinckerinck indeed likened the entire Devout way of life for Sisters to such a book in which a person inscribed on the heart good exercises and thoughts year after year so as to have a "great book" from which to read in old age.[74]

Scholars have considered the *rapiarium*, this scrapbook or personal florilegium, a distinctive mark of the Modern-Day Devout. The form, Staubach has shown, arose from common school practice, a bundle of loose papers in which boys scribbled everything from lesson helps to jokes and charms.[75] What the Devout did was turn this everyday schoolboy practice into a spiritual instrument. John Cele, schoolmaster at Zwolle, friend of Grote and fellowtraveler with the Devout, "dictated to the whole school passages from the saints for individuals to write in their notebooks (*rapiaria*)."[76] That exercise may mark an early or inbetween stage. A manuscript copied several years later (now Cologne, Historisches Stadtarchiv, GB 8⁰ 76: see Figure 18), Vennebusch has argued persuasively, is based upon a *rapiarium* drawn up by Cele himself.[77] Indeed the term had, we may see (though now strangely erased), its own abbreviation (**Ꝛ**). In practice each of the Devout personalized these scrapbooks, their inner lives inscribed here, a text to which they could return again and again—an exercise Mertens has called "reading with the pen."[78] These "grab-bags" might contain almost anything. One disciple of Florens, John Vos (later prior of Windesheim, 1391–1424), copied significant portions of Bernard on the Song of Songs into his, while another, John of Kempen (brother of Thomas), chose to copy different portions of the same text.[79] As, literally, personal scrapbooks, the only authentic examples to survive date from well into the sixteenth century.[80]

Most scrapbooks likely contained, among a host of possibilities, the spiritual and moral exercises a Brother set for himself, referred to as "points" (*puncta*). "Frequently inspect your little book," Thomas of Kempen instructed, "so you may more clearly become aware of your internal progress and defects."[81] They mostly contained "sayings of the saints," materials selected for copying out, against which to measure one's intent or practice or fervor. Some books were laid out with headings (fear of God, love of God, purity of heart, humility, and so on), others proceeding randomly with passages copied over time. For Brothers of greater literary or spiritual power these notebooks could become more. Hen-

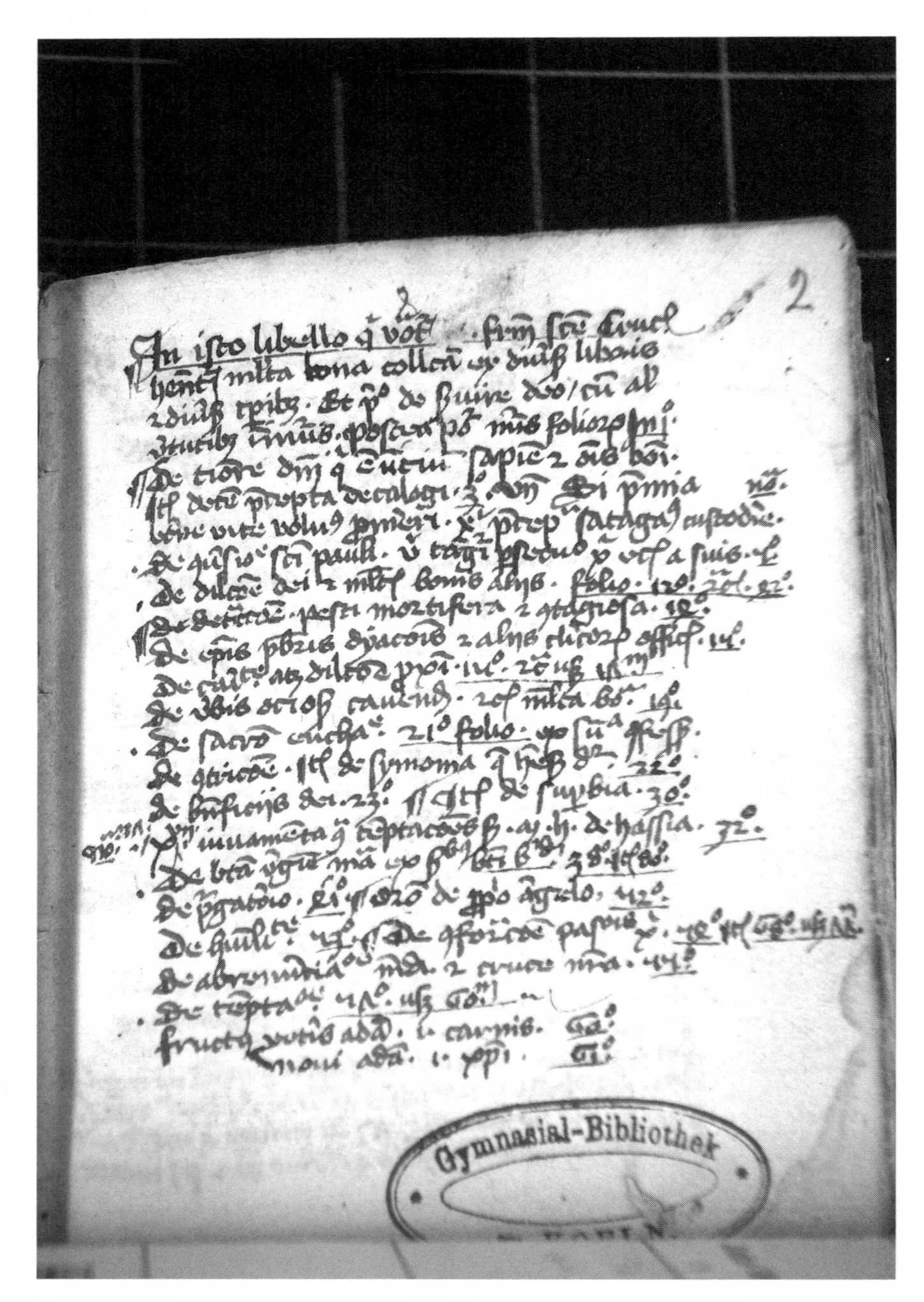

Figure 18. Opening of a *rapiarium*, possibly a copy of that drawn up by John Cele of Zwolle (d. 1417), the schoolmaster and close ally of Geert Grote. Its title rubric included a symbolic abbreviation (Ŗ) for the term "rapiarium," subsequently erased for reasons unknown. Cologne, Historisches Stadtarchiv, GB 8° 76, f. 7r.

drik Mande (d. 1431), a court scribe for the count of Holland, was converted by Grote, eventually becoming a *redditus* (lay oblate) at Windesheim. From him we have twelve works in the vernacular, in good part his elaborations upon materials copied out from authors such as Jan Ruusbroec, best viewed, Mertens has argued, as all growing out of his *rapiarium*.[82] A contemporary cleric from Deventer who went through Master Florens' House to end up at Windesheim, Gerlach Peters (d. 1411), left quires and notes scattered all around his room which Prior John Vos mandated Gerlach's confident John Scutken (the Bible translator) to pull into order, this yielding the *Breviloquium* (part resolutions, part exercises) and the *Soliloquium*, spiritual teachings partly mystical in character. Copied authorities were purged out or submerged, the work standing as original writing, if still scrap-like, reflections generated on individual quires.[83] The manuscript from Alijt Bake's own convent containing her own spiritual conferences written in with sermons from Tauler and other figures might also have arisen from something like a *rapiarium*. This effort could also become communal. Florens' still unpublished gathering of texts (*omnes, inquit, artes*)[84] and his *Tractatulus devotus* underpinned Zerbolt's reworking of these same materials into his "Reformation of the Powers of the Soul" and "Spiritual Ascents." Here was no master lecturing, schoolmaster dictating, or preacher delivering a homily, or readings at table (which they had), or author dictating to a secretary. Individuals worked together to build up a body of texts for reading, texts out of which they could together construct lives.

Exhortation in Public and Correction in Private

Brothers assumed a public presence in their towns as preachers, delivering *collationes*, vernacular exhortations offered especially on Sunday and feastday afternoons. Preaching was a privilege reserved in principle for the local curate, delegated in practice to friars and only rarely to others. Geert Grote, a deacon, died fighting a suspension of his right to preach after critiquing the local clergy, particularly for their female hearthmates. In the Late Middle Ages preaching played a huge role in public culture: towns in Italy and Germany hiring gifted orators for Lenten sermons, friars touring widely to instruct and to admonish. For Brothers to move in this direction too was hardly surprising. They were sensitive to suspicions their independent public preaching/teaching might arouse, and did in the 1390s, but persisted in it while denying that it was "preaching." Zerbolt wrote two tractates (V and VI) justifying their practices, the second responding to criticism,[85] these positioned in *Circa modum* immediately after communal life (I–IV), suggesting its prominence in their self-conception and in the charges raised against them.

Brothers claimed to engage in "charitable admonition and fraternal reproach" (*caritatiue ammonicione et fraterna correpcione*), rubrics that described their practices and also deliberately blurred the private and the public. They knew the difference, also inside their own households. The rector, an ordained priest and head of community, was to undertake no "public" preaching, one customary stipulated, apart from the Brothers's own permission.[86] Zerbolt drew upon several authorities (including a biblical gloss on 1 Cor. 2:4) to distinguish between admonition, also called "erudition," delivered "to a few" as a "private" or personal word, and the "public" sermon addressed to a church. He drew this distinction in part, interestingly, from Thomas Aquinas's discussion of whether women could preach. The first form, an act of instruction (*erudicio*) or in-house admonition (*familiaris admonitio*), as Zerbolt characterized it, was allowed to women (thus to laypeople), the second only to male prelates.[87] Zerbolt also invoked yet again Innocent's decretal *Cum ex iniuncto* of 1199. It had distinguished two kinds of exhortation with respect to handling early Waldensians: a public form restricted to licensed priests and preachers, and a private form open to all including laypeople, it dealing in moral, not doctrinal, matters. What Innocent had meant as a concessive gesture Zerbolt again treated as declarative permission, the pope rhetorically allowing at one point that instruction was good, even to be commended.[88] In an encyclopedic (and most interesting) gloss known to Zerbolt, the influential jurist Henry Boyck in the early fourteenth century surveyed in detail which clerics might preach under what circumstances. In passing, a mere half-sentence, he also noted that "private admonition" was open to "all,"[89] as indeed Thomas Aquinas earlier had opened "colloquy" to women.[90] Zerbolt turned this tiniest of openings into a positive principle: In private circumstances (*familiari colloquio*) such admonition was licit and meritorious, also for women. More, it must go on, an expression of true charity.

Such exhorting to good *mores* might take place in a house or on a city-street, not just in a church,[91] quoting at length from Jerome, Gregory, Bede and Chrysostom on the virtue of admonition, which Brothers and Sisters now appropriated as their charge. But what then of *correpcio*, that authoritative reproach more closely identified with priestly authority? Again Zerbolt posited a distinction. That which pertains to the common good and restrains others from doing evil represents an act of public justice reserved for prelates with the power to punish. But private correction offered erring individuals is open to any; indeed as an act of charity it was expected of all.[92] All this, he claimed, was self-evident from the discussion of fraternal correction in moral casuists like John of Freiburg and Thomas (*Summa* II/II q. 33). In reality Zerbolt's move marked a bold extension. Those friars had presumed the "obligatory" and "weightier" role of prelates in exercising "correction," then asked additionally whether other forms of admonition might exist beyond such authoritative roles. Yes, they said, on occasion when individuals delivered it as an act of charity. Zerbolt again took a small opening and exploited it to justify this public practice of admonitory preaching. To this end he cited the Gospel, Bernard, and Chrysostom—general passages about exhorting fellow believers not to do evil, blurring here public office into personal act.

This move effectively turned a voluntary Christian virtue into a licit community practice, side-stepping the hierarchy and religious orders. Though deft, it might not have seemed such a stretch for someone familiar with the activities of town and student societies, their kinds of mutual "admonishing." But it annoyed lawyers and churchmen who saw the argument's intent quite differently. Zerbolt responded in a further tractate (VI), presumably written a little later. Critics ("certain people") had invoked Christ's word (John 18:20) saying to Pilate that he had always taught openly in the synagogue and temple, never in secret. This very text was also cited by Innocent III and to the same purpose in his *Cum ex iniuncto*, though that passage not normally reproduced in legal collections. It appeared to offer an apt rebuke to any (Waldensians or Devout) cultivating their own reading and exhortation circle, here invoked, as Zerbolt noted, to foreclose entirely the Devout practice of private or personal instruction and admonition (*nulla erudicio uel ammonicio priuata sit licita*). So he undertook a further interpretation of Scripture. Quoting Augustine and Chrysostom on this verse, he objected back: what could be more foolish than to imagine that Christ never taught while sitting in a home or at a well or while walking down a street? Again he offered distinctions, with Augustine's help separating out different forms of "privy" teaching. Any "secret" teaching that was genuinely occult, dubious, or heretical Christ never engaged in and neither should anyone else, but he did explain the obscure, also a form of "secret" teaching. So the Devout might and should admonish others in Scripture or the spiritual life, instructing according to their audience's capacity for understanding (and in their language).[93] On this issue the jurist consultants reacted variously, and revealingly. Foec rephrased the question to suit himself (or make it intelligible to himself), namely, whether "fraternal correction was a precept," that is, a command and thus applicable to all. Drawing nearly all his arguments and authorities from Thomas's question on the topic, he affirmed the point,[94] but entirely avoided the central issue of public collations held as licit private acts—an ingenious lawyerly move by someone mildly empathetic with the Devout, yet distantly wary of their unusual practices. They had publicly stretched the limits of the known and the permitted.

Theoretical justifications aside (ingenious and even novel as they were), to get at actual Devout practices we must triangulate three bits of evidence: statutes, lives, and those fragments of collations that remain.[95] The surviving stipulations in customaries differ far beyond the usual local adjustments, indicating that this activity played out variously in towns and houses. The text from Zwolle distinguished three relatively distinct kinds of activities: collations, admonitions, and reproaches. The third ("reproach") referred to a kind of chapter of faults held periodically, among Sisters on Fridays, the second ("admonition") to public preaching for students and laypeople, and the first ("collations") to open conversation among the Brothers on a read text.[96] The term "collation" went back to monastic practice, a short talk on a reading held at day's end. In Dominican practice this became expanded talks on *mores*, reflection together on cases likely to come up in guiding lives, thus part training, part edification.[97] For the Brothers, influenced in part by Cassian's *Collationes patrum*, it referred first of all to a "charitable" or "mutual" conversation (*caritatiuum colloquium*) held on feastdays. The "guardian" of the collation (or "keeper of the book") read out a passage to be discussed in common. They were not to proceed in the disputatious method of the schools or any vain show of rhetoric but with each modestly proposing something edifying suggested by the text, a spiritual discussion, an exercise intended for learning (*scientia*) as well as inspiration (*accendimur ad feruorem*). Readings were not officially assigned, though Zwolle refers to a *Collacionale*, almost certainly meaning Dirk's, which survives in both Latin and Dutch. Among the men every house staged it slightly differently, though always on Sundays and feastdays: at Zwolle for an hour after the midday meal and then again after the evening meal, in 'sHertogenbosch only after the evening meal, at Deventer/Gouda in the evening after compline, at Emmerich only after the midday meal. This was communal discourse (*colloqui communiter de materia*), with no notice taken of rank or priestly office, the gathering engaged in mutual edifying conversation about a chosen reading.

On Sundays and feastdays they also convened to deliver "admonitions" to schoolboys and interested laypeople (*scolares et alii boni uiri*). This was their preaching in effect, though deliberately personalized in method. A text was read out in the vernacular, something accessible (*plana*) on the vices and virtues or the fear of God, useful for stirring people to improvement. At that point any of the Brothers (again not just priests or rectors) could address any of the visitors, as a single group or in smaller separate groups or one on one. This they did as exhortation, not, the customary says explicitly and defensively, as a sermon (*non quidem per modum predicationis sed simplicis exhortationis*). If they judged it useful or necessary they could carry on in a private or personal talk (*priuata et familiaris allocutio*), even with counsel in their own cell/room, though never longer than half an hour, to prevent rumors. At Zwolle and Deventer/Gouda this happened following vespers at the parish church, students and laypeople walking over afterward to the Brothers' house.[98] At Herford this took place at the fourth hour, thus following morning mass, though Brothers were urged not to take up the faults of the church in talking before students and laypeople.[99] Throughout we find a delicate maneuvering around the rules for preaching, avoiding any explicit rivalry with the parish rector: the read passages selected more or less randomly, Brothers contributing according to their insights or inspiration, groups forming collectively or informally, individuals instructed personally.

These practices went back to the beginnings of the Brotherhood. Already in the 1380s Florens reserved a room in his house for delivering admonitions on the fear and love of God.[100] From 1391 laypeople in Deventer gathered at his new and larger house to hear sacred readings (*sacram lectionem*) in the vernacular (Scripture and other readings) as well as "fervent admonitions" from the Brothers. The lay Brother John Kessel (d. 1398) delivered admonitions to students in the entry hall of the house.[101] When the Brothers were driven into exile during the interdict, they continued delivering readings and admonitions in the vernacular at the guesthouses in their new locales.[102] So central was this activity that references to it permeate the lives of Brothers. Peter Horn (d. 1479) spoke so penetratingly on any vice or virtue, it was remembered, that his words cut to the marrow, be it in mutual colloquies among Brothers or in collations for students.[103] Brother Rutger in Zwolle, caretaker of the student hostel, was remembered as devout and easy (*facundus*) with words, having a good knowledge of Scripture (*bonus biblicus*).[104] Brother Dirk (d. 1475), the librarian at Zwolle, was remembered as excellent in composing and delivering collations owing to his fine memory.[105] John of Hattem at Deventer, longtime procurator, claimed to be a simple man and so would only read things to hearers. He, we are told, preferred stories of the saints, the four last things, chastity, and contempt for the world. He proceeded in a kindly way, no showy distinctions like public preachers (meaning, friars).[106] A Brother Peter (d. 1483) was judged unfit for leadership of the student hostel, interestingly, because he proved too shy to deliver collations and admonitions.[107] This pattern of admonition extended as well into the circles of converted laypeople, Devout associates. Those who took students into their houses discussed with them (*conferre*: the verb from which *collatio* comes) the vices and virtues.[108]

About the effect of the Brothers' exhortations we have only scattered anecdotal evidence. Brother Albert at Zwolle, said to penetrate other's interiors, would use the evening collation on feastdays to rail against vices he knew some in his audience were harboring, though without being specific. Some hearers found him harsh and took it poorly, making light of what he said (especially the guilty, the narrator says), while others grew terrified that such faults might lurk in them.[109] This same Brother, the son of a learned adviser to the duke of Cleve, when himself a boy in the hostel, had mocked these collations, thinking, "You have not caught me yet." But frightened once by a talk on hell, he began to listen, then to read, and finally turned to the Brothers.[110] These performances were intended not as sermons but admonitions, and so written down for memory and meditation as "points" or "sayings" (*dicta*). Meant to be memorable, they cut to the quick, thus: "There is little difference between a woman and another person. But if a woman makes a diligent effort, she often gains more grace and becomes more uplifted before our dear Lord than a man."[111] Such sayings, many of them spiritual commonplaces, some pointed, some enlightening, set the basic tone inside these gatherings, informing the admonitions they delivered to one another and to schoolboys and interested laypeople. Theirs was a cultivation of the apt word, some proverbial point, a spiritual insight, easily heard, easily passed on.

In the Sisters' houses admonitions came formally from the Brother who acted as their father-confessor, the Sisters at Emmerich remembering theirs as good (*scoen*) preachers.[112] At Diepenveen the Sisters took notes on and wrote up John Brinckerink's collations in the 1410s,[113] as they did Brother Rudolph's in the 1440s at Master Geert's House,[114] and Brother Jasper's in the 1380s/90s and Brother Claus van Euskirchen's in the 1510s.[115] They labeled their transcribed notes "good points" gathered from the collations. The texts read as points, not as sermonic discourse. Sisters also acted themselves, though our sources are more limited. They gathered among themselves on feastday evenings for mutual collations, the Mothers speaking and teaching (*wat goedes toe verkallen, leerden ons vol guedes*) while encouraging the women to address one another. This proved more effective than reading from a large book, Mother Ide (d. 1487) said.[116] According to Sister Heilwich (d. 1481), coming together on feastday evenings to "say something good to one another" was good old custom.[117] Sister Griet (d. 1479), longtime procuratrix, was widely remembered for her "good points."[118] The early sisters in Deventer were said to read in books and then converse mutually (*onderlinge callinge*) about how best to progress in virtue.[119] Sister Hadewich (d. 1434), one of the earliest there and strict in manner, said Sisters should talk only about one of four things, about Scripture or holy writings, about the lessons read during meals, or what they had taken away from the collations, or the virtues of fellow Sisters.[120] But Sister Griete (d. 1444), for instance, held collations on the angels.[121]

About the addresses Brothers delivered or read we have a mix of evidence, though no study has yet tried systematically to survey the major themes. Dirk of Herxen (d. 1457) compiled a book of exemplary collations in Latin and in Dutch, "materials useful and apt for turning over in the memory and in the collations held on feastdays." Organized by topics, correspondent in part to those of Florens' foundational compilation (*Omnes inquit artes*), each was made up of materials drawn mainly from early authors. It focused, as had Florens, on devotional and moral themes, not theological or mystical.[122] The collection began, pragmatically, with a person knowing the "end" of their life-plan, that notion (*scopos*) and the text taken from Cassian.[123] Dirk's collection then went on to the fear of God, the four last things, scripture and reading, temptation, leaving father and mother, simple clothing, manual labor, sin, speech, the seven vices, penance, alms, moral discipline, prayer, the cardinal virtues, poverty, chastity, prudence, perseverance, admonition (drawing on Zerbolt and his texts), correction, not seeking ordination to priesthood (Zerbolt again), the ten commandments, and the gifts of the Spirit. In general, while the Modern-Day Devout innovated in their organizational structures and means, they stayed closer to the mainstream in their spiritual themes, one reason they were never accounted heretics in the end. Toward the end of Dirk's collection came the collation on communal life or a "good society" noted in Chapter 6, also one on the "true nature of Christian perfection." It consisted in "progress in the virtues, not the glory of miracles." The faithful and spiritual people in his era, Dirk argued, were suspicious of miraculous signs, including wonders happening with women (meaning Brigitte or Joan or some such figure), especially those full of ostentation. The point was to know one's purpose, to strive toward "purity of heart or reforming the faculties of the soul," Zerbolt's manuals thus informing not only Devout life but the collations delivered to laypeople and schoolboys.

We come closest to their actual themes, also their practice of admonition, in my view, by examining their "points" or "sayings," a study hardly undertaken as yet, in part because they can seem so random, even commonplace. A visiting Brother became the occasion to hear a "word" from him—a distant, and perhaps self-conscious, echo of Desert Father practices. Peter Horn kept a record of such sayings he heard around the house in Deventer.[124] This suggests the informality, even "democracy," of this admonition, not just in encounters with schoolboys or laypeople, but especially in mutual conversation. Sayings ascribed to Grote and Florens were passed down inside the community (in differing forms, this still not sorted out). One exhorted Brothers to flee all worldly people, especially priests and women. Uppity priests thus represented potentially as great a temptation as women—this one suppressed by Thomas of Kempen (himself later a priest-canon).[125] Admonitions offered a mix of worldly and spiritual wisdom, thus: Whatever you expect from someone, do not inject yourself if honor or vainglory or advantage or carnal love is attached. In a work of God and for a

Brother advance securely, however, even where you expect scorn and no personal comfort. Or again: Flee to your cell as to a lady friend. There compel and coerce yourself; there you are secure.[126] Or this for people who were in part devising their own rhythm of prayer, work, and worship: Frequently to be in church for a long time is rarely useful. For if you pray a long time, and tedium sets in, you will be made sleepy and turn your ears and eyes to empty things, and return to prayer less willingly.[127] One "point" was marked as an admonition for schoolboys:

> You must carefully look out lest you become attracted to scholastic teaching, because worldly learning is very alluring (*affectiua*). But you must go to the Lord through it as a means (*medium*). This is like someone who sets off for Utrecht for a great bit of gold or silver and passes through woods and forests, as if not noticing the way until he can rest at ease when he arrives. Look to it therefore that you do not remain caught in the means.[128]

In these apodictic sayings we come closest to what collations were in practice, homespun advice guiding people toward a distinct lifestyle, often articulated in Latin among the Brothers, always in the vernacular among Sisters and for laypeople. It came closer to lay or parish religious culture in tone and style than to an elitist monastic or mystical circle. This also held for their chosen themes, the focus on virtues and vice, on the four last things, on penance. This must have been deliberate, reflecting the audience or indeed the Sisters and Brothers themselves. Still, the themes and materials drew ultimately in good part from early monastic teachers such as Cassian or Gregory, here rediscovered and made accessible. It was the genius of Thomas of Kempen in the four pamphlets that came to make up his *Imitatio Christi* to shape these sayings and proverbial points, many he inherited or would have heard growing up around the Brothers, into something suppler and more thematically organized—and along the way trimming off the edgier points at times

Spiritual Guidance and Mutual Reproof

The Brothers offered spiritual guidance as well, another infringement upon acts ordinarily reserved to curates or friars. Letters in the summer of 1398 noted their need to stay in Deventer despite the plague and always cited the same reason, to hear confessions and comfort people, also avoid causing scandal by leaving.[129] To churchmen or the inquisitor, people choosing to disclose their sins to the

Devout participated in a usurpation of the power of the keys, the Brothers illicitly intruding into the internal forum, priestly jurisdiction over confession. Zerbolt defended this too (IX), but was careful in his formulation of their practice: whether someone in "receiving counsel" might also "reveal their sins" to a person possessing neither keys (priestly powers) nor jurisdiction. This hints at what was actually going on, spiritual guidance that blurred into a confessional mode, this an illicit move, some charged.[130]

As always, Zerbolt first recognized the letter of the law, then exploited an opening. He presented his case so carefully, so laced with authorities, that its revolutionary force may easily escape a reader. He acknowledged first and last that the ruling *Omnis utriusque*, Lateran IV's requirement of annual confession to a person's own priest, defined ruling law. Even within a communal household (*prefatis societatibus*), so he closed his presentation, priests were permitted to absolve one another or others in any full sacramental sense only with special permission. He drew key distinctions, however. From the main Franciscan casuist (Asteranus) and the jurist Heinrich Boyck, he seized upon one accepted distinction to open up an alternative vision of "giving counsel" or "disclosing sins." In a brief passage near the beginning of Boyck's commentary, taken over from Asteranus, the jurist had recognized confession as also being a virtue (*Uno modo, prout est opus uirtutis*). As a matter of virtue, anyone could humble himself in confession to any cleric or layperson apt for offering prayer or advice (*hoc modo confessio potest fieri cuilibet qui potest adiuuare instruendo uel orando*).[131] Zerbolt then culled out further authorities, including Innocent IV who had earlier noted two kinds of "non-sacramental confession." Anyone, the pope had allowed, might function as a "*minister dei*" in times of necessity or in cases of venial sins (this disputed by some theologians). Further, one could always make confession, he remarked, as a way of seeking aid and counsel (*ut consilium uel auxilium ab aliquo recipiant, dicunt sibi peccatum suum*)[132]—exactly the service the Devout saw themselves as fulfilling.

These had been concessions to spiritual and human practice, never intended to undercut the unique claims of priestly authority in the confessional. But Zerbolt transformed them into a platform for distinctive Modern-Day Devout practices. He declared "non-sacramental confession" or "simple disclosure of sins" something "most useful," and with respect to at least four ends. First, a kind of remitting could take place. On the basis of what authorities had said about pardoning venial sins, he concluded that private confession could remit them, the more so if done devoutly and to enhance contrition.[133] Second, non-sacramental confession enriched a person's understanding of spiritual life, especially his personal struggles with virtue and vice. The person to whom disclosures were made could help discern the virtues and suggest antidotes to vices (a medical metaphor common in confession), Zerbolt here alluding to texts from Cassian and Bernard. What's needed for this nonsacramental disclosure, he proclaimed, was not a power of the keys but a spirit of discernment, not so much a learned man (*literatum*) as someone expert in offering spiritual guidance (*expertum*). Third, any person who made this form of "confession" customary practice would find himself held back from falling easily in fear of embarrassment, of having to tell them again. Lastly, regularly to "open up" about temptations and failings might more quickly liberate a person from them—this supported with a story drawn from Cassian.[134] Zerbolt's exposition of nonsacramental confession sketches out the Devout program for spiritual guidance. But it also offers a potentially alternative vision of confession. While the entire sacramental structure remained in place unchallenged, this practice, drawn in part from monastic example, might effectively supplant it in daily lived experience, a private disclosure of sins and temptations practiced regularly as a virtue. This was altogether licit in a private religious society, Zerbolt argued, and spiritually effective besides.

The arguments were almost certainly Zerbolt's own. Abbot Arnold simply paraphrased them, as did the jurists in Cologne in January 1398. Deacon Foec again went his own way. He supported a Devout practice of mutual counsel and disclosure, and said so.[135] But the case he argued mixed in elements pertinent to *correpcio* and something like a chapter of faults, practices related to obedience and yielding to the head of the household, activities he probably heard about with respect to the women's communities. As for any charge that the Devout illicitly practiced a form of sacramental penance, he tactfully avoided it, as a good lawyer might. Interestingly, this key dimension of Modern-Day Devout practice came to expression in house customaries only in their version of a chapter of faults, even though it proved central to community life, permeating their sayings and exercises. No virtue was so prized as "freely disclosing" one's faults and temptations, no spiritual gift so admired as that of listening and finding an apt word in response.

As for actual practice distinct matters confusingly overlap here, mutual reproof inside a gathering and spiritual guidance directed to persons inside and outside the house. We begin with mutual reproof, speaking to someone else's and your own faults. Sisters, to judge from our one set of surviving statutes, were to gather each Friday for "collation," which here meant the Mother and the senior Sisters exhorting the community about violations of "good order" in keeping house ordinances; after which any Sister could speak to the same, and those faulted were to confess their failings.[136] Brothers for their part held a monthly meeting led by the rector which served essentially the same end as the Sisters' weekly gathering.[137] This looked like a chapter of faults—what Foec had in mind, knowing the women's communities around Utrecht better than the men's in the Oversticht. On the more personal plane, also on Friday, each Sister was to approach another, permitted to reproach the other's faults (*geoorloft is gebreken te vermaenen*), with the other asking to have her faults named. The Sister reproached was to admit her fault, neither bearing grudges, neither acting out of false motives, the reproof (*vermaenen*) not delivered harshly.[138] Brothers spoke of this "reproof" (*correptio*) as an "act of fraternal charity necessary for the preservation of discipline."[139] They were to reproach one another about violations of their house customs, about harsh or foolish talk, empty gossip mongering and storytelling, infringements on silence or on communal goods, all "public vices." To promote openness or ease (*liberiores*) in doing so, each Brother, in this case biweekly, was to go to another and ask personally for reproof. In Deventer/Gouda the general meeting was to begin with a critique delivered by the junior Brother, not the rector or the senior. To get at the real purpose and meaning of mutual reproof in these communities we must listen to the words attributed to Brother Nicholas in the 1510s by the Sisters at Master Geerts House:

> Our old fathers [four named] used to say: "People professed in orders have harsh disciplines and heavy penalities if they go astray. But we have nothing other than one little point, which is reproof (*vermaninge*)." It behoves us therefore to be faithful in it, because if reproof is forgotten among us, then our estate will also perish.[140]

With no Rule or obedience, this mutual reproof was finally, as he said so tellingly, the discipline which kept their life together from dissolving into chaos or self-serving.

As a practice either personal or collective it can never have been easy among people living so closely together. It called for a daunting laying bare of the self in close communities leaving in any case little space for the truly personal. Twenty years after the house at Emmerich had been regularized, Mother Geertruijt (d. 1491) was still encouraging everyone to say openly what needed improving, quite particularly to teach the young in the good ways of the house.[141] Sister Ide (d. 1477), not professed in 1469 because "not strong in the head and also a cripple," was once "sharply chaptered" for some fault, such that those who observed cried, and two nieces also in the house went away hurt and despondent. Ide bore it without a word, and consoled her nieces: "What was done here was not really done to me; be at peace, time here is short and eternity long."[142] This practice, emotionally often very difficult, received interestingly almost no attention in the spiritual manuals. There the focus was on self-examination and self-reproof. Florens set the tone: People should be firm (*severus*) first of all with themselves in reproaching faults, then with those around them, always in kindness and compassion, never out of rancor or scorn.[143] As personal resolve constituted a community and mutual reproach was to sustain it, so self-examination alone could finally ground both the personal resolve and the individual's relation to the whole.

Distinct from mutual reproof as a community-sustaining exercise were spiritual guidance as well as sacramental confession. Sisters had a father-confessor, and it was to him they were to turn in a formal sense for sacramental confession. At Emmerich these Brother-confessors were remembered as treating them kindly, encouraging open-hearted confession, not scolding. These figures were placed first in the memorial book, a mark of deference but also respect.[144] Still, Mother Mechtheld (d. 1476), the last to rule before their regularization, was remembered for intervening with the father-confessor if she heard he had been sharp with anyone in confession.[145] As important in practice, however, was the guidance Sisters provided one another. This was formalized in the *spreekzuster* (literally, "talk-sister"), a spiritual confident to whom one could talk and from whom one could seek guidance. Younger Sisters were to choose one for themselves, intriguingly, and thereby often formed life-long spiritual bonds. This same Mother Mechtheld told younger Sisters to be "open-hearted toward their *spreekzuster* and humbly confess their faults and seek counsel as necessary, so they might become perfect."[146] The word for confess (*belijen*) here was the same as that used for the sacramental act. In effect the Sisters had an alternative system inside the house, aimed at instituting the young in spiritual life, a "non-sacramental confession" as Zerbolt described it. Some Sisters were remembered for humility or submissiveness toward their *spreekzuster*, intimating that this person served in her own way as an authority figure.[147] A Sister Beel (d. 1481) who "taught many devout inward points" had one Sister confess to her she would rather die than spend any more time spinning (their main daily work) and another that she could not pray the Our Father with outstretched arms at night because it caused her too much pain—and she helped them sort out these dilemmas.[148] Sister Griete (d. 1444) at Deventer served many in this role. A woman accounted naturally wise, she would sit on her bed on holy days, and Sisters would come seeking counsel about their passions and faults, she handing out apt remedies like a pharmacist.[149]

Beyond mutual reproof and spiritual counsel inside the gatherings Sisters also acted as counselors to laypeople. Mother Mechthelt was sought out by them for counsel and comfort—she being, Egbert of Deventer said, the wisest person between Dordrecht and Cologne.[150] Laypeople who spoke with her successor Mother Ide about their "desires" said they found solace (*troest*) and help from

God.[151] But this happened with ordinary Sisters too. Whenever laypeople and their children came into the Sisters' "yard" (*were*) at Emmerich, Sister Henrick (d. 1469) would ask them after their guardian angel or apostle, and bestow one if they had none. She was regarded as a veritable saint: She bore suffering patiently (she was sickly); rarely said a word that was not good or useful; comforted, enlightened, and taught with spiritual wisdom any who came to her for help or advice; treating thoughtfully any laypeople who came into their house and yard.[152] Laypeople who were despondent or suffering also went to Sister Beel, an especially gifted person whom many Sisters asked to have attend and console them on their deathbeds.[153] These Sisters were effectively offering ministerial services more typically associated with priests.

Among Brothers we find the same intense concern with mutual reproof and personal guidance. But their situation was more complex, some being priests and many clerics. Priest-Brothers who served as father-confessors to Sisters or schoolboys or interested laypeople, providing they were locally licensed, did so in principle within the normal workings of the church. Indeed a Windesheim canon named Arnold Gheyloven, originally from Rotterdam, professed at Groenendael, in 1423 prepared a *summa* of moral theology specifically for guiding schoolboys at Deventer and Louvain, which he entitled, very notably, "Know Yourselves" (*Gnotosolitos*).[154] But even here the line was surprisingly blurred. In the unpublished sayings of John Hattem (d. 1485), priest and longtime procurator at Deventer, the very first enjoined listeners to "reveal your passions" to the father (rector, always a priest) or instructor (thus boys in the hostels) or your "spiritual Brother" (the equivalent of the *spreekzuster*)—three choices! And he told this story. A local artisan (*mechanicus*) was accustomed to "lament his faults" to the Brothers (*conqueri*: thus avoiding the term "confess"). When the devil plagued him with a certain passion, he threatened to go see them, even putting on his cloak, whereupon the devil disappeared.[155] Students young and old, we are told, ran to Hattem seeking medicine for their souls, indeed coming into his room, where several at a time would climb up on his bed to fit in.[156] He was also said to advise a student after his formal confession, sacramental absolution and spiritual guidance being thus quite distinct.[157] This sort of thing had been happening from the beginning, many laypeople coming into the room of Brother Henry (d. 1410) at Deventer "to receive comfort."[158] Nor were such practices restricted to the priests in the house. A lay Brother at Zwolle would sit in his writer's chair copying books in Dutch and there receive laypeople to whom "he gave counsel like our priests and clerics."[159] In offering counsel Brothers labored to be scrupulous. Godfrey (d. 1450) at Deventer said that whenever someone died who had come to him for confession and guidance a certain horror gripped him: he might not have been diligent enough, and thus put the person at eternal risk.[160]

The guidance offered grew out of their reading, their scrapbook making, their sayings, their mutual admonition. To those grown despondent in their spiritual exercises John Hattem said, "It's not all oil, not all unguent," and told the story of a master caring for a wounded horse, first with ungent, but also with a stinging purgative. To another suffering at night with insupportable fears about the future, he reminded him that the past was past, the future not yet, the present to be focused on, and if God be for him no one could be against him.[161] The Brothers above all saw themselves as passing out remedies or antidotes, these drawn from their reading, their admonishing and their sayings. To combat gluttony, the most primal of animal desires, one had to counterpose the forces of interiority, along with a desire for things heavenly; best was to cultivate sobriety, not too much food, not too much fasting. To combat lust, in the body or spirit, required a long struggle, aided by a continuous moderate fast, and also not allowing the soul or hands to be idle.[162] These were traditional notions in fact, gleaned in this case primarily from the Franciscan David of Augsburg. What the Brothers developed an instinct for, even if their stance often appeared firm and ascetic, was moderation, sensing the realities of the human condition. That arose from what they most insisted upon, self-examination and self-knowledge, the touchstone of their whole conversionary endeavor.

Modern-Day Devotion: Examining the Self, Making Progress, Experiencing Peace

Converts, Zerbolt taught, were to become imperious rulers of their own personal universe (*rigidus imperator tui microcosmi*), judges of themselves in their own tribunal.[163] The end of all this reading and admonishing and spiritual guidance was finally to cultivate an inner life (another oft-repeated Devout term), to learn to know yourself (*teipsum disce agnoscere*) and to care for yourself (*cura tui ipsius*).[164] Thomas of Kempen, trying to win schoolboys away from clerical posts and university learning, stated simply: "This is the very highest and most useful learning (*lectio*, Middle-English *redinge*), the true knowledge and despising of yourself."[165] This built on teachings going back to the twelfth century. Within Devout circles, however, it acquired its own distinctive ways and tones. Knowing came by way of constant self-examination. Despising, linked obviously to "contempt for the world" traditions, aimed primarily in this case at realistic self-assessment, personal honesty about the vagaries of the heart and passions. This self-knowing served as the pendant to the "resolving" (*proposita*) that animated their conversionary intent. An independently arranged religious life would fail apart from keen self-knowing, even a despising (*despectio, versmadenisse*) of the lingeringly unsatisfactory self. In an influential letter, copied out by Thomas and by Busch, Florens instructed one of his converts to "place before his eyes" every morning and everyday after the mid-day meal all his evil customs, principle vices, and the virtues toward which he was striving.[166]

To reform the powers of the soul a person had first vigorously to "have it out" with himself (*teipsum diligenter discucias*), truly see what he was (*teipsum uides, ut qualis fueris discas*).[167] Converts were to examine themselves each day anew, preferably at day's end, in Zerbolt's view: to see where older customs held on, tawdry thoughts slipped in, attention during prayer strayed, time at work got wasted, and so on.[168] This extended to a "most severe" exam of the soul's powers (intellect, memory, will), and especially the affections: what you love or hate, what saddens or gladdens you, what upsets you.[169] Admonition and mutual colloquy inside the house helped facilitate this, that is, seeing yourself through others' eyes, preserving your self from self-deception. This, he added, could yield the self-knowledge of saints.[170] But the most efficacious way to know yourself (*efficacius ad tui cognicionem promotiuum*) was finally to take up personal battle with your vices, confront first-hand their resistance, come thus truly to know what you were made of, even, as it were, to touch it.[171] Only after you had acquired this experiential knowledge would you become fit to counsel others.[172] For if such knowledge came only from books, Zerbolt remarked, it would be a "tinkling cymbal" (1 Cor. 13:1). To admonish and guide fittingly and compassionately, "a sweet and indivisible concord must arise in a person from holy writing and experience."[173]

Examining the self was accordingly built into the day. After the house closed and silence descended at the end of day, each person was to "hold chapter with themselves," according to the customaries, a notion borrowed from the twelfth century.[174] Exactly the same was enjoined in women's statutes, with the same reference to "Bernard." For them it was an exercise undertaken at the foot of their bed evenings after the *Salve regina*: to investigate (*ondersuecken*) themselves and their conscience, whether during that day they had advanced in virtue.[175] This exercise also could involve writing. Master Geert reportedly wrote his faults down on scraps, these dutifully destroyed at his death. In the Münster customary tradition a Brother resolved to note down his faults each night on wax tablets after self-examination, then to consult them before going to confession, ordinarily once a week.[176] In a text that may come from Florens (more likely Zerbolt), two times were recommended as best for "meditating and exercising," at vespers around eight before sleeping and in the morning on rising, before matins.[177] Self-examination thus served as a kind of *basso continuo* that underlay and sustained nearly all other spiritual and communal exercises among the Modern-Day Devout. This medieval "self-knowing" and "self-care" pre-dated and prepared the way for any Renaissance "self-fashioning," whatever sixteenth-century innovations ensued. Thomas More, the figure Greenblatt began with, entirely presumed and cultivated such traditions of knowing the soul and caring for the self, including its self-despising or "self-cancelling."[178] "Self-fashioning" built upon deep medieval roots, mainly monastic, and the Modern-Day Devout self-consciously adapted that tradition, even transformed it, so as to create religious life, communal and personal, outside the cloister.

Souls face to face with God, stripped of all masks or guises: this was the heart of the matter. This might also be conceived as earnest, lifelong preparation for death. The presence of Plague made that actual, taking their founder at age forty-four, Zerbolt their thinker and writer at age thirty-one, a host of Brothers and Sisters in 1429, then in 1458 some fifty-five sisters in Deventer, thirty alone in Master Geert's House. But we must be careful of easy causal connections. A computerized study has found the word "death" in two percent of all sentences in the Sisters' lives at Deventer, about the same rate of occurrence as the words "holy" and "ardent," but far less frequent than the words "humble" (5 percent) and "virtue" (4 percent).[179] Death was an important reality, but thoughtful preparation for it was more so. The Devout concern with spiritual preparation arose at the same time that Jean Gerson, along with others, set in motion the "Memento Mori" tradition that would take the fifteenth century by storm. In those relatively short texts, soon accompanied by dramatic illustrations that carried over into print, a person was to dispel self-delusion in the face of death, exactly the point of the daily Devout self-examination, by examining one's faith, doubt, pride, patience, and so on.

In nearly all Devout lives or chronicles, the *agon*, the final struggle with death became a set-piece. As someone approached the end, often sensing and announcing it themselves, Sisters or Brothers attended them, called to the deathbed by a house bell, gathered round to encourage, chant penitential psalms, attend last rites, place the resurrection candle in the hands of a departing companion. They observed a person with whom they had lived in a life-long "society of friends" (*amicitia socialis*) now facing down the final enemy. They took for granted a natural fear of death, so too a dread of "agonic" pain and divine judgment, but also looked toward the reward for a lifetime of readying and remaking. The mix would differ by individual. We find peace and humor, a book brought for reading, a favored *spreekzuster* brought in, a woman stripping to meet her bridegroom naked (these noted previously). Often they refused any softening or privileges. John of Hattem (d. 1485), disabled by growing pain, refused a more pleasing dish prepared by Sisters. He also walked in the Brothers' garden, visited the nearby house where his life as a Brother had begun, later asked two novices whether they would like to go with him to Jerusalem, also insisted on attending the monthly colloquy. Asked if he wanted to live longer, he said that he had lived long enough, even if he had barely begun to take real care to improve in virtue (*parum heu me emendare curaui*). Asked if he was content in his conscience, he quoted a saying: "I do not fear to die, since we shall have a good Lord." On the last day he asked for food, recalled in Dutch a saying at meals from his mother, then asked to be placed in a chair, where he sat up praying until his head nodded in death.[180] Hattem was not alone in being at peace. A Sister Katherynna (d. 1470) of Emmerich, asked on her deathbed how it was with her conscience, replied: "so well that I have no words for it."[181]

Equally revealing, however, is the (still unpublished) story of Brother Albert (d. 1492), a layman who entered the house in Deventer at age thirty to serve as tailor and cook and died eight years later of fevers then sweeping the region. Though entering as an adult layman, he engaged in sacred reading, offered antidotes to Brothers who came to him with their vices, spoke up aptly at the collations, and admonished students. When he was struck down by high fever, he examined his conscience thoroughly in preparation for death and then grew exceedingly anxious about two items somehow not purged, whether hidden or insufficiently confessed: the purchase of a kitchen work-table beyond costs allowed by the leadership, and making loans to poor relatives and neighbors caught in famine (arranged either on his own, or on the Brothers' collateral, both forbidden). The Brothers tried to reassure him with hymns and good cheer, but he became convinced that he was damned. His father came in to say he would repay the money—but to no avail. In his fevered state he cried out "hellish" words, and suffered a vision of being called before the Tribunal and damned. Thereafter he never regained full consciousness, though the Brothers asked for a consoling sign. They saw his death as "most horrible," beyond any precedent they could recall, and attributed it largely to the fevers (that human realism again). They were nonetheless deeply shaken, and hoped the form of his death had done him "no harm" (*non obfuere*). They also found it profitable (*profuisse*), as many others set out thoroughly to reexamine themselves.[182] We must recognize here too, for all the human realism and words of mercy, an anxiety sewn implicitly in the conscience by this constant call for self-examination, a lurking fear of entering the divine presence impure, insufficiently confessed, unfit for heavenly companionship.

Unlike people who took vows and grew slack, "un-exercised and unknowing of themselves" (*inexercitati et sibi ipsis manent incogniti*),[183] the Modern-Day Devout, living out their resolve, filled their day with spiritual exercises. This "exercising" turned their resolve into action over a lifetime. Almost any act—humbling the self, praying, working, meditating—could count as "exercise," working the self, making it spiritually fit.[184] But it came linked most often to meditation and to living out the conversionary resolve. The way of life they adopted had finally to operate from within or it could not be sustained. Their exercises, though widely varying, turn the day's structure into a personal plan, this often written down, if only a few survive, one being a very early example linked directly to Florens or more probably Zerbolt (See Figure 19). This reads: "rise at the third hour" and "prepare yourself for matins" by reading through the materials for meditation "as I wrote them out." There follow notes such as "I want to avoid an excess of talking and conversation," to keep silent in the kitchen and hall, and so on. Rising at three rather than four places this text well back in the 1390s, and referring to "what I wrote" about meditation could point to either Zerbolt or Florens, this manuscript a copy dated to 1400. Intriguingly, a subsequent hand rendered all its singular verbs (I, you) as plurals, adapting the personal to the communal.[185] Another text, subsequently titled "the customs of our house," offered such an exercise in far greater detail, its day and intentions offering rich anticipations of later patterns; this being, in Klausmann's view, Florens's own exercise transformed into house customs.[186] However that may be, the life of the community hinged upon the inner life of the individual, each member turning each step of the day into a personal resolution. That is exactly what we find commended to Sisters as well in Salome Sticken's "Formula for a way of life." Hers was not an impersonal description of how to set up or conduct community life but an injunction to each to do this or intend that as they lived out their day, the collective hinging upon the personal.[187] Brothers and Sisters thus brought to communal life a considerably different sensibility than that of the professed, who operated out of obedience, submitting themselves to an external Rule. For the Devout these exercises, not the customs, drove the life, even if by definition the personal and interior also had to fit within the communal structure, the house customs.

Exercises also meant those meditations each Brother or Sister might sustain on their own, whether in private or as part of the whole. In one set of exercises central to the men's house at Deventer the day ended and began anew with meditating on topics and readings each Brother set for himself.[188] Florens's "Little Tractate" suggested a set of meditations on the four last things (death, judgment, hell, heaven). One should think how death would come suddenly; what natural terror it would bring; what remorse of conscience, the past suddenly flooding the memory; how quickly a lifetime had disappeared; how awful the separation from loved ones and earthly goods; the look of a dying person; how one entered this unknown region; burial in the ground; lasting oblivion.[189] Rehearsing this at night before retiring was said to be useful for driving away any

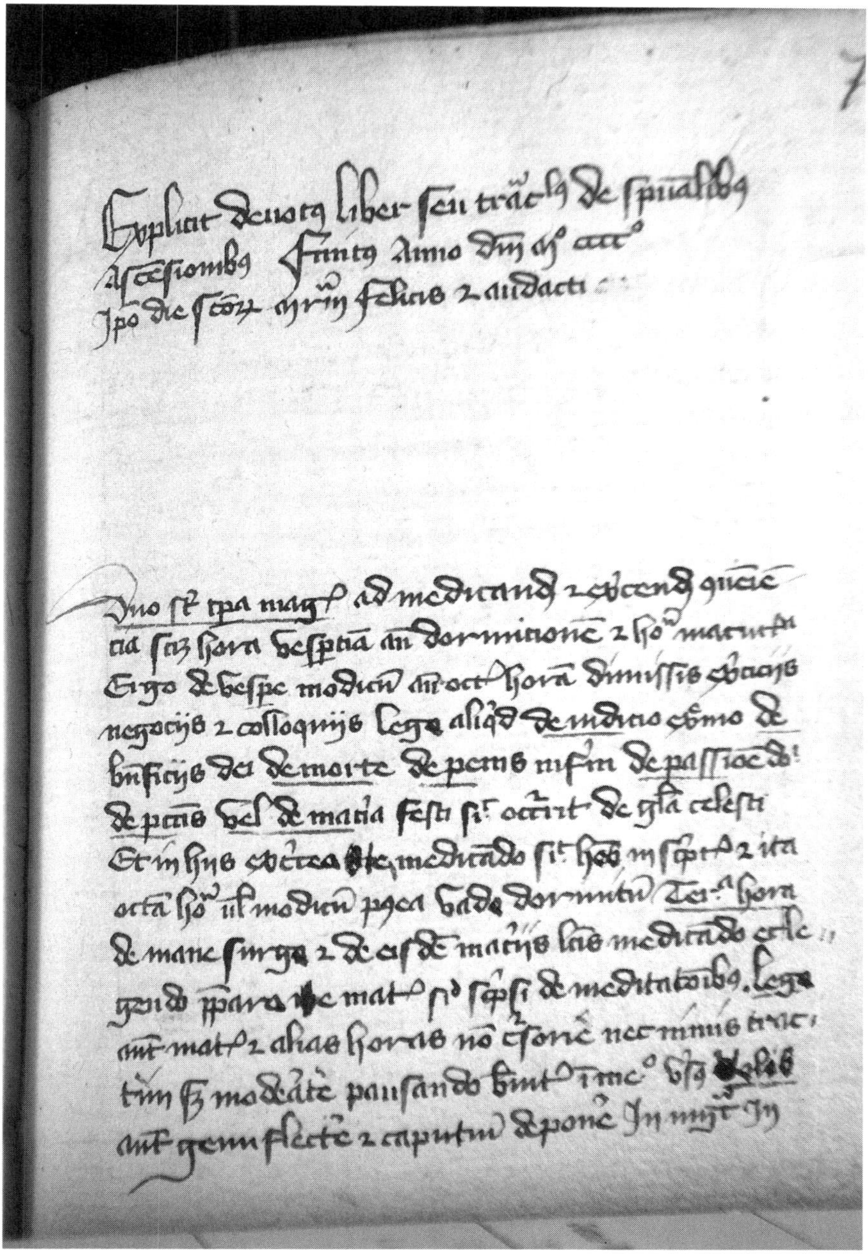

Figure 19. A copy from the year 1400 of personal spiritual exercises possibly first composed by Zerbolt (in the mid- to later 1390s), appended to the earliest extant copy of his *Spiritual Ascents*. A slightly later hand altered the exercise from "I" to "you" (thus *me* to *te*, *habeo in scriptis* to *habes*, *surgo* to *surges*, and so on). Cologne, Historisches Stadtarchiv, MS 8° 145, f. 75r.

alien thoughts that otherwise might invade.[190] Meditating on the passion, by contrast, to be done all through the day, was understood to elicit love rather than fear.[191] Zerbolt set out "little bundles" of passion meditations, possibly taken over from Grote.[192] Bonaventure, ps-Bonaventure and Liudolf as well as Suso had suggested ordered approaches, but the Devout now practiced a more systematic method, anticipating, it is often said, what would emerge among the Jesuits.[193] The person was to "revolve in the mind" all they had read or could "give shape to" (*si ibi non est expressum, ex teipso formare*)[194] For each day of the week three "points" were to be drawn from the passion story, turned to (*converte te*) for then turning over within, the person to see, think (*cogita*), place before the eyes, bend and bow with, feel with. For these meditations the Devout spiritual manuals drew on materials widely available in the Later Middle Ages, even if they also lent them distinctive emphases and tones. The point in all this was quite simply to "transform affections and mores" from within.[195]

The Devout set up their way of life in an age when visual images enlivened the walls of churches (inside and out) as well as chapels and shrines. Sacred paintings and sculptures were now becoming widely obtainable in commercial markets, at the high end or low, not only for side altars but an individual's inner chambers. Devotion and the visual became so interlinked that the one could hardly be imagined without the other, the practice of devotion without images to focus or inspire it, the production of images without a large ecclesiastical and devotional market to finance it. Amid all this the Modern-Day Devout privileged texts over images. This was not a confrontational stance like some Lollards across the channel. They aimed at simplicity, with no hint of iconoclasm. But it is one reason why, despite endless attempts to link them to the flourishing Netherlandish art of this period, few or no connections have ever successfully been established.[196] To be sure, the Devout worked as illuminators in making books, and their houses, we occasionally hear, contained a sculptured image of the house patron, and their meditations in some sense presumed images (the shepherds, the crown of thorns). But in their communities spiritual life turned on texts, and their energy went into mental imaging.[197] They were enjoined to think, to feel, to consider, to move the affections of the heart, but not to focus on a certain image, even if that was sometimes presupposed (no absolute dichotomy here). Zerbolt's chapter on passion meditation has a careful choice of verbs: people were to reflect on points in the passion story and direct them to their utility, to consider them, thoroughly to occupy themselves with them (*pertractes*), turn them over in the mind (*in mente tua reuoluis*), represent them to the mind (*in mente tua representetur*). To feel with the suffering meant to turn it over in the mind (*semper in mente tua reuoluere*), forming the details in yourself from readings or from within.[198] This was not an image-less meditation, the goal for some earlier and contemporary mystical writers. Still, the intent was not to immerse themselves in passion images, but to enter mentally into the passion so it could overcome their passions, counter their trouble or despair, act as an antidote to anxiety or pain or evil.[199]

Meditation aimed too at sharpening self-examination (*exacuere in circumspectione sui*).[200] Still, resolutions and exercises and meditations were not ends in themselves, large as they loomed in Devout spiritual literature. They were means to an end, and that end was steadily to advance in virtue, or as they kept reminding themselves, to persevere to the end and be saved (Matt. 10:22, 24:13). With the Franciscan David of Augsburg Florens and Zerbolt defined virtue as an "affection of the mind." And so to purge the heart and reform the powers of the soul was finally to plant (*inserere*) virtues in the mind and heart.[201] This was to be undertaken day by day, point by point, vice after vice, virtue after virtue, methodically if you like, then examined at the end of each day and the results perhaps inscribed in your scrapbook. This was truly to know and care for yourself. Striking, again, was not the material but the method. The Devout proposed to proceed pragmatically, like setting a shop or city in order:

> There are many who wanting to wipe out the vices confusedly go to war against all, fighting against all but defeating none, running about uncertainly and striking empty air. There are others who proceed against one vice today and fight another tomorrow, who, since they pursue none properly, follow none to its destruction. You, however, advance not thus but as an ordered line into battle. For you ought to take up one vice that is most troublesome (*molestum*) to you, and pursue it until it surrenders, directing against it all your effort and mind's intent. Whenever you meet resistance, start again, praying often for its extinction, emitting ardent sighs, pouring out tears, though not giving yourself so totally to the effort against this one as to be ruined by others.[202]

What the Sisters and Brothers looked for was "spiritual carpentry" (*geestliker tymmeringe*)[203]—a remarkable phrase for "self-fashioning" employed in one of the memorial lives. Each Devout convert was to build or re-build the self to render it useful for work and prayer, for teaching and advising, a "carpentered spiritual self," so to speak.

This was serious business. About John Kassel (1398), a layman, they noted that he "fought fiercely against himself" the first four years, becoming at times somewhat depressed (*contristari*).[204] At the heart of it was the moral struggle. Expositions about carnal desire (*luxuria*), based in part on David of Augsburg, were unblushingly clear. This "beast" made itself manifest in titillations and movements of the flesh, also in affections and inclinations of the soul. It blinded a person, springing up merely at the sight of a woman or through pleasing talk. It required multiple remedies: fasting, avoiding idleness, stirring up spiritual desires to counter carnal desire, a firm resolution manfully to avoid any sexual act.[205] Notably, only this vice got singled out for treatment in the statutes. Contact with women was to be avoided, especially easy or enticing talk; conversation kept short, with no direct eye contact.[206] In the Münster tradition this generated an additional resolve (*proponimus*): no care of women or hearing confessions (obviously not observed in fact), no Sisters' washing the men's clothes, no mutual invitations for meals (or at least minimized)[207]—all of which suggests steady and familiar contact. The customary from Deventer/Gouda added a cautionary provision as well against meeting with students or young men for spiritual guidance behind closed doors.[208]

Experience and honesty entered in here. Brothers in particular had regular contact with laypeople attending collations, with schoolboys, and with members of their own families as did women producing textiles for market or upon attending church. Secular clerics and adolescent students, the chief recruitment ground for Brothers, were moreover, as everyone knew, regular clients of medieval prostitutes, they also present in towns like Deventer, one of them someone John Brinckerink tried to recruit for the Sisters.[209] Memorials at Deventer sometimes noted that, to the best of their knowledge (*ex veresimili coniectura*), a Brother had died a virgin, this also said of the rector Godfrey (d. 1450), a former lector.[210] So few young people (men or women), they claimed, actually kept chaste anymore, "fewer than most people would believe"—this likely echoing their work as spiritual guides or perhaps their own experience.[211] The chronicle from Doesburg tells of a man who left the Brotherhood to join a Cistercian monastery because he could not resist carnal temptation apart from the discipline and walls of a cloister, also of two Brothers who left together after being attracted to one another (*inordinato amore se copulantes*), and a father-confessor who became involved with Sisters and finally left with one of them.[212]

At the heart of this Modern-Day Devotion were texts and lives, reading to shape lives, lives then memorialized in texts. So too their most original form of writing came in the shape of personal exercises and scrapbooks on the one hand and memorial lives on the other, both deeply informed by the routines of continuous self-examination and mutual reproof. Those stories have informed this entire study (see Figure 16 for the table of contents of the Sisterbook for Master Geerts House, so often cited in this study). We must pause for a moment finally to consider their characterizations, always remembering edifying intentions. For all their spiritual aspirations, as in Zerbolt's systematic "ascents," the Devout harbored a sober, sometimes slightly dark, view, and along with it a kind of human realism born of their own self-examination. They started with the human as they found it, that is, what they observed in the emotional and mental predispositions of companion Brothers or Sisters. As Zerbolt explained it, a convert had to organize his battle against vice in a way correspondent to his "general inclination." Some, he explained, are by nature scrupulous, others perplexed, some timid, some happy, some sad, some brash; and so each must arrange their spiritual exercises accordingly.[213] By living in communal households they grew keenly alert to such features in one another. A Sister Wibbe (d. 1412) was "simple" by nature but, they said, turned that simplicity to good effect in their way of life. Sister Stijne (d. 1435), lively by nature, found the life's disciplines hard, and suffered considerable anxiety at first adjusting to its ways. Sister Mynte (d. 1444) was naïve and good-hearted, so much so that her good cheer could prove irritating. Sister Wibbe (d. 1449) was happy and willing by nature, so much so that she had little understanding of evil.[214] Writing all these remarkable memorial lives was no accident. The lives represented the fruition of the enterprise, born of that steady drive to deepen human inwardness, that daily struggle to do battle with vicious passions, to advance bit by bit in virtue, to cultivate devotional affections. At Deventer someone drew up a list of themes for collations: the four last things, the seven vices, and so on. Under each rubric he then copied stories taken over from the memorial lives of their own recently departed Brother-companions, not sayings from church fathers, not points from the long-departed Grote or Florens, not examples drawn from saints, not wondrous miracles.[215] Their own lives could serve as paradigmatic exemplars for vices combatted and virtues lived out.

In an age full of talk about reform of the church in head and members, of religious orders, of social estates, of kingdoms and statutes—the Modern-Day Devout focused on knowing, examining, caring for, and methodical re-making the self, or in Zerbolt's titles the "reformation of the powers of the soul" and undertaking "spiritual ascents." For them the end was not to lose the self in the abyss (Marguerite) or in a common divine life of union without intermediating means (Ruusbroec) or in the ground of being prior to being (Eckhart). These options were still around, still read, still followed by some, but they had grown wary of them, and not only because the church was prickly about them. It comes down to what spoke to them, what attracted them. What we find most commonly in their texts and lives was a moral vision, all the emphasis upon virtue and vice, the concern with merit, the preoccupation with daily examining and measuring. In the larger world around them this took the genre form of "mirrors," literary representation of what upright or holy people should be and do. As much as Devout organization emulated that of the professed religious and their reading turned back to monastic fathers (late antique or twelfth century), the tone they adopted was closer in many ways to the parish and to townspeople than to the cloister, as in their craftsman-like approach to "spiritual carpentry." What lent tension and dynamism to their conversionary zeal was their attempt simultaneously to live and work in towns and to cultivate a probing interior life. This leads to the second point. What they sought was to "live quietly," to be "at peace," and to share that peace with others (captured by Thomas in the epigraph). Theirs was a yearning for "quietude" and "apartness," in their form of life as well as their spiritual interiors, to be fostered nonetheless outside vows and cloisters amid all the clamor (*strepitus*) around them. These Sisters and Brothers lived just off narrow city streets and markets and still attended church in parishes. They had to create an inner cell, possible only with constant self-care and disciplined effort. Theirs was a distinctive and in its way original outlook, fixed on re-making the person in this world, if always in preparation for the next, pursued in very practical ways like the people they lived among, if relentlessly spiritual and disciplined in its form of life.

Our historical vision of late medieval society must hold in tension a full-blooded world and a passionate asceticism, privileged legal hierarchies and inventive private societies, people who enjoyed life to the full and people possessed of a powerful sense of suffering. The Modern-Day Devout created a way to pursue a life filled with self-examination and advancing in virtue, filling their day with self-supporting work and their minds with meditation schemes. This experience looked to the personal and the inwardly-directed, retold in Latin or the mother-tongue in the lives of their companions. Conversion and care of the self demanded every day anew, even of those entering too young or as unwilling or inapt participants, that they return daily to the exercises and the scrapbook, the long hours of labor, the reading and writing, the self-examining and self-critique, in hopes of knowing and possibly expressing what it was like to experience a deepest self, the heart and all the affections, "glued to the deity" as Sister Stijne put it. Such an "inward" and "devout" person could, Thomas of Kempen held, bringing our story full circle, "freely turn/convert himself toward God" (*libere conuertere*, *vry te God keren*) and "lift himself above himself" and "rest in the enjoyment" (*fruitiue quiescere*, *rusten inden ghebruken*, *reste fruybly*), that "fruition of peace" echoing the term Ruusbroec used for the highest contemplative experience of God, not rapture but peace and "enjoyment."[216]

Conclusion: Private Gatherings and Self-Made Societies in the Fifteenth Century

To PASSERSBY IN fifteenth-century Netherlandish towns, the Modern-Day Devout might have looked on occasion like an overgrown artisanal household laboring at textiles or book-making, or a religious house with its life inside focused on liturgical prayer and collective discipline, or a parish house offering townspeople and students preaching and spiritual guidance. Each perception had truth in it. Yet Devout households were none of these, at least not exactly, and that puzzled contemporaries, sometimes irritating them. To the inquisitor they looked like a sect, a conventicle in flagrant violation of papal law. To friars the Modern-Day Devout looked like a self-made religious order. To local parish rectors their gatherings ("congregations") looked like potential rivals offering alternative and apart ministries. To city aldermen such gatherings looked all too likely to slip away into ecclesiastical immunity. Yet the Modern-Day Devout survived, even flourished in places, and secured privileges to protect this way of life. In defending these arrangements during the late 1390s Zerbolt regularly employed the terms "private" (*privati*: meaning not a public corporation) and "house" (*domus*: like a household with its paterfamilias or materfamilias) and "gathering" (*congregatio, vergadering*: freely assembled people). That language and what it represented would persist to the end—as would varying degrees of suspicion and harassment it provoked. To make sense of this we need to look back one last time, and in a broader way. But we begin, as ever with the Devout and in the fifteenth century, with a particular case.

The house at Herford, founded with three other clerics by a priest from Münster through the usual *donatio inter vivos* in 1427/28, reached its peak, like other Devout houses, around 1500 with at least seventeen Brothers and a hostel for schoolboys. When Evangelical Reformers took control of the city their preachers moved in 1532 to close the house. The Brothers, then twelve in number, responded with a rationale for their way of life ("Grundt des Fraterlevendes"), nineteen dense pages written in their Low German vernacular.[1] All the essential formulas, now under threat, persisted. They, to quote, had firmly resolved (*vorgesat*) in Christian freedom to live chastely and in common from the work of their hands, not to beg, and to wear simple clothing. The New Testament had counseled chastity, they explained to these Reformers, and so they had freely resolved to live this out in common, as an estate in society (*standt des levendes*) above reproach.[2] Cleverly, in the face of new Protestant ordinances and New Testament religion, they characterized their special estate as a life in house churches (*huskercken*).[3] What most disturbed the city's Evangelical pastors and magistrates emerges by implication from the "Grundt": chastity first of all (which most of these preachers had just given up); a communal life (defended from Scripture and Augustine, the Reformers' favored church father); a gathering ("congregation") set up independently and engaged in preaching and sacraments (existing apart from the now Protestant city congregation); unusual clothing (defended as the way plain folks used to dress); and self-made household statutes. These objections were virtually the same raised by medieval churchmen in the 1390s, if now on different theological and legal grounds. The Protestant preachers (*Predyckstul*), like Dominican preachers a generation earlier, charged the Brothers with being a sect, a planting outside Christ's vineyard.[4] Confronted with the Brothers' apologia, they turned it over in bewilderment to Luther—where medieval critics ordinarily would have turned to a bishop or an inquisitor or a pope. Doctor Martin Luther at Wittenberg wrote back in his own hand. He found nothing "unchristian" in this "little book," and asked that these preachers spare the Brothers. Their upright way of life pleased him extraordinarily (*auss der massen gefaln*), he said. Melanchton added in Latin, cutting quickly to the legal and theological questions at stake, that their "society" should be adjudged "licit" (legally acceptable) rather than "counseled" or "perfect" (theological notions Reformers were repudiating).[5]

Luther had encountered the Devout briefly as a teenager in Magdeburg and in 1520/21 had written a laudatory preface for the publication of John Pupper's theological fragments. Here he noted that the Brothers' house possessed certain public rights (*das ist öffentlich, dass sie Pfarrecht haben*) going beyond those of a simple household (*Hausgesind*), namely their right to offer sacramental ministries under certain circumstances. But the city would now no longer tolerate, as the Brothers explained it to Luther in September 1534, their "living in Christian freedom apart from vows," nor their efforts to "reform young people to the image of Christ." This elicited a further and angry response from Luther in October 1534. He saluted the Brothers on their way of life (*vestrum vivendi institutum*). These "hypocrites of the new Gospel" had no right to lay new burdens on them, a plan, for instance, to compel them to serve as schoolmasters without pay as a condition for survival. Monasteries were once schools, in Luther's new vision of the medieval past, thus institutions founded with public and princely monies under public law, hence to be returned to public service (a version of fifteenth-century disendowment notions). But your gathering, he said to the Brothers, making a distinction, is a private house (*Vestrum collegium privata domus*), its services underwritten by your own labors, "like a private citizen taking care to teach his own children" (alluding to their care for schoolboys).[6] At least on these points, and actually on more, Luther was thinking still in fifteenth-century terms. He saw the Brothers as a private gathering, not a public religious institution, but one that had obtained certain public privileges, such as to hold communion among themselves and to provide spiritual care to young people. By the 1530s most Protestant leaders, pressing Luther's own rebellion against the medieval public church, aimed to ban all religion-like estates outside the congregational parish. The English king, whatever his motivations, would proceed to dissolve all monasteries four years after this exchange. And the post-Tridentine papacy a generation later (1568) would repudiate any halfway or inbetween state. But as for the Brothers in Herford, to complete that story, they survived on Luther's word (until 1802), uniquely among Devout houses becoming a household for chaste Lutheran men considering or entering ministry.

It is the fifteenth-century world we must understand if we wish to grasp the houses and the way of life of the Modern-Day Devout.[7] From the 1370s—crucial for Grote, Wyclif, Catherine of Siena, papal schism, conciliar approaches to reform and government, the Observant movement, Italian humanists, vernacular poets like Langland and Chaucer, the visionary Julian, the diffusion of universities, and much more—European society sparkled with new religious and cultural agendas and experimented with new political forms, many of which remained in play until about 1530. This "long fifteenth century" is the era of the Modern-Day Devout, and has recently emerged as deserving of closer attention for its own tones and emphases, still decidedly medieval, but also creative and distinct, not just "autumnal." From it has sprung interest now in Lollards or women visionaries (Joan of Arc) or reformist streams in English literature as well as careful attention to new holy blood cults (Bynum), visual images (Hamburger), and a new "devotional theology" (Hamm).[8] Making sense of the Modern-Day Devout is of a piece with making sense of this long fifteenth century, something we have only begun to do in all its complexity. It is to recognize, as Luther on occasion did, Erasmus too (not choosing between "Evangelicals" or "Romans," "humanists" or "religious"), a layered environment in which multiple and contradictory options competed and coexisted. When scholars argue about whether Luther was "medieval" still, or Erasmus a "Christian" humanist, or Machiavelli "republican" in spirit, they point to roots deep in this long fifteenth century. Europe as a whole, however much ink is spilled over Germany in the 1520s, did not transform society and culture into something definitively other until after 1530. Sisters and Brothers peaked in numbers in the 1490s, also in expansion of their complexes, and withered dramatically after about 1525.

Brothers and Sisters defended their way of life, their "estate" in fifteenth-century society, as lying outside the public sphere, as a "private" society. To get at what that meant is not easy, our notions of "public" and "private" having formed in the wake of John Locke and the nineteenth century. Burckhardt set out claims in the 1860s for an emerging Renaissance "individual," and Duby a generation ago for a developing fifteenth-century private space. Both notions have been seriously tempered by historical recognition of pervasive familial, guild, and corporate interests as still shaping human life, not to speak of oversight by local churches or towns, whence even the bedroom or marriage-making was not in the modern sense "private."[9] Neither was, we must be clear, the making of a religious society. And yet in the fifteenth century there was an expanding personal sphere, evident for instance in domestic space, separate bedrooms, say, in wealthy lay households, and in religious orders (that to which the Observants were reacting) separate rooms or expense accounts or even "vacations," and for wealthy or pious individuals more generally personal books of hours to pray the liturgy, Grote himself making this possible in Dutch in the Netherlands.[10] Italian merchants now kept diaries and books of instruction as legacies for their heirs, even as the Devout would design personal spiritual exercises, and lay persons of a religious bent acquired books and images for their inner chambers.[11] Brothers led their lives in their own rooms, and Sisters had a kind of personal space in and around their beds. In historical fact the Modern-Day Devout stood in a dialectical relationship to this fifteenth-century culture. They were its beneficiaries in designing their own religious lives, even as they critiqued the personal excesses they perceived in orders and among the worldly. This broader culture, while central to the sociocultural ambience, does not precisely get at what Zerbolt meant by "private" in the 1390s, or Luther in the 1530s, as applied to gatherings and ways of life able to form and survive in this socioecclesiastical context.

Zerbolt often invoked the notion of a household. An urban household with its own internal social or familial or labor patterns was in some sense private, and yet decidedly not private but embedded in all the ordinances and expectations that came with the larger urban society. Brothers and Sisters could not simply withdraw from society into their own private sphere. There were questions about jurisdiction civil and ecclesiastical, about taxes, about parish duties, about products entering the local marketplace, indeed about their *mores*, any unusual way of life inviting the scrutiny of town or church. So "private," while benefiting from an expanding sense of the personal or domestic, ultimately meant in social or political or ecclesiastical reality those liberties or privileges a person or group could acquire for themselves, those pieces of the "public," so to speak, they could gain a right to make "particular" for themselves. This may sound abstract, but its practice was entirely concrete, hinging upon what a person or group could gain by concession or negotiation, or alternatively what might be denied them, Brothers and Sisters for instance denied a private chapel distinct from the local parish for a full century. Beyond an intense localism in all this, one key characteristic of the fifteenth century was a kind of free-for-all in negotiating privileges, also at the highest levels, kings, for instance, winning unprecedented concessions from a beleaguered papacy. It is this milieu which the Modern-Day Devout ingeniously availed themselves of, making possible their gatherings and societies. Not all bargaining succeeded, of course; some groups and practices were shut down. But rather than to begin with binary expectations (orthodoxy/repression), historians need to discern what was possible, what in play, whether initiatives were contingent or carefully negotiated, whether outcomes proved circumstantial or revealing of larger patterns, with some new groups or initiatives becoming viable, others shut down, even brutally, some issues discussable, some not.

In drawing up his defense Zerbolt appropriated materials from standard encyclopedic works of law and theology, then exploited small points to create larger openings, an intricate dialectic between innovative practice and inherited law. In the end he generated an innovative work of social theory, advancing his own theses more by way of rhetorical questions than blanket assertions. He envisioned a way of being religious without professing religion, postulating a private society organized as a communal household for devotional purposes, thereby unsettling critics. He appropriated the notion of a self-contracted "society" introduced into church law from Roman law. Societies had the right to organize; what better than a society whose purpose was devotion? Societies could manage their own goods, thus a merchant society; what better way for the Devout to manage goods than on the communal model of the early church and natural reason? Household societies could establish internal customs; what better than a likeminded household of devout people acting according to a common purpose? Christians could admonish, teach, counsel, and correct one another; how better than in a household society that facilitated such action as voluntary works of charity and carried them out in the people's own language? Zerbolt located a place for the Devout legally and conceptually in the interstices of late medieval society. His successors, sometimes reluctantly, sometimes determinedly, acquired particular "licenses" and privileges to guarantee public rights for these private practices. The inquisitors found it all infuriating, the bishop and his advisers too initially puzzled or cautious.

The tone set within these communal societies was complex, egalitarian and deferential at the same time. Matters hung on common counsel, whether in electing leaders or choosing members or working side by side. Yet each was to bow in humility and voluntary obedience to the other and ultimately to an elected rector or mother—or the entire enterprise risked collapse. The Brothers referred to theirs as a "companionate" society and took over terms both legal and antique, an *amicitia socialis*. It was a bond, but voluntary rather than obligatory, making members allies in a joint venture. But whereas commercial societies died with the venture or the loss of a member, these private devotional societies were specifically designed to perpetuate themselves, the "joint-holders" of books or goods or a house replaced by election on a member's death or departure. In principle members were free, not bound by vows or institutions, but in practice subject to mutual reproof and common decision-making. Sisters had little true personal privacy in fact inside their households, Brothers a good deal more in their rooms. As communities they took upon themselves everything from cycles of prayer and patterns of work to chapters of fault and spiritual advising, most centrally their communal holding of goods and income. More, many matters regarded as largely reserved to and regulated by the public sphere of authorized religion they took up as private household arrangements. Spies invoked the term *genossenschaftlich* for beguine communities in Frankfurt, a word hoary with nineteenth-century ideologies, to be sure, but not inapt, conveying a fitting sense of self-made associations held together by a common purpose.[12] What the Modern-Day Devout undertook was consonant with widespread moves in the fifteenth century toward participation and consultation, from town councils to church councils.

The Modern-Day Devout were converts, and lived to make more converts. Their vision, what one memorial life called so expressively "spiritual carpentry," what their documents and manuals referred to as "living quietly" or "at peace," pervaded this way of life and its literature. Though their originality proved great in making and rethinking structures, their aims lay in remaking souls. Hence the resolutions, the exercises, the reading, the meditations, the self-examination, the scrapbook-keeping, the mutual reproof, all taken on voluntarily. The converted and "carpentered" soul was finally to know peace, not rapture, but also not doubt or anxiety or scrupulosity. Busy lives in community, long days engaged in manual labor, and worried self-examinations may doubtless sometimes have made it otherwise. But this too drew from deeper human and cultural inclinations in the fifteenth century, a search for quiet amid society's clamor and busyness. We should not forget the large readership for Petrarch's "on the solitary life," or the fifteenth-century humanist exploration of platonic theology, or the deep and wide resurgence, as Constable showed, of twelfth-century spiritual writing in fifteenth-century manuscripts (and print).

Sisters and Brothers accounted their initiatives ultimately purer and more authentic because conceived and undertaken in Christian liberty, understanding themselves to act out of desire and not obligation. Authorities in church or town had the power to create obligation, and presumed an obligatory society, one based on law, individuals assuming obligations by citizenship or birth, by vow or baptism. But free gatherings constituted as a private society possessed no obligatory power as such, beyond whatever rights an individual voluntarily assigned to it, say, resigning all goods to it. In forming communities and spiritual lives freely, proceeding from "liberty of will" rather than obligatory obedience, the Modern-Day Devout resonated to a broader fifteenth-century inclination to place the will ahead of reason as the predominant human faculty, a predilection as true for whole wings of scholastic philosophy (especially the *via moderna*) as it was for humanist moral discourse. Among the Devout this could, under pressure from Dominican critics, provoke an even stronger claim: that acting in freedom was more meritorious than acting under obligation, exactly the reverse of what Friar Thomas Aquinas had taught in the thirteenth century and what was indeed widely presumed, certainly in theology but to a degree as well in social attitudes. In a deferential society obeying could seem inherently meritorious. For the Devout, however, life turned on intention and interiority, personal resolves continuously sustained over time as a form of life.

From the beginning these societies resolved to support themselves by the work of their own hands. For the men this took the form of book-making as a commercial venture, for the women textile-production, each also upholding and maintaining their own houses and victuals. In social terms this too surprised, since many of the men were clerics and some of the women patrician. Here too the Modern-Day Devout resonated to fifteenth-century religious and social attitudes. Much as people counted on the professed for intercessory prayer and spiritual services, they resented the leisured lifestyle of most religious, whether as propertied gentry or begging mendicants. Sisters, Brothers and Tertiaries, also canons in their early days, determined to support themselves, and largely did, even if over time they also accrued properties and incomes. And they never stopped working, manual labor in fact dominating their day. All this comported with urban expectations where we find decreasing tolerance for beggars, especially able-bodied beggars, how many in the fifteenth century looked upon beguines and Tertiaries and any self-made religious prepared to accept alms.

The Modern-Day Devout had their greatest impact in these towns arguably on teenagers, though women's houses were often very large too. The Brothers aided hundreds of schoolboys with lessons, worked persistently (oppressively, some said) to form their characters, strove to sensitize them to spiritual life. The Sisters served hundreds of young women who found in their houses a safe and quasiliterate environment in which to lead stable and productive lives. Self-consciousness about forming the young (the Latin word, whether the overtones were educational or moral or religious, was *instituere*, "educating" and "training" them) resonated across fifteenth-century societies, among humanists preparing a new elite lay leadership for Italian towns, and Gerson looking to future church leaders, noblemen too rethinking aristocratic society (the new "courtier" or gentlemen emerging from this long fifteenth century). Focusing on the young, especially "training" the young, met with resistance, many, whether lay or clerical, perceiving it as imposing too great a yoke too soon. It seemed novel, whether in fact or in the methods proposed—striking since from the sixteenth century onward it would become altogether standard in church and education and society. Fifteenth-century figures saw two human realities demanding this initiative: adults hardened in their ways, unchangeable, uneducable, their evil customs pulling down church or society or culture; and young people still in some sense blank slates, capable of being shaped, "instituted" so as to become productive or reformed or refined. All this was happening, we should also remember, even if it is hard to document, as literacy rates were rising, especially at local levels and in lower schools, even if reading and writing were still reserved, relatively speaking, for an elite.

Reading emerged as central to the spiritual program undertaken in these private gatherings. All across Europe at the beginning of this long fifteenth century writing in the vernacular took off. We have tended understandably to study the literary masters, but fully three-fourths of the production, at least in extant manuscripts, was devotional prose. In Germanic lands the Devout led the way defending and distributing vernacular writing. This was not accidental, nor was it in any way set against the role of Latin, Brothers operating in both Latin and Dutch. Texts, and access to texts, were essential tools for "instituting" the young, also for animating adults striving to remake themselves and their society. Brothers are unintelligible apart from texts, their exercises, their scrapbooks, their spiritual manuals, their mutual discussion of readings (this true for Sisters too, if less visible)—as unintelligible indeed as humanists apart from theirs. The movement had begun with youthful copyists and a "commune" of books. Brothers, like Gerson, and like the humanists, preferred to go back to "originals," to whole books and venerated antiques, in their case the Scriptures (corrected and copied), the Desert Fathers, Cassian and Jerome, twelfth-century fathers like Bernard and William. Theirs was an active form of reading, "reading with the pen," transforming the student notebook into the convert's spiritual diary.

The Devout instinctively stayed away from topics electric with heretical danger. Though the eucharist seems quite understated in their manuals (whether or not deliberately so), and all their emphasis to fall upon personal preparation and spiritual communion, they never challenged eucharistic teaching, and often sought as one of their first particular privileges the right to a portable altar. Similarly, Geert Grote worried more about the schism in human hearts than in the papal office, and while the Devout were instinctively more inclined to conciliar or republican ways of doing business they never challenged the reigning ecclesiology, many in the Oversticht going into exile for six years rather than to violate a papal interdict. Again, though they defended reading in the vernacular and continued to read Ruusbroec, Tauler, and scattered sermons of Eckhart, they transformed that intense longing for emptying the self into divine union, articulated so dramatically and persuasively by a previous generation, into a kind a quietism fostered by constant self-examination and a disciplining of affections, a searching for solace and peace. But they nonetheless challenged a reigning orthodoxy, first of all in practice, then in theory. They deliberately reconceived the estate of the perfect, its privileging of vows and of a merit born of obedience. They elevated private spiritual interiors over public religious structures.

The inquisitor had found these Modern-Day converts and their private gatherings heretical, violating anti-beguine legislation, forming illicit or subversive "conventicles." They responded, as beguines had, by contending, and indeed with law and in the courts, that their form of conversion was licit, then securing privileges for distinct practices (such as communal living or electing a paterfamilias) thereby exempting them from the general law, and also repeatedly covering themselves in the mantle of Gregory XI's description of an acceptable convert as described in 1374 in *Ex iniuncto*. What actually protected them, and came closest to describing their real conversionary practices, was the privilege of 1401 issued by the bishop at Utrecht. When Friar Matthew Grabow sought a decade later to ground new objections theologically in the rights and merits reserved for the estate of religion, the tables got turned at the Council of Constance and the Dominican was found heretical. At stake were the theological foundations for an exclusive caste of sworn religious, any higher merit for those acting under vowed obligation, a perfection defined more or less exclusively as three specific Gospel counsels (poverty, chastity, obedience) pursued within religious orders. John Wyclif and Jean Gerson, both secular masters, also challenged this position in the fifteenth century, the first with a raging and sometimes foul-mouthed repudiation of "private religious sects" (meaning chiefly mendicants), the second with a tightly-argued theological critique that used and overturned Aquinas's arguments. No one thought so deeply and so hard about what what constituted "religion" than the Devout authors Zerbolt in the 1390s and John Pupper in the 1460s/70s. While some of Wyclif's theses were condemned at Constance (as were Grabow's on the other side) and some Hussites mobilized their convictions by emptying out and even destroying religious houses, this issue did not grab headlines in fifteenth-century Europe as did the eucharistic and ecclesiological flashpoints. Yet it was being talked about everywhere—also by humanists like Salutati and Valla—and no one pushed it harder, in theory or in practice, than the Modern-Day Devout, though they too early on protected themselves by founding a front organization, the canons of Windesheim, who in practice rapidly overshadowed them to become, ironically, the most successful new religious order of the fifteenth century.

A good deal was at stake here, the conception and structure of sanctity in a world that defined and ordered itself in terms of religion. Protestant Reformers would move early to shut down thousand-year old monasteries and religious orders and to redefine Christian sanctity as located in laypeople, indeed married laypeople and the nuclear family, this too anticipated by the fifteenth-century cults of Joseph and Anne and the Holy Family. The Modern-Day Devout did not agree with the Reformation move, and were in fact shut down by Reformers in their home region, the founding house in Deventer turned into the town library (books, in other words, still at the center). And yet they had raised the issue pointedly, in practice and in theory. The stance of the Modern-Day Devout was probing but also paradoxical, characteristic one might say of the fifteenth century. Gerson, even Wyclif, never denied the notion of the counsels of perfection, but tried to appropriate them as well for the laity. The Modern-Day Devout tried to live them, but apart from vows, even refusing to be turned into a "college of canons." Apart from vows they worked all the harder to set up a self-instituted communal poverty based on New Testament Jerusalem and to discipline themselves into chastity and to humble themselves in loving obedience to one another. Moreover, they organized a chapter of Tertiaries and founded Windesheim and encouraged schoolboys to consider religious life (Erasmus says in the 1480s dunned them into it). Yet they rejected the professed state (the priesthood too) as inherently higher. Zerbolt first, John Pupper too, insisted that higher merit accrued to religious life only by way of interiority, acting in freedom. More, they insisted on the legitimacy and merit inherent in the estate they had conceived and put in practice, even as their actions and arguments implicitly undermined the estate system that for a thousand years had ranked sworn religious as the premiere and perfect caste in medieval society. With Gerson, and with Wyclif, they proposed a single "Christian" religion, not Benedictine or Augustinian, living under the "Abbot Christ" and the "Rule/law of the Gospel."

This was an era, finally, consumed with talk about how to live, what in English literature circles at the moment is being called "exemplarism." It pervaded writing and preaching, and its emblem was the "mirror" literature

(*Spieghel* in Dutch), texts modeling and exhorting to the moral, often with respect to persons according to their "estate" in life. Not only in intense religious circles like the Devout did people turn from the mystical or the wondrous (those also still present) to modeling the moral. It is what we find among humanists too, a turn broadly from metaphysics to moral philosophy, from logic to rhetoric, from disputing to persuading. Gerson, in so many ways an emblem of this age, moved decisively in the same direction in Latin and French, in prose and poetry. Fifteenth-century literature has sometimes been neglected or even dismissed for its moralizing affect, so workaday compared to the raptures of the mystical or the depths of the metaphysical or the wit of the satirical. But for the historian the issue is to recognize cultural patterns, to acknowledge its address to widespread felt need for guidance in how to live. In one computerized survey of word choice in Devout memorial lives (for Master Geert's House) "humility" and "virtue" ranked first. Humility was central to their vision, and implementation, of a holy life, and its goal was "progress in virtue." For the Modern-Day Devout this took distinctly religious tones, going back to the texts of the monastic fathers, but as well a practical burgher tone, their tackling one vice at a time, methodically checking their progress in virtue daily or weekly or yearly. Benjamin Franklin in eighteenth-century Philadelphia, born in Puritan Boston, would propose taking on one vice or virtue seriatim, now with an enlightened and secularizing cast of mind, echoing at nearly four centuries' distance what we first find articulated among the Modern-Day Devout.

The Question of an Afterlife

Groups like the Modern-Day Devout exploited the opportunities afforded by the fifteenth century, and fitted their forms of life, their spiritual aspirations and literary forms, into the niches and interstices of this remarkably complex society. That possibility would not survive the Reformation turn. From the 1560s all sides tightened down on what might count as religion and practice within their territories. That spelled the end for the Modern-Day Devout (including Tertiaries, despite their claims to a "Rule")—excepting only the remnants of the Windesheim canons in the Catholic Low Countries. Yet it was not the end. The spirit of the Modern-Day Devout survived, infiltrating early modern religious culture in quite remarkable ways. This question, first contested, then often simply ignored in the wake of exaggerated claims made by scholars like Hyma and their near total dismissal by others like Post, has rarely known nuanced discussion. Here, to conclude, we can offer only a tease. Four of the dominant figures in the sixteenth century—Erasmus, Martin Luther, John Calvin, Ignatius Loyola—all were touched in some way by the spirit or work of the Modern-Day

Devout, and Thomas of Kempen's *Imitatio Christi* utterly permeated the early modern religious world in print, Protestant and Catholic, so much so that one scholar has reckoned it more a modern than a medieval success.[13] Because Brothers and Sisters were finally not an institutionalized order, their spirit could quickly disappear obviously, as their houses did, but also the more easily infiltrate new and different settings and situations.

In 1522/23 Friar Martin Luther (1483–1546), anonymously, wrote a letter prefacing John of Pupper's *Fragments*. There he named him a true German and learned theologian, alongside John Tauler and Wessel Gansfort, and looked forward to a time free of Thomists and Scotists and Ockhamists, all thinkers being in fact "simple children of God and brother Christians."[14] In September 1521 Friar Martin Luther had himself tackled John's central theme in his own "theses concerning vows," followed two months later by a full treatise on the subject, he still formally an Augustinian friar, which he had been for over fifteen years.[15] He would not marry until 1525. The second work began, as did John's *Freedom*, with Psalm 76:12, the text medieval theologians understood to authorize religious profession. Luther's position was strikingly close to John's: religious vows were not found in Scripture; evangelical poverty meant in truth desiring nothing in spirit; chastity must come from grace and the will, not obligation; profession is not a second baptism nor does it make people "better" than the ordinary baptized.[16] His driving preoccupation was likewise with intent: Not one in a thousand, he posited, had vowed "piously" in "these unfaithful times"; most had acted out of fear or to secure rewards.[17] That did injury to the original and more fundamental baptismal vow (his emphasis here stronger than John's). Baptismal promises were compatible with liberty, left choice; an obligatory vow did not.[18] We have no proof that Luther had read John as yet, though, chronologically, it was just possible. They were thinking through an issue crucial to the structure of medieval life (and to their own!) on, at the very least, parallel tracks. Luther still held that a profession made in "faith" was authentic and good—it being simply altogether rare. Where John impugned "obligation," Luther impugned "works." But the real difference was practical and "medieval." John, having never taken vows, fought the arrogant assumptions and extra merit of an elevated estate of the perfect. Friar Martin Luther agreed, but was preoccupied with another, more personal, point: A vow taken "unfaithfully" had no validity before God, rather the reverse, and was not binding. That person could therefore leave, probably should, perhaps even choosing to take vows again "faithfully." He did not argue as yet for emptying religious houses. But he held that most of the professed had taken vows in the wrong spirit, with the wrong expectations (undoubtedly speaking in some way about himself); so they were in fact, despite church law and theological argument, free to leave, to make choices in liberty.

John Pupper and Martin Luther were thinking, on the issue of religion conceived as vows, in large part alike. But in Luther's "Christian Freedom" of 1520 the matter turned entirely on freedom from sin before God, freedom with respect to ecclesioreligious structures reduced to something secondary or tertiary. Luther too held, however, that being free and truly Christian had all to do with the interior, the spiritual, not things external.[19] But here we have no talk of "Gospel law," law/works being what terrorized a soul. As Luther described it, by "faith" the soul was united, virtually absorbed in, the "promises of God," even conjugally joined to Christ (*animam copulat cum Christo, sicut sponsam cum sponso*),[20] yielding a freedom that made people kings and priests. The stuff of monasteries, of profession and estates, had to do with subjection. A free person (Luther wrote still as an Augustinian friar) should hear any commands and counsels coming out of them, accordingly, as self-interested, as extinguishing Christian freedom.[21] Yet their importance persisted, as instruments, not ends, for taming ourselves as one tames the youth[22]—echoing Thomas on vows and sounding like the Brothers on schoolboys. It was, he argued, through a faith that came by hearing (Rom. 10:17, *fides ex auditu*) that a person was "consoled and exalted."[23] What Luther described sounds remarkably like what people had sought in medieval conversion: consolation (*consolacio*), comfort, God's own solace, being at peace. It was still the same world as John's, with similar dilemmas, yet rapidly becoming a very different world. It should come as no surprise that many in the 1520s were growingly confused.

John of Brussels (Mauburnus), ca. 1460–1501, entered the house at Agnietenberg outside Zwolle roughly ten years after Thomas of Kempen's death there in 1471. Formed there in religious life, exchanging ideas with Wessel Gansfort on the "ladder of meditation," he was sent to France where he worked as a reformer of canons regular, including the venerable house of St. Victor (where the Windesheim canons, paradoxically, had first turned for guidance when they began). Mauburnus provided that house and others with a set of spiritual exercises derived ultimately from the Brothers, including daily self-examination, daily work as copyists, continuous combat against vices and progress in virtue, even a list of books for reading.[24] Out of this all came as well his *Rosary of spiritual exercises and sacred meditations*, a giant compendium of materials with his own extensive elaboration of Devout spirituality, first printed at Zwolle in 1494, a definitive edition at Paris in 1510.

Another figure from the Low Countries, Jean Standonck, born in Malines in 1443 and exposed to Devout circles, earned his doctorate in theology at Paris and then formed a community there, much like the Brothers' hostels, for poor students. In 1483 he aided in reforming the Collège de Montaigu, securing for it a special endowment for eighty-six poor students, twelve in theology, the rest in arts preparatory to divinity; its statutes survive from 1499. Standonck, famous for his rigor, extended operations to Cambrai, Malines, Louvain, Valenciennes, and elsewhere.[25] In each town he established a version of the Brothers' hostels, now for university or pre-university students, with austere prescriptions for shaping their moral, religious, and academic lives. Standonck and Mauburnus crossed paths in Paris, and the *Rosetum* entered into the college's spiritual reading, as did the works of Thomas of Kempen. In 1495 Erasmus spent a year at the college, and later satirized its unrelenting spiritual rigor, for him worse even than what he had experienced growing up under Brothers at Deventer and Gouda.

Both Ignatius Loyola and John Calvin spent time at the Collège de Montaigu (along with other major figures such as the Scots conciliarist John Major), where they came under the influence of its spirit and exercises. John Calvin (b. 1509) was sent to college/university in his early teens, arriving with financial support so he could take a room among the "rich," the paying students. Like Erasmus, therefore, he spent his teenage years (ca. 1521/23–ca. 1528) learning the arts in a spiritual atmosphere partly set by the Modern-Day Devotion, Calvin himself destined at that point for the priesthood. He left in 1528 when he turned to law. Loyola arrived in 1528 as a poor man already thirty-seven years old, living externally but following the College's classes and exercises. Both figures would place a searching interiority at the center of their religious visions, and in the later sixteenth century their disciples would battle for spiritual leadership in Europe. To be sure, an intense preoccupation with the interior, shaping or reshaping the soul in the presence of the divine, marked fifteenth-century religious life generally, and in the sixteenth century was not peculiar to Protestant or Catholic, monk or layperson. But the Modern-Day Devout had shown the way, their spirit and texts part of the ferment, and indisputably touching the lives of Calvin and Ignatius at a formative moment.

In his constitutions of 1540 Loyola chose, notably, to call his band a "society," not an order, and for its end he used the term *scopus*, the Greek word Brothers had taken over from Cassian to speak of their spiritual ends. Jesuits likewise adopted a form of religious life that remained in the world, as had Sisters and Brothers, and what he prescribed for shaping and sustaining their spiritual lives within that world was "exercises," again like Brothers and Sisters. More, the reading assigned to Jesuit novices was Thomas's *Imitatio Christi*, men in the Society of Jesus expected to carry it around with them. Ignatius was exposed to Devout materials even before arriving in Paris. The works of Thomas but also Zerbolt's *Spiritual Ascents* and Mauburnus' *Rosetum* had deeply influenced the reforming Catalan abbot Garcia de Cisernos at Monserrat (1493–1510), this particularly evident in his own *Exercitatorio de la vida espiritual* (1500), that work made available to Ignatius Loyola there in 1522.

John Calvin put *pietas* at the center of his religious vision, an echo in neoclassical Latin—possibly distant and unconscious, others say direct—of the *devotio* in which he was trained during his teenage years in Paris. Breaking fundamentally with Luther on this point, Calvin also put sanctification at the center of his religious system, a much-read section of his *Institutes* on the Christian life, its tones deeply reminiscent of the Devout tones, often circulating separately as his "Golden Booklet" on spiritual life. That self-conscious Reformed/Calvinistic cultivation of a holy life would of course generate the whole set of practices we associate with Puritanism and (more complexly) with continental pietism. In all such circles Thomas's *Imitatio* was widely read and reprinted (among the earliest books printed in Boston, for instance), albeit with the sections on monastic life and sometimes those on the eucharist altered or excised. Even so Richard Baxter would eventually recover for those circles deeper traditions of self-examination and meditation, silently taking them over from medieval and Catholic authors, often by way of Bishop Hall, a highly influential Anglican spiritual author from ca. 1600, who took his meditation schemes in part (and again to a degree silently) from Mauburnus.

We close with Erasmus, who spent nearly ten years under the Brothers' care in Deventer and Gouda, then later skewered them for their asceticism, their lack of literary sophistication, their pushing young boys into the spiritual life. Ironically, he joined the canons regular at age eighteen (while Brothers and Sisters professed no vows) and early wrote a tract on "contempt for the world" (a genre they did not formally indulge). The tensions between influence and antipathy could form the subject of another chapter, if not a book. A few simple observations, which go to the paradox of Erasmus and the Modern-Day Devout. Erasmus, nearing fifty, appealed for relief from his vows and his habit in 1517 (blaming his woes in part on the Brothers), but he lived a life, before and after, that was "inbetween" in ways not so different from the Brothers. We should take care not to imagine him solely in that marvelous Holbein portrait but as going around much of his life in, at least in principle, his canon regular habit. Erasmus made his reputation as an editor and close reader of the New Testament and the church fathers, a return to sources not so unlike the Brothers, and for all his critique of the Brothers' literary skills critiqued humanists in his day fixated on antique paradigms. Erasmus would focus an enormous amount of his literary effort on composing his "adages," a mix of learned commentary on and compilation of antique sayings, arguably a highly sophisticated and literate form of the Brothers' scrapbooks, evolved into witty moral essays. Erasmus impugned theology, as they did, emphasized intentions, satirized the church's wholesale confusion of the material and the spiritual, focused on a relatively simple "philosophy of Christ," even wrote a "handbook" to instruct the young, all as they did. The structural parallels are breathtaking.

This leaves Thomas's *Imitation of Christ,* which returns us to the fifteenth century. Nearly nine hundred manuscripts survive, far more than any other non-service book (bible or liturgy), with hundreds of editions and dozens of translations produced from the sixteenth century onward. Thomas wrote his four pamphlets (originally distinct) while still near to his teenage experience of the early Brothers and Sisters and their societies ca. 1393–1406. His proverbial sayings resonate with their enterprising vision of conversion, of turning inward to an interior life, creating a cell within, turning away from the clamor of the world, winning over the still malleable young, finding peace and living peaceably in the presence of God. But Thomas wrote ca. 1420 in a cloister just outside Zwolle (though he would continue to follow the Brothers and Sisters and their houses closely in his chronicle to the end of his life). The hundreds of proverb-like sayings that made up his four pamphlets, supple and balanced, simple and accessible, came wrapped now in a kind of gauze, safe from the hurly-burly of towns and household societies and schoolboys. That protective distance, psychological and literary, allowed him to write in such a way as to generalize rather than particularize the originating experience, smoothing out the rough-hewn admonitions which gave them birth. In this new form they could more easily travel across differing landscapes, useful still for recruiting or forming novices in the fifteenth and sixteenth centuries (close to their original purpose), but also subsequently for touching more remote souls, Protestants in the early modern period, Victorian readers in hugh numbers, and so on into the present. But how could the same work appeal to Jesuits and metaphysical English poets? to John Wesley and George Eliot? Or to one of Richardson's eighteenth-century female characters in *Clarissa* sassing another about "Kempis" ("you will find excellent things in that little book")? Despite the gauze, its suppleness and smoothness, these sayings breathed still the atmosphere of religion lived potentially outside religion—this, intriguingly despite Thomas's own entry into professed life and appeal for it at the end of Book I. Even a former Methodist and Victorian freethinker like George Eliot could sense in its deeper structures the call to create an interior life of one's own making, an inner cell or space for living quietly, a place where the soul and the Ultimate could meet, within and private, apart from the world. But those sayings had originated in tension with the world, coming out of a way of life not finally separate from the world, to be sustained daily amid the world. This was a dynamic, a sensibility future readers could recapture for themselves, in its origin a conversionary appeal envisioned by devotees of a present-day devotion lived in the middle of fifteenth-century Netherlandish towns.

NOTES

INTRODUCTION: THE DEVOTIO MODERNA AND MODERN HISTORY

1. A depiction of the "common people" at the time Master Geert began his preaching, this from a *vita* that belonged to the Sisters in his house: Brinkerinck, "Biografien van beroemde mannen," p. 416.

2. *Vita Egberti*, ed. Dumbar, *Analecta*, pp. 162–65.

3. *Van onsen oelden zusteren* 20, ed. de Man, p. 54.

4. The emblematic book was Ullmann, *Reformatoren*. But it was then, for instance, that Grote's works first began to be edited, editions on which we are still dependent.

5. Hyma, *The Christian Renaissance*, pp. 6–7 (closing sentence of his introduction).

6. Post, *Modern Devotion*, expressed his purpose in his subtitle, a "Confrontation with Reformation and Humanism." For an appreciation of Post's strengths, limitations, and influence as a historian, see Rogier, "De historicus."

7. For the extensive older literature see the fine surveys by Alberts, "Zur Historiographie der Devotio Moderna," and Elm, "Die Brüderschaft," and the running bibliography in *OGE*.

8. Elm, "Die Brüderschaft," and "*Vita regularis sine regula*," and "Die 'Devotio moderna' und die neue Frömmigkeit," the last a wonderful summing up of his life's work, complete with bibliography. For attempts to nuance and expand upon Elm's vision, see J. Van Engen, "Friar Johannes Nyder," and Staubach, "Zwischen Kloster und Welt?" as well as the conclusion of this book.

9. Weiler, "Recent Historiography" for a review of recent historiographical questions, his own contribution specifically on pp. 173–76. A student of Post, Weiler has contributed throughout his life, from an edition in 1974 to his volume of the *Monasticon* in 2005 (see bibliography), and a study and translation of a moral *summa* out of Devout circles, *Het morele veld van de Moderne Devotie*, with an edition of this text in the works.

10. Mertens, general editor of *OGE*, and a scholarly editor of Middle Dutch texts beginning with the Devout author Hendrik Mande, has made many signal contributions; note especially his edited volume *Boeken voor de eeuwigheid* and his essays "Lezen met de pen" and "Collatio und Codex."

11. Staubach has published pioneering articles over the past fifteen years, beginning in 1991 (see the bibliography), and three important dissertations appeared under his direction: Kock, *Die Buchkultur*, Klausmann, *Consuetudo*; and Lesser, *Johannes Busch*; with another begun there, Bollmann, *Frauenleben*.

12. See Goudriaan, "De derde orde" and "Het monasticon" for the beginning and endpoint of this project. Important dissertations to come out of it were H. Van Engen, *De derde orde*, and Van Luijk, *Bruiden van Christus*, along with the research instrument "monasticon" by Sabrina Corbellini.

13. Van Dijk, *De constituties*, and Scheepsma, *Deemoed and Devotie.*

14. The term ("Pre-reformer" = "Vorreformatoren"), much employed in the nineteenth century and in earlier confessional polemics, gained new currency indirectly by way of Hudson, *The Premature Reformation*, and from there returned to the continent. See now the essays in Šmahel, *Häresie und vorzeitige Reformation*, and Frank-Niewöhner, *Reformer als Ketzer*. On the term itself, a history and a critique, see the excellent essay by Mahlmann, "Vorreformatoren." For its return now to the continent, see the essays in Derwich and Staub, *Die "Neue Frömmigkeit"*.

15. The essential works are the three-volume *Monasticon Windeshemense* for the regular branch, and the *Monasticon Fratrum Vitae Communis* for the Brothers (1977: Belgium, 1979: Germany, 2004: Netherlands). The Dutch volume appeared in a provisional form: Weiler, *Volgens de norm.* There is no volume on the Dutch Sisters except the outdated work of Schoengen, *Monasticon*; for the German Sisters, see Rehm, *Die Schwestern*; and for the Tertiaries now the important work of H. Van Engen, *De derde orde*. For the entire movement the foundational work was (and is) Acquoy, *Klooster te Windesheim*. The most interesting access in many ways comes in the exhibition catalogue *Moderne Devotie* (1984), and the pithy introduction by Alberts, *Moderne Devotie*. I offered an introduction in English, with translated sources, *Devotio Moderna*.

16. See the highly influential article by Ditsche, "Zur Herkunft und Bedeutung," generated by a graduate seminar in 1958 with Herbert Jedin, and echoed by most subsequent scholars. A reformist narrative only matured over a generation or two. Johan Busch, who joined Windesheim at age 18 in 1417 and wrote the preface to his history about 1457/58, expressed something more complex, ancient miracles made new in modern wonders: *De origine moderne deuotionis*, ed. Grube p. 245. Compare Staubach, "Wunder" (1996).

17. Pomerius, *De origine* II.8, ed. de Leu, p. 288.

18. This opening sentence of Pomerius' prologue is rhetorically charged, and the word not easy to translate. The Middle Dutch translator, as I see it, changed the sense of the sentence, lessening some of the charge and rendering the word instead as "extraordinary interiority." That may reveal what the translator thought was distinctive about the Devout, but it is not what Pomerius said. The relevant phrase is *Nochtans want devoten herten sonderlinge ynnichheit* [= *noua singularitas*] *van sommigen sancten is als een ontfunckende cole.* Verdeyen, "De middelnederlandse vertaling," p. 115.

19. Pomerius, *De origine*, prologus, ed. de Leu, pp. 263, 264.

20. Thomas, *Dialogus* I, ed. Pohl VII, p. 30.

21. For a general critique, especially of the "crisis" rubric, see Kaminsky, "From Lateness to Waning," with recent bibliography; and Meuthen, "Gab es ein spätes Mittelalter?"

22. See now Krul, "In the Mirror of van Eyck," and Peters and Simons, "The New Huizinga."

23. Shuster, "Die Krise des Spätmittelalters," among others, has questioned the socioeconomic evidence for "crisis."

24. See, for instance, Huizinga, *Herfstij*, pp. 191–93. His Dutch used language laden with overtones, mostly implicitly disparaging.

25. For basic orientation to the transmission of the *Imitatio*, Neddermeyer, "*Radix studii et speculum vitae*" and "Verbreitung und Wirkung." See also now the essays in *Aus dem Winkel*.

CHAPTER I. CONVERTS IN THE MIDDLE AGES

Epigraphs. *Clem.* 3.11.1, ed. Friedberg 2.1170; *Extravagantes* 3.9.1, ed. Friedberg, 2.1279.

1. On Geert Grote we have two biographies, Van Zijl, *Gerard Groote*, and Épiney-Burgard, *Gérard Grote*, here pp. 20–30; now, importantly, as well Van Dijk, *Prologomena* (to a critical edition) with a complete bibliography (pp. 633–90); on which see Van Engen, "Geert Grote." For the supplications, see Courtenay, *Rotuli Parisienses* II, pp. 231, 248, 315, 434; as well as Deniflé, *Chartularium* III, pp. 91–93; and Fierens, *Suppliques d'Urbain V*, p. 615 (n. 1610). Grote's surname is one later to become common in Dutch (de Groot, Middle-Dutch "Groete"), in his case conventionally rendered as "Geert Grote." While its ur-meaning would have been something like "the elder" (in contrast with the younger, de Jong), his disciples interpreted it as "the great" (Gerardus Magnus). In the only extant original charter from him (Figure 4), the document begins ("Ic Gherijt de Grote").

2. *Piers Plowman*, ll. 83–84, ed. Pearsall, p. 33.

3. Grote, *Epistola* 12, ed. Mulder, p. 40, 41.

4. His spiritual heirs made up for it with a series of contradictory and confusing stories, derived likely from him or those around him. Illness may have precipitated his turn. Van Zijl, *Gerard Groote*, pp. 72–116, Épiney-Burgard, *Gérard Groote*, pp. 37–44; and Post, *Modern Devotion*, pp. 176–96; also the stimulating, if erratic, account of Van Ginnekin, *Geert Groote's Levensbeeld*, pp. 113–201.

5. The text transmitted by way of Thomas, *Dialogus*, ed. Pohl, 7.87–107, trans. Van Engen, *Devotio Moderna*, pp. 65–75. Southern, *Western Society*, pp. 331–52 characteristically spotted its interest. For its influence, see Kock, *Buchkultur*, pp. 123ff.

6. The text may have come together in parts, but that paraphrased here must be dated to before his relinquishing all church posts (by fall 1375), since he resolves to seek "no more" (*primum est, nullum amplius beneficium desiderare*: p. 88), suggesting he had yet to give them all up. Épiney-Burgard, *Gérard Grote*, pp. 37–44 remains sensible on the date.

7. Grote, *Epistola* 56, ed. Mulder, pp. 212–13. Van Dijk, *Prologomena*, p. 533. Busch, *De viris illustribus* 38, ed. Grube, pp. 105–9 devoted a chapter to Berthold, and began with this letter. The land on which Windesheim was built came by way of Berthold's father, a gift valued at three thousand pounds (!). Berthold was among the first six canons invested there in 1387, along with Thomas of Kempen's older brother John (see Acquoy, *Klooster te Windesheim*, III, p. 267). Busch describes him as losing his health and mind after entering upon a period of extreme asceticism. Grote and Berthold were likely kin (Mulder, p. 213, with n. 3) through Grote's mother, a Van der Basselen of wealth and property around Zwolle.

8. Grote, *Epistola* 20, ed. Mulder 72–77 for this paragraph; Van Dijk, *Prologomena*, pp. 498–99 for dating.

9. See Mulder, "Guillaume de Salvarvilla," on William (ca. 1327–ca.1385), a native of Rouen, long in Paris, deeply drawn to Grote, later facilitating Grote's appeal to Rome when suspended from preaching, and author of a posthumous *laudatio* edited as *Epistola* 65, Mulder, pp. 256–57. See further Grote, *De simonia*, ed. De Vreese, pp. 41–48.

10. Abelard, *Collationes* 7, ed. Marenbon-Orlandi, pp. 8–10.

11. Kieckhefer, "Convention and Conversion; Van Engen, "Conversion and Conformity."

12. Bernard, *De conversione* 1, ed. Leclercq, p. 70

13. Van Engen, "Religious Profession," for profession and marriage in law; see also Birkmeyer, *Ehetrennung und monastische Konversion.*

14. Venarde, *Robert of Arbrissel* for the texts in English.

15. Guibert, *De uita sua* 11, ed. Labande, p. 72.

16. Bernard, *De conversione* 4, 9, 18, 20, ed. Leclercq, pp. 334, 346, 366, 370.

17. See Elm, *Reformbemühungen und Observanzbestrebungen*, and his programmatic essay "Verfall und Erneuerung," as well as the thoughtful overview of D. Mertens, "Monastische Reformbewegungen."

18. Thomas, *Imitatio* I.11.

19. *Seuses Leben* Prologue, ch. 1, in *Deutsche Schriften* ed. Bihlmeyer, pp. 8, 9, 10.

20. . . . *quem circa conversionis suae initia quaedam tristitia inordinata tam letaliter oppressit, ut nec legere vel orare vel quidquam boni pro tunc facere posset. . . . Horologium Sapientiae* I.14, ed. Künzle, p. 495. On Suso, see Hamburger, "Medieval Self-Fashioning."

21. *Seuses Leben* c. 3, ed. Bihlmeyer, p. 13.

22. For the text, *Oerloy der ewigher wijsheit*, ed. van de Wijnpersse; for its circulation among the Devout, Hoffmann, "Die volkssprachliche Rezeption."

23. Basic now is Lesser, *Johannes Busch*, and Jostes, *Die Historisierung der Devotio Moderna*, pp. 17–134.

24. Busch, *De reformatione monasteriorum* I.1, ed. Grube, pp. 393–95.

25. The Book of Margery Kempe 1, 2, ed. Meech and Allen, pp. 3–4.

26. Ibid., c. 62, 69, ed. Meech and Allen, pp. 153, 167.

27. Ibid., 18, ed. Meech and Allen, pp. 43, 44.

28. Ibid., c. 15, ed. Meech and Allen, p. 32.

29. Ibid., p. 43.

30. Ibid., c. 16, ed. Meech and Allen, p. 37.

31. Grundmann, *Religious Movements*, with an important introduction by Robert Lerner to this English translation. The aptness of Grundmann's term "women's religious movement" for the twelfth century has been questioned; see Wehrli-Johns, "Voraussetzungen und Perspektiven," who prefers the medieval category "penitents." Degler-Spengler, "Die Beginen" and Wehrli-Johns, "Mittelalterliche Beginentum," also dispute Grundmann's notion of a twelfth-century "women's movement." Grundmann took the concept over from Bücher, *Die Frauenfrage*, for whom it was then very current. In the Netherlands the phenomena treated in this book increasingly are labeled a "second women's movement."

32. Constable, *Reformation of the Twelfth Century.*

33. For religious impulses that may have informed Foucauld's thinking, see *Religion and Culture*, ed. Carrette.

34. See representatively Kieckhefer, *Unquiet Souls*, and Weinstein and Bell, *Saints and Society.*

35. See now Luongo, *Saintly Politics.*

36. J. Van Engen, "Conversion and Conformity."

37. J. Van Engen, "Dominic and the Brothers," and "From Canons to Preachers," where I emphasize historic discontinuity in the quest for an "apostolic life."

38. Mulder-Bakker, *Lives of the Anchoresses.*

39. Zarri, *Le sante vive*, and Benvenuti Pappi, *In castro poenitentiae.*

40. See Rüther, *Bettelorden* for Strassburg, esp. pp. 183–222 on financial matters; Neidiger, *Mendikanten* for Basel, especially financial arrangements; also Müller, *Bettelorden* on Hildesheim, especially their integration into citylife.

41. Simons, *Bedelordekloosters.*

42. For Dominican houses in the north, see Wolfs, *Middeleeuwse dominicanenkloosters*; for Franciscan houses in Holland, Henderikx, *De oudste bedelordekloosters.*

43. Rudolf, *Vitae fratrum*, ed. Dumbar, *Analecta*, p. 4.

44. Walsh, *A Fourteenth-Century Scholar*, and "Die Rezeption der Schriften."

45. *Reformation Kaiser Siegmunds*, ed. Koller, pp. 204–6.

46. For the deeper historiography, see Greven, *Die Anfänge der Beginen*; Simons, "The Beguine Movement"; Wehrli-Johns and Opitz, *Fromme Frauen oder Ketzerinnen?*; Reichstein, *Das Beginenwesen*, pp. 5–30.

47. Jacques of Vitry noted all differing names meant primarily to mock and discourage: "*Hec uult esse 'beguina' (sic enim nominantur in Flandria et Brabancia), uel "papelarda' (sic enim appellantur in Francia), uel 'humiliata' (sicut dicitur in Lumbardia), uel 'bizoke' (secundum quod dicitur in Ytalia), uel 'coquennune' (ut dicitur in Theotonia), ita deridendo eas et quasi infamando nituntur eas retrahere a sancto proposito.*" Here cited from Greven, "Ursprung des Beginenwesens," pp 44–45. On origins, see Neel, "Origins of the Beguines," and now Miller, "What's in a Name?"

48. Gysseling, "De herkomst."

49. See Simons, *Cities of Ladies*, pp. 122–23, with a slightly different interpretation.

50. The literature on beguines has become enormous. See Koorn, *Begijnhoven* for Holland, Simons, *Cities of Ladies* for the Southern Low Countries, and Reichstein, *Das Beginenwesen* for Germany, the latter two with rich bibliographies. I have also learned from Spies, *Beginengemeinschaften* for Frankfurt; Degler-Spengler, "Die Beginen" and "Die religiöse Frauenbewegung" for Basel; and Wilts, *Beginen im Bodenseeraum* for the region of Lake Constance. Still important are McDonnell, *The Beguines and Beghards*; Asen, "Die Beginen in Köln"; Phillips, *Beguines in Medieval Strasburg*; Mens, *Oorsprong en betekenis*. For visual materials, see Oliver, *Gothic Manuscript Illumination* and Ziegler, *Sculpture of Compassion.*

51. Neumann, *Rheinisches Beginen- und Begardenwesen*, pp. 72ff.

52. See Ziegler, "The *curtis* beguinages."

53. Simons, *Cities of Ladies*, p. 104.

54. See Simons, *Cities of Ladies*, pp. 253–313; Reichstein, *Das Beginenwesen*, pp. 40–52; Wilts, *Beginen im Bodenseeraum*, pp. 275–470.

55. Bériou, "La prédication au béguinage."

56. See Simons, *Cities of Ladies*, pp. 48–60.

57. Ibid., p. 55 (the source of his title).

58. Ibid., p. 82, 193.

59. Ibid., p.114. Simons found this marvelous document but reads it somewhat differently.

60. *Quellen Köln*, ed. Ennen, vol. 2, no. 301, p. 306. See Reichstein, *Das Beginenwesen*, p. 93.

61. Humbert, *Sermones ad status 54*, Bibliothica patrum 25, p. 483.

62. Critiques compiled by Simons, *Cities of Ladies*, pp. 118ff, Reichstein, *Das Beginenwesen*, pp. 100ff, McDonnell, *Beguines*, pp. 417–29, 439–73, 505–15.

63. Miller, "What's in a Name?" emphasizes this to contextualize the fate of Marguerite Porete.

64. Guibert, *Collectio*, ed. Stroick, p. 61.

65. *Reformation Kaiser Siegmunds*, ed. Koller pp. 216–18.

66. *Osnabrücker Urkundenbuch* 4, no. 674 (Reichstein, p. 91).

67. Reichstein, *Das Beginenwesen*, pp. 88ff. No modern edition or study of this text, cited here from p. 90, n. 461.

68. Schannat-Hartzheim, *Concilia* 3.603.

69. *Osnabrücker Urkundenbuch* 4, no. 674.

70. Simons, "Staining the Speech." I would argue, perhaps even more than he, that scholars must take care using these three quite exceptional writers for general statements about beguines.

71. For this work, see now the wonderful edition of M. Kors, with its extensive introduction (CCCM 107). All scholars agree that this work is disjunctive. The title piece, which effectively only makes up the first 867 lines (pp. 5–85) and ends with an "Amen," might have arisen in a time when Ruusbroec was closer still to the beguine community in Brussels. On this text, cp. Warnar, *Ruusbroec*, pp. 79–80.

72. Ruusbroec, *Vanden XII beghinen* I.48–49, ed. Kors, p. 9.

73. This is the emphasis of Wehrli-Johns, "Voraussetzungen," pp. 299–303, and Reichstein, *Das Beginenwesen.*

74. Meersseman, *Dossier*, Doc. 2, p. 42.

75. Ibid., Doc. 1, p. 41.

76. Ibid., Doc. 4, p. 45.

77. Ibid., Doc. 15, pp. 51–52 (1236), 31, p. 62 (1251).

78. Osheim, "Conversion."

79. Meersseman, *Dossier*, Doc. 32, pp. 62–63 (1251).

80. The emphasis of Thompson, *Cities of God*, ch. 2.

81. The characterization is mine; the basic treatment now is Burr, *Spiritual Franciscans.*

82. *Clem.* 5.3.3, ed. Friedberg 2.1183–84. Basic on this legislation is Tarrant, "The Clementine Decrees."

83. Lerner, *The Heresy of the Free Spirit* is the fundamental starting point. For the Low Countries, see Wormgoor, "De vervolging."

84. Wehrli-Johns, "Mystik und Inquisition."

85. Ibid., pp. 231ff. The letter is found in the marvelous corpus of materials assembled by Patschovsky, "Strassburger Beginenverfolgungen," pp. 133–41; on the manual of Friar Eymeric and its influence, see Heimann, *Nicolaus Eymeric.*

86. Porete, *Mirror* c. 91, trans. Colledge (1999), p. 116. I have largely followed this

translation but worked from the edition of Verdeyen, *Speculum simplicium animarum*, pp. 256–59. See Hollywood, *Soul as Virgin Wife*, pp. 87–119.

87. Ibid., cc. 95, 133, 134, ed. Verdeyen, pp. 264, 392–95.

88. Patschovsky, "Beginenverfolgungen," with the documents edited, pp. 133–48, here p. 147, his discussion, pp. 92–101.

89. Ibid., pp. 134, 136, 141.

90. Wehrli-Johns, "Mystik und Inquisition," p. 243.

91. See now McGinn, *The Harvest*, with repeated discussion of Eckhart's debt to, and interaction with, Porete's thought.

92. See Ubbink, *De receptie van Meister Eckkart* for the reception of Eckhart in Middle Dutch, and pp. 62–95 for the sermon.

93. Schweitzer, *Meister Eckhart und der Laie*, p. 96.

94. Ibid., p. 106

95. Ibid., pp. 17–18.

96. See now Van Dijk, *Prolegomena*, pp. 206–7.

97. Post, "De statuten," pp. 9–12.

98. Grote, *Epistolae* 31, 36, 37, ed. Mulder, pp. 133–37, 149–52. On these letters, see van Dijk (2003), pp. 515–17, and on the incident, Épiney-Burgard, *Gérard Grote*, pp. 190–94.

99. Pomerius, *De origine* II. 18, ed. de Leu, p. 296. This episode has generated a large literature. See Warnar, "Tauler in Groenendael," who creates a plausible case for a 1346 meeting and an echo of it in the Friends' later "*Meisterbuch*" (which remains unedited). On Tauler, orientation to an enormous literature in McGinn, *The Harvest*, pp. 240–96, and Gnädinger, *Johannes Tauler*.

100. See especially Mertens, "Ruusbroec onder de godsvrienden," and now Williams-Krapp, "*Ein puch verschriben ze deutsche*," both with further bibliography. Further connections noted now by Scheepsma "Überregionale Beziehungen."

101. Williams-Krapp, p. 45. For the case of Mechthild of Magdeburg (originally writing in Low German), see now Gottschall, "Basel als Umschlagplatz."

102. Best introduction is Steer, "Merswin, Rulman," with bibilography; in English now the fine chapter by McGinn, *The Harvest*, pp. 407–31.

103. To get at documents and the earlier claims, see Schmidt, *Die Gottesfreunde* and Jundt, *Les Amis de Dieu*, reviewed freshly by Gorceix, *Amis de Dieu*. Very helpful is Steer, "Die Stellung des 'Laien'."

104. Merswin, *Vier Jahren seines anfangenden Lebens*, ed. Strauch, p. 3.

105. Ibid., p. 18.

106. Ibid., p. 22.

107. Thus the inscription at the front of the manuscript, inserted into the community's so-called *Briefbuch*, pp. 1–2, and Strauch's discussion, pp. v–vi.

108. Ibid., p. 3, authenticated with his seal.

109. *Des Gottesfreundes Fünfmannenbuch*, ed. Strauch, with introductory material on its supposed origins, pp. 28–29.

110. See now Warnar, "Tauler in Groenendael," and McGinn, *The Harvest*, pp. 420–23.

111. A point deserving of more attention; see Wand-Wittkowski, "Mystik und Distanz," with an interesting list on pp. 130–31. The works of story and dialogue have on the whole no analogues or sources, unlike the more or less borrowed mystic teachings.

112. On this issue, widely discussed in the nineteenth century, see Gorceix, *Amis de Dieu*, pp. 98–113; McGinn, *The Harvest*, pp. 418–20.

113. Merswin, *Vier Jahren seines anfangenden Lebens*, ed. Strauch, p. 22.

114. Steer, "Die Stellung des 'Laien'," p. 649.

115. The work translated into Latin. For manuscripts and editions (no edition of the Latin and only a partial edition of the Middle Dutch text)," see Steer, "Merswin, Rulman," p. 428, its visionary and mystical dimensions treated by McGinn, *The Harvest*, pp. 423–27.

116. Merswin, *Neun-Felsen-Buch*, ed. Strauch, p. 18.

117. Ibid., p. 20.

118. Ibid., pp. 61–62.

119. Ibid., p. 77.

120. Ibid., p. 93.

121. Ibid., pp. 127–28.

122. Ibid., p. 1.

123. Ibid., pp. 67, 68.

124. The language is woven into the narrative of the *Memorial* c. 4, ed. Schmidt 1854, *Die Gottesfreunde*, pp. 38–39 but seems to echo a founding document.

125. *Fünfmannenbuch*, ed. Strauch, pp. 52, 76. See Steer, "Die Stellung des 'Laien'," p. 645.

126. Well set out by McGinn, *The Harvest*, pp. 408–14.

127. *Neun-Felsen-Buch*, ed. Strauch, pp. 28–29.

128. Ibid., pp. 33, 34.

129. Ibid., p. 37.

130. This text, actually extant at one time in eight differing German or Latin versions (three now lost), deserves more intense study, since its array of literature and documents was plainly meant to serve, after Merswin's death in 1382, as the foundation for the actual community at Green Isle. See the bibliographical and manuscript data in Steer, "Merswin, Rulman," pp. 424–25.

131. Ibid., c. 5, ed. Schmidt, pp. 39–46.

132. Ibid., c. 8, p. 48.

133. The argument of Warnar, *Ruusbroec* (2003) passim, esp. pp. 130ff. For related arguments Warnar, "Mystik in der Stadt."

134. There is an enormous literature, much of it in Dutch and theological in caste, but a good biography/literary history now by Warnar, *Ruusbroec*, with a full bibliography.

135. Ruusbroec, *Spieghel*, ed. de Baere, ll. 1420–32, pp. 333–35.

136. Ibid., 1491–1506, pp. 341–43.

137. Ruusbroec, *Vanden blinkenden steen*, ed. Noë, p. 109.

138. Ibid., pp. 119–23.

139. On this see Verdeyen, "Oordeel van Ruusbroec."

140. On origins and family, see the recent summary of Warnar, *Ruusbroec* (2003), pp. 17–38 and Warnar, "Jan van Ruusbroec." The crucial work on local history was done by Martens, "Une ville en expansion (1291–1374) and "Hedwige Blomart face au mystique Jean van Ruysbroec."

141. On the household and family of Ruusbroec's legendary bête-noire, see Martens,

"Hedwige Blomart," and cp. Warnar, *Ruusbroec*, pp. 69–80. I am not personally persuaded by Warnar's attempted identification of her with Hadewijch, the poet and mystic.

142. Pomerius, *De origine* 2.5, ed. de Leu, p. 286.

143. Ruusbroec, *Die geestelike brulocht* b2411–14, ed. Alaerts p. 551 (the previous paraphrased from lines beginning at b2294, p. 539.

144. Ruusbroec, *Spieghel* ll. 1520–90, 1253–59, ed. de Baere, pp. 345–51, 317.

145. Ibid., pp. 127–29.

146. Ibid., p. 129.

147. Ibid., p. 131.

148. Ibid., p. 133.

149. Ibid., pp. 135, 137.

150. On the meaning of this term in Ruusbroec, and its possible echo in Grote, see De Baere, "Het 'ghemeine leven'."

151. A story told by Pomerius, *De origine* 1.13, ed. de Leu, p. 275; also by Sayman of Wijc, ed. Dykmans, p. 1.

152. Groenendael's earliest founding documents appear to be lost; see *Monasticon Windeshemense* I pp. 47, 62–63. Compare *Monasticon Belge* 4, pp. 1067, 1075–77. We are reliant primarily upon the later narratives of Sayman and of Pomerius, *De origine* 1.10, 1.15 (on the dedication of the chapel in 1344).

153. Pomerius, *De origine* 1.16, I.17, ed de Leu, pp. 277, 278.

154. See Dykmans, *Obituaire*, p. 234.

155. Grote, *Epistola* 24, ed. Mulder, pp. 107–8.

156. Best on this remains Épiney-Burgard, *Gérard Grote*, pp. 104–41. See now Grote, *Ornatus spiritualis desponsationis*, ed. Hofman (CCCM 172), with a good introduction, and the text here p. 3.

157. Grote, *Epistola* 54, ed. Mulder, p. 208–9.

158. Van Dijk, *Prolegomena*, pp. 565–83.

159. J. Van Engen, "Brabantine Perspective," p. 39.

160. Lateran Council IV, c. 13, entered into church law as *Decretales* 3.36.9, ed. Friedberg 2.607. Legal commentators took it to mean what it said, thus Johannes Andreae a good century later, "*nouam religionem prohibit in personis et locis*" (*Novella Commentaria* in 3.36.9, ed. 1581 p. 186). What was to be avoided was, thus Hostiensis, *Commentaria* in 3.39.9, ed. p. 138a, a multiplicity of customs and observances: *sic et alias arguitur multitudo consuetudinum et diuersarum observantiarum in ecclesia dei.*

161. Lyon Council II c. 27 (*Religionum diuersitatem nimiam*), entered into church law as *Liber Sextus*, 3.17.1, ed. Friedberg 2.1054–55.

162. The title above the gloss states: "*Mulieres statum beguinarum sectantes et de nouo assumentes, ac religiosi in hoc dantes consilium uel fauorem, ipso facto sunt excommunicati. Status tamen penitentialis per hoc non interdicitur, secundum Paulum*" *Clementines* (1584) 2.154. For at least one commentator, Paulus de Lazariis, the "penitential" estate was allowed but not the "beguine." For glosses and commentaries, see Bertram, "Clementinenkommentare."

163. *Sed hic protestor quod, quandocumque in sequentibus dixeres beginarum statum uel beghardorum fore licitum, nequaquam intelligere uolo de istis qui et que condempnati sunt . . . Sed quia uulgus eciam alios uiros et feminas deo in seculo seruientes, presertim eos qui sunt extra matrimonium, communiter uocat beginas et begardos, idcirco ex accomodacione usus eisdem nomi-*

nibus uti cogor, quamquam uideatur origo huius denominacionis in personas bonas derisorie iniectus. Deridetur enim iusti simplicitas apud mundanos homines faciliter, et sunt deuoti pauperes. . . . Nyder, *De secularium religionibus* 4, here as in Basel, Universitätsbibliothek B III 15, ff. 5–6.

164. Fundamental, in a large literature, are the works by Lerner, *The Heresy of the Free Spirit*; Kieckhefer, *Repression of Heresy*, pp. 19–52; Tarrant, "The Clementine Decrees"; Reichstein, *Das Beginenwesen*, pp. 100–14.

165. Entered into church law as *Clem.* 3.11.1, ed Friedberg 2.1169–70.

166. *Item, quod begine conuentum habere non debent, set queuis filiam uel neptam in domo sua nutriat et custodiat prout potest.* Tarrant, "The Clementine Decrees." p. 302.

167. *Clem.* 5.3.3, ed. Friedberg 2.1183–84 (placed under the title on "heresy," not on "religious persons and houses" as was *Cum de quibusdam*).

168. *Extravagantes Johannis XXII* 3.8.2, ed. Friedberg 2.1277–78 (the title "De regularibus").

169. See the elaborate data of Reichstein, *Das Beginenwesen*, reduced to a schematic on pp. 374–78. The same in a remarkable graph by Wilts, *Beginen im Bodenseeraum*, p. 275. The same seems true for the data and graph presented by Simons, *Cities of Ladies*, pp. 49–50, though he is inclined to interpret it otherwise, pp. 135–37.

170. This in *Lecte coram nobis*, in answer to the bishop of Strasburg: Patschovsky, "Beginenverfolgungen," p. 151.

171. *Extravagantes* 3.9.1, ed. Friedberg 2.1279–80.

172. Koorn, *Begijnhoven*, pp. 16–24; Simons, *Cities of Ladies*, pp. 132ff. The large community at Brussels turned to the pope in Avignon, dated 23 May 1319: Frédéricq, *Corpus*, no. 47, pp. 78–79.

173. Reichstein, *Das Beginenwesen*, pp. 111–13 emphasizes its importance. Frédéricq, *Corpus*, p. 81 had already drawn attention to it for the Low Countries.

174. Frédéricq, *Corpus* no. 45, II, pp. 74–76.

175. From an unpublished charter, *Regesten Utrecht* I.778, Act of 1323, Vidimus of 1422.

176. *Regesten Utrecht* I.779, addressed to "*Consulibus nostre ciuitatis predicte in virtutem sancte obediencie.*" Under threat of excommunication they are enjoined to protect the women.

177. Patschovsky, "Beginenverfolgungen," on whose editions this next section mostly relies, here p. 101.

178. *Lecte coram nobis et fratribus nostris* [that is, the bishop's letter was read out before the pope and his cardinals at court in Avignon], ed. Ibid., pp. 148–53.

179. . . . *hucusque execucionem huiusmodi circa reprobacionem dicti status beginagii non duximus faciendam; propter quod, sicut experienca nos docuit, scandala et pericula in populo nobis sunt suborta.* Ibid., pp. 153–54.

180. Ibid.

181. Ibid., pp. 155–56.

182. Ibid., pp, 156–61.

183. Phillips, *Beguines in Medieval Strasburg*, passim, esp. pp. 222–32.

184. Meersseman, *Dossier*, no. 47, 48, 46 pp. 71–72, 73, 71.

185. On Kerlinger, and on the situation in Erfurt, see Erbstösser-Werner, *Ideologische Probleme*.

186. Vones, *Urban V* is inclined to see this from the papal perspective, placing it in the

context of Urban V's reform of the orders, thus his "Papst Urban V. (1362–1370)." I see the initiative coming from zealous Dominicans. A proper edition of the parallel imperial decrees does not exist, but see Tönsing, "'Contra hereticam pravitatem'."

187. Patschovsky, "Beginenverfolgungen," pp. 110ff, and pp. 161–65 for the empowering document; also in Kurze, *Quellen zur Ketzergeschichte*, pp. 64–66. See Kieckhefer, *Repression of Heresy*, pp. 24ff.

188. Patschovsky, "Beginenverfolgungen," p. 170; Kurze, *Quellen zur Ketzergeschichte*, p. 65.

189. Mosheim, *De Beghardis*, pp. 351–54; for the earlier language, pp. 357, 368. Tönsing, "'Contra hereticam pravitatem'," pp. 292ff has a different interpretation.

190. A Franciscan chronicle cited in Reichstein, *Das Beginenwesen*, p. 122.

191. Lerner, *Heresy of the Free Spirit*, pp. 55–57.

192. For the text, see Schmidt, "Tractatus contra Hereticos"; on Master Johan, see Kieckhefer, *Repression of Heresy*, pp. 44, 125.

193. This is a famous case, with a growing literature. For Mulberg's tractate, see now the edition and study by von Heusinger, *Johannes Mulberg OP*; for interpretation, see Schmitt, *Mort d'une hérésie* and Patschovsky, "Beginen, Begarden und Terziaren."

194. Johan Wasmud, ed. Schmidt, "Tractatus," p. 365

195. Ibid., p. 361.

196. Ibid., p. 382.

197. Ibid., p 366.

198. See Patschovsky, "Beginenverfolgungen," pp. 171–75 for the document.

199. This connection first made by Patschovsky, Ibid., pp. 89–92.

200. Ibid., p. 185. The proposed or fictive exchange, quite remarkably, armed priests to argue in the streets.

201. Patschovsky, "Beginenverfolgungen," pp. 176–81 for the friars' protest letter.

202. Ibid., pp. 182–84.

203. Ibid., pp. 191–95: the appeal and a copy of *Ex iniuncto*.

204. Ibid., p. 194. See Frédéricq, *Corpus* no. 220, p. 229, where the four people representing this constitution before the *officialis* in Strassburg (the bishop's chief legal officer) are from Koblenz, Brussels, Liège, and Trier.

205. Ibid., no. 241, p. 257.

CHAPTER 2. MODERN-DAY CONVERTS IN THE LOW COUNTRIES

Epigraphs: *Vitae fratrum* ed. Dumbar, *Analecta*, p. 31; *Van onsen oelden zusteren* 13, ed. de Man, p. 31.

1. Thomas of Kempen, *Chronicon* c.1, ed. Pohl, 7.336–37.

2. Vita I, lines 43, 46, 57, 102, 193, ed. Brandsma, "Twee berijmde levens," pp. 33, 34, 36.

3. Busch, *De viris illustribus* 52, ed. Grube, pp. 149–55. Grote, *Epistola* 29, ed. Mulder, pp. 234–31, on which cp. Van Dijk, *Prolegomena*, pp. 509–10. I translated the full letter, *Devotio Moderna*, pp. 78–83.

4. Busch, *De viris illustribus* 53, ed. Grube, pp. 154–55.

5. Grote, *Epistola* 15, ed. Mulder, p. 50.

6. Grote, *Epistola* 27, ed Mulder, pp. 119–21 (see Job 7:1).

7. . . . *fuissent sufficientes cause et raciones de non intrando ordinem sed non de exeundo, saltem post professionem.* Grote, *Epistola* 69, ed. Mulder, pp. 269–70.

8. Grote, *Epistola* 74, ed. Mulder p. 74.

9. Grote, *Epistola* 10, ed. Mulder, pp. 37–38.

10. Grote, *Epistola* 61, ed. Mulder, pp. 229–30.

11. Grote, *Epistola* 51, ed. Mulder p. 197.

12. This storyline was massively promoted by Busch's chronicles; see now Lesser, *Johannes Busch*, pp. 230–58.

13. In the first version of this work (begun in the mid-1450s) he had set out to write a history of his own house at Windesheim and of the Brothers and Sisters who lay behind it. His title was: *Liber deuotus de origine monasterii in Wyndesem ordinis canonicorum regularium traiectensis dyocesis, et omnium deuotorum presbiterorum, clericorum, et sororum totius patrie regionis Almannie* (Brussels, Royal Library, MS IV, 110). When he polished and revised the work six years or so later, now at a great distance from Windesheim, he reconceived it as a history of the entire movement, and his title began: *Liber de origine moderne deuocionis omnium deuotorum presbyterorum, clericorum, et sororum siue beginarum tocius nostre patrie regionis Almanie, et consequenter de origine processu et consummacione temporali et spirituali monasterii nostri in Windesem ordinis canonicorum regularium Traiectensis diocesis, ac de origine et consummacione capituli nostri generalis.*

14. Busch, *De viris illustribus* 15, ed. Grube, p. 41

15. Busch, *De viris illustribus* 18, ed. Grube, 48. This sermon (pp. 48–52), though recorded and improved upon by Busch (*Sermo in forma meliori*), deserves attention as perhaps our earliest witness (1424) to the community's sense of historical identity. Busch heard it from Prior Johan Vos as a young canon, and claimed he was enjoined to take it down and distribute it. It similarly claims a religious transformation of their homeland: "*Florencius et sui confratres, itinera magistri sui [Grote] recto tramite insequentes, talia ac tanta in hac nostra provincia in novis monasteriis, devotis congregactionibus apte construendis, et idoneis personis pro religione servanda debite instituendis, maximis suis laboribus et expensis perfecerunt, ut vix aliqua in hac nostra terra civitas, oppidum, aut villa magna et notabilis repperiatur, quin ibi aut regularium monasteria aut clericorum congregaciones seu sororum beginaria cernantur iam erecta et in suis temporalibus spritualibusque bonis competenter bene fundata*" (p. 49).

16. *Epistola Wilhelmi Vornken* 5, ed. Acquoy, *Klooster te Windesheim* 3.238: *De ortu noue deuocionis in terra nostra.* This rubric was possibly added by a scribe rather than William himself.

17. Ibid., 3.255.

18. Pomerius, *De origine* II.8, ed. de Leu, p. 288; in Middle Dutch, ed. Verdeyen, "De middelnederlandse vertaling," p. 142

19. *Epistola Wilhelmi Vornken*, ed. Acquoy, *Klooster te Windesheim*, pp. 237–38.

20. For this broad definition, see Blockmans, *LMA* 10.1141–42, and for more context the study of de Schepper, *Belgium Nostrum*. The best starting point, with extensive bibliographies, is the *Algemene geschiedenis der Nederlanden*, vol. 3 and 4 (1980).

21. On Guicciardini, see now *Guicciardini Illustratus*, with a full bibliography. I have used the first edition, published at Antwerp in 1567.

22. Guicciardini, *Paesi Bassi*, p. 2.

23. For Van den Keere we have a modern reprint, *Germania Inferior*, with an introduction by Koeman. Its text in Latin, by Petrus Montanus (van den Berghe), rested in part on Guicciardini, amplified with humanist learning.

24. A helpful overview down to the early 1970s, with a summary of the main historical positions in Rutgers, "Gelre," pp. 27–33. The dispute between Pirenne and Geyl, the Southerner and the Northerner, is well known to early modern historians. Perhaps less well known, because in Dutch, is Johan Huizinga's description of the Kingdom of Burgundy as the immediate "pre-history" of a distinctive Netherlandic nation and culture, "Uit de voorgeschiedenis," the real setting for his "autumn" of the Middle Ages.

25. Huizinga, "Mittlerstellung," pp. 284–303 (a lecture first given in Germany in 1933).

26. The oldest maps of the Low Countries as a unit (done by Gastaldi in 1548 and by Jakob van Deventer ca. 1565) project it as just such an angle. See Van der Heijden, "Oude kaarten," p. 198 (fig. 1), pp. 202–3 (fig. 2).

27. On links between England and the Low Countries in the later middle ages, see the volume of that title edited by Barron and Saul.

28. Guicciardini, *Paesi Bassi*, p. 27.

29. Ibid., pp. 27–29.

30. On notions of "territorial consciousness," compare now Nijsten, *In the Shadow*. On this subject in general see the essays in *Raumerfassung*, especially that by Stabel on the Flemish cities.

31. Busch, *De viris illustribus* 15, ed. Grube, p. 42.

32. Thomas, *Dialogus* 2.15, ed. Pohl, 7.76.

33. For this southern perspective, J. Van Engen, "Brabantine Perspective," now elaborated upon by Jostes, *Die Historisierung der Devotio Moderna*, pp. 135–371.

34. See Slicher van Bath, "Overijssel," and the essays in Petri and Alberts, *Gemeinsame Probleme.*

35. Eloquent on this, Nijsten, *In the Shadow*.

36. Guicciardini, *Paesi Bassi*, p. 165.

37. See now Schneider, *Deventer*, for background and bibliography.

38. Hugenholtz, "Particularistische burgerijen."

39. Vitaefratrum, p. 65.

40. An overview in the collection edited by Rutgers, *De Utrechtse bisschop*; there especially Muller and Slicher van Bath; and cp. Rutgers, "Gelre," pp. 37–38.

41. Busch, *De origine moderne devotionis* 6, ed. Grube, pp. 266, 267.

42. J. Van Engen, "Managing," p. 137, where I edited this document, the folio reproduced there as fig. 4.

43. *Ubi uero splendor tante claritatis per universum mundum diffundi cepit, ultimas etiam mundi partes, terram quodammodo inhabitabilem, Hollandiam loquor, attigit et usque ad ciuitatem Goudensem deuenit.* For this charter at Gouda, see Streekarchief Midden-Holland, Kloosters Gouda, inv. nr. 95.

44. *Satisfactio nostra*, in Emmerich, Stadtarchiv MS 13, f. 75v.

45. A rubric employed, for instance, by Hagemeijer, "Devote vrouwen," Van Luijk, *Bruiden van Christus*, and "Devote vrouwen," also Koorn, "Hollandse nuchterheid?".

46. For Amsterdam the fundamental work remains Van Eeghen, *Vrouwenkloosters en*

begijnhof, a weighty piece of archival work, with a register of documents and materials for each; for Zwolle and Leiden now, Van Luijk, *Bruiden van Christus*, with a summary overview, pp. 29–38.

47. See Hagemeijer, "Devote vrouwen," and Koorn, "Hollandse nuchterheid?"

48. Schoengen, *Monasticon Batavum*, vol. 2, passim.

49. Goudriaan, *De derde orde,* with a provisional list, pp. 239–42. The fundamental work is now H. Van Engen, *De derde orde*, pp. 411–14 for a complete list.

50. Carnier, "De reguliere vrouwelijke derde orde."

51. Ypma, *Het generaal kapittel van Sion* sketched out the broad lines of development (pp. 1–17), but without a listing of houses.

52. Good on this: Rehm, *Die Schwestern*, pp. 31–32.

53. Koorn, "Ongebonden vrouwen" remains the best comparison between beguines and the new converts.

54. *Oorkondenboek van Amsterdam* n. 529, p. 351.

55. *Van onsen oelden zusteren* 13, ed. De Man p. 31.

56. Busch, *Liber de origine* 43, ed. Grube, pp. 364.

57. *Susteren van Diepenveen* 2, ed. Brinkerink, pp. 39, 49, 55.

58. Verhoeven, "De kronieken," pp. 137–39.

59. Ibid., pp. 124–25 (the entire chronicle to p. 135).

60. For orientation to family and social history, see now Walter Prevenier in *Prinsen en Poorters* (1998), pp. 184–231, with extensive bibliography, pp. 401–4.

61. Still women in the Low Countries probably had more room to maneuver, an essential consideration in the founding of these households. See now Hutton, "On Herself and All Her Property."

62. Dumbar, *Deventer* (1731), p. 548. The document still exists; see a reproduction in *Geert Grote* (1984), p. 9.

63. *In sijn huys, dat hij totter ere Godes gegeven hadde, moeste hij oelde vrouwen nemen, omdat hij gene jonferen en conde gecrigen.* Compare *Van onsen oelden zusteren* 9, ed de Man, p. 26.

64. For a general introduction to the role of aldermen in Netherlandish urban history, see now Van Leeuwen, "Schepeneden in de Lage Landen," a study of the oaths they took upon entering office.

65. Post, "De statuten," p. 21. Two versions have come down, both in later copies, a shorter one dated 16 July 1379, a longer one 13 July 1379, a complication raising questions about authenticity. See Post, "De statuten," Weiler, "Geert Grote en begijnen (1995," and Klausmann, "Die ältesten Satzungen." I will deal with it further in *Making Private Religion* ch. 1.

66. Exemplary now on these civic tensions in Zwolle is Van Luijk, "Voorbede versus verzet."

67. Dumbar, *Deventer*, pp. 550–51.

68. Koorn, "Hollandse nuchterheid?" pp. 107–14, a wonderful piece of archival research.

69. Rudolph, *Vitae fratrum*, ed. Dumbar, *Analecta*, pp. 32–33.

70. The documents for this, what became a house of Tertiaries dedicated to St. Margaret, are at Gouda, Streekarchief Midden-Holland, Kloosters Gouda, inv. nr. 95. Basic orientation in Van Heel, "Het Sint Margareta Klooster" and Goudriaan, "Gouda."

71. The document will be edited, along with the inquisitorial records, and given a full exposition in my *Making Private Religion*, ch. 1.

72. See now its entry in the *Monasticon Trajectense*.

73. I draw here upon my transcription of the document from Rhenen, found in the Rijksarchief, Utrecht, Kleine Kapittelen en Kloosters 1224 = 31, St. Agnieten Klooster te Rhenen, a cartularium of the sixteenth century prepared by a Sister Van Brakel in 1540. The positioning of the Knights, the parish church, and the Sisters' household can still be discerned on the "map" of Rhenen drawn up by Jacob of Deventer in the mid-sixteenth century.

74. *Oorkondenboek van Amsterdam tot 1400*, n. 528, pp. 348–50.

75. What follows draws upon the foundation document: RA Alkmaar, Archief Klooster de Oude Hof, Inv. nr. 1. My gratitude to Dr. Sabrina Corbellini for making available to me her transcription. For more on this foundation see her entry in the *Monasticon Trajectense*.

76. For another example, its foundation documents also fairly brief, see those for the Adamanshuis in Zutphen, dated to December 1397 and August 1398, edited by Doornink-Hoogenraad, *Adamanshuis*, pp. 93–96. See also Van Luijk, "Devote vrouwen," pp. 48–49 for examples from Leiden.

77. I am reediting the two reports; for now see Frédéricq, *Corpus*, II, pp. 153–56, 167–81.

78. Vornken and his companion (Henry Walvisch) were both invested at Windesheim in 1398. See Acquoy, *Klooster* III, p. 268.

79. Busch, *De viris illustribus* 47, ed. Grube 137.

80. *Epistola* 19, ed. Mulder, pp. 65–71 for the text of what follows. See Van Dijk, *Prolegomena*, pp. 497–98.

81. *Est quidam qui multa luctatus est in regimine curarum, qui est in pleno proposito faciendi secundum hoc scriptum de consilio meo.* Grote, *Epistola* 51, ed. Mulder, p. 199. Scholars have not noted that "*hoc scriptum*" implies that Grote included a copy of the document Mulder edited as *Epistola* 19.

82. We have three independent, yet interrelated, memorials of Henry (d. 1410, buried in Windesheim): a *vita* in Ms. B, edited by Schoengen, *Narratio*, pp. LXVI–LXXI (by far the richest source); an echo of it in Thomas, *Chronicon* 17, ed. Pohl, pp. 505–7; and a notice in Jacobus, *Narratio* 2, ed. Schoengen, pp. 13–17.

83. Busch, *De viris illustribus* 18, 33, ed. Grube, pp. 49, 90; Busch, *De origine* 18, ed. Grube, p. 297.

84. The reference here is to "dominus," the term of respect comparable to "sir" used for priests in the Later Middle Ages—as in the English "Dom," retained in Dutch for Reformed ministers as "Dominee." I use the current priestly title "Father" in my text, though it does not have the same powerful resonance.

85. Thomas, *Chronicon* 17, ed. Pohl pp. 505–7.

86. "*and prestis . . . shulden be pore as Crist*": orientation to this complex theme in Hudson, *Premature Reformation*, pp. 344–58.

87. J. Van Engen, "Managing the Common Life."

88. *Et residuum summe reseruetur ad dictamen domini Henrici et Celie si debeat ad utilitatem seruitorum Campensium distribui, uel ad dictamen Florencii et Gherardi si debeat ad ultilitatem Deventrie Dei seruitorum deputari.* Grote, *Epistola* 19, ed. Mulder, p. 70. This Cecelia was the founder of the women's household in Kampen.

89. Petrus Horn, *Vita Gerardi* 13, ed. Kühler, p. 361.

90. Thus Rudolph of Muiden, an early member of the House and long-time procurator (that is, in charge of administrative matters, including documents), in his *Vitae fratrum*, ed. Dumbar, *Analecta*, p. 9: *Libros vero suos, quos in copia non parva habuit, communicavit domino Florencio et domino Iohanni de Gronda, ea condicione quod semper permanerent tres pro conservacione librorum, ut si quando unus decederet reliqui duo eligerent aliquem in locum defuncti.* This, though a narrative text, echoes the previous legal agreements and likely a lost document.

91. *Vitae fratrum*, ed. Dumbar, *Analecta*, p. 11.

92. Ibid. p. 71.

93. For the Brothers' retrospective memories of this house, see Johannes Hattem *Scriptum* I.1, VI.1, ed. J. Van Engen, "Managing," pp. 149, 156.

94. *Copie*, ff. 9r–10v = pp. 17–20, with editions by Dumbar, *Deventer*, pp. 562–63, and Van der Wansem, *Het ontstaan*, pp. 179–82. Van der Wansem, pp. 68–74 saw this as the "common life" already in place, and failed to grasp the legal arrangement at work here.

95. These documents were edited by Schoengen, *Narratio*, pp. 279–84.

96. Ibid., p. 9.

97. See Weiler, *Volgens de norm*, pp. 173–83, with bibliography and references.

98. Ibid., pp. 184–91.

99. Van der Wansem, *Het onstaan*, p. 183.

100. An agreement of January 1391 approved by the city aldermen: Van der Wansem, *Het ontstaan*, pp. 183–87. Compare Hattem, *Scriptum* I.1, ed. Van Engen, "Managing," p. 149.

101. Van der Wansem, *Het onstaan*, p. 184.

102. Rudolph, *Vitae fratrum*, ed. Dumbar, *Analecta*, p. 16.

103. The original is lost; Van der Wansem, *Het ontstaan*, pp. 188–89.

104. . . . *die nun in der tijt ende hier namaels bewaren ende besitten zolen zeligher ghedechtenisse meyster Gheerdes des Groten ende heren Iohans van den Gronde* [d. 1392] *boken ende hore boken; ende oec dat huys dat ghelegen is inder stad van Deventer . . . ende dat nu gheheten is Meyster Florens Huys*. *Copie*, f. 1r (21 February 1397). See Johannes Hattem's *Scriptum* I.3, ed. J. Van Engen, "Managing," p. 149.

105. *Copie*, f. 2r.

106. Grote, *Epistola* 51, ed. Mulder, p. 198 (in December 1382 or 1383).

107. See, for instance, *The Parish*, and French, *The People of the Parish*, with further references.

108. The positive reading of Duffy, *Stripping the Altars*, which represented his assertive response to the negative assessments common from the 1960s on, and compare my "The Christian Middle Ages." In their zeal the Modern-Day Devout were quite prepared, however, to condemn routinely what they saw around them as laxity and indifference.

109. Keiser, "Noght how lang man lifs," p. 145. Many of the essays in *De cella in seculum*, ed. Sargent, are pertinent here.

110. For an approach to the Middle Dutch materials, see especially *Boeken voor de eeuwigheid*, ed. Mertens, with his estimate of "70 to 80 percent" of the prose as "geestelijk," religious or devotional.

111. The collations were edited by Moll, "Acht collationiën." See now Mertens, "Postuum auteurschap" on the text and transmission. On the sister, *Susteren van Diepenveen*, ed. Brinkerink, pp. 253–54. The basic work on Brinckerink remains Kühler, *Johannes Brinckerink.*

112. . . . *sonder enich waeromme ende sonder eneghen loen van gratien often van glorien.* Beatrice, *Seven manieren* ll. 81–82, ed. Vekeman-Tersteeg (1970), p. 36 (the "second manner').

113. Moll, "Acht collatiën," pp. 111–12, 113, 115, 118, 119, 121.

114. The two works ascribed to Florens barely survived, in single copies. See now the edition of the *Tractatulus* by Legrand, with an introduction by Mertens. For the florilegium, see the study by Van Woerkum, "Het libellus '*Omnes, inquit, artes.*'"

115. Zerbolt, *De reformatione*, ed. Legrand; *De ascensionibus*, ed. Legrand. On Zerbolt see Van Rooij, *Gerard Zerbolt*, and Gerrits, *Inter timorem et spem*. For a partial translation of *De spiritualibus ascensionibus*, see J. Van Engen, *Devotio Moderna*, pp. 243–315.

116. Grote, *Epistola* 20, ed. Mulder, p. 74.

117. *Istud est uere et spiritualiter conuerti, uires scilicet anime et affectiones, a Deo et recto statu suo auersas deordinatas et indispositas, ad debitum statum suum conuertere reducere et reformare; in isto est uera perfectio.* Zerbolt, *De reformacione* 3, ed. Legrand, p. 106 (earlier cc. 1, 2, pp. 94–98).

118. Ibid., 3, ed. Legrand, p. 104.

119. Florens, *Tractatulus* 1, ed. Legrand, p. 62 (with the citation to David of Augsburg).

120. Ibid., 5, p. 5.

121. Zerbolt, *De reformacione* 9, ed. Legrand, p. 124.

122. Ibid., 10, p. 128.

123. Ibid., 20, p. 160.

124. Thomas, *Dialogus* IV.14, pp. 318–19.

125. Ibid., IV.12, p. 295.

126. Ibid., IV.13, ed. Pohl, pp. 292, 295–96, 307, 313–14, 317.

127. See *Monasticon Windeshemense* III, pp. 37–41; *Monasticon fratrum* III, pp. 35–40.

128. Thomas, *Dialogus* I, ed. Pohl VII, pp. 4–30. Basic orientation now to this work, with manuscripts, in Sudmann, "Der 'Dialogus noviciorum'."

129. Thomas, *De imitatione Christi* II.1.7

130. Ibid., II.3.1, II.3.3.

131. Thomas, *De imitatione Christi* II.4.

132. Ibid., II.5.2.

133. Thomas, *De imitatione Christi* III.42.2, III.56.1.

134. Grote, *De simonia*, ed. De Vreese, p. 1. See Épiney-Burgard, *Gérard Grote*, pp. 217–24.

135. Grote, *De simonia*, ed. De Vreese, pp. 26, 27.

136. Compare Van Luijk, *Bruiden van Christus*, pp. 43–48, who reviews various explanations, especially the "excess of women" idea, articulated already in the nineteenth century, and which she mostly rejects.

CHAPTER 3. SUSPICION AND INQUISITION

Epigraphs: *Vitae fratrum*, ed. Dumbar, *Analecta*, pp. 29–30; *Vitae fratrum*, ed. Dumbar, *Analecta*, pp. 29–30.

1. A document dated 30 April 1401: Schoengen, *Narratio*, pp. 512–14, here, p. 512.

2. See the text in Post, "De Statuten," p. 4

3. Ibid., (c. 5).

4. Ibid., pp. 6, 8, 15–17 (cc. 10, 12, 25–27).

5. Thomas, *Dialogus* 4.1, ed. Pohl VII, p. 216.

6. Rudolph, *Vitae fratrum*, ed. Dumbar, *Analecta*, p. 13. Busch has John Vos, a young copyist for Grote, report (1424) that on his deathbed Master Geert exhorted the men to keep up their recently begun communal life: . . . *cum suis clericis et presbyteris ceterisque devotis communem vitam nuper inchoatam in debita forma firmissime servaret*. . . . Busch, *De viris illustribus* 18, ed. Grube, pp. 48–49.

7. Busch, *De origine moderne devocionis* 2, ed. Grube, pp. 253–54.

8. See Wolfs, *Middeleeuwse dominicanenkloosters*, p. 316.

9. The third chapter title has notable variants in its first edition: *De fratribus mendicantibus communem uitam modernorum deuotorum reprobantibus* [*reprobare conantibus*, Grube], *sed a magistro Gerardo magno iuridice* [*publice*, Grube] *conuictis*. This follows immediately upon Busch's extravagant statement in chapter two of wondrous growth, ending with a declaration of approval for their way of life: *Huiusmodi ergo fratres et sorores deuotarum congregacionum . . . in statu sunt eterne salutis, cum iuxta primitiue ecclesie institucionem* [*sine solempni professione, add.* Grube] *uita uiuant sepius enarrari et certis documentis ecclesiasticis* [*om.* Grube] *id eciam* [*similiter*] *comprobari* [*approbari*, Grube] *frequenter audiuimus*. The key point about "no vows" appears in Busch's previous sentence: . . . *preter numerosas illas* [Grube, *trans.*] *presbiterorum, clericorum et sororum deuotarum congregaciones, more patrum primitiuorum sine aliqua certa regula professa, in uera obediencia humilitate et simplicitate* [*carencia proprii et continencia*, Grube], *et in regula Christi caritate deo fideliter* [trans. Grube] *seruientes*. Busch, *De origine* 2, ed. Grube 256 (here following the first edition, MS Br IV, 110, f. 3v). In general, interestingly, his second edition made the Brothers' novel stance and practices more explicit.

10. Busch, *De origine* 3, ed. Grube pp. 256–59.

11. Busch, *De origine* 3, ed. Grube 259. Note that the vulnerable Devout here are women (*quas*).

12. *Gerardi Opera omnia* I, ed. Van Dijk, *Prolegomena*, pp. 51, 70, 72, 75, 76. Some titles were repeated from one compiler to another; others are inferences drawn from Busch's account, then with the title *De uita in communi degentium*.

13. This was a copy, subsequently entered into a manuscript containing other materials relevant to the Brothers' case. Florens nonetheless possessed an original, complete with the episcopal seal: *Habuit et in manibus suis tenuit quasdam litteras sigillo reverendi in Christo patris ac domini, domini Florencii, diuina providencia episcopi traiectensis*. . . . Liège, Grand Séminaire, MS 6 F 2, ff. 254v–258r and MS 6 B 14, ff. 220v–222v.

14. Haarlem, Kerkvoogdij 561C, original transumpt. See also H. Van Engen, *De derde orde*, pp. 87–88.

15. Thomas, *Dialogus* 3, Prologue, ed. Pohl p. 118. For basic studies and bibliography on Florens Radewijns, see Gerretsen, *Florentius*; Épiney-Burgard, "La vie et les écrits"; and Van Woerkum, "Florent Radewijns," the latter two with full bibliographies. Important remain Van Woerkum, "Florentius Radewijns," and "Het libellus '*Omnes, inquit, artes*'."

16. Rudolph, *Vitae fratrum*, ed. Dumbar, *Analecta*, p. 52 ; Busch, *De origine* 6, ed. Grube, pp. 266, 267.

17. Thomas, *Dialogus* 3.27, ed. Pohl, p. 186.

18. Ibid., 3.24, p. 177.

19. Ibid., 3.11, ed. Pohl, p. 142.

20. Ibid., 3.18, p. 162.

21. Thomas, *Dialogus* 3.22, ed. Pohl, p. 172 speaks to his reputation, and *Chronica*, p. 495 emphasizes the respect shown at his death. An issue is his title, as in that of the house named after him, "Heer-Florens-Huis." The title *Heer* = *Dominus* = "lord" or "sir" applied to priests, though it also applied to a master, and Florens was both. Geert Grote was only a master; so the meaning was clear, Master Geert. Florens was both, and I use both titles contextually. For that there is evidence even in Thomas's rhyming prose: *Itaque communem uitam sectando et fraternam caritatem omnibus exhibendo, non alta de se sapiendo sed humilibus semper consentiendo, iam non ut magister rigidus metuebatur sed sicut amabilis pater diligebatur.* . . . Thomas mostly called him "*Magister*," as did many contemporary documents.

22. Post, *Modern Devotion*, p. 204 n. 1. He must have spent the latter 1370s in Prague.

23. Thomas, *Dialogus* 3.4, ed. Pohl, p. 127. Compare Van der Wansem, *Het ontstaan*, p. 52, and Moll, *Kerkgeschiedenis*, II, pp. 289ff.

24. Thomas, *Dialogus* 3.6–7, ed. Pohl, pp. 130–33. In Grote's correspondence Florens appears as an associate sparingly, and only in the last year of his life, late 1383–August 1384, though he was the person who then handled materials and funds for Master Geert's appeal to Rome: *Epistola* 59, ed. Mulder, p. 219.

25. On these vicarages, see Dumbar, *Deventer*, pp. 345–415. Tradition held that Grote only ever recommended one of his followers as worthy enough for advancement to the priesthood, then sent him outside the diocese for a legitimate ordination, and that was Florens; see Thomas, *Dialogus* 3.10, ed. Pohl, pp. 138–40. There is no absolute proof, but Grote, *Epistola* 6, ed. Mulder, p. 11 is usually connected to this, the recommendation of someone for ordination, described as "*magistrum N . . . socium meum, secundum eundum amorem ualde michi preelectum uirum simplicem et rectum.*"

26. Thomas, *Dialogus* 3.24, ed. Pohl, p. 177.

27. In the culminating chapter of his biography Thomas makes canons the epitome and paradigm for the entire movement, something for which there is no evidence in Grote himself or in any of the Brothers' writings: *Dialogus* 2.15, ed. Pohl, pp. 74–78, here, pp. 77–78. This passage has had a disproportionate and distorting influence. See Lesser, *Johannes Busch*, pp. 230–58 on the "Mythos Windesheim," and now Jostes, *Die Historisierung der Devotio Moderna*, pp. 55–75.

28. Vornken, *Epistola*, in Acquoy, *Klooster*, III, p. 245.

29. Busch, *De origine moderne devotionis* 5, ed. Grube, pp. 263–66.

30. . . . *fundati nimirum a primo fratrum in Dauentria rectore, domino scilicet et magistro Florentio, quemadmodum litere fundationis domus nostre in presentiarum testantur.* From a sermon to the Brothers at Delft in June 1475, ed. Acquoy, *Klooster*, III, p. 331.

31. *Ista fuit causa mouens ad instituendum religiosos, quia in simplici communi uita timebant sustinere persecutiones ab emulis, ut si aliquibus existentibus religiosis multi fratres deuoti non professi religione tuerentur, seu laterent sub professis religionem.* Rudolph, *Vitae fratrum*, ed. Dumbar, *Analecta*, p. 13.

32. Busch, *De origine moderne devotionis*, 6, 16, ed. Grube 266, 267, 290.

33. On Windesheim, the essential work remains Acquoy, *Klooster te Windesheim*, with a list of surviving documents at III, pp. 256ff. A full bibliography in *Monasticon Windeshemense*

3, pp. 467–512, with a basic history on pp. 497ff. The earliest documents edited by Acquoy, III, pp. 262–64.

34. Busch, *De origine moderne devotionis* 6, ed. Grube, pp. 267–68.

35. The best version in Van Zijl, "Bisschoppelijke goedkeuring," pp. 337–41.

36. See Jocqué, "De Victorijnse wetgeving."

37. Busch, *De origine moderne devotionis* 5, ed. Grube, p. 264.

38. *Susteren van Diepenveen*, ed. Brinckerink, p. 44. The document from the city acknowledges that Zwedera appeared, together with "Joncker Zweder van Rechter en Wynold van Arnhem," her "legal heirs" (*gherechte erfghenamen*); and because they four "prayed and desired" this in a "godly, reasonable, and honorable way," the magistrates "approved and consented." Van der Wansem, *Het ontstaan*, pp. 183–84.

39. Ibid., pp. 183–87 for the whole, which is based upon Dumbar, *Deventer*, pp. 604–6, who apparently had access still to the original.

40. Even Grote, though following the Roman allegiance, was uncharacteristically cautious and even-handed when asked for an opinion, one of his lengthier and better-known letters: *Epistola* 21, ed. Mulder, pp. 78–93.

41. On this election, see Post, *Kerkgeschiedenis*, I, pp. 297–99. For Frederick himself, his election and political ambitions, Schmedding, *De Regeering*. For his actions against Waldensians in Strassburg, De Lange and Utz Tremp, *Friedrich Reiser*, pp. 189–204; and allegedly against beguines, Lerner, *Heresy*, p. 99 n. 38

42. Busch claimed that it was a golden era for lands subject temporally to the bishop (*tunc Traiectensi patrie aurea secula*) in *De origine moderne devotionis* 34, ed. Grube, p. 332. Frederick did play a key role with respect to the Tertiaries, on which see H. Van Engen, *De derde orde*, passim.

43. Schmedding, *De Regeering*, pp. 168–275. On Utrecht's participation in the Council of Pisa, Van Asseldonk, "Het bisdom Utrecht," pp. 61–68.

44. Busch, *De origine* 38, ed. Grube, p. 347.

45. On the *consilia* relating to the Devout, see also Makowski, *A Pernicious Sort*, pp. 143ff.

46. The best introduction to Foec is Van den Hoven van Genderen, "Evert Foec," and *Heren van de kerk*, pp. 128, 305, 346, 626, and passim on the cathedral chapter. H. Van Engen, *De derde orde*, pp. 406–7, with further references, finds him more firmly in the Devout camp than I do.

47. Important *consilia* concerning the bishop's temporal claims to Groningen, not edited, and his role in handling benefices, may be traced through Muller, *Regesten*, no. 1657–59, 1714.

48. For the will, extant in multiple copies, see Utrecht, Rijksarchief, Oudmunster inv. 220–21

49. Grote, *Epistola* 38, ed. Mulder, p. 153, who mistakenly identified this as "Gerardus," Foec's uncle.

50. . . . *ille dominus qui satagit in suis sermonibus uel scriptis statum beghinarum tanquam perniciosum uel defectuosum reprobare. . . .* Ibid., p. 168. This and the following paragraph based upon the text in Frédéricq, *Corpus*, II, pp. 167–69, supported by my work on a new edition. I know four manuscripts, set out in *Making Private Religion*, ch. 4. The rubric for this *consilium*, supplied by the Devout, possibly by Zerbolt, says it was directed against

"*quemdam, qui in sermonibus suis publice consueuit detrahere deuotis personis in congregacionibus cohabitantibus.*"

51. Van den Hoven van Genderen, *Heren van de kerk*, p. 417.

52. *Sic quod examinare uitam et conuersacionem talium spectat ad officium ordinariorum singulorum locorum et non ad inferiores. Temerarie ergo presumit inferior. . . .* Frédéricq, *Corpus*, p. 169.

53. On other occasions, the same core group commonly acted together, even if some were now professed: *Cum autem pauci tunc adhuc essent, dominus Florencius in Davantria rector congregacionis cum certis suis presbyteris capitulo eorum* [that is, the chapter of the professed canons] *communiter tunc interesse consueverunt. . . .* Busch, *De origine* 37, ed. Grube p. 344.

54. Schoengen, *Narratio*, p. 500, who drew upon Hofman, "Broeders van het Gemene Leven," pp. 225–29, who claimed to publish on the basis of the original document.

55. See Acquoy, *Windesheim*, III, p. 281, who published the document on pp. 303–5. At least according to Bush, writing sixty years later, the bishop took a very active hand in sorting out legal details with respect to organization. Busch, *De origine* 38, ed. Grube, pp. 346–47.

56. Basic orientation now in Van den Hoven van Genderen, "Gerrit van Bronkhorst." His post in Deventer noted in Busch, De *origine* 38, ed. Grube, p. 346. He acted for the provost in matters pertinent to spiritual jurisdiction as distinguished from temporal. See also Van den Hoven van Genderen, *Heren van de kerk*, pp. 201–2, 286.

57. Van Zijl, "Bisschoppelijke goedkeuring," p. 341, among four witnesses the only churchman, the other three of the knightly class.

58. Schoengen, *Narratio*, pp. 289–91.

59. Rijksarchief Utrecht, Archief Oudmunster, inv. 160–62 (dated 1 September 1403).

60. Thomas, *Chronica*, ed. Pohl, p. 354.

61. I have found two copies of this, in Liège, Grand Seminaire, MS 6 F 2, f. 257v–259v and MS 6 B 14, ff. 220v–222v.

62. WFA Hoorn, oud-archief Hoorn, inv. Nr. 770. See H. Van Engen, *De derde orde*, p. 71 and n. 12.

63. Thomas, *Dialogus* 4.8, ed. Pohl, p. 279

64. See Kock, "Zerbolt incognito," pp. 173–79.

65. Thomas, *Dialogus* 4.8, ed. Pohl, p. 281. Arnold Willemz, a Benedictine, studied in Paris and Bologna (Magister, 1391), served as abbot of Dickninge in Drenthe (1395–1406), then went to St. Paul's in Utrecht, and worked regularly with Foec; see now H. Van Engen, *De derde orde*, pp. 407–8.

66. This was the most widely distributed of his tractates, and the subject of J. Van Engen, "Late Medieval Anticlericalism."

67. Rudolph, *Vitae fratrum*, ed. Dumbar, *Analecta*, p. 48.

68. Thomas, *Dialogus* 4.8, ed. Pohl, pp. 281–82.

69. See Revius, *Daventriae* I, p. 36; on which see Staubach, "Gerhard Zerbolt," pp. 228–29.

70. See Kock, "Zerbolt incognito" now for an excellent edition: the Latin text (based on five mss), pp. 188–212; the later Dutch version done by Dirk of Herxen (based on two mss), pp. 212–35.

71. Frédéricq, *Corpus*, II, p. 196.

72. On clothing and status, see, for instance, Eisenbart, *Kleiderordnungen*; on sumptuary law, see Killerby, *Sumptuary Law*.

73. That is, a distinct hood, if nothing else: . . . *insuper dedit togas superiories, tunicas, et capucia de nouo panno formata iuxta modum deuotorum in Dauentria*. Rudolph, *Vitae fratrum*, ed. Dumbar, *Analecta*, p. 25.

74. Ibid., p. 13.

75. Kock, "Zerbolt incognito," p. 192.

76. Ibid., p. 197.

77. Ibid., p. 199.

78. Ibid., p. 199.

79. Ibid., p. 200.

80. My summary of Ibid., pp. 199–201, followed by Zerbolt's extended rebuttal, pp. 201–7.

81. Ibid., p. 201.

82. Ibid., pp. 201–2.

83. The best orientation is Staubach, "Gerhard Zerbolt." Honeman is promising a critical edition; see his studies "Zu Interpretation" and "Textvarianz." For the three Latin versions, see Revius (1650), pp. 41–60, partial and possibly tendentious; Hyma, "The 'De libris teutonicalibus'," a poor transcription of our only manuscript; and Hyma, "Het Traktat 'Super modo'," pp. 56–71, the seventh book of Zerbolt's *Circa modum*. For an edition of the Dutch version, see Deschamps, "Middelnederlandse vertalingen," who then did not yet know what may be the best manuscript, Kalamazoo, Library, Institute of Cistercian Studies, MS 18. The question of authorship, long under debate, is now regarded as settled. See Jostes, "Die Schriften" for the older position, and then Hyma, "Is Gerard Zerbolt of Zutphen the Author." But even a new edition may not settle entirely which version grew out of which.

84. When the women come under critique for their vernacular books, their father-confessor in the Brothers' house, John Brinckerink, fetched out Zerbolt's tractate, read and preached from it, but did not hand it over for them to read and use, possibly an issue of control, more likely because it was still in Latin. For the reference, see n. 91 below.

85. Hyma, "The 'De libris teutonicalibus'," p. 45 (the opening sentence); Deschamps, "Vertalingen," p. 179. Where the Latin has "devout books" (*libros deuotos in uulgari ydiomate*), the Middle Dutch reads "good and inward books" (*goede ende ynnighe boecke die in deutscher talen*); and where the Latin has a stern "reproach, avoid, and eliminate" (*debere reprehendi fugari pariter et eliminari*) with respect to lay readers, the Middle Dutch speaks of books not "useful or permitted" (*niet oerberlic, nutte, of gheoerlofi*) for lay readers. Assuming the Latin version was done first, responding to objections from churchmen, it reported tougher charges and posed a tougher tone than that taken subsequently in presenting this apologia, positively, to lay people, above all, women converts.

86. Frédéricq, *Corpus* I, no. 224, pp. 236–37. This is item "o" in Friar Hinrich's manuscript, as set out by Patschovsky, "Zeugnisse des Inquisitors," p. 252.

87. For orientation to this immense topic, still not fully studied, see Weiler, *Getijden van eeuwige wijsheid, Moderne Devotie* (1984), pp. 93–120, and now Van Dijk, *Prolegomena*, pp. 583–85, with essential bibliography. For an edition of the text, see Van Wijk, *Het getijdenboek van Geert Grote*.

88. Thomas, *Chronicon* c. 19, ed. Pohl, p. 509.

89. The text of Kalamazoo MS 18, ff. 266r–267r, cited in Staubach, "Gerhard Zerbolt," p. 250.

90. Hyma, "The 'De libris teutonicalibus'," p. 65.

91. This taken from a still unedited Diepenveen vita of John Brinckerink, Deventer, Stads-or Athenaeumsbibliotheek, Suppl. 198 (101 E 26), ff. 31–32. See Stooker-Verbeij, " 'Uut Profectus'," pp. 478–79 for the text. Their study was of the distribution of the *Profectus* in Middle Dutch among the Devout.

92. *Decretales* 7.7.12, ed. Friedberg 2, p. 784–87. This appears in the church law's title on "heresy" and treats a gathering in Metz (probably Waldensians) referred to as a "conventicle," a word applied to "sects" and as well to the Devout.

93. Hyma, "The 'De libris teutonicalibus'," p. 62.

94. The best introduction to the structure and argument of this work is Staubach, "Gerhard Zerbolt," pp. 233–53, but see n. 98 below.

95. Hyma, "The 'De libris teutonicalibus'," p. 47.

96. Ibid., pp. 47–48, 49, 50.

97. Ibid., pp. 52, 53.

98. Staubach treats these last paragraphs as "appendices," whereas I see them as the punchline of the argument.

99. Hyma, "The 'De libris teutonicalibus'," pp. 66–67.

100. Ibid., p. 68.

101. Ibid., p. 69.

102. Ibid., p. 70.

103. These documents were first published by Lindeborn, *Historia*, pp. 97–103 and Dumbar, *Deventer*, pp. 606–9, and have since gone missing; accessible now in Van der Wansem, *Het ontstaan*, pp. 188–92.

104. . . . *adhuc plurimi in seculo remanserunt, qui quibusdem corporis uel anime defectibus prepediti, religionem ingredi non ualebant; aut certe alterius propositi aut aliter diuinitus inspirati—nam diuersa sunt dona et modi uocationum—religionem ingredi non ualebant seu non intendebant. . . .* Ibid., p. 191.

105. See J. Van Engen, "Brabantine Perspective," passim.

106. . . . *illos sub permissione huiusmodi ab aliis molestari non patiantur. . . .* The document is known only because it was kept, along with other letters and constitutions, by Friar Hinrich Schoenvelt in a codex, now Wolfenbüttel 315 Helmst, here f. 205ra–va, later in the possession of the protestant church historian Mathias Flacius Illyricus. See Patschovsky, "Zeugnisse des Inquisitors," p. 252, item "l," the text first edited by Mosheim, *De beghardis*, pp. 409–10, taken over by Frédéricq, *Corpus* I, nr. 238, pp. 253–54.

107. Ibid., pp. 254–56.

108. Ibid., pp. 256–57, based on Mosheim, *De beghardis*, pp. 409–10, appearing as item "m" in Hinrich's list. The copy of *Ex iniuncto* appeared last, item "u," copied on the basis of a 1396 transumpt, it noted here as a "*noua bulla Beghardorum.*"

109. This appeared as item "c" in Hinrich's list, ed. Frédéricq, *Corpus*, pp. 221–22, on the basis of Mosheim, *De beghardis*, pp. 364–66.

110. This appeared as item "p" in Hinrich's list, ed. Frédéricq, *Corpus*, pp. 222–24, and p. 256 (its new frame), on the basis of Mosheim, *De beghardis*, pp. 380–84.

111. Basic work was done on Schoneveld by Wilmans, "Zur Geschichte der römischen

Inquisition," pp. 205–7; Ribbeck, "Beiträge zur Geschichte der römischen Inquisition, Kieckhefer, *Repression of Heresy*, pp. 26, 123–24, 147, and Lerner, *Heresy of the Free Spirit*, pp. 149–51, 198–99; but the starting point is now Patschovsky, "Zeugnisse des Inquisitors," pp. 261ff.

112. The claims in most literature for dating his intervention to 1393/94 appear to go back to Frédéricq, and have no evidentiary basis. J. Michael Raley, recently graduated from the University of Chicago, argues that other Dominican inquisitors were also at work, for instance Adam of Gladbach, and will explore this in future articles.

113. Rudolph, *Vitae fratrum*, ed. Dumbar, *Analecta*, pp. 29–30 (see epigraph).

114. Lerner, *Heresy of the Free Spirit*, pp. 149–51; Kieckhefer, *Repression of Heresy*, pp. 122–23.

115. See now Patschovsky, "Zeugnisse des Inquisitors." The inquisitorial report is found in Wolfenbüttel Helmst. 315, ff. 216r–217r, its text edited by Mosheim, *De beghardis*, pp. 443–50, taken over by Frédéricq, *Corpus*, 2.181–85. I am re-editing it and the other report in *Making Private Religion* ch. 1.

116. Frédéricq, *Corpus*, p. 181, here, importantly, corrected from the manuscript (*Gherarditarum*, not *Gherardinorum*!).

117. The final sentence, re-edited from the manuscript: *Prout hec omnia supra dicta coram notario et testibus sunt inquisitori predicto mediante iuramento delata ab illis que hiis omnibus personaliter interfuerunt et conscie extiterunt.* Soest, Stadtbibliothek MS 14b, f. 217r.

118. My account is a summary of the findings, wonderfully set out, of Michael, *Die mittelalterlichen Handschriften*, pp. 102–10.

119. Patschovsky, "Beginenverfolgungen," pp. 127–42

120. Stadtbibliothek Soest Cod. 14b, ff. 98v–100r, described by Michael (1990), pp. 106–10. The other copy of Eymeric, with handwritten glosses by Soest, is Cod. 14a, described, pp. 102–6. This was first edited by Ribbeck, "Beiträge zur Geschichte der römischen Inquisition," pp. 138–44, taken over by Frédéericq, *Corpus*, pp. 153–56. On Jacob of Soest, see Beckmann, *Studien zum Leben*. On Eymeric see Heimann, *Nicolaus Eymeric*.

121. Post, "De statuten," c. 20, p. 12, naming the bishop, archdeacon (legal officer), parish rector, and aldermen, along with the inquisitor, as people to whom the Sisters should be open to inspection.

122. With differing emphases, see Lansing, *Power and Purity*, esp. pp. 145ff and Thompson, "Lay versus Clerical Perceptions of Heresy."

123. De Puig i Oliver, "Nicholás Eymerich, un inquisitor discutido."

124. Beckmann, *Studien zum Leben*, pp. 25–50.

125. Forrest, *The Detection of Heresy*.

126. A standing part of church law from 1298: *Liber Sextus* 5.2.17, ed. Friedberg, II, p. 1076.

127. *Clem.* 5.3.1, ed. Friedberg II, p. 1181.

128. Bernard Gui, *Practica inquisitionis* 4, ed. Douais, p. 188.

129. *Et omnia et plura alia inueniri poterunt ab eismet que in congregacionibus existent, si super hiis debite inquirantur.* Soest, Stadtbibliothek MS 14b, f. 217r.

130. *Vitae fratrum*, ed. Dumbar, *Analecta*, p. 31.

131. A first description in J. Van Engen, "Devout Communites," pp. 48–54; a full presentation, with two more manuscripts, in J. Van Engen, *Making Private Religion*, ch. 4.

132. See J. Van Engen, "Privileging the Devout," and "Friar Johannes Nyder," on Nyder's knowledge of the Devout.

133. The rubric: *Dubia orta super uita laycorum communiter uiuencium, non tamen mendicancium sed tantum uictum sine mendicitate acquerencium.* Nuremberg, Stadtbibliothek, Cent II, 10, f. 272ra. The text is Foec's, as in Frédéricq, *Corpus* II, pp. 160–66, breaking off at the bottom of p. 162.

134. Grote, *Epistola* 38, ed., Mulder, p. 154, n. 4. A canon of St. Peter's of that name was a jurist in contact with Grote.

135. . . . *simul habitare, manibus laborare, etcetera nequaquam faciant eas diffamatos de heresi uel suspectos nec aliquo modo includat heresim, ymo uero uitam christianam et christiformem. Sequitur autem quod nisi aliunde sint suspecti de heresi, nequaquam super modo predicto potest procedere ad inquerendum et propter talia aliquem iudicare malum, precipue autem hereticum, que sunt simpliciter licita. Magis est temerarium iudicium omnibus cauendum quam debitum examen iudiciarium.* Nuremberg, Stadtbibliothek, Cent II, 10, f. 273ra.

136. The general conclusion, in effect: *Ex quibus omnibus, saluo semper melius sapientium iudicio et sanio consilio expertorum, apparet quod isti homines secundum omnia iura possunt inquisicionem recusare ne contra eos possit procedere ad inquirendum.* Ibid., ff. 273rb–273va.

137. Ibid., f. 273va.

138. *Potest enim dicere: Domine, non potestis contra me in istis designatis capitulis uel articulis inquirere. In his non sum de uestra iurisdicione uel sub uestra potestate.* Ibid.

139. *Valde enim absonum esset si quociens inquisitori placeret, posset alicui heresim imponere et eam per inquisicionem tanquam suspectam de heresi diffamare.* Ibid., f. 274vb.

140. *Absit absit ut propter susurracionem uel rumorem, presertim maliuolorum contra bonos, debeat inquiri. Absit ut propterea boni sint uel debeant iudicari suspecti de heresi, quoniam sunt mentibus carnalibus aduersi et hominibus secularibus odiosi et despecti.* Ibid. 274vb–275ra.

141. Frédéricq, *Corpus* II, p. 169. The rubrics vary slightly in manuscript. Hannover, MS I, 182 describes the work as written "*contra quosdam eis iniuste detrahentes uel molestantes.*"

142. Frédéricq, *Corpus* II, p. 170.

143. *Que in diuersis domibus singulas marthas habentibus simul in communi sub cura et regimine earumdem martharum degunt. Nec aliquid proprii siue peccuniam siue uestem uel quamcumque rem in singulari sed omnia in communi habentes. Partim de laboribus manuum, pro maiori autem de eleemosynis ad modum religiosorum uiuunt.* Ibid., p. 182, re-edited against the manuscript. In Friar Hinrich's summary this appears first, with no mention at all of communal life in Friar Jacob's.

144. Ibid., p. 170.

145. Ibid., pp. 172, 171

146. Ibid., pp. 171–72. Often, but not always, a "shorthand" reference (here to the "*vitas patrum*") seems to presuppose Zerbolt's fuller text.

147. Ibid., p. 160.

148. For Abbot Arnold's *consilium* we have one manuscript witness, the least of any, the basis for Frédéricq, *Corpus* II, pp. 173–76. But we also have of it our only independent copy in the form of a transumpt, edited by Korth,"Die ältesten Gutachten"

149. Thus the concluding sentence of Foec's *consilium*: *Ecce quomodo clarissime est ostensum quod predicti homines utriusque sexus insimul commorantes et in communi extra religionem uiuentes non sunt de iurisdicione inquisitorum, sed solum et immediate subiecti iurisdicioni dy-*

ocesanorum in prouinciis supradictis per specialem constitucionem dicte extrauagantis. Ex iniuncto. . . . Frédéricq, *Corpus* II, p. 166.

150. For the text of the first and second, see Schoengen, *Narratio*, pp. 503–8, 508–11, based upon a copy made and presented to Cardinal Pierre d'Ailly, entered fragmentarily into the cartulary for the Brother's house in Zwolle. For all three see a copy made from a transumpt, now Nuremberg, Stadtbibliothek, Cent II, 10, ff. 270r–272r.

151. Here translated from Schoengen, *Narratio*, p. 503.

152. *Nec urget obiectus aduersariorum arbitrancium statum sic simul habitancium et in communi uiuencium a iure dampnatum, cum omnia collegia sint illicita nisi probarentur concessa* . . . [the adveraries' charge]. . . . *Nam hee persone, de quibus queritur, non uiuunt collegialiter nec per modum collegii sed congregacionis caritatiue omni iure licite in communi.* . . . Frédéricq, *Corpus*, p. 161. Compare Arnold's position, p. 173.

153. Ibid., p. 160.

154. Schoengen, *Narratio*, pp. 506–8.

155. On this see now *Monasticon fratrum* III, p. 61.

156. Ibid., p. 59; Dumbar, *Deventer*, p. 626; and especially Van Kalveen, "Problemen rond de oudste geschiedenis."

157. The rubric: *Determinacio dubiorum ortorum super uita laycorum in communi absque mendicacione tamen uiuencium. Et est decisio facta in uniuersitate coloniensi per doctores utriusque iuris infra nominatos qui sigilla sua infrascriptis apposuerunt.* Nuremberg, Stadtbibliothek, Cent. II, 10, f. 270r.

158. *Sequentes questiones cum suis solucionibus super causa qui sequitur sunt scripte et formate ex responsionibus et determinacionibus uenerabilium dominorum et magistorum legum et decretorum doctorum infrascriptorum, quas requisiti dederunt anno domini M°CCC°XCVIII°, sicut in litteris eorum sigillis roboratis continetur* . . . Frédéricq, *Corpus* II, pp. 176–77, based on Mosheim, *De beghardis*, pp. 433–42, but here following my own transcription.

159. "*pro munime Beghardorum*" was inserted by Friar Hinrich or his source after the word "*formate*," this taken over by Mosheim, then Frédéricq, and thus the only way the text has been known. The Devout did not call themselves "Beghards"; inquisitors did.

160. *Habent enim quasdam informaciones pro defensione status sui contra inquisitores, quas reor esse supradictas doctorum Coloniensium determinaciones, satis tamen impertinenter pro eis factas et per pretactum presbyterum, ipsarum gubernatorem, in uulgari malo utentem consilio cum auctoritatibus et allegationibus translatas.* Frédéricq, *Corpus* II, p. 184,

161. Ibid., p. 184.

162. *Quod falsem esse, imo dictam determinationem ad munimen eiusdem inproprie et contra intencionem ipsorum determinancium retorqueri* . . . My transcription, cp. Ibid., pp. 181–82.

163. Ibid., I, pp. 260–61. This (*Sancte inquisicionis officium*) was item "r," or effectively the last in the series, prior to two imperial edicts and the alternative form of *Ex iniuncto*, in Friar Hinrich's list: Patschovsky, "Zeugnisse des Inquisitors," p. 252. This ordering and the specific mention of Eylard strongly suggests that the list of papal laws was first drawn up by him and taken over by his successor.

164. Frédéricq, *Corpus* II, p. 162.

165. The "chariot-drivers of the divine raceway" (*loquentes et comedentes cum illis qui*

deberent esse aurige currus dominici, scilicet N., qui non senciunt nobis) were most likely movers and shakers among churchmen, indeed one of the key jurists. But it is also possible to hear in this a glancing reference to Dominicans. *Epistolae fratrum* 4, ed. J. Van Engen, p. 148.

166. Ibid., 1 ed. J. Van Engen, p. 144. He was awaiting word, he says, from the two most prominent lawyers and officials at the bishop's court, Evert Foec and John of Arnhem.

167. Ibid., 2, ed. J. Van Engen, p. 146.

168. Ibid., 4, ed. J. Van Engen, p. 148.

169. . . . *etiam nos* . . . *in fauorem pacem et tranquillitatem dictarum personarum, nostrum dignaremur adhibere consensum, ac eciam (si qua opus esset) predicte auctoritatis et commissionis licentiam et approbationem impertiri.* Schoengen, *Narratio*, p. 513.

170. This from Liège, Grand Séminaire, MS 6 F 2, f. 260r.

171. *Considerantes autem easdem litteras personas diuersorum locorum a se distancium tangere, et propter uiarum discrimina ad singula loca tute deferri non posse, ad supplicacionem dicti domini Amilii ipsas litteras per notarium infrascriptum transumi publicari fecimus et transcribi.* Ibid, f. 260r, the entire document ff. 260r–262r.

CHAPTER 4. FROM CONVERTS TO COMMUNITIES: TERTIARIES, SISTERS, BROTHERS, SCHOOLBOYS, CANONS

Epigraphs: *Van onsen oelden zusteren*, ed. De Man, pp. 245–46; Thomas, *Imitatio* I.17.

1. See Elm, "*Vita regularis sine regula*," a summary of his argument, with a retrospective bibliography.

2. For an attempt to nuance Elm's view, see J. Van Engen, "Friar Johannes Nyder.

3. Elliott, *Proving Woman*, passim.

4. In *Wonderful Blood* Bynum has now turned her attention to the local (northern Germany) and to practices and theologies associated with host and blood cults.

5. H. Van Engen, *De derde orde*, a wonderful study, is now fundamental, with an extensive bibliography and a list of houses on pp. 411–14. He is preparing a *bullarium*, provisionally available online (= *Bronnen*). A *Monasticon* is underway by Sabina Corbellini, also provisionally available online. The first to open this topic up anew was Koorn, "Het Kapittel van Utrecht." Important among earlier studies were De Kok, *Bijdragen*, Van Heel, *De tertiarissen*, and Ypma, *Het generaal kapittel van Sion*. The new work arose from a research project directed by Goudriaan, "De derde orde." See now the articles gathered into *Ons Geestelijk Erf* 74 (2000) and its conclusion in *Trajecta* 14.2 (2005). On the central archive of the chapter, see H. Van Engen, "Het archief." For a summary of what the project achieved, see Goudriaan, "Het monasticon," with bibliography and wider perspectives.

6. H. Van Engen, *De derde orde*, pp. 111–24.

7. See Van Heel, *De tertiarissen*, p. 22, and De Kok, *Bijdragen*, pp. 103–6.

8. This evidence collected by H. Van Engen, *De derde orde*, p. 119.

9. H. Van Engen, *Bronnen* no. 35, 38.

10. Ibid., p. 205.

11. Ibid., p. 217.

12. H. Van Engen, *Bronnen* no. 128, 136, and his discussion, *De derde orde* on pp. 214–31.

13. Koorn, "Het Kapittel van Utrecht," pp. 134, 138. The document is: Streekarchief Westfriese Gemeenten te Hoorn, stadsarchief Hoorn, inv. 769.

14. De Kok, *Bijdragen*, p. 169.

15. For these statutes, still not readily accessible, see H. Van Engen, *De derde orde*, pp. 34ff.

16. Verhoeven, "De kronieken," pp. 129–30, pointed to by H. Van Engen, ibid., pp. 115–16 n. 15.

17. This, for instance, deliberately echoed when the Ursulaconvent in Purmurend and the Ceceliaconvent in Hoorn joined the chapter on 13 and 30 April 1401 respectively; see H. Van Engen, *Bronnen*, no. 36, 37.

18. See H. Van Engen, *Bronnen* no. 41, 43, 44, who in his interpretation (for instance, pp. 166–70) sees more consensus about, even yearning for, uniform ordinances. I sense more tension and difficulty in making this transition.

19. . . . *hucusque proteximus tam diuersis graciis et priuilegiis muniendo quam ora latrantium contra eundum per censuram ecclesiasticam compescendo. . . .* Ypma, *Het generaal kapittel van Sion*, p. 122. I have read "*latrantium*" (from the apparatus) rather than "*lactancium.*" A future edition in *Bronnen* no. 62.

20. A suggestion of Van Luijk, *Bruiden van Christus*, p. 11 taken over by H. Van Engen, *De derde orde*, p. 111.

21. H. Van Engen, *De derde orde*, pp. 236–37, 242–43 provides a list.

22. Ibid., p. 224.

23. H. Van Engen, *Bronnen* no. 42, 68.

24. Ibid. no. 90.

25. This document, to be reedited by H. Van Engen, *Bronnen* no. 35, quoted here from Wadding, *Bullarium* IX. 569–70.

26. A crucial point, noted indirectly in H. Van Engen, *De derde orde*, p. 286.

27. Kühler, *Johannes Brinckerinck*, p. 37; Van Luijk, *Bruiden van Christus*, pp. 46–50. This distinction is not clear in the historical exposition of Rehm, *Die Schwestern*, who treats all sixty-seven houses as "Sisters," though all, sooner or later, became regularized as Tertiaries or Augustinians. Thus the foundation charters he summarizes (pp. 110–12) appear mostly appropriate to Devout communities, that is, to their originating status, while the statutes he publishes (pp. 252–317) apply to their movement into regular status, though perhaps with many holdovers from their founding status.

28. Rehm, *Die Schwestern*, pp. 161–79.

29. Rehm (Ibid., pp. 26–59, esp. 53–54), studying "German" houses, suggested these criteria to identify a house as of "the common life": (1) a common life apart from profession; (2) belonging to a colloquy; (3) under the pastoral care of Brothers (occasionally canons); (4) founded by "Sisters" (what I call the Devout) ; (5) not incorporated into the Tertiaries or Windesheim canonesses; (6) statutes distinct from Windesheim canonesses; (7) their origins not predating the Devout. Van Luijk, *Bruiden*, studied all women's houses in two cities, Zwolle and Leiden, and offers a chart of their typology, pp. 48–49, with six of eight in Zwolle accounted "Sisters of the Common Life" and three of nineteen in Leiden, that is, for at least a time. The brief sections in Post, *Modern Devotion*, pp. 259–72, 495–501 (esp. 495) offered approximations, as he knew, and should be treated cautiously.

30. Fundamental orientation to them now in Bollmann, *Frauenleben*, pp. 43–136.

31. The basic work is Doornink-Hoogenraad, *Adamanshuis.*

32. Van Dijk, "Het vrouwenklooster Diepenveen," pp. 21–22; Van Luijk, *Bruiden*, pp. 171–72; H. Van Engen, *De derde orde*, pp. 325–30.

33. Weiler, "De intrede," and Van Luijk, *Bruiden*, pp. 178–79, summarizes older literature, and offers her own findings, pp. 182–92, from houses of all types in Leiden and Zwolle.

34. Rehm, *Die Schwestern*, pp. 219–24.

35. Van Luijk, *Bruiden*, pp. 175–92.

36. Bollmann, *Frauenleben* , pp. 304–5, n. 99.

37. For evidence of its regular use still in many other houses, Van Luijk, *Bruiden*, p. 76–79.

38. *Van onsen oelden zusteren*, ed. de Man, p. 4.

39. Ibid., pp. 27–28.

40. *Schwesternbuch Emmerich* 58, ed. Bollmann and Staubach, p. 252. The highlighted terms are stronger than my English quite conveys: "*schemel*" is related ultimately to the word "shame" and the word of choice for the lower end of commoners; *noetdroefte* a term for economic hardship.

41. Weiler, "De intrede," p. 404.

42. Rehm, *Die Schwestern*, pp. 212–24, esp. pp. 214–15, 213, 217.

43. Van Luijk, *Bruiden*, p. 68 (with numbers, much smaller, for other houses). If the other houses together had about that many, thus seventy or eighty Sisters in total (not counting beguines or Tertiaries or regulars), and the population of Zwolle was ca. 4,000 (a middle number from estimates between 3,200 and 5,000), the number of Sisters there would have come in far below one percent, notable given the vociferous complaints they provoked (Chapter 6).

44. Ibid., p. 68.

45. From an unpublished letter: *Et ab eadem peste obierunt in Dauentria in diuersis domibus lii sorores*. The Hague, Royal Library, MS 128 G 16, f. 203v–204r.

46. Van Vloten, *Vijftal lezingen*, p. 168; cp. Bollmann, *Frauenleben*, p. 157.

47. The sources and history of Diepenveen set out in the *Monasticon Windeshemense* IV, pp. 592–614. Compare the essays in *Het ootmoedig fundament* and Scheepsma, *Medieval Religious Women*. Beyond archival materials, we have a cartulary: Van Slee, "Het necrologium."

48. *Van onsen oelden zusteren*, ed. De Man, pp. 25–26.

49. Bollmann, *Frauenleben*, pp. 69–70.

50. The fundamental work on these memorials is now Bollmann, Ibid.

51. This was worked out explicitly by Rehm, *Die Schwestern*, pp. 222–24 (with a map) for Emmerich. The book from Deventer is much less explicit about social or geographical origins.

52. Bollmann, *Frauenleben*, p. 305.

53. *Van onsen oelden zusteren*, ed. De Man, pp. 231–35.

54. Bollmann, *Frauenleben*, p. 304, n. 98 for Master Geert's House. Van Luijk, *Bruiden*, pp. 182–85 notes too the pattern of family links in female religious houses.

55. This reconstructed from the lives themselves and the opening footnote for each prepared by Bollmann and Staubach, *Schwesternbuch Emmerichs*.

56. *Van onsen oelden zusteren*, ed. De Man, pp. 165ff, 32ff.

57. Ibid., pp. 245–46 (translated in the opening epigraph).

58. Explicitly so in *Schwesternbuch Emmerichs* 65, ed. Bollmann and Staubach, p. 290 (*mer X iaer oelt*).

59. Ibid., 67, p. 297 (*een volwassen maget*). For Leiden and Zwolle Van Luijk, *Bruiden*, pp. 192–94 could find little about age but pointed as well to 15 or 16 as a median age.

60. *Van onsen oelderen zusteren*, ed. de Man p. 130 (*een oelde maget, al boven oer twijntich jaeren, doe si totten zusteren quam*), p. 192. Compare p. 147 where a girl dying at 15 is said to have come in "very young."

61. *Schwesternbuch Emmerichs* 5, ed. Bollmann and Staubach, p. 5.

62. Ibid., 46, p. 203.

63. Ibid., 13, p. 17

64. *Van onsen oelden zusteren*, ed. De Man, pp. 54–57.

65. Ibid., pp. 166, 171–72 (this passage largely overlooked until now). But Van Luijk, *Bruiden*, pp. 194–99 finds a similar range of motivation, and reviews earlier discussions.

66. *Van onsen oelden zusteren*, ed. de Man, pp. 171–72.

67. Ibid., 8, 21, 23, 29, 38, 40, 43, 48, 50, 53, 54, 62, 68, 69; pp. 109, 140, 143, 155, 176, 184, 192, 210, 217, 228, 232, 272, 301, 304.

68. Ibid., 21, p. 140, and regularly.

69. Ibid., 9, 43, pp. 119, 192.

70. Thus Ibid., 8, p. 109, and more often.

71. *Schwesternbuch Emmerichs* 25, 61, pp. 149, 268.

72. Ibid., 35, 45, pp. 167, 200. And cf. ibid., 56, p. 240, the mother remarrying; 7, 63, pp. 103, 276, the father remarrying.

73. Ibid., 45, 6, pp. 152–53, 82. On mothers' "abandoning" children to pursue their own spiritual life, see the perceptive essay by Newman, "Crueel Corage," though here of course it was neither hagiography nor romance.

74. Ibid., 20, p. 155.

75. *Van onsen oelderen zusteren*, ed. de Man, pp. 243–45.

76. Ibid., p. 172.

77. Ibid., 48, p. 210.

78. Ibid., 23, p. 143.

79. Ibid., 19, 37, 24, 67, pp. 136, 172, 145–47, 297–99.

80. *Van onsen oelden zusteren*, ed. De Man, p. 172.

81. Ibid., pp. 105–7, esp. 107.

82. Ibid., p. 49. The same held for Sister Eefce (d. 1422), gentry from Mark; ibid., p. 54.

83. Van den Elsen and Hoevenaars, pp. 172–79. Van Luijk, *Bruiden van Christus*, pp. 81–94 deals with this as set out in extant rules, especially that for the houses of Sion.

84. Ibid., pp. 53–80, esp. 65–68 (again from Sion); Rehm, *Die Schwestern*, pp. 204–8; and Van Dijk, *De constituties* I, pp. 325–67 (for offices among canonesses and the sources of this legislation) and II, pp. 539–706 (for the influence of these statutes).

85. Ibid., pp. 196–202.

86. *Schesternbuch Emmerichs* 4, ed. Bollmann and Staubach, pp. 64–70, here 65.

87. For work on this to date, see Scheepsma, *Deemoed en Devotie*, pp. 75–100; Van Luijk, *Bruiden*, pp. 102–11.

88. *Van onsen oelden zusteren* 46, p. 154.

89. *Schwesternbuch Emmerichs*, ed. Bollmann and Staubach, p. 89.

90. *Si was ongeleert ende en conde die heilige schrief[t] niet leesen, noch si en leerden der oec nije hoer dage. Schwesternbuch Emmerichs*, 24, ed. Bollmann and Staubach, p. 145.

91. *Si hadde groete mynne ende liefde tot her heiliger schrief[t] toe leesen ende toe studieren. Ende die plach si wael toe onthalden, ende si konde si wttermaten wael enen anderen voert seggen ende oec leeren. Want si hadde alte guet verstant ende seer kloeke siene.* Ibid., 28, p. 152. Whether the teaching (*oec leeren*) should be taken metaphorically or more literally is unclear.

92. Ibid., p. 154.

93. Ibid., 18, pp. 51, 46, 47.

94. Ibid., 61, p. 233.

95. Ibid., 60, pp. 224, 230.

96. Ibid., 33, p. 163.

97. *Van onsen oelden zusteren* 10, ed. De Man, p. 27.

98. *Dit was oer studieren, hier plegen si die boeck omme te lesen, ende dat was oer onderlinge callinge als si tesamen quemen: hoe si in den doechden mochten vorderen ende enen anderen mede herden . . . Ende die de alrevuerigeste were, die weren die alrevlijgtichsten in desen punten.* Ibid., 22, p. 61, 63. This was part of a retrospective chapter on the virtues of the first generation, written more than a generation later, expressive of the ideals of the late 1450s when it was written.

99. Ibid., 26, p. 91.

100. Ibid., 35, p. 126–27.

101. Basic now is the *Monasticon fratrum vitae communis* in three volumes: (Belgium (1977), Germany (1979), and the Netherlands (2004). Weiler, *Volgens de norm* rendered the Dutch volume more narrative, with a good short general introduction, pp. xiii–xxvi. See also Faix, *Gabriel Biel*, pp. 7–33, and the still useful sketch by Lourdaux, "De Broeders." Where not otherwise noted, my data is gleaned and pulled together from the various entries in the *Monasticon*.

102. Brussels, Royal Library 8849–59, ff. 252r–55r (I have an edition underway).

103. For a broad view, see Thompson, *The English Clergy*; for parish priests in Brabant, the excellent study of Bijsterveld, *Laverend tussen kerk en wereld*.

104. *Vitae fratrum embricensium*, ed. Alberts and Ditsche, passim. The local student, one of three described as the "*primum fructum noue domus nostre*," attended the local Latin school and was under their care before joining the house (ibid., p. 48).

105. *Vita Petri Horn*, ed. Dumbar, *Analecta*, p. 149.

106. Thus Brother Gerard Brant at Zwolle (d. ca. 1412) fulfilled all four jobs and was remembered as "very clever" (*magni ingenii*) and highly useful (*utile*), though a laymen (*quamuis layci*): Schoengen, *Narratio*, p. 67. Though written as praise, even a communal household could not entirely overcome the lay-clerical distance among men, located in part in a Latin education.

107. Brother Arnold at Zwolle (d. ca. 1451), very learned in writings for a layman, as the memorial put it (*in scripturis satis eruditus quantum ad laicum spectat*), copied books in Dutch and counseled lay adherents like a cleric or priest (*habens accessum deuotorum laicorum quibus more sacerdotum et clericorum nostrorum monita salutis dabat*): ibid., p. 96.

108. Ibid., p. 117.

109. Ibid., pp. 74–75.

110. *De ortu*, ed. Weilers, p. 28.

111. The priest-friend, Peter of Ghent (d. 1484), later father-confessor to the Sisters in Emmerich, was memorialized by them in Dutch: *Schwesternbuch Emmerichs* 2, ed. Bollmann and Staubach, pp. 44–54. I am editing the life of Matthew (d. 1459): Brussels, Royal Library, MS 8849–59 ff. 60r–66r.

112. A sampling of names drawn from contemporary documents may be found at the opening section for each house in the *Monasticon fratrum*. At Deventer from about 1450 the most common designation was the "*gemynen priesteren, clercken, ende broders*" or some variation thereon.

113. Van der Wansem, *Het ontstaan*, p. 189 (dated 1396).

114. Schoengen, *Narratio*, p. 274, 410–11.

115. The reporting continues: for 1501 seven priests, eight clerics, three laymen, and five father-confessors; for 1523, thirteen priests, three clerics, three laymen, two father-confessors; and for 1558 (the last such entry) eight priests, six clerics, three laymen, and four father-confessors. *De ortu*, ed. Weiler (1974), pp. 67, 74, 100, 150.

116. Erasmus, *Epistola* II.447, ed. Allen, pp. 286, 299, 305. See Weiler, *Volgens de norm*, p. xxv.

117. Thomas, *Dialogus*, ed. Pohl, pp. 87–107.

118. Acquoy, *Klooster te Windesheim* III, pp. 321–29

119. See now Lesser, *Johannes Busch*, pp. 182–208.

120. Klausmann, *Consuetudo*, pp. 387–91.

121. Handy charts by Weiler, *Volgens de norm*, p. xiii, and Faix, *Gabriel Biel*, p. 16.

122. Godet, *La congrégation de Montaigu.*

123. Basic still is Post, *Scholen en onderwijs*, and for Zwolle Schoengen, *Die Schule von Zwolle.*

124. *De stadsrekening*, p. 76.

125. See now Van Dijk, *Prolegomena*, pp. 478–563 for the letters.

126. Thomas, *Dialogus* 3.24, ed. Pohl, p. 177.

127. Busch, *De uiris illustribus* 35, ed. Grube, p. 95.

128. Ibid., cc. 68–71, pp. 204–22.

129. Van der Wansem, *Het ontstaan*, p. 145.

130. *Vitae fratrum*, ed. Dumbar, *Analecta*, pp. 23–25.

131. Ibid., pp. 47, 53.

132. Ibid., p. 39.

133. Basic, despite his interpretative stance, is Post, "Studiën," and *Modern Devotion*, passim, esp. 251–58, 346–51, 564ff. The essential data on schools and hostels respectively were gathered in the *Monasticon fratrum* under the rubrics 3.4.2 and 3.4.3, with full references to the extant archival and secondary literature (most of the latter fragmentary at best). In the Dutch volume edited by Weiler (but also the Belgian volume) these sections offer the basis for future research.

134. For these figures, see *Monasticon fratrum* III, pp. 81, 369, 416–17, 295–96, 142.

135. Rudolph, *Vitae fratrum*, ed. Dumbar, pp. 39–41. Compare *Monasticon fratrum* III, pp. 142–44. An independent cartulary survives from the house: Zwolle, Rijksarchief, Inv. Nr. 78. See also an itemized register in Levelt, "Regestenlijst."

136. The Hague, Royal Library 70 H 75, ff. 26, 27 (Arabic numbering).

137. *Monasticon fratrum* I, pp. 39, 83ff.

138. Taal, *De Goudse kloosters*, pp. 37–38, Carlier, "Het Fraterhuis," pp. 57–58.

139. *Monasticon fratrum* III, pp. 292–97, and esp. 407–18 (Zwolle), contains important original research by Weiler. Compare his *Volgens de norm*, pp. 39–47, 102–5.

140. . . . *instituendis pueris quaestum factitant*. Erasmus, *Epistola* 447 (August 1516), ed. Allen, p. 295.

141. Schoengen, *Narratio*, p. 155.

142. Ibid., p. 155.

143. Ibid., pp. 194–95.

144. Ibid., p. 211.

145. On this phenomenon, little studied or understood, see Hoenen, "The 'Reparationes librorum'," pp. 309ff.

146. *Monasticon fratrum* III, pp. 140–41.

147. *Vitae fratrum*, ed. Dumbar, *Analecta*, pp. 64, 66, 143–44.

148. Schoengen, *Narratio*, pp. 177, 88.

149. *Vitae fratrum*, ed. Dumbar, *Analecta*, p. 66 (*ex promotione domini Florencii in scholis Daventrie legerant*); Schoengen, *Narratio*, p. 175 (*procuratione domini Theoderici Herxen cogniti sui, ordinatus est ad tempus aliquot lector in scholis*).

150. The house there was founded twenty years earlier, explicitly on the model of Deventer, Zwolle, 'sHertogenbosch, and Louvain, the founding document quoted in Lourdaux, *Moderne devotie*, p. 273.

151. Ibid., p. 275.

152. *Monasticon fratrum* I, pp. 74, 56ff, 29, 93–94, 37.

153. *Monasticon fratrum* III, pp. 364–67.

154. *Met Erasmus naar school*; Bedaux, *Hegius poeta*; Agricola, *Letters* 21, 36, 42, 43, ed. Van der Laan and Akkerman, esp. p. 310; *Monasticon fratrum* III, pp. 140–41.

155. On Erasmus's youth, education, and attitude toward the Brothers much dispute has raged, with a large literature now judiciously brought together by Weiler in *Monasticon fratrum* III, pp. 144–47.

156. Beriger, "Rutger Sycamber," pp. 129, 139–41.

157. *Collatio Johannis Brugman*, ed. Van Dijk, *Verspreide sermoenen*, p. 156.

158. *Collatio Johannis Brugman*, ed. Van Dijk, p. 157.

159. *Oratio de laudibus fratrum clericorum*, ed. Beriger, "Rutger," pp. 137–38.

160. Beriger, "Rutger Sycamber," p. 133.

161. *Collatio Johannis Brugman*, ed. Van Dijk, p. 161.

162. See Meuthen, "Bursen und Artesfakultät."

163. Karras, *From Boys to Men*, pp. 67–108.

164. Vergerio, *De ingenuis moribus*, ed. Kallendorf, p. x. This exemplary edition and translation, pp. 1–91, is complemented by the edition of three others. Piccolomini's "Education of Boys" (pp. 126–259) of about 1450 makes religion a significant part of the program.

165. Ibid., pp. 14–28.

166. Gerson, *Pro pueris ecclesie parisiensis*, ed. Glorieux, *Opera* IX, pp. 686–89.

167. Gerson, *Pro pueris*, ed. Glorieux, *Opera*, pp. 686–89.

168. The basic study of the legacy itself, superseding earlier work, is Hoenen, "'Ut pia

testatoris uoluntas observetur'." The phrase is repeated three times. For the text of the statutes, Marx, *Nikolaus von Cues*, pp. 238–43. I give chapter numbers in the text.

169. . . . *in eorum reditu eis lectiones repetere, et eos in sciencia bona, et modestia, humilitate, et ceteris uirtutibus congruis instruere, atque eos cum omni obedientia tenere ad instar scolarium in domo Fratrum diciti opidi residencium.* Ibid. p. 240 (c. 3).

170. Ibid., p. 214.

171. *Collatio Johannis Brugman*, ed. Van Dijk, pp. 159, 161–65.

172. Emmerich, Stadtarchif MS 13, ff. 74–75.

173. Erasmus, *Epistola* 447, ed. Allen, p. 295.

174. Busch, *de origine devotionis moderne* 47, ed. Grube p. 372–73 (this peroration added in 1464, only to the second edition). See Lesser, *Johannes Busch*, passim.

175. John Vos in a valedictory sermon of 1424, preached in Busch's hearing: Busch, *De viris illustribus* 18, ed. Grube, pp. 48–52. Busch constructs a succession in leadership, part retrospective fiction, part fact, from the founder Grote d. 1384 (*origo fuit et pater primus omnium hominum moderne deuocionis huius patrie*) to Florens d. 1400 (*primus rector congregacionis clericorum in Daventria*) to John Vos Prior of Windesheim d. 1424 (*ita deuotus pater noster . . . eorum fidelis factus est successor in cura consulendi auxiliandi et defendendi*). Ibid. 15, ed. Grube, p. 41. By contrast in Zwolle they accounted their rector Dirk of Herxen (1410–57) the successor to Florens as leader of the Devout Brothers and Sisters, and in Deventer they accounted Egbert (1450–83) as his successor as general leader of the Devout.

176. *Liber de origine* 4, *De viris illustribus* 3, ed. Grube, pp. 262–64, 12–14.

177. See J. Van Engen, "Brabantine Perspective," and now in great detail Jostes, *Die Historiserung des Devotio Moderna*, pp. 135–371.

178. The best overview now, with a table, is by Van Dijk and Hendrikman, "Tabellarium Chronologicum."

179. On the house see Weiler, *Volgens de norm*, pp. 110–19, here, p. 112; *Monasticon fratrum* III, pp. 171–93, here p. 189. The key sources are its chronicle, *De ortu domus fratrum*, ed. Weiler, pp. 36–37, and the *Vita Egberti*, ed. Dumbar, *Analecta*, pp. 174–75.

180. *De ortu*, ed. Weiler, p. 37.

181. *Vita Egberti*, ed. Dumbar, *Analecta*, p. 175.

182. For authors in the Windesheim Congregation, the best point of departure is: *Petri Trudonensis catalogus.*

183. See J. Van Engen, "The Work of Gerlach Peters (d. 1411)."

184. Hedlund, *Epistola de vita* is the place to begin, but cp. now also Lesser, *Johannes Busch*, pp. 182–208.

185. See H. Van Engen, *De derde orde*, pp. 233–96, who made it the endpoint of his story under the rubric "Het process van verkloostering" (the process of cloistering/monasticizing). He did all the hard archival work on this and lists the houses (pp. 246–47). See also his "*Speciosus forma*," with a full edition of the document at pp. 241–43.

186. Basic is Makowski, *Canon Law*; for good historical sense, see too Gill, "Scandala."

187. H. Van Engen, *De derde orde*, pp. 256–64 (with an image on p. 257).

188. H. Van Engen, "*Speciosus forma*" for an edition and discussion.

189. See H. Van Engen, *De derde orde*, p. 250.

190. There is almost no serious historical study of this phenomenon outside Prim, *De Kloosterslot-beweging* and De Keyser and Trio, "De *inclusio*."

191. Its chapter titles may be found in Prim, *De Kloosterslot-beweging*, pp. 8–9, itself more a summary of the chronicle than an analytic historical examination. For the *Chronicon* I have consulted the autograph manuscript, Vienna, Nationalbibliothek, MS 12,816. On this author see J. Van Engen, "Brabantine Perspective."

192. *Chronicon* III.1.3, Vienna, Nationalbibliothek MS 12,816 fol. 78v–80r.

193. Paraphrased from Leiden, gemeentelijke archief, archief van de kloosters no. 597 = Reg. no. 979, done in 1451. See De Keyser and Trio, "De *inclusio*," pp. 199–202 for an edition of that from Mello in 1447, each with common formulas but stipulations worked out specifically for the individual house.

194. Busch, *Liber de origine* 46, ed. Grube pp. 370–72.

195. The best list is now in De Keyser and Trio, "De *inclusio*," pp. 196–97.

196. The agreement for Melle defines the precinct in terms of four parish churches, possibly because the canons ministered or preached there, but at any rate a reasonably generous realm for enclosure, considering all the streets in between. Ibid., p. 200.

197. Ympens, *Chronicon* III.2.9–10 (still unedited), Vienna, Nationalbibliothek 12,816 fol. 82r–88r.

198. *Sed diligenter aduertendum quod ista sequestracio uel solitudo intelligenda est et accipienda non tam quoad consortium et cohabitacionem hominum corporalem uel exteriorem quam secundum conuersationem interiorem seu eque uel magis de solitudine mentis quam corporis.* This and the foregoing drawn from *Tractatus de laude inclusionis religiosorum*, in Utrecht, Universiteitsbibliotheek MS 332, ff. 95–139.

CHAPTER 5. INVENTING A COMMUNAL HOUSEHOLD: GOODS, CUSTOMS, LABOR, AND "REPUBLICAN" HARMONY

Epigraphs: The personal *propositum* suggested for anyone joining the Brothers' house in Münster: Klausmann, *Consuetudo*, p. 387 for the Latin text; Thomas, *Sermones ad novicios* II, ed. Pohl VI, p. 14.

1. Mattheus, *De squaloribus curie* 7, as in *Quellen zur Kirchenreform* I, p. 92.

2. See Mixson, *Professed Proprietors* for our only nuanced look at this phenomenon.

3. This is a subject studied, if at all, primarily by looking backward from the 1960s or by way of the Israeli kibbutz. For two sociological accounts, with brief historical prefaces, see Zablocki, *Alienation and Charisma*, and Schehr, *Dynamic Utopia*.

4. Among Taborites, from 1419–20, an elected priest was to oversee the distribution of common funds; see still Kaminsky, *The Hussite Revolution*, pp. 384ff.

5. The title, as I reconstruct it in my forthcoming edition, was: *Circa modum uiuendi quorundam deuotorum dominum qui simul in suis domibus uel conductis hospiciis commorantur.* Each of its eleven tractates began with a "question." See J. Van Engen, "Devout Communities," pp. 97–99 for a preliminary edition of the table of contents.

6. See Klausmann, *Consuetudo*, pp. 345–65 for an edition, pp. 113–20 for discussion.

7. See Faix, *Gabriel Biel*, pp. 347–68 for the edition, pp. 60–68 for discussion; compare Klausmann, *Consuetudo*, pp. 345–65, 134–47.

8. Gerson, *De simonia*, ed. Glorieux VI, pp. 167–74, here p. 170. Dated to October 1415, thus during the Council at Constance.

9. Excellent on this paradoxical dialectic, with its inherent reversals, is Freedman, *Images of the Medieval Peasant*: the serf is either contemptible brute or ideal Christian.

10. Rudolph, *Vitae fratrum*, ed. Dumbar, *Analecta*, p. 13 seems the most reliable testimony, but compare Peter Horn, *Vita Gerardi*, ed. Kühler p. 362. Most secondary literature repeats a version of Hyma, *Christian Renaissance*, pp. 44–46, 364–65.

11. Gemeentearchief Zwolle, Kerkelijke Archieven, Archief Agnietenbergklooster, Inv. KAOO12 (cartularium), ff. 1–2. For a précis, see *Monasticon fratrum* III, p. 38.

12. Schoengen, *Narratio*, pp. 1, 9, 13, 24–25, 27. The complex origins in Zwolle, often misconstrued from a simplifying narrative, are set out by Weiler in *Monasticon fratrum* III, pp. 423–26.

13. See J. Van Engen, "Managing," where I first laid this all out; an enhanced version will appear in *Making Private Religion*, ch. 2.

14. Schoengen, *Narratio*, pp. 420–24, here p. 421–22.

15. Stupperich, *Das Fraterhaus*, p. 142 (*Grundt des Fraterlevendes*, 18 February 1532).

16. Zerbolt, *Circa modum* III, ed. Hyma, p. 3.

17. Zerbolt drew this distinction from commentary surrounding *Decimas* (C.16 q.1 c.47), and quite explicitly from the influential teacher at Bologna called the "archdeacon," Guido de Baysio (d. 1313), whose *Rosarium decretorum* represented an astute and widely used encyclopedic commentary on Gratian's Decretum. Zerbolt was probably led to it by commentary on *Quoniam* (X 3.1.9, ed. Friedberg II.450–51), a decretal ascribed to Gregory VII, though probably from Alexander III (1159–81). It spoke explicitly of clerics living in common (*ut bona eorum ueniant in commune et in una domo uescantur atque sub uno tecto dormiant et quiescant*). Zerbolt likewise used the comparable encyclopedic commentary on the *Decretales*, that by Henry of Bohic, *Commentarii.*

18. In the opening sentence of *Circa modum* Zerbolt cited explicitly the "archdeacon" on C.16 q.1 c.47, Guido de Baysio, *Rosarium* II pp. 253f), but the argument was actually clearest in Henry of Bohic on *Quoniam ut ait* (*Commentarii.* II, pp. 371–72), where those living in common are given a right to a hearing under a bishop if they strike a clergyman, thus a privilege usually reserved for benefit of clergy. Zerbolt, or his legal advisers, may have noted especially the mention of "*clerici*" (i.e., minor or student clerics) living in the same house off a common purse (*Si clerici, tunc aut uiuunt ut singuli scholares in bursa communi et in domo communi manentes*). That is, they were in effect still lay in law but specially privileged and protected by reason of living in common. A few pages later in fact (ed. Hyma, p. 10) Zerbolt conceded that this was about clerics living a common life, but insisted that these jurists had not explicitly objected to living as one in a society: *Nullus tamen eorum contradicit societati simul uiuencium non collegialiter uel conuentualiter. . . .*

19. Zerbolt, *Circa modum*, ed. Hyma, p. 10.

20. A technicality, but a very important one, in medieval life and institutions; for orientation to a contested subject, see Landau, "Was war ein Kollegium."

21. Innocent IV, Apparatus ad X 5.31.14, ed. pp. 526–28; Hostiensis, *Summa*, ed. 65v: "'*quid societas' . . . Est autem permissum causa religionis.*"

22. Zerbolt, *Circa modum* I, ed. Hyma, pp. 3, 4, 5.

23. Frédéricq, *Corpus* II, p. 161.

24. Zerbolt, *Circa modum*, ed. Hyma, p. 42 (the concluding assertion of that section).

25. For all this see Innocent ad X 3.31.14, ed. pp. 526–28; Hostensis, *Summa,* p. 65v, Johannes Andreae ad X 3.31.14, p. 155. Zerbolt, *Circa modum*, ed. Hyma, p. 4 appears at times to claim for a *societas* what Innocent IV would have reserved for a *collegium*, and this may be why his adversaries were persistent on this point.

26. In Van Engen, "Managing," p. 129, I noted this but had not yet fully grasped the essential connection to the legal dispute distinguishing a "college" from a "society."

27. Zerbolt, *Circa modum*, ed. Hyma, pp. 42–43.

28. Ibid., p. 5.

29. *Quoniam ut ait* (X 3.1.9), as in n. 18 above; *Preter hoc* (d.32 c.6), a decree of Pope Alexander II (1061–73) on enforcing clerical chastity and a common life as a means to that end; *Decimas* (C.16 q.1 c.47), a decree of Pope Paschal II against laymen seizing tithes from clerics living in common; *In omnibus* (De cons. D.5 c.34), a Carolingian forgery on clerics eating and sleeping in common. Most crucial of all, and treated apart was *Dilectissimis* (C.12 q.1 c.2), another Carolingian forgery that mandated common life as necessary to all (*Communis uita omnibus est necessaria*), and especially those who served others such as clergymen.

30. This pithy presentation of six "reasons" for a communal life caught Dirk of Herxen's eye, and is what he took over to begin his "collation" on this subject. See Klausmann, *Consuetudo*, pp. 346–50 for the text.

31. *Essetque fatuum dicere quod hoc modo religiose uiuere in propria domo . . . fore reprobatum. Non enim potest alicui prohibere; quin potest sancte et religiose uiuere.* Zerbolt, *Circa modum*, ed. Hyma, p. 18–20, here p. 18.

32. Hostiensis, *Summa* ("quis est regularis"), f. 173v: *Sed et largo modo dicitur religiosus qui in domo propria sancte et religiose uiuit, licet non sit professus . . . et dicitur talis religiosus non ideo quod astrictus sit alicui regule certe sed respectu uite quam arctiorem et sanctiorem ducit quam ceteri seculares qui omnino seculariter, idest dissolute, uiuunt.* Elm repeatedly emphasized the importance of this passage as establishing a kind of constitution for the "semireligious"; see especially "*Vita regularis sine regula.*"

33. Zerbolt, *Circa modum*, ed. Hyma, p. 20.

34. *Modum autem ille necessario varius est secundum uarios status hominum.* Henricus, *Quodlibeta* 3.20, ed. p. 134v. Henry had six types too, but differently worked out; Zerbolt's formulation was his own, if partly suggested by Henry's.

35. Probably known to him through commentary on "custom" as outlined by Gratian at the opening of church law: *Decretum* dd. 8–9, ed. Friedberg, pp. 1.12–18.

36. . . . et *mortaliter peccat qui hoc modo res sibi appropriat uel suo usui solummodo applicat. Usus enim rerum debet esse communis. . . . Presertim in neccessitate. . . .* Zerbolt, *Circa modum*, ed. Hyma p. 25. Thomas, *Summa* II–II q. 66, aa. 6–7 by contrast affirmed ownership as a better arrangement for society and criticized communal arrangements as unworkable.

37. Tierney, *Medieval Poor Law* remains fundamental.

38. Zerbolt, *Circa modum*, ed. Hyma, p. 26.

39. . . . *ita uidelicet quod conuiuentes uel cohabitantes habeant quilibet rerum suarum amministracionem et potestatem procurandi et alienandi, et tamen quod usum faciant communem non solum in necessitate, sed quandocumque amicicia exigit uel caritas postulat seu racio dictat aliorum usui applicant et condistribuunt ad utendum. Hoc enim proprium est amicicie.* Ibid., p. 28. This may well be our best description of what the earliest Devout, male and female, often did, before stricter forms came in place.

40. *Manifestum est autem secundum doctores quod consilia ewangelica nullum certum statum* [Thomas's argument, ironically, against the seculars!] *sed solam disposicionem requirunt in obseruante, et sunt libere et uniuersaliter tradita.* Ibid., p. 29. See Chapter 7.

41. Zerbolt drew his conclusion from natural reason: *Ergo, si qui sunt qui habent appetitum ad bonum commune, qui possunt uiuere in communi, illis expedit, et est meritorium et caritatiuum.* Ibid., p. 31.

42. *Sed hec raciones* [Thomas, *Summa* II/II q.66 a.2; Innocent IV ad X 3.34.8: defense of private property] *non habent locum nisi propter maliciam hominum uel caritatis defectum, que omnia negligit et discordia causatur et confusionem introducit. Sed hec locum non habent inter aliquos inter quos caritas et amicicia uiget.* . . . And then the crux and conclusion of a longer passage, close to the heart of Zerbolt: *Ergo, sequitur quod sit meritorium sic in amicicia et caritate simul uiuere hiis, qui sciunt communia propriis preponere uel sicut propria curare.* Ibid., p. 32.

43. Ibid., p. 33.

44. Ibid., p. 34.

45. Ibid., p. 37.

46. Ibid., pp. 40, 41.

47. Ibid., pp. 39, 40.

48. *Decretum* C.12 q.1 c.2, ed. Friedberg, 1.676–77.

49. *Cons.*-Wesel, ed. Klausmann, p. 397.

50. Thus *Cons.*-Deventer/Gouda, ed. Hyma, p. 441, 466; *Cons.*-Zwolle, ed. Schoengen, pp. 264–65, 267; *Cons.*-Herford, ed. Stupperich, p. 59. See also *Cons.*-Münster, ed. Klausmann, p. 387 and *Cons.*-Wesel, ed. Klausmann, p. 407, and the defense of canonical status in Hildesheim, ed. Doebner, *Annalen,* pp. 209–12.

51. . . . *proposuimus in domo nostra abdicare omnem proprietatem ita quod nullus nostrum proprium aliquid possideat sed sint nobis omnia communia. Sit communis bursa, sit communis archa, sit mensa et prouisio communis.* . . . *Cons.*-Zwolle, ed. Schoengen, p. 266; *Cons.*-Deventer/Gouda , ed. Hyma, p. 467.

52. *Cons.*-Herford, ed. Stupperich, p. 58.

53. *In signum etiam uite communis quisque diceret: tunica nostra, toga nostra, etcetera.* *Cons.*-Emmerich, ed. Alberts and Ditsche, p. 83.

54. Klausmann, *Consuetudo,* pp. 394–95, 410–12, with an echo in *Cons.*-Herford, ed. Stupperich, p. 59. Several points listed at Münster as "*conclusiones pro communi proposito nostro*" were subsequently blended in at Wesel as part of "preserving concord."

55. *Cons.*-Zwolle, ed. Schoengen, pp, 267–68; *Cons.*-Deventer/Gouda , ed. Hyma, pp. 467–68. *Cons.*-Münster, ed. Klausmann, pp. 393–94; *Cons.*-Wesel, ed. Klausmann, pp. 409–10; *Cons.*-Herford, ed. Stupperich, pp. 58–59.

56. *Cons.*-Zwolle, ed. Schoengen, p. 264; also *Cons.*-Deventer/Gouda, ed. Hyma, p. 466.

57. *Cons.*-'sHertogenbosch cc.32–34, ed. Van den Elsen and Hoevenaars, pp. 184–85.

58. Rehm, *Die Schwestern,* p. 266.

59. *Schwesternbuch Emmerichs,* ed. Bollmann and Staubach 31, 47, 56, pp. 159, 207, 241.

60. Klausmann, *Consuetudines,* p. 376 = *Consuetudines,* ed. Alberts, p. 13.

61. Here a translation of my transcription of Brussels, Royal Library MS IV 124 ff. 127–128r.

62. Thomas, *Sermones ad novicios* II, ed. Pohl VI, pp. 14–20, here 14–16.

63. Thomas's introduction hardly makes it clear whether they were composed or collected by him, seemingly the latter: *Sermones quos per modum dulcis collationis pro nouiciis nostris diuersis quidem temporibus in unum collegi. . . .* Ibid., p. 3.

64. Ibid., pp. 17–20.

65. Thomas, *Dialogus*, ed. Pohl, pp. 87–107 (Grote's: discussed above pp.), 260–67 (Lubbert's *exercitia*), 306–17 (John Kessel's *exercitium et propositum*: discussed above pp. 79–80).

66. Klausmann, *Consuetudo*, pp. 144–70, with a reedition of the text on pp. 369–76. This text, it should be noted, was not identified as coming from Florens, and one that is (Wüstenhoff, "*Florencii parvum et simplex exercitium*") was plainly written for or by a canon. See Klausmann, pp. 367–68, for another he ascribes to Florens, and Kors, "Het propositum bij de Moderne Devoten" for an overview of the genre and the edition of an anonymous example.

67. Rehm, *Die Schwestern*, p. 181.

68. Zerbolt, *Circa modum*, ed. Hyma p. 88.

69. Ibid., pp. 89, 90.

70. That formulation is Zerbolt's. Hostiensis, *Summa*, p. 15, set out four "species," with nearly no attention to the last or most particular.

71. Zerbolt, *Circa modum*, ed. Hyma p. 92.

72. Ibid., p. 93.

73. This is the rubric heading Tractate XI (though not identified as such by Hyma).

74. Bernard, *De precepto* 6–7, ed. SC 457, pp. 158–60.

75. Zerbolt, *Circa modum*, ed. Hyma, p. 94, 95, 96.

76. Ibid., p. 96.

77. Bernard, *De precepto* 2, ed. SC 457, p. 150.

78. Zerbolt, *Circa modum*, ed. Hyma p. 99, 100.

79. The basic work is now Klausmann, *Consuetudo*, who reviews the editions and dating.

80. These statutes, first edited by Hyma, *Christian Renaissance*, pp. 440–74, based on the only manuscript (The Hague, Royal Library, MS 73 G 22), have been the subject of much scholarly dispute, partially settled by Lem, "De consuetudines" and refined by Klausmann, *Consuetudo*, pp. 239–49. I take a slightly different stance, to be argued elsewhere, namely, that they came from, or were written for, Gouda (which first entered the Colloquy in 1456) on the basis of the statutes of Deventer, whence my designation Deventer/Gouda.

81. Doebner, *Annalen*, pp. 209–45; see Klausmann, *Consuetudo*, pp. 273–84.

82. Rehm, *Die Schwestern*, pp. 180–89, here p. 180. Rehm edited a series of statutes (pp. 251–309), and signaled a few others in his notes, but from women's houses at the point they became regularized.

83. *Van onsen oelden zusteren*, ed. De Man, pp. 196–97.

84. Heidemann, "Die Beginenhäuser Wesels"; Van den Elsen and Hoevenaars, *Analecta*, (1907), pp. 172–92. See Rehm, *Die Schwestern*, p. 181.

85. Kühler, *Johannes Brinckerinck*, pp. 360–80; and Bollmann, *Frauenleben*, pp. 164–72

86. *Cons.*-Wesel, ed. Klausmann, p. 407.

87. *Cons.*-Herford, ed. Stupperich, p. 57.

88. This not entirely worked out yet, and perhaps variable, but see Lourdaux, "Kartuizers-Moderne Devoten."

89. The same sentence, which must go back to an earliest layer, is found in *Cons.*-Zwolle, ed. Schoengen, p. 239 and *Cons.*-Deventer/Gouda, ed. Hyma, p. 441–42: *Et licet non obligamus nos uota uel professione ad obseruantiam istarum consuetudinum uel alicuius religionis, non est tamen sine culpa in huiusmodi negligens uel inobediens inueniri, turbare pacem domesticam, et occasionem dare uite remissioris.*

90. . . . *collegi et conscripsi pro consuetudinibus dicte domus et pro quodam directorio morali. . . .* At Wesel he dropped the word "customs" (an implicit legal claim): . . . *infrascripta collegi pro quodam directorio morali pro personis dicte domus et eorum successoribus, quibus ego in exordio dicte domus in cura domestica, licet heu satis debiliter, deseruiui . . . .* Klausmann, *Consuetudo*, pp. 377, 397.

91. Twice in 1398 the *Epistolae fratrum* refer to forming the spirit and practices of the house, in V and more remarkably in VI, about the still entirely malleable young students in need of molding: *Ecce iuuenes ad nos recipiemus adhuc inexpertos, nulli firmiter affixos, nec sentire nec uidere nec uelle nec nolle alicui fortiter adherentes. Nichil adhuc in eis est depictum uel saltem induratum, sed sunt depingibiles et trahibiles et informabiles ad quidlibet.* Ed. Van Engen, *Epistolae fratrum*, pp. 152, 153.

92. *Vitae fratrum*, ed. Dumbar, *Analecta*, pp. 85–86.

93. Ibid., p. 55.

94. *Vita Petri Horn*, ed. Dumbar, *Analecta*, pp. 155–56.

95. *Schwesternbuch Emmerichs* 8, ed. Bollmann and Staubach, p. 117.

96. Ibid., 37, p. 174.

97. *Van onsen oelden zusteren*, ed. De Man, p. 60.

98. Ibid., p. 250.

99. Post, "De statuten," p. 3.

100. Biel, *De communi uita*, ed. Faix, pp. 348–50.

101. Thomas, *Summa* II/II q. 186 a.1; Henry of Ghent, *Quodlibeta* 3. q. 15.

102. On this see J. Van Engen, "Religious Profession."

103. Zerbolt, *Circa modum*, ed. Hyma, pp. 21–22.

104. Ibid., pp. 59–60.

105. *Nec excusantur racione societatis . . . quoniam non mutant statum nec religionem assumunt, quare eque manent sub suis superioribus.* Zerbolt, *Circa modum,* ed. Hyma, p. 72.

106. Ibid., p. 73.

107. . . . *de facione autem societatis est magis equalitas uel paritas. Nec debent eligere superiores quibus se hoc modo ad obediendum obligent uel obedienciam promittant, quia hoc magis pertinet ad religionem uel collegium.* Ibid.

108. Bernard, *De precepto*, ed. SC 457, pp. 142–83, with an extensive introduction, pp. 21–140.

109. While the distinction was probably suggested by Thomas, Zerbolt's four elements may be found implicitly in Bernard, *De precepto* 6, 16, 32, ed. SC 457, pp. 158, 178–82, 216–18.

110. Zerbolt, *Circa modum*, ed. Hyma p. 74.

111. Ibid., p. 75. Cf. William Durandus, *Speculum iudiciale* IV, De iudiciis §§11–12 (the example, as so often in dealing legally with "societies," is of students, one of whom proves disruptive).

112. Bernard, *De precepto* 2, ed. SC 457 p. 150.

113. . . . *eciam ex humilitate et caritate obedit suo equali uel inferiori. Et quantum ad hanc obedienciam possunt prefati homines, uel quicumque alii, sibiinuicem uel cuicumque alteri meritorie ad licita et honesta obedire* . . . Ibid., p. 77.

114. Ibid., p. 78.

115. Ibid., p. 79.

116. Ibid., pp. 79–80, citing Bede, *In Lucam* PL 92.331 and Augustine, *In Johannem*, Tractatus 51.13.

117. Schoengen, *Narratio*, p. 507.

118. *Cons.*-Zwolle, ed. Schoengen, pp. 265–66; *Cons.*-Deventer/Gouda, ed. Hyma, p. 467; *Cons.*-Herford, ed. Stupperich, pp. 60–61.

119. *Cons.*-Münster, ed. Klausmann, p. 387; *Cons.*-Wesel, ed. Klausmann, p. 407.

120. *Van onsen oelden zusteren*, ed. de Man, p. 28.

121. Ibid., 133.

122. *Schwesternbuch Emmerichs* 47, ed. Bollmann and Staubach, p. 208.

123. Salome Sticken, *Formula vivendi*, ed. Kühler, *Johannes Brinckerink*. pp. 371, 370.

124. *Vitae fratrum*, ed. Dumbar, *Analecta*, p. 13.

125. Salome Sticken, *Formula vivendi*, p. 369.

126. Brinckerink, *Collatiën* 3, ed. Moll, pp. 127, 132–33.

127. Ibid., 4, pp. 134–37.

128. Biel, *Tractatus*, ed. Faix, p. 361.

129. *Scriptum*, ed. J. Van Engen, "Managing," p. 149.

130. Zerbolt, *Circa modum* XI, ed. Hyma, pp. 97–100, where the issue is to do work in an orderly way, as part of house customs. In *De reformacione virium anime* 39, ed. Legrand, pp. 246–52 it appears as part of the reform of the will in its battle with carnal vice which flourishes amid leisure. This built upon, in a different way, Florens, *Tractatulus devotus* 24, ed. Legrand, pp. 108–10, where it is presented as a matter of balance with spiritual labor. Both cited Guillaume de St.-Thierry's *Golden Epistle* 157 (as Bernard), which recommended labor befitting monks such as book-copying, ed. Déchanet SC 223, p. 266.

131. Post, "De Statuten," pp. 12–13 (c. 21).

132. *Cons.*- Zwolle, ed. Schoengen, p. 244; *Cons.*-Deventer/Gouda, ed. Hyma, p. 445, *Cons.*-Herford, ed. Stupperich, p. 67.

133. *Vita Petri Horn*, ed. Dumbar, *Analecta*, pp. 150–51.

134. *Van onsen oelden zusteren*, ed. De Man, p. 27–28.

135. *Schwesternbuch Emmerichs* 57, ed. Bollmann and Staubach, p. 57.

136. Ibid., 52, pp. 224–25.

137. Salome Sticken, *Formula vivendi*, ed. Kühler, p. 376.

138. Ibid., p. 375.

139. *Cons.*-Zwolle, ed. Schoengen, pp. 244–45; *Cons.*-Deventer/Gouda, ed. Hyma, pp. 445–56; *Cons.*-Herford, ed. Stupperich, pp. 67–68.

140. *Cons.*-'sHertogenbosch cc.26–27, ed. Van den Elsen and Hoevenaars, pp. 182–83.

141. Rehm, *Die Schwestern*,, pp. 288–89.

142. *Van onsen oelden zusteren*, ed. De Man pp. 69, 81.

143. Van Vloten, *Vijftal lezingen*, p. 168; see Bollmann, *Frauenleben*, pp. 156–57.

144. Rehm, *Die Schwestern*, pp. 234–39.

145. Klug, *Armut und Arbeit*, pp. 167–88 has now gleaned what she could from the lives and compared it to general information about textile operations in the later middle ages.

146. *Schwesternbuch Emmerichs*, ed. Bollmann and Staubach, p. 111.

147. Basic remains the work of Kruitwagen, *Laat-middeleewsche paleografica*, esp. pp. 1–78 for the Brothers as copyists.

148. This famously set out in the statutes: *Cons.*- Zwolle, ed. Schoengen, pp. 252–55; *Cons.*-Deventer/Gouda, ed. Hyma, p. 454; *Cons.*-Herford, ed. Stupperich, pp. 75–77; *Cons.*-Münster, ed. Klausmann, pp. 379–80, *Cons.*-Wesel, ed. Klausmann, pp. 399–400. For basic orientation, see Staubach, "Pragmatische Schriftlichkeit" and Kock, *Die Buchkultur*. This is a much-interpreted passage, especially by scholars of manuscript production; see, for instance, Rouse, *Authentic Witnesses*, pp. 449ff, and compare Wierda, *De Sarijshandschriften*.

149. Schoengen, *Narratio*, p. 164.

150. Gerson, *De laude scriptorum*, ed. Glorieux IX, pp. 1423–34 (dated by Glorieux to April 1423).

151. Ibid., pp. 425–26. Typically he noted the regulars (meaning, the canons), not the Brothers or Sisters.

152. Ibid., p. 429.

153. Ibid., 433. See Kruitwagen, "Het schrijven op feestdagen"

154. Klug, *Armut und Arbeit*, pp. 89–113 has now assembled selected texts on this topic from the Devout tradition.

155. Brinckerink, *Collatiën* VII, ed. Moll, p. 156.

156. Grote, *Epistola* 32, 68, ed. Mulder pp. 138–39, 266–67.

157. *Vitae fratrum embricensium*, ed. Alberts and Ditsche, p. 31.

158. Kock, *Die Buchkultur*, pp. 79–121.

159. Van Engen, "Managing" and *De ortu*, ed. Weiler, pp. 158–92.

160. See Wierda, *De Sarijshandschriften*.

161. For Gouda, see Hensen, "Henric van Arnhem's kronyk," p. 17 (*scribentes pro pecio*), p. 28 (*uiuens in magna egestate de laboribus manuum*). For Emmerich, *Vitae fratrum Embricensium*, ed. Alberts and Ditsche, p. 33. Kock, *Die Buchkultur*, pp. 84–85 also points to evidence of book-copying as prominent in hard times.

162. Kock, *Die Buchkultur*, pp. 100–108.

163. J. Van Engen, Managing," pp. 149–59.

164. Schoengen, *Narratio*, p. 166.

165. The best approach to this complex bibliography is now by way of section 3.2.4 for each house in *Monasticon fratrum* III.

166. Schoengen, *Narratio*, p. 165.

167. The shifting rubrics reveal movement here, as well as some uneasiness about how to label what is happening: *Cons.*-Zwolle, ed. Schoengen, p. 262 speaks of the "quality of the brothers"; *Cons.*-Münster, ed. Klausmann, p. 384 of "receiving a brother for permanent residence"; *Cons.*- Wesel, ed. Klausmann, p. 406, of "receiving a brother"; *Cons.*-Herford, ed. Stupperich, pp. 92–94 more elaborately of testing and instituting novices; and *Cons.*-Deventer/Gouda, ed. Hyma, pp. 461–65, also elaborately, of receiving, instituting, and accepting novices (the "receiving" essentially the same text as Zwolle's "quality"). After a generation or so the houses plainly were moving toward a form of novitiate.

168. *Cons.*-Zwolle, ed. Schoengen, p. 262; *Cons.*-Deventer/Gouda, ed. Hyma, p. 462; *Cons.*-Herford, ed Stupperich, p. 92.

169. The final sentence says, of the notarized resignation: *Et quam primum possumus, capimus instrumentum a fratre recepto secundum formam aliorum receptorum fratrum. Cons.*-Münster, ed. Klausmann, p. 384 and *Cons.*-Wesel, ed. Klausmann, p. 406 (same text).

170. Here again the language of the rubrics varied, from Zwolle/Deventer's "*propter que uidetur aliquis reiici posse*" to Henry of Ahus's "*Casus expulsionis.*" See *Cons.*-Zwolle, ed. Schoengen, pp. 263–64; *Cons.*-Deventer/Zwolle, ed. Hyma pp. 465–66; *Cons.*–Herford, ed. Stupperich, pp. 95–96; *Cons.*-Münster/Wesel, ed. Klausmann, pp. 384–85, 406–7.

171. *Item, racione huiusmodi societatis tenetur quod, si quis de societate recesserit, quod partem rerum communium repetere non potest. . . . .* Zerbolt, *Circa modum*, ed. Hyma p. 76.

172. J. Van Engen, "Managing," pp. 121–22, 159–62.

173. *De ortu domus*, ed. Weiler p. 34.

174. Ibid., pp. 19, 30, 72.

175. Ibid., p. 28.

176. Ibid., pp. 35–36.

177. Ibid., p. 45.

178. Ibid., pp. 54–55.

179. Ibid., pp. 57–58.

180. Ibid., p. 72.

181. Ibid., pp. 91–92.

182. *Cons.*-Deventer/Gouda, ed. Hyma, pp. 462–63; *Cons.*-Herford, ed. Stupperich, pp. 92–94 (far more elaborate).

183. Jacobus, *Narratio* 64, ed. Schoengen, pp. 163–65.

184. Ibid., 39, p. 181.

185. *Schwesternbuch Emmerichs* 54, ed. Bollmann and Staubach, p. 232.

186. Ibid., 37, pp. 172–75.

187. *Cons.*-Zwolle, ed. Schoengen, pp. 260–62; *Cons.*-Deventer/Gouda, ed. Hyma, pp. 460–61; *Cons.*-Herford, ed. Stupperich, pp. 89–90. The following paragraph based on these texts, which are virtually identical.

188. The same text in Zwolle and Herford (*solemus conuenire*). But *Cons.*-Deventer/Gouda, ed. Hyma, p. 460, reflecting a later era and a tightening sense of structure, says: . . . *solent fratres qui acceptati sunt, uel alias a communi colloquio non segregati, conuenire. . . .* Some in the house have not yet been accepted into the society, while some were away (father-confessors serving women's houses).

189. *Epistolae* VIII, IX, ed. Van Engen.

190. Jacobus, *Narratio*, ed. Schoengen, p. 164.

191. For the text, see Hyma; for interpretation, J. Van Engen, "Late Medieval Anticlericalism."

192. *Cons.*-Deventer/Gouda, ed. Hyma, p. 450; *Cons.*-Zwolle, ed. Schoengen, pp. 248–49; *Cons.*-Herford, ed. Stupperich, p. 71. The Low German version at Herford (p. 118) renders this as "*gemeinheit,*" a community.

193. Klausmann, *Consuetudo*, p. 339 for an edition of this anonymous text.

CHAPTER 6. DEFENDING THE MODERN-DAY DEVOUT: PUBLIC EXPANSION UNDER SCRUTINY

Epigraph: *Vita Petri Horn*, ed. Dumbar, *Analecta*, pp. 154–55.

1. For the text, see Hudson, *English Wycliffite Writings*, pp. 24–29, and compare the essays in *Lollardy and the Gentry*.

2. See now Kerby-Fulton, *Books Under Suspicion*, pp. 397–401.

3. A recent authoritative summary in Šmahel, *Die Hussitische Revolution* II, pp. 876–930.

4. This text in Van Engen, "Sayings of the Fathers," p. 303.

5. See now the essays by Watson and Riddy in *Voices in Dialogue*, pp. 394–455; also Staley, *Dissenting Fictions*.

6. *The Book of Margery Kempe* c. 15, ed. Meech and Allen, p. 35.

7. Ibid. c. 16, pp. 36–37.

8. Ibid. c. 57, p. 139.

9. Ibid. c. 18, pp. 42, 43.

10. Ibid. cc. 48, 49, pp. 116, 119.

11. For background I am indebted to Schmedding, *De Regeering van Frederik*, pp. 203–4; De Vries, "Gildenwoelingen en interdict"; Berkenvelder, "Zwolle," and Van Luijk, *Bruiden van Christus*, pp. 222–25.

12. Berkenvelder, "Zwolle," p. 38, n. 3.

13. *Monasticon fratrum* III, pp. 406–15, with bibliography.

14. Zwolle, Gemeente archief inv. OAAZ nr. 60, fol. 35, par. 276. See Berkenvelder, "Zwolle," p. 43. An edition in Dozy, *De oudste stadrechten*, p. 153.

15. Good on all this, a lively article, is De Vries, "Gildenwoelingen en interdict"

16. De Vries, "Gildenwoelingen en interdict," p. 64.

17. Schoengen, *Narratio*, pp. 17–18, 107ff.

18. Schoengen, *Narratio*, pp. 47–51, 229–35. In general on Dirk of Herxen, see still Knierim, *Dirc van Herxen (1381–1457)*.

19. At what age he joined is not clear. In 1400 and 1401 he made gifts to the house, but along with his entire family and acting in part for his sister and mother. In May 1406, at age twenty-five, he asked that the family land (Noortberge, in Wijhe, near Windesheim) be freed of its temporal obligations to the bishop (specifically the castle in Colmschate), so he would be free for ordination to the priesthood (that is, not have temporal familial responsibilities), a document of which the house had a transumpt made in September. Then in January 1407 Dirk gave his familial property irrevocably to the four men who constituted the house's joint-holders: Schoengen, *Narratio*, pp. 297–99, 301–2. The document's prominence in house records indicates his fiscal importance to it.

20. Ibid., p. 76.

21. Ibid., p. 58.

22. Dozy, *De oudste stadrechten*, par. 231–38, pp. 138–41.

23. De Vries, "Gildenwoelingen en interdict," p. 66.

24. A highly detailed account, from extant records, in Ibid., pp. 67–74.

25. Ibid., pp. 75–77; Berkenvelder, "Zwolle," p. 45.

26. Thus in Van Luijk, *Bruiden van Christus*, pp. 224–25.

27. Schoengen, *Narratio*, pp. 274–78, based on Hofman, "Broeders van het Gemene Leven" who saw still the original.

28. Schoengen, *Narratio*, pp. 300–301, 302–4.

29. . . . *hoc ex littera illa originali probari uel uerificari non poterit.* The original document, issued in Dutch by the curate Reynold, referred repeatedly to the three clerics (the joint–holders) with whom the agreement was struck: Schoengen, *Narratio*, pp. 275, 289–90.

30. Schoengen, *Narratio*, p. 277.

31. Ibid., p. 425.

32. Ibid., pp. 427–28.

33. The text was first uncovered, and the historical connection made, by Lourdaux, "Dirk of Herxen's Tract," the edition then made by Haverals, "*Contra detractores monachorum.*" See also Klausmann, *Consuetudo*, pp. 116–18, who (n. 107) added three manuscripts to Haverals' three.

34. The chronicler says, perhaps exaggerating, that Dirk avoided steady contact with people as much as possible, though aware of the need for good relations: Schoengen, *Narratio*, p. 54.

35. Listed in the chronicle as "*Disputacio et obiuracio cuiusdam qui detrahebat deuotis personis,*" a description, not an incipit or title. Ibid., p. 235.

36. Dirk, *Contra detractores*, ed. Haverals, pp. 286–87.

37. Ibid., pp. 278, 286. Compare Lourdaux, "Dirk of Herxen's Tract," p. 318.

38. Dirk, *Contra detractores*, ed. Haverals, pp. 249, 253, 258, 263, 267, 271–72, 276, 279.

39. Ibid., p. 282.

40. Ibid., p. 284.

41. Ibid., 250–51.

42. Ibid., p. 249.

43. Ibid., 252–53.

44. Ibid., 262.

45. Ibid., 270.

46. Ibid., 272–73, 275.

47. Ibid., 276, 277, 281.

48. Ibid., 282–83.

49. Ibid., 284.

50. Dirk, *De paruulis*, in Cologne, Historisches Stadtarchiv GB 4° 60, f. 32r–v.

51. Gerson, *De paruulis ad Christum trahendis*, ed. Glorieux IX, pp. 669–86. On this tractate, see McGuire, *Jean Gerson*, pp. 174–77, who emphasizes disproportionately, I think, defensiveness over sexual issues: it was larger than that. The treatise became widely circulated in the Late Middle Ages (unlike his little program for Paris, of which there are only one or two manuscripts). Dirk must have learned of it almost right away. It was also printed at Zwolle in the same year (1479) and by the same press as Dirk's work (see *Monasticon fratrum* III, p. 401).

52. Gerson, *De paruulis*, ed. Glorieux, pp. 671, 673–74.

53. Gerson, *De paruulis*, ed. Glorieux, pp. 674, 675, 678.

54. Ibid., p. 676.

55. Ibid., 679.

56. Ibid., 682–83.

57. My titles follow Cologne, *Historisches Stadtarchiv* GB 4° 60, which distinguishes the four tractates more accurately. To date most scholars have followed Utrecht, Universiteitsbibliothek MS 380, ff. 1–71. The first tractate was printed at Zwolle in 1479. For studies see Épiney-Burgard, "Die Wege der Bildung" and "Les idées pédagogiques," and Bange, *Spiegels der Christenen*, pp. 62–64, with a summary of the first tractate.

58. For the first tractate I cite the incunable edition, Dirk, *Speculum iuvenum* (The Hague, Royal Library 171 G 88), with arabic page numbering supplied by me, here p. 1.

59. Ibid., 2. The basic image comes from Gerson, *De paruulis ad Christum trahendis*, ed. Glorieux IX, p. 670 (*primitias florentis etatis*), but is much stronger in Dirk. He also took over from Gerson the guiding scriptural verse, Lamentations 3:27: "It is good for a man that he bear the yoke in his youth."

60. Dirk, *De parvulis*, The Hague, Royal Library 171 G 88, pp. 4, 5, 7.

61. Ibid., pp. 8–10.

62. *De laudabili studio*, Utrecht, Universiteitsbibliothek, MS 380, ff 41r–71r, here 43v, 47r.

63. Ibid., 55r.

64. Schoengen, *Narratio*, p. 107 (no date, no identification, and so possibly at any point in Dirk's lifetime).

65. The basic works on Grabow are: Keussen, "Der Dominkaner Matthäus Grabow" for the texts, Wachter, "Matthäus Grabow" for a detailed reading, and now Staubach, "Zwischen Kloster und Welt?" pp. 397–426 for new texts and interpretations. I treat this incident at greater length in "Illicit Religion" and in future in *Making Private Religion* ch. 5.

66. For the Dominican house in Groningen, see Bakker, *Bedelorden en begijnen*, pp. 48–73 and passim. There are no in-house documents pertaining to Grabow. For the key position of lector in a Dominican convent, see Mulchahey, "*First the Bow Is Bent in Study.*"

67. On the battle in Basel, see Patschovsky, "Beginen, Begarden und Terziaren," and now above all Von Heusinger, *Johannes Mulberg OP*, pp. 39–89. Schmitt, *Mort d'une hérésie*, highlighted the social resentments.

68. This I take to be the meaning of his phrase: . . . *aliaque multa peiora et enormia facere dampnabili temeritate presumunt, prout certis documentis super hoc habitis. . . .* Staubach, "Zwischen Kloster und Welt?" p. 412.

69. Both complexes disappeared after the Reformation, but images of them reproduced in Bakker, *Bedelorden en begijnen*, p. 54, 56, 58–59 (Jacobijnenklooster) and esp. p. 137 (Olde Convent). See now H. van Engen, *De derde orde*, pp. 74–76.

70. The relevant document is in *Oorkondenboek Groningen* II, pp. 313–14 (no. 1098), with corrections by H. Van Engen, *De derde orde*, p. 75 n. 60.

71. This from a document addressed by Grabow to Pope Martin V later in the legal wranglings: Keussen, "Der Dominkaner Matthäus Grabow," p. 34.

72. Grabow's *sollicitatio* (as I call it) edited in Staubach, "Zwischen Kloster und Welt?" p. 412.

73. Its *incipit*: *Suppono primo quod non intendo infrascripta neque quelibet alia pertinaciter defendere sed tantum scolastice inquirendo procedere, nec aliqua ponere scienter que sunt contra fidem.* Keussen, "Der Dominkaner Matthäus Grabow," p. 46.

74. See now Hobbins, "The Schoolman as Public Intellectual" and "Jean Gerson's Authentic Tract."

75. Rudolph Buschmann's "positions," all we have left from him, edited now by Von Heusinger, *Johannes Mulberg OP*, pp. 131–32, recorded by Dominican adversaries as a defense of "Lollards and Beguines and Tertiaries" who wished to beg, though able bodied.

76. Mulberg spoke to the clergy of Basel assembled in the cathedral choir: Ibid., p. 133.

77. *Item, episcopi Argentinenses Johannes, Lampertus, Fridericus in suis executoriis processibus contra beginas expresse asserunt eas per constitucionis iuris communis fore excommunicatas et absolucione indigere. . . .* Ibid., p. 166. This is the only evidence I know for Frederick turning against beguines as bishop of Strassburg.

78. *Ponunt eciam in fine sui libri quem dicunt se de meo copiasse "Explicit tractatus contra fratres et sorores tertii ordinis," quod in toto fingunt. . . .* Keussen, "Der Dominkaner Matthäus Grabow," p. 40.

79. Ibid., p. 40.

80. The most accessible text of these twenty-four sentences is Frédéricq, *Corpus* II, pp. 219–20.

81. This apologetic brief may be found in Keussen, "Der Dominkaner Matthäus Grabow," pp. 37–41.

82. *Infrascriptos articulos seu conclusiones uerisimilter credo esse in tractatu meo, et ex una illarum, que est principalis, omnes alie deducuntur exceptis paucis. . . .* Ibid., p. 37. The Devout had placed his "fundamental" proposition fifteenth in their list.

83. H. Van Engen, *De dere orde*, p. 130 notes that Grabow was first demonstrably active in the diocese (named in a document) in September 1414.

84. See now Staubach, "Zwischen Kloster und Welt?" pp. 411–15 for an edition of this *sollicitatio* based on two manuscripts; one copy, known earlier but without attribution to Grabow, edited by Finke, *Acta* IV, pp. 676–80. Its petitionary character has tended to get overlooked.

85. Thus his closing sentence: *Spiritus sanctus corda uestra* [the council fathers to whom this is addressed] *illuminet et inspiret pro extirpacione secte predicte.* Ibid., p. 415.

86. The bishop's language appears to be taken over from the priors' document: . . . *nulla umquam ad audienciam nostram sinistra fama peruenerit quod heresim, sectam, scisma aliaque a sacris canonibus prohibita attemptarent. . . .* Ibid., pp. 416–20.

87. Two of these also edited in Ibid., pp. 421–26.

88. From an anonymous piece first edited in Ibid., pp. 416–20, here p. 417.

89. Ibid., pp. 423–26; first edited by Wachter, "Matthäus Grabow," pp. 365–68.

90. Staubach, "Zwischen Kloster und Welt?" pp. 431–33.

91. Keussen, "Der Dominkaner Matthäus Grabow," p. 35.

92. Ibid., pp. 35–36.

93. Ibid., p. 41.

94. Ibid., 37.

95. Ibid., pp. 37–41.

96. *Scriptus Constantie propria manu, die tertia Aprilis, anni millesimi quadringentesimi decimi octaui.* Gerson, *Opera* (1484), f. 10

97. Ibid..

98. Scholars have not noted that the opinions of these other eleven were summarized by Friar John Nyder roughly ten years later in a still unpublished work, which I will edit in *Making Private Religion*, ch. 5.

99. . . . *maturo multorum prelatorum in theologia et utroque iure magistorum et doctorum necnon aliorum peritorum communicato consilio.* . . . Keussen, "Der Dominkaner Matthäus Grabow," p. 45

100. Ibid., pp. 41–42.

101. Gerson, *Opera* (1484), f. 10.

102. I am re-editing this text, but for now see Ibid., pp. 390–91.

103. See J. Van Engen, "Friar Johannes Nyder" for a first attempt to get at this intriguing pair of texts.

104. For this "episcopal schism," see De Hullu, *Bijdragen*, and Post, *Geschiedenis der utrechtsche bishopsverkiezingen*, pp. 126–63.

105. *Van onsen oelden zusteren*, ed. De Man, pp. 67–87.

106. Ibid., p. 68

107. Ibid., p. 70.

108. This revealed indirectly: . . . *die zusteren meer onghehorsam weren dan in die ander vergaderinge, soe wasset hem* [the "schepenen": aldermen] *onverdrachlick te liden*. Ibid., p. 73.

109. Ibid., p. 75–76.

110. Ibid., pp. 79–80.

111. Ibid., p. 80.

112. Ibid., p. 82.

113. Ibid., pp. 86–87.

114. The fundamental study of this memorial book now is Bollmann, *Frauenleben*, pp. 271–393.

115. *Van onsen oelden zusteren*, ed. De Man, pp. 67, 83, and passim.

116. This noted already by Schoengen, *Narratio*, pp. clxxxvi–vii.

117. See Korth, "Die ältesten Gutachten," pp. 23–25, for an edition of the document.

118. Ibid., pp. 25–27.

119. Acquoy, *Klooster te Windesheim* III, p. 243; compare J. Van Engen, "Privileging," pp. 961–62. We have, so far as I know, no other witness to this affair.

120. *Van onsen oelden zusteren*, ed. De Man, pp. 95–101, here, p. 96.

121. Kaminsky, *Simon de Cremaud*, pp. 66–67 commenting on this as "property."

122. Schmugge, *Kirche, Kinder, Karrieren* treats this example and also illumines one dimension of the papal court, that of "supplications."

123. Schoengen, *Narratio*, pp. 512–13.

124. Van Luijk, *Bruiden van Christus*, pp. 144–55.

125. For 'sHertogenbosch the resume of a document in Vanden Elsen and Hoevenaars, *Analecta*, pp. 192–93, plainly the same more or less as a document preserved in full at Emmerich, in *Schwesternbuch Emmerichs*, ed. Bollmann and Staubach, p. 335. The latter was issued by the German papal legate for Germany from Basel; the former is said to have come from Pope Eugene IV.

126. *Schwesternbuch Emmerichs*, ed. Bollmann and Staubach, pp. 337–38. For the same a little later at 'sHertogenbosch, granted by the bishop of Liège, Van den Elsen and Hoevenaars, *Analecta*, p. 193.

127. Schoengen, *Narratio*, pp. 501–11, this copied into the cartulary for Zwolle.

128. For the texts, see Miraeus, *Regulae*, pp. 8–10.

129. For the text and documentation, see Schoengen, *Narratio*, pp. 515–18. A much later

text (ca. 1470) claimed this was obtained without any fee; see Van Engen, "Privileging," p. 961.

130. Miraeus, *Codex regularium*, pp. 11–13. The best introduction now in Faix, *Gabriel Biel*, pp. 18–28 (with the older literature).

131. Doebner, *Annalen*, p. 259.

132. Ibid., pp. 206–7.

133. The best study remains Barnikol, *Die Brüder*, pp. 112–55, with a summary in Post, *Modern Devotion*, pp. 453–63. We have two versions of the Münster records: Doebner, *Annalen*, pp. 242–82, and Rehm, "Quellen," pp. 25–45.

134. Doebner, *Annalen*, pp. 248–49.

135. Ibid., p. 252.

136. Schoengen, *Narratio*, p. 534.

137. *De ortu*, ed. Weiler, p. 19.

138. *Monasticon fratrum* III, p. 216. See the relevant letter in Taal, *De Goudse kloosters*, p. 201.

139. For the documents, see Schoengen, *Narratio*, pp. 519–25.

140. See *Acta Cusana* Nr. 1631–39 for texts and sources.

141. *Et ualde ad tempus timuit ne status noster et communis uite noua plantatio penitus, ut quidam minabantur, eradicaretur. Vita Egberti*, ed. Dumbar, *Analecta*, p. 173. See the *Acta Cusana* (1996) nr. 1629. Despite some skepticism about this report, there is in fact an independent witness; see n. 163 below.

142. Brugman, *Epistola* I, ed. Moll, *Johannes Brugman* II, p. 204.

143. Elm, "Die Brüderschaft." The text is in Emmerich, Stadtarchiv, HS 13, ff. 59v–76v; on this manuscript see J. Van Engen, "Privileging," pp. 952–53.

144. For a contrary view, see Klausmann, *Consuetudo*, pp. 124–30.

145. *Petis a me, karissime, ut paucis tibi annotare curem, quid respondere habeas allocutoribus et derogatoribus super modo uite nostre quo presbyteri et clerici uiuimus in communi.* Emmerich, Stadtarchiv MS 13, f. 59v.

146. . . . *qui cauillantur nos approbacionem sedis apostolice non habere et ex hoc iudicant illicitum esse sic uiuere.* . . . Ibid. f. 61r.

147. Brugman, *Epistola* I.1, 8, ed. Moll, pp. 199, 205–6.

148. *Hanc itaque satisfacionem nostram non in derogacionem quorumcumque conceptam, si pia corda admittere dignum duxerint, bene quidem. Sin autem, uideant sibi ne notentur uerbo apostoli dicentis: Omnia munda mundis; coninquinatis autem et immundis, nichil est mundum.* Emmerich, Stadtarchiv, MS 13, f. 76v. (The concluding lines of the tractate. For the scriptural reference, see Titus 1:15).

149. Schoengen, *Narratio*, pp. 408–10 (with notice of all the transfixed episcopal confirmations that exist or are attested); Miraeus, *Codex regularium*, pp. 3–4.

150. Miraeus, *Codex regularium*, pp. 4–5. This same privilege extended to Zwolle in 1464: Schoengen, *Narratio*, pp. 434–37. Earlier episcopal confirmations made no mention of a common seal.

151. For an edition, J. Van Engen, "Managing," p. 163. One may pursue information about seals at paragraph 4 in Weiler's *Monasticon fratrum* III. Most examples listed there date from much later, and the information was compiled without consideration of the issue raised here.

152. Miraeus, *Codex regularium*, pp. 6–7. We have at least two full manuscript copies of this joint set of privileges, as in n. 154 below.

153. See *Monasticon fratrum* III, pp. 55, 259–60.

154. We possess at least two important fair copies of these privileges, one for 'sHertogenbosch, Provinciaal archief Paters Cupucijnen Nr. 3 (its contents set out in Ibid., pp. 259–60), another for Brussels (now Brussels, Royal Library MS 16515), it the basis for the edition by Miraeus, *Regulae*, pp. 3–17.

155. *Schwesternbuch Emmerichs* 5, ed. Bollmann and Staubach, p. 73–74. See their comments and further references on p. 10 n. 30.

156. Ibid., pp. 264, 265.

157. *Schwesternbuch Emmerichs* 56, ed. Bollmann and Staubach, pp. 240–47.

158. *Vita Egberti*, ed. Dumbar, *Analecta*, pp. 171–73 for what follows. Note that the *vita* moves out of chronological sequence, telling this story, explicitly dated to 1470 first, then the story of the confrontation with Cusa in 1451. Dumbar, *Deventer*, pp. 599–600, appears to be a version of this same narrative, though Bollmann, *Frauenleben*, pp. 110–14, who also saw the significance of this episode, treats it as an independent source.

159. *Vita Egberti*, Dumbar, *Analecta*, p. 172.

160. That Brugman's long letter was written to Pieter Horn, not Egbert, is clear from a collation of all five extant manuscripts. Moll happened to work from the one that ascribed it to Egbert. On Brugman and his works, see Van den Hombergh, *Leven en werk*, here pp. 94–96.

161. Brugman, *Epistola*. I.3, 5, 6, 12, 13, ed. Moll, pp. 200, 201, 202, 203, 210, 211. I have read Moll's edition of these two letters against the extant manuscripts, particularly important for this first letter.

162. Ibid. II.3, 4, 5, ed. Moll, p. 219, 220.

163. *Spero firmiter quod radix et mater domus, scilicet domini Florencii, finaliter non peribit.* Ibid II.5, ed. Moll, p. 220.

164. Ibid., II, p. 219.

165. Brugman, *Epistola* I.13, ed. Moll, p. 211.

166. Van Engen, "Privileging," p. 962–93.

167. Faix, *Gabriel Biel*, pp. 33–59, supersedes earlier literature (all noted there).

168. The rubric for his first foundation, Marienthal, in 1467: here the name for the group already seemed fixed. Ibid., p. 38.

169. Ibid., pp. 347–68 (an exemplary edition), 60–67 (introduction).

170. Ibid., pp. 349, 352, 351.

171. *Et accepimus formam primitiue ecclesie in auctoritatem, et exhortationem consilii trahimus in obligationem precepti, et gerimus nos pro his qui tacite et expresse renunciauerunt propriis et professionem communis uite susceperunt. Nec aliquem in nostrum consortium recipimus nisi expresse resignatione renunciauerit propriis et cautionem fecerit de non repetenda proprietate.* Ibid., p. 355.

172. Ibid., p. 351

173. *Utinam autem multi ex hiis . . . saltem ingrati non existerent hiis ipsis fratribus communis uite, a quibus primum tanti profectus tanteque utilitatis beneficium susceperunt.* Ibid., 360.

174. See the documents in the house cartularium, The Hague, Royal Library, MS 70 H

75, f. 70r, treated in J. Van Engen, "Managing," p. 144 with Pl. 9. The document at Deventer was labeled on its reverse (dorso): "*Copie litterarum separacionis nostre et dismembracionis.*"

175. Schoengen, *Narratio*, p. 540.

176. Ibid., pp. 533–37, 538.

CHAPTER 7. PROPOSING A THEOLOGICAL RATIONALE: THE FREEDOM OF "CHRISTIAN RELIGION"

Epigraphs: John Pupper, *Dialogus*, ed. Walch, p. 187; ibid., p. 185; John Pupper, *De libertate* IV.5, ed. Pijper, pp. 237–38.

1. Thomas, *Imitatio* I.1.

2. Gabriel Biel, *Collatio*, ed. Faix, pp. 375–77.

3. See now Weiler, "The Dutch Brethren,"pp. 310–17, with further literature.

4. See Lourdaux, *Christelijke humanisme.*

5. Basic orientation, with literature, in the *Lexikon des Mittelalters* VIII, pp. 44ff. Its articles focus primarily on social estates, "*Stände*" in German. On "mirrors" in Dutch, see Bange, *Spiegels der Christenen.*

6. On the resonance of this last idea, see Van Engen, "God Is no Respecter of Persons."

7. Clear and useful orientation to Thomas with bibliography in Pocquet du Haut -Jussé, *La vie religieuse.*

8. *Unde status pertinet proprie ad libertatem uel seruitutem, siue in spiritualibus siue in ciuilibus.* Thomas, *Summa theologie* II-II q. 182 a.1.

9. Ibid., q.184 a.3.

10. Excellent orientation, especially for the thirteenth century, in L. Hödl, "Evangelische Räte," in *LMA*, IV. 131–35.

11. Thomas, *Summa theologie* II-II q. 186 a.6.

12. *Sic ergo et in statu perfectionis proprie dicitur aliquis esse non ex hoc quod habet actum dilectionis perfecte sed ex hoc quod obligat se perpetuo cum aliqua solemnitate ad ea que sunt perfectionis.* Ibid., q. 184 a.4.

13. Ibid., II-II q. 88, a.6.

14. Ibid., q. 184 a.7.

15. Despite all the recent work on Wyclif and the Lollards, this particular topic has received little systematic attention. For orientation, see Lohse, *Mönchtum und Reformation*, pp. 176–93.

16. *English Wycliffite Sermons* IV, p. 121.

17. *The Lollard Disendowment Bill*, ed. Hudson, *Selections*, p. 137.

18. Wyclif, *De religionibus vanis monachorum*, ed. Buddensieg, p. 437–38.

19. Wyclif, *De perfectione statuum* 2, ed. Buddensieg, p. 453.

20. Ibid., 6, pp. 479–80.

21. *Sermon* 36, ed. Gradon and Hudson, I, p. 374 (Also I, p. 644).

22. *Sermon* 123, ed. Gradon and Hudson, II, p. 342; *Sermon* 100, ed. Gradon and Hudson II, p. 247.

23. William Thorpe, in *Two Wycliffite Texts*, ed. Hudson, pp. 26–28.

24. . . . *sicut est religio privata claustralis perfectorum, sic est vel potest esse religio privata*

secularis sive exclaustralis perfectorum. Et a pari est vel potest esse religio privata, tam claustralis quam exclaustralis imperfectorum. Wyclif, *De religione privata I* c. 8, ed. Buddensieg 515, 516.

25. Wyclif, *Speculum ecclesie militantis* 25, p. 52.

26. Ibid., 26, p. 54.

27. John Wycliffe, *De ordinatione fratrum* 3, ed. Buddensieg, pp. 95–96.

28. *Novitas autem istorum ordinum impedit plenitudinem observancie legis Cristi, quia multi ingrediuntur hos novos ordines quibus non convenit hec rudis observancia.* Ibid., p. 96.

29. Wyclif, *De oratione et ecclesiae purgatione* 5, ed. Buddensieg 352–53, where similarly strong language is repeated several times.

30. It is transmitted both as "*De religione privata II*," ed. Buddensieg, pp. 524–36, and as Sermon, ed. Loserth, III. pp. 224–39. See Thomson, *The Latin Writings*, pp. 155–56.

31. This paragraph taken from *De religione privata II*, as in the foregoing note.

32. Denzinger, *Concilium Constantiense Sessio XV*, pp. 398–402, here item no. 23. In authorizing "interrogations" of possible Wycliffites, the bull of 22 February 1418 (*Inter cunctas*) formulated one question (n. 30) on this issue: *utrum credat religiones ab ecclesia approbatas a sanctis patribus rite et rationabiliter introductas.*

33. On Gerson in general, see now McGuire, *Jean Gerson.* On this issue, cp. Abramowski, "Die Lehre von Gesetz," Burger, *Aedificatio, Fructus, Utilitas*, pp. 178–83, Brown, *Pastor and Laity*, pp. 73–78; and Corcoran, *John Gerson.*

34. Gerson, *De consiliis euangelicis et statu perfectionis* ed. Glorieux, III, pp. 10–26. On the date, otherwise unattested, see Glorieux, *Oeuvres*, 10, p. 584 "between August 25 and Sept. 29, 1393."

35. Ibid., pp. 11, 12–13, 14, 15, 18, 19.

36. Ibid., 16, 17. In 1408 a Franciscan named Jean of Gorello would harry the university with these issues anew, but scholars have generally placed this quodlibet several years earlier; see Burger, *Aedificatio, Fructus, Utilitas*, pp. 160–64.

37. . . . *etsi consilia euangelica plurimum expediant et ualeant ad perfectionem uite spiritualis conquerendam, non tamen necessario requiruntur ad eam, quoniam in omni statu sexu ordine gradu perfecti uiri inuenti sunt. . . . Ex istis infero quod obligatio preceptorum maior est et efficacior quam obligatio uotorum.* Ibid., p. 20.

38. Ibid., 21.

39. . . . *Ulterius sequitur quod status perfectissimus in ecclesia militante est status episcoporum. . . . quia hominem iam perfectum requirit.* Ibid., pp. 22, 23.

40. . . . *curati ordinati sunt ad bonum commune, religiosi uero uacant bono priuato et singulari et sacre stationi; bonum uero commune diuinius est et melius bono priuato.* Ibid., 25.

41. *Infero ultra quod status curatorum, sicut et episcoporum, est de primaria et ordinaria Christi institutione.* Ibid.

42. Gerson, De *perfectione cordis*, ed. Glorieux VIII, pp. 116–33.

43. Ibid., p. 117.

44. . . . *ut secundum legem dei, que regula est generalis omnium christiane religionis professorum sub uno abbate Christo. . . .* Gerson, *De uita spirituali*, ed. Glorieux III, p. 170.

45. Gerson, *De perfectione cordis*, ed. Glorieux VIII pp. 118–20, with this conclusion: *Concludimus igitur ad unum quod solus status religionis christiane sub abbate Christo est status perfectionis, sicut solus est charitatis et salutis, extra quem neque salus stat neque perfectio. . . .*

46. Ibid., p. 122.

47. The soul's conclusion, the previous one coming from the theologian: . . . *in omni statu perfectos homines inuenire contingit . . . secundum quam in seculo dici possunt obedientes et in matriomonio casti et in maximis diuitiis pauperes spiritu. Ac exinde perducuntur ex his mediis ad augmentum et perfectionem charitatis supra multos in religione in celibatu in mendicitate uiuentes.* Ibid., p. 121.

48. A very fine edition by Ullman, *De seculo et religione.* Good on this remains Trinkaus, *In Our Image and Likeness*, pp. 651–82, here pp. 654ff; see now also Staubach, "*Christianam sectam arripe*" for comparisons between the Devout and the early humanists.

49. Salutati, *De seculo*, ed. Ullman, p. 111; cp. p. 163. In general I find this work more subtle than readers, shocked by a humanist chancellor promoting the religious life, have often found.

50. Ibid., p. 111.

51. Ibid., p. 112.

52. *Quare si philosophi ipsi suum illum morem diversa sentiendi diverseque vivendi "sectas" appellarunt, non debes tu mirari. . . . Nam quid est aliud esse religiosum quam esse christianum, et quidem vere christianum?* Valla, *De professione*, ed. Cortesi, pp. 18–19. Her introduction to this edition is exceptionally good on contextual matters.

53. Ibid., 45–46.

54. Ibid., 51–54.

55. *Et enim omnis ratio voti, omnis indictio ieiunii, omne iusiurandum, omnis denique lex (est autem professio lex quedam), propter metum inventa est, idest ut apertius loquar, propter malos.* Ibid., 62.

56. Ibid., p. 60.

57. Valla too, himself a cleric, like Gerson elevated the secular clergy, now in humanist Latin: *fratres, qui ad populum habentes orationem (quod erat munus episcoporum sacerdotumque et esse debet), mares feminasque a uitiis revocant, a pravis opinionibus liberant, ad pietatem scientiamque perducunt, in quo eos ego maxime apostolorum imitatores existimo.* Ibid., p. 65.

58. *Ego sic sentio omnes qui christianam religionem servant esse religiosos, nec recte se professos esse solos religiosos dicere, cum alii tales sint et quidem non minus quam ipsi.* This from Valla's "defense," quoted by Cortesi in her introduction, p. L.

59. The starting point for John Pupper's life is now Van Kalveen, "Johan Pupper van Goch," subsequently built upon by Weiler, "The Dutch Brethren of the Common Life," which refutes the false arguments of Post, *Modern Devotion*, pp. 469–76. The basic work remains Clemen, *Johann Pupper.*

60. That history now set out in *Monasticon fratrum* III, pp. 55–69, here pp. 63–65. The account from Gouda makes clear that he belonged to the house at Amersfoort: . . . *fratres suos de Amersffordia quia frater domus erat. . . .* Henrik, *De primo ortu*, ed. Hensen, pp. 26, 27.

61. *Monasticon fratrum* III, pp. 195–220, here pp. 214–16. The founding documents edited in Vorstman, here p. 47 for the key clause: . . . *qui ibidem exercebunt et facient more solito diebus festiuis de uespere deuotas collationes ac exhortationes pro communi populo deseruientes.*

62. *Monasticon fratrum* III, pp. 216–17. Documents edited in Vorstman (NAKG 7 [1848], p. 78).

63. Henrik, *De primo ortu*, ed. Hensen (1899), p. 17. See Taal, *De Goudse kloosters*, pp. 345–38.

64. Herp, subsequently a Franciscan preacher and mystical writer for thirty years (1450–78), best known for his "Mirror of Perfection" which borrowed heavily from Ruusbroec and Merswin, would, ironically, end up in the same city as John Pupper, namely, Malines. Basic is the edition by Verschueren, *Spieghel der volcomenheit*, with an extensive introduction.

65. . . . *ita ut pusillanimis factus statum suum mutauit et locum. . . .* Henrik, *De primo ortu*, ed. Hensen, p. 23.

66. Ibid., pp. 25–26. This person, notably, was his spiritual director.

67. *Ex hiis satis pusillanimis factus est Johannes prefatus, hesitans et in se deliberans quid melius faceret . . . uiuens in magna egestate de laboribus manuum quantum ipse et fratres sui ex lucris laborum suorum habere poterant.* Ibid., p. 28.

68. Ibid., pp. 26, 28.

69. This document edited by Taal, *De Goudse kloosters*, p. 201.

70. Henrik, *De primo ortu*, ed. Hensen pp. 31–32.

71. See Clemen, *Johann Pupper*, p. 27.

72. Ibid., pp. 34–45, citing two early modern chronicles, the oldest reading: . . . *Priester ende Pater van het Klooster van S. Maria Magdalena tot Sluys, van waer hy gebrocht heeft vier gewylde Nonnekens, vier Donatinnen, ende vijf Conversinnen . . .* (n. 2). The second chronicle claims likewise that he came with thirteen women (. . . *is gekomen mit derthien religieusen van dry staeten . . . de welcke waeren religieusen in een seer goet en deughdelyck klooster in de stadt van Cleve*) but from three places around Cleve, thus near his hometown of Goch. Beyond misinformation or confusion, at issue may be the location of "Sluis," the best-known town of that name being in the far west, then Flanders, today Zeeland. But the name is not uncommon, and may refer to a site around Cleve or Goch. John Pupper would then have returned to the area of his hometown after study at Cologne, and taken a position as father-confessor to a nascent group of converted sisters (four professed nuns, four "*donatae*," five "*conversae*").

73. Clemen, *Johann Pupper*, p. 37. I see no evidence, however, that John Pupper himself professed as a canon; quite the contrary.

74. Basic is *Monasticon Belge*, pp. 581–85.

75. Van Kalveen, "Johan Pupper van Goch," p. 113, n. 49, which would seem to refute the suggestion of Weiler, "The Dutch Brethren of the Common Life," p. 318 that he left the brotherhood.

76. Clemen, *Johan Pupper*, pp. 34–35 n. 3.

77. Foppens, *Bibliotheca belgica*, pp. 714–15. He listed the two main works under consideration here first and last, *De libertate christianae religionis* and *De uotis et obligationibus*, and probably referred to the Letter as *de scripturae sacrae dignitate.*

78. John Pupper's theology was central to Ullmann's *Reformatoren*. But the basic work remains Clemen, *Johann Pupper*. See also Abramowski, "Die Lehre von Gesetz" and "Johann Gerson," and Steinmetz, "*Libertas Christiana*." By contrast Post, "Johann Pupper von Goch," is largely a negative polemic. Pithy and good now is Staubach, "Zwischen Kloster und Welt?" pp. 392–96.

79. Both Post and Staubach have expressed reservations about the editions as possibly contaminated by Reformation polemics. While this is possible, it became for Post a way to

explain away what he found disagreeable as "not medieval." But in 1520/21 in the Low Countries (Antwerp, Zwolle) a reformation party had not yet separated from the church nor had censorial bans gone into place until the Edict of Worms, June 1521. Here I use the *Dialogus de quattuor erroribus circa legem euangelicam exortis et de religionibus facticiis* (hereafter: *Dialogus* as edited by Walch from the edition ca. 1521); and for *De libertate* see n. 94 below.

80. *Litere charitatis uestre dudum mihi directe innotuerunt quod quidam . . . dicant euangelice legis libertatem ab exordio ecclesie sub obligatione uoti fore conclusam et limitatam, nullumque absque uoti obligatione ad ipsius perfectam obseruantiam posse sufficere. . . . . . . dicunt apostolos et totam primiuitam ecclesiam legem euangelicam non nisi sub uoto obseruasse. Dialogus* ed. Walch, pp. 75–76.

81. *Vestra tamen fraternitas dignum duxit a me expostulare ut contra huiusmodi recentes errores, dudum quidem sepultos, nunc uero de sepulchro uenenatum caput erigentes, aliqua scripturarum testimonia in unum coadunarem. . . .* Ibid. 76.

82. In its first edition (also ca. 1521) the text was prefaced with twenty-two rubrics (*Index titulorum Dialogi*), whether by John or the editor, subsequently interspersed in the text itself in ways that actually impede rather than aid understanding.

83. *Dialogus*, ed. Walch, p. 90.

84. *Dialogus*, ed. Walch p. 105, and see p. 99.

85. *Amor enim sibi ipsi retributio est, ipse sibi soli sufficit, et preter se uel extra se nihil aliud querit.* Ibid., pp. 107, 108.

86. *Si uero appetitus tuus pondere diuini amoris sursum eleuatur, a se et suis naturalibus exit et eleuatur et in Deum transfertur, ac sui penitus oblitus in eum quem amat totus resoluitur, ita ut proprie utilitatis ac delectationis immemor. . . . Hoc denique ueri amoris exercitium est. . . . Amans enim nihil aliud querit nisi amari ab amato.* Ibid., pp. 106–7.

87. . . . *ad perfectiora opera legis euangelice facienda libertatem spiritus secundum interiorem motum fidei non sufficere contendunt, sed ad hoc obligationem uoti necessario requiri impie dogmatisare non erubescunt, ita ut libertatem euangelicam in seruitutem obligatoriam redigentes, a pharisaica superstitione non multum distare reperiantur. Hic est error nostri temporis. . . .* Ibid., p. 109.

88. Ibid., p. 113 See Thomas, *Summa* II-II q. 88 a. 6.

89. . . . *bonum humane uoluntatis tanto uicinius ad conformitatem diuine uoluntatis accedit quanto ex maiori libertate procedit. Dialogus*, ed. Walch, p. 121.

90. Ibid., pp. 134, 137.

91. Ibid., pp. 147, 149.

92. Ibid., p. 154.

93. Ibid., p. 182.

94. The title is one point where we probably have an intervention from 1520/21, conscious or unconscious. John's title was "*Tractatus* de *libertate christiane religionis*" (with or without the "tractatus"), as can be seen from the opening rubric apparently copied from a manuscript (Pijper, p. 41). But Cornelius Grapheus printed it as "*De libertate christiana*" (Pijper, p. 33). The difference is crucial: John Pupper was writing about "religion" in the medieval sense. In 1908 Pijper took over Grapheus's title. In English I will refer to the work as "The Freedom of the Christian Religion," cited in the notes as "*De libertate.*" See also Clemen, *Johann Pupper*, pp. 43–50.

95. *De libertate* I.1, ed. Pijper, pp. 42–43.

96. *Quintum erit de uouente et non uouente, et de differentia uel identitate actuum eorum.* Ibid., p. 42.

97. *De libertate,* ed Pijper, p. 94.

98. See Clemen, pp. 50–54 on the text and editions. I cite that of Pijper, pp. 284–95. In March 1520 Grapheus claimed to have received a copy of the letter from Nicholas den Bosch, who said the manuscript was in John Pupper's own hand and from forty-six years earlier: *libellum hunc . . . ante annos ferme sex et quadraginta . . . conscriptum . . . idque preuetusto charactere propria ipsius autoris manu (ut affirmabas) exaratum. . . .* Ed. Pijper, p. 345.

99. *Libellus cuiusdam fratris ordinis Predicatorum una cum literis charitatis tue suscepi et legi, qui contra christiane religionis libertatem editus. . . . . . . ammiratio non modica mihi coepit exoriri. . . . quod uos, quibus canonica scriptura nota est, sermo tam uolatilis et inanis mouere uideatur. Epistola,* ed. Pijper, p. 284–85.

100. . . . *libelli prefati fratris sententia erronea posset breuiter et faciliter canonica ueritate refelli. . . .* Ibid., p. 290.

101. At issue was the unwilling professed: . . . *quia qui inuite agit quod precipitur simulachrum habet uirtutis sed non uirtutem. Epistola,* ed. Pijper, p. 295.

102. John Pupper, *De libertate* 25, ed. Pijper, p. 93.

103. Baudry, *La querelle,* p. 216 for this text, and passim for the dispute, with a chronology in the introduction.

104. See Wolfs, *Studies,* pp. 60, 68, 81–83, 90–105, and Kaeppeli, *Scriptores* I, pp. 367–68.

105. Clemen, *Johann Pupper,* p. 49 n.1.

106. See nn. 80, 99. Further: *Sextum* [distinctionem] *erit responsio ad quendam tractatum a quodam doctore ordinis predicatorum nomine Engelberto compositum, qui pro parte Thome partem nititur tenere affirmatiuam. De libertate* I.1, ed. Pijper, pp. 42–43.

107. . . . *ut dicant euangelice legis libertatem ab exordio ecclesie sub obligatione uoti fore conclusam et limitatam, nullumque absque uoti obligatione ad ipsius perfectam obseruantiam posse sufficere non erubescant dogmatisare. Ad sui erroris robur scripturam repugnantem allegantes, dicunt apostolos et totam primitiuam ecclesiam legem euangelicam non nisi sub uoto obseruasse. Dialogus,* ed Walch, pp. 75–76. Again: *Nam dicere quod absque obligatione uoti consilia euangelica quoad summam eorum perfectionem obseruari non possint, quid aliud uidetur sonare quam quod gratia legis euangelice per se ad hoc non sufficiat? Dicite mihi quorum hec est opinio?* Ibid., p. 110. Much of John's work can be understood as reacting to these positions.

108. *Dialogus,* ed. Walsch, pp. 76–77.

109. *Quamquam ergo per mille uota ad bonum se quis obligauerit, ex ipsa obligatione nihil meretur nisi ipsum bonum ad quod se obligauit per libertatem spiritus operatur. Epistola,* ed. Pijper, p. 292.

110. One difficulty is the reported dating of the letter. But we have no way of knowing what the claim of "46 years earlier" refers to, or on what basis.

111. See J. Van Engen, "Ralph of Flaix," for twelfth-century background.

112. Thomas, *Summa* II-I, q. 106–8 specifically on the "new law of the gospel."

113. Ibid., q. 108 a.1 ad secundum. John will instinctively dispute this notion.

114. *Epistola,* ed. Pijper, p. 293.

115. *De libertate* IV.1, ed Pijper, p. 227.

116. Ibid., IV.5, pp. 236–37.

117. *Et hanc reor esse causam erroris quorundam circa libertatem euangelice legis. . . . Presumunt multi quod quicunque facit quod in euangelio scriptum statim habeat charitatem a deo cordi inscriptam. Et non attendunt quantum interest inter bonum facere et bonum bene facere. Bonum faciunt qui faciunt quod deus precepit, sed bonum bene faciunt qui faciunt quod deus precepit ex amore iustitie.* Ibid., ed Pijper, p. 237–38.

118. Ibid. ed. Pijper pp. 235–36. See Thomas, *Summa* I-II q.106 a.1 (*secundario autem est lex scripta*), where at first glance the similarities seem much greater than the differences, including use of Augustine's *De spiritu et littera*, the key source for much of John Pupper's theology. But the attack is less on Gospel law as something written down in the New Testament than as written within the human (that is, the notion of "habitus"), thus Thomas, ad secundum: *Alio modo est aliquid inditum homini quasi superadditum per gratie donum. Et hoc modo lex noua est indita homini, non solum indicans quid sit faciendum sed etiam adiuuans ad implendum.*

119. *Dialogus*, ed. Walch, p. 187. These are passionate convictions, which he attempts to set up as a syllogism.

120. Ibid., p. 184.

121. The fundamental arguments, implicitly informing this entire debate, are in Thomas, *Summa*, II-II q. 88 a. 6, summarized above pp. 242–44.

122. *Votum religionis est per positiuam constitutionem ecclesie christiane religioni superadditum et ordinatum, non ad alicuius defectus christiane religionis suppletionem sed ad ipsius religionis perfectissime tradite necessariam et compulsiuam obseruationem quoad substanciam actus exterioris. Dialogus*, ed. Walch, p. 183.

123. Ibid., p. 185.

124. Ibid., p. 186.

125. Ibid., pp. 189–90.

126. Ibid., pp. 192–93.

127. *Sed habere interiorem affectus preparationem ad faciendum summum actum euangelice perfectionis, cum necessitas uel opportunitas se offeret est summi premii meritorium. Ergo in omni statu christiane religionis potest summum mereri premium eterne felicitatis. De libertate*, ed. Pijper p. 193.

128. *De libertate* II.20, ed. Pijper, p. 125; again, p. 123.

129. Ibid., II.23, p. 126.

130. *Sic et nunc dicimus cum apostolo et Augustino quod gratia est illa charitas que per spiritum sanctum cordibus fidelium infunditur.* Ibid, p. 127. John had first argued this extensively in the first distinction.

131. Ibid., II.25, p. 133.

132. Ibid., II.30, p. 145.

133. Ibid., II.26, 27, pp. 134, 135.

134. Ibid., II.37, 39, pp. 159, 160.

135. Ibid., III.4, p. 191.

136. *Votum ergo non potest facere actus alios* [chastity, etc] *esse maioris meriti quam essent sine uoto, quia ipsum ex se non est meritorium nisi inquantum producitur a gratuita uoluntate tanquam a principio merendi et ordinatur per rectam intentionem in deum tanquam in finem principalem.* Ibid., III.4, pp. 191–92. cp. Ibid. III.5, ed. p. 195

137. Ibid., III.12, ed. p. 216. Compare Hamm, *Promissio, pactum, ordinatio*, passim.

138. *Et tamen nescit homo utrum amore an odio dignus sit, sed omnia in futurum seruantur incerta. . . . Hec est unica sollicitudo piarum mentium qua anxiatur in nobis spiritus noster et cor nostrum turbatur, donec de fide sublati ad speciem sciamus quid de operibus nostris acceptum sit apud deum. . . .* Ibid. III.12, pp. 215, 216.

139. Ibid., III.13, p. 223.

140. This dominates the account of Ullman, *Reformatoren*, pp. 59ff and passim, as it has many subsequent interpreters. Much better is Steinmetz, "*Libertas Christiana*," pp. 195–205.

141. *Epistola*, ed. Pijper, pp. 285, 288–89; *De libertate* I.1, ed Pijper, p. 43.

142. Ibid., II, prologue, p. 92.

143. See Courtenay, "The Bible in the Fourteenth Century" and J. Van Engen, "Studying Scripture."

144. *Cetera scripta omnia tantam habent auctoritatem quantam cum scriptura canonica conformitatem. De hac dicit Augustinus ad Hieronymum. . . .* [there follows the text from *Decretum* d.9 c.5, ed. Friedberg 1.17]. *De libertate* I.1, ed. Pijper, p. 43 This cited again, not explicitly, in I.16, p. 69 on the question of relative authority of texts.

145. *Unde que cum diuine uoluntati seu canonice scripture seu diuinis legibus postponenda censentur. . . .* Gratian, *Decretum* D. 9 d.p. c.11, ed. Friedberg, p. 18. The fundamental work on this subject remains Schüssler, *Der Primat der Heiligen Schrift*, here pp. 11–17.

146. Since the printed text of 1584 is not readily available, readers may usefully consult the translation undertaken by Thompson and Gordley, *The Treatise on Law*, pp. 29–32.

147. Oberman, *The Harvest*, pp. 361–422 moved this issue centrally into discussion, whether or not his "Tradition I" and "Tradition II" was the best way to approach it historically. See also Oberman, *Forerunners*, pp. 51–120 for further discussion and representative texts.

148. Thus disputing any reception of grace simply by virtue of taking vows, a widely held notion throughout the middle ages: *De profitentibus uero aliquam religionem in antiquorum patrum sententiis nusquam simile legi, licet in aliquorum modernorum doctorum dictis aliqua magna de huiusmodi religionibus inserta reperiantur; que, quia in canonicis scripturis fundamentum non habent, eadem facultate contemnuntur qua probantur. Dialogus*, ed Walch, p. 239 (the concluding sentence of the entire work!)

149. *Ex hiis uerbis beati Augustini* [*Decretum* d.9 c., ed. Friedberg 1.] *colligitur manifeste quod sola scriptura canonica inirrefragabilem habeat auctoritatem. Ceterorum uero quorumcumque doctorum scripta, cuiuscunque fuerit sanctitatis uel doctrine, nullius reputat auctoritatis nisi per reductionem eorum ad scripturam canonicam, sicut eciam* [corrected from *enim*] *in scripturis philosophicis ueritas naturalis cognoscitur per reductionem eorum ad prima principia per se nota ex apprehensione terminorum. De libertate* I.16, ed. Pijper, p. 69.

150. See esp. ibid., I.14–15, pp. 65–69.

151. Thomas, *Dialogus*, ed. Pohl, pp. 97–98.

152. *Cons.*-Zwolle, ed. Schoengen, *Narratio,* p. 243.

153. *De libertate* III.10, ed. Pijper, p. 209.

154. Ibid., I.1, ed. p. 50

155. *Talis est ueritas eterna in scripturis sanctis reuelata. Unde ex nulla alia scriptura potest directe sumi auctoritas quam ex scriptura sancta uel ex scripturis patrum quas auctoritates sanctarum scripturarum roborauerunt.* Ibid., I.14, ed p. 67.

156. Ibid., IV., ed. p. 226.

157. Ibid., IV. 7, p. 242.

158. Ibid. IV. 9, ed. p. 245. The reference is to Thomas, *Summa* I-II q.108 a. 4.

159. *Dicendum ergo quod sentire quod lex euangelica addit consilia supra precepta est falsum et erroneum, quia concilia sic sunt de lege euangelica sicut precepta, et ad euangelice legis summam perfectionem omnibus indifferenter necessaria. Sed quia hoc multis nouum fortassis uidebitur, ideo rogo ut attente legant et sane intelligant. . . .* Ibid., IV.10, p. 247.

160. *Patet ergo ex omnibus premissis quod precepta et concilia euangelica sunt una lex euangelica, et sunt una perfectio euangelica et non due, omnibus christifidelibus pro loco et tempore ad obseruandum a Christo instituta. . . . Et quia in hiis duobus preceptis charitatis* [love God and neighbor] *omnibus indifferenter christifidelibus omnis euangelica perfectio a Christo precipitur, que potest alia excogitari perfectio ad quam aliquis christifidelis non teneatur?* Ibid., IV.10, p. 249.

161. *Dialogus,* ed. Walch, p. 109.

162. *Ad quod respondetur quod uoti obligatio non facit homines unius esse uoluntatis, et simul in una domo habitantes omnia habere communia et diuidere singulis prout cuique opus est, sicut hoc maxime patet in monasteriis mendicantium et uagorum religiosorium ita manifeste ut nulla possit tergiversatione celari. De libertate* I.5, ed. Pijper, p. 50.

163. *Dialogus,* ed. Walch, pp. 158–59

164. Ibid., p. 171.

165. *Sic etiam uotum religionis ab eccesia ordinatur, non quia est magnum bonum in se, sed quia multis infirmis et negligentibus potest esse melioris boni occasio.* Ibid., pp. 164–65.

166. *Votum igitur religionis propter infirmos et instabiles eclesia ordinauit qui ad perfectam legis euangelice obseruantiam sub communi institutione christiane religionis aliter induci non poterant. . . .* Ibid., p. 167.

167. *Vita sacerdotalis secundum eminentiam status sacerdotalis et dignitatem ordinis regulata est uere et simpliciter apostolica et summa perfectio religionis christiane. . . . status sacerdotalis esse summus status ecclesie militantis.* Ibid., p. 199.

168. Ibid., pp. 201–4.

169. *Et ideo sacerdos ad maiorem perfectionem acquirendam non indiget ad quemcumque statum ecclesie se transferre, quia ad omnem perfectionem potest sibi status sacerdotalis sufficere, tantum ut digne suo statu studeat conuersari.* Ibid., p. 204.

170. Ibid., p. 207.

171. *Instituit ergo Augustinus monasterium clericorum, idest sacerdotum, qui nunc dicuntur canonici. Et coepit uiuere secundum regulam sub sanctis apostolis constitutam, quia apostoli habebant talem modum communem uitam gerere cum suis discipulis, sicut manifeste patet de Petro Paulo et Ioanne, secundum modum quem Christus habuit cum discipulis suis. Quem modum sancti patres, Hieronymus, Martinus, Augustinus, et alii tanquam totius religionis christiane perfectissimum elegerunt imitari. Unde liquet quod sacerdotes secundum consilia euangelica sub episcopo communem uitam gerere et sacerdotaliter uiuere fuit ab exordio chrisiane religionis uere uita apostolica et Christi uite simillima, tam quoad summum actum exteriorem quam ad interiorem affectum.* Ibid., pp. 211–12.

172. Ibid., p. 211.

173. *Temporalia igitur habere non est diminutio sanctitatis perfecte. Nam Christus loculos habuit et apostoli temporalia habuerunt.* Ibid., p. 214.

174. *De libertate* II. 42, ed. Pijper, p. 172.

175. Ibid., pp. 172–73.

176. Ibid., p. 173.

177. *Quod uita communis sit a primitiua ecclesia obseruata sub libertate charitatis et non sub obligatione uoti ita canonice ueritati innititur, ut pertinaciter contrarium tenere hereticum sentiatur. Dialogus*, ed. Walch, p. 227.

178. Ibid., pp. 228–29.

179. *Ex his uidetur absolute dicendum quod magis perfectum est temporalia retinere et continue pauperibus dare quam simul omnia relinquere. . . .* Ibid., p. 234.

180. *. . . duplex est proprietas, scilicet proprietas iuris et amoris. Proprietas iuris potest stare cum summa perfectione euangelica; proprietas amoris est omnibus christianis per preceptum charitatis simpliciter illicita et interdicta. . . . Non enim res sed inordinatus usus et amor rerum appetitum mentis inquietat et a spirituali profectu retardat.* Ibid., pp. 234–35.

181. Ibid., p. 235.

182. The opening or thesis sentence of this whole closing section: *Vita communis, quamuis requirit omnimodam proprietarii amoris a rebus temporalibus abdicationem; non tamen requirit proprietarii iuris resignationem de necessitate perfectionis. Requirit tamen hec omnia propter infirmos.* Ibid., p. 226.

CHAPTER 8. TAKING THE SPIRITUAL OFFENSIVE: CARING FOR THE SELF, EXAMINING THE SOUL, PROGRESSING IN VIRTUE

Epigraphs: Thomas of Kempen, *Imitatio Christi*, I.11, II.3.

1. See now Pansters, *De kardinale deugden*, pp. 165–202, placing the Devout emphasis within a larger late medieval Netherlandish literature on the cardinal virtues.

2. Oberman, *Harvest*, pp. 129–45, 468, and passim.

3. Thomas, *imitatio* II.5 (also citing a middle-Dutch translation from Thomas's lifetime, ed. De Bruin, p. 93).

4. Rudolph, *Vitae fratrum*, ed. Dumbar, *Analecta,* pp. 22–23.

5. A frequent triad in Jacob's chronicle for Zwolle, whether his own formulation (*orando, studendo, scribendo*: it corresponds to the statutes) or simply a commonplace in the houses, all of it characterized as the "spiritual exercises" defining a house: *. . . tempora exerciciis deputata ipse sicut alii strennue obseruabat orando, studendo, scribendo, scolaribus uacando etcetera.* Schoengen, *Narratio*, p. 178.

6. Ibid., p. 208.

7. Thomas, *Dialogus* 3.1, ed. Pohl, pp. 214–17, here 216.

8. Erasmus, *De recta pronunciatione*, ed. Cytowska, p. 28.

9. Doebner, *Annalen*, p. 29.

10. Zerbolt, *Circa modum* II, ed. Hyma, p. 22.

11. Ibid., p. 23.

12. Biel, *Tractatus de communi vita*, ed. Faix, pp. 366–68.

13. See *Die Amanduskirche*, pl. 1, where interestingly Gerson's presumed role in approving the Brotherhood was commemorated by carving him in a pulpit alongside three church fathers (pl. 2).

14. The best orientation to this now in Kors, "Die Bibel für Laien"; for a census of manuscripts and works, the starting point is now Stooker and Verbeij, *Collecties op orde.*

15. This is a complicated issue, with questions still about dating and provenance; a complete bibliography in Kors, "Die Bibel für Laien," pp. 244–45.

16. Busch, *De origine* 25–26, ed. Grube, pp. 310–13.

17. For this number see Van Dijk, *Die Prolegomena*, p. 615, who, for now, has excluded it from the plan for an *Opera omnia* of Geert Grote.

18. Stooker and Verbeij, " 'Uut Profectus' "

19. This is still not properly studied, but Wybren Scheepsma has an essay forthcoming.

20. Zerbolt, *Circa modum*, ed. Hyma, pp. 56–64.

21. *Decretales* 5.7.12 (*Cum ex iniuncto*), ed. Friedberg 2.785.

22. Zerbolt, *Circa modum*, ed. Hyma, pp. 56–71, pp. 56–64, on it being licit, here pp. 57, 64. To this must be compared the independent and prior, but widely overlapping, "De libris teutonicalibus." Best on all this now is Staubach, "Gerhard Zerbolt von Zutphen."

23. See Suntrup, "Der Gebrauch der Quellen," for general orientation to what he summarizes as forty quotations from twenty (mostly patristic) authors.

24. Frédéricq, *Corpus* I, pp. 163–64.

25. Ibid., pp. 174–75.

26. Ebbinge Wubben, *Over middelnederlandsche vertalingen*, p. 70; on which see Kors, "Die Bibel," p. 254 (who reads the two groups differently than I do).

27. Ebbinge Wubben, *Over middelnederlandsche vertalingen* pp. 73, 74.

28. Ibid., pp. 84, 90; see Kors, "Die Bibel," p. 258.

29. Zerbolt, *De libris teutonicalibus*, ed. Hyma, p. 56.

30. Zerbolt, *Circa modum*, ed. Hyma, pp. 64–67.

31. Zerbolt, *De libris teutonicalibus*, ed. Hyma, p. 48.

32. Ibid., pp. 48–50, here p. 50.

33. Ibid., pp. 51–54.

34. Ibid., p. 54.

35. Ibid., p. 55.

36. Ibid., p. 59.

37. Frédéricq, *Corpus* I, pp. 215–17. I agree with Kors, "Die Bibel," p. 259, n. 70, against Staubach, that this does not refer to Scripture as such, or at least not in the first instance.

38. Zerbolt, *Circa modum*, ed. Hyma, pp. 67–69.

39. Zerbolt, *De libris teutonicalibus*, ed. Hyma, pp. 62–64.

40. Ibid., pp. 61–62.

41. Ibid., pp. 64–66.

42. Schoengen, *Narratio*, p. 243; *Cons.*-Deventer/Gouda, ed. Hyma, pp. 444–45; *Cons.*-'sHertogenbosch, ed. Vanden Elsen and Hoevenaars, p. 97.

43. Klausmann, *Consuetudo*, pp. 387, 408 (*pro deuocione quilibet quod placeat legendo*)

44. Rudolph, *Vitae fratrum*, ed. Dumbar, *Analecta, p.* 69.

45. Schoengen, *Narratio*, p. 246.

46. *Post hoc studebo in studio meo donec signum fiat ad requiem.* Klausmann, *Consuetudo*, p. 389.

47. . . . *singule materie singulis diebus reuoluende, iterum recollectioni et studiis sacrarum literarum uacabitur.* . . . Doebner, *Annalen*, p. 203.

48. Florens, *Tractatulus* 7, ed. LeGrand, p. 76. While there is a reference to Augustine, *De doctrina Christiana* I.40, the formuation is Florens's who, interestingly, alludes to passages quoted in Zerbolt's *Circa modum.*

49. Willim of St.-Thierry, *Epistola* 120–121, ed. Déchanet, pp. 238–40. Compare Florens, *Tractatulus* 7, ed. Legrand, p. 78; Zerbolt, *De reformatione* 15, ed. LeGrand, pp. 142–46; Zerbolt *De ascensionibus* 44, ed. Legrand, pp. 276–82.

50. Florens, *Tractatulus* 7, ed. Legrand, p. 78.

51. Ibid., 6, p. 74, here following the prologue to Bonaventure's *De triplici uia,* a very influential book in Devout devotional schemes.

52. Zerbolt, *De reformatione* 14–15, ed. Legrand, pp. 138–46.

53. Zerbolt, *De ascensibonibus* 44, ed. Legrand, pp. 276–82.

54. For work on this to date, see Scheepsma, *Deemoed en devotie,* pp. 75–100; Van Luijk, *Bruiden van Christus,* pp. 102–11.

55. On this see for now Corbellini, "Mannenregels voor een vrouwenwereld," pp. 186–88 (with images from the manuscript); she has an edition underway.

56. See for editions Moll, "Boekerij" and Stooker en Verbeij, *Collecties op orde,* pp. 298–301, as well as Corbellini, "Mannenregels," pp. 182–83 (with an image). For Doesburg with 66 titles, see Janse, "Het religieuze leven"; and for Warmond with 36 titles, Brinkman, *Dichten uit liefde,* pp. 287–88.

57. Van Heel, "Het Sint Margareta Klooster," pp. 85–87.

58. The best introductions to this rich subject are Lourdaux, "Het boekenbezit en boekengebruik," and Kock, *Die Buchkultur,* the latter with extensive bibliographies.

59. Lourdaux, "Boekenbezit en boekengebruik," pp. 251–65 assembled the key references to Grote and his obsession with books.

60. Grote, *Epistola* 13, ed. Mulder, p. 42.

61. Obbema, *Een Deventer bibliotheekatalogus.*

62. *Cons.*-Deventer/Gouda, ed. Hyma, p. 455; *Cons.*-Zwolle, ed. Schoengen, p. 253; *Cons.*-Herford, ed. Stupperich, p. 77; *Cons.*-Hildesheim, ed. Doebbner, p. 231; *Cons.*-Münster, ed. Klausmann, pp. 379; *Cons.*-Wesel, ed. Klausmann, p. 399.

63. Staubach, "Pragmatische Schriftlichkeit," pp. 418–28 opens with this "janus-like" attitude, interpreted as a devotional instrumentality. I would emphasize as well their closeness to the Latin schools and competition for the students' attention or rather intentions.

64. *Vita Petri Horn,* ed. Dumbar, *Analecta,* p. 117. Horn says this was forced by Rector Godfrey, against resistance, himself a former lector in the school.

65. Orientation to this famous list of St. Martin's in Kock, *Die Buchkultur,* pp. 225–47 (with extensive literature), and to the unedited catalogue on pp. 137ff, 154–85.

66. Thomas, *Dialogus,* ed. Pohl, pp. 97–98. The best study now, with earlier literature, Ibid., pp. 125ff.

67. Schoengen, *Narratio,* pp. 493–94.

68. *Item, quia precipue uolo niti pro reformacione interioris hominis, idest uirium anime mee, uolo eciam habere libellum qui incipit "Beatus uir" uel "homo quidam," qui pro tali materia multum deseruit . . . et illum diuidere mihi per singulos dies in particulas. . . .* *Cons.*-Münster/Wesel, ed. Klausmann, pp. 388, 409.

69. The best study and edition now by Kock, *Die Buchkultur,* pp. 136–50.

70. *Cons.*-Herford, ed. Stupperich, p. 58.

71. *Vitae fratrum Embricensium*, ed. Alberts, p. 41.

72. *Van onsen oelden zusteren*, ed. de Man, p. 31.

73. Busch, *De uiris illustribus* 62, ed. Grube, p. 188.

74. Brinckerink, *Collatien*, ed. Moll, p. 112.

75. See Staubach, "*Diversa raptim undique collecta,*" and as well Mertens in *Moderne devotie*, pp. 152–67.

76. Busch *De viris illustribus* 78, ed. Grube, p. 207, almost certainly reporting from his own experience as a schoolboy under Cele.

77. Vennebusch, *Die theologischen Handschriften*, p. 220, and Staubach, p. 137, n. 56.

78. Mertens, "Lezen met de pen."

79. Busch, *De viris illustribus* 35, ed. Grube, pp. 95–96.

80. For an attempt at systematizing what little we know, see Mertens, *Moderne Devotie*, pp. 153–56; Staubach, "*Diversa raptim undique collecta,*" p. 133–41

81. Thomas, *Libellus spiritualis exercitii*, ed Pohl, II, p. 331–32.

82. The basic work is Mertens, *Hendrik Mande*. See the memorial by Busch, *De viris illustribus* 43, ed. Grube, pp. 122–25.

83. On this see J. Van Engen, "The Work of Gerlach Peters." On the context, Busch, *De viris illustribus* 54–55, ed. Grube, pp. 156–64

84. See still Van Woerkum, "Het libellus '*Omnes, inquit, artes*'"

85. Zerbolt, *Circa modum*, ed. Hyma, pp. 46–56.

86. This specified in *Cons.*- Herford, ed. Stupperich, p. 72.

87. Ibid., pp. 46–47. See Thomas, *Summa* II-II q. 177 a. 2.

88. *Licet autem desiderium intelligendi diuinas scripturas, et secundum eas studium adhortandi, reprehendum non sit sed potius commendandum. Decretales* 5.7.12, ed. Friedberg, II.785.

89. Bohic, *Commentarii* 2, p. 136: *de secreta predicatione, non per modum predicationis sed per uiam monitionis, quam quilibet potest facere, etiam monachus.*

90. *Et quantum ad hoc* [*priuate ad unum uel paucos familiariter colloquendo*], *gratia sermonis potest competere mulieribus.* Thomas, *Summa* II-II q.177 a.2. For a fuller discussion of women's preaching, see now Kerby-Fulton, *Books Under Suspicion*.

91. Zerbolt, *Circa modum*, ed. Hyma, p. 48, 49.

92. Ibid., p. 51. The key discussion in Thomas, echoed here, is in II-II q.33 a.3, which Zerbolt took from John of Freiburg's *Summa confessorum* III.9 q.5.

93. Zerbolt, *Circa modum*, ed. Hyma pp. 53, 55.

94. *Hoc est querere, prout michi uidetur, utrum fraterna correctio cadat sub precepto.* Fredéricq, *Corpus* I, p. 164.

95. The best work remains Mertens, "Collatio und Codex."

96. *Cons.*-Deventer/Gouda, ed. Hyma, pp. 447–48; *Cons.*-Zwolle, ed. Schoengen, pp. 246–48; *Cons.*-Herford, ed. Stupperich, pp. 63–64. While extensive passages read the same, with the usual borrowings, the local adjustments are greater, perhaps a measure of this topic's importance.

97. Mulchahey, *First the Bow Is Bent in Study*, pp. 194–203.

98. Schoengen, *Narratio*, p. 247.

99. This appears in the vernacular version of the statutes, not an exact translation of the Latin: *Cons.-Herford, ed.* Stupperich, pp. 107–8.

100. *Vitae fratrum*, ed. Dumbar, *Analecta*, p. 8.

101. Ibid., p. 38.

102. Ibid., p. 75.

103. *Vita Petri Horn*, ed. Dumbar, *Analecta*, p. 153.

104. Schoengen, *Narratio*, p. 158.

105. Ibid., p. 164.

106. *Vita Johannis Hattem*, ed. Dumbar, *Analecta,* pp. 184–85.

107. Schoengen, *Narratio,* p. 197.

108. Ibid., pp. 23–23, 24.

109. Ibid., p. 128.

110. Ibid., pp. 120–21.

111. Brinckerink, *Collatiën* VI, ed. Moll, p. 150.

112. *Schwesternbuch Emmerichs* 2, 3, ed. Bollmann and Staubach, pp. 51, 58.

113. Basic (with literature) is Mertens, "Postuum auteurschap." The only edition remains Moll, "Acht collatiën."

114. This done by Sisters Lutgert (d. 1453) and Mette (d. 1452): *Van onsen oelden susteren*, ed. De Man, pp. 230, 235; these unfortunately have not survived.

115. The text of the latter in Brinkerink, "Goede punten." For the manuscripts, see Mertens, "Collatio Under Codex," pp. 176, 179.

116. *Schwesternbuch Emmerichs* 6, ed. Bollmann and Staubach, pp. 91, 98.

117. Ibid., 54, p. 234; cp. c. 69, p. 306.

118. Ibid., 8, p. 116.

119. *Van onsen oelden zusteren* 22, ed. De Man, p. 61.

120. Ibid., 33, p. 113.

121. Ibid., 46, p. 157.

122. *Tabula de materiis circa quas utiliter et opportune uersari potest memoria et collacio in diebus festiuis*. . . . Brussels, Royal Library, MS IV, 124, here f. 1. There is no full study, but see Mertens, "Collatio Under Codex," pp. 170–71, and *Moderne Devotie*, pp. 139–42.

123. Cassian, *Collationes* I.2, which provides the opening for Florens's text.

124. For a study and edition, see J. Van Engen, "The Sayings of the Fathers."

125. De Vregt, "Eenige ascetische tractate," p. 431. Thomas, *Dialogus*, ed. Pohl, p. 200 edited this down to "*Fuge seculares magnates and conuiuantes*."

126. De Vregt, "Eenige ascetische traktaten," p. 433.

127. Ibid., p. 428. This one too edited out by Thomas.

128. Ibid., p. 436.

129. *Epistolae fratrum* III, IV, ed. J. Van Engen, pp. 147, 149.

130. Zerbolt, *Circa modum*, ed. Hyma, pp. 80–87.

131. Ibid., pp. 80–81, directly quoting Boyck 2.241.

132. Ibid., pp. 81–82. See Innocent IV ad *Decretales* 5.12.38, ed. p. 546 where, again, what was a minor concession in Innocent's presentation became an opening for Zerbolt to justify Devout practices.

133. Zerbolt, *Circa modum*, ed. Hyma pp. 83, 84.

134. Ibid., pp. 84, 85–86.

135. *Patet ergo quod supradicti homines licite possent a se mutuo, uel ab aliis curam domus habentibus, consilia recipere, et eciam aliquibus, quamquam clauibus et iurisdictione carentibus,*

temptaciones et passiones anime gracie captandi consilii et auxilii reuelare. Frédéricq, *Corpus* I, p. 163.

136. *Cons.*-'sHertogenbosch 18, ed. Vanden Elsen and Hoevenaars, p. 179–80.

137. *Cons.*-Deventer/Gouda, ed. Hyma, p. 460; *Cons.*-Zwolle, ed. Schoengen, p. 260–61; *Cons.*-Herford, ed Stupperich, p. 89; *Cons.*-Hildesheim, pp. 243–45.

138. *Cons.*-'sHertogenbosch 11, 21, ed. Vanden Elsen and Hoevenaars, pp. 177, 181–82.

139. Virtually the same text in *Cons.*-Zwolle, ed. Schoengen, p. 248 and in *Cons.*-Herford, ed. Stupperich, pp. 62–63. A more expanded version in *Cons.*-Deventer/Gouda, ed Hyma, pp. 448–49.

140. Brinkerinck, "Goede punten," p. 237.

141. *Schwesternbuch Emmerichs* 7, ed. Bollmann and Staubach, p. 105.

142. Ibid., 46, pp. 205–6.

143. Florens, *Tractatulus* 46, ed. Legrand, p. 148.

144. Ibid., 1, 2, 3, pp. 43, 48, 50–51, 58.

145. Ibid., 5, p. 77.

146. Ibid., p. 75.

147. Ibid., 38, p. 176.

148. Ibid., 56, pp. 245–46.

149. *Van den oelden zusteren*, ed. De Man, pp. 157, 154.

150. *Schwesternbuch Emmerichs* 5, ed. Bollmann and Staubach, p. 76.

151. Ibid., 6, p. 94.

152. Ibid., 39, pp. 181–82.

153. Ibid., 56, pp. 244, 246.

154. Weiler, *Het morele veld* has now interpreted this work (in one of its two forms), and translated it into Dutch (there with further literature), with an edition of the Latin text forthcoming.

155. Brussels, Royal Library, MS 8849–59, f. 156v.

156. *Vita Johannis Hattem*, ed. Dumbar, *Analecta*, pp. 184, 185.

157. Brussels, Royal Library, MS 8849–59, f. 158r.

158. *Vitae fratrum*, ed. Dumbar, *Analecta*, p. 68.

159. Schoengen, *Narratio*, p. 96.

160. *Dicta patrum* 10, ed. Van Engen, "Sayings," pp. 305–6.

161. Brussels, Royal Library, MS 8849–59, f. 163v–164r, 157r.

162. Zerbolt, *De reformatione* 45, 46, 48, ed. Legrand, pp. 270–74, 280–82.

163. Ibid., 5, p. 108.

164. Ibid., 4, p. 108.

165. Thomas, *Imitatio* I.2. The key words are "*lectio*" (*les* in Middle Dutch), the core of school-acquired knowledge, as contrasted with "*sui ipsius uera cognitio*" (*warachtich bekennis . . . dijns selfs*).

166. Florens, *Epistola*, ed. Legrand, p. 180.

167. Zerbolt, *De reformacione* 4, ed. Legrand, p. 108. For a general introduction to meditation and self-examination among the Modern-Day Devout, see Goossens, *De meditatie*, and Van Dijk, "Thematische meditatie."

168. Zerbolt, *De ascensionibus* 6, 7, 8, ed. Legrand, pp. 118–32.

169. Zerbolt, *De reformacione* 5, ed. Legrand, p. 110.

170. Ibid., 7, pp. 114–16.

171. Ibid., 8, pp. 116–20.

172. Ibid., 10, p. 126.

173. Ibid., p. 128.

174. *Cons.*-Zwolle, ed. Schoengen, *Narratio,* p. 246; *Cons.*-Deventer/Gouda, ed. Hyma, p. 447; *Cons.*-'sHertogenbosch, ed. Van den Elsen and Hoevenaars, p. 99. It is ascribed to Bernard, but actually came from the *Speculum monachorum* (PL 184.1176), a favorite Devout text. The same point made by Florens, *Tractatulus* 12, ed. Legrand, p. 88.

175. *Cons.*-'sHertogenbosch 13, 14, ed. Vanden Elsen and Hoevenaars, p. 178.

176. *Propono omni uespere post completorium signare in tabula defectus meos, ne obliuiscar in quibus excessi, et inspiciam quando debeo confiteri ut reducam defectus meos ad memoriam.* Ed. Klausmann, *Consuetudo,* p. 388. For Grote, *Vitae fratrum,* ed. Dumbar, *Analecta,* pp. 9–10.

177. Klausmann, *Consuetudo,* p. 367.

178. Greenblatt, *Renaissance Self-Fashioning,* pp. 11–73.

179. Breure, "Het devote sterven," p. 442, and in general, *Doodsbeleving en levenshouding.*

180. *Vita Johannis Hattem,* ed. Dumbar, *Analecta,* pp. 218–23 (written by two Brothers who identified themselves as his disciples).

181. *Schwesternbuch Emmerichs* 41, ed. Bollmann and Staubach, p. 188.

182. The following is based upon Brussels, Royal Library, MS 8849–59, ff. 252r–255r which I am editing.

183. *Epistola,* ed. Hedlund, pp. 90–91.

184. The Modern-Day Devout may have been the most systematic exemplars of this initiative, but they were hardly alone in the fifteenth century. For English circles, see now Bryan, *Looking Inward* (which also focuses in part on a "private self."

185. For an edition of this text, see Klausmann, *Consuetudo,* p. 367, with his discussion (attributing it probably to Florens) on pp. 156–60, and a helpful general discussion of exercises on pp. 32–94.

186. A new edition of this text at Ibid., pp. 369–76.

187. Salome Sticken, *Formula vivendi,* ed. Kühler, pp. 360–80.

188. Klausmann, *Consuetudo,* p. 369.

189. Florens, *Tractatulus* 16 (*Generalis modus meditandi de morte*), ed. LeGrand, pp. 94–96. Notably this is not grounded in Cassian or Bernard or David of Augsburg or Bonaventure. Meditations on hell and judgment owed more to those earlier authors, thus Ibid., 17, pp. 98–100. But this would appear to come from that human realism found among the Devout.

190. Ibid., 14, p. 90.

191. Ibid., 51, p. 158.

192. Zerbolt, *De reformacione* 29–34, ed. Legrand, pp. 214–28.

193. This remains a contested issue, on which see Debongnie, *Jean Mombaer* and Goossens, *De meditatie.*

194. Florens, *Tractatulus* 28, ed. Legrand, p. 210.

195. Ibid., 36, p. 134. This topic is not as widely studied as one might expect, in part

perhaps because Devout originality lay more in method than in materials; but see Van Dijk, "*Ascensiones in corde disponere.*"

196. See now the sober and important appraisal of Veelenturf, "Inleiding," and all the essays in *Geen povere schoonheid.*

197. Good on this now is Van Dijk, "Thematische meditatie," though he works still to make as many links as possible to visual imaging.

198. Zerbolt, *De reformacione* 38, ed. Legrand, pp. 200–12.

199. *Schwesternbuch Emmerichs* 24, ed. Bollmann and Staubach, p. 148

200. Florens, *Tractatulus* 13, ed. Legrand, p. 90.

201. Ibid. 5, p. 70; Zerbolt, *De reformacione* 3, pp. 104–6.

202. Zerbolt, *De reformacione* 41, pp. 254–56.

203. *Van onsen oelden zusteren* 67, ed. De Man, p. 250.

204. Rudolph, *Vitae fratrum*, ed. Dumbar, *Analecta,* p. 37.

205. Zerbolt, *De reformacione* 47–48, ed. Legrand, pp. 278–82; *De ascensionibus* 57, ed. Legrand, pp. 334–40.

206. *Cons.*-Zwolle, ed. Schoengen, p. 268; *Cons.*-'sHertogenbosch, ed. Van den Elsen and Hoevenaars, pp. 110–11; *Cons.*-Deventer/Gouda, ed. Hyma, p. 468–69.

207. *Cons.*-Münster, ed. Klausmann, p. 395; *Cons.*-Wesel, ed. Klausmann, p. 412.

208. *Cons.*-Deventer/Gouda, ed. Hyma, p 469.

209. *Dicta patrum* 24, ed. Van Engen, "Sayings," p. 309. The Brother, contesting with her in frustration reportedly said, "no hundred men would satisfy her."

210. *Vitae fratrum*, ed. Dumbar, *Analecta,* pp. 118, 146, 147.

211. *Dicta patrum* 23, ed. Van Engen, "Sayings," p. 309.

212. *De ortu*, ed. Weiler, pp. 33, 62–63, 72.

213. Zerbolt, *De reformacione* 41, ed. Legrand, p. 256.

214. *Van onsen oelden zusteren*, ed. De Man, pp. 15, 127, 162, 208.

215. See Van Engen, "*The Virtues, the Brothers*" for an edition. For the explicit repudiation of miracles as necessary to show sanctity, see Busch, *De viris illustribus* 72, ed. Grube, pp. 222–26.

216. Thomas, *De imitatione Christi* II.1, ed. Pohl 2.62; the contemporary Middle Dutch (ed. de Bruin, p. 90) and Middle English (ed. Biggs 42) translations capturing in their language the deeper associations of the Latin text.

CONCLUSION: PRIVATE GATHERINGS AND SELF-MADE SOCIETIES IN THE FIFTEENTH CENTURY

1. Stupperich, *Das Fraterhaus*, pp. 142–59.

2. Ibid., pp. 142, 148, 149.

3. Ibid., p. 154.

4. Ibid., 160.

5. Ibid., pp. 167, 161.

6. This all from a correspondence wonderfully edited by Stupperich, Ibid., nn. 28, 32, 47, 47a, 49, pp. 222–24. 226–27, 240–42, 242–43, 244.

7. Subsequent to finishing this book I wrote a broader article on this subject, J. Van Engen, "Multiple Options."

8. See Bynum, *Wonderful Blood*; Hamburger, *The Visional and the Visionary*; Hamm, *The Reformation of Faith*; and much else, which I take up in my "Multiple Options."

9. This nicely summarized, and very nicely put now, by McSheffrey, "Place, Space, and Situation."

10. On the latter, see for instance Lentes, "*Vita perfecta* zwischen *Vita communis* und *Vita privata*," where the Devout serve as an important example, as does Suso.

11. This is getting considerable attention in English literary circles at the moment, thus Bryant, *Looking Inward* (with additional bibliography).

12. Spies, *Beginengemeinschaften*, esp. pp. 101–25

13. Neddermeyer, "*Radix studii et speculum vitae.*"

14. See Luther, *Werke* II, pp. 327–30.

15. Luther, *Themata de votis* and *De votis monasticis*, in: *Werke* VIII, pp. 323–35, 577–669. Lohse, *Mönchtum und Reformation* remains the basic work, though not altogether satisfactory, for he failed to recognize the "medieval monk" still in Luther and therefore did not fully grasp its meaning in context.

16. Luther, *De votis monasticis*, pp. 578, 587, 611, 595.

17. Luther, *Themata de votis*, p. 325

18. Ibid., pp. 331–32.

19. *Primum autem interiorem hominem apprehendimus uisuri qua nam ratione iustus, liber uereque christianus, hoc est spiritualis, nouus, interior homo, fiat. Et constat nullam prorsus rerum externarum, quocumque censeantur nomine, aliquid habere momenti ad iustitiam aut libertatem christianam. . . .* Luther, *De libertate christiana*, p. 50.

20. Ibid., pp. 53, 54.

21. Ibid., pp. 67–68.

22. Ibid., p. 71.

23. Ibid., p. 64.

24. The basic work remains Debongnie, *Jean Mombaer*, with an edition of the "*tabula librorum praecipue legendorum*" on pp. 320–31.

25. The basic work remains Godet, *La congrégation de Montaigu,* the statutes edited on pp. 143–70.

BIBLIOGRAPHY

ABBREVIATIONS

AGKKN = Archief voor de Geschiedenis van de Katholieke Kerk in Nederland.

AGAU = Archief voor de geschiedenis van het Aartsbisdom Utrecht.

Busch, *De origine moderne deuotionis* = Johan Busch, *De origine deuocionis omnium deuotorum presbyterorum clericorum et sororum siue beginarum tocius nostre patrie regionis Almanie* in *Des Augustinerpropstes Iohannes Busch Chronicon Windeshemense und Liber de reformatione monasteriorum*, ed. Karl Grube (Halle 1886; rprt 1968), pp. 245–375.

Busch, *De reformationibus* = Johan Busch, *De reformationibus monasteriorum ordinum diuersorum*, in *Des Augustinerpropstes Iohannes Busch Chronicon Windeshemense und Liber de reformatione monasteriorum*, ed. Karl Grube (Halle 1886; rprt 1968), pp. 379–799.

Busch, *De viris illustribus* = Johan Busch, *Liber de uiris illustribus ordinis canonicorum regularium monasterii in Windesem diocesis Traiectensis*, in *Des Augustinerpropstes Iohannes Busch Chronicon Windeshemense und Liber de reformatione monasteriorum*, ed. Karl Grube (Halle 1886; rprt 1968), pp. 1–244.

CCCM = Corpus christianorum Continuatio mediaevalis.

Clem. = *Clementinae*, in Friedberg, 2.1133–1200

Cons. = *Consuetudines.*

Cons.-Deventer/Gouda = Albert Hyma, *The Christian Renaissance: A History of the "Devotio Moderna"* (Grand Rapids 1924), pp. 441–74.

Cons.-Emmerich = *Fontes historiam domus fratrum Embricensis aperientes*, ed. Jappe Alberts, Wybe and Ditsche, Magnus (Groningen 1969), pp. 81–115.

Cons.-Herford = *Das Fraterhaus zu Herford II: Statuten, Bekenntnisse, Briefwechsel*, ed. Robert Stupperich (Münster 1984), pp. 55–132.

Cons.-Hildesheim = *Annalen und Akten der Brüder des Gemeinsamen Lebens im Lüchtenhove zu Hildesheim*, ed. Richard Doebner (Hannover 1903), pp. 209–45.

Cons.-Münster = Theo Klausmann, *Consuetudo consuetudine vincitur: Die Hausordnungen der Brüder vom gemeinsamen Leben im Bildungs- und Sozialisationsprogramm der Devotio moderna* (Frankfurt 2003), pp. 377–95.

Cons-'sHertogenbosch = G. Van den Elsen and W. Hoevenaars, ed. *Analecta Gysberti Coeverinx* 2 vols. ('sHertogenbosch 1907).

Cons.-Wesel = Theo Klausmann, *Consuetudo consuetudine vincitur: Die Hausordnungen der Brüder vom gemeinsamen Leben im Bildungs- und Sozilisationsprogramm der Devotio moderna* (Frankfurt 2003), pp. 397–412.

Cons.-Zwolle = Schoengen, *Narratio*, pp. 239–73.
Copie = The Hague, Royal Library, MS 70 H 75.
Decretales = Friedberg 2.5–928
Dumbar, *Analecta* = Gerhard Dumbar, *Analecta seu vetera aliquot scripta inedita* (Deventer 1719).
Dumbar, *Deventer* = Dumbar, Gerhard, *Het kerkelyk en wereltlyk Deventer*, 2 vols. (Deventer 1731, 1788).
Extravagantes = Friedberg 2.1205–1312.
Friedberg = *Corpus iuris canonici*, 2 vols., ed. Emil Friedberg (Leipzig 1879)
Henrik, *De primo ortu* = Hensen, A. H. L. "Henric van Arnhem's kronyk van het Fraterhuis te Gouda," *Bijdragen en Mededeelingen van het Historisch Genootschap* 20 (1899), pp. 1–46.
Liber Sextus = Friedberg 2.937–1124.
LMA = *Lexikon des Mittelalters.*
OGE = *Ons geestelijk erf.*
De ortu = Weiler, Anton G., *Necrologie, kroniek en cartularium c.a. van het Fraterhuis te Doesburg (1432–1559)* (Leiden 1974), pp. 11–152.
SC = Sources chrétiennes.
Schoengen, *Narratio* = *Jacobus Traiecti alias de Voecht Narratio de inchoatione domus clericorum in Zwollis, met akten en bescheiden betreffende dit fraterhuis*, ed. M. Schoengen (Amsterdam 1908).
Schwesternbuch Emmerichs = *Schwesternbuch und Statuten des St. Agnes-Konvents in Emmerich*, ed. Anne Bollmann and Nikolaus Staubach (Emmerich 1998)
Susteren van Diepenveen = *Van den doechden der vuriger ende stichtiger susteren van Diepen Veen ("'Handschrift D")*, ed. D. A. Brinkerink (Leiden 1904).
Thomas, *Dialogus* = Thomas of Kempen, *Dialogus noviciorum*, in Thomas Hemerken à Kempis, *Opera omnia*, ed. Michael Josephus Pohl, 7 vols. (Freiburg 1910–1922), VII, pp. 1–329.
Van onsen oelden zusteren = *Hier beginnen sommige stichtige punten van onsen oelden zusteren*, ed. D. de Man (Den Haag 1919).
Vitae fratrum = Dumbar, *Analecta*, pp. 1–148.
Vitae fratrum Embricensium = *Fontes historiam domus fratrum Embricensis aperientes*, ed. Jappe Alberts, Wybe and Ditsche, Magnus (Groningen 1969), pp. 1–78.
Zerbolt, *Circa modum* = Albert Hyma, "Het traktaat '*Super modo vivendi devotorum hominum simul commorantium,*' door Gerard Zerbolt van Zutphen," *AGAU* 52 (1926), pp. 1–100.

PRIMARY SOURCES

Abelard, Peter. *Collationes*, ed. John Marenbon-Giovanni Orlandi (Oxford 2001).
Acta concilii Constanciensis, vol. IV, ed. Heinrich Finke (Münster 1928).
Acta Cusana: Quellen zur Lebensgeschichte des Nikolaus von Kues, ed. Erich Meuthen and Hermann Hallauer (Hamburg 1996).

Annalen und Akten der Brüder des Gemeinsamen Lebens im Lüchtenhove zu Hildesheim, ed. Richard Doebner (Hannover 1903).

Agricola, Rudolph, *Letters*, ed. Adrie van der Laan and Fokke Akkerman (Assen 2002)

Beatrice van Nazareth. *Van seven manieren van heiliger minnen*, ed. H. W. J. Vekeman and J. J. Th. M. Tersteeg (Zutphen 1970).

Bedaux, J. C. *Hegius poeta: het leven en de latijnse gedichten van Alexander Hegius* (Deventer 1998).

Bernard of Clairvaux. *Ad clericos de conversione*, ed. J. Leclercq, with an introduction by J. Miethke (SC 457, Paris 2000).

———. *Liber de precepto et dispensatione*, ed. J. Leclercq, with an introduction by C. Friedlaender, G. Tacti, and J. Regnard (SC 457, Paris 2000).

Bernardo Guidonis. *Practica inquisitionis heretice prauitatis*, ed. C. Douais (Paris 1886).

Biel, Gabriel. *Tractatus de communi vita clericorum*, ed. Faix, *Gabriel Biel*, pp. 347–68.

———. *Collatio de vita communi*, ed. Faix, *Gabriel Biel*, pp. 369–77.

Henricus Bohic. *In quinque Decretalium Libros Commentarii* (Venice 1571).

Brinkerink, Dirk Adrianus, "Biografiën van beroemde mannen uit de Deventer kring," *AGAU* 27 (1901), pp. 400–423; 28 (1902), pp. 1–37, 225–76, 321–43; 29 (1903), pp. 1–39.

———. "Goede punten uit de collatiën van Claus van Euskerken," *Nederlandsch archief voor kerkgeschiedenis* 3 (1905), pp. 225–64, 353–95.

Consuetudines fratrum vitae communis, ed. Wybe Jappe Alberts (Fontes minores medii aevi 8, Groningen 1959).

Courtenay, William J. and Goddard, Eric D. *Rotuli Parisienses: Supplications to the Pope from the University of Paris*, vol. II, *1352–1378* (Leiden 2004).

Corpus documentorum inquisitionis haereticae pravitatis neerlandicae, ed. Paul Frédéricq, vols. I–II (Ghent-The Hague 1896).

Corpus iuris canonici (2 vols.), ed. Emil Friedberg (Leipzig 1879).

Denifle, Henricus. *Chartularium universitatis parisiensis*, vol. III (Paris 1894).

Denzinger, Henricus. *Enchiridion symbolorum, definitionum, et declarationum de rebus fidei et morum* (33rd ed. Barcinone 1965)

Deschamps, Jan. "Middelnederlandse vertalingen van 'Super modo vivendi' (7de hoofstuk) en 'De libris teutonicalibus' van Gerard Zerbolt van Zutphen," *Koninklijke Zuidnederlandse Maatschappij voor Taal- en Letterkunde en Geschiedenis, Handelingen* 14 (1960), pp. 67–108, 15 (1961), pp. 175–220.

De Vregt, J. F. "Eenige ascetische Tractate, afkomstig van de Deventersche Broederschap van het Gemeene Leven, in verband gebragt met het Boek van Thomas à Kempis *De Navolging van Christus*," *AGAU* 10 (1882), pp. 321–498.

Dozy, Gaultherus Jacob. *De oudste stadrechten van Zwolle* (Zaltbommel 1867).

Durandus, Guillelmus. *Speculum iudiciale* (Basel 1574; rprt 1975)

English Wycliffite Sermons I–V, ed. Pamela Gradon and Anne Hudson. (Oxford 1983–96).

Erasmus. *Opus epistolarum*, 12 vols., ed. P. S. Allen (Oxford 1906–58).

Florens Radewijns. *Petit manuel pour le dévot moderne, Tractatulus deuotus*, ed. Francis Joseph Legrand, with an introduction by Thomas Mertens (Turnhout 1999).

Fontes historiam domus fratrum Embricensis aperientes, ed. Wybe Jappe Alberts and Magnus Ditsche (Groningen 1969).

Das Fraterhaus zu Herford: Vol II: *Statuten, Bekenntnisse, Briefwechsel*, ed. Robert Stupperich (Münster 1984).

Gerardi Magni [cited as Grote]. *Epistolae*, ed. Willelmus Mulder (Antwerp 1933).

———. *Ornatus spiritualis desponsationis*, ed. Rijklof Hofman (CC CM 172; Turnhout).

Gerlaci Petri Opera Omnia, ed. Mikel Mario Kors (CC CM 155, Turnhout 1996).

Gerson, Jean. *Opera Omnia*, 4 vols. (Cologne 1484)

———. *Oeuvres complèts*, vols. 1–10, ed. Palémon Glorieux (Paris 1960–73)

———. *De consiliis euangelicis et statu perfectionis*, ed. Glorieux, III, pp. 10–26.

———. *De laude scriptorum*, ed. Glorieux IX, pp. 1423–34.

———. *De paruulis ad Christum trahendis*, ed. Glorieux IX, pp. 669–86.

———. De *perfectione cordis*, ed. Glorieux VIII, pp. 116–33.

———. *Pro pueris ecclesie parisiensis*, ed. Glorieux IX, pp. 686–89.

———. *De simonia*, ed. Glorieux VI, pp. 167–74.

———. *De uita spirituali*, ed. Glorieux III, p. 170.

Des Gottesfreundes Fünfmannenbuch, in *Schriften aus der Gottesfreund-Literatur 1*, ed. Philipp Strauch (Halle 1927).

Gratian. *The Treatise on Law*, trans. Augustine Thompson and James Gordley (Washington, D.C. 1993).

Grote, Geert. *De simonia ad beguttas: De middelnederlandsche tekst opnieuw uitgegeven met inleiding en aantekeningen*, ed. Willem De Vreese ('sGravenhaage 1940).

Grube, Karol. *Des Augustinerpropstes Iohannes Busch Chronicon Windeshemense und Liber de reformatione monasteriorum*, ed. Karl Grube (Halle 1886; rprt 1968).

Guibert, *De uita sua, siue monodiae*, ed. Edmond-René Labande (Les classiques d'histoire de France 34, Paris 1984).

Guibert of Tournai. *Collectio de scandalis ecclesiae*, ed. A. Stroick, *Archivum Franciscanum Historicum* 24 (1931), pp. 33–62.

Guicciardini, Lodovico. *Descrittione . . . di tutti I Paesi Bassi, altrimenti detti Germania inferiore* (Antwerp 1567).

Guido de Baysio. *Rosarium decretorum* (Lyon 1549)

Johannes Hattem. *Scriptum de bonis et redditibus domus nostre*, ed. J. Van Engen, "Managing," pp. 149–62.

Hedlund, Monica. *Epistola de vita et passione domini nostri: Der lateinische Text mit Einleitung und Kommentar* (Leiden 1975).

Henricide Segusio Cardinalis Hostiensis in decretalium libros commentaria (Venice 1581, rprt 1965).

Henricus de Segusio Cardinalis Hostiensis Summa (1537, reprt Aalen 1962).

Henricus de Gandavo, *Quodlibeta*, 2 vols. (Paris 1518; rprt Louvain 1961).

Hensen, A. H. L. "Henric van Arnhem's kronyk van het Fraterhuis te Gouda," *Bijdragen en Mededeelingen van het Historisch Genootschap* 20 (1899), pp. 1–46.

Herp, Hendrick. *Spieghel der volcomenheit*, ed. P. Lucidius Verschueren 2 vols. (Antwerp 1931).

Hier beginnen sommige stichtige punten van onsen oelden zusteren, ed. D. de Man (The Hague 1919).

Humbert. *Sermones ad status* (Bibliotheca patrum 25, Lyon 1576).

Hyma, Albert. "The 'De libris teutonicalibus' by Gerard Zerbolt of Zutphen," *Nederlandsch Archief voor Kerkgeschiedenis n.s.* 17 (1924), pp. 42–70.

———. "Het traktaat 'Super modo vivendi devotorum hominum simul commorantium', door Gerard Zerbolt van Zutphen," *AGAU* 52 (1926), pp. 1–100.

Innocent IV. *Commentaria in V Libros Decretalium* (1570; rprt 1968).

Jacobus Traiecti alias de Voecht Narratio de inchoatione domus clericorum in Zwollis, met akten en bescheiden betreffende dit fraterhuis, ed. M. Schoengen (Amsterdam 1908).

Johannis Andreae in decretalium libros novella commentaria (Venice 1581, rprt 1965).

Kallendorf, Craig W. *Humanist Educational Treatises* (Cambridge, Mass. 2002).

Keere, Pieter van den. *Germania inferior*, intro. C. Koeman (Amsterdam 1966).

The Book of Margery Kempe, ed. Sanford Brown Meech and Hope Emily Allen (London 1940).

Kock, Thomas, "Zerbolt incognito: Auf den Spuren des Traktats 'De vestibus pretiosis'," in: *Kirchenreform von Unten*, pp. 165–235.

Kühler, Wilhelmus. "De 'Vita magistri Gerardi Magni' van Petrus Horn (in M.S. no. 8849–59 van de Koninklijke Bibliotheek te Brussel)," *NAKG* 6 (1909), pp. 325–70.

Lindeborn, Jan. *Historia sive notitia episcopatus Daventriensis ex ecclesiarum membranis, monasteriorum tabulis, authenticis annotatis et classicis authoribus eruta ac publici iuris facta* (Cologne 1670).

Luther, Martin. *Werke: Kritische Gesamtausgabe* (Weimar 1897).

———. *Themata de votis, in: Werke* vol. VIII (1889), pp. 313–35.

———. *De votis monasticis*: in *Werke* Vol. VIII (1889), pp. 564–669.

Merswin, Rulman. *Buch von den vier Jahren seines anfangenden Lebens*, ed. Philipp Strauch (Altdeutsche Textbibliothek 23, Halle 1927).

———. *Neun-Felsen-Buch* (*Das sogenannte Autograph*), ed. Philipp Strauch (Altdeutsche Textbibliothek 27, Halle 1929).

Miraeus, Aubert. *Codex regularium et constitutionum clericalium* (Antwerp 1638).

Moll, Willem. "Acht collatiën van Johannes Brinckerink: Eene bijdrage tot de kennis van den kanselarbeid der broeders van het gemeene leven, uit handschriften der vijftiende en zestiende eeuw," *Kerkhistorisch Archief* 4 (1866), pp. 99–167.

Obituaire du monastère de Groenendael dans la forêt de Soignes, ed. Marc Dykmans (Brussels 1940).

Oorkondenboek van Amsterdam tot 1400, ed. P. H. J. van der Laan (Amsterdam 1975).

Osnabrücker Urkundenbuch IV, ed. Max Bär (Osnabrück 1902)

Pez, Bernard. *Bibliotheca ascetica antiquo-nova* (Regensburg 1725).

Petri Trudonensis catalogus scriptorium Windeshemensium, ed. W. Lourdaux, E. Persoons (Louvain 1968).

Piers Plowman by William Langland, an Edition of the C-Text, ed. Derek Pearsall (Berkeley, Calif. 1978).

[Pomerius]. "De origine monasterii viridisvallis et de gestis patrum et fratrum in primordiali fervore ibidem degentium," ed. J. B. de Leu. *Analecta Bollandiana* 4 (1885), pp. 263–322.

Porete, Marguerite. *The Mirror of Simple Souls*, trans. Edmund Colledge, J. C. Marler, and Judith Grant (Notre Dame, Ind. 1999).

———. *Margarete Porete Speculum simplicium animarum*, ed. P. Verdeyen (Corpus Christianorum 69, Turnhout 1986).

Pupper, John, of Goch. *De quatuor erroribus circa legem evangelicam exortis et de votis et religionibus facticiis dialogus*, ed. Christian W. F. Walch in *Monumenta Medii Aevi* I.4 (Göttingen 1760), pp. 74–239.

———. *Epistola apologetica*, ed. F. Pijper, *Geschriften Johann Pupper van Goch* in Bibliotheca Reformatoria Neerlandica 6 ('sGravenhage 1910), pp. 284–95.

———. *De libertate christiana*, ed. F. Pijper, Ibid., pp. 41–255.

Quellen zur Geschichte der Stadt Köln, ed. Leonard Ennen and Gottfried Eckertz, vol. 2 (Cologne 1863).

Quellen zur Ketzergeschichte Brandenburgs und Pommerns, ed. Dietrich Kurze (Berlin 1975).

Quellen zur Kirchenreform der grossen Konzilien des 15. Jahrhunderts, ed. Jürgen Miethke and Lorenz Weinrich, 2 vols. (Darmstadt 1995, 2002).

Reformation Kaiser Siegmunds, ed. Heinrich Koller (Monumenta germaniae historica, Staatsschriften des späteren mittelalters 6, Stuttgart 1964).

Regesten van het Archief der bisscoppen van Utrecht (722–1528), ed. S. Muller (Utrecht 1917), 2 vols.

Revius, Jakobus, *Daventriae illustratae sive historiae urbis Daventriensis libri sex* (Leiden 1650).

Ruusbroec, Jan. *Die geestelike brulocht*, ed. J. Alaerts (CCCM 103, Turnhout 1988).

———. *Vanden blinkenden steen*, ed. H. Noë, (CCCM 110, Turnhout 1991), pp. 5–216.

———. *Vanden XII beginen*, ed. M. M. Kors (Opera omnia 7A = CCCM 107A, Turnhout 2000).

———. *Een spieghel der eeuwigher salicheit*, ed. G. de Baere (Opera omnia 8 = CCCM 108, Turnhout 2001).

Salome Sticken. *Formula vivendi*, ed. Kühler, *Johannes Brinckerink*, pp. 360–80.

Salutati, Coluccio. *De seculo et religione*, ed. Berthold L. Ullman (Florence 1957).

Schannat, J. F., and Hartzheim, J. *Concilia Germaniae*, vol. 3 (Cologne 1760; rprt 1970).

Schmidt, Aloys. "Tractatus contra hereticos Beckardos, Lulhardos et Swestriones des Wasmud von Homburg," *Archiv für mittelrheinsiche Kirchengeschichte* 14 (1962), pp. 336–86.

Schweitzer, Franz Josef. *Meister Eckhart und der Laie: Ein antihierarchischer Dialog des 14. Jahrhunderts aus den Niederlanden* (Berlin 1997).

Schwesternbuch und Statuten des St. Agnes-Konvents in Emmerich, ed. Anne Bollmann, Nikolaus Staubach (Emmerich 1998).

Selections from English Wycliffite Writings, ed. Anne Hudson (2nd ed. Toronto 1997).

Seuse, Heinrich. *Deutsche Schriften*, ed. Karl Bihlmeyer (Stuttgart 1907).

Heinrich Seuses Horologium Sapientiae, ed. Pius Künzle (Spicilegium Friburgense 23, Freiburg 1977).

De stadsrekening van Deventer, ed. G. M. de Meyer (Groningen 1968).

Suso, Henricus. *Oerloy der ewigher wijsheit*, ed. Hildegarde van de Wijnpersse (Groningen 1938).

Suppliques d'Urbain V (1362–70), ed. Alphonse Fierens (Rome 1914).

Thomas Aquinas. *Summa theologiae*, 3 vols. (Taurini 1952).

Thomas of Kempen, *The Imitation of Christ: The First English Translation of the "Imitatio Christi"*. Ed. B. J. H. Biggs (Early English Text Society 309, Oxford 1997).

Thomas Hemerken à Kempis. *Opera omnia*, ed. Michael Josephus Pohl, 7 vols. (Freiburg 1910–1922).

———. *De imitatione Christi*, ed. Pohl, *Opera omnia* 2.3–264

———. *Sermones ad novitios*, ed. Pohl, *Opera omnia* 6.1–314.
———. *Libellus spiritualis exercitii*, ed. Pohl, *Opera omnia* 2.329–56.
———. *De middelnederlandse vertaling van De imitatione Christi (Qui sequitur)*, ed. C.C. de Bruin (Leiden 1954)
Two Wycliffite Texts: The Sermon of William Taylor 1406, The Testimony of William Thorpe 1407, ed. Anne Hudson (Early English Text Society 301, Oxford 1993).
Valla, Lorenzo. *De professione religiosorum*, ed. Mariarosa Cortesi (Padua 1986).
Van den doechden der vuriger ende stichtiger sustern van Diepen Veen "Handschrift D", ed. D. A. Brinckerink (Leiden 1904).
Van den Elsen, G., Hoevenaars, W., ed. *Analecta Gysberti Coeverinx*, 2 vols. ('sHertogenbosch 1907).
Van Dijk, R.Th. M. *De constituties der Windesheimse vrouwenkloosters vóór 1559: Bijdrage tot de institutionele geschiedenis van het Kapittel van Windesheim* (Nijmegen 1986).
Van Engen, John. "Epistolae fratrum," in *Kirchenreform von unten*, pp. 143–61.
Verspreide Sermoenen van Jan Brugman, ed. A. van Dijk (Antwerp 1948).
Vita Egberti, ed. Dumbar, *Analecta*, pp. 162–78.
Vita Johannis Hattem, ed. Dumbar, *Analecta*, pp. 179–223.
Vita Petri Horn, ed. Dumbar, *Analecta*, pp. 148–62.
Wadding, L., ed. *Annales Minorum seu trium ordinum a S. Francisco institutorum* (Lyon 1625–54).
Walter Hilton's "Mixed Life" Edited from Lambeth Palace MS 472, ed. S. J. Ogilvie-Thomson (Salzburg 1986).
Weiler, Anton G. *Necrologie, kroniek en cartularium c.a. van het Fraterhuis te Doesburg (1432–1559)* (Leiden 1974).
Wüstenhoff, D. J. M. "*Florencii parvum et simplex exercitium*: Naar een Berlijnsch handschrift medegedeeld," *Nederlandsch Archief voor Kerkgeschiedenis* 5 (1894), pp. 89–105.
Wyclif, John. *De oratione et ecclesiae purgatione*, ed. Rudolf Buddensieg, *John Wiclif's Polemical Works in Latin* (London 1883), pp. 342–54.
———. *De ordinatione fratrum*, ed. Rudolf Buddensieg, *John Wiclif's Polemical Works in Latin* (London 1883), pp. 88–106.
———. *De perfectione statuum*, ed. Rudolf Buddensieg, *John Wiclif's Polemical Works in Latin* (London 1883), pp. 449–82.
———. *De religione privata I*, ed. Rudolf Buddensieg, *John Wiclif's Polemical Works in Latin* (London 1883), pp. 491–518.
———. *De religione privata II*, Rudolf Buddensieg, *John Wiclif's Polemical Works in Latin* (London 1883), pp. 524–36.
———. *De religionibus vanis monachorum*, ed. Rudolf Buddensieg, *John Wiclif's Polemical Works in Latin* (London 1883), pp. 437–40.
———. *Speculum ecclesiae militantis*, ed. A.W. Pollard (London 1892)
———. *Sermones*, ed. Johann Loserth, 4 vols. (London 1887–90).
Zerbolt, Gerhart, of Zutphen. *Manuel de la réforme intérieure, Tractatus deuotus de reformacione uirium anime*, ed. Francis Joseph Legrand (Turnhout 2001).
———. *La montée du coeur, De spiritualibus ascensionibus*, ed. Francis Joseph Legrand (Turnhout 2006).

SECONDARY SOURCES

Abramowski, Luise. "Die Lehre von Gesetz und Evangelium bei Johann Pupper von Goch im Rahmen seines nominalistischen Augustinismus," *Zeitschrift für Theologie und Kirche* 64 (1967), pp. 83–98.

———. "Johann Gerson, De consiliis evangelicis et statu perfectionis," in *Studien zur Geschichte und Theologie der Reformation: Festschrift für Ernst Bizer*, ed. L. Abramowski and J. F. G. Goeters (Neukirchen 1969), pp. 63–78.

Acquoy, J. G. R. *Het Klooster te Windesheim en zijn invloed*, 3 vols. (Utrecht 1875–1880; reprt. 1984).

Alberts, W. Jappe. "Zur Historiographie der Devotio Moderna und ihrer Erforschung," *Westfälische Forschungen* 11 (1958), pp. 51–67.

———. *Moderne devotie* (Bussum 1969).

Algemene geschiedenis der Nederlanden, vol. 3 and 4 (Haarlem 1980).

Die Amunduskirche in Bad Urach, ed. Friedrich Schmidt (Sigmaringen 1990).

Anecdota ex codicibus hagiographicis Iohannis Gielemans canonici regularis (Brussels 1895).

Arts, Mathias. *Het dubbelklooster Dikninge* (Assen 1945).

Asen, Johannes. "Die Beginen in Köln," *Annalen des historischen Vereins für den Niederrhein* 111 (1927–1928), pp. 81–180; 112 (1927–1928), pp. 71–148; 113 (1927–1928), 13–19.

Aus dem Winkel in die Welt: Die Bücher des Thomas von Kempen und ihre Schicksale (Frankfurt 2006).

Bakker, Folkert Jan. *Bedelorden en begijnen in de stad Groningen tot 1594* (Assen 1988).

Bange, P. *Spiegels der Christenen: Zelfreflectie en ideaalbeeld in laat-middeleeuwse moralistisch-didactische traktaten* (Nijmegen 1986).

Barnikol, Ernst. *Die Brüder vom Gemeinsamen Leben in Deutschland* (Diss. Marburg 1916)

Barron, Caroline-Saul. Nigel, *England and the Low Countries in the Late Middle Ages* (1995).

Baudry, Léon. *La querelle des futurs contingents (Louvain 1465–75): textes inédits* (Paris 1950)

Beckmann, Josef Hermann. *Studien zum Leben und literarischen Nachlass Jakobs von Soest, O.P., 1360–1440* (Leipzig 1929).

Belozerskaya, Marina. *Rethinking the Renaissance: Burgundian Arts Across Europe* (Cambridge 2002).

Benvenuti Papi, Anna. *"In castro poenitentiae": Santità e società femminile nell'Italia medievale* (Italia sacra, Studi e documenti di storia ecclesiastica 45, Rome 1990).

Beriger, Andreas. "Rutger Sycamber von Venray: Rede zum Lob der Brüder vom gemeinsamen Leben (1501)," *OGE* 68 (1994), pp. 129–43.

———. *Windesheimer Klosterkultur um 1500: Vita, Werk, und Lebenswelt des Rutger Sycamber* (Tübingen 2004).

Berkenvelder, F. C. "Zwolle ten tijde van Thomas à Kempis," in *Bijdragen over Thomas à Kempis en de Moderne Devotie* (Brussels-Zwolle) 1971), pp. 38–54.

Bériou, Nicole. "La prédication au béguinage de Paris pendant l'année liturgique 1272–73," *Recherches augustiniennes* 13 (1978), pp. 105–229.

Bertram, Martin. "Clementinenkommentare des 14. Jahrhunderts," *Quellen und Forschungen aus italienischen Archiven und Bibliotheken* 77 (1997), pp. 144–75.

Bijsterveld, A.-J. *Laverend tussen kerk en wereld: die pastoors in Nord-Brabant, 1400–1570* (Amsterdam 1993).

Biller, Peter. "Words and the Medieval Notion of 'Religion'," *Journal of Ecclesiastical History* 36 (1985), pp. 351–69.

Birkmeyer, Regine. *Ehetrennung und monastische Konversion im Hochmittelalter* (Berlin 1998).

Blockmans, Wim. "Verwirklichungen und neue Orientierungen in der Sozialgeshichte der Niederlande im Spätmittelalter," in *Niederlande und Nordwestdeutschland,* ed. W. Ehbrecht and H. Schilling (Cologne 1983), pp. 41–60.

Blockmans, Wim and Prevenier, Walter. *The Promised Lands: The Low Countries Under Burgundian Rule, 1369–1530* (Philadelphia 1999).

Boeken voor de eeuwigheid: Middelnederlands geestelijk proza, ed. Thomas Mertens (Amsterdam 1993).

Bollmann, Anne M. "'Mijt dijt spynnen soe suldi den hemel gewinnen': Die Arbeit als normierender und frömmigkeitszentrierender Einfluss in den Frauengemeinschaften der Devotio moderna," in *Normative Zentrierung = Normative Centering,* ed. Suntrup, R. and Veenstra, J. R. (Frankfurt 2002), pp. 85–124.

———. *Frauenleben und Frauenliteratur in der Devotio moderna: Volkssprachige Schwesternbücher in literarhistorischer Perspektive* (Groningen 2004).

Brandsma, Titus. "Twee berijmde levens van Geert Groote," *Ons Geestelijke Erf* 16 (1942), pp. 5–51.

Breure, L. *Doodsbeleving en levenshouding: Een historisch-psychologische studie betreffende de Moderne Devotie in het IJsselgebied in de 14e en 15e eeuw* (Hilversum 1987).

———. "Het devote sterven als menselijke ervaring," *OGE* 59 (1985), pp. 435–56.

Brinkman, Herman. *Dichten uit liefde: Literatuur in Leiden aan het einde van de Middeleeuwen* (Hilversum 1997).

Bryan, Jennifer. *Looking Inward: Devotional Reading and the Private Self in Late Medieval England* (Philadelphia 2008).

Bücher, Karl. *Die Frauenfrage im Mittelalter* (Tubingen 1910).

Brown, D. Catherine. *Pastor and Laity in the Theology of Jean Gerson* (Cambridge 1987).

Burger, Christoph. *Aedificatio, Fructus, Utilitas: Johannes Gerson als Professor der Theologie und Kanzler der Universität Paris* (Tubingen 1986).

Burr, David. *The Spiritual Franciscans: From Protest to Persecution in the Century After Saint Francis* (University Park, Pa. 2001).

Bynum, Caroline Walker, *Holy Feast and Holy Fast: The Religious Significance of Food to Medieval Women* (Berkeley, Calif. 1987)

———. *Wonderful Blood: Theology and Practice in Late Medieval Northern Germany and Beyond* (Philadelphia 2007)

Carlier, J. J. "Het Fraterhuis of Collatiehuis op de Jerusalemstraat," *Bijdragen oudheidkundige kring 'Die Goude'* 5 (1947), pp. 50–77.

Carnier, Marc. "De reguliere vrouwelijke derde orde in de zuidelijke Nederlanden," *Trajecta* 14 (2005), pp. 205–20.

De cella in seculum: Religious and Secular Life and Devotion in Late Medieval England, ed. Michael G. Sargent (Cambridge 1989).

Clemen, Otto. *Johann Pupper von Goch* (Leipzig 1896).

Der Codex im Gebrauch, ed. Christel Meier, Dagmar Hüpper, and Hagen Keller (Munich 1996).

De codicibus hagiographicis Iohannis Gielemans canonici regularis in Rubea Valle prope Brusellas adiectis anecdotis (Brussels 1895).

Constable, Giles. *The Reformation of the Twelfth Century* (Cambridge 1995).

Corbellini, Sabrina. "Mannenregels voor een vrouwenwereld: De spirituele opvoeding van zusters in derde-ordegemeenschappen," *Trajecta* 14 (2005), pp. 177–92.

Corcoran, Charles J. *John Gerson, Champion of Parish Priest: A Study in the History of the States of Perfection* (Rome 1944).

Courtenay, William J. "The Bible in the Fourteenth Century: Some Observations," *Church History* 54 (1985), pp. 176–87.

Creytens, Raymond. "L'obligations des constitutions dominicaines d'après le B. Jean Dominici O.P.," *Archivum Fratrum Praedicatorum* 23 (1953), pp. 195–235.

De Baere, Guido. "Het 'ghemeine leven' bij Ruusbroec en Geert Grote," *OGE* 59 (1985), pp. 172–83.

De Hullu, J. *Bijdrage tot de geschiedenis van het Utrechtsche schisma* ('sGravenhaage 1892).

De Keyser, R. and Trio, P. "De *inclusio* van Melle uit 1447: bijdrage tot de insluiting van Windesheimse kloosters," in *Serta devota*, pp. 189–202.

De Kok, David. *Bijdragen tot de Geschiedenis der Nedelandsche Klarissen en Tertiarissen vóór de Hervorming* (Utrecht 1927).

De Lange, A. and Utz Tremp, K. *Friedrich Reiser und die "waldensisch-hussitische Internationale" im 15. Jahrhundert* (Heidelberg 2006).

De Schepper, H. *Belgium Nostrum 1500–1650: over integratie en desintegratie van het Nederland* (Antwerp 1987).

De Vries, Th. J. "Gildenwoelingen en interdict te Zwolle 1413–16: Een bijdrage tot de kennis van het anticlericalisme in de middeleeuwen," *Verslagen en Mededelingen van de Vereeniging ter beoefening van Overijssels Regt en Geschiedenis* 2de reeks 60 (1945), pp. 54–90.

Debongnie, Pierre. *Jean Mombaer de Bruxelles, abbé de Livry: ses écrits et ses réformes* (Louvain 1928).

Degler-Spengler, Brigitte. "Die Beginen in Basel," *Basler Zeitschrift für Geschichte und Altertumskunde* 69 (1969), pp. 5–83, 70 (1970), pp. 29–118.

———. "Die religiöse Frauenbewegung des Mittelalters," *Rottenburger Jahrbuch für Kirchengeschichte* 3 (1984), pp. 75–88.

Deutsche Mystik im abendländischen Zusammenhang: Neu erschlossene Texte, neue methodische Ansätze, neue theoretische Konzepte, ed. Walter Haug and Wolfram Schneider-Lastin (Tübingen 2000).

Ditsche, Magnus. "Zur Herkunft und Bedeutung des Begriffes Devotio Moderna, *Historisches Jahrbuch* 79 (1960), pp. 124–45.

Doornink-Hoogenraad, M. M. *Adamanshuis: een zusterhuis van de moderne devotie in Zutphen* (Zutphen 1983).

Duffy, Eamon. *The Stripping of the Altars: Traditional Religion in England 1400–1580* (New Haven, Conn. 1992).

Dumbar, Gerhard. *Het kerkelyk en wereltlyk Deventer*, 2 vols. (Deventer 1731, 1788).

Ebbinge Wubben, C. H. *Over Middelnederlandsche vertalingen van het Oude Testament: Bouwstoffen voor de geschiedenis der Nederlandsche Bijbelvertaling* ('sGravenhage 1903).

Eisenbart, L. C. *Kleiderordnungen der deutschen Städte zwischen 1350 und 1700: Ein Beitrag zur Kulturgeschichte des deutschen Bürgertums* (Göttingen 1962).

Elliott, Dyan. *Proving Woman: Female Spirituality and Inquisitional Culture in the Later Middle Ages* (Princeton, N.J. 2004)

Elm, Kaspar. "Verfall und Erneuerung des Ordenswesens im Spätmittelalter: Forschungen und Forschungsaufgaben," in *Untersuchungen zu Kloster und Stift* (Göttingen 1980) 188–238.

———. "Die Brüderschaft vom gemeinsamen Leben: Eine geistliche Lebensform zwischen Kloster und Welt, Mittelalter und Neuzeit," *OGE* 59 (1985), pp. 470–96.

———. "*Vita regularis sine regula*: Bedeutung, Rechtsstellung and Selbstverständnis des mittelalterlichen und frühneuzeitlichen Semireligiosentums," in *Häresie und vorzeitige Reformation im Spätmittelalter*," ed. František Šmahel (Munich 1998), 239–73.

———. "Die 'Devotio moderna' und die neue Frömmigkeit zwischen Spätmittelalter und früher Neuzeit," in *Die "Neue Frömmigkeit*," pp. 15–29.

Épiney-Burgard, Georgette. *Gérard Grote (1340–84) et les débuts de la Dévotion moderne* (Wiesbaden 1970).

———. "Florens Radewijns," in *Verfasserlexicon* (1989), VII, 968–72.

———. "La vie et les écrits de Florent Radewjns en langue vernaculaire," *OGE* 63 (1989), pp. 370–83.

———. "Die Wege der Bildung in der Devotio Moderna," in *Lebenslehren und Weltentwürfe im Ubergang vom Mittelalter zur Neuzeit*, ed. Hartmut Boockmann, Bernd Moeller, and Karl Stackmann (Göttingen 1989), pp. 181–200).

———. "Les idées pédagogiques de Dirc van Herxen," in *Serta Devota*, pp. 295–304.

Martin Erbstösser and Ernst Werner. *Ideologische Probleme des mittelalterlichen Plebejertums: Die freigeistige Häresie und ihre sozialen Wurzeln* (Berlin 1960).

Faix, Gerhard. *Gabriel Biel und die Brüder vom gemeinsamen Leben: Quellen und Untersuchungen zum Selbstverständnis des Oberdeutschen Generalkapittels* (Tübingen 1999).

Foppens, Jean François, *Bibliotheca belgica, sive virorum in Belgio vita scriptisque illustrium catalogus* (Brussels 1739), 2 vols.

Forrest, Ian. *The Detection of Heresy in Late Medieval England* (Oxford 2005).

G. Frank and F. Niewöhner. *Reformer als Ketzer: heterodoxe Bewegungen von Vorreformatoren* (Stuttgart 2004).

Freedman, Paul. *Images of the Medieval Peasant* (Stanford, Calif. 1999).

French, Katherine. *The People of the Parish: Community Life in a Late Medieval English Diocese* (Philadelphia 2001).

Fromme Frauen oder Ketzerinnen? Leben und Verfolgung der Beginen im Mittelalter, ed. Martina Wehrli-Johns and Claudi Opitz (Freiburg 1998).

Geen Povere Schoonheid: Laat-middeleeuwse kunst in verband met de Moderne Devotie, ed. Kees Veelenturf (Nijmegen 2000).

Gerretsen, J. *Florentius Radewijns* (Nijmegen 1891).

Gerrits, Gerrit H. *Inter timorem et spem: A Study of the Theological Thought of Gerard Zerbolt of Zutphen (1367–98)* (Leiden 1986).

Gerwing, Manfred. *Malogranatum oder der dreifache Weg zur Vollkommenheit* (Munich 1986).

Gill, Katherine. "Scandala: Controversies Concerning *Clausura* and Women's Religious Communities in Late Medieval Italy," in *Christendom and Its Discontents*, ed. Scott Waugh and Peter Diehl (Cambridge 1996), pp. 177–203.

Gnädinger, Louis. *Johannes Tauler: Lebenswelt und mystische Lehre* (Munich 1993).

Godet, Marcel. *La congrégation de Montaigu, 1490–1580* (Paris 1912).

Goossens, Mathias, *De meditatie in de eerste tijd van de Moderne Devotie* (Haarlem-Antwerp 1954).

Gorceix, Bernard. *Amis de Dieu en Allemagne au siècle de Maître Eckhart* (Paris 1984).

Gottschall, Dagmar. "Basel als Umschlagplatz für geistliche Literature: Der Fall des *Fliessenden Lichts der Gottheit* von Mechthild von Magdeburg," in *University, Council, City*, pp. 137–70.

Goudriaan, Koen. "Gouda en de Moderne Devotie," *Holland, regional-historische tijdschrift* 11 (1997), pp. 130–41.

———. "De derde orde van Sint Franciscus in het bisdom Utrecht: Een voorstudie," *Jaarboek voor Middeleeuwse Geschiedenis* 1 (1998) 205–60.

———. "Het monasticon: een nuttig instrument? Bij de presentatie van het *Monasticon Trajectense*," *Trajecta* 14 (2005), pp. 133–46.

Greven, Joseph. *Die Anfänge der Beginen: Ein Beitrag zur Geschichte der Volksfrömmigkeit und des Ordenswesens im Hochmittelalter* (Vorreformationsgeschichtliche Forschungen 8, Turnhout 1912).

———. "Der Ursprung des Beginenwesens: Eine Auseinandersetzung mit Godefroid Kurth," *Historisches Jahrbuch* 35 (1914), pp. 26–47, 291–318.

Grosse, Sven. *Heilsungewissheit und scrupulositas im späten Mittelalter: Studien zur Johannes Gerson und Gattungen der Frömmigkeitstheologie seiner Zeit* (Tübingen 1994).

Grundmann, Herbert. *Religious Movements in the Middle Ages* (Notre Dame, Ind. 1995), German original in 1935.

Guicciardini Illustratus: De karten en prenten in Lodovico Guicciardini's Beschrijving van de Nederlanden, ed. Henk Deys, Mathieu Franssen, Vincent van Hezik, Fineke te Raa, and Erik Walsmit (Utrecht 2001).

Gysseling, Maurits. "De herkomst van het woord begijn," *Heemkundig Nieuws* 13 (1985), pp. 9–12.

Hagemeijer, P. "Devote vrouwen in Holland omstreeks 1400," in *In de schaduw van de eeuwigheid: tien studies over religie en samenleving in laatmiddeleeuws Nederland, aangeboden aan prof. dr. A. H. Bredero*, ed. N. Lettink and J. J. van Moolenbroek (Utrecht 1986), pp. 224–41, 299–302.

Hamburger, Jeffrey. "Medieval Self-Fashioning: Authorship, Authority, and Autobiography in Suso's *Exemplar*," in his *The Visual and the Visionary: Art and Female Spirituality in Late Medieval Germany* (New York 1998).

Hamm, Berndt. *Promissio, pactum, ordinatio: Freiheit und Selbstbindung Gottes in der scholastischen Gnadenlehre* (Tübingen 1977).

———. "Was ist Frömmigkeitstheologie? Uberlegungen zum 14. bis 16. Jahrhundert," in *Praxis Pietatis: Beiträge zu Theologie und Frömmigkeit in der Frühen Neuzeit, Wolfgang Sommer zum 60. Geburtstag* (Stuttgart 1999), pp. 9–45.

———. *The Reformation of Faith in the Context of Late Medieval Theology and Piety: Essays by Berndt Hamm*, ed. Robert J. Bast (Leiden 2004).

Die Handschriften der Klosterbibliothek Frenswegen (Wiesbaden 1994).

Häresie und vorzeitige Reformation im Spätmittelalter, ed. František Šmahel (Munich 1998).

Haverals, Marcel. "*Contra detractores monachorum* alias *De utilitate monachorum* van Dirk van Herxen," in *Serta devota* 1, pp. 241–94.

Heidemann, J. "Die Beginenhäuser Wesels," *Zeitschrift des Bergischen Geschichtsvereins* 4 (1867), pp. 85–114.

Heimann, Claudia. *Nicolaus Eymeric (vor 1320–1399): Predicator veridicus, inquisitator intrepidus, doctor egregius: Leben und Werk eines Inquisators* (Münster 2001).

Helmrath, Johannes. *Das Basler Konzil 1431–1449, Forschungsstand und Probleme* (Cologne 1987).

Henderikx, P. A. *De oudste bedelordekloosters in het graafschap Holland en Zeeland* (Dordrecht 1977).

Heusinger, Sabine von. *Johannes Mulberg OP (gest. 1414): Ein Leben im Spannungsfeld von Dominikanerobservanz und Beginenstreit* (Berlin 2000).

Hillenbrand, Eugen. "Die Observantenbewegung in der deutschen Ordensprovinz der Dominikaner," in *Reformbemühungen*, pp. 219–72.

Hobbins, Daniel. "The Schoolman as Public Intellectual: Jean Gerson and the Late Medieval Tract," *American Historical Review* 108 (2003), pp. 1308–35.

———. "Jean Gerson's Authentic Tract on Joan of Arc: *Super facto puellae et credulitate sibi praestanda* (14 May 1429)," *Mediaeval Studies* 67 (2005), pp. 99–155.

Hoenen, Maarten J. F. M. "The 'Reparationes librorum totius naturalis philosphiae' (Cologne 1494) as a Source for the Late Medieval Debates between Albertistae and Thomistae," *Documenti et studi sulla tradizione filosofica medievale* 4 (1993), pp. 307–44.

———. " 'Ut pia testatoris uoluntas observetur': Die Stiftung der *bursa cusana* zu Deventer," in *Conflict and Resolution: Perspectives on Nicholas of Cusa*, ed. Inigo Bocken (Leiden 2004), pp. 53–73.

Hoffmann, W. J., "Die volkssprachliche Rezeption des 'Horologium sapientiae' in der Devotio moderna," in *Heinrich Seuses Philosophia spiritualis: Quellen, Konzept, Formen und Rezeption*, ed. R. Blunrich and Ph. Kaiser (Wiesbaden 1994), pp. 202–54.

Hofman, J. "De broeders van het Gemene Leven en de Windesheimse kloostervereniging," *AGAU* 2 (1875), pp. 217–75; 5 (1878), pp. 80–152.

Hofman, Rijklof. "De functionaliteit van handschriften uit de Moderne Devotie," in *Geen Povere Schoonheid*, pp. 169–91.

Hollywood, Amy. *The Soul as Virgin Wife* (Notre Dame, Ind. 1995).

Honemann, V. "Zu Interpretation und Uberlieferung des Traktats 'De libris teutonicalibus'," in *Opstellen voor Dr. Jan Deschamps*, 3 vols., ed. E. Cockx-Indestege and F. Henrickx (Louvain, 1987), III, pp. 113–23.

———. "Textvarianz im Milieu der Devotio moderna: Zur Genese der verschiedenen Fassungen von 'Super modo vivendi devotorum hominum simul commorantium' und 'De libris teutonicalibus'," in *Lingua theodisca: Beiträge zur Sprach- und Literaturwissenschaft, Jan Goossens zum 65. Geburtstag*, ed. J. Cajot, L. Kreme, and H. Niebaum (Munster-Hamburg, 1995), pp. 969–78.

Hudson, Anne. *The Premature Reformation: Wycliffite Texts and Lollard History* (Oxford 1988).

Hugenholtz, F. W. N., "Particularistische burgerijen," in *Postillen* (1964), pp. 27–38.

Huizinga, Johan. "Der Mittlerstellung der Niederlande zwischen West- und Mitteleuropa," *Verzamelde Werken* II, pp. 284–303.

———. "Uit de voorgeschiedenis van ons nationaal besef," *Verzamelde Werken* II, pp. 95–160.

———. *Herfstij der Middeleeuwen: Studie over levens- end gedachtenvormen der veertiende en vijftiende eeuw in Frankrijk en de Nederlanden* (Groningen 1985; original 1919)

———. *Verzamelde Werken*, 7 vols. (Haarlem 1948).

Hutton, Shennan. "'On Herself and all Her Property': Women's Economic Activities in Late-Medieval Ghent," *Continuity and Change* 20 (2005), pp. 325–49.

Hyma, Albert. "Is Gerard Zerbolt of Zutphen the Author of the 'Super modo vivendi'?" *Nederlandsche Archief voor Kerkgeschiedenis n.s.* 16 (1921), 107–28.

———. *The Christian Renaissance: A History of the "Devotio Moderna"* (Grand Rapids 1924).

Janse, A. "Het religieuze leven in het Grote Convent te Doesburg," *OGE* 74 (2000), pp. 84–104.

Jedin, H. J. "Thomas von Kempen als Biograph und Chronist," in *Universitas: Festschrift Dr. A Stohr* (Mainz 1960) II, pp. 69–77.

Jocqué, Luc. "De Victorijnse wetgeving als inspiratiebron voor de constituties van Windesheim, *OGE* 59 (1985), pp. 211–24.

Jostes, Aloysia Elisabeth, *Die Historiseriung der Devotio Moderna im 15. und 16. Jahrhundert: Verbandsbewusstsein und Selbstverständnis in der Windesheimer Kongregation* (dissertation, Groningen, 2007).

Jostes, F. "Die Schriften des Gerhard Zerbolt van Zutphen 'De libris teutonicalibus'," *Historisches Jahrbuch* 11 (1890), pp. 11–22, 709–17.

Jundt, Auguste. *Les Amis de Dieu au quatorzième siècle* (Paris 1879).

Kaeppeli, Thomas. *Scriptores Ordinis Praedicatorum Medii Aevi* vol. I (Rome 1970).

Kaminsky, Howard. *A History of the Hussite Revolution* (Princeton 1967).

———. *Simon de Cramaud and the Great Schism* (New Brunswick, N.J. 1983)

———. "From Lateness to Waning to Crisis: The Burden of the Later Middle Ages," *Journal of Early Modern History* 4 (2000), pp. 85–125.

Karras, Ruth Mazo. *From Boys to Men: Formations of Masculinity in Late Medieval Europe* (Philadelphia 2003).

Keiser, George, R. "'Noght how lang man lifs, bot how wele': The Laity and the Ladder of Perfection," in *De cella*, pp. 145–60.

Kerby-Fulton, Kathryn. *Books Under Suspicion: Censorhip and Tolerance of Revelatory Writing in Late Medieval England* (Notre Dame, Ind. 2006).

Keussen, Hermann. "Der Dominkaner Matthäus Grabow und die Brüder vom gemeinsamen Leben," *Mitteilungen aus dem Stadtarchiv von Köln* 13 (1887), pp. 29–47.

Kieckhefer, Richard. *Repression of Heresy in Medieval Germany* (Philadelphia 1979).

———. *Unquiet Souls: Fourteenth-Century Saints and Their Religious Milieu* (Chicago 1984).

———. "Convention and Conversion: Patterns in Late Medieval Piety," *Church History* 67 (1998), pp. 32–51.

Killerby, Catherine Kovesi. *Sumptuary Law in Italy, 1200–1500* (Oxford 2002).

Kirchenreform von unten: Gerhard Zerbolt von Zutphen und die Brüder vom gemeinsamen Leben, ed. Nikolaus Staubach (Frankfurt 2004).

Klausmann, Theo. *Consuetudo consuetudine vincitur: Die Hausordnungen der Brüder vom gemeinsamen Leben im Bildungs- und Sozilisationsprogramm der Devotio moderna* (Frankfurt 2003).

———. "Die ältesten Satzungen der Devotio moderna," in *Kirchenreform von unten* (2004), pp. 24–43.

Klug, Martina B. *Armut und Arbeit in der Devotio moderna: Studien zum Leben der Schwestern in niederrheinsichen Gemeinschaften* (Münster 2005).

Knierim, Philippina. *Dirc van Herxen (1381–1457): Rector van het Zwolsche Fraterhuis* (Amsterdam 1926).

Kock, Thomas. *Die Buchkultur der Devotio moderna: Handschriftenproduktion, Literaturversorgung, und Bibliotheksaufbau im Zeitalter des Medienwechsels* (Frankfurt 1999, 2nd ed. 2002).

———. "Selbstvergewisserung und Memoria in der Devotio Moderna: Die Traditionscodices der brabantischen Augustiner-Chorherrenstifte," in *Medieval Narrative Sources: A Gateway into the Medieval Mind,* ed. Werner Verbeke, Ludo Milis, Jean Goosens (Louvain 2005), pp. 181–204.

Koorn, Florence W. J. *Begijnhoven in Holland en Zeeland gedurende de middeleeuwen* (Assen 1981).

———. "Ongebonden vrouwen: Overeenkomsten en verschillen tussen begijnen en zusters des Gemenen Levens," *OGE* 59 (1985), pp. 393–402.

———. "Hollandse nuchterheid? De houding van de Moderne Devotie tegenover vrouwenmystiek en-ascese," *OGE* (1992), pp. 97–114.

———. "Het Kapittel van Utrecht," in *Windesheim*, pp. 131–42.

———. "Von der Peripherie ins Zentrum: Beginen und Schwestern vom Gemeinsamen Leben in den nördlichen Niederlanden," in *Fromme Frauen*, pp. 53–94.

Kohl, Wilhelm."Die Windesheimer Kongregation," in *Reformbemühungen*, pp. 83–106.

Korth, Leonard. "Die ältesten Gutachten über die Brüderschaft des gemeinsamen Lebens," *Mitteilungen aus dem Stadtarchiv von Köln* 13 (1887), pp. 1–27.

Kors, Mikel. "Het propositum bij de Moderne Devoten: Over de verschriftelijking van een kernbegrip uit de vadertijd," *OGE* 71 (1997), pp. 145–80.

———. "Die Bibel für Laien: Neuansatz oder Sackgasse? Die Bibelübersetzer von 1360 und Gerhard Zerbolt von Zutphen," in *Kirchenreform von unten*, pp. 243–63.

Kruitwagen, Bonaventura. "Het schrijven op feestdagen in den middeleeuwen," *Tijdschrift voor Boek- en Bibliotheekwezen* 5 (1907), pp. 97–120.

———. *Laat-middeleeuwse paleographica, paleotypica, liturgica, kalendalia, grammaticalia* ('sGravenhage 1942).

Krul, Wessel. "In the Mirror of van Eyck: Johan Huizinga's Autumn of the Middle Ages," *Journal of Medieval and Early Modern Studies* 27 (1997), pp. 353–84.

Kühler, W. J. *Johannes Brinckerinck en zijn klooster te Diepenveen* (Amsterdam 1908)

———. "De betrouwbaarheid der geschiedeschrijving van Thomas à Kempis." *Nederlandsch Archief voor Kerkgeschiedenis* n.s. 25 (1932), pp. 49–64.

Laienlektüre und Buchmarkt im späten Mittelalter, ed. Thomas Kock and Rita Schlusemann (Frankfurt 1997).

Landau, Peter. "Was War um 1300 ein Kollegium?" in *Königliche Töchterstämme, Königswähler, und Kurfürsten*, ed. Armin Wolf (Frankfurt 2002), pp. 485–95.

Lansing, Carol. *Power and Purity: Cathar Heresy in Medieval Italy* (New York 1998).

Lem, Constant A. M. "De consuetudines van het Collatiehuis in Gouda," *OGE* 65 (1991), pp. 125–43.

Lentes, Thomas. "*Vita perfecta* zwischen *vita communis* und *vita privata*: Eine Skizze zur klösterlichen Einzelzelle," in *Das Öffentliche und Private in der Vormoderne*, ed. Gert Melville and Peter von Moos (Cologne 1998), pp. 125–64.

Lerner, Robert. *The Heresy of the Free Spirit in the Later Middle Ages* (Princeton, N.J. 1972).

Lesser, Bertam. *Johannes Busch, Chronist der Devotio moderna: Werkstruktur, Überlieferung, Rezeption* (Frankfurt 2005).

Levelt, H. "Regestenlijst van het cartularium, toebehoorend het Meester Florenshuis en het Arme Klerkenhuis binnen Deventer," *Verslagen en mededeelingen Vereeniging tot beoefening van Overijsselsche Regt en Geschiedenis* 41 (1918), pp. 289–319.

Logan, Donald. *Runaway Religious in Medieval England, c.1240–1540* (Cambridge 1996).

Lohse, Bernhard. *Mönchtum und Reformation: Luthers Auseinandersetzung mit dem Mönchsideal des Mittelalters* (Gottingen 1963).

Lollardy and the Gentry in the Later Middle Ages, ed. M. Aston and C. Richmond (Stroud 1997).

Lourdaux, W. "Kartuizers-Moderne Devoten: Een problem van afhankelijkheid," *OGE* 37 (1963), pp. 402–18.

———. *Moderne devotie en christelijk humanisme: de geschiedenis van Sint-Maarten te Leuven van 1433 tot het einde der XVIe eeuw* (Louvain 1967).

———. "De Broeders van het Gemene Leven," *Bijdragen: Tijdschrift voor Filosofie en Theologie* 33 (1972), pp. 372–416.

———. "Het boekenbezit en het boekengebruik bij de Moderne Devoten," in *Studies over het Boekenbezit en Boekengebruik in de Nederland vóór 1600* (Archives et bibliothèques de Belgique 11, Brussels 1974), pp. 247–325.

———. "Dirk of Herxen's Tract *De utilitate monachorum*: A Defence of the Lifestyle of the Brethren and Sisters of the Common Life," in *Pascua Medievalia: Studies voor Prof. J. M. de Smet*, ed. R. Lievens, E. van Mingroot, W. Verbeke (Louvain 1983), pp. 312–36.

Luongo, F. Thomas. *The Saintly Politics of Catherine of Siena* (Ithaca, N.Y. 2006).

Mahlmann, Theodor. "'Vorreformatoren', 'vorreformatorisch', 'Vorreformation': Beobachtungen zur Geschichte eines Sprachgebrauchs," in *Die "Neue Frömmigkeit"*, pp. 13–55.

Makowski, Elizabeth. *Canon Law and Cloistered Women: Periculoso and Its Commentators, 1298–1545* (Washington, D.C. 1997).

———. *"A Pernicious Sort of Woman": Quasi Religious Women and Canon Lawyers in the Later Middle Ages* (Washington, D.C. 2005).

Martens, M. "Une ville en expansion (1291–1374), in *Histoire de Bruxelles*, ed. M. Martens (Toulouse 1976), pp. 99–138.

———. "Hedwige Blomart face au mystique Jean van Ruysbroec: leurs milieus familiaux à l'éprouve des assertions de Pomerius, visant la Bloemardinne (1350–XVe siècle)," *Cahiers bruxellois* 31 (1990), pp. 1–107.

Marx, Jakob. *Nikolaus von Cues und seine Stiftungen zu Cues und Deventer* (Trier 1906).

McDonnell, Ernest. *The Beguines and Beghards in Medieval Culture, with Special Emphasis on the Belgian Scene* (New Brunswick 1954).

McGinn, Bernard. *Anti-Christ: Two Thousand Years of the Human Fascination with Evil* (New York 1994).

———. *The Mystical Thought of Meister Eckhart: The Man from Whom God Hid Nothing* (New York 2001).

———. *The Harvest of Mysticism in Medieval Germany* (New York 2005).

McGuire, Brian Patrick. *Jean Gerson and the Last Medieval Reformation* (University Park, Pa. 2005).

McSheffrey, Shannon. "Place, Space, and Situation: Public and Private in the Making of Marriage in Late-Medieval London," *Speculum* 79 (2004), pp. 960–98.

Meersseman, G. G. *Dossier de l'ordre de la pénitence au XIIIe siècle* (Spicilegium Friburgense 7, Fribourg 1961).

Mens, Alcantara. *Oorsprong en betekenis van de nederlandse beginen- en begardenbeweging* (Louvian 1947).

Mertens, Dieter. "Monastische Reformbewegungen des 15. Jahrhunderts: Ideen-Ziele-Resultate," in Ivan Hlaváček-Alexander Patchovsky, ed., *Reform von Kirche und Reich zur Zeit der Konzilien von Konstanz (1414–1418) and Basel (1431–1449)* (Constance 1996), pp. 157–81.

Mertens, Thom. *Hendrik Mande (d. 1431): teksthisorische en literairhistorische studies* (Nijmegen 1986).

———. "Lezen met de pen: ontwikkelingen in het laatmiddeleeuws geestelijk proza," in *De studie van de Middelnederlandse letterkunde: stand en toekomst*, ed. Frits van Oostrom-Frank Willaert (Hilversum 1989), pp. 187–200.

———. "Texte der modernen Devoten als Mittler zwischen kirchlicher und persönlicher Reform," *Niederdeutsches Wort* 34 (1994), pp. 63–74.

———. "Postuum auteurschap: De collaties van Johannes Brinckerinck," in *Windesheim* (1996), pp. 85–97.

———. "Ruusbroec onder de godsvrienden," in *Die spätmittelalterliche Rezeption niederländischer Literatur im deutschen Sprachgebiet*, ed. R. Schlusemann and P. Wackers (Amsterdam 1997), pp. 109–30.

———. "Collatio und Codex im Bereich der Devotio moderna, in *Der Codex*, pp. 163–82.

Met erasmus naar school: Handschriften, boeken en voorwerpen uit de tijd van Alexander Hegius als rector van de Latijnse school in Deventer (Deventer 1998).

Meuthen, Erich. "Gab es ein spätes Mittelalter?" in *Spätzeit: Studien zu den Problemen eines historischen Epochenbegriffs*, ed. J. Kunisch (Berlin 1990), pp. 91–135.

———. "Bursen und Artesfakultät der alten Kölner Universität," in *Philosophy and Learning: Universities in the Middle Ages*, ed. Maarten J. H. Hoenen, Josef Schneider, and Georg Wieland (Leiden 1995), pp. 225–45.

Michael, Bernd, *Die mittelalterlichen Handschriften der wissenschaftlichen Stadtbibliothek Soest* (Wiesbaden 1990).

Miller, Tanya Stabler. "What's in a Name? Clerical Representations of Parisian Beguines (1200–1328)," *Journal of Medieval History* 33 (2007), pp. 60–86.

Mills, Kenneth and Grafton, Anthony. *Conversion: Old Worlds and New* (Rochester, N.Y. 2003).

———. *Conversion in Late Antiquity and the Early Middle Ages: Seeing and Believing* (Rochester, N.Y. 2003).

Mixson, James. *Professed Proprietors: Ownership and Mortal Sin at the Origins of the Observant Movement* (forthcoming Leiden 2009).

Moderne Devotie: Figuren en facetten (Nijmegen 1984).

Moll, Willem. *Johannes Brugman en het godsdienstig leven onzer vaderen in de vijftiende eeuw* (Amsterdam 1854).

———. "De boekerij van het St. Barbara-klooster te Delft in de tweede helft der vijftiende eeuw: Eene bijdrage tot de geschiedenis der middeleeuwsche letterkunde in Nederland," *Kerkhistorische archief* 4 (1866), pp. 209–85.

———. *Kerkgeschiedenis van Nederland vóór de hervorming*, 2 vols. (Arnhem 1867).

Monasticon Belge IV (Liège 1970).

Monasticon Fratrum Vitae Communis, ed. W. Leesch, E. Persoons, A. G. Weiler, 3 vols. (1977, 1979, 2004).

Monasticon Trajectense, at: www.let.vu.nl/project/monasticon.

Monasticon Windeshemense, ed. W. Kohl, E. Persoons, A. G. Weiler, 3 vols. (Brussels, 1976, 1977, 1980), with an index volume (1984).

Morrison, Karl, *Understanding Conversion* (Charlottesville, Va. 1992).

Mosheim, J. L., *De Beghardis et Beguinabus commentarius*, ed. G.H. Martini (Leipzig 1790).

Mulchahey, M. Michèle, *"First the Bow Is Bent in Study": Dominican Education before 1350* (Toronto 1998).

Mulder, Wilhelmus, "Guillaume de Salvarvilla," *OGE* 5 (1931), pp. 186–211.

Mulder-Bakker, Anneke. *Lives of the Anchoresses: The Rise of the Urban Recluse in Medieval Europe* (Philadelphia 2005).

Muldoon, James. *Varieties of Religious Conversion in the Middle Ages* (Gainesville, Fla. 1997).

Peter Müller. *Bettelorden und Stadtgemeinde in Hildesheim im Mittelalter* (Hannover 1994).

Muller, S. *Regesten van het archief der biscoppen van Utrecht, 722–1528* (Utrecht 1917).

Neddermeyer, Uwe. "*Radix studii et speculum vitae*: Verbreitung und Rezeption der 'Imitatio Christi' in Handschriften und Drucken bis zur Reformation," in *Studien zum 15. Jahrhundert: Festschift für Erich Meuthen zum 65. Geburtstag*, ed. Johannes Helmrath, Heribert Müller and Helmut Wolff (Munich 1994), I, pp. 457–81.

———. "Verbreitung und Wirkung der 'Imitatio Christi' in Handschriften und Drucken vom 15. bis zum 18. Jahrhundert," in *Kempner Thomas-Vorträge* (Kempen 2002), pp. 55–83.

Neel, Carol. "The Origins of the Beguines," *Signs* 14 (1989), pp. 321–41.

Neidiger, Bernhard. *Mendikanten zwischen Ordensideal und städtischer Realität: Untersuchungen zum wirtschaftlichen Verhalten der Bettelorden in Basel* (Berliner Historische Studien 5, Berlin 1981).

Die "Neue Frömmigkeit" in Europa im Spätmittelalter, ed. Marek Derich and Martial Staub (Gottingen 2004).

Neumann, Eva Gertrud. *Rheinisches Beginen- und Begardenwesen: ein Mainzer Beitrag zur religiösen Bewegung am Rhein* (Meisenheim am Glam 1960).

Newman, Barbara. " 'Crueel Corage': Child Sacrifice and the Maternal Martyr in Hagiography and Romance," in her *From Virile Woman to WomanChrist: Studies in Medieval Religion and Literature* (Philadelphia 1995), pp. 76–107.

Nijsten, Gerard. *In the Shadow of Burgundy: The Court of Guelders in the Late Middle Ages* (Cambridge 2004).

Northern Humanism in European Context, 1469–1625: From the "Adwert Academy" to Ubbo Emmius, ed. F. Akkerman, A. J. Vanderjagt, A. H. van der Laan (Leiden 1999).

Obbema, P. F. J. *Een Deventer bibliotheekcatalogus van het einde der vijftiende eeuw: Een bijdrage tot de studie van laat-middeleeuwse bibliotheek catalogi* (Brussels 1973).

Oberman, Heiko. *The Harvest of Medieval Theology* (Cambridge, Mass. 1963).

———. *Forerunners of the Reformation: The Shape of Late Medieval Thought Illustrated by Key Documents* (1966; rprt 1981 Philadelphia).

Oliger, P. "De relatione inter Observantium querimonias constantienses (1415) et Ubertini Casalensis quoddam scriptum," *Archivum Franciscanum Historicum* 9 (1916), pp. 22–53.

Oliver, Judith. *Gothic Manuscript Illumination in the Diocese of Liège (c. 1250–c. 1350)* (Louvain 1988).

Het ootmoedig fundament van Diepenveen: zeshonderd jaar Maria en Sint-Agnesklooster, 1400–2000, ed. Wybren Scheepsma (Kampen 2002).

Osheim, Duane J. "Conversion, *Conversi*, and the Christian Life in Late Medieval Tuscany," *Speculum* 58 (1983) 368–90.

Pansters, Krijn. *De kardinale deugden in de Lage Landen, 1200–1500* (Hilversum 2007).

The Parish in English Life, 1400–1600, ed. Katherine French, Gary Gibbs, Beat Kümin (Manchester 1997).

Patschovsky, Alexander. "Strassburger Beginenverfolgungen im 14. Jahrhundert," *Deutsches Archiv* 30 (1974), pp. 56–198.

———. "Zeugnisse des Inquisitors Hinrich Schoenvelt in einer Nicolaus Eymericus-Handschrift," in *Vera Lex Historiae. Studien zu mittelalterlichen Quellen. Festschrift für Dietrich Kurze zu seinem 65. Geburtstag am 1. Januar 1993*, ed. Stuart Jenks, Jürgen Sarnowsky, Marie-Luise Laudage (Cologne 1993), pp. 247–275.

———. "Beginen, Begarden und Terziaren im 14. und 15. Jahrhundert: Das Beispiel des Basler Beginenstreits (1400/04–1411)," in *Festschrift für Eduard Hlawitschka zum 65. Geburtstag*, ed. Karl Rudolf Schnith and Roland Pauler (Münchener Historische Studien. Abteilung Mittelalterliche Geschichte 5, Kallmünz 1993), pp. 403–18.

Peters, Edward and Simons, Walter. "The New Huizinga and the Old Middle Ages," *Speculum* 74 (1999), pp. 587–620.

Petri, F. and Jappe Alberts, W. *Gemeinsame Probleme deutsch-niederländischer Landes- und Volksforschung* (Groningen 1962).

Phillips, Dayton. *Beguines in Medieval Strasburg: A Study of the Social Aspect of Beguine Life* (Stanford, Calif. 1941).

Pocquet du Haut-Jussé and Laurent-Marie. *La vie religieuse d'après Saint Thomas d'Acquin* (Paris 1999).

Post, R. R. *Geschiedenis der utrechtsche bishopsverkiezingen tot 1535* (Utrecht 1933).

———. "Studiën over de Broeders van het Gemeen Leven," *Nederlandsche Historiebladen* 1 (1938), pp. 304–35, 2 (1939), pp. 136–62.

———. "De statuten van het Mr. Geertshuis te Deventer," *AGAU* 71 (1952), pp. 1–46.

———. *Scholen en onderwijs in Nederland gedurende de middeleeuwen* (Utrecht 1954).

———. *Kerkgeschiedenis van Nederland in de middeleeuwen* 2 vols. (Utrecht 1957).

———. "Johann Pupper von Goch," *NAK* 47 (1965/66), pp. 71–97.

———. *The Modern Devotion: Confrontation with Reformation and Humanism* (Leiden 1968).

Postillen over kerk en maatschappij in de vijftiende en zestiende eeuw, aangeboden aan Dr. R. R. Post (Nijmegen 1964).

Praedicatores Inquisitores I: *The Dominicans and the Medieval Inquisition* (Rome 2004).

Prevenier, Walter, *Prinsen en poorters: Beelden van de laat-middeleeuwse samenleving in de Bourgondische Nederlanden, 1384–1530* (Antwerp 1998).

Prim, Florens, *De Kloosterslot-beweging in Brabant in de XVe eeuw* (Mededeelingen van de

Koninklijke Vlaamsche Academie voor wetenschappen, letteren en schoone kunsten van Belgie, Klasse der Letteren VI.1, Antwerp 1944).

Das Publikum politischer Theorie im 14. Jahrhundert, ed. J. Miethke (Schriften des Historischen Kollegs 21, Munich 1992).

de Puig i Oliver, Jaume. "Nicholás Eymeric, un inquisitor discutido," in *Praedicatores Inquisitores* I (2004), pp. 545–93.

Raumerfassung und Raumbewusstsein im späteren Mittelalter (Vorträge und Forschungen 49, Stuttgart 2002).

Reformbemühungen und Observanzbestrebungen im spätmittelalterlichen Ordenswesen, ed. Kaspar Elm (Berlin 1989).

Rehm, Gerhard. *Die Schwestern vom gemeinsamen Leben im nordwestlichen Deutschland* (Berlin 1985).

Reichstein, Frank-Michael. *Das Beginenwesen in Deutschland, Studien und Katalog* (Berlin 2001).

Religion and Culture: Michel Foucault, ed. Jeremy R. Carrette (New York 1999).

Ribbeck, W. "Beiträge zur Geschichte der römischen Inquisition in Deutschland," *Zeitschrift für vaterländische Geschichte und Alterthumskunde* 46 (1888), pp. 129–56.

Riddy, Felicity. "Text and Self in *The Book of Margery Kempe*," in *Voices in Dialogue*, pp. 435–57.

Rieder, Karl. *Der Gottesfreund vom Oberland: Eine Erfindung des Strassburger Johanniterbruders Nikolaus von Löwen* (Innsbruck 1905).

Rogier, L. J. "De historicus en hoogleraar R. R. Post," in *Postillen* (1964), pp. 1–24.

Rouse, Richard and Mary Rouse. *Authentic Witnesses: Approaches to Medieval Texts and Manuscripts* (Notre Dame, Ind. 1991).

Rutgers, C. A. "Gelre: een deel van 'Nederland'?", *Tijdschrift voor Geschiedenis* 88 (1975), pp. 27–38.

———. *Van Standen tot Staten* (Utrecht 1975).

———, ed. *De Utrechtse bisschop in de middeleeuwen* (The Hague 1978).

Rüther, Andreas. *Bettelorden in Stadt und Land: Die Strassburger Mendikantenkonvente und das Elsass im Spätmittelalter* (Berliner Historische Studien 26, Berlin 1997).

Scheepsma, Wybren. *Deemoed en Devotie: De koorvrouwen van Windesheim en hun geschriften* (Amsterdam 1997).

———. *Medieval Religious Women in the Low Countries: The "Modern Devotion," the Canonesses of Windesheim, and Their Wiritings* (Rochester, N.Y. 2004).

———. "Überregionale Beziehungen zwischen dem Rheinland und Brabant in der mysttischen Literatur des 14. Jahrhunderts," in *University, Council, City*, pp. 247–76.

Schehr, Robert C. *Dynamic Utopia: Establishing Intentional Communities as a New Social Movement* (Westport, Conn. 1997).

Schlotheuber, Eva. "'Nullum regimen difficilius et periculosius est regimine feminarum': Die Begegnung des Beichtvaters Frederik van Heilo mit den Nonnen in der Devotio moderna," in *Spätmittelalterliche Frömmigkeit zwischen Ideal und Praxis*, ed. Berndt Hamm and Thomas Lentes (Tubingen 2001), pp. 45–84.

Schmedding, L. *De Regeering van Frederik van Blankenheim Bisschop van Utrecht* (Leiden 1899).

Schmidt, Alois. "Tractatus contra Hereticos, Beckardos, Lulhardos et Swestriones des Wasmud von Humburg," *Archiv für mittelrheinische Kirchengeschichte* 14 (1962), pp. 336–86.

Schmidt, Charles. *Die Gottesfreunde im 14. Jahrhundert: Historische Nachrichten und Urkunden* (Jena 1854).

Schmitt, Jean-Claude. *Mort d'une hérésie: l'Église et les clercs face aux béguines et aux béghards du Rhin supérieur du XIVe au XVe siècles* (Paris 1978).

Schmugge, Ludwig. *Kirche, Kinder, Karrieren: Päpstliche Dispense von der unehelichen Geburt im Spätmittelalter* (Zurich 1995)

Schneider, Reinhold. *Deventer zwischen dem Stift Utrecht und dem Herzogtum Gelderen vom 13. bis zum späten 14. Jahrhundert: Möglichkeiten und Grenzen städtischer Aussenpolitik im Kräftespiel zweier Territorien* (Münster 1993).

Schnittpunkte: Deutsche-Niederländische Literaturbeziehungen im späten Mittelalter, ed. Angelika Lehmann-Benz, Ulrike Zellmann, Urban Küsters (New York 2003).

Schoengen, Michael. *Die Schule von Zwolle von ihren Anfängen bis zur Einführung der Reformation, 1582* (Freiburg 1898).

———. *Jacobus Traiecti alias de Voecht Narratio de inchoatione domus clericorum in Zwollis, met akten en bescheiden betreffende dit fraterhuis* (Amsterdam 1908).

———. *Monasticon Batavum*, 3 vols. (Amsterdam 1941–42).

Schüssler, Hermann. *Der Primat der Heiligen Schrift als theologisches und kanonistisches Problem im Spätmittelalter* (Wiesbaden 1977).

Serta devota in memoriam Guillelmi Lourdaux, ed. Werner Verbeke, Marcel Haverals, Rafael de Keyser, Jean Goosens (Mediaevalia Lovaniensia ser.1, Studia 20/21; Louvain 1992, 1995).

Shuster, Peter. "Die Krise des Spätmittelalters: Zur Evidenz eines sozial-und wirtschaftsgeschichtlichen Paradigmas in der Geschichtschreibung des 20. Jahrhunderts," *Historische Zeitschrift* 269 (1999), pp. 19–55.

Simons, Walter. *Bedelordekloosters in het graafschap Vlaanderen: Chronologie en topografie van de bedelordenverspreiding in het graafschap Vlaanderen vóór 1350* (Bruges 1987).

———. *Stad en apostolaat: De vestiging van de bedelorden in het graafschap Vlaanderen (ca. 1225–ca.1350)* (Brussels 1987).

———. "The Beguine Movement in the Southern Low Countries: A Reassessment," *Bulletin de l'institut historique belge de Rome* 59 (1989), pp. 63–105.

———. *Cities of Ladies: Beguine Communities in the Medieval Low Countries, 1200–1565* (Philadelphia 2001).

———. " 'Staining the Speech of Things Divine': The Uses of Literacy in Medieval Beguine Communities," in *The Voice of Silence: Women's Literacy in a Men's Church*, ed. T. de Hemptinne and M. E. Góngora (Turnhout 2004), pp. 85–110.

Slicher van Bath, B. H. "Overijssel tussen west en oost (1250–1350)," in his *Herschreven Historie: Schetsen en studien op het gebied der middeleeuwse geschiedenis* (Arnhem 1978).

Šmahel, František. *Die Hussitische Revolution*, trans. Thomas Krzenck, ed. Alexander Patschovsky, 3 vols. (MGH Schriften 43, Hannover 2002).

Sneller, Z. W. *Deventer: Die Stadt der Jahrmarkte* (Weimar 1936).

Southern, Richard, *Western Society and the Church in the Middle Ages* (Harmondsworth 1970).

Spies, Martina. *Beginengemeinschaften in Frankfurt am Main: Zur Frage der genossenschaftlichen Selbstorganisation von Frauen im Mittelalter* (Dortmund 1998).

Stabel, Peter. "Urbanisation and its Consequences: Spatial Developments in Late Medieval Flanders," in *Raumerfassung* (2002), pp. 179–202.

Staley, Lynn. *Margery Kempe's Dissenting Fictions* (University Park, Pa. 1994)

Staubach, Nikolaus. "Pragmatische Schriftlichkeit im Bereich der Devotio moderna," *Frühmittelalterliche Studien* 25 (1991), pp. 418–61.

———. "Von der persönlichen Erfahrung zur Gemeinschaftsliteratur: Entstehungs-und Rezeptionsbedingungen geistlicher Reformtexte im Spätmittelalter," *OGE* (1994), pp. 200–228.

———. "*Christianam sectam arripe*: Devotio moderna und Humanismus zwischen Zirkelbildung und gesellschaftlicher Integration," in *Europäischen Sozietätsbewegimg und demokratische Tradition*, ed. Klaus Garber and Heinz Wismann (Tubingen 1996), pp. 112–67.

———. "Das Wunder der Devotio Moderna: Neue Aspekte im Werk des Windesheimer Geschichtsschreibers Johannes Busch," in *Windesheim 1395–1995: Kloosters, teksten, invloeden*, ed. A. J. Hendrikman, P. Bange, R. T. M. van Dijk, A. J. Jelsma (Nijmegen 1996).

———. "Der Codex als Ware: Wirtschaftliche Aspekte der Handschriftenproduktion im Bereich Devotio Moderna," in *Der Codex* (1996), pp. 143–62.

———. "Gerhard Zerbolt von Zutphen und die Apologie der Laienlektüre in der Devotio moderna," in *Laienlektüre* (1997), pp. 221–89.

———. "*Memores pristinae perfectionis*: The Importance of the Church Fathers for *Devotio moderna*," in *The Importance of the Church Fathers in the West, from the Carolingians to the Maurists*, 2 vols. (Leiden 1997) I, pp. 405–69.

———. "*Diversa raptim undique collecta*: Das Rapiarium im geistlichen Reformprogramm der Devotio moderna," in *Florilegien-Kompilationem-Kollektionem: Literarische Formen des Mittelalters*, ed. Kaspar Elm (Wolfenbüttler MittelalterStudien 15, Wiesbaden 2000), pp. 115–47.

———. "Zwischen Kloster und Welt? Die Stellung der Brüder vom gemeinsamen Leben in der spätmittelalterlichen Gesellschaft, in *Kirchenreform von unten*, ed. Staubach (2004), pp. 368–426.

Steer, Georg. "Merswin, Rulman," *Verfasserlexikon: Die deutsche Literatur des Mittelalters* 6 (1987), pp. 420–42.

———. "Die Stellung des 'Laien' im Schrifttum des Strassburger Gottesfreundes Rulman Merswin unter der deutschen Dominikanermystiker des 14. Jahrhunderts," in *Literatur und Laienbildung im Spätmittelalter und in der Reformationszeit*, ed. Ludger Grenzmann and Karl Stackmann (Stuttgart 1984), pp. 643–60.

Steinmetz, David. "*Libertas Christiana*: Studies in the Theology of John Pupper of Goch (d. 1475)," *Harvard Theological Review* 65 (1972), pp. 191–230.

Stooker, Karl and Verbeij, Theo. "'Uut Profectus': Over de verspreiding van Middelnederlandse kloosterliteratuur aan de hand van de 'Profectus religiosorum' van David van Augsburg," in *Boeken voor de Eeuwigheid* (1993), pp. 318–40, 476–90.

———. *Collecties op orde: Middelnederlandse handschriften uit kloosters en semi-religieuze gemeenschappen in de Nederlanden*, 2 vols. ((Louvain 1997)

Sudmann, Stefan. "Der 'Dialogus noviciorum' des Thomas von Kempen: Textgestalt und Textüberlieferung," in *Aus dem Winkel*, pp. 188–201.

Suntrup, Rudolph. "Der Gebrauch der Quellen in der Argumentation von 'De libris teutonicalibus'," in *Kirchenreform von unten*, pp. 264–76.

Taal, J. *De Goudse kloosters in de middeleeuwen* (Hilversum 1960).

Tarrant, Jacqueline. "The Clementine Decrees on the Beguines: Conciliar and Papal Versions," *Archivum Historiae Pontificiae* 12 (1974), pp. 300–308.

Thompson, A. Hamilton. *The English Clergy and Their Organization in the Later Middle Ages: The Ford Lectures for 1933* (Oxford 1947).

Thompson, Augustine. "Lay Versus Clerical Perceptions of Heresy: Protests Against the Inquisition in Bologna, 1299," in *Praedicatores inquisitores I* (2004), pp. 701–30.

———. *Cities of God: The Religion of the Italian Communes 1125–1325* (University Park, Pa. 2005).

Thomson, Williel R. *The Latin Writings of John Wyclif: An Annotated Catalogue* (Toronto 1983).

Tierney, Brian. *Medieval Poor Law: A Sketch of Canonical Theory and its Application in England* (Berkeley, Calif. 1959).

Tönsing, M. "'Contra hereticam pravitatem': Zu den Luccheser Ketzererlassen Karls IV. (1369)," in *Studia Luxemburgensia: Festschrift Heinz Stoob zum 70. Geburtstag*, ed. F. B. Fahlbusch and P. Johannek (Warendorf 1989), pp. 285–311.

Trinkaus, Charles. *In Our Image and Likeness: Humanity and Divinity in Italian Humanist Thought* (Chicago 1971).

Ubbink, R. A. *De receptie van Meister Eckkart in de Nederlanden gedurende de middeleeuwen: een studie op basis van middelnederlandse handschriften* (Amsterdam 1978).

Ullmann, Carl. *Reformatoren vor der Reformation* 2 vols. (Hamburg 1841).

University, Council, City: Intellectual Culture on the Rhine (1300–1550), ed. Laurent Cesalli, Nadja Germann, and Maarten J.F.M. Hoenen (Turnhout 2007)

Van Adrichem, D. "Explicatio primae regulae s. Clarae auctore s. Ioanne Capistranensi (1445)," *Archivum Historicum Franciscanum* 22 (1929), pp. 32–51.

Van Asseldonk, G. A. "Het bisdom Utrecht en de concilies van Pisa en Constanz," in *Postillen* (1964), pp. 61–84.

Van den Bosch, Pieter. "Die Kreuzherrenreform des 15. Jahrhunderts: Urheber, Zielsetzung und Verlauf," in *Reformbemühungen* (1989), pp. 72–82.

Van den Hombergh, F. A. H. *Leven en werk van Jan Brugman O.F.M.* (Groningen 1967).

Van den Hoven van Genderen, B. "Gerrit van Bronkhorst (1320/1340–1412), kannunik en steunpilaar van de Moderne Devotie, in *Utrechtse biografieën 1: Levensbeschrijvingen van bekende en onbekende Utrechters*, ed. J. Aalbers (Utrecht 1994), pp. 31–34

———. *Heren van de kerk: De kannunniken van Oudmuster te Utrecht in de laate Middeleeuwen* (Zutphen 1997).

———. "Evert Foec," *Utrechtse biografieën* 4 (Utrecht 1997), pp. 71–76.

Van der Heijden. H. A. M., "Oude kaarten van de Nederlandse bisdommen, 1559–1801," *Trajecta* 8 (1999), pp. 195–265.

Van der Wansem, C. *Het ontstaan en de geschiedenis der Broederschap van het Gemene Leven tot 1400* (Louvain 1958).

Van Dijk, Rudolf Th. M., "Het vrouwenklooster Diepenveen in zijn historische context: Bijdrage aan de geschiedenis van de religieuze vrouwen in de Modern Devotie," in *Het ootmoedig fundament*, pp. 15–40.

———. "*Ascensiones in corde disponere*: Spirituelle Umformung bei Gerhard Zerbolt von Zutphen," in *Kirchenreform von unten*, pp. 287–305.

———. "Thematisiche meditatie en het beeld: visualiteit in *De spiritualibus ascensionibus* van Gerard Zerbolt van Zutphen (1367–1398), in *Geen povere schoonheid*, pp. 43–66.

———. *Prolegomena ad Gerardi Magni Opera omnia* (CC CM 192, Turnhout 2003).

Van Dijk, R.Th.M. and Hendrikman, A. J. "Tabellarium Chronologicum Windeshemense: De Windesheimse kloosters in chronologisch perspectief," in *Windesheim 1395–1995* (1996), pp. 186–210.

Van Eeghen, Isabella Henriette. *Vrouwenkloosters en begijnhof in Amsterdam van de 14e tot het eind der 16e eeuw* (Amsterdam 1941).

Van Engen, Hildo. "Het archief van het Kapittel van Utrecht," *OGE* 74 (2000), pp. 33–49.

———. "*Speciosus forma*: Het Kapittel van Utrecht en de invoering van de clausuur," *Jaarboek voor Middeleeuwse Geschiedenis* 5 (2002), pp. 206–46.

———. "Met het volste recht: De juridische pretenties van de tertiarissen van het Kapittel van Utrecht," *Trajecta* 14 (2005), pp. 147–60.

———. *De derde orde van Sint-Franciscus in het middeleeuwse bisdom Utrecht* (Hilversum 2006).

———. *Bronnen met betrekking tot het Kapittel van Utrecht van de derde orde van Sint-Franciscus (1256–1579)*, provisionally available at: http://www.bkvu.nl.

Van Engen, John. *Devotio Moderna: Basic Writings* (New York 1988).

———. "The Virtues, the Brothers, and the Schools: A Text from the Brothers of the Common Life," *Revue Bénédictine* 98 (1988), pp. 178–217.

———. "A Brabantine Perspective on the Origins of the Modern Devotion: The First Book of Petrus Impens' *Compendium Decursus Temporum Monasterii Christifere Bethleemitice Puerpere*," in *Serta Devota in memoriam Guillelmi Lourdaux, Pars Prior: Devotio Windeshemensis* (Louvain1992), pp. 3–78.

———. "'God Is No Respecter of Persons': Sacred Texts and Social Realities," in *Intellectual Life in the Middle Ages: Studies for Margaret Gibson*, ed. Leslie Smith and Benedicta Ward (London 1992), pp. 243–64.

———. "Late Medieval Anticlericalism: The Case of the New Devout," in *Anticlericalism in Late Medieval and Early Modern Europe*, ed. Peter Dykema and Heiko Oberman (Studies in Medieval and Reformation Thought 51, Leiden 1993), pp. 19–52.

———. "Studying Scripture in the Early University," in *Neue Richtungen in der hoch- und spätmittelalterlichen Exegese*, ed. Robert Lerner (Schriften des Historischen Kollegs, Kolloquien 32, Munich 1996), pp. 17–38.

———. "Religious Profession: From Liturgy to Law," *Viator* 29 (1998), pp. 323–43.

———. "Dominic and the Brothers: *Vitae* as Life-Forming *Exempla* in the Order of Preachers," in *Christ Among the Medieval Dominicans*, ed. Kent Emery, Jr. and Joseph Wawrykow (Notre Dame, Ind. 1998), pp. 7–25.

———. "Privileging the Devout: A Text from the Brothers at Deventer," in *Roma, magistra mundi, Itineraria culturae medievalis: Mélanges offerts au Père L.E. Boyle à l'occasion de son 75e anniversaire* (Louvain-la-Neuve, 1998), pp. 951–63.

———. "Friar Johannes Nyder on Laypeople Living as Religious in the World," in *Vita Religiosa im Mittelalter: Festschrift für Kaspar Elm zum 70. Geburtstag* (Berlin 1999), pp. 583–615.

———. "Managing the Common Life: The Brothers at Deventer and the Codex of the Household (The Hague, MS KB 70 H 75)," in *Schriftlichkeit und Lebenspraxis im Mittelalter*, ed. Hagen Keller, Christel Meier and Thomas Scharff (Munich, 1999), pp. 111–69.

———. "The Work of Gerlach Peters (d. 1411), Spiritual Diarist and Letter-Writer, a Mystic Among the Devout," *OGE* 73 (1999), pp. 150–77.

———. "The Sayings of the Fathers: An Inside Look at the New Devout in Deventer," in *Continuity and Change: The Harvest of Late Medieval and Reformation History. Essays Presented to Heiko A. Oberman on his 70th Birthday*, ed. Robert J. Bast and Andrew Colin Gow (Leiden 2000), pp. 279–302, with "A Working Edition of the *Dicta patrum*," pp. 303–20.

———. "Ralph of Flaix: The Book of Leviticus Interpreted as Christian Community," in *Jews and Christians in Twelfth-Century Europe* (Notre Dame, Ind. 2001), ed. John Van Engen and Michael Signer, pp. 150–70.

———. "Conversion and Conformity in the Early Fifteenth Century," in *Conversions Old and New*, ed. Kenneth Mills and Anthony Grafton (Rochester 2003), pp. 30–65.

———. "Devout Communities and Inquisitorial Orders: The Legal Defense of the New Devout," in *Kirchenreform von unten* (2003), pp. 44–101.

———. "From Canons to Preachers: A Revolution in Medieval Governance," in *Domenico di Caleruega e la nascita dell'ordine dei Fratri Predicatori* (Todi 2005), pp. 261–95.

———. "Multiple Options: The World of the Fifteenth-Century Church," *Church History* 77 (2008).

Van Ginnekin, Jacobus. *Geert Groote's levensbeeld naar de oudste gegevens bewerkt* (Verhandelingen der Nederlandsche Akademie van Wetenschappen, Afdeeling letterkunde, n.r. 47, 2; Amsterdam 1942).

Van Heel, Damian. "Het Sint Margareta klooster te Gouda," *Oudheidkundige kring 'Die Goude'* 6 (1949), pp. 55–95.

———. *De tertiarissen van het Utrechtsche kapittel* (Utrecht 1939).

Van Kalveen, C. A. "Johan Pupper van Goch en de Broeders des Gemenen Levens," *AGKKN* 20 (1978), pp. 103–13.

———. "Problemen rond de oudste geschiedenis van het fraterhuis en van het Nieuwe Gasthuis te Amersfoort," *Jaarboek Oud-Utrecht* (Utrecht 1981), pp. 101–24.

Van Leeuwen, Jacoba. "Schepeneden in de Lage Landen: Een eerste verkenning vun hun betekenis, overlevering en formulering (dertiende tot zestiende eeuw)," *Jaarboek voor Middeleeuwse Geschiedenis* 6 (2003), pp. 112–60.

Van Luijk, M. "Devote vrouwen tijdens de tweede religieuze vrouwenbeweging in de laatmiddeleeuwse Noordelijke Nederlanden," *Tijdschrift voor Sociale Geschiedenis* 27 (2001), pp. 33–56.

———. *Bruiden van Christus: De tweede religieuze vrouwenbeweging in Leiden en Zwolle 1380–1580* (Zutphen 2004).

———. "Voorbede versus verzet: Relaties tussen vrouwenhuizen en magistraat in laatmiddeleeuws Zwolle," *Trajecta* 14 (2005), pp. 161–76.

Van Oostrom, Frits. *Court and Culture: Dutch Literature, 1350–1450* (Berkeley, Calif. 1992).

Van Rooij, J. *Gerard Zerbolt van Zutphen: Leven en geschriften* (Nijmegen-Utrecht 1936).

Van Slee, J. C. "Het necrologium en cartularium van het convent der reguliere kanunnikessen te Diepenveen," *AGU* 33 (1908), pp. 318–415.

Van Vloten, J. *Vijftal lezingen over de working en ontwikkeling der stad en gemeente Deventer* (Zutphen 1866)

Van Wijk, N. *Het getijdenboek van Geert Grote naar het Haagse handschrift 133 E 21 uitgegeven* (Leiden 1940).

Van Woerkum, Martin. "Florentius Radewijns: Schets van zijn leven, geschriften, persoonlijkheid en ideeën," *OGE* 24 (1950), pp. 337–64.

———. "Het libellus '*Omnes, inquit, artes*': Een rapiarium van Florentius Radewijns," *OGE* 25 (1951), pp. 113–58, 225–68.

———. "Florent Radewijns," *Dictionnaire de spiritualité ascétique et mystique* (1964), VII, pp. 427–34.

Van Zijl, Th. P. *Gerard Groote, Ascetic and Reform (1340–84)* (Washington, D.C. 1963).

———. "Bisschoppelijke goedkeuring van Windesheim," *AGKKN* 8 (1966), pp. 327–41.

Veelenturf, Kees. "Inleiding," in *Geen povere schoonheid*, pp. 9–30.

Venarde, Bruce, ed. and trans. *Robert of Arbrissel: A Medieval Religious Life* (Washington D.C. 2003).

Vennebusch, J. *Die theologischen Handschriften des Stadtarchivs Köln, 2: Die Quarthandschriften der Gymnasialbibliothek* (Cologne 1980).

Verdeyen, Paul. "De middelnederlandse vertaling van Pomerius' werk 'De origine monasterii viridisvallis'," *OGE* 55 (1981), pp. 105–65.

———. "Oordeel van Ruusbroec over de rechtgelovigheid van Margaretha Porete," *OGE* 66 (1992), pp. 88–96.

Verhoeven, Gerrit. "De kronieken van de Delftse tertiarissenconventen," *OGE* 74 (2000), pp. 105–52.

Voices in Dialogue: Reading Women in the Middle Ages, ed. Kathryn Kerby-Fulton and Linda Olson (Notre Dame, Ind. 2005).

Vones, Ludwig. *Urban V.: Kirchenreform zwischen Kardinalkollegium, Kurie und Klientel* (Päpste und Papsttum 28, Stuttgart 1998).

———. Papst Urban V. (1362–1370) und die dominikanische Inquisition," in *Praedicatores Inquisitores* (2004), pp. 495–511.

Von Heusinger, Sabine. *Johannes Mulberg OP (d. 1414): Ein Leben im Spannungsfeld von Dominkanerobservanz und Beginenstreit* (Berlin 2000).

Wachter, Stephan. "Matthäus Grabow, ein Gegner der Brüder vom gemeinsamen Leben," in *Festschrift zum 50-jährigen Bestandsjubiläum des Missionshauses St. Gabriel Wien-Mödling* (Vienna-Mödling 1939), pp. 289–376.

Walsh, Katherine. *A Fourteenth-Century Scholar and Primate: Richard FitzRalph in Oxford, Avignon, and Armagh* (Oxford 1981).

———. "Die Rezeption der Schriften des Richard FitzRalph (Armachanus) im lollardisch-hussitischen Milieu," in *Das Publikum politischer Theorie* (1992).

Wand-Wittkowski, Christine. "Mystik und Distanz: Zur religiösen Erzählungen Rulman Merswins," *Mediaevistik* 13 (2000), pp. 117–34.

Warnar, Geert. "Jan van Ruusbroec and the Social Position of Late Medieval Mysticism," in *Showing Status: Representations of Social Positions in the Late Middle Ages*, ed. W. Blockmans and A. Janse (Turnhout 1999), pp. 365–86.

———."Mystik in der Stadt: Jan van Ruuxbroec (1293–1381) und die niederländische Literatur des 14. Jahrhunderts," in *Deutsche Mystik* (2000), pp. 683–702.

———. *Ruusbroec: literatuur en mystiek in de veertiende eeuw* (Amsterdam 2003).
———. "Tauler in Groenendael: Mystik und Gelehrtheit in der niederländischen Literatur des 14. Jahrhunderts," in *Schnittpunkte* (2003), pp. 55–66.
Watson, Nicholas. "The Making of *The Book of Margery Kempe*," in *Voices in Dialogue*, pp. 395–434.
Wehrli-Johns, Martina. "Voraussetzungen und Perspektiven mittelalterlicher Laienfrömmigkeit seit Innozenz III: Eine Auseinandersetzung mit Herbert Grundmanns "Regliösen Bewegungen," *Mitteilungen des Instituts für Österreichische Geschichtsforschung* 104 (1996), pp. 286–309.
———. "Das mittelalterliche Beginentum: Religiöse Frauenbewegung oder Sozialidee der Scholastik?" in Wehrli-Johns and Optiz (1998), pp. 25–52.
———. "Mystik und Inquisition: Die Dominikaner und die sogenannte Häresie des Freien Geistes," in Haug (2000), pp. 223–52.
Weiler, A. G. "Recent Historiography on the Modern Devotion: Some Debated Questions," *AGKKN* 26 (1984), 161–79.
———. *Getijden van eeuwige wijsheid naar de vertaling van Geert Grote* (Baarn 1984).
———. "De intrede van rijke weduwen en arme meisjes in de leefgemeenschappen van de Moderne Devotie," *OGE* 59 (1985), pp. 403–20.
———. "La systématique de la théologie morale selon Arnold Geilhoven, in *Vocabulaire du livre et de l'écriture au moyen âge* (Turnhout 1987, 2 vols.), I, pp. 11–18.
———. "La construction du soi dans les milieux de la devotio moderna," in *La dévotion moderne dans les pays bourguignons et rhénans des origines à la fin du XVI*[e] siècle, ed. Jean-Marie Cauchie (Neuchâtel 1989), pp. 9–16.
———. "De constructie van het zelf bij Geert Grote," in *Serta* (1992), pp. 225–40.
———. "Geert Grote en begijnen in de begintijd van de moderne devotie," *OGE* 69 (1995), pp. 114–32.
———. *Volgens de norm van de vroege kerk* (Nijmegen 1997).
———. "The Dutch Brethren of the Common Life: Critical Theology, Northern Humanism, and Reformation," in *Northern Humanism* (1999), pp. 307–32.
———. *Het morele veld van de Moderne Devotie, weerspiegeld in de* Gnotosolitos parvus *van Arnold Gheyloven van Rotterdam, 1423: Een Summa van moraaltheologie, kerkelijk recht en spiritualiteit voor studenten in Leuven en Deventer* (Hilversum 2006)
Weinstein, Donald and Bell, Rudolph. *Saints and Society: The Two Worlds of Western Christendom, 1000–1700* (Chicago 1982).
Wierda, Lydia, *De Sarijshandschriften: Laatmiddeleeuwse handschriften uit de IJsselstreek* (Zwolle 1995).
Williams-Krapp, Werner. "*Ein puch verschriben ze deutsche in brabantzer zunge*: Zur Rezeption von mystischem Schrifttum aus dem *niderlant* im *oberlant*," in *Schnittpunkte* (2003), pp. 41–53.
Willibrord en het begin van Nederland, ed. Marieke van Vlierden (Utrecht 1995).
Wilmans, R. "Zur Geschichte der römischen Inquisition in Deutschland während des 14. und 15. Jahrhunderts," *Historische Zeitschrift* 41 (1879), pp. 193–228.
Wilts, Andreas. *Beginen im Bodenseeraum* (Sigmaringen 1994).
Windesheim 1395–1995: Kloosters, texten, invloeden, ed. A. J. Hendrikman (Nijmegen 1996).

Witt, Ronald. *Hercules at the Crossroads: The Life, Works, and Thought of Coluccio Salutati* (Durham, N.C. 1983).

———. *In the Footsteps of the Ancients: The Origins of Humanism from Lovato to Bruni* (Leiden 2000).

Wolfs, S. P. *Studies over Noordnederlandse dominicanen in de middeleeuwen* (Assen 1973).

———. *Middeleeuwse dominicanenkloosters in Nederland* (Assen 1984).

I. Wormgoor. "De vervolging van de Vrijen van Geest, die begijnen en begarden," *Nederlands Archief voor Kerkgeschiedenis* 25 (1985), pp. 107–30.

Ypma, E. *Het generaal kapittel van Sion: zijn oorsprong, ontwikkeling en inrichting* (Nijmegen 1949).

Zablocki, Benjamin. *Alienation and Charisma: A Study of Contemporary American Communes* (New York 1980).

Zarri, Gabriella. *Le sante vive: profezie di corte e devozione femminile tra '400 e '500* (Turin 1990).

Ziegler, Joanna. "The *Curtis* Beguinages in the Southern Low Countries and Art Patronage: Interpretation and Historiography," *Bulletin de l'institut historique belge de Rome* 57 (1987), pp. 31–70.

———. *Sculpture of Compassion: The Pietà and the Beguines in the Sourthern Low Countries c. 1300–c. 1600* (Brussels and Rome 1992).

INDEX

ACKNOWLEDGMENTS

Just over twenty years ago I spent an academic year living with my family in the beguine court in Louvain, where, courtesy of a fellowship from the John Simon Guggenheim Foundation, I began research on a project dealing with thirteenth-century religious life. Evenings, however, I translated texts from the Devotio Moderna. As I set about choosing pieces for that volume (published in 1988) I realized that Devout texts were not easy of access outside the Low Countries or a major research library; more, that many were not properly edited, some hardly studied. Digging deeper into these manuscripts and archives yielded uncommon satisfaction, and so I persisted off and on over the years, never thinking of it as my main writing project, still advancing on other topics while also sustaining an administrative position. What I published on the Devout mostly took the form of essays with accompanying texts newly found or newly edited. This suggested a larger project: to edit or re-edit a body of materials essential for understanding the Devotio Moderna (including key texts underpinning this book), a laborious editorial project still underway. My graduate students meanwhile suggested that I gather up the completed essays, particularly since many had appeared in places out of the way for most North American medievalists. I took up their suggestion, and Brill has graciously agreed to publish them under the title *Making Private Religion*, a volume of published as well as unpublished studies, nearly all with edited texts, to appear in the near future. But as I worked at gathering and correcting these individual studies, I sensed the outlines of a larger story, a narrative that went beyond textbook commonplaces about the Devotio Moderna. And so, beginning in earnest in January 2003, I wrote a new book, this book.

In years now of scholarly work I have found only helpfulness at libraries and archives across the Low Countries and Germany, their staffs consistently gracious to an American scholar coming for a day or two and then disappearing for a year or two. My special gratitude to, in alphabetical order: the Gemeente Archief, Amsterdam; the Universiteitsbibliotheek, Amsterdam; the Royal Archives, Brussels; the Royal Library, Brussels; the Historisches Archiv in the city of Cologne; the Stads-en Atheneum Bibliotheek in Deventer; the Streeksarchief Midden-Holland in Gouda; the Stadsarchief in Haarlem; the Koninglijke Bibliotheek in The Hague; the Gemeente archief in Léiden; the Grand Séminaire in Liège; the Stadtsbibliothek in Soest; the Rijksarchief in Utrecht; the Universiteitsbibliotheek in Utrecht; and the Historisch Centrum Overijssel in Zwolle (combining the former Stadsarchief Zwolle and Rijksarchief Overijssel). Their holdings and accessibility made this study possible.

Repeated trips to archives, also the gathering of microfilms and digital images, requires considerable material support, and the University of Notre Dame has been exceptionally generous, primarily by way of research funds attached to the Andrew V. Tackes Chair in Medieval History. The publication of this book was also supported in part by the Institute for Scholarship in the Liberal Arts, College of Arts and Letters, University of Notre Dame. The book itself grew to maturity in the welcoming environment of Notre Dame's Medieval Institute and Library directed by Thomas Noble and its History Department chaired by John McGreevy. Among many wonderful colleagues in a department full of fine minds and good people I note fondly conversations with James Turner, Sabine MacCormack, and Olivia Remie Constable.

For reading this manuscript in whole or in part, and at various stages, I am grateful to many; to Lisa Wolverton of the University of Oregon, once student, now colleague, who lent her acuity to both its larger logic and its syntactical detail; to Robert Sullivan of the University of Notre Dame, who prodded me to help the reader move out of the kitchen into the dining room; to Walter Simons, who made me think again about beguines and Sisters; to an anonymous reader for the Press who wisely pointed up matters large and small requiring attention or correction; to Gordon Thompson for drawing the map of the medieval Low Countries (Figure 1); at the very end to J. Michael Raley, reading early Devout texts for his doctoral dissertation at the University of Chicago, for encouraging reactions; and to Marcella Kliçova Perett, presently a graduate student at Notre Dame, for proofreading the whole. In addition, Ruth Mazo Karras, as editor of this series, gave firm but altogether apt advice about streamlining the manuscript, while offering steady support. If this work is still too long, it is not her fault, nor that of any other readers. Beyond perceiving the need for a broader interpretation, I sought to uncover the historical life latent in all the human, organizational, legal, and religious detail—as did, as I see it, if I may allude to models from a generation ahead of mine, Robert Brentano and Giles Constable. Jerome Singerman, as general editor, has proved both patient and encouraging, in just the right measure.

My four sons, Hans, Stefan, Lucas, and Abram, playing soccer with me in Leuven's begijnhof when I first meandered into this subject, have been waiting all along to see the other work begun there, and schemed in the meantime about what size backpacks they could market to carry around the book that finally emerged from that research. Their enterprise will have to wait a little still. I hope they can make peace for now with this book. Their teasing and heartfelt encouragement has meant all to me, over long and sometimes trying stretches.

Kathryn Kerby-Fulton read and commented on every word of this manuscript, gently urging me on, drawing out points too easily overlooked in the myopia of close research. She gave me heart to tell the big story, to let the Modern-Day Devout come to life—as do the religious visionaries and literate social critics who people her deeply learned work. There she showed the courage to go her own way, to recover aspects of later medieval culture overlooked or neglected, a prodigious manuscript scholar and sensitive literary reader able to speak tellingly as well to Europe's historical and religious past, someone whose imagination truly is not bounded by disciplinary shackles. This book is for her.